W9-BGO-754

Physical Science

Tom Hsu, Ph.D.

FIRST EDITION
Cambridge Physics Outlet
Peabody, Massachusetts 01960

The cover is an evocative montage of historic scientific achievements that demonstrate the incredible persistence of the human intellect. Around the border, DaVinci's graphics represent the start of an evolving tapestry of conceptual thinking. His fantastical mechanisms become the modern bicycle, a quintessential machine, which rolls into a graphical interpretation of wavelength division multiplexing on a fiber optic. These images follow 500 years of scientific and technological innovation. The Earth and DNA serve to remind us that this technological innovation will always remain deeply connected to the natural world. On the back cover, the elegant geometry of the chambered nautilus folds into a spiral defined by the Golden Rectangle. The interplay of organic and architectural forms represents the balance we seek between the power of technology and the fragility of our lives and our world. I hope this colorful interplay of images will inspire interest and excitement about the discovery of science.

Bruce Holloway - Senior Creative Designer

Foundations of Physical Science

ISBN 1-58892-005-4
3 4 5 6 7 8 9 - QWE - 05 04 03

Cambridge Physics Outlet
26 Howley Street
Peabody, MA 01960
(800) 932-5227
http://www. cpo.com

Printed and Bound in the United States of America

CPO Science Development Team

Tom Hsu, Ph.D. – Author, President

Ph.D., Applied Plasma Physics, Massachusetts Institute of Technology

Nationally recognized innovator in science and math who has taught in middle and high school, college, and graduate programs. Personally held workshops with more than 10,000 teachers and administrators to promote teaching physics using a hands-on approach. CPO was founded by Dr. Hsu to create innovative hands-on materials for teaching math and science.

Lynda Pennell – Educational Products and Training, Vice President

B.A., English, M.Ed., Administration, Reading Disabilities, Northeastern University; CAGS Media, University of Massachusetts, Boston

Nationally known in high school restructuring and for integrating academic and career education. Has served as the director of an urban school with seventeen years teaching/administrative experience.

Thomas Narro – Product Design, Vice President

B.S., Mechanical Engineering, Rensselaer Polytechnic Institute

Accomplished design and manufacturing engineer; experienced consultant in corporate re-engineering and industrial-environmental acoustics.

Scott Eddleman – Curriculum Manager

B.S., Biology, Southern Illinois University; M.Ed., Harvard University

Taught for thirteen years in urban and rural settings; nationally known as a trainer of inquiry-based science and mathematics project-based instruction; curriculum development consultant.

Laine Ives – Curriculum Writer

B.A., English, Gordon College; graduate work, biology, Cornell University, Wheelock College

Experience teaching middle and high school, here and abroad, and expertise in developing middle school curriculum and hands-on activities.

Mary Beth Abel – Curriculum Writer

B.S., Marine Biology, College of Charleston; M.S., Biological Sciences, University of Rhode Island

Taught science and math at an innovative high school; has expertise in scientific research and inquiry-based teaching methods.

Erik Benton – Professional Development Specialist

B.F.A. Universty of Massachusetts

Taught for eight years in public and private schools, focusing on inquiry and experiential learning environments.

Irene Baker – Senior Curriculum Writer

B.S., Chemistry, B.S., Humanities, MIT; M.Ed., Lesley University

Experience is in scientific curriculum development, in educational research and assessment, and as a science consultant.

Bruce Holloway – Senior Creative Designer

Pratt Institute, N.Y.; Boston Museum School of Fine Arts

Expertise is in product design, advertising, and three-dimensional exhibit design; winner of National Wildlife 1999 Stamp Award.

Polly Crisman – Graphic Designer and Illustrator

B.F.A., University of New Hampshire

Graphic artist who has worked in advertising and marketing and as a freelance illustrator and cartoonist.

Patsy DeCoster – Professional Development Manager

B.S., Biology/Secondary Education, Grove City College; M.Ed., Tufts University

Curriculum and professional development specialist. Taught science for twelve years. National inquiry-based science presenter.

Curriculum Contributors

Thomas Altman – Teaches physics at Oswego High School, NY, and invented the Altman Method for making holograms in the classroom.

Julie Dalton – Has worked as a copy editor for major Boston newspapers. She has also worked as a sports writer and editor and taught secondary English.

Gary Garber – Teaches physics and math at Boston University Academy, and is a researcher at the BU Photonics Center; past president of the Southeast section of the American Association of Physics Teachers.

Matt Lombard – Marketing manager, oversees marketing and public relations activities for CPO; expertise is in photography of equipment and curriculum materials.

Catalina Moreno – Taught eight years at East Boston High School as a bilingual science and math teacher. Also an expert resource for the American Astronomical Society.

David Bliss – Teaches life, physical, and Earth science at Mohawk Central High School. Has been a teacher for 34 years.

Consultants

Tracy Morrow – technical consultant
James Travers – illustration and graphic designer
John Mahomet – graphic designer
Dexter Beals – Beals Dynamics

Kent Dristle – physics teacher, Oswego (NY) High
Kelly Story – assessment specialist
Cerise Cauthron – teaching consultant
Debbie Markos – teaching consultant

Greg Garcia – Spanish glossary
Mike Doughty – intern, Endicott College
Jennifer Lockhart – intern, Endicott College

Product Design

Jeff Casey – experimental physicist
Roger Barous – machinist

Kathryn Gavin – quality specialist
Agnes Chan – manufacturing engineer

Greg Krekorian, Shawn Greene – production team

Reviewers

Bell, Tom
Curriculum Specialist
Cumberland County Schools
North Carolina

Chesick, Elizabeth
Head of Science Department
Baldwin School
Pennsylvania

Curry, Dwight
Assistant Director of Physical Science
St. Louis Science Center
Missouri

Gharooni, Hamid
Program Director, Math & Science
Madison Park Technical-Vocational High School
Massachusetts

Haas, Jack
Principal Reviewer, Chemistry
Professor of Chemistry
Gordon College
Massachusetts

Inman, Jamie
Physics Teacher
North Carolina

Lamp, David
Associate Professor
Physics Department
Texas Tech University
Texas

Leeds, Susan
Science teacher, eighth grade
Howard Middle School
Florida

Lowe, Larry
Physics and Electricity Teacher
Masconomet Regional High School
Massachusetts

Madar, Robert
Senior Consultant and Trainer
Impact Consulting
Oregon

Nelson, Genevieve M.
Head of Science Department
Germantown Friends School
Pennsylvania

Ramsay, Willa A.
Science Education Consultant
California

Susan Schafer
Principal Investigator
College of Engineering
Texas Tech University
Texas

Scott, Janet
Curriculum Specialist
Durham Public Schools
North Carolina

Les Sewall
Science Education Consultant
Georgia

Tally, Michael
Science Supervisor
Wake County Public Schools
North Carolina

Texas, Leslie A.
Senior Consultant and Trainer
Impact Consulting
Kentucky

Thompson, Gaile B.
Director of Science Collaborative
Region 14 ESC
Texas

Woodring, Kathleen
Physics Teacher
Industrial High School
Texas

Science Through Discovery

The universe is like a safe to which there is a combination, but the combination is locked up in the safe.
Peter de Vries

In many learning situations, you are expected to study prescribed materials and come up with correct answers by yourself. Usually, you read the information and then, in a laboratory, you try out the knowledge you acquired. With the CPO program, you will find that science is an opportunity for you to discover and solve problems—though they sometimes seem like mysteries more than "problems"—while working with others as a team.

Working with your fellow students, you will use very accurate equipment to answer key questions, decide if your findings can be backed up with data and facts, and learn how to prove and justify your end results.

What you learn in school should be connected to what you know about the world around you. These connections will contribute to your success in life, sometimes in obvious ways, and many times in quite surprising ways. In today's workplace and in future educational pursuits, you will need to ask insightful questions, plan and organize your work, look for and analyze information, try out your ideas, and then be able to rethink a problem and try again. You must also be able to work on a team, to come up with a system for organizing information, and to feel comfortable about tackling new problems.

The CPO program provides the opportunity for you to practice answering questions, working with others, and finding your own system for solving problems. In the student text, you will find knowledge and skills needed to answer key questions and explore a variety of science topics. Along with each reading, you will complete an investigation activity so that part of your discovery of science is done with others. Some people may think exactly like you, while others might find different ways of approaching the same problem.

Finally, the ability to communicate effectively is one of the most valued skills in the world today. As a result, analyzing and communicating your findings to others in written, verbal or illustration form will be a major part of the learning process throughout the CPO program.

About the Student Text

There are *Nine* Major Science Units covered in the CPO student text. Each Unit contains *Chapters* which are divided into three or four *sections*. The chapters and sections are organized so that you will learn basic skills and then build your knowledge to more complex understanding. You will notice that many of the important science concepts are repeated in different ways throughout the sections. Numerous illustrations, charts, graphs, and data tables support your reading and assist you in grasping its content. Also, there are short subheadings on the left margin of each page to help you study the main ideas and find information quickly.

Student Text Main Components

Main text: In addition to reading about science concepts and skills, you will discover brief stories about important scientists, inventions, real world connections, environmental issues, and interesting facts.

Chapter pages: Each chapter starts with two pages that outline what you will learn in the chapter. These pages provide you with a brief summary, the key questions for each Investigation, vocabulary, and learning goals.

Review questions: After each section, there are review questions that evaluate what you have learned and support you and your teacher in choosing what needs to be reviewed and which concepts to discuss further.

Glossary: The glossary is where you will find the meaning of words that are important science concepts and essential vocabulary. You can also find references to important people who are discussed in your reading.

Index: This section helps you find more specific topic information by giving page numbers that refer to the topic. You can use the index while studying to find information.

Reference Tables: A quick reference guide provides you with safety information, problem solving techniques (dimensional analysis), a conversion chart, table of formulas, and a list of physical constants. The inside back cover of the book is a quick reference periodic table and explanation of how to interpret it.

Student Text Pages

Sidenotes (idea headers): In the left margin of each page you will find phrases, short sentences, and questions to guide you in understanding the most important ideas. These sidenotes will also help you skim the text and quickly find information when you are reviewing and studying for tests.

Illustrations: Use the illustrations, graphs, charts, and data tables to help you understand the reading. These reading tools help most students improve their understanding of the key concepts.

Vocabulary words: The vocabulary words are highlighted in blue. You need to understand their meanings to be successful in science and will find the same vocabulary used in many contexts and repeated throughout the text. The definitions can be found in the glossary.

Data tables: These tables will help you understand complex information, organize numerical data, and provide examples of how to collect and present data.

Figure number/captions: As you are reading, notice the references to the word *Figure* followed by a number. These figures are found on the right side of the page in the form of an illustration, picture, or chart. The figure number indicates which figure goes with the text you are reading and gives you another way to understand the information in the reading.

STUDENT TEXT PAGES

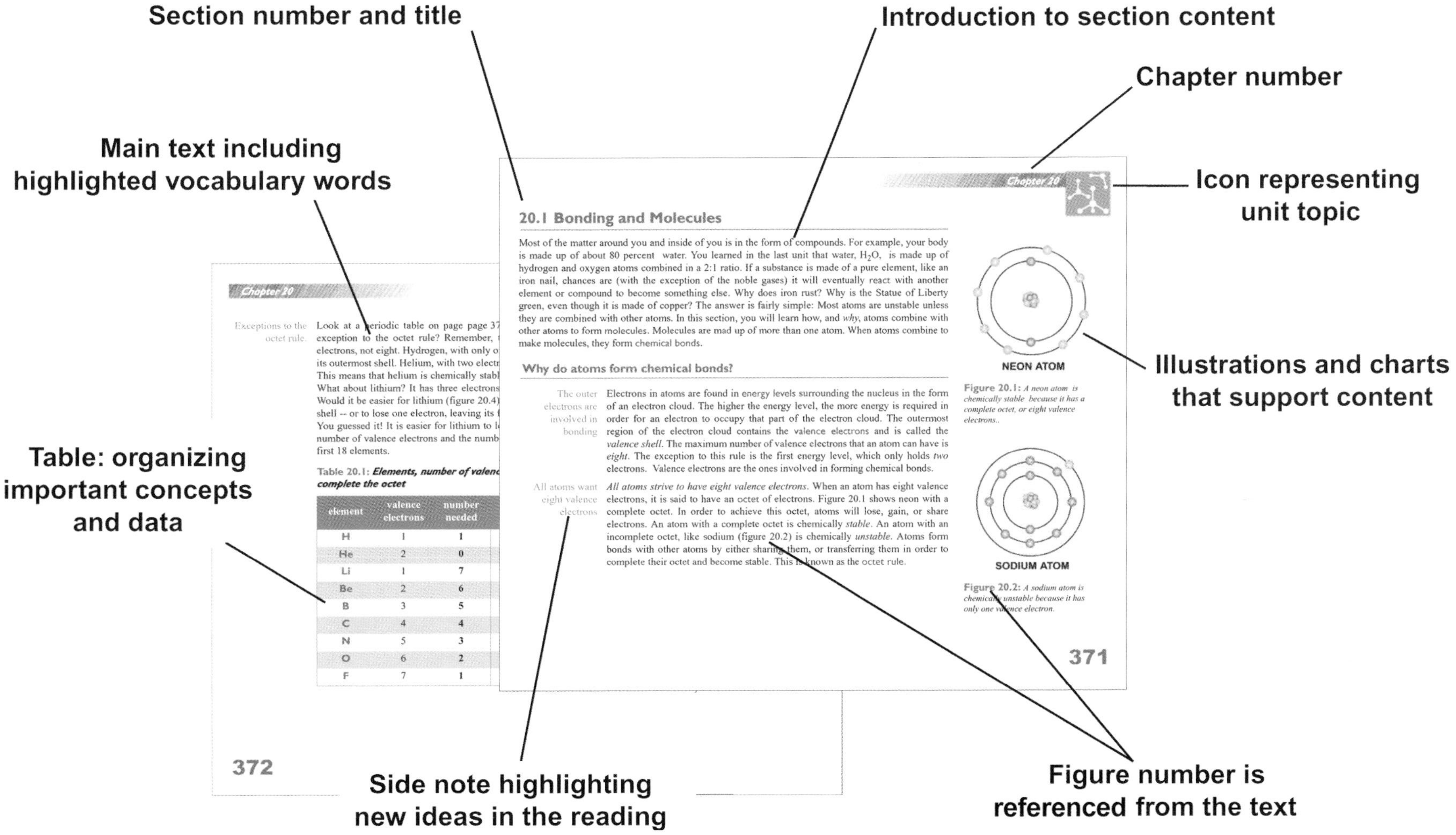

Section number and title

Introduction to section content

Chapter number

Icon representing unit topic

Main text including highlighted vocabulary words

Illustrations and charts that support content

Table: organizing important concepts and data

Side note highlighting new ideas in the reading

Figure number is referenced from the text

Chapter 20

Exceptions to the octet rule.

Look at a periodic table on page page 37 exception to the octet rule? Remember, electrons, not eight. Hydrogen, with only o its outermost shell. Helium, with two electr This means that helium is chemically stabl What about lithium? It has three electrons Would it be easier for lithium (figure 20.4) shell -- or to lose one electron, leaving its You guessed it! It is easier for lithium to l number of valence electrons and the numb first 18 elements.

Table 20.1: ***Elements, number of valenc complete the octet***

element	valence electrons	number needed
H	1	1
He	2	0
Li	1	7
Be	2	6
B	3	5
C	4	4
N	5	3
O	6	2
F	7	1

372

Chapter 20

20.1 Bonding and Molecules

Most of the matter around you and inside of you is in the form of compounds. For example, your body is made up of about 80 percent water. You learned in the last unit that water, H_2O, is made up of hydrogen and oxygen atoms combined in a 2:1 ratio. If a substance is made of a pure element, like an iron nail, chances are (with the exception of the noble gases) it will eventually react with another element or compound to become something else. Why does iron rust? Why is the Statue of Liberty green, even though it is made of copper? The answer is fairly simple: Most atoms are unstable unless they are combined with other atoms. In this section, you will learn how, and *why*, atoms combine with other atoms to form molecules. Molecules are mad up of more than one atom. When atoms combine to make molecules, they form chemical bonds.

Why do atoms form chemical bonds?

The outer electrons are involved in bonding

Electrons in atoms are found in energy levels surrounding the nucleus in the form of an electron cloud. The higher the energy level, the more energy is required in order for an electron to occupy that part of the electron cloud. The outermost region of the electron cloud contains the valence electrons and is called the *valence shell*. The maximum number of valence electrons that an atom can have is *eight*. The exception to this rule is the first energy level, which only holds *two* electrons. Valence electrons are the ones involved in forming chemical bonds.

All atoms want eight valence electrons

All atoms strive to have eight valence electrons. When an atom has eight valence electrons, it is said to have an octet of electrons. Figure 20.1 shows neon with a complete octet. In order to achieve this octet, atoms will lose, gain, or share electrons. An atom with a complete octet is chemically *stable*. An atom with an incomplete octet, like sodium (figure 20.2) is chemically *unstable*. Atoms form bonds with other atoms by either sharing them, or transferring them in order to complete their octet and become stable. This is known as the octet rule.

NEON ATOM

Figure 20.1: *A neon atom is chemically stable because it has a complete octet, or eight valence electrons.*

SODIUM ATOM

Figure 20.2: *A sodium atom is chemically unstable because it has only one valence electron.*

371

Investigation Text

Hear and you forget;see and you remember; do and you understand.

Confucius

Investigations are hands-on activities that accompany the student text. For each section of the text, you will complete a hands-on activity, answer key questions, and find results. The *Investigation Manual* is a softcover book that contains Investigation activities that accompany each section you are reading. Sometimes you will read the student text before doing an Investigation activity, but usually you will complete the Investigations before you read the section.

The Investigations are the heart of the CPO program. We believe that you will learn and remember more if you have many opportunities to explore science through hands-on activities that use equipment to collect data and solve problems. Most of the Investigations rely on the use of CPO equipment to collect accurate data, explore possibilities and answer the key question. The equipment is easy to set up, and your teacher will help you learn how to use the equipment properly.

Features of the Investigation

Key question: Each Investigation starts with a key question that conveys the focus of the lesson. This question tells you what information you need to collect in order to answer the questions at the end of the Investigation.

Data tables: Data tables help you collect and organize your data in a systematic manner.

Learning objectives (goals): At the top of each investigation are the learning goals. These statements will explain what you will have learned and what you be able to do after completing the Investigation.

Brief introduction: This information helps you understand why the exercise is important to complete and, in most cases, how it connects to other sections of your reading.

Icons and section title: The icon is a reminder of the unit that you are studying. The section title corresponds to the reading in your student text.

Numbered steps: The Investigation sequence numbers point out the sequence of steps you will need to follow to successfully complete the Investigation. These steps highlight specific stages of the scientific method such as: following directions, completing hands-on experiments, collecting and analyzing data and presenting the results. The *Applying your Knowledge* step asks you to reflect on what you have learned and to explain your findings.

Illustrations: The illustrations support your understanding of the Investigation procedures.

Fill-in answer sheets: Your teacher will provide you with answer sheets to fill in the data tables and written responses. At times your teacher may collect this data to compile class results. You can also use the sheets to reinforce your reading in your student text.

INVESTIGATION PAGES

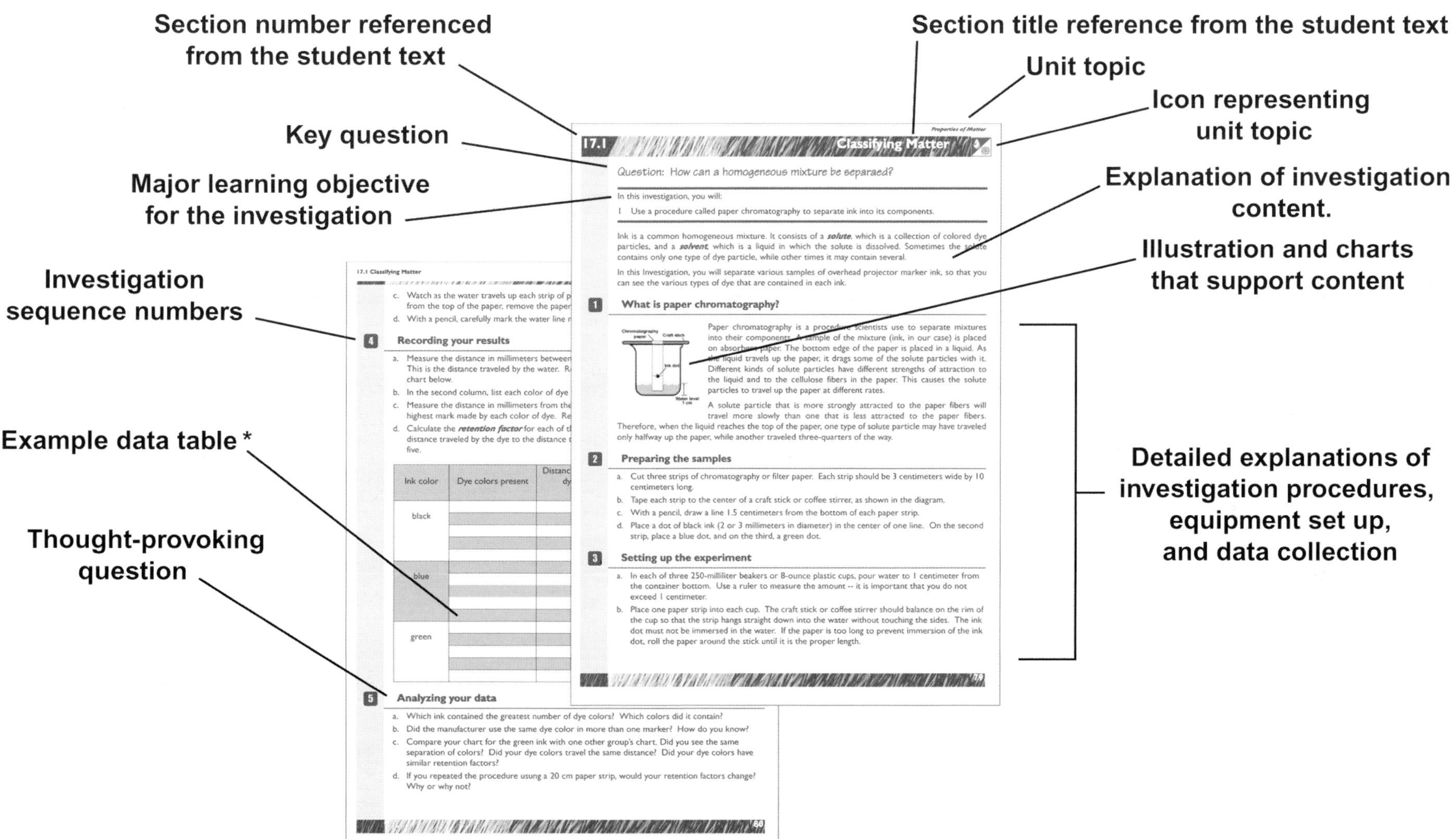

* Note: All data and answers to questions will be written on a separate fill-in answer sheet.

Student Text Chapter Pages

Each *Unit* has several sections which make up a *Chapter*. *Chapter pages* outline what you will learn in the Chapter and the Investigations (hands-on activities) that complement the readings. The Chapter pages serve as a map that directs you to the major concepts that will be covered. It is important to refer back to these pages to help you focus your learning on the most important ideas introduced in the chapter.

Features of the Chapter Pages

Introduction: The Chapter page introduction summarizes what you will have learned when you finish all the sections and Investigations. Refer back to this summary after you finish the chapter to check your understanding, and use this summary when studying for exams.

Chapter contents and Investigations: This listing with the chapter numbers outlines the key questions and the content of the Investigations that accompany your student readings. When you read the questions and Investigation descriptions, you will be able to see how the Investigations help you understand the skills and concepts introduced in each chapter.

Learning goals: These goals are the major ideas that you will explore throughout the chapter. You should check your learning by going back to this page to make sure you can explain each of these concepts in writing or to another person.

Vocabulary: The list of vocabulary words at the beginning of the chapter will familiarize you with the words in the chapter. Understanding the science vocabulary will help you learn the concepts in the readings. Thinking and guessing about the meaning of the words before reading and then seeing how close you were to the correct meaning is a good learning tool.

Unit Icons Guide

Unit icons are used to identify what unit topic you are studying. You will see these icons on the Chapter and Investigation corners.

F = ma	Unit One: Force and Motion		Unit Six: Properties of Matter
	Unit Two: Work and Energy		Unit Seven: Changes in Matter
	Unit Three: Electricity and Magnetism		Unit Eight: Water and Solutions
	Unit Four: Sound and Waves		Unit Nine: Heating and Cooling
	Unit Five: Light and Optics		

CHAPTER PAGES

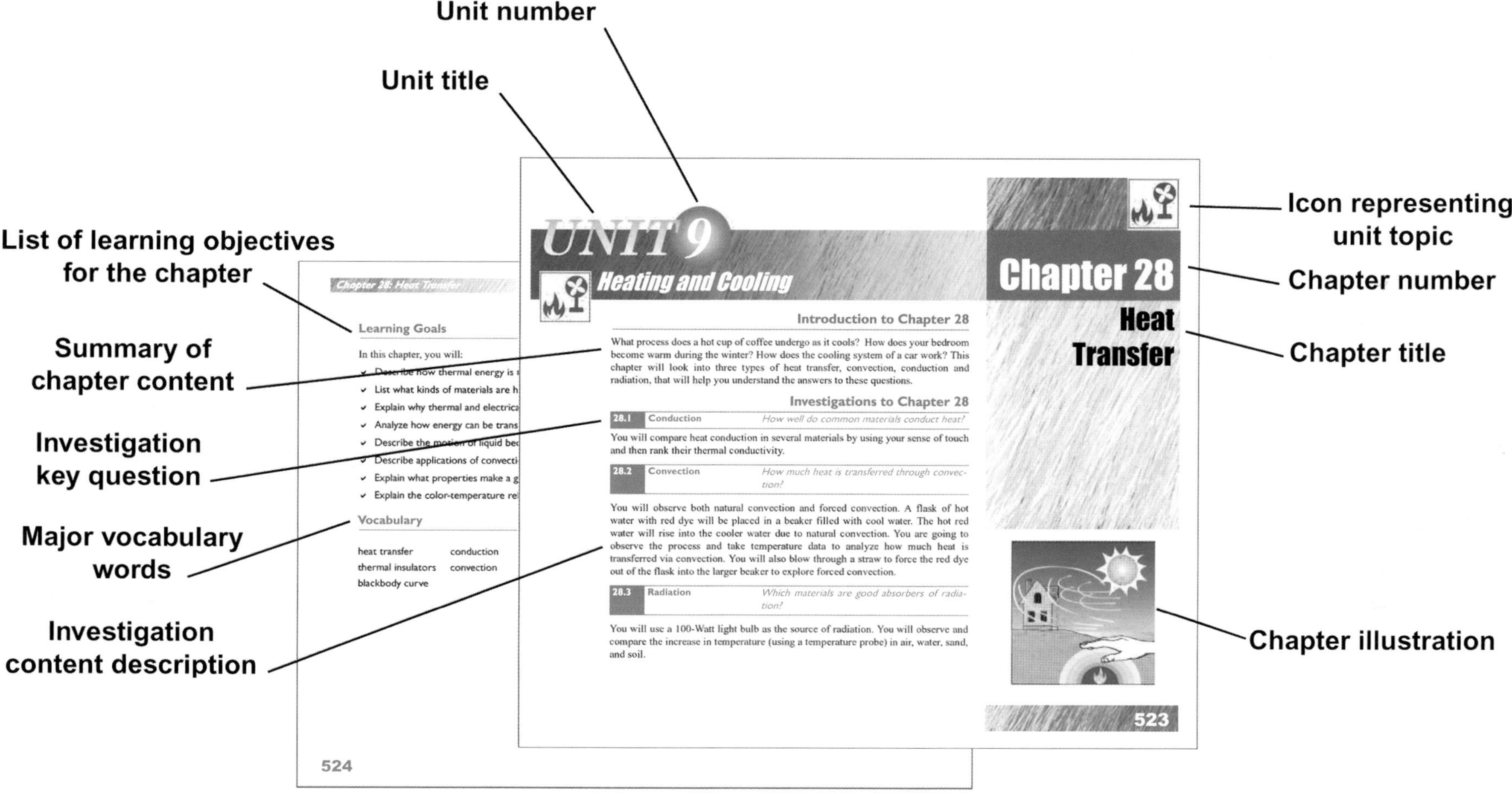

Unit number
Unit title
List of learning objectives for the chapter
Summary of chapter content
Investigation key question
Major vocabulary words
Investigation content description
Icon representing unit topic
Chapter number
Chapter title
Chapter illustration
UNIT 9
Heating and Cooling
Chapter 28
Heat Transfer
Introduction to Chapter 28
What process does a hot cup of coffee undergo as it cools? How does your bedroom become warm during the winter? How does the cooling system of a car work? This chapter will look into three types of heat transfer, convection, conduction and radiation, that will help you understand the answers to these questions.
Investigations to Chapter 28
28.1 Conduction How well do common materials conduct heat?
You will compare heat conduction in several materials by using your sense of touch and then rank their thermal conductivity.
28.2 Convection How much heat is transferred through convection?
You will observe both natural convection and forced convection. A flask of hot water with red dye will be placed in a beaker filled with cool water. The hot red water will rise into the cooler water due to natural convection. You are going to observe the process and take temperature data to analyze how much heat is transferred via convection. You will also blow through a straw to force the red dye out of the flask into the larger beaker to explore forced convection.
28.3 Radiation Which materials are good absorbers of radiation?
You will use a 100-Watt light bulb as the source of radiation. You will observe and compare the increase in temperature (using a temperature probe) in air, water, sand, and soil.
523
Chapter 28: Heat Transfer
Learning Goals
In this chapter, you will:
List what kinds of materials are h
Explain why thermal and electrica
Analyze how energy can be trans
Describe applications of convecti
Explain what properties make a g
Explain the color-temperature re
Vocabulary
heat transfer
conduction
thermal insulators
convection
blackbody curve
524

Using Icons to Locate Information

The mind is not a vessel to be filled but a fire to be kindled
Plutarch

Icons are small pictures that convey meaning without words. In the CPO program, we use icons to point out things such as safety considerations, real-world connections, and when to find information in the reference pages, complete a writing assignment, or work in a team. The chart below lists the icons that refer to instruction and safety and the meaning of each one:

Icon	Meaning	Icon	Meaning
	Reading: you need to read for understanding.		**Real-world connections:** you are learning how the information is used in the world today.
	Hands-on activity: you will complete a lab or other activity.		**Teamwork:** you will be working in a team to complete the activity.
	Time: tells how much time the activity may take.		**Economics:** you are learning how science impacts the economy.
	Research: you will need to look up facts and information.	a/b	**Formula:** you are reading information about a formula or you will need to use an equation to solve a problem.
	Setup: directions for equipment setup are found here.		**Use extreme caution:** follow all instructions carefully to avoid injury to yourself or others.
	History: you are reading historical information.		**Electrical hazard:** follow all instructions carefully while using electrical components to avoid injury to yourself or others.
	Environment: you are reading information about the environment or how to protect our environment.		**Wear safety goggles:** requires you to protect your eyes from injury.
	Writing: you need to reflect and write about what you have learned.		**Wear a lab apron:** requires you to protect your clothing and skin.
JAN FEB MAR	**Project:** you need to complete an assignment that will take longer than one day.		**Wear gloves:** requires you to protect your hands from injury from heat or chemicals.
	Apply your knowledge: refers to activities or problems that ask you to use your skills in different ways.		**Clean-up:** includes cleaning and putting away reusable equipment and supplies, and disposing of leftover materials.

Unit 1: Forces and Motion

Unit 2: Work and Energy

Unit 3: Electricity and Magnetism

CONTENTS

Unit 4: Sound and Waves

Unit 5: Light and Optics

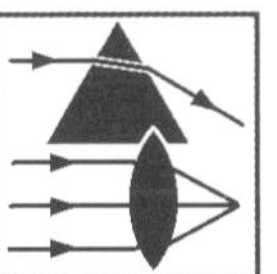

Unit 6: Properties of Matter

Unit 7: Changes in Matter

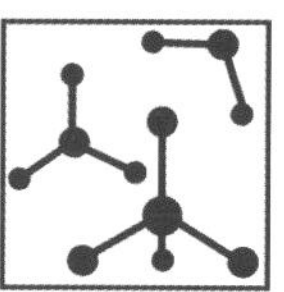

Unit 8: Water and Solutions

Unit 9: Heating and Cooling

UNIT 1 Forces and Motion

Chapter 1 Science and Measurement

Introduction to Chapter 1

This chapter is about measurement and how we use measurements and experiments to learn about the world. Two fundamental properties of the universe that we want to measure are time and distance. A third important measurement, speed, tells us how time and distance relate to the motion of objects.

Investigations for Chapter 1

1.1	Time and Distance	*How do we measure and describe the world around us?*

In the first Investigation, you will use electronic timers and other measuring tools to explore precision measurement of the fundamental quantities of time and distance.

1.2	Investigations and Experiments	*How do we ask questions and get answers from nature?*

Investigating a car rolling down a ramp may seem simple, but it is difficult to understand what is really happening. The key is learning to design careful experiments that test our ideas with observations. In this Investigation, you will examine the motion of a car on a ramp to explore the action of variables in experiments.

1.3	Speed	*What is speed and how is it measured?*

The words *fast* and *slow* are not precise enough for many questions in science. We need to know how fast is fast. You will learn to determine the speed of moving objects with great accuracy. This Investigation of speed will be the foundation for answering many questions about motion.

Learning Goals

In this chapter, you will:

- ✔ Accurately measure time using electronic timers and photogates.
- ✔ Use decimals to represent fractions of a second.
- ✔ Develop a research question or hypothesis that can be tested.
- ✔ Identify the variables that affect motion.
- ✔ Develop an experimental technique that achieves consistent results.
- ✔ Draw conclusions from experimental results.
- ✔ Accurately measure distance.
- ✔ Identify metric and English units of distance.
- ✔ Convert between units of distance.
- ✔ Calculate speed in units of inches per second, feet per second, and centimeters per second.

Vocabulary

cause and effect	experimental technique	metric system	time
control variables	experimental variable	procedure	trial
controlled experiment	hypothesis	research question	variables
distance	investigation	scientific evidence	velocity
English system	length	scientific method	
experiment	measurements	second	

1.1 Time and Distance

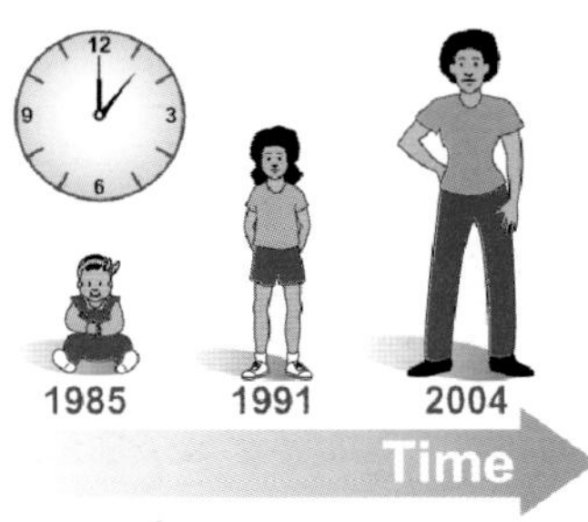

Figure 1.1: *The flow of time is an important part of our experience of life. To understand nature we need to investigate how things change with time.*

In this section, you will learn about two fundamental properties of the universe: time and distance. Learning about how things change with time motivates much of our study of nature. We are born and our bodies change as time passes. The steady forward movement of time creates a present, a past, and a future.

Another important quality of the universe is that it has three dimensions. To observe and learn about objects, their sizes, and their motion in the universe, we need units of length. Common measures for length are inches and meters. Other units of length are used for very small distances like atomic sizes and very large distances like those between cities.

Two ways to think about time

What time is it? There are two ways we think about time (figure 1.2). One meaning for time is to identify a particular moment. If we ask "What time is it?" we usually want to know time relative to the rest of the universe and everyone in it. For example, 3:00 PM, Eastern Time, on April 21 tells the time at a certain place on Earth.

How much time? Another meaning for time is a quantity, or interval of time. The question "How much time?" is asking for an interval of time with a beginning and end. For example, we might measure how much time has passed between the start of a race and when the first runner crosses the finish line.

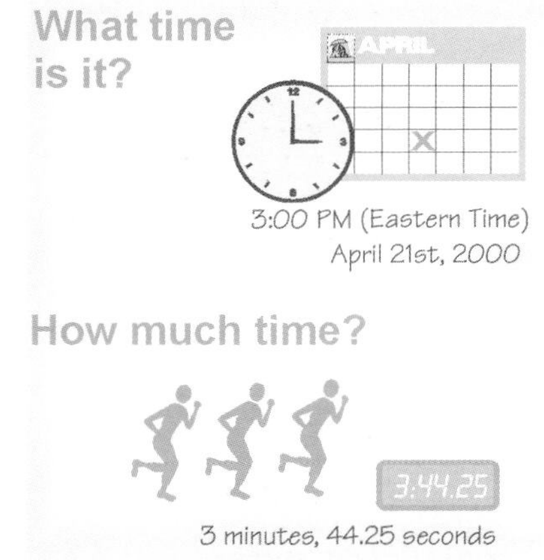

Figure 1.2: *There are two different ways to understand time.*

How is time measured? For most of physical science we measure and record time in seconds. Some other units of time you may see are hours, minutes, days, and years. Choose the unit most suited to the time you want to measure. Short races are best measured in seconds while the age of a person is best measured in years.

Time comes in mixed units

Many calculations require that time be expressed in seconds. However, seconds are very short. Hours and minutes are more convenient for everyday time measurement. As a result, time intervals are often in mixed units, such as 2 minutes and 15 seconds. If you have a time interval that is in mixed units you will have to convert it to seconds before doing calculations. Table 1.1 gives some useful relationships between units of time.

Table 1.1: *Some units for time*

Time Unit	How Many Seconds	How Many Days
1 second	1	0.0001157
1 minute	60	0.00694
1 hour	3,600	0.0417
1 day	86,400	1
1 year	31,557,600	365.25
1 century	3,155,760,000	36,525

Why we have different units for time

How many seconds have there been since you were born? From the table you should see that for every year there are 31,557,600 seconds. To give your age in seconds would be silly. The number would be too big and change too fast. Years is a better unit for describing people's ages.

How do you read a timer?

Most timing equipment (including digital timers) displays time in three units: hours, minutes, and seconds. Colons separate the units into hours, minutes, and seconds. The seconds number may have a decimal that shows fractions of a second. To read a timer you need to recognize and separate out the different units. Figure 1.3 shows a timer display that reads 1 hour, 26 minutes, and 31.25 seconds.

How do you convert to seconds?

To convert a time to seconds you have to first separate out all the different units. For physics problems, the starting units will often be hours, minutes, and seconds. Follow the list below to convert any amount of time to seconds.

1 Separate the total time into the amount of time in each unit.

2 Convert each separate quantity of time to seconds.

3 Add all the seconds.

Figure 1.3: *Electronic timers have displays that show mixed units. Colons (:) separate the units.*

Example:

Convert the time in figure 1.3 to seconds.

Solution:

Separate time into each unit.

1 hour

26 minutes

31.25 seconds

Convert each different unit into seconds.

1 hour × 3,600 seconds/hour = 3,600 seconds

26 minutes × 60 seconds/minute = 1,560 seconds

Then add all the seconds.

$$\begin{array}{r} 3{,}600.00 \\ 1{,}560.00 \\ +\quad 31.25 \\ \hline 5{,}191.25 \text{ seconds} \end{array}$$

Measuring distance

Distance is measured in units of length

Distance describes how far it is from one point to another. Distance is measured in units of length. Like other measurements, distance always has a number and a unit. It is hard to say precisely how far something has moved without units. It would be silly to ask someone to walk 25. They would ask, "Twenty-five what?" There is a big difference between 25 feet and 25 miles! Without units, distance measurements are meaningless.

There are two common systems

There are two common systems of units that are used for measuring distance. You need to understand both systems. The English system uses inches, feet, and miles. The metric system uses millimeters, centimeters, meters, and kilometers.

Reading the English ruler

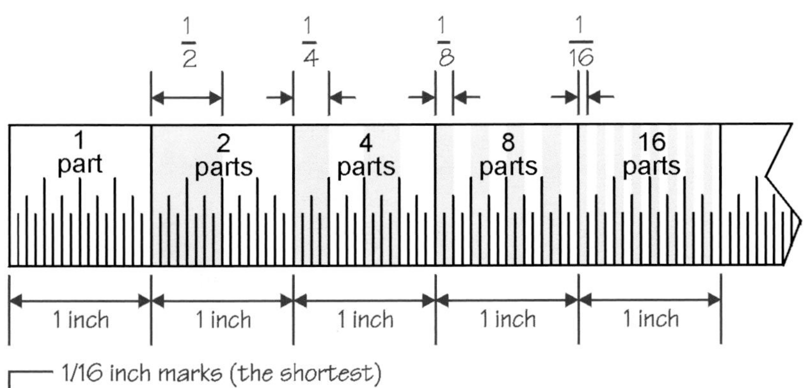

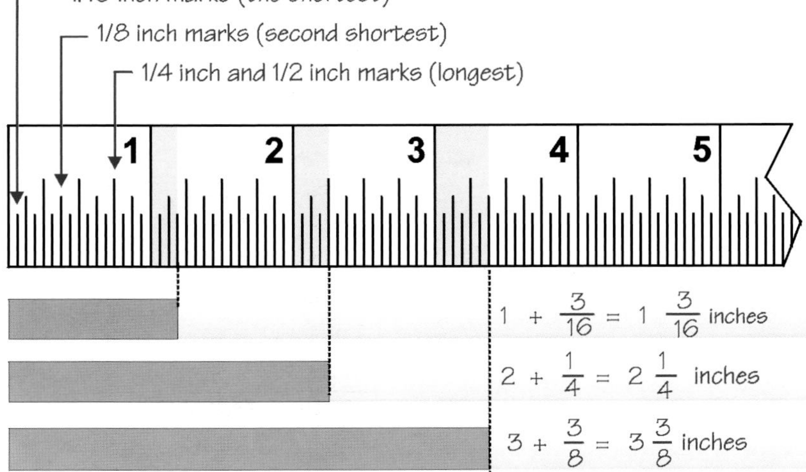

Reading the metric ruler (meter stick)

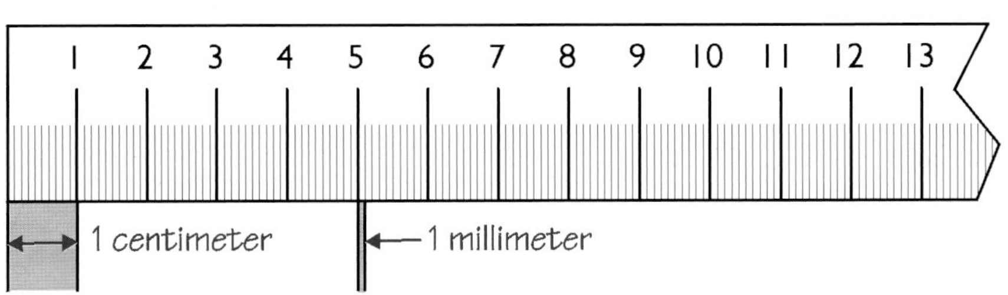

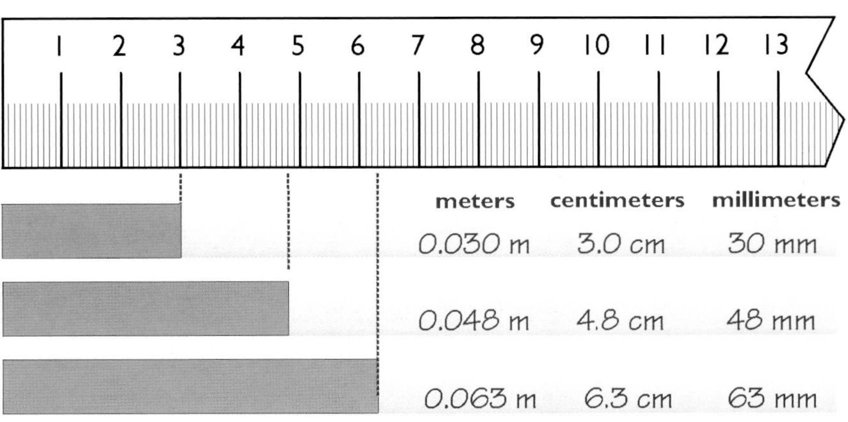

Why are there so many different ways to measure the same thing?

Why units were invented

Units were invented so people could communicate amounts to each other. For example, suppose you want to buy 10 feet of rope. The person selling the rope takes out a ruler that is only 10 inches long (instead of 12 inches) and counts out 10 lengths of the ruler. Do you get your money's worth of rope? Of course not! For communication to be successful, everyone's idea of one foot (or any other unit of measure) must be the same. Figure 1.4 illustrates a hot dog vendor trying to sell a foot-long hot dog that is only 10 inches long. If the girl were to buy a hot dog, would she be getting what the sign says that she is paying for?

Figure 1.4: *The hot dog vendor and the girl have different ideas about how long a foot is.*

Scientists use metric units

Almost all fields of science use metric units because they are so much easier to work with. In the English system, there are 12 inches in a foot, 3 feet in a yard, and 5,280 feet in a mile. In the metric system, there are 10 millimeters in a centimeter, 100 centimeters in a meter, and 1,000 meters in a kilometer. Factors of 10 are easier to remember than 12, 3, and 5,280. The diagram below will help you get a sense for the metric units of distance.

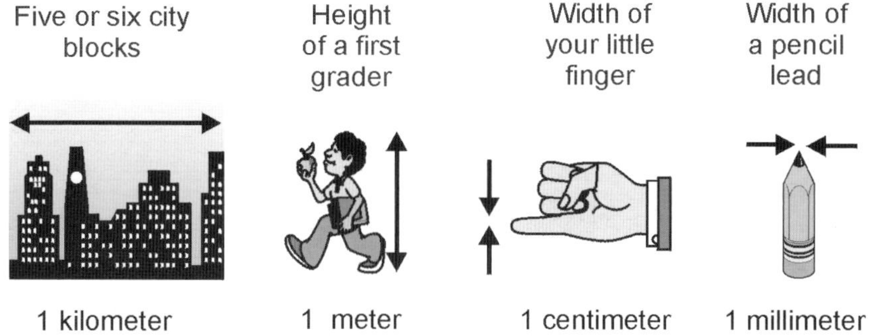

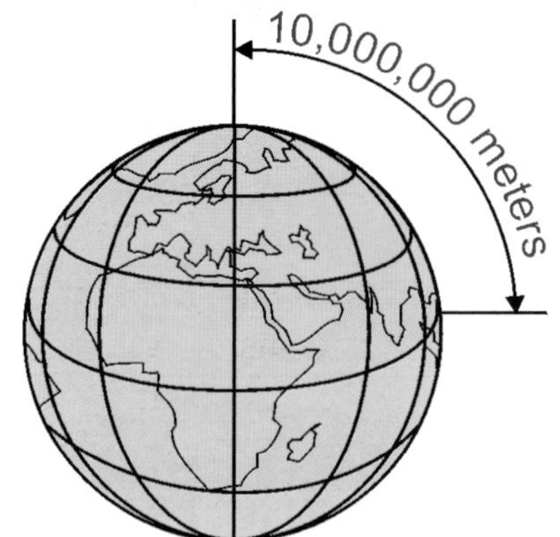

Figure 1.5: *In 1791, a meter was defined as 1/10,000,000 of the distance from a pole of Earth to its equator. Today the meter is defined more accurately using wavelengths of light.*

We use units every day

In your life, and in this book, we use both English and metric units. We measure some quantities, like power and wavelength, in metric units. We measure other quantities, like weight and speed, in both metric and English units. Science measurements are always metric, but you may use units of pounds and miles per hour in your daily experience. In many other countries, people use metric units for everyday measurements.

1.2 Investigations and Experiments

Science is about figuring out cause and effect relationships. If we do something, what happens? If we make a ramp steeper, how much faster will a car roll down? This is an easy question. However, the process we use to answer this question is the same process used to answer more difficult questions, like what keeps the moon in orbit around the Earth?

The rules of nature are often well hidden. We ask questions about nature and then design experiments to find clues. A series of one or more experiments that helps us answer a question is called an **investigation**. In this section you will learn how to design investigations using the scientific method.

Designing experiments

What is an experiment? An **experiment** is any situation we set up to observe what happens. You do experiments every day. You might wear your hair a new way to see if people treat you differently. That is an experiment.

Measurements can be recorded In science, we usually plan our experiments to give us **measurements**, which are observations we can record and think about. You might ask 10 friends if they like your hair the new way or the old way. That would be a way of collecting data from your experiment. From the results of the survey, you might decide to leave your hair the new way, or change it back. We usually do experiments for a reason, because we want to know something.

Experiments start with questions Experiments usually have a question associated with them. The question might be "Will people like my short hair better?" Sometimes you are aware of the question and sometimes you are not. If you push a door to see if it opens, that is an experiment. You often do it without thinking about the question. But the question is still there. What will happen if I push on this door?

Answers from nature Experiments are the way we ask questions of nature. You might want to know if salt water freezes at a lower temperature than fresh water. To answer the question you do an experiment. Place containers of salt water and fresh water in a freezer. Observe the water samples, and when ice forms measure and record the temperature of the sample. You can now compare the freezing points. Nature answers our questions about how things work through the results of experiments.

Figure 1.6: *Changing your hairstyle to see what people think is an experiment. You are setting up a situation to see what happens. We all do experiments every day.*

The process of science

How did people learn science?

Have you ever wondered why people know so much about the world? Nobody told Sir Isaac Newton about how force and motion worked. There was no physics course he could take to learn it. Newton did his own experiments and figured it out. Once he knew, he told others, who told others, and now this course will tell *you*. But, we understand force and motion today because people did the original experiments to figure it out.

Scientists learn new information

Learning new information about the world—and the universe—is the most important thing scientists do. It is also important to *you*. Every day you have to figure out how to solve problems, like how to get your car to start in the cold. Science is a way of collecting information that can help you solve problems.

Experiments provide clues

Suppose your car will not start. You probably check obvious things first. Looking at your gas gauge is a simple experiment to test if there is any gas in your tank. Another experiment is to check the battery by trying the lights. If you are a mechanic, every experiment provides a clue. You keep doing experiments until you have enough clues to figure out what's wrong with the car.

Why doesn't the car start?

Is there any gas?
Is the battery dead?
Are the wires loose?

Scientific evidence

Every experiment you do provides you with evidence. If you are a good mechanic you might try each experiment a couple of times to be sure of your evidence. For example, you might test the lights two or three times to see if the battery is really dead or maybe you just did not turn the switch all the way the first time. Scientific evidence is any observation that can be repeated with the same result.

The Earth is round?

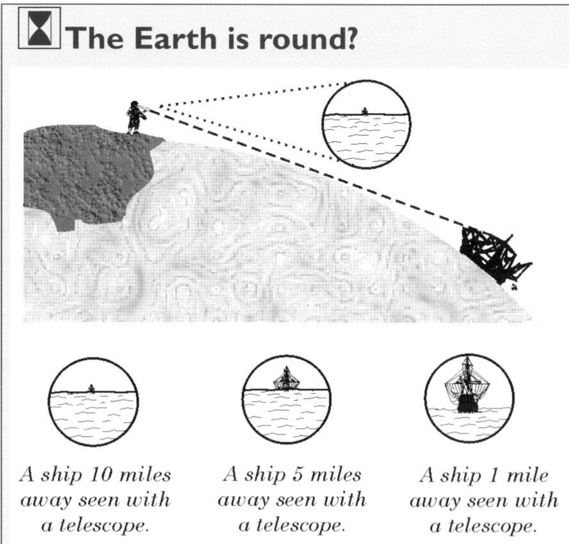

A ship 10 miles away seen with a telescope. *A ship 5 miles away seen with a telescope.* *A ship 1 mile away seen with a telescope.*

A good example of science is how people figured out the Earth is round. If you look out your window, you don't see a round Earth. The Earth looks flat. People figured out it was round by thinking scientifically about what they saw and experienced.

People saw that the tops of ships appeared first as the ships approached shore. This could be explained if the Earth was round.

Over a period of time people collected all kinds of evidence that suggested the Earth was round. The evidence did not make sense if the Earth was flat. When there was enough evidence, people were convinced and understood that the Earth really is round.

The scientific method

The scientific method The process you use to figure out what is wrong with your car is an example of the scientific method. As you try to fix your car, you ask yourself questions (Is there any gas? Is the battery dead?) and formulate ideas (or hypotheses) about what is wrong. By testing your ideas, you are experimenting and collecting data. You may be able to use this data to fix the car. Even if you conclude that the car can't be fixed, you have learned information to use the next time you are faced with a similar problem. Table 1.2 shows the steps of the scientific method.

Steps in the scientific method

Table 1.2: *Steps in the scientific method*

Step	Example
1 Ask a question.	Why doesn't the car start?
2 Formulate a hypothesis.	Maybe the battery is dead.
3 Design and conduct an experiment.	Turn the lights on to test the battery.
4 Collect and analyze data.	The lights go on.
5 Make a tentative conclusion.	Battery is OK.
6 Test conclusion, or if necessary, refine the question, and go through each step again.	Are the ignition wires loose or wet?

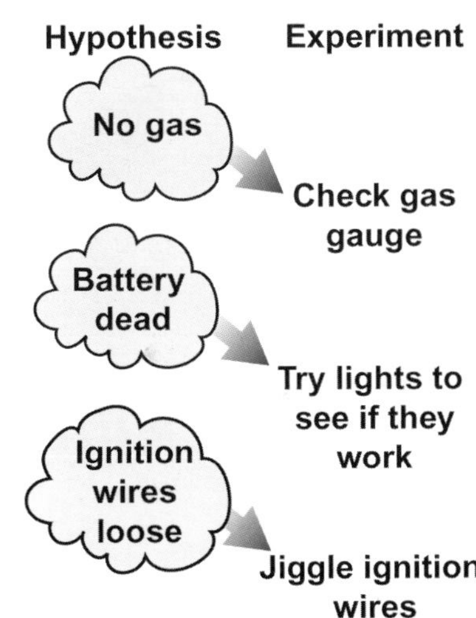

Figure 1.7: *Science is a process of collecting information through observation and experiment. The information is used to solve problems and test ideas about how things work.*

The research question and hypothesis

A research question

Suppose you are interested in how the angle of a hill affects the speed of a car rolling down. Your **research question** could be, "How is the speed of the car down the ramp affected by changing the steepness of the hill?"

The hypothesis

It is often useful to start with a guess (or hunch) about how something will happen. For example, you might start with a guess that making the ramp steeper will make the car roll faster. Your guesses or intuitions can take the form of a **hypothesis**, a prediction that can be tested by experiment. A good hypothesis might be: "Steeper hills result in cars with faster speeds." The hypothesis represents the tentative answer to the question "How is the speed of the car down the ramp affected by the angle of the hill?"

Hypothesis:
Cars go faster on steeper hills.

A hypothesis is an educated guess about what will happen.

Making a good hypothesis or research question

Forming a good hypothesis or research question depends on already knowing a little about how things might happen. You need to do a little experimenting before trying to form a hypothesis. For this reason, the word "hypothesis" is also defined as "an educated guess." Your experience with how objects roll down a smooth surface will help you make a hypothesis for a car and ramp experiment. However, don't worry if you cannot think of a hypothesis before you start your experiment. A good hypothesis can only be formed when you know a little about what is going to happen. The more experience you have, the better your hypothesis will be. It may be helpful to keep in mind that good hypotheses and research questions are those that you can test with an experiment.

Happy accidents

Not all discoveries in science are made using the scientific method! In fact, many important new discoveries and inventions happen by trial and error, a lucky experiment, or by accident.

The discovery of a way to waterproof fabric is a good example. Scientists tried to stretch Teflon® a special kind of plastic into thin films. The plastic kept breaking. One day, in frustration, one scientist just ripped a piece very fast. It stretched without breaking! The resulting thin plastic film was waterproof but let water vapor through.

Stretched Teflon® film eventually became a breathable waterproof fabric called GoreTex®, used for outdoor clothing.

Designing experiments

Start with a good question

Will a car roll faster down a steeper hill?

This is a good research question because we can test it with an experiment. We could set up ramps at different angles and measure the speeds of cars as they roll down the ramp. Once you have a good question, you can design an experiment to help you find the answer.

Suppose you find that a car on a steep ramp rolls faster than a car on a ramp at a lower angle. Can you say that your experiment proves steeper ramps make cars go faster?

Identify all the factors when designing experiments

Maybe, and maybe not. Before you can design a good experiment, you must identify all the factors that affect how fast the car moves down the ramp. Maybe you pushed the car on one ramp. Maybe one car was heavier than another. Your observation of higher speed *because* the angle was steeper *could* be correct. Or, the speed could be higher for another reason, like a push at the start.

Variables

Factors that affect the results of an experiment are called variables. You can think about variables in terms of cause and effect. The weight of the car is one variable that may have an effect on the speed of the car. Some other variables are the angle of the ramp and how far down the ramp you measure the speed.

Change one thing at a time

When you can identify more than one variable that could affect the results of your experiment, it is best to change *only one variable at a time*. For example, if you change both the weight of the car and the angle of the ramp, you won't know which of the two variables caused your speed to change. If you want to test the effect of changing the angle, keep ALL the other variables the same.

Control variables and experimental variables

The variable that you change is called the experimental variable. The variables that you keep the same are called control variables. When you change one variable and control all of the others, we call it a controlled experiment. Controlled experiments are the preferred way to get reliable scientific evidence. If you observe that something happens (like the car goes faster), you know *why* it happened (because the ramp was steeper). There is no confusion over which variable caused the change.

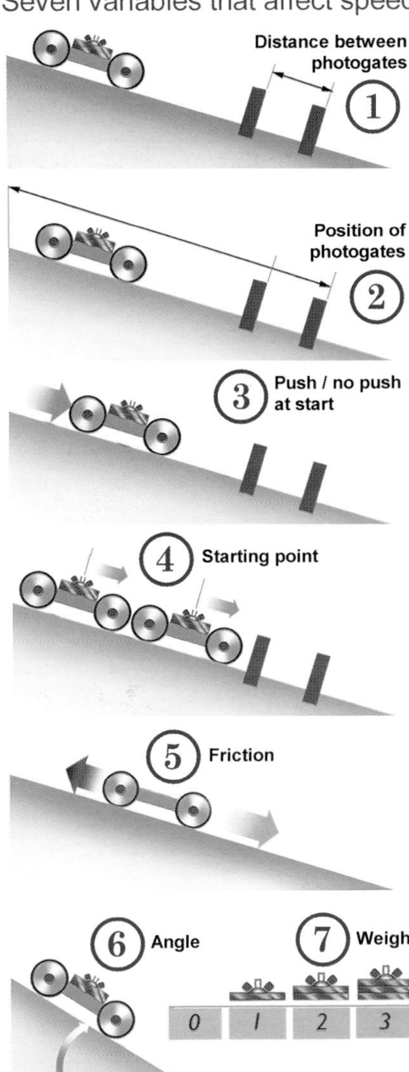

Figure 1.8: *Variables that affect a car rolling down a ramp.*

Experimental techniques

Experiments often have several trials

Many experiments are done over and over with only one variable changed. For example, you might roll a car down a ramp 10 times, each with a different angle. Each time you run the experiment is called a trial. To be sure of your results, each trial must be as close to identical as possible to all the others. The only exception should be the one variable you are testing.

Experimental technique

Your experimental technique is how you actually do the experiment. For example, you might release the car using one finger on top. If this is your technique, you want to do it the same way every time. By developing a good technique, you make sure your results accurately show the effects of changing your experimental variable. If your technique is sloppy, you may not be able to tell if any results are due to technique or changing your variable.

Procedures

The procedure is a collection of all the techniques you use to do an experiment. Your procedure for testing the ramp angle might have several steps (figure 1.9). Good scientists keep careful track of their procedures so they can come back another time and repeat their experiments. Writing the procedures down in a lab notebook is a good way to keep track (figure 1.10).

Scientific results must always be repeatable

It is important that your experiments produce measurements that are reliable and accurate. What good would a new discovery or invention be if nobody believed you? Having good techniques and procedures is the best way to be sure of your results.

Scientific discoveries and inventions must always be able to be tested by someone other than you. If other people can follow your procedure and get the same results, then most scientists would accept your results as being true. Writing good procedures is the best way to ensure that others can repeat and verify your experiments.

1. Drop the car from the top using one finger to release.

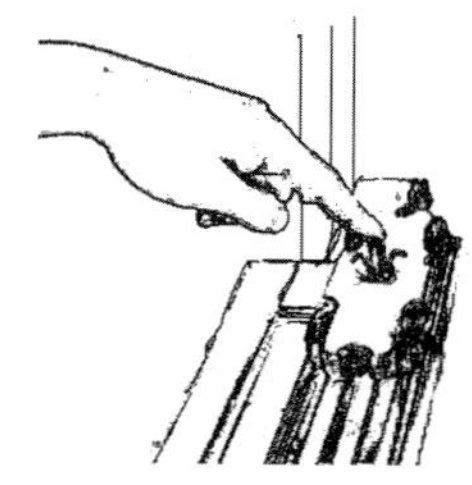

2. Use photogates to measure speed every 10 centimeters.

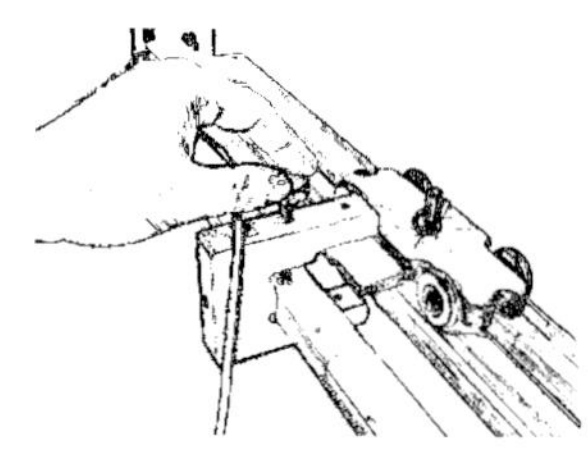

Figure 1.9: *A procedure is a collection of all the techniques that someone else would need to repeat your experiments in order to confirm your results.*

Measure from the bottom of the ramp and set the distance to 12" between photogates.
Use only one weight on the car.
Have timer set to measure with both photogates.

12"

Figure 1.10: *A notebook keeps your observations and procedures from getting lost or being forgotten.*

1.3 Speed

Just saying that something is fast is often not enough description for a scientist. You can easily walk faster than a turtle, yet you would not say walking was fast compared with the speed of driving a car. In this section, you will learn how to be very precise about speed.

What do we mean by speed?

- Exactly how fast are you walking?
- How many meters do you walk for each second?
- Do you always walk the same number of meters every second?

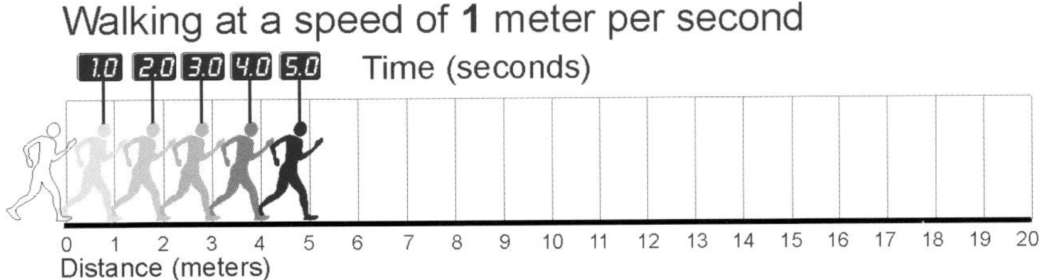

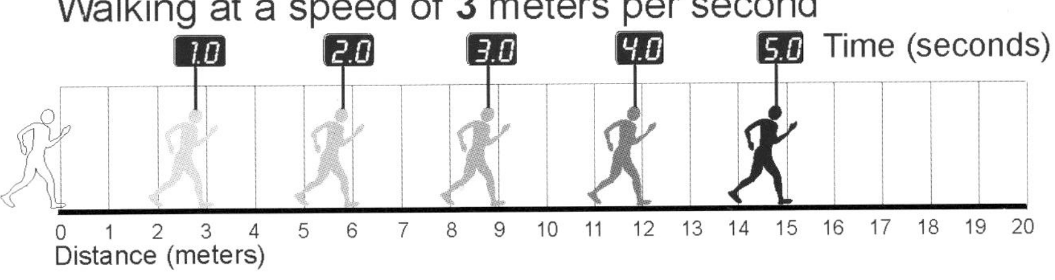

What is speed?

Objects in the world are rarely at rest for very long. Describing movement from place to place naturally leads you to think about speed. The speed of an object is a measure of how quickly the object gets from one place to another. Speed is a characteristic of all objects. Even objects that are standing still have a speed of zero.

Fast trains

Fast trains are being used for transportation in several countries. In Japan, where cities are crowded, people have to travel from far away to reach their jobs. Japan's 500 Series train is the world's fastest, operating at a speed of 300 km/h (186 mph).

In France, the TGV goes almost as fast. In the United States, Amtrak runs high-speed trains from Boston to Washington. Fast trains are also being considered in California and the Midwest.

Fast trains offer benefits like performance and friendliness to the environment. As airports become more crowded, the use of fast trains for long-distance travel will probably increase.

Calculating speed

Calculating speed

There are several ways to look at the concept of speed. In the simplest interpretation, speed is the distance traveled divided by the time taken. For example, if you drive 90 miles in 1.5 hours (figure 1.11), then your speed is 90 miles divided by 1.5 hours, equal to 60 miles per hour. To determine a speed, you need to know two things:

- The distance traveled
- The time taken

Speed is calculated by taking the distance traveled divided by the time taken.

Units for speed

Since speed is a ratio of distance over time, the units for speed are a ratio of distance units over time units. If distance is in miles and time in hours, then speed is expressed in miles per hour (miles/hours). We will often measure distance in centimeters or meters, and time in seconds. The speeds we calculate would then be in units of centimeters/second or meters/second. Table 1.3 shows many different units commonly used for speed.

What does "per" mean?

The word "per" means "for every" or "for each." The speed of 60 miles per hour is really a shorthand for saying 60 miles *for each* hour. When used with units, the "per" also means "divided by." The quantity before the word per is divided by the quantity after it. For example, if you want speed in meters per second, you have to divide meters by seconds.

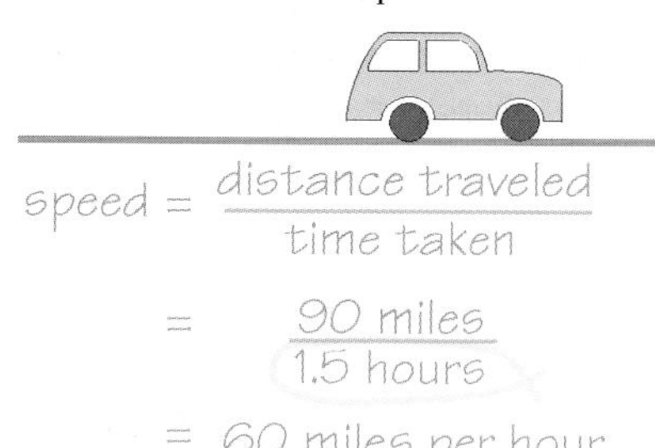

Problem:
A car goes 90 miles in one hour and 30 minutes. What is the speed of the car?
speed = distance traveled / time taken
= 90 miles / 1.5 hours
= 60 miles per hour

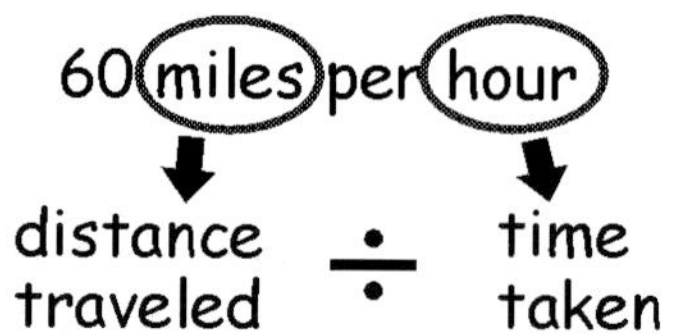

Figure 1.11: *If you drive 90 miles in 1.5 hours, your speed is 60 miles per hour. This is calculated by dividing the distance traveled (90 miles) by the time taken (1.5 hours).*

Table 1.3: ***Some Common Units for Speed***

Distance	Time	Speed	Abbreviation
meters	seconds	meters per second	m/sec
kilometers	hours	kilometers per hour	km/h
centimeters	seconds	centimeters per second	cm/sec
miles	hours	miles per hour	mph
inches	seconds	inches per second	in/sec, ips
feet	minutes	feet per minute	ft/min, fpm

Relationships between distance, speed, and time

How far did you go if you drove for 2 hours at 60 mph?

Mixing up distance, time, and speed

This seems like a fair question. We know speed is the distance traveled divided by the time taken. Now we are given the time and the speed. We are asked to find the distance. How do you take the new information and figure out an answer?

Let the letter v stand for "speed," the letter d stand for "distance traveled," and the letter t stand for "time taken." If we remember that the letters stand for those words, we can now write our definition of speed much faster.

Speed

$$v = \frac{d}{t}$$

Speed (m/sec) → v; d ← Distance traveled (meters); t ← Time taken (seconds)

Using formulas

Also remember that the words or letters stand for the values that the variables really have. For example, the letter t will be replaced by the actual time when we plug in numbers for the letters. You can think about each letter as a box that will eventually hold a number. Maybe you don't know what the number is yet. Once we get everything arranged according to the rules we can fill the boxes with the numbers that belong in each one. The last box left will be our answer. The letters (or variables) are the labels that tell us which numbers belong in which boxes.

Three forms of the speed formula

There are three ways to arrange the three variables that relate distance, time and speed. You should be able to work out how to get any of the three variables if you know the other two.

Equation	Gives you...	If you know...
v = d/t	speed	time and distance
d = vt	distance	speed and time
t = d/v	time	distance and speed

Why *v* is used to represent speed in an equation.

When we represent speed in a formula, we use the letter v. If this seems confusing, remember that v stands for velocity.

For this chapter, it isn't important, but there is a technical difference between *speed* and *velocity*. Speed is a single measurement that tells how fast you are going, like 60 miles per hour.

Velocity really means you know both your speed, and also what direction you are going. If you told someone you were going 60 mph straight south, you told them your velocity. If you just told them you were going 60 mph, you told them your speed.

How to solve science problems

An example An airplane is flying at a constant speed of 150 meters per second. After one hour, how far has the plane traveled?

Solution There is a five-step process that works for almost all science problems.

Step 1 Identify what you are asked.

The problem asks for the distance.

Step 2 Write down what you are given.

You are given time and speed.

Step 3 Write down any relationships you know that involve any of the information you are asked, or given.

$v = d/t$, 1 hour = 3,600 seconds.

Step 4 Pick which relationship to start with and try to arrange it to get the variable you want on the left-hand side of an equals sign.

$d = vt$

Step 5 Plug in the numbers and get the answer.

$d = vt = (150 \text{ m/sec}) \times (3{,}600 \text{ sec})$
$= 540{,}000$ meters
$= 540$ kilometers

For this example, you may have figured out the answer in your head. Other problems may not be obvious. It is worth going through the whole process (all five steps) with an easy problem so you know how to approach a harder problem.

Solving science problems

There is a step-by-step approach that can solve almost any science problem. It may not always be the fastest way, but it will always get you started and on the right path to the answer.

Step 1

Read the problem carefully and figure out what it is asking for.

Step 2

Read the problem again and write down all the information you are given, such as speed and distance.

Step 3

Write down all the relationships or formulas that apply to either the answer or the information you are given.

Step 4

Choose, combine, or rearrange the relationships until you get the variable you want (the answer) by itself on one side of an equals sign.

Step 5

Plug in the numbers and calculate the answer.

Chapter 1 Review

Vocabulary review

Match the following terms with the correct definition. There is one extra definition in the list that will not match any of the terms.

Set One

1. time
2. second
3. distance
4. length
5. English system

a. How far it is from one point to another
b. A system of measuring that uses length units of inches, feet, and miles
c. A type of distance measurement
d. A measurement that describes the interval between two events; the past, present, and future
e. A system of measuring time based on the Babylonian number system
f. A common unit used in measuring time

Set Two

1. metric system
2. investigation
3. experiment
4. measurement
5. scientific evidence

a. A series of experiments connected to a basic question
b. An observation that can be recorded and thought about
c. An observation that can be repeated with the same result
d. An observation that is reported in a newspaper
e. A situation that is set up in order to observe what happens
f. A system of measuring that uses length units of millimeters, centimeters, meters, and kilometers

Set Three

1. scientific method
2. research question
3. hypothesis
4. variables
5. cause and effect

a. An educated guess about what will happen
b. When one variable affects another
c. A process used to solve a problem or test an idea about how things work
d. A process used to build a device
e. Factors that affect the result of an experiment
f. A question that can be answered by an experiment or series of experiments

Set Four

1. experimental variable
2. control variable
3. controlled experiment
4. trial
5. experimental technique

a. A variable that is kept the same in an experiment
b. How an experiment is done
c. The running of an experiment
d. A variable that is not important in an experiment
e. An experiment in which one variable changes and all other variables are kept the same
f. A variable that is changed in an experiment

Concept review

1. Units of time include seconds, minutes, hours, days, and years. Why are there so many units for time?
2. To make sense, a measurement must always have a _______ and a _______.
3. How are an investigation and an experiment related to each other?
4. Experiments usually have a question associated with them. True or false?
5. List the steps of the scientific method.
6. When doing an experiment, you must change only one________ at a time.
7. A hypothesis is a random guess. True or false?
8. Scientific discoveries and inventions must always be verified by more than one person. True or false?
9. What is the definition of speed?
10. How are speed and velocity different? Use each in a sentence.
11. Write the speed equation that you would use in each of the following scenarios:
    a. You know distance and speed.
    b. You know time and distance.
    c. You know speed and time.
12. What is the speed of an object that is standing still?
13. Describe, in your own words, how you determine the speed of an object.

Problems

1. Which one of the following times is equal to 75 seconds?
    a. 3 minutes (3:00)
    b. 1 minute, 15 seconds (1:15)
    c. 1 minute, 25 seconds (1:25)
2. How many seconds are in half an hour? Show your work.
3. Match the measurement in the first column to the corresponding equal measurement in the second column:

a) 1 centimeter	1) 12 inches
b) 1 foot	2) 1 meter
c) 5, 280 feet	3) 10 millimeters
d) 1000 millimeters	4) 1 mile

4. A student is 5 feet, 2 inches tall. What is her height in meters?
5. A model car is 30 cm in length. How many inches long is it?

6. What is the correct order of the following lengths from shortest to longest? Show your work.

a.	16 inches	c.	1.1 feet
b.	26.6 centimeters	d.	0.4 meters

7. You would like to find out whether a sports drink or plain water is better for an athlete. You have several friends on the field hockey team and the soccer team. You conduct an experiment at practice one day. You give the field hockey players the plain water and the soccer players the sports drink.

   Did you run a controlled experiment? Why or why not?

8. You have heard that plants grow better in response to music. You have permission to do an experiment to find out if this is true. You have 20 small plants and two rooms that face the same direction. Each room has a window that gets the same amount of light. Describe the experiment you would do to see if music affects plants. Write down your question, your hypothesis, and the procedure you would follow in your experiment.

9. Three groups of students are doing car and ramp experiments. Each group does three identical releases of the car and measures the following times from photogate A to photogate B.

Group 1	Group 2	Group 3
0.2315 seconds	0.2442 seconds	0.2315 seconds
0.2442 seconds	0.2437 seconds	0.2202 seconds
0.3007 seconds	0.2443 seconds	0.2255 seconds

Which group did the best experiment and why do you think so? Be sure that you include the term *variable* in your answer.

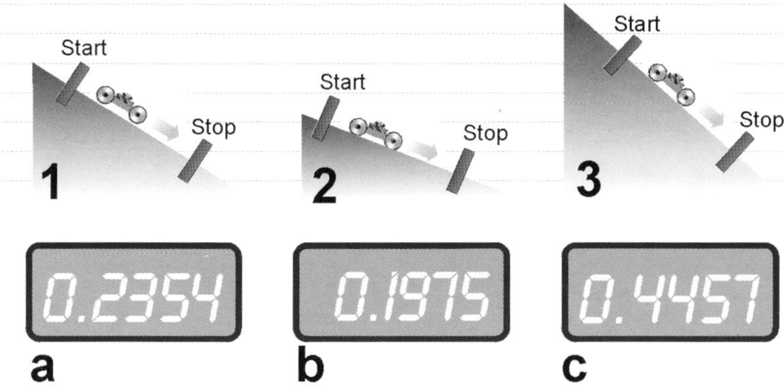

10. Match the timer with the corresponding ramp in the diagram above. You may assume that only the angle of the ramp is different, and all of the other variables are the same.

    a. Timer A corresponds to ramp # ________.

    b. Timer B corresponds to ramp # ________.

    c. Timer C corresponds to ramp # ________.

11. An armadillo is a peculiar animal that is common in the southwestern United States. You are a wildlife biologist and you observe an armadillo that moves 5 feet in 1 minute.

    a. Calculate the speed of the armadillo in feet/minute.

    b. Calculate the speed of the armadillo in inches/second.

    c. Calculate the speed of the armadillo in centimeters/second.

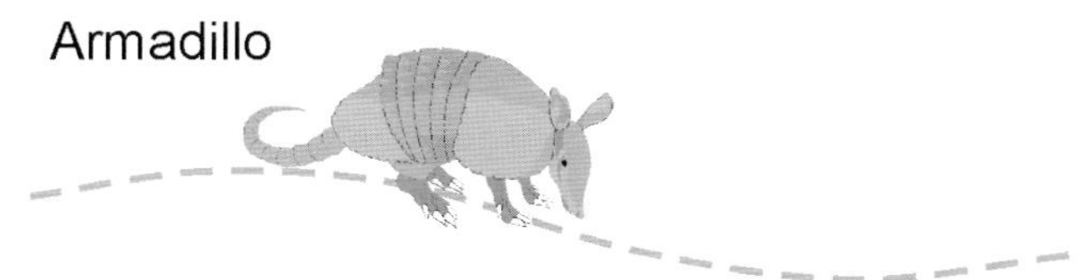

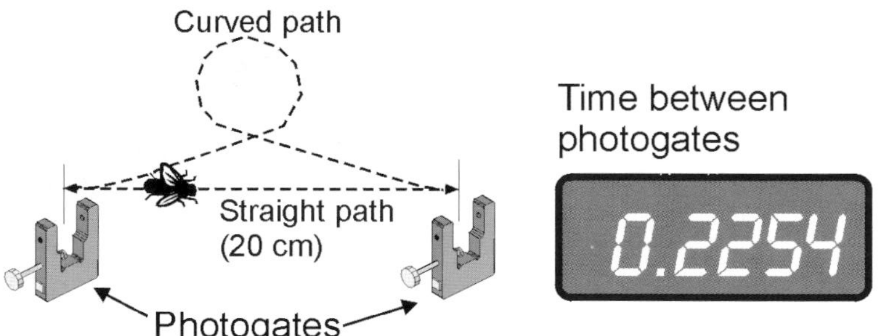

12. A bumblebee flies through two photogates that are spaced exactly 20 centimeters apart. The timer shows the measurement made for the time between gates in seconds.
    a. Calculate the speed of the bumblebee assuming it flies a straight line between the two light beams. Show your work.
    b. If the bumblebee flies a curved path in the same amount of time, will its actual speed be different? Explain your reasoning.

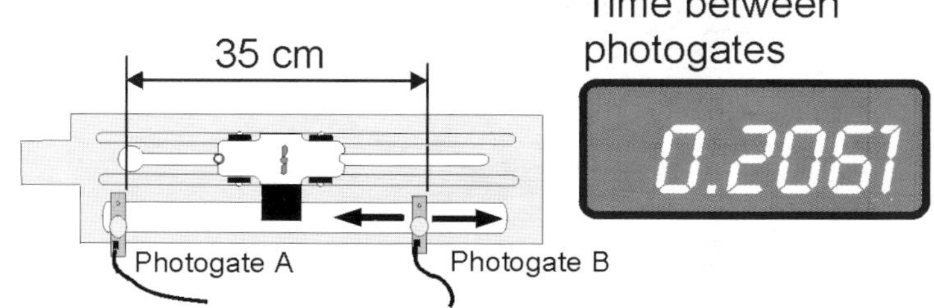

13. A car was timed as it passed through two photogates. The distance between the photogates is 35 centimeters. Calculate the speed of the car as it passed through the two photogates. The timer displays time in seconds.
14. A group of students is doing a speed experiment, and they measure the speed of a car rolling down a ramp five times at the exact same location on the ramp. Review their data below:

    66.7 cm/sec; 70.5 cm/sec; 64.9 cm/sec; 67.8 cm/sec; 69.1 cm/sec

    What factors could explain the variability in their data?

Applying your knowledge

1. Many old number systems were based on 12's because of the following way of counting with the hands:
    - By using the thumb on one hand, a person can easily count to twelve on the four fingers by touching the tip and then the first two joints of each finger.
    - By using the same method on the other hand, the same person could keep track of how many times he or she reached 12 on the first hand.

    Try out this method and calculate how high it is possible to count using this method.
2. Research the number system and units of an ancient civilization and write a short report on what you learned.
3. Read an article in a science magazine and try to identify how scientists have used the scientific method in their work.
4. Research the speeds of many kinds of animals and make a table showing slowest to fastest.
5. Prepare a short report on important speeds in your favorite sport.

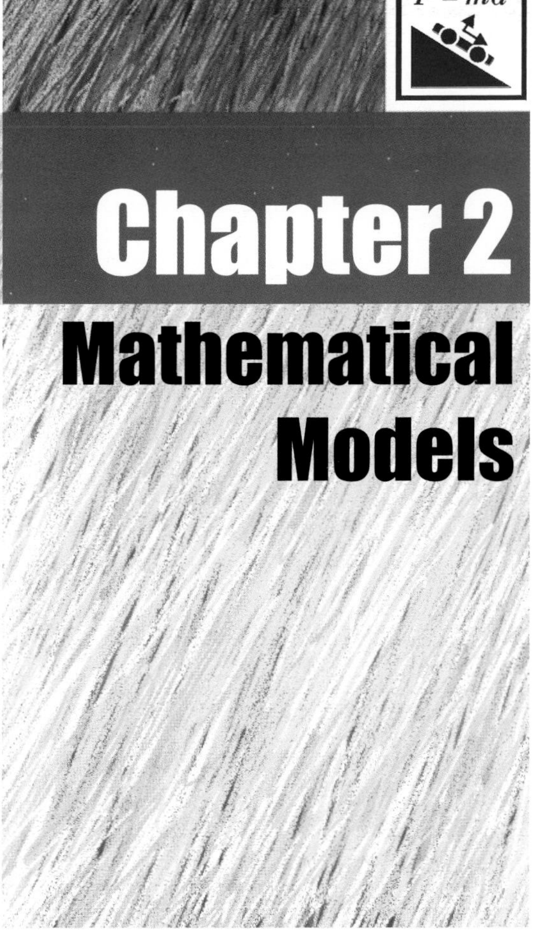

Introduction to Chapter 2

This chapter is about graphing data from your experiments with the car and ramp. You will learn that graphs are mathematical models used for making predictions and solving equations.

Investigations for Chapter 2

2.1	Using a Scientific Model to Predict Speed	*How can you predict the speed of the car at any point on the ramp?*

In this Investigation you will create a graphical model that you can use to predict the speed of the car at any point on the ramp. You will do this by determining the speed of the car at six points along the ramp and then graphing the speed of the car against the distance traveled.

2.2	Position and Time	*How do you model the motion of the car?*

In this Investigation you will make a distance vs. time graph from the data you collect with the car and ramp. You are going to model the motion of one trip of the car down the ramp. To get enough data to model motion, you will collect data at 10 or more points along the ramp. Your teacher will assign your group's ramp angle.

2.3	Acceleration	*How is the speed of the car changing?*

Since acceleration depends on the angle of the hill, a car and ramp make a good tool to discover the behavior of *uniform acceleration*, or when speed changes at a constant rate. Shallow (nearly level) angles will give very little acceleration, and the increasing speed is easy to observe. Steep (nearly vertical) angles resemble *free fall* or motion that is entirely under the influence of gravity.

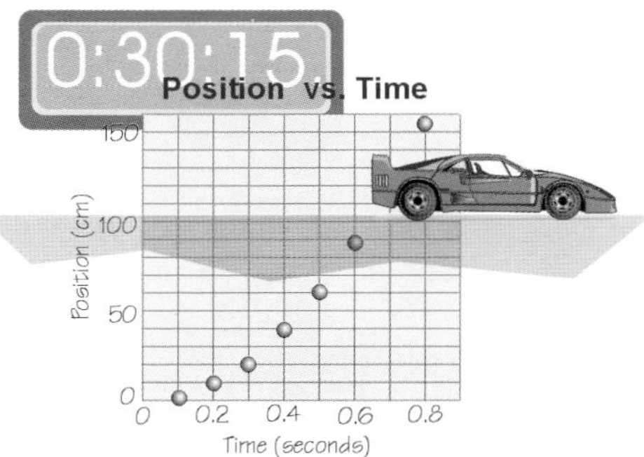

Learning Goals

In this chapter, you will:

- ✔ Construct a speed vs. distance graph.
- ✔ Use a graph to make a prediction that can be quantitatively tested.
- ✔ Calculate the percent error between a measurement and a prediction.
- ✔ Create and analyze a distance vs. time graph.
- ✔ Determine the slope of a line.
- ✔ Distinguish between linear and nonlinear graphs.
- ✔ Distinguish between speed and acceleration.
- ✔ Calculate acceleration from a formula.
- ✔ Calculate acceleration from the slope of a speed vs. time graph.

Vocabulary

accelerate
acceleration
average speed
conceptual model
deceleration
dependent variable
free fall
graphical model
gravity
independent variable
instantaneous speed
physical model
scientific model

2.1 Using a Scientific Model to Predict Speed

In this section, you will learn how to make a model that will accurately predict the speed of a car. Making models is an important part of science and engineering. For a given situation, models tell us how all the variables, like speed, distance, and time, fit together. If we have a model, we can predict what will happen because we know how changes in one variable affect the others.

Why make models?

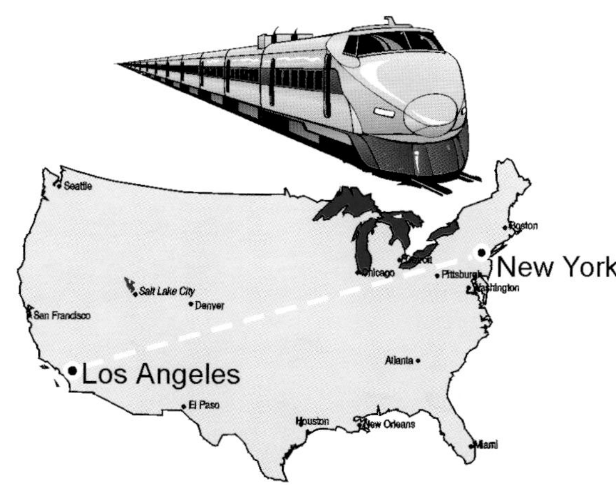

Suppose it is your job to design a train to go from New York to Los Angeles in the shortest possible time. Your train would have to go up and down hills and across flat plains carrying 1,000 people.

How powerful a motor do you need?
How powerful do the brakes need to be?
How much fuel do you need to carry?

There are many things you have to know. You want the answers to the questions *before* you build the train. How do you get answers to a complicated problem such as how to design a high-speed train?

The way we answer complicated questions is to break them down into smaller questions. Each smaller question can be answered with simple experiments or research. One question might be how fast a train will roll down a hill of a given angle. You might do an experiment with a miniature train to get some data on downhill speeds that would help you design the brakes for the train. Other questions might be answered with research, in order to learn how other people solved similar problems.

You can often use the results of an experiment to produce a model that tells how each of the variables in the experiment are related. One model you might make is a graph showing how fuel efficiency depends on the size of the engine. If you know the engine size needed to climb the steepest hill, the model tells you how much fuel you have to carry on the train. Once you have models for each part of the train, you can evaluate different choices for your design.

Big complex question

How can I design a high-speed train that can cross the United States?

Smaller questions

How powerful does the train's motor need to be to go up hills?

How good do the train's brakes need to be to go down hills?

How much fuel should the train carry?

Experiment and research

Design experiments, collect data, do research, and create models for each question. Then figure out how all the systems of the train work together.

Figure 2.1: *We solve complex questions by breaking them down into smaller problems. Each small problem is solved and the results are used to solve the larger question.*

Scientific models

What do experiments tell us?

An experiment tells us about the relationship between variables. If we roll a car downhill to learn about its motion, we will need to measure its speed at several distances from the top. Speed and distance are the variables.

We will be looking for a way to connect these variables. We need to know exactly how much speed is gained by the car for every centimeter it rolls down the ramp. We collect experimental data to figure out the relationship between the variables.

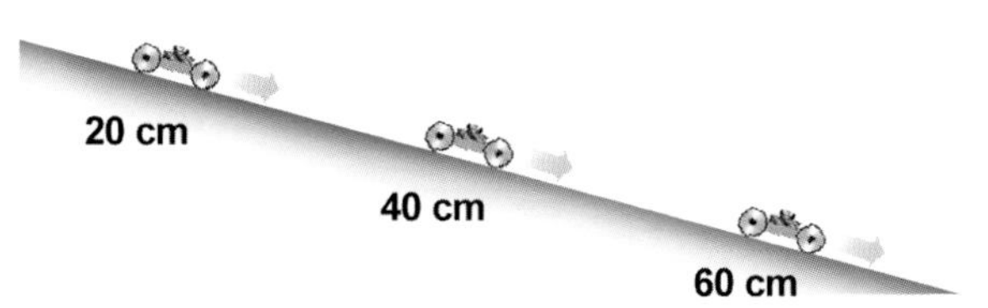

Distance	Speed
20 cm	80 cm/sec
40 cm	120 cm/sec
60 cm	160 cm/sec

What is a scientific model?

We then take the results and make a scientific model that shows how each variable relates to another. For example, how does the distance traveled relate to the speed? The data above shows that for every 20 centimeters traveled, the speed increased by 40 cm/sec. If we graph this data, we can use it to make predictions about the speed of the car at other places along the ramp. A similar process could be used in the train design. A graphical model could answer the question "If the hill is longer by a kilometer, how much faster will the train go if the brakes fail?"

Solving the big question

Once we have models for the smaller relationships, we can put them together to solve the bigger question of how to design the train. Experiments and research have given us enough information to create and test models that tell us how each part will work. Once we know how each part of the train will work, we can design a train where all the parts work together.

Accurate measurements

Instruments like an electronic timer allow you to make *very* accurate measurements of speed. The more accurate your measurements, the better your model will be. By using very accurate data to make the graphical model, you can be sure that your predictions will be accurate also.

Variables

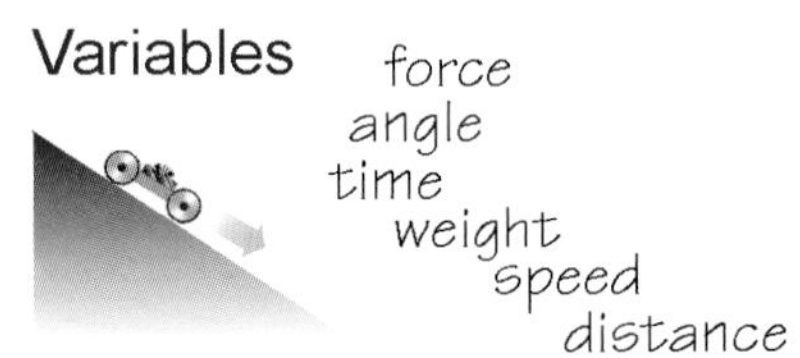

Experiment

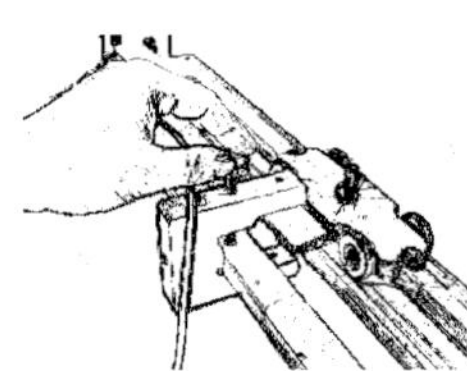

Distance (cm)	Speed (cm/sec)
10	100
20	140
30	171
40	198
50	221
60	242
80	280
90	297

Model

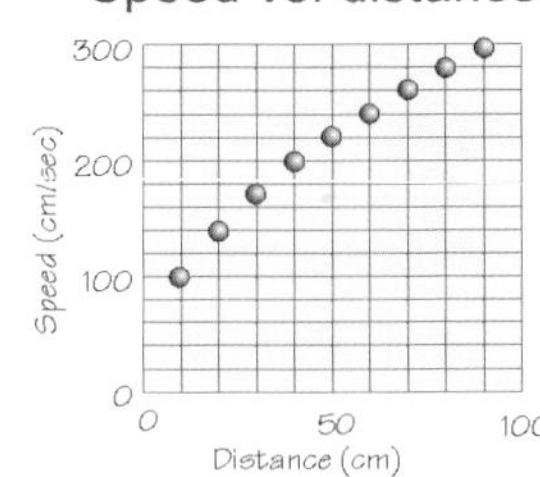

Prediction

At 55 centimeters, the speed of the car will be 231 cm/sec.

Figure 2.2: *A model is something we make that identifies the relationships between the variables. The model can answer questions like "If I change the distance down the ramp, how much will the speed change?"*

We all make mental models

Our models of nature can take many forms. For example, suppose you want to kick a soccer ball into the goal. In your mind, you know how the ball moves on the grass of the field or through the air because of your previous experience. This mental image is a kind of model you use to make adjustments in how you kick the ball toward the goal.

Figure 2.3: *Mental models help us imagine how something will happen. Soccer players make accurate models in their minds when they shoot the ball at the goal.*

Physical models

Some models are physical. **Physical models** are models that we can look at, touch, feel, and take measurements from. Engineers often construct scale models of bridges and evaluate them for strength and design. The word *scale* means that lengths on the model are proportional to lengths on the real object. For example, a scale of 1 inch = 10 feet (120:1) means that every inch on the model represents 10 feet in real life. It is much easier to do experiments on scale models than it is to build full-size bridges! If properly constructed, models tell the engineers about the behavior of the real bridge, and help them avoid dangerous mistakes.

Early civilizations believed the Earth was covered by a dome on which the sun, stars and planets moved.

In the Middle Ages people thought the sun, stars, and planets circled the Earth which sat in the center.

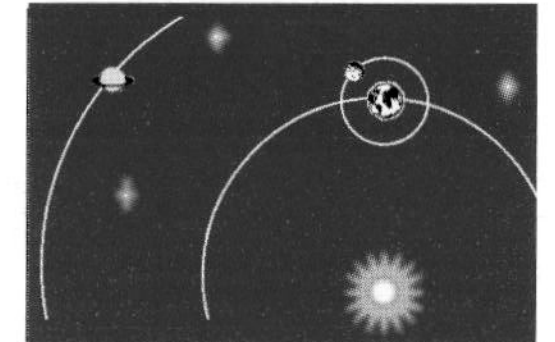

Today we know the Earth and planets orbit around the sun and the stars are very far away.

Conceptual models

Much of our scientific understanding of nature is expressed in the form of **conceptual models**. These types of models are *descriptive*, that is, we use them to describe how something works. For example, in 1543, Nicholas Copernicus, the great astronomer, described a conceptual model of the heavens in which the Earth revolves in an orbit around the sun. Copernicus's conceptual model was a major revolution in our understanding of astronomy, since most people of his time believed in Ptolemy's model in which the sun moved around the Earth. Other astronomers added to Copernicus' model. Galileo invented the telescope in 1609, and Johannes Kepler used the telescope to work out detailed orbits for other planets. In 1687, Isaac Newton's law of universal gravitation finally provided a model that explained why planets move in orbits. Our models improve as our understanding grows.

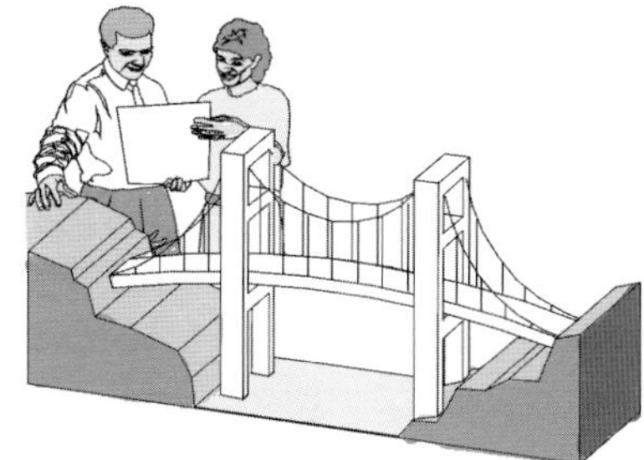

Figure 2.4: *Some models are physical, like this model of a bridge. Models can tell engineers and architects a lot about how a project will be built.*

Making a graphical model

Graphical models

While conceptual models are very useful, often they are only the first step toward making a model that can make predictions. The next step is often a graph. A graph shows how two variables are related with a picture that is easy to understand. A **graphical model** uses a graph to show a relationship between the variable on the *x*-axis and the variable on the *y*-axis. Because a graph uses numbers it is also known as a mathematical model.

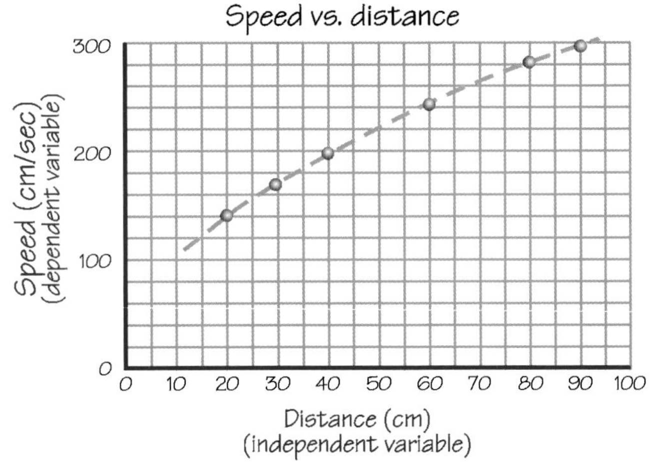

Distance (cm)	Speed (cm/sec)
20	140
30	171
40	198
60	242
80	280
90	297

The dependent variable

The graph shows how the speed of a rolling car changes as it rolls downhill. We expect the speed to change. Speed is the **dependent variable** because we think the speed *depends* on how far down the ramp the car gets.

The independent variable

The distance is the **independent variable**. We say it is *independent* because we are free to make the distance anything we want by choosing where on the ramp to measure.

Choosing *x* and *y*

People have decided to always put the independent variable on the horizontal *(x)* axis. You should too, since this is how people will read any graph you make. The dependent variable goes on the vertical (*y*) axis.

How to Make a Graph

1 Decide what to put on *x* and *y*.

Each box = 1   Each box = 10   Each box = 20

Letting each box = 20 fits the biggest data point (297 cm/sec)

2 Make a scale for each axis by counting boxes to fit your largest value. Count by multiples of 1, 2, 5, or 10 to make it easier to plot points. Make the graph big, try to use as much of the graph paper as you can.

3 Plot your points by finding the *x* value, and drawing a line up until you get to the right *y* value. Put a dot for each point.

4 Draw a smooth curve that shows the pattern of the points. Don't simply connect the dots.

5 Make a title for your graph.

Reading a graph

Why are graphs useful? One purpose of making a graph is to organize your data into a model you can use to make predictions. Pictures are much easier to understand than tables of data (figure 2.5). By making a graph, you are making a picture that shows the exact relationship between your variables.

Making predictions from a graph Suppose you want to find out what the speed of the car would be 50 centimeters from the start. You did not measure the speed there. Yet the graph can give you an answer.

1 To predict the speed, start by finding 50 centimeters on the *x*-axis.
2 Draw a line vertically upward from 50 centimeters until it hits the curve you drew from your data.
3 Draw a line horizontally over until it reaches the *y*-axis.
4 Use the scale on the *y*-axis to read the predicted speed.
5 For this example, the model graph predicts the speed to be 220 cm/sec.

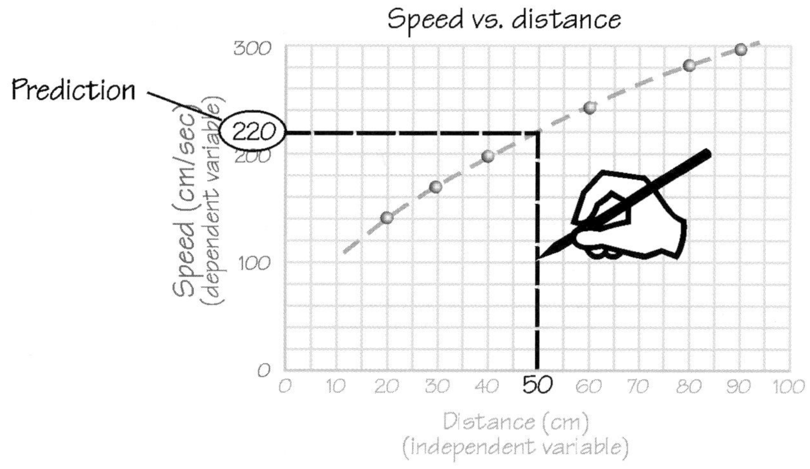

Checking the accuracy of a model If the graph is created from accurate data, the prediction will also be accurate. You could check by doing another experiment and measuring the speed of the car at 50 centimeters. You should find it to be very close to the prediction from your graph.

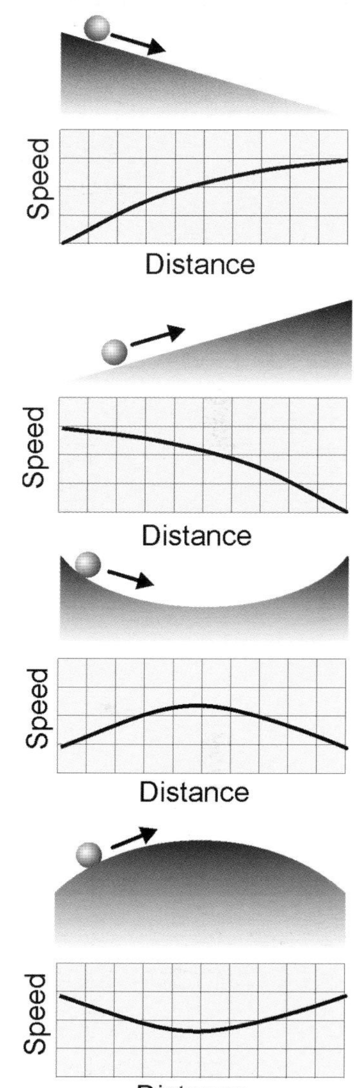

Figure 2.5: *Some different shapes for ramps and their corresponding speed vs. distance graphs.*

Cause and effect relationships

Cause and effect relationships

In many experiments we are looking for a cause and effect relationship. How does changing one variable effect another? Graphs are a good way to see whether there is a connection between two variables or not. You cannot always tell from looking at tables of data. With a graph, the connection is clear.

Patterns indicate relationships

When there is a relationship between the variables the graph shows a clear pattern. The speed and distance variables show a strong relationship. When there is no relationship the graph looks like a collection of dots. No pattern appears. The number of musical groups a student listed in one minute and the last two digits of his or her phone number are an example of two variables that are not related.

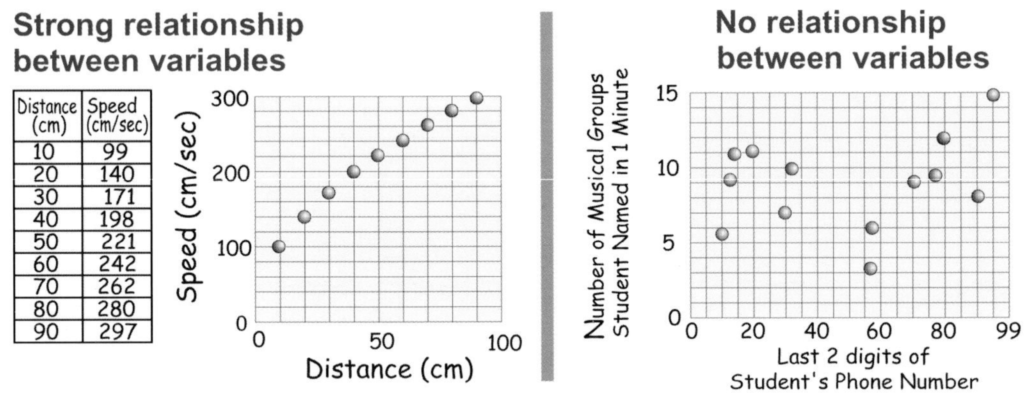

Distance (cm)	Speed (cm/sec)
10	99
20	140
30	171
40	198
50	221
60	242
70	262
80	280
90	297

Strong and weak relationships

You can tell how strong the relationship is from the pattern. If the relationship is strong, a small change in one variable makes a big change in another. If the relationship is weak, even a big change in one variable has little effect on the other. In weak relationships, the points may follow a pattern but there is not much change in one variable compared to big changes in the other (figure 2.6)

Inverse relationships

Some relationships are inverse. When one variable increases, the other decreases. If you graph how much money you spend against how much you have left, you see an inverse relationship. The more you spend, the less you have. Graphs of inverse relationships always slope down to the right (figure 2.7).

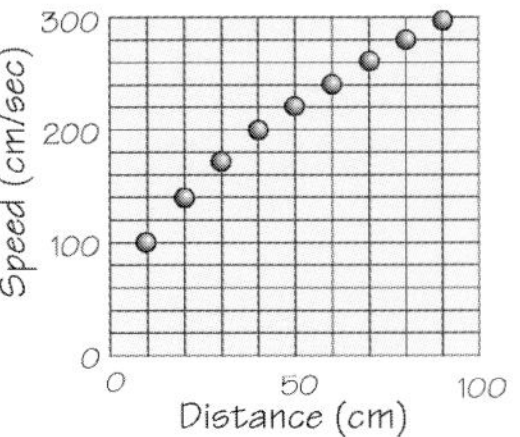

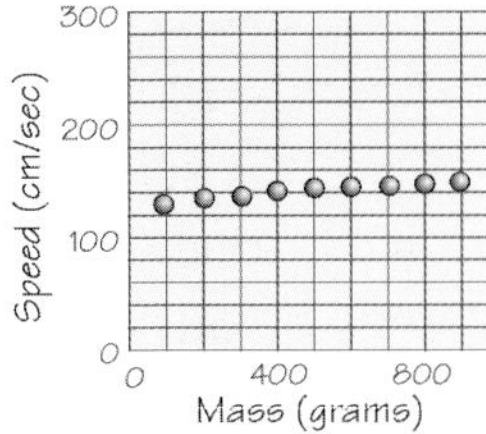

Figure 2.6: *In a strong relationship (top), a big change in distance creates a big change in speed. In a weak relationship (bottom), a big change in mass makes almost no change in speed.*

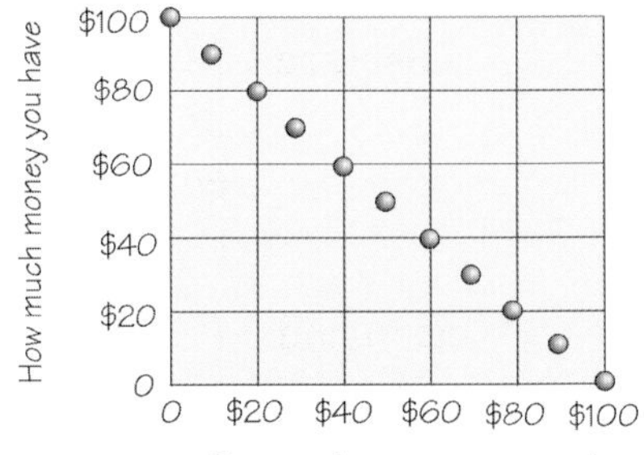

Figure 2.7: *A typical graph for an inverse relationship.*

2.2 Position and Time

Distance (cm)	Speed (cm/sec)
10	100
20	140
30	171
40	198
50	221
60	242
80	280
90	297

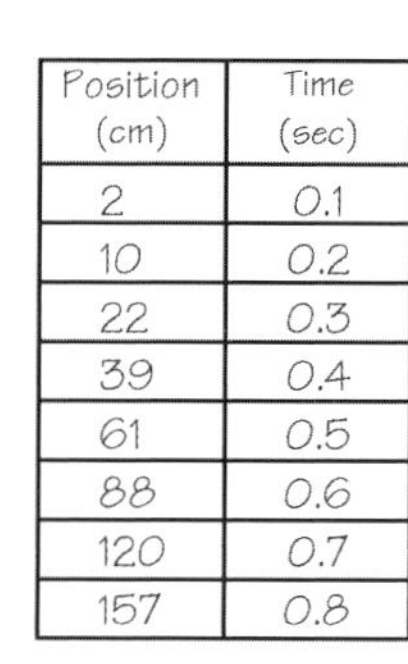

Position (cm)	Time (sec)
2	0.1
10	0.2
22	0.3
39	0.4
61	0.5
88	0.6
120	0.7
157	0.8

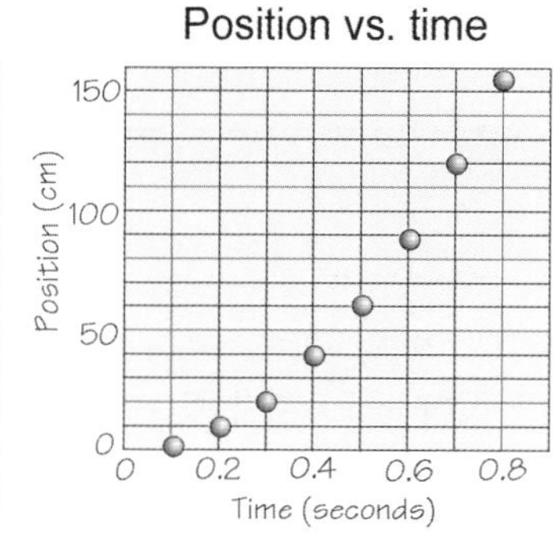

Time	Position
1:00	0 (start)
2:00	3 km
3:00	6 km
4:00	7 km
5:00	5 km
6:00	3 km
7:00	1 km

Figure 2.8: *You leave at 1:00 and walk away from school in a straight line until 4:00. Then you turn around and walk back. At 7:00, you are still 1 kilometer away from school.*

Graphical models like the speed vs. distance graph are good for organizing data so you can make predictions. In this section, you will learn how to model motion with another graph: position vs. time. The position vs. time graph offers a new way to find the speed of a moving object. The position vs. time graph will also be our example as we explore different ways to use and interpret graphs. The techniques you learn in this section will help you understand acceleration, the next important idea in motion.

Position

Position In physics, the word **position** means where something is compared with where it started, including direction. As things move their position changes. If you walked in a straight line away from your school, your position would keep getting larger (figure 2.8). If you stopped walking, your position would stop changing.

Distance Distance is an interval of length without regard to direction. You can walk a distance of 10 miles in a circle and end up exactly where you started. If you walk a curved path, the distance you walk could be much greater than the distance between where you started and where you end up (figure 2.9).

Position and distance Position and distance are different. If you are 7 kilometers north of school, that is a statement of your position. If you walk back towards your school, your position decreases. If you get back to where you started, your position is zero even though the distance you walked is 14 kilometers (7 km away plus 7 km back)!

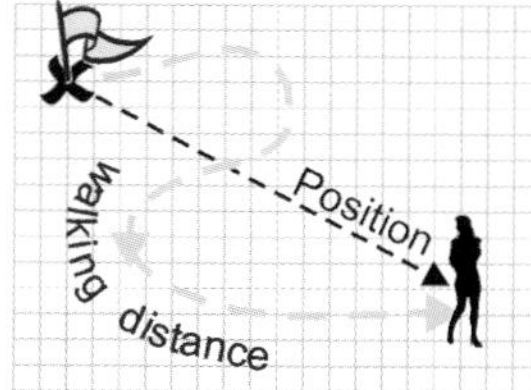

Figure 2.9: *If there are turns, the position might be different from the distance you travel.*

The position vs. time graph

What does the graph tell you? The position vs. time graph shows where things are at different times. If things have moved, it is easy to see from the graph. You might think giving the speed is enough description of how things have moved. But speed does not always give you enough information.

A car trip with a rest For example, suppose you take a car trip that includes 1.5 hours of driving and a half-hour rest stop, for a total time of 2 hours. You drive a total distance of 90 miles in a straight line. At the end you call your friends to tell them it took you 2 hours and they calculate your speed to be 45 mph (90 miles divided by 2 hours).

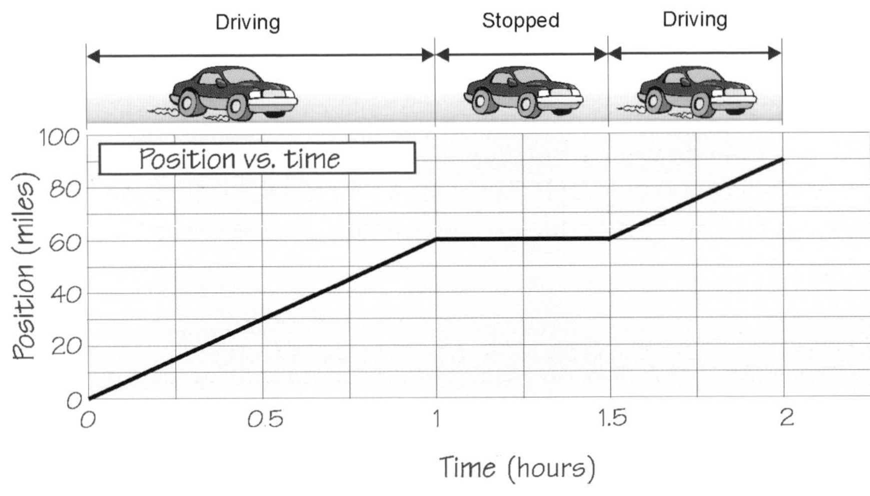

Actually, you drove a lot faster than 45 mph to make up for the half-hour rest stop. You really covered the 90 miles in 1.5 hours, at a speed of 60 mph. You stopped (with zero speed) for a half hour.

The graph is a better picture of the trip The position vs. time graph shows your trip much more accurately than saying you covered 90 miles in 2 hours. For the first hour, your position gradually increases from zero (start) until you are 60 miles away. Your position stays the same between 1 hour and 1.5 hours because you stopped. Then you get going again and cover the last 30 miles in a half hour. The position vs. time graph shows a complete history of your trip including your stop.

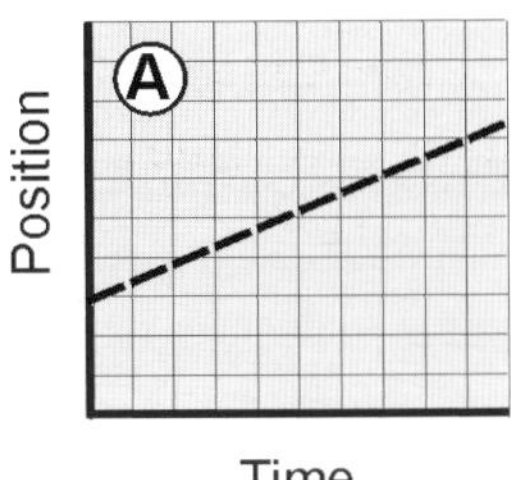

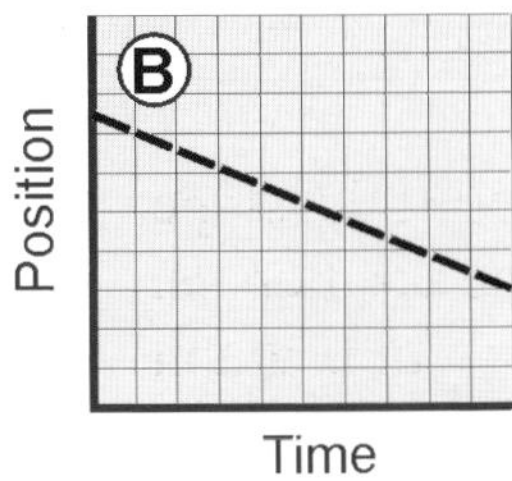

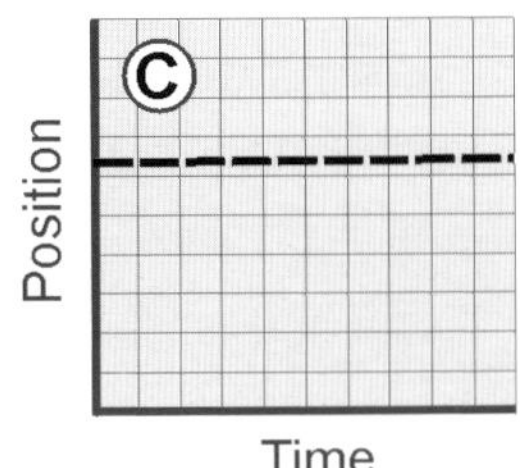

Figure 2.10: *Examples of graphs showing different speeds.*
Graph A shows movement away from start.
Graph B shows movement back toward start.
Graph C shows no motion. The object is stopped with zero speed.

Determining speed from the slope of a graph

Look at the distance vs. time Let's take a closer look at the first hour of your driving trip (figure 2.11). You drove at a constant speed of 60 mph. The position vs. time graph shows the position of your car on the highway as it changes with time. The line on the graph represents the motion of the car. If the graph is a complete description of the motion, you should be able to figure out the speed of the car from the graph.

The definition of slope The definition of slope is the ratio of "rise" (vertical change) to the "run" (horizontal change) of the line. The rise is determined by finding the height of the triangle shown. The run is determined by finding the length along the base of the triangle. For this graph, the x-values represent time and the y-values represent position.

Speed is the slope of the position vs. time graph Speed is the distance traveled divided by the time taken. The distance is really the difference in position between where you finished and where you started. This is equal to the rise (vertical distance) on the graph. The run on the graph is the time taken for the trip. The slope is rise over run, which is the distance traveled over the time taken, which is the speed.

Driving at constant 60 mph in a straight line

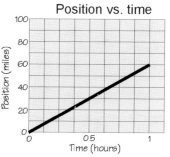

Position vs. time

Figure 2.11: *The first hour of the driving trip. The car has a constant speed of 60 mph.*

Speed is the slope of the position vs. time graph.

The slope of a graph

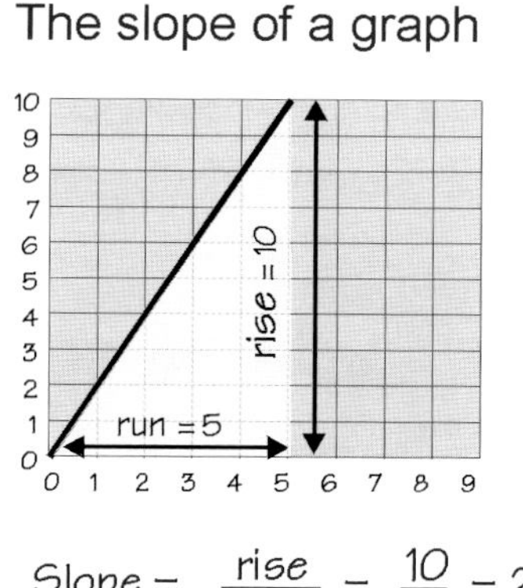

Speed from the slope of the position vs. time graph

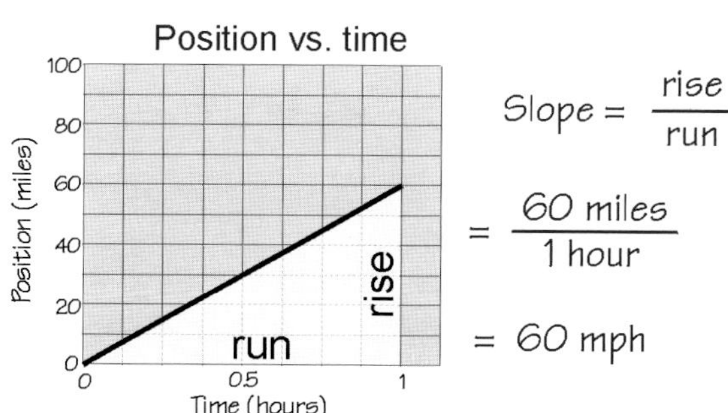

Instantaneous and average speed

Speed does not usually stay constant

Does your speed stay exactly the same during a real trip? The answer is, of course not. Your speed is almost always changing. You slow down for stop lights, and speed up to pass people. For the next example, consider taking a bicycle trip. You may remain on flat ground for moment, but eventually you come to a hill. As you climb the hill, you slow down. As you go down the hill, you speed up.

Average speed

There are two ways you should think about speed. If it takes you 2 hours to ride 50 kilometers, your average speed is 25 kilometers per hour (25 km/h). To calculate average speed, you simply take the total distance traveled divided by the total time taken.

Instantaneous speed

At some points along the way, you may go slower, or faster than average. The instantaneous speed is the speed you have at a specific point in your journey. You might go uphill at 10 km/h and downhill at 60 km/h, with an average speed of 25 km/h even though your speed was never exactly 25 km/h at any time in the trip!

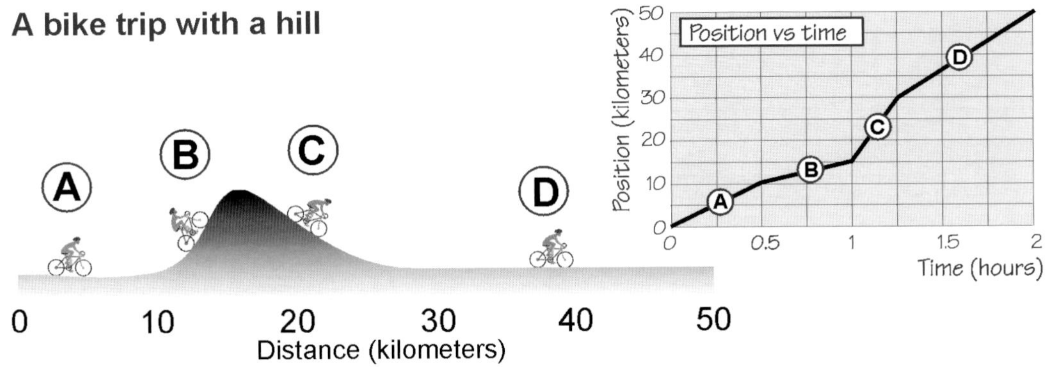

The position vs. time graph

The real story is told by the position vs. time graph. The graph captures both the instantaneous speed and the average speed. If the slope of the graph is steep (**C**), you have lots of position changing in little time (figure 2.12) indicating a high speed. If the slope is shallow (**B**), relatively little position changes over a long time, giving a slow speed. If the graph is level the slope is zero, so the speed is also zero, indicating you have stopped and are not moving.

Part A

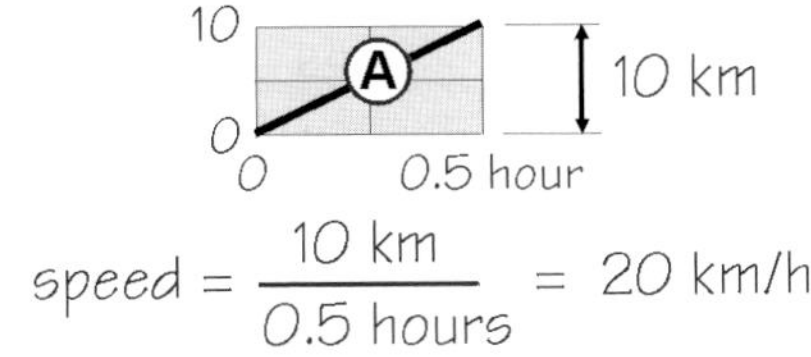

Part B

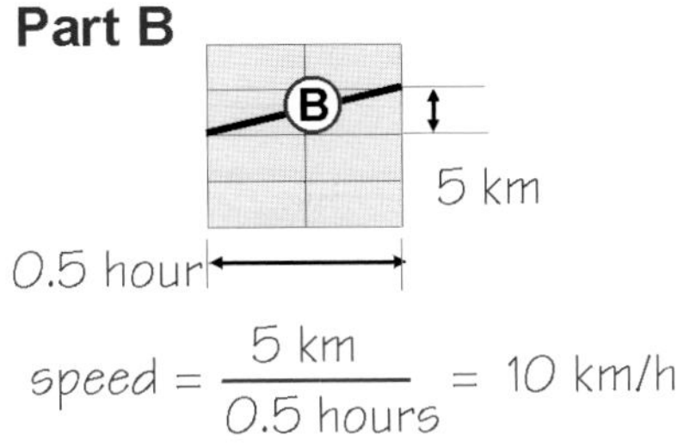

Part C

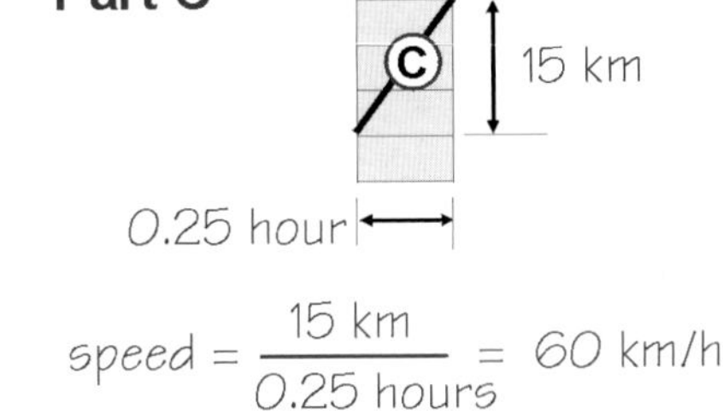

Part D

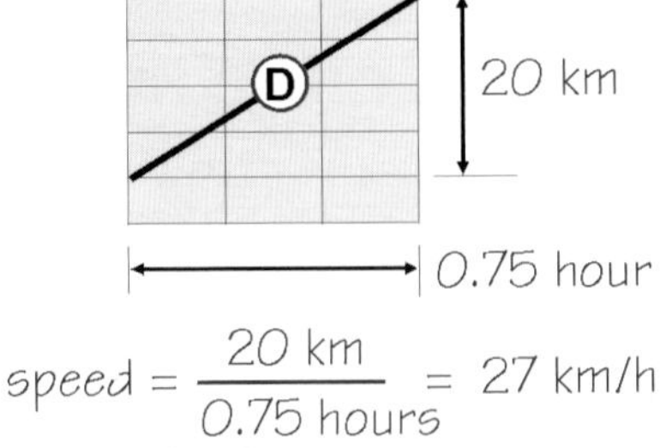

Figure 2.12: *Calculating the speed of each part of the trip.*

2.3 Acceleration

The speed of things is always changing. Your car speeds up and slows down. If you slow down gradually, it feels very different from slamming on the brakes and stopping fast. In this section we will learn how to measure and discuss changes in speed. Specifically, we will investigate objects rolling downhill. You already know that an object rolling downhill speeds up. The rate at which its speed changes is called **acceleration**.

Acceleration

You accelerate coasting downhill

What happens if you coast your bicycle down a long hill without pedaling? You accelerate, that is your speed increases steadily. If your bike has a speedometer you find that your speed increases by the same amount every second!

Time	Speed
0 (start)	0 (start)
1 second	1 mph
2 seconds	2 mph
3 seconds	3 mph
4 seconds	4 mph
5 seconds	5 mph

Time	Speed
0 (start)	0 (start)
1 second	2 mph
2 seconds	4 mph
3 seconds	6 mph
4 seconds	8 mph
5 seconds	10 mph

Steeper hills

On a steeper hill, your findings are similar. Your speed increases every second, but by a bigger amount. On the first hill your speed increased by 1 mph every second. On the steeper hill you find your speed increases by 2 mph every second.

Acceleration is the amount that your speed increases, compared to how long it takes. Increasing speed by 1 mph every second means you accelerated at 1 mph per second. Every second your speed increased by 1 mile per hour. It is common to describe acceleration in units of speed (changed) per second.

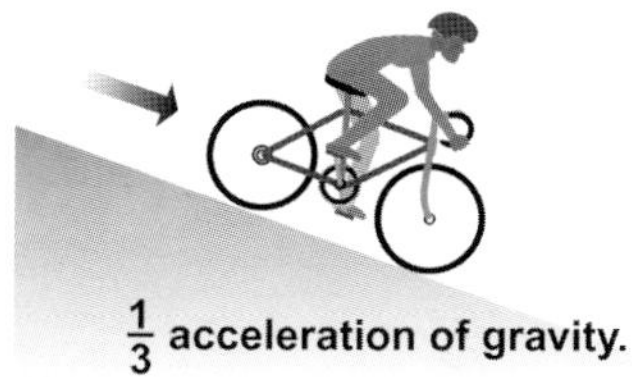

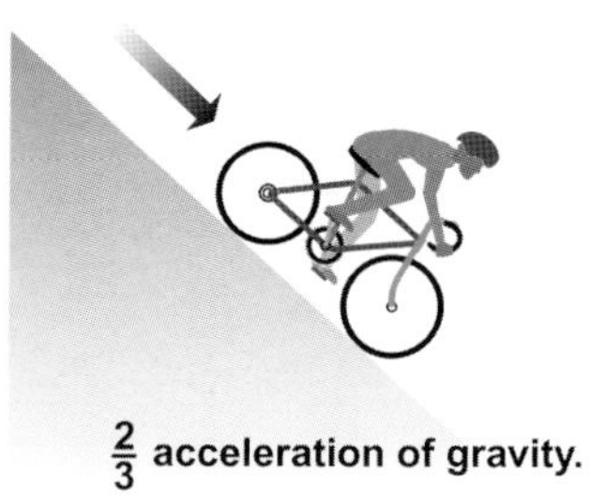

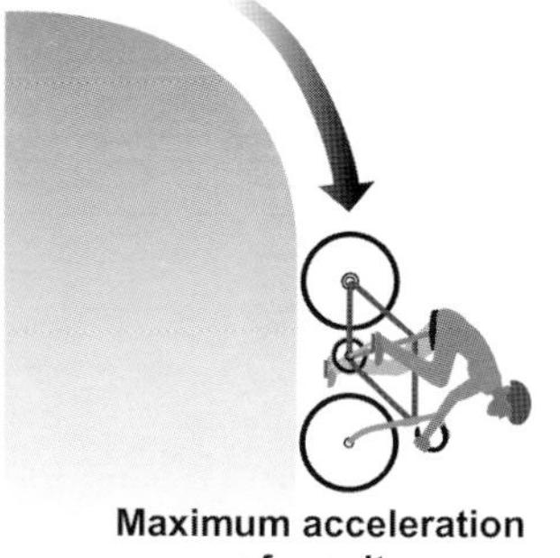

Figure 2.13: *How much of the acceleration of gravity you experience depends on the angle of the hill.*

Acceleration when speed is in miles per hour

Acceleration Acceleration is the rate of change in the speed of an object. Rate of change means the ratio of the amount of change divided by how much time it took to change.

The acceleration of the car is 10 mph/sec

Time 0:00:00 — 20 mph — Speed increase — Time 0:00:04 — 60 mph

An example of acceleration Suppose you are driving and your speed goes from 20 mph to 60 mph in four seconds. The amount of change is 60 mph minus 20 mph, or 40 miles per hour. The time it takes to change is 4 seconds. The acceleration is 40 mph divided by 4 seconds, or 10 mph/sec. Your car accelerated 10 mph per second. That means your speed increased by 10 miles per hour each second. Table 2.1 shows how your speed changed during the four seconds of acceleration.

Table 2.1: ***Watching your speed while accelerating***

Time	Speed
0 (start)	20 mph
1 second	30 mph
2 seconds	40 mph
3 seconds	50 mph
4 seconds	60 mph

Thinking about acceleration

Aristotle
365 BC

Newton
1686

People have been thinking about acceleration for a long time. In the fourth century BC two Greek scientists, Aristotle and Strato, described free fall as acceleration. In the 1580s European scientists Simon Stevinus and Galileo determined that all objects fall equally fast, if other forces do not act on them.

About 100 years later, Isaac Newton figured out the three laws of motion. Newton's attempts to fully describe acceleration inspired him and others to develop a whole new kind of math, called *calculus*. We will not be learning about calculus in this course, but we will follow some of Newton's experiments with acceleration.

Acceleration in metric units

The units of acceleration The units of acceleration can be confusing. Almost all of the calculations of acceleration you will do will be in metric units. If we measure speed in cm/sec, then the change in speed is expressed in cm/sec as well. For example, 2 cm/sec is the difference between a speed of 3 cm/sec and a speed of 1 cm/sec.

Calculating acceleration Acceleration is the change in speed divided by the change in time. The units for acceleration are units of speed over units of time. If speed is in cm/sec and time in seconds, then the units for acceleration are cm/sec/sec, or *centimeters per second per second.* What this means is that the acceleration is the amount that the speed changes in each second. An acceleration of 50 cm/sec/sec means that the speed increases by 50 cm/sec *every second.* If the acceleration persists for three seconds then the speed increases by a total of 150 cm/sec (3 seconds × 50 cm/sec/sec).

What do units of *seconds squared* mean? To make matters confusing, an acceleration in cm/sec/sec is written cm/sec^2 (centimeters per second squared). Likewise, an acceleration of m/sec/sec is written m/sec^2 (meters per second squared). If you use the rules for simplifying fractions on the units of cm/sec/sec, the denominator ends up having units of seconds times seconds, or sec^2. Saying *seconds squared* is just a math-shorthand way of talking. The units of square seconds do not have physical meaning in the same way that square inches mean surface area. It is better to think about acceleration in units of speed change per second (that is, centimeters per second *per second*).

$$\text{Acceleration} = \frac{\text{Change in speed}}{\text{Change in time}}$$

How we get units of cm/sec^2

plug in values / clear the compound fractions / final units

$$= \frac{50\,\frac{cm}{sec}}{sec} = \frac{50\,\frac{cm}{sec} \times \frac{sec}{}}{sec \times sec} = \frac{50\,\frac{cm}{\cancel{sec}} \times \cancel{sec}}{sec^2} = 50\,\frac{cm}{sec^2}$$

Acceleration in m/sec^2 Many physics problems will use acceleration in m/sec^2. If you encounter an acceleration of 10 m/sec^2, this number means the speed is increasing by 10 m/sec every second.

Example

A car rolls down a ramp and you measure times and distances as shown. Calculate the acceleration in cm/sec^2.

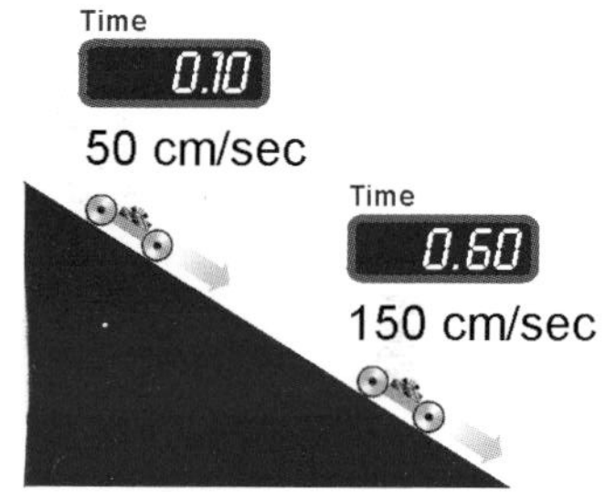

Change in speed

$$150\text{ cm/sec} - 50\text{ cm/sec} = 100\text{ cm/sec}$$

Change in time

$$0.60\text{ sec} - 0.10\text{ sec} = 0.50\text{ sec}$$

$$\text{Acceleration} = \frac{\text{Change in speed}}{\text{Change in time}} = \frac{100\text{ cm/sec}}{0.50\text{ sec}} = 200\text{ cm/sec}^2$$

Figure 2.14: *An example of calculating acceleration for a car on a ramp.*

Different examples of acceleration

Any change in speed means acceleration

Acceleration means changes in speed or velocity. *Any* change in speed means there is acceleration. If you put on the brakes and slow down, your speed changes. In the example of slowing down, the acceleration is in the negative direction. We also use the term **deceleration** to describe this situation. *Acceleration occurs whenever the speed changes, whether the speed increases or decreases.*

Zero acceleration

An object has zero acceleration if it is traveling at constant speed in one direction. You might think of zero acceleration as "cruise control." If the speed of your car stays the same at 60 miles per hour, your acceleration is zero.

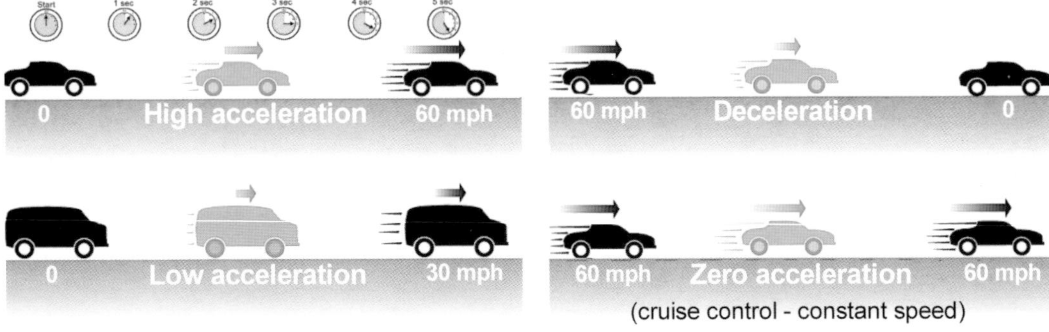

Acceleration when turning

If you change direction, some acceleration happens. When you turn a sharp corner in a car you feel pulled to one side. The pull you feel comes from the acceleration due to turning. To explain this, you need to remember velocity encompasses speed *and direction*. Any time you change either speed or direction, you are accelerating.

Steep hills and acceleration

You have probably noticed that the steeper the hill, the faster you accelerate. You may already know this effect has to do with **gravity**. Gravity pulls everything down toward the center of the Earth. The steeper the hill, the greater the amount of gravity pulling you forward, and the greater your acceleration.

Free fall

If you drop something straight down it accelerates in free fall. The speed of a free falling object in a vacuum increases by 9.8 meters per second for every second it falls (figure 2.15). This special acceleration is called the acceleration of gravity because it is the acceleration of objects under the influence of the Earth's gravity. The acceleration of gravity would be different on the moon or on other planets.

Free Fall

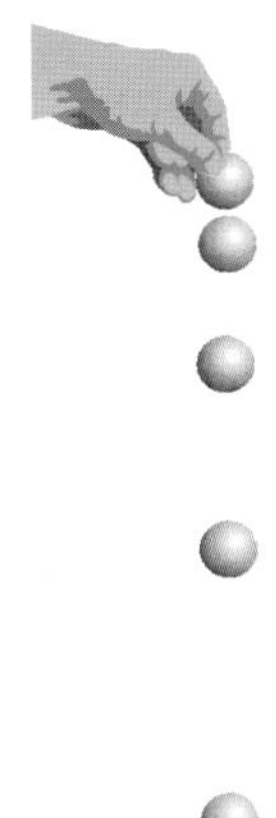

Time	Speed
0 (start)	0
1 second	9.8 m/sec
2 seconds	19.6 m/sec
3 seconds	29.4 m/sec
4 seconds	39.2 m/sec

The speed of free falling objects increases by 9.8 m/sec every second they fall.

This is how we know the acceleration of gravity is 9.8 m/sec^2 at the surface of the Earth.

Figure 2.15: *In free fall, the speed of objects increases by 9.8 m/sec each second. Free fall is most accurately measured in a vacuum, since air friction changes the rate of fall of different objects in different ways.*

Acceleration and the speed vs. time graph

The speed vs. time graph

Another motion graph we need to understand is the graph of speed vs. time. This is the most important graph for understanding acceleration because it shows how the speed changes with time.

The graph below shows an example from an experiment with a car rolling down a ramp. The time is the time between when the car was first released and when its speed was measured after having moved farther down the ramp. You can see that the speed of the car increases the longer it rolls down.

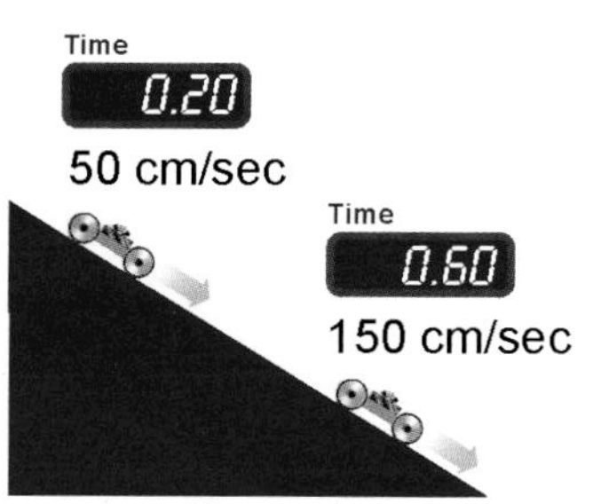

Time (sec)	Speed (cm/sec)
0.1	25
0.2	50
0.3	75
0.4	100
0.5	125
0.6	150
0.7	175
0.8	200

Speed vs. time

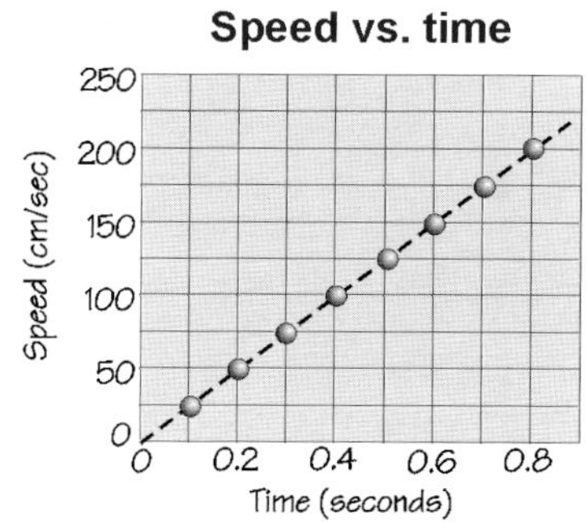

The graph shows a straight line

The graph shows a straight line. This means that the speed of the car increases by the same amount every second. The graph (and data) also shows that the speed of the car increases by 25 cm/sec every one-tenth (0.1) of a second.

Acceleration

You should be thinking of acceleration. This graph shows an acceleration of 250 cm/sec/sec or 250 cm/sec^2. This is calculated by dividing the change in speed (25 cm/sec) by the change in time (0.1 seconds).

Seeing acceleration on a graph

If you see a slope on a speed vs. time graph, you are seeing acceleration. Figure 2.16 shows some examples of graphs with and without acceleration. *Any time* the graph of speed vs. time is not perfectly horizontal, it shows acceleration. If the graph slopes down, it means the speed is decreasing. If the graph slopes up, the speed is increasing.

Positive acceleration
(speeding up)

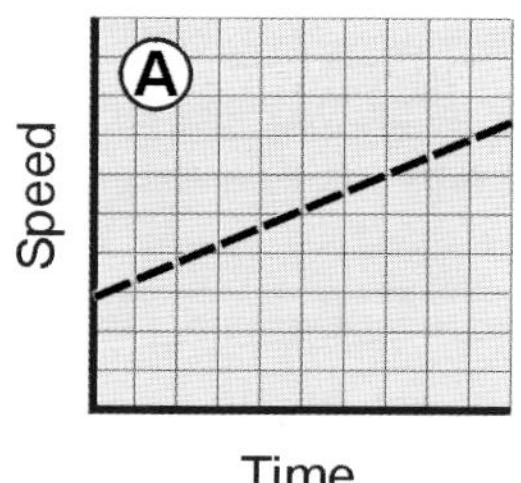

Negative acceleration
(slowing down)

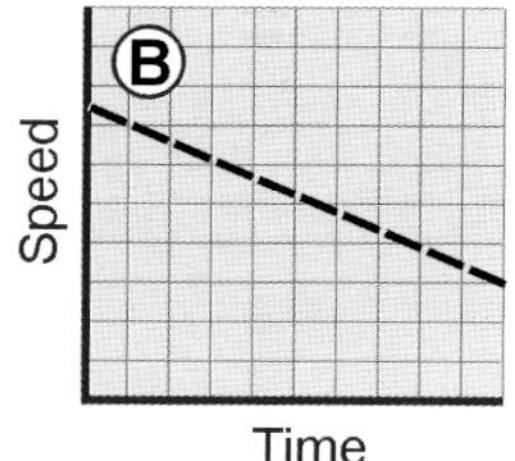

No acceleration
(constant speed)

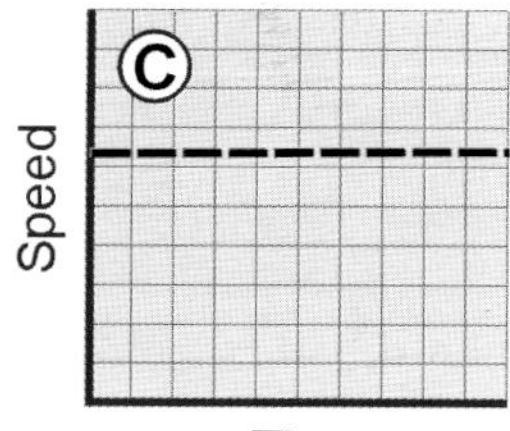

Figure 2.16: *Examples of graphs with different amounts of acceleration.*
Graph **A** *shows positive acceleration, or speeding up.*
Graph **B** *shows negative acceleration, or slowing down.*
Graph **C** *shows zero acceleration.*

Calculating acceleration from the speed vs. time graph

Slope From the last section, you know that the slope of a graph is equal to the ratio of *rise* to *run*. On the speed vs. time graph, the rise and run have special meanings, as they did for the distance vs. time graph. The *rise* is the amount the speed changes. The *run* is the amount the time changes.

Acceleration and slope Remember, acceleration is the change in speed over the change in time. This is *exactly the same* as the rise over run for the speed vs. time graph. The slope of the speed vs. time graph is the acceleration.

Acceleration is the slope of the speed vs. time graph

The slope of a graph

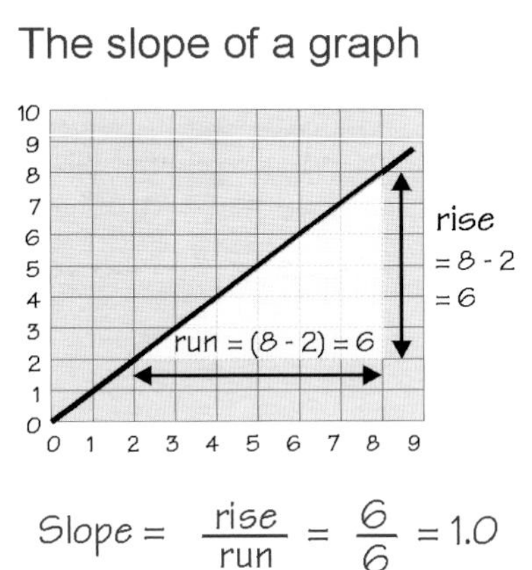

Acceleration from the slope of the speed vs. time graph

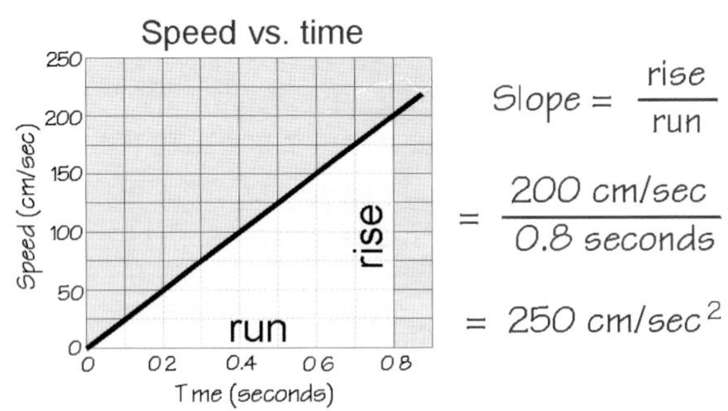

Make a triangle to get the slope To determine the slope of the speed vs. time graph, take the rise or change in speed and divide by the run or change in time. It is helpful to draw the triangle shown above to help figure out the rise and run. The rise is the height of the triangle. The run is the length of the base of the triangle.

Complex speed vs. time graphs You can use slope to recognize when there is acceleration in complicated speed vs. time graphs (figure 2.17). Level graphs mean the speed does not change, which means the acceleration is zero.

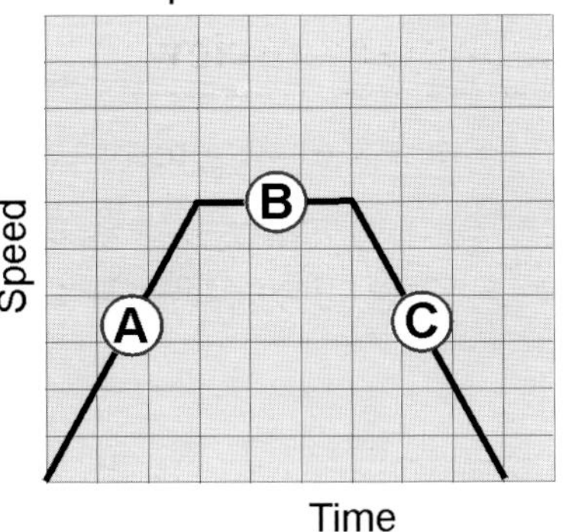

(A) Positive acceleration

(B) Zero acceleration

(C) Negative acceleration

Figure 2.17: *How to recognize acceleration on speed vs. time graphs.*

(A) Positive slope means positive acceleration (speeding up)

(B) No slope (level) means zero acceleration (constant speed)

(C) Negative slope means negative acceleration (slowing down)

Chapter 2 Review

Vocabulary review

Match the following terms with the correct definition. There is one extra definition in the list that will not match any of the terms.

Set One

1. scientific model
2. conceptual model
3. graphical model
4. dependent variable
5. independent variable

a. A way to show how something works that is descriptive in nature
b. A variable that changes in response to another variable
c. A variable that doesn't change during an experiment
d. A variable that we set in an experiment
e. A way to show how variables are connected
f. A graph that shows how variables are connected

Set Two

1. position
2. slope
3. average speed
4. instantaneous speed
5. acceleration

a. Total distance traveled divided by total time elapsed
b. The amount of time elapsed during an experiment
c. How speed changes over time
d. A measurement of a line on a graph, equal to vertical change divided by horizontal change
e. Where something is compared with where it started
f. Speed at one moment in time

Set Three

1. deceleration
2. gravity
3. free fall

a. A measurement of a line on a graph, equal to horizontal change divided by vertical change
b. A force that tends to pull things toward the center of the earth
c. A decrease in speed over time
d. An object that is moving freely towards the center of the Earth exhibits this type of motion

Concept review

1. One of the early conceptual models of the solar system showed the other planets and the sun orbiting around the Earth. Copernicus developed a new model of the solar system that shows the Earth and other planets orbiting around the sun. Draw a picture of these two models of the solar system.

2. The following terms and phrases refer to the two axes of a graph. Divide the terms and phrases according to which group they belong in.

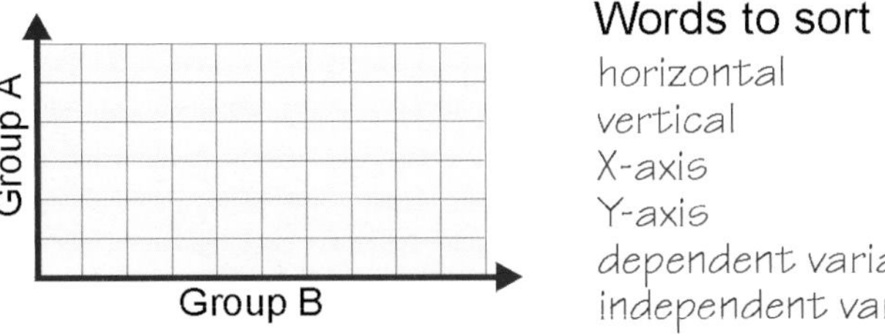

Words to sort
horizontal
vertical
X-axis
Y-axis
dependent variable
independent variable

Group A	Group B

3. Which of the following types of scientific models is frequently used to make numerical predictions that you can test with measurements? You may choose more than one.

   a. a graph

   b. an equation

   c. a conceptual model

   d. a physical model

4. You take a walk from your house to your friend's house around the block. If you graph your position during your walk, the longest distance on the graph is 15 meters. But you actually walked 20 meters. Explain why your position (distance from start) and the actual distance you walked were different.

5. You know the average speed of a trip, and you have a position versus time graph of the trip. Which gives you more information about the trip? Explain your answer.

6. The slope of a position vs. time graph is equal to ____________.

7. What is the difference between *average speed* and *instantaneous speed*? Use a real-life example to help you explain.

8. Is it possible for an object to simultaneously have a speed of zero but an acceleration that is not zero? Answer with an example.

9. What is the acceleration of a car that is going at a steady speed of 60 mph?

10. Does a car accelerate when it goes around a corner at a steady speed? Explain your answer.

11. Does the speedometer of a car give you the average speed or the instantaneous speed of the car? Explain your answer.

12. The slope of a speed vs. time graph is equal to ____________.

Problems

1. Engineers propose to build a bridge that is 30 meters in length. They build a model of the bridge that is 3 meters in length. What is the scale of the model? Express your answer in the form 1:x, where x is the corresponding number of meters on the bridge, when compared with 1 meter on the model.

2. You do an experiment where you measure the height of plants and calculate their growth rate. The growth rate is the amount each plant gets taller per day. You collect the following data on height and growth rate:

Week	Height of plant (cm)	Average daily growth rate (mm/day)
start	2.2	
1	7.9	8.1
2	11.8	5.6
3	15.2	4.9
4	17.7	3.6
5	19.9	3.1
6	21.2	1.9
7	22.1	1.3
8	22.3	0.3

   a. Graph the above data with height on the x-axis and growth rate on the y-axis.

   b. Does the data show (you may choose more than one):

      1) a strong relationship between variables
      2) a weak relationship between variables
      3) an inverse relationship between variables
      4) a direct relationship between variables

3. A woman goes to a store three blocks away from her home. She walks in a straight line and at a steady pace. Draw a position vs. time graph of her walk. Regard home as start.

4. A woman leaves a store and goes to her home three blocks away. She walks in a straight line and at a steady pace. Draw a position vs. time graph of her walk.

5. A car rolling down a ramp starts with a speed of 50 cm/sec. The car keeps rolling and 0.5 seconds later the speed is 150 cm/sec. Calculate the acceleration of the car in cm/sec^2.

6. Think about the relationship between the amount of gas you have in your car and how far you can travel. Make a graphical model of this relationship. Which is the dependent variable (the effect)? Which is the independent variable (the cause)?

7. The data table below contains information from an experiment where a car was rolling down a ramp. You suspect some of the numbers are incorrect. Which numbers are suspect? Make a graph that demonstrates how you found the bad data.

Distance (cm)	Speed (cm/sec)
10	110
20	154
30	205
40	218
50	243
60	266
80	275
90	327

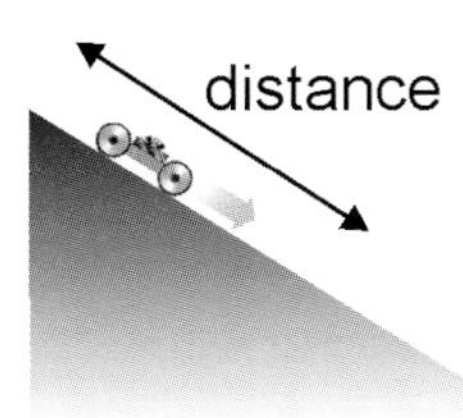

8. Use the graph below to predict the speed of the car at the following distances: 20 cm, 35 cm, 60 cm, 80 cm

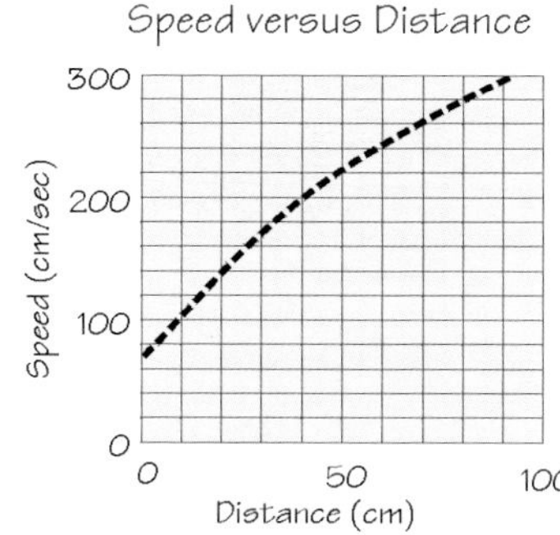

9. Arrange the four points on the distance vs. time graph in order from slowest to fastest.

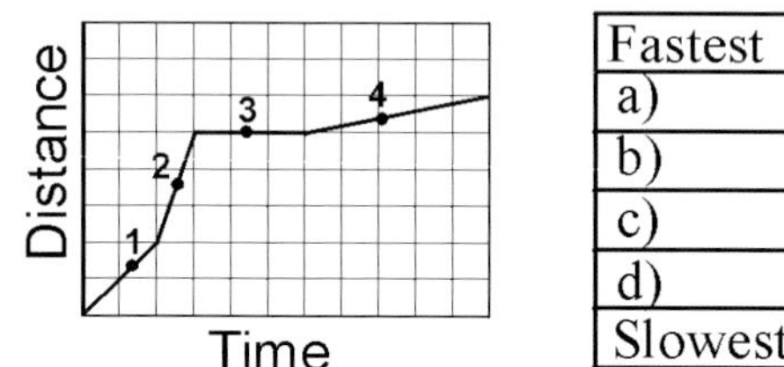

Fastest
a)
b)
c)
d)
Slowest

10. A bicyclist, traveling at 30 miles per hour, rides a total of 48 miles. How much time did it take?

11. A turtle is moving in a straight line at a steady speed of 15 cm/sec for 3 hours. How far did the turtle travel?

12. Match each of the three distance vs. time graphs with the corresponding speed vs. time graph. All three distance vs. time graphs contain only straight-line segments.

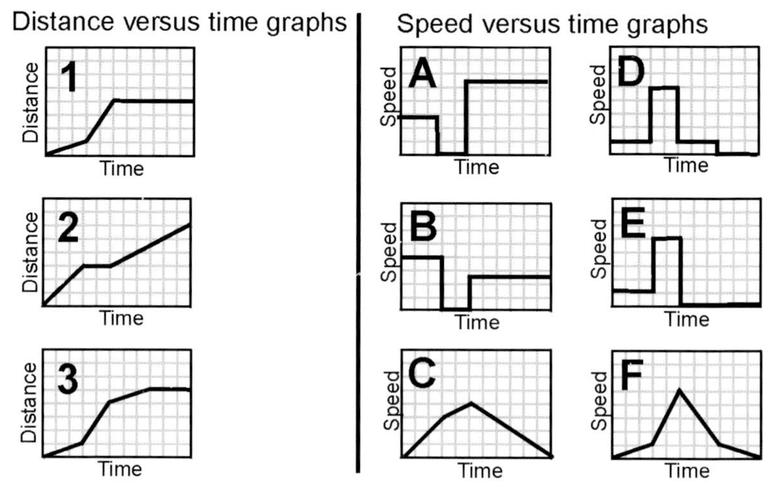

13. Calculate speed from the position vs. time graph on the left. Show all of your work.

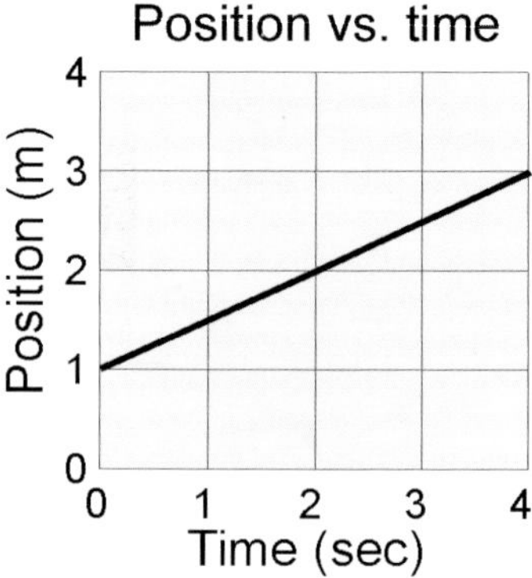

Applying your knowledge

1. Research the following: What is the fastest acceleration in a human in a sprint race? What is the fastest acceleration of a race horse? Which animal is capable of the fastest acceleration?

2. How fast do your fingernails grow? Devise an experiment to determine the answer. How would you represent your measurement? What units would you use to represent the speed?

Chapter 3

Forces and Motion

Introduction to Chapter 3

Things in the universe are always moving, but what gets them going? In this chapter you will follow Sir Isaac Newton's brilliant discoveries of the link between force and motion. Newton's three laws of motion have become a foundation of scientific thought.

Investigations for Chapter 3

3.1	Force, Mass, and Acceleration	*What is the relationship between force, mass and acceleration?*

In this Investigation you will devise ways to measure force and acceleration. By graphing force, mass, and acceleration, you will deduce Newton's second law of motion.

3.2	Weight, Gravity, and Friction	*How does increasing the mass of the car affect its acceleration?*

Do heavier objects fall faster? And if so, why? In this Investigation you will measure the Earth's gravity and learn why perpetual motion machines are impossible.

3.3	Equilibrium, Action and Reaction	*What is Newton's third law of motion?*

For every action there is an equal and opposite reaction. What does this famous statement really mean? In this Investigation you will explore how Newton's third law of motion explains the interaction and motion of everyday objects.

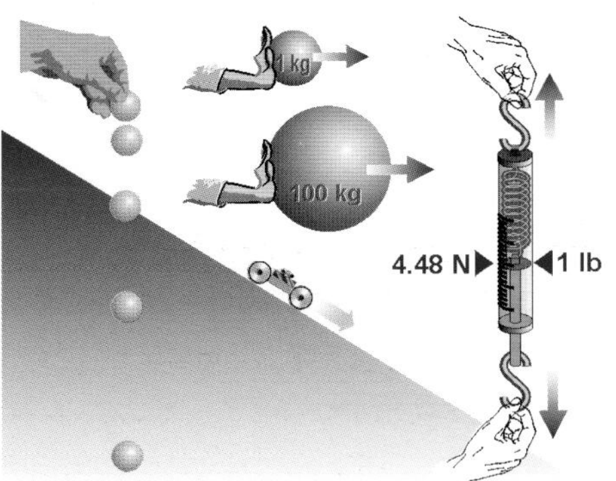

Learning Goals

In this chapter, you will:

- ✔ Explain the meaning of force.
- ✔ Show how force is required to change the motion of an object.
- ✔ Use a graph to identify relationships between variables.
- ✔ Explain and discuss Newton's second law and the relationship between force, mass, and acceleration.
- ✔ Describe how changing the mass of the car affects its acceleration.
- ✔ Draw conclusions from experimental data.
- ✔ Demonstrate qualitatively how friction can affect motion.
- ✔ Explain Newton's third law of motion.
- ✔ Identify action-reaction pairs of forces.
- ✔ Recognize how Newton's third law of motion explains the physics behind many common activities and useful objects.

Vocabulary

air friction	inertia	newton	rolling friction
equilibrium	law of conservation of momentum	Newton's first law of motion	sliding friction
force	mass	Newton's second law of motion	viscous friction
friction	momentum	Newton's third law of motion	weight
gravity	net force	pounds	

3.1 Force, Mass, and Acceleration

Sir Isaac Newton discovered one of the most important relationships in physics: the link between the force on an object, its mass, and its acceleration. In this section, you will learn about force and mass, and then apply all that you have learned to complete an important Investigation on acceleration. Through your experiments and data analysis, you will follow the path taken by one of history's most innovative thinkers.

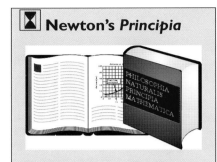

Introduction: Sir Isaac Newton's laws of motion

Sir Isaac Newton Sir Isaac Newton (1642-1727), an English physicist and mathematician, is one of the most brilliant scientists in history. Before the age of 30, he formulated the basic laws of mechanics, discovered the universal law of gravitation, and invented calculus! His discoveries helped to explain many unanswered questions, such as how do the planets move? What causes the tides? Why doesn't the moon fall to the Earth like other objects?

Table 3.1: *Newton's Laws of Motion*

The Three Laws	What Each One Says	In Other Words...
Newton's first law of motion	An object at rest will remain at rest unless acted on by an unbalanced force. An object in motion will continue with constant speed and direction, unless acted on by an unbalanced force.	Unless you apply force, things tend to keep on doing what they were doing in the first place.
Newton's second law of motion	The acceleration of an object is directly proportional to the force acting on it and inversely proportional to its mass.	Force causes an object to accelerate, while the object's mass resists acceleration.
Newton's third law of motion	Whenever one object exerts a force on another, the second object exerts an equal and opposite force on the first.	For every action, there is an equal and opposite reaction. If you push on the wall, you feel the wall pushing back on your hand.

Newton's *Principia*

Published in England in 1687, Newton's *Principia* is possibly the most important single book in the history of science. The *Principia* contains the three laws of motion and the universal law of gravitation.

Force

If your teacher asked you to move a cart containing a large, heavy box, would you: (a) push it; (b) pull it; or (c) yell at it until it moved (figure 3.1)?

Of course, the correct answer is either (a) push it or (b) pull it!

You need force to change motion

Every object continues in a state of rest, or of motion, unless force is applied to change things. This is a fancy way of saying that things tend to keep doing what they are already doing. There is no way the cart with the heavy box is going to move unless a force is applied. Of course, the force applied has to be strong enough to actually make the cart move.

Once the cart is set into motion, it will remain in motion, unless another force is applied to stop it. You need force to start things moving and also to make any change in their motion once they are going.

What is force?

A force is what we call a *push or a pull*, or *any action that has the ability to change motion*. This definition does not, however, mean that forces always change motion! If you push down on a table, it probably will not move. However, if the legs were to break, the table *could* move.

Force is an action that has the ability to change motion.

Pounds and newtons

There are two units of force that are commonly used: pounds and newtons (figure 3.2). Scientists prefer to use newtons. The newton is a smaller unit than the pound. There are 4.48 newtons in one pound. A person weighing 100 pounds would weigh 448 newtons.

The origin of the pound

The origin of the pound is similar to the origin of many standard units of length. Merchants needed a standard by which to trade goods without dispute. Weight is an obvious measure of quantity so the pound was standardized as a measure of weight. The oldest known standard weight was the *mina* used between 2400 and 2300 BC. One *mina* was a little more than one modern pound.

Figure 3.1: *Which action will move the cart, yelling at it or applying force to it?*

Unit	Equivalents
1 newton	0.228 pounds
1 pound	4.48 newtons

Figure 3.2: *Units of force.*

Example:

A person stands on a scale and measures a weight of 100 pounds. How much does the person weigh in newtons?

Solution:

(1) Multiply by conversion factors

$$100 \text{ lbs} = 100 \text{ lbs} \times \left(\frac{4.48 \text{ N}}{1 \text{ lb}}\right)$$

(2) Cancel units

$$= \frac{448 \cancel{\text{lb}} \times \text{N}}{\cancel{\text{lb}}}$$

(3) Answer = 448 N

The difference between force and mass

The origin of the newton The metric unit of force, the newton, relates force and motion. One newton equals 1 kilogram multiplied by 1 meter per second squared. This means that a force of one newton causes a 1-kilogram mass to have an acceleration of 1 m/sec^2. In talking about force, "newton" is easier to say than "1 kilogram · m/sec^2."

Use the correct units in formulas Force and mass have different units. Force units are pounds or newtons. Mass units are grams or kilograms. To get the right answer when using formulas that include force or mass, you need to use the correct units!

Defining force and mass Force is a push or pulling action that can change motion. Mass is the amount of "stuff" or matter in an object. Mass is a basic property of objects. Mass resists the action of forces by making objects harder to accelerate.

Weight is different from mass The weight of a person can be described in pounds or newtons. On Earth, a child *weighs* 30 pounds or about 134 newtons. In other words, the force acting on the child, due to the influence of Earth's gravity, is 134 kilograms · m/sec^2.

Your mass is the same everywhere in the universe, but your weight is different A child that weighs 30 pounds on Earth has a *mass* of about 14 kilograms because on Earth 2.2 pounds equals 1 kilogram. Because mass is an amount of matter, mass is independent of the force of gravity. Therefore, the mass of a person is the same everywhere in the universe. However, the *weight* of a person on Earth is different from what it would be on the moon or another planet because the force of gravity is different at these other places.

Units of force and mass can describe a quantity Mass and weight are commonly used to describe the quantity of something. For example, a kilogram of bananas weighs 2.2 pounds. You can describe the quantity of bananas as having a mass of 1 kilogram, or a weight of 2.2 pounds. Using two different kinds of measurement to describe the same quantity of bananas does *not* mean pounds and kilograms are the same thing.

Different units can describe the same quantity We often use different units to describe a quantity. For bananas, you can use a unit of mass (kilograms) or a unit of force (pounds). Likewise, buying one gallon of milk is the same as buying 8.4 pounds of milk. Pounds and gallons both describe the same quantity but one unit is a measure of volume (gallons) and one is a measure of force (pounds).

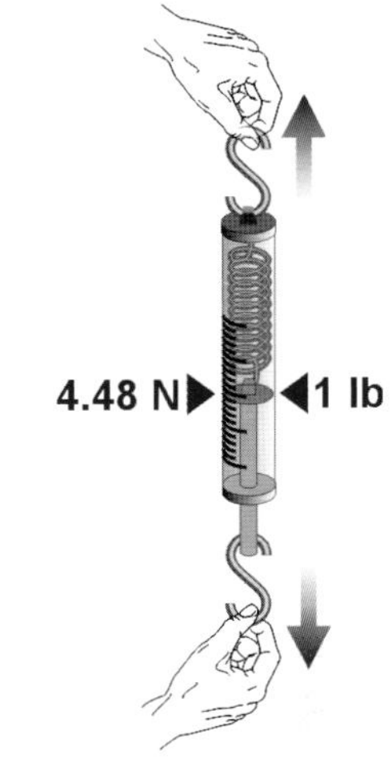

Figure 3.3: *A spring scale is a tool for measuring force. A force of 1 pound is the same as a force of 4.48 newtons.*

Newton

A newton is the metric unit of force.

A force of 1 newton
on a mass of 1 kilogram ...
creates an acceleration of 1 m/sec^2.

A force of one newton acting on a mass of 1 kilogram produces an acceleration of 1 m/sec^2.

Mass and inertia

Newton's first law

Newton's first law is also called the *law of inertia.* **Inertia** is defined as the property of an object to resist changing its state of motion. An object with a lot of inertia takes a lot of force to start or stop. Big trucks have more inertia than small cars, and bicycles have even less inertia.

Figure 3.4: *A large truck has more inertia than a small car. As a consequence it is much harder to push a truck than to push a car.*

Discussion question:

What part of a bicycle or car is designed to overcome the law of inertia?

Inertia is a property of mass

The amount of inertia an object has depends on its mass. **Mass** is a measure of the inertia of an object. Mass is what we usually think of when we use words like "heavy" or "light." A heavy object has a large mass while an object described as "light as a feather" has a small mass. We can also define mass as the amount of matter an object has.

The kilogram

Mass is measured in **kilograms**. The kilogram is one of the primary units of the metric system, like the meter and second. For reference, 1 kilogram has a weight of about 2.2 pounds on the Earth's surface. That means gravity pulls on a mass of 1 kilogram with a force of 2.2 pounds.

Bunch of bananas
1 kilogram

Cat
5 kilograms

Person
55 kilograms

Motorcycle
200 kilograms

You feel inertia by moving things

Which is harder to push: a ball that has a mass of 1 kilogram, or a ball that has a mass of 100 kilograms (figure 3.5)? Once you get each ball moving, which is easier to stop? Of course, the 100 kilogram ball is harder to start and harder to stop once it gets moving. This is a direct example of the law of inertia in action.

Which has more inertia?
Which is easier to push?

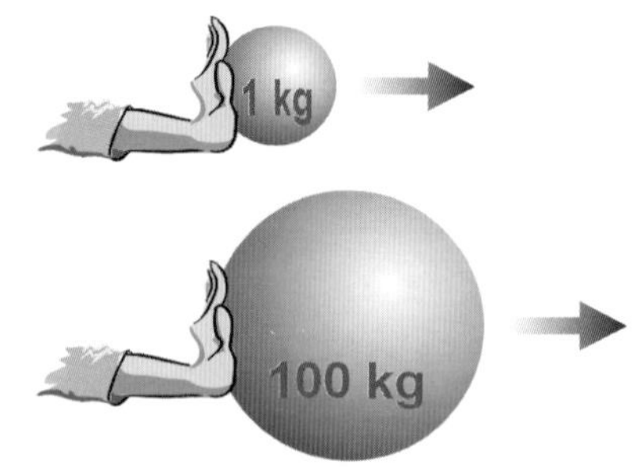

Figure 3.5: *The 100 kilogram ball has much more inertia, which makes it much harder to push.*

Mass is a constant property of an object

The mass of an object does not change, no matter where the object is, what planet it is on, or how it is moving. The only exception to this rule is when things go extremely fast, close to the speed of light. For the normal world, however, mass is an unchanging property of an object. The only way to change the mass is to physically change the object, like adding weights or breaking off a piece.

F = ma

Newton's second law of motion

Newton's second law

Newton's second law relates the applied force on an object, the mass of the object, and acceleration.

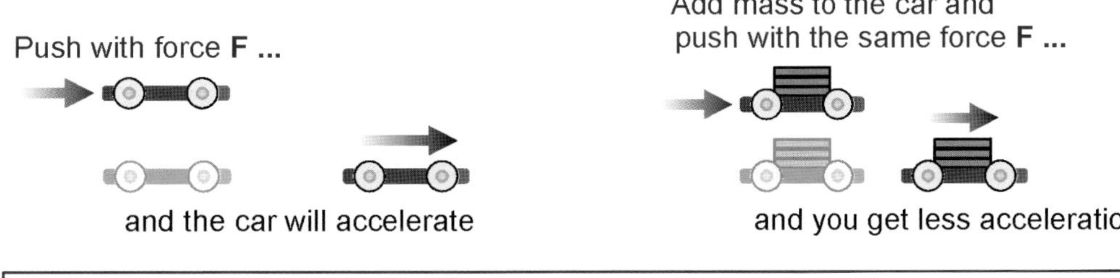
Push with force F ...
and the car will accelerate
Add mass to the car and push with the same force F ...
and you get less acceleration

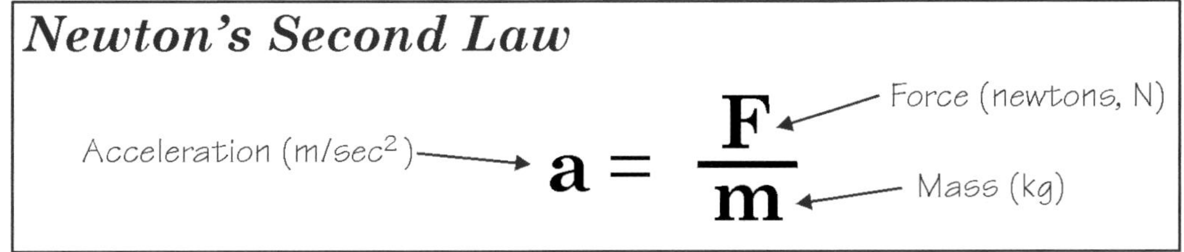
Newton's Second Law
Acceleration (m/sec²)
a = F/m
Force (newtons, N)
Mass (kg)

What the second law tells us

Newton's second law is one of the most famous equations in physics. It says that:

- Force causes acceleration.
- Mass resists acceleration.
- The acceleration you get is equal to the ratio of force over mass.

The second law is common sense when you think about it. If you make something very heavy (more mass), it takes proportionally more force to cause acceleration. It does not matter whether the acceleration is a speeding up or a slowing down.

Force is related to acceleration

There are many examples that demonstrate why force should be linked to acceleration. Force isn't necessary to keep an object in motion at constant speed. An ice-skater will coast for a long time without any outside force. However, the ice-skater does need force to speed up, slow down, turn or stop. Recall that changes in speed or direction all involve acceleration. *Force* causes *acceleration*; this is how we create changes in motion.

Example:

A car rolls down a ramp and you measure a force of 2 newtons pulling the car down. The car has a mass of 500 grams (0.5 kg).

Calculate the acceleration of the car.

m = 0.5 kg (500g)

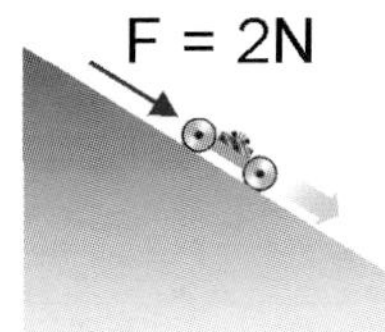
F = 2N

Solution:

(1) What are you asked for?

The acceleration

(2) What do you know?

Mass and force

(3) What relationships apply?

$a = F/m$

(4) Solve for what you need.

$a = F/m$

(5) Plug in numbers. Remember that $1\ \text{N} = 1\ \text{kg·m/sec}^2$.

$a = (2\ \text{N}) / (0.5\ \text{kg})$

$= (2\ \text{kg·m/sec}^2) / (0.5\ \text{kg})$

(6) Cancel units. In this case, kilogram cancels. The car's acceleration is:

$= 4\ \text{m/sec}^2$

Using the second law of motion

Writing the second law The formula for the second law of motion uses *F*, *m*, and *a* to represent force, mass, and acceleration. The way you write the formula depends on what you want to know. Three ways to write the law are summarized in table 3.1.

Table 3.1: *The three forms of Newton's second law*

Form of Newton's second law	if you want to know...	and you know....
a = F/m	the acceleration (**a**)	the mass (**m**) and the force (**F**)
F = ma	the force (**F**)	the mass (**m**) and the acceleration (**a**)
m = F/a	the mass (**m**)	the force (**F**) and the acceleration (**a**)

Units for the second law One newton is the amount of force that causes an acceleration of 1 meter/sec^2 for a body of 1-kilogram mass. To use Newton's second law in calculations, you must be sure to have units of meters/sec^2 for acceleration, newtons for force, and kilograms for mass. In these calculations, remember that *m* stands for *mass* in the formula. In the units for acceleration, *m* stands for *meters*.

Applications of the second law Newton's second law is frequently used by scientists and engineers to solve technical problems. For example, for an airplane to take off from a runway, it has to reach a minimum speed to be able to fly. If you know the mass of the plane, Newton's second law can be used to calculate how much force the engines must supply to accelerate the plane to take off speed.

Applying the second law to cars Cars offer another example. If a car engine can produce so much force, the second law is used to calculate how much acceleration the car can achieve. To increase the acceleration, car designers can do two things: reduce the mass by making the car lighter, or increase the force by using a bigger engine. Both options are based directly on the Newton's second law.

Example:

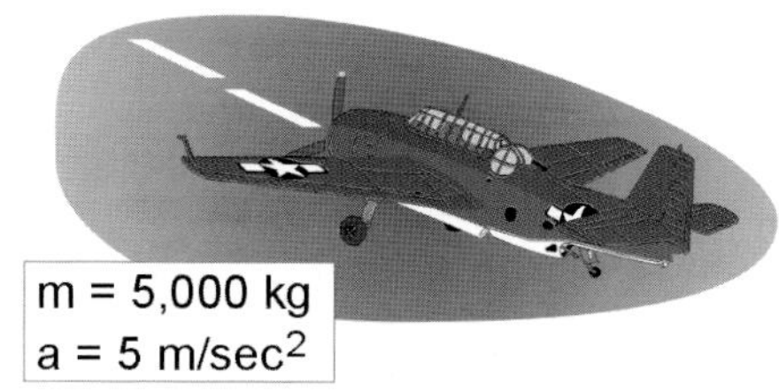

An airplane with a mass of 5,000 kilograms needs to accelerate at 5 m/sec^2 to take off before it reaches the end of the runway. How much force is needed from the engine?

Solution

(1) What are you asked for?

The force

(2) What do you know?

Mass and acceleration

(3) What relationships apply?

a = F/m

(4) Solve for what you need.

F = ma

(5) Plug in numbers. Remember that 1 N = 1 kg·m/sec^2.

F = (5,000 kg) x (5 m/sec^2)

= 25,000 kg·m/sec^2

(6) Convert the units to newtons. The force needed is:

= 25,000 N

Balanced and unbalanced forces

Net force The motion of an object depends on the *total* of all forces acting on the object. We call the total of all forces the **net force**. To figure out the net force, we usually have to make some forces positive and some negative so they can cancel out. Choose a direction to be positive, and be consistent about treating forces in the opposite direction as negative (figure 3.6).

What is equilibrium? When forces on an object are balanced, the net force is zero, and we say that the object is in **equilibrium**. In equilibrium there is no change in motion. An object at rest stays at rest, and an object already moving keeps moving at the same speed.

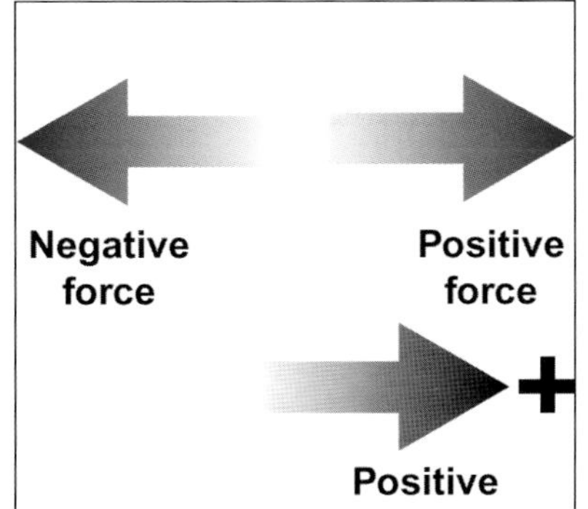

Figure 3.6: *Assigning positive and negative values to forces in opposite directions.*

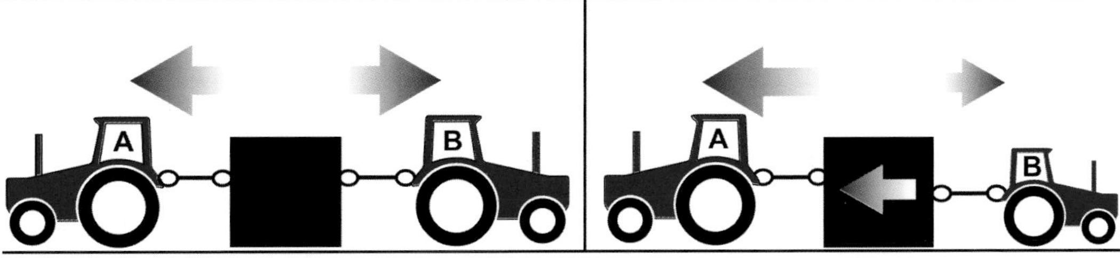

An example of equilibrium and nonequilibrium The diagram above illustrates the difference between balanced and unbalanced forces. Imagine a giant box being pulled on both sides by tractors. If the tractors are equal, the forces are equal, the box is in equilibrium and does not move. If tractor A is 10 times stronger than tractor B, the forces are *not* in equilibrium. The net force points toward tractor A, so the box accelerates toward tractor A.

The second law refers to net force The force that appears in the second law is really the net force acting on an object. Acceleration is caused by a net force that is *not* zero. For motion to change, the forces acting on the object have to be unbalanced. In other words, a force acting on one side of the object has to be greater than the force acting on the other side of the object.

Solving force problems We often use equilibrium and the second law to prove the existence of forces. If we see that an object is at rest, we know its acceleration is zero. That means the net force must also be zero. If we know one force (like weight), we know there is another force in the opposite direction to make the net force zero (figure 3.7).

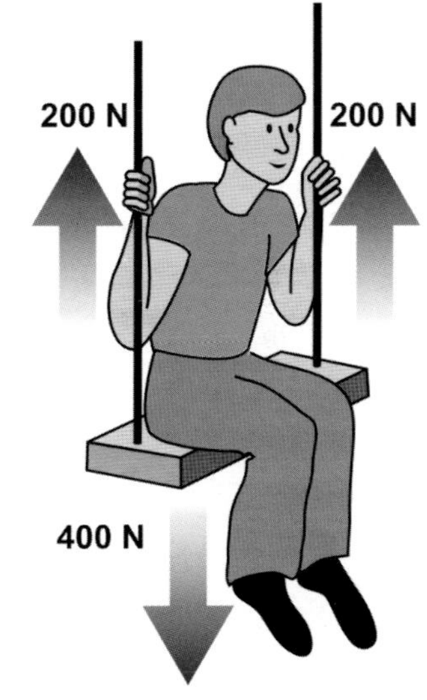

Figure 3.7: *This swing is not moving so the net force must be zero. If the weight of the person is 400 N, then each rope must pull upwards with a force of 200 N to make the net force zero.*

3.2 Weight, Gravity, and Friction

Suppose you and a friend are riding your bicycles in San Francisco. You both reach the top of a hill and stop to take in the view. You decide to coast to the bottom of the hill without pedaling. If you both push off at the same time, and with the same amount of force, will you both reach the bottom of the hill at the same time? Who will accelerate the fastest? In this section, you will learn about weight and friction. These two forces determine who gets down the hill first.

Gravity

What is gravity

What is the force that causes an object like a car to accelerate down a ramp?

You probably know **gravity** is involved. Gravity is a force that pulls every mass toward every other mass. Since Earth is the biggest mass around, gravity pulls everything toward the center of Earth. Ask someone the meaning of the word *down* and they point toward the center of Earth. Down is the direction of the force of gravity.

Gravity depends on mass

The force of gravity depends on how much mass you have. If you have more mass, gravity pulls on you with more force. That is why we can use force to measure mass. When you use a digital balance to measure the mass of a sample, you are really measuring the force of gravity acting on your sample. If you are on the surface of Earth, every kilogram of mass creates a gravitational force of 9.8 newtons. You may recognize this number—9.8 newtons is the same as 9.8 m/sec^2, the acceleration of gravity. We will talk more about the relation between newtons and the acceleration of gravity on the next page.

Mars' gravity is weaker than Earth's

If you were on Mars, your force/mass balance would have to be adjusted. The planet is much smaller than Earth and therefore Mars's gravity is weaker. Every kilogram of mass on Mars results in a gravity force of only 3.8 newtons (figure 3.8). The larger the planet you are on, the greater the force of gravity. On Jupiter, the largest planet, gravity has a force 2.6 times stronger than on the surface of Earth. If you weighed 110 pounds on Earth, you would weigh 286 pound on Jupiter!

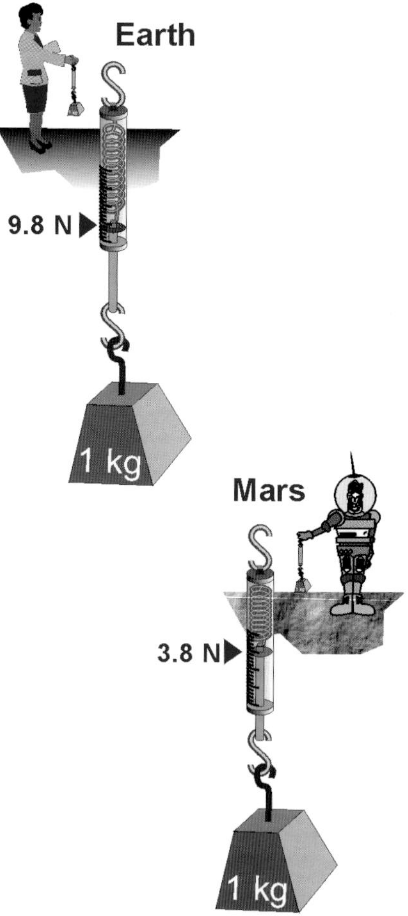

Figure 3.8: *Weight is a force that comes from gravity pulling on mass. The weight depends on how strong gravity is. Earth is bigger than Mars and has stronger gravity. A kilogram weighs 9.8 newtons on Earth but only 3.8 newtons on Mars.*

Mass and weight

What is weight? Weight is what we call the force created by gravity on objects. The weight of an object depends on its mass. Your mass is constant throughout the universe, but your weight changes depending on what planet you happen to be on. For example, because the gravitational force on Mars is less than that on Earth, you *weigh* less on Mars than on Earth, but your *mass* is the same at both locations!

How to calculate weight If you know the mass of an object, you can calculate its weight using Newton's second law. When you drop something on Earth, gravity causes it to accelerate at 9.8 m/sec^2. Because there is acceleration, you know there must be a force. You also know the force is exactly equal to mass times acceleration. The force we call weight is equal to an object's mass times the acceleration of gravity (9.8 m/sec^2).

Weight in formulas Since weight is a force, we use the letter F to represent it. To remind us that we are talking about the weight force, we add a little w next to the F. The w is called a subscript, and we would say "F sub w" if we wanted to tell someone what we were writing. The F and w always stay together since they are really one symbol for the weight force.

Weight

$$F_w = mg$$

Weight force (N) → F_w; mass (kg) → m; Acceleration of gravity (9.8 m/sec^2) → g

DON'T use kilograms for weight Because we live and work on the surface of Earth, we tend to use weight and mass interchangeably. Heavy objects have lots of mass and light objects have little mass. Boxes and people are "weighed" in both kilograms and pounds. This is OK for everyday use, but you must remember the difference when doing physics. Physics is about the true nature of how the universe works and mass is truly a fundamental property of an object. Force often depends on outside influences, like gravity. You cannot interchange force and mass in a formula; doing so would be like substituting a fork for a spoon when you are trying to eat soup. In physics, force and mass are different quantities with different units.

Example

A legend has it that, around 1587, Galileo dropped two balls from the Leaning Tower of Pisa to see which would fall faster.

a) Calculate the weight of each ball.

b) Calculate the acceleration of each ball's fall.

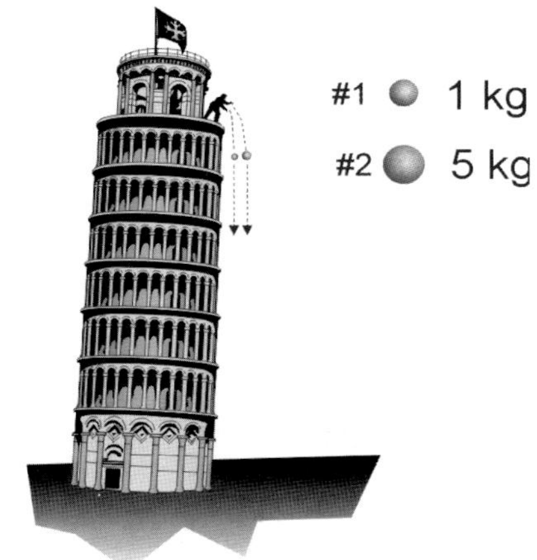

Part a)

#1 $F_w = mg$
$= (1\ kg) \times (9.8\ m/sec^2)$
$= 9.8\ N$

#2 $F_w = (5\ kg) \times (9.8\ m/sec^2)$
$= 49\ N$

Part b)

#1 $a = F/m$
$= (9.8\ N)/ 1\ kg$
$= 9.8\ m/sec^2$

#2 $a = (49\ N)/ 5\ kg$
$= 9.8\ m/sec^2$

The acceleration of both balls is the same!

Newton's law of universal gravitation

Why does the moon orbit Earth? Mars and Earth are two massive objects that orbit the sun. Similarly, Earth's moon is a massive object that orbits around Earth. The same gravity that gives you weight is what holds Earth and its moon together. If you could simply drop the moon, it would fall to Earth just like an apple falls down from a tree. That does not happen because the moon is moving quite fast in a direction perpendicular to Earth's attractive gravity. The force of gravity bends the path of the moon toward the center of Earth, resulting in a nearly circular orbit.

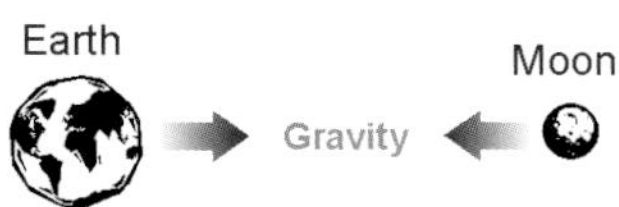

Gravity attracts the Moon to the Earth and the Earth to the Moon.

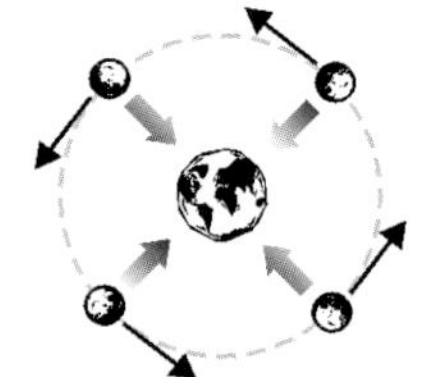

The velocity of the Moon is perpendicular to its distance from the Earth. Because gravity pulls toward the center of the Earth, the Moon's path is bent into a (nearly) circular orbit.

Figure 3.9: *The attractive force from gravity between objects of ordinary mass is incredibly small.*

What is the law of universal gravitation? Gravity is a force of attraction that exists between any two objects that have mass. This idea is known as the law of universal gravitation. The force of attraction increases when the mass of the objects increases. The force of gravity also increases when the objects get closer together. Given this information, does this mean that we feel forces of attraction between ourselves and other objects?

Law of universal gravitation:
The force of attraction between two objects is directly related to the masses of the objects and inversely related to the distance between them.

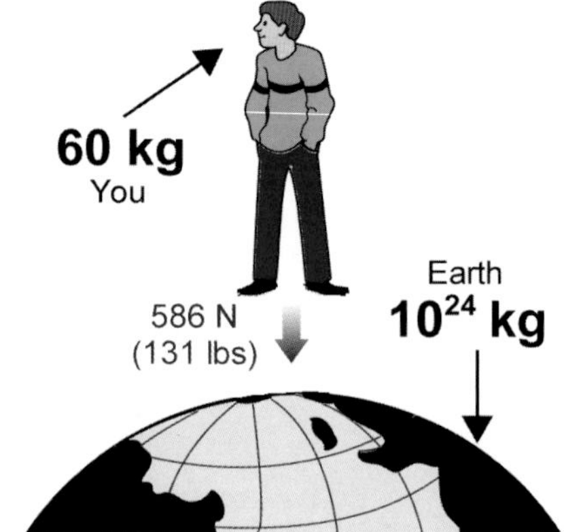

Figure 3.10: *You feel weight because the mass of Earth is large enough to create significant gravity forces.*

It takes a lot of mass to create gravity you can feel You may feel attracted to a chocolate cake, but gravity has nothing to do with it! The force of gravity between ordinary masses is so weak that you can't really feel it (figure 3.9). We notice the effects of gravity because the mass of one particular object (Earth) is huge, and relatively close to us. For gravity to create noticeable forces between two objects, the mass of at least one of them must be very large, like a planet or a star (figure 3.10).

Calculating the gravitational force between objects

Calculating the force of gravity

You can calculate the gravity force between two objects using the equation for universal gravitation. The attractive force between two objects is equal to 'G' times the product of their masses divided by the square of the distance between them. 'G' is the gravitational constant, and is the same everywhere in the universe. This one equation describes gravity for small things, like people and chocolate cakes. It also works for huge things like galaxies, stars, and planets.

Equation of Universal Gravitation:

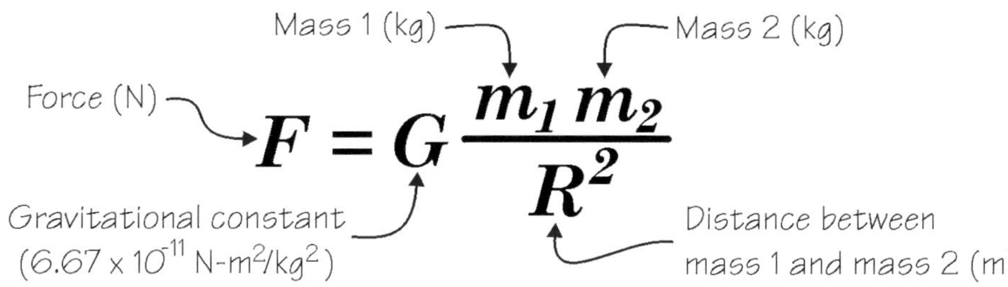

Example

The mass of Jupiter's third largest moon, Io, is 8.9×10^{22} kg. The radius of Io is

$$F = G \times \frac{m_1 \times m_2}{R^2}$$

1,815 kilometers. Use the equation of universal gravitation to calculate your weight if you were on the surface of Io and had a mass of 50 kilograms.

1) Use the formula for the universal law of gravitation.

2) Plug in values.

$G = 6.7 \times 10^{-11}$ kg/m-sec^2; $m_1 = 50$ kg; $m_2 = 8.9 \times 10^{22}$kg; $R = 1{,}815{,}000$ m

$= [(6.7 \times 10^{-11}$ kg/m-sec$^2) \times (50$ kg$) \times (8.9 \times 10^{22}kg)] \div (1{,}815{,}000$ m$)^2$

$= 91$ N or 20 lbs (4.448 N = 1 lb)

Your weight on Io is about 20 pounds! On Earth your weight would be 110 pounds. With such a small weight, you could jump 13 meters (43 feet) high on Io.

Historical Perspective

Many people associate the discovery of the law of gravitation with a falling apple. As the story goes, Newton observed an apple fall from a tree and was inspired to wonder if the moon experienced a similar force that affected its motion around Earth. Newton deduced that the force responsible for accelerating a falling apple is the same force involved in keeping the moon in orbit. As Newton developed his theories about motion, he concluded that gravity is a force that behaves the same throughout the universe—it's universal!

Friction

How is space travel different from Earth travel? When Newton was developing the law of universal gravitation, he realized that with enough speed, an object would orbit forever as long as nothing slowed it down. For an object like a space shuttle, orbiting around Earth can be nearly effortless because there is no air resistance in space. Air resistance "resists" forward movement of cars and other objects on Earth. Air resistance is a kind of force kind called friction.

What is friction? Friction is a term that is used to describe forces that result from relative motion between objects (like the wheel and axle of a car). *Frictional forces always work against the motion that produces them.* For example, when a model car rolls down a ramp frictional forces resist the motion. Friction is a force that holds the car back. Axles and ball bearings are inventions that help reduce friction.

What causes friction? Friction comes from two surfaces moving against each other. Surfaces of objects that appear smooth and shiny actually have microscopic hills and valleys. As the surfaces slide across each other the hills and valleys interfere causing friction.

Friction and wear Objects that continuously rub against each other cause wear. Wear refers to how moving parts can erode each other. In old cars, the parts are often so worn down due to friction that they are too loose and no longer fit correctly.

Kinds of friction We use the word *friction* to describe any force that is caused by motion and that acts to slow motion down. Some examples of friction include:

- Air Friction: The air moving around moving objects creates an opposing force. This is why many cars have rounded, *aerodynamic* shapes. A rounded design reduces air friction, allowing cars to go faster and get better gas mileage.
- Sliding Friction: When two surfaces rub against each other, we get sliding friction. Sliding friction is caused by irregularities in the surfaces.
- Viscous Friction: Objects that move in water or other fluids create this type of friction. Oil changes sliding friction to viscous friction and helps reduce wear.
- Rolling Friction: This type of friction is caused by one object rolling over another, like a wheel rolling over the road. Ball bearings in wheels are designed to reduce the effect of rolling friction.

Figure 3.11: *Sliding friction is caused by microscopic hills and valleys on the surface of materials.*

Figure 3.12: *The wheels of the car have ball bearings to reduce sliding friction. Even ball bearings have rolling friction and may also have viscous friction from oil.*

Friction and motion

How does friction affect acceleration?

Friction is a force that always opposes motion. That means the force of friction is opposite whatever force is causing motion. For a car rolling downhill, gravity supplies a force pulling down the hill. Friction opposes motion, so it pushes the car up the hill while gravity is pulling the car down the hill.

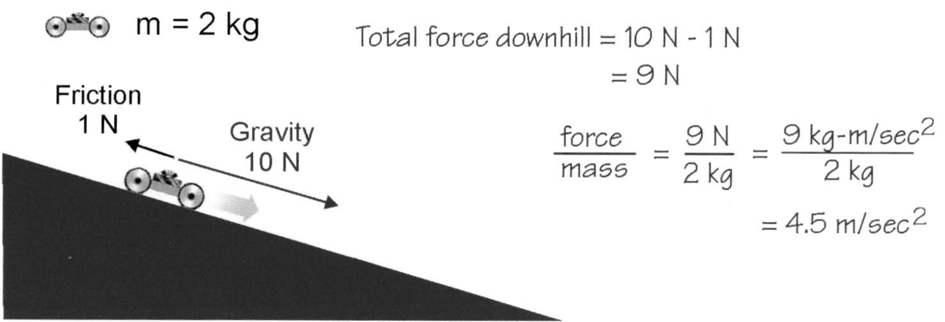

The net force

The F that appears in Newton's second law stands for the total force acting on the car. This includes gravity and friction. To find out the total force we need to subtract the friction force from gravity. What is left is often called the net force. When talking about forces, the word *net* means total.

Friction reduces acceleration

The acceleration we observe will always be less than it would have been if there were no friction. This is because the friction force partly cancels some of the gravity force pulling the car down.

All machines have friction

All true machines have friction. That means there are always forces that tend to oppose motion. Unless you continually supply force, eventually, friction slows everything to a stop. Bicycles have very low friction, but even the best bicycle slows down if you coast on a level road.

Perpetual Motion

Throughout history, many people have claimed to have invented a machine that will run forever with no outside force. We call them perpetual motion machines and none have ever worked.

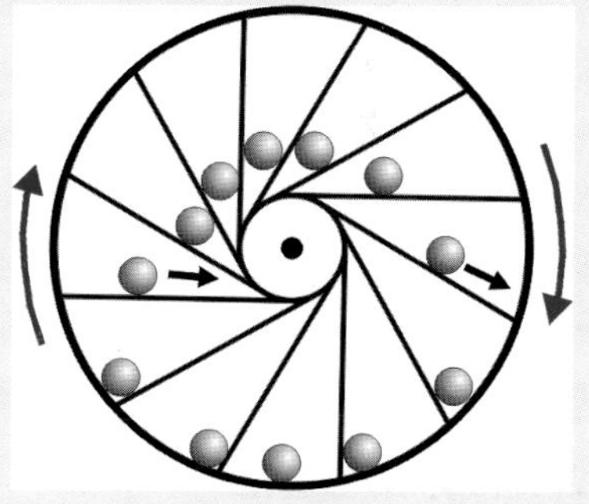

Perpetual motion machines never work because there is always some friction. Friction always opposes motion so sooner or later everything slows down.

If someone shows you a device that seems to go without stopping, be suspicious. There is no escape from friction. Somewhere, you will always find a hidden plug or battery supplying force.

3.3 Equilibrium, Action and Reaction

In this section, you will come to understand the truth behind the phrase "For every action there is an equal and opposite reaction." This statement is known as Newton's third law of motion and it explains the interaction and motion of objects. You will learn that forces are always at work when the motion of an object changes. However, this is not to say that objects at rest experience no forces. What keeps your book perfectly still on a table as you are trying to read it (figure 3.13)? Why would your book fall to the ground if you lifted the table at one end? "Force" is a good answer to both of these questions.

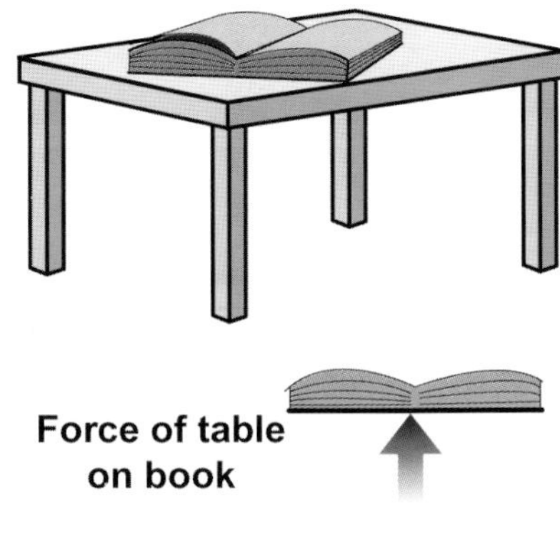

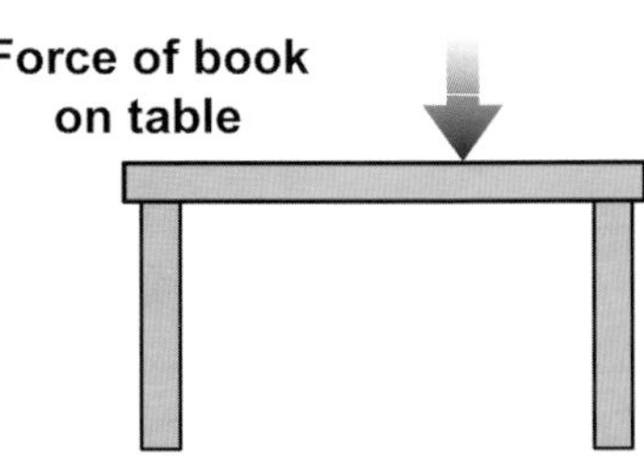

Figure 3.13: *Even when things are not moving there are forces acting. Gravity pulls the book down with a force. The table pushes back up with an equal and opposite force. The book stays still because the two forces are balanced*

Newton on a skateboard

An imaginary skateboard contest

Imagine a skateboard contest in which each person has to move his or her skateboard without their bodies touching the ground. Neither their feet nor their hands may touch the ground. How would you win this contest? How would you move your skateboard? Here are some possible strategies.

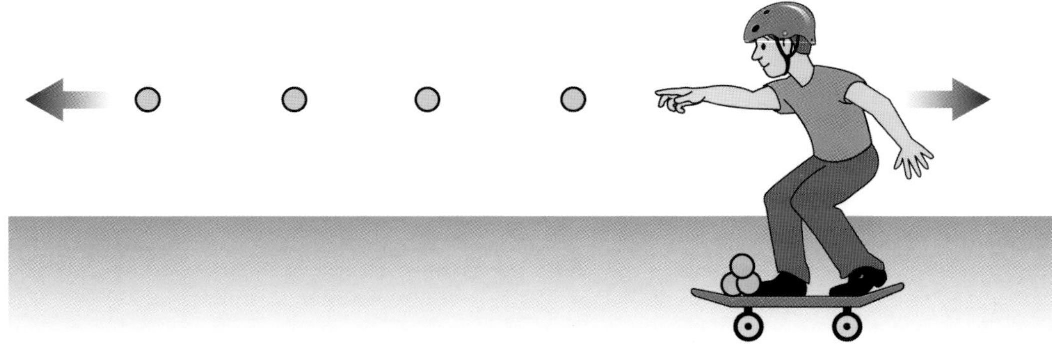

- Wave your arms back and forth.
- Walk from one end of the skateboard to the other.
- Start the contest at the top of an inclined plane.
- Stuff tennis balls in your pockets and throw them away from you.

Which strategies would work? Can you think of any others? Newton's third law of motion explains why you use your feet in the first place to get a skateboard moving. This law also explains why you can move a skateboard even if you don't use your hands or feet.

Newton's third law of motion

Review the first and second laws The first and second laws apply to single objects. For example, the first law states that an object will remain at rest or in motion at constant velocity unless acted upon by an external force. The second law states that the acceleration of an object is directly proportional to force and inversely proportional to the mass.

The third law operates with pairs of objects In contrast to the first two laws, the third law of motion deals with pairs of objects. This is because *all forces come in pairs*. Newton's third law states that for every action force there has to be a reaction force that is equal in magnitude (in size) and opposite in direction to the action force.

For every action force, there is a reaction force equal in strength and opposite in direction

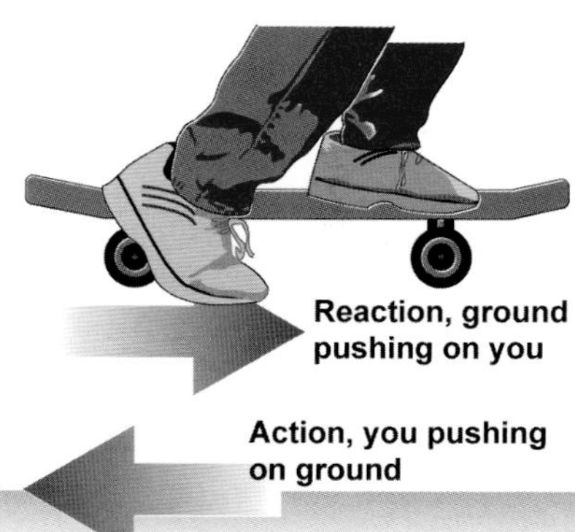

Figure 3.14: *All forces come in pairs. When you push on the ground (action), the reaction of the ground pushing back on your foot is what makes you move.*

The third law applied to a skateboard The action/reaction forces act on separate objects, *not* the same object. For example, the action-reaction pair that is required to move your skateboard includes your foot and the Earth. Your foot pushing against the ground is the action force. The ground pushing back on you is the reaction force. The reaction force makes you move because it acts on *you* (figure 3.14). If you were on slippery ice, you could push just as hard, but without a reaction force you would not move.

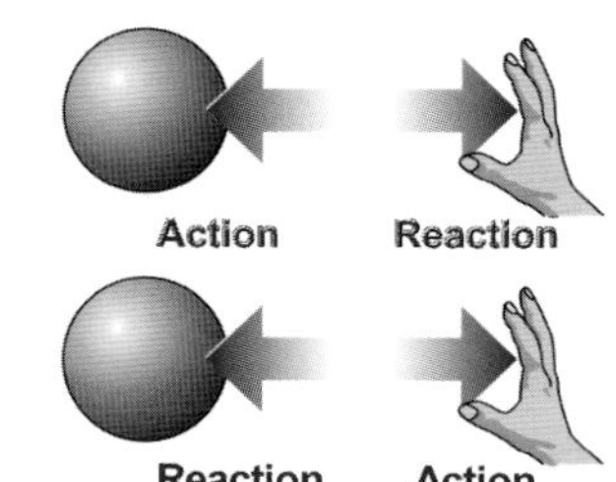

Figure 3.15: *It doesn't matter which force you call the action and which the reaction. The action and reaction forces are interchangeable.*

Stopping action and reaction confusion It is easy to get confused thinking about action and reaction forces. Why don't they always cancel each other out? The reason is that the action and reaction forces act on different objects. When you throw a ball you apply the action force to the ball, creating acceleration of the ball. The reaction is the ball pushing back against your hand. The forces don't cancel because they act on different objects.

Momentum

The motion of objects

When two objects exchange forces in an action-reaction pair, their motions are also affected as a pair. If you throw a ball from your skateboard you must apply a force to the ball. The third law says the ball exerts an equal and opposite force on you. Your force makes the ball accelerate in one direction and the reaction makes you accelerate in the opposite direction.

What happens if you throw faster or heavier balls?

Because of the third law, the speed at which you and the ball move away from each other are related in a special way. If you throw the ball away very fast, your backward acceleration is higher than when you throw the ball away slowly. If you throw a heavier ball away fast, your backward acceleration is greater than if you throw a lighter ball (figure 3.16). The backward acceleration from the reaction force is called **recoil**.

Momentum is mass times velocity

Momentum is the mass of an object multiplied by its speed or velocity. If you increase the mass or the speed of an object, you increase its momentum. The units for momentum are kilograms-meters per second or kg-m/sec.

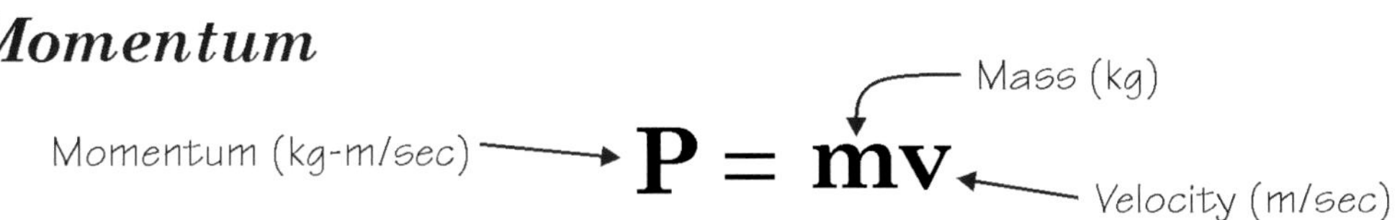

The law of conservation of momentum

Because of the third law, the momentum of you and the ball are connected. If the ball takes away momentum to the left, you must take away an equal amount of momentum to the right. This rule is an example of the **law of conservation of momentum**. The law of conservation of momentum says that as long as interacting objects are not influenced by outside forces (like friction), the total amount of momentum cannot change.

Figure 3.16: *The speed and mass of the ball you throw affect your backward acceleration (recoil).*

Using positive and negative

When talking about momentum we usually need to use positive and negative to tell the direction of motion (figure 3.17). That means momentum can also be positive (moving to the right) or negative (moving to the left).

Before you throw the ball, your speed (and the ball's) is zero. Since momentum is mass times speed, the total momentum is also zero. The law of conservation of momentum says that *after* you throw the ball, the total momentum *still* has to be zero.

An example of the conservation of momentum

If the ball has a mass of 1 kilogram and you throw it at a speed of -20 m/sec to the left, the ball takes away -20 kg-m/sec of momentum. To make the total momentum zero, *you* must take away +20 kg-m/sec of momentum. If your mass is 40 kg and you ignore friction, then your speed is +0.5 m/sec to the right (figure 3.18).

Rockets and jet planes

Rockets and jet planes use the law of conservation of momentum to move. A jet engine pushes exhaust air at very high speed out of the back of the engine. The momentum lost by the air going backward must be compensated by the momentum gained by the jet moving forward. A rocket can accelerate in space without touching anything because it throws mass at high speed out the end of the engine. The forward momentum of a rocket is exactly equal to the momentum of the escaping mass ejected from the end of the engine.

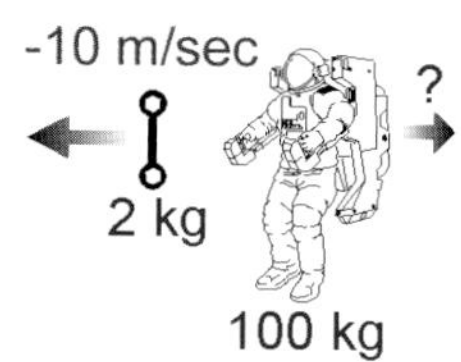

Example: An astronaut in space throws a 2-kilogram wrench away from him at a speed of -10 m/sec. If the astronaut's mass is 100 kilograms, at what speed does the astronaut move backward after throwing the wrench?

Solution: (1) You are asked for the speed. Since the astronaut is in space, we can ignore friction.

(2) You are given the mass and speed of the wrench and the mass of the astronaut.

(3) This is enough to apply the law of conservation of momentum.

$$m_1 v_1 + m_2 v_2 = 0$$

(4) Plug in numbers.

$$[2\text{ kg} \times (-10\text{ m/sec})] + [(100\text{ kg}) \times v_2] = 0$$

$$v_2 = +20 / 100 = +0.2\text{ m/sec}$$

The astronaut moves backward at a speed of +0.2 m/sec.

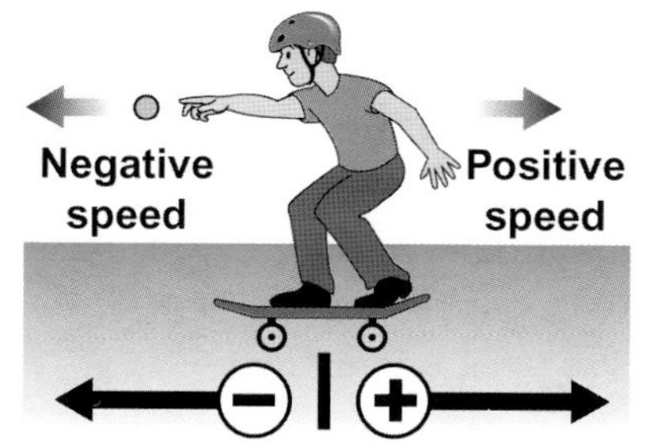

Figure 3.17: *The direction is important when using the law of conservation of momentum. We use positive and negative numbers to represent opposite directions.*

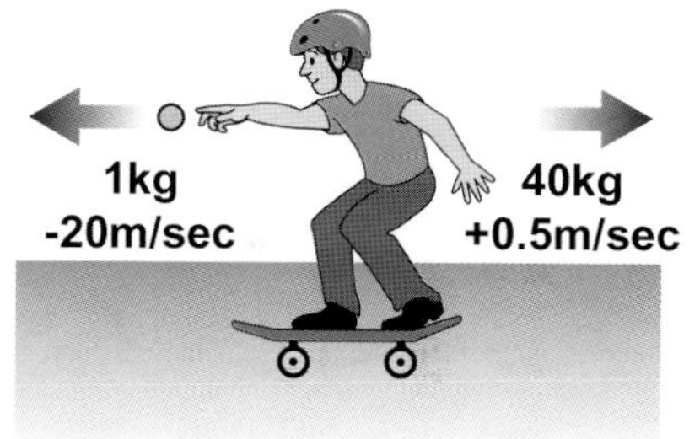

Figure 3.18: *The result of the skateboarder throwing a 1-kg ball at a speed of -20 m/sec is that he and the skateboard with a total mass of 40 kg move backward at a speed of +0.5 m/sec if you ignore friction. If you account for friction, would the calculation for speed of the skateboarder on the skateboard end up being less or more than 0.5 m/sec?*

Chapter 3 Review

Vocabulary review

Match the following terms with the correct definition. There is one extra definition in the list that will not match any of the terms.

Set One

1. force	a. The metric unit of force
2. pound	b. Objects at rest stay at rest, and objects in motion stay in motion, unless acted on by a force
3. newton	c. The English unit of force
4. Newton's first law of motion	d. An object that is in a state of motion
5. inertia	e. An action that has the ability to change motion
	f. The property of a body to resist changing its state of motion

Set Two

1. mass	a. When an object has a net force of zero acting on it
2. kilogram	b. A measurement of the amount of matter
3. Newton's second law of motion	c. The total forces acting on an object
4. net force	d. Force causes an object to accelerate, while the object's mass resists acceleration
5. equilibrium	e. When an object has a net force acting on it
	f. The metric unit of mass

Set Three

1. gravity	a. Forces that result from chemical reactions
2. weight	b. A force that pulls every mass toward every other mass
3. friction	c. For every action, there is an equal and opposite reaction
4. wear	d. Forces that result from the relative motion between objects
5. Newton's third law of motion	e. The grinding away of moving parts that are in contact with each other
	f. The force created by gravity on objects

Set Four

1. viscous friction	a. Friction caused by the movement of two surfaces against each other
2. sliding friction	b. Friction caused by one object rolling over another
3. rolling friction	c. Friction caused by the movement of air around moving objects
4. air friction	d. Friction caused by the movement of an object through a liquid
5. momentum	e. The mass of an object multiplied by its acceleration
	f. The mass of an object multiplied by its velocity

Concept review

1. Define the term *force*, and give some examples of forces.
2. Give an example of Newton's first law acting in everyday life.
3. Which has more inertia, a 1-kilogram ball or a 10-kilogram ball?
4. An object with more inertia is both harder to __________ and to __________.
5. Give an example of Newton's second law acting in everyday life.
6. Explain how the unit of 1 newton is defined.
7. Any object with mass exerts a force on any other object with mass. This force is called __________.
8. On the surface of the Earth, the force of gravity acting on one kilogram is:
   a. 9.8 pounds
   b. 3.8 newtons
   c. 9.8 newtons
   d. varies according to your mass
9. What is the difference between the *mass* of an object and the *weight* of an object?
10. According to the law of universal gravitation, what two factors are important in determining the force of gravity between two objects?
11. Name a unit for measuring:
    a. force
    b. mass
    c. weight
12. The net force acting on a car rolling down a ramp is the addition of two forces.
    a. Name the two forces on the car.
    b. Which of the two forces helps the motion of the car?
    c. Which of the two forces opposes the motion of the car?
13. Give an example of Newton's third law acting in everyday life.
14. Fill in the blanks in the following statements:
    a. Forces always occur in __________.
    b. Each force in an action-reaction pair of forces is equal in __________.
    c. Each force in an action-reaction pair of forces is opposite in __________.
15. The momentum of an object depends on what two factors?
16. Give an example of the law of conservation of momentum from everyday life.

Problems

1. A company uses a ramp to slide boxes of parts to a shipping area. Each box weighs about 10 kilograms. When sliding down the ramp, the boxes accelerate at a speed of 0.1 m/sec^2. What is the force acting on each box? For this problem, ignore the effects of friction acting on each box.
2. You have an object that has a mass of 4.4 kilograms.
   a. What is its weight in newtons?
   b. What is its weight in pounds?
3. You drop an object from a second-floor window.
   a. Describe the speed of the object after 1 second.
   b. Describe the speed of the object after 2 seconds.
4. A heavy block of lead is placed on a table. The block of lead has a weight, or a force, of 500 newtons. Explain why it doesn't fall through the table.
5. From the text you learned that a 110-pound person would weigh 20 pounds (89 N) on Jupiter's moon Io. The mass of Jupiter is 1.9 x 10^{27} kg and its diameter is 142, 984 km. Would this same person weigh more on Io or on Jupiter? Explain your answer. What would this person weigh on Jupiter?
6. In the supermarket you return a cart to the cart area. You stand still and push the cart towards the other carts. You've just learned that the cart pushes back on you too, according to Newton's third law.
   a. Explain why the cart moves and you do not.
      Hint: Consider the cart and yourself separately. Also consider all the forces acting on you and on the cart.
   b. Which object is in equilibrium, you or the cart?
7. What is the momentum of a 0.5-kilogram object traveling at 4 m/sec?

Applying your knowledge

1. You learned in this chapter that an object in motion will stay in motion unless acted on by a force. However, in everyday life, friction always slows things down. Research ways that people reduce friction in machines, such as by using ball bearings.
2. Joints like knees and elbows are designed to move freely. Find out how friction is reduced in a joint.
3. Research the effects of weightlessness on people and what astronauts do to counter those effects.
4. When an ice skater is on ice, a small amount of melting occurs under the blades of the skates. How does this help the skater glide? Your answer should discuss two different types of friction.

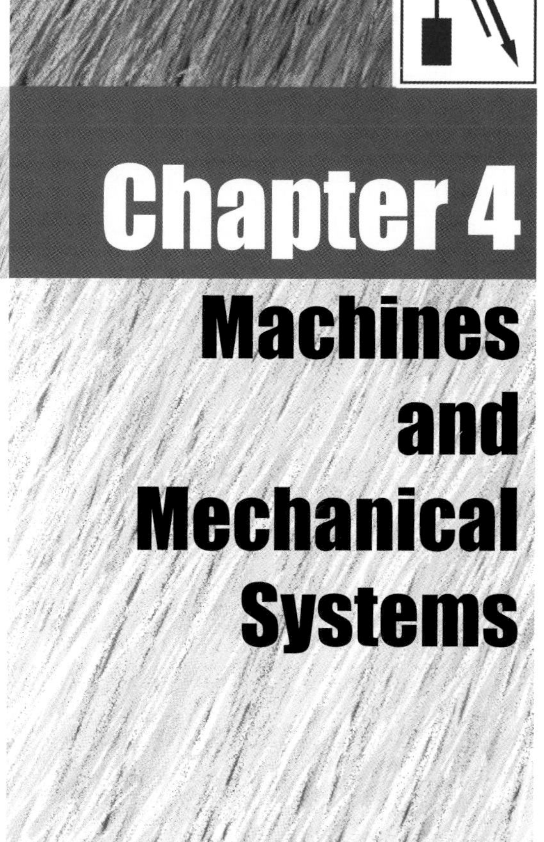

Introduction to Chapter 4

Engineering is the process of applying science to solve problems. Technology is the word we use to describe machines and inventions that result from engineering efforts. The development of the technology that created computers, cars, and the space shuttle began with the invention of simple machines. In this chapter, you will discover the principles upon which simple machines operate. You will study several simple machines closely and learn how machines can multiply and alter forces.

Investigations for Chapter 4

4.1	**Forces in Machines**	*How do simple machines work?*

Machines can make us much stronger than we normally are. In this Investigation, you will design and build several block and tackle machines from ropes and pulleys. Your machines will produce up to six times as much force as you apply. As part of the Investigation you will identify the input and output forces, and measure the mechanical advantage.

4.2	**The Lever**	*How does a lever work?*

Archimedes said "Give me a lever and fulcrum and I shall move the Earth." While the lever you study in this Investigation will not be strong enough to move a planet, you will learn how to design and build levers than can multiply force. You will also find the rule which predicts how much mechanical advantage a lever will have.

4.3	**Designing Gear Machines**	*How do gears work?*

Many machines require that rotating motion be transmitted from one place to another. In this Investigation, you will learn how gears work and then use this knowledge to design and build a gear machine that solves a specific problem.

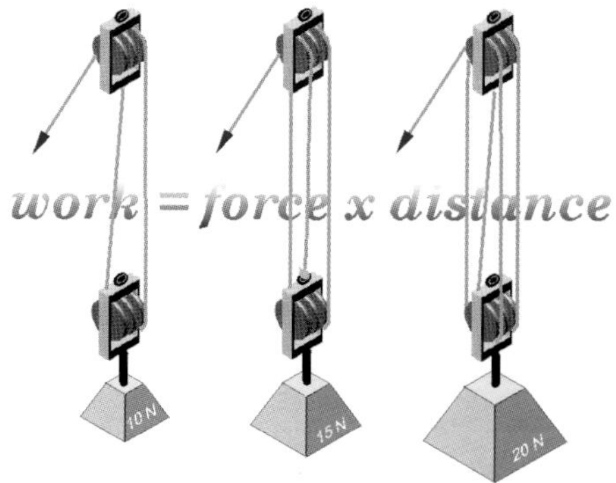

Learning Goals

In this chapter, you will:

- ✔ Describe and explain a simple machine.
- ✔ Apply the concepts of input force and output force to any machine.
- ✔ Determine the mechanical advantage of a machine.
- ✔ Construct and analyze a block and tackle machine.
- ✔ Describe the difference between science and engineering.
- ✔ Understand and apply the engineering cycle to the development of an invention or product.
- ✔ Describe the purpose and construction of a prototype.
- ✔ Design and analyze a lever.
- ✔ Calculate the mechanical advantage of a lever.
- ✔ Recognize the three classes of levers.
- ✔ Build machines with gears and deduce the rule for how pairs of gears turn.
- ✔ Design and build a gear machine that solves a specific problem.

Vocabulary

engineering	gear	lever	output arm
engineering cycle	input	machine	output force
engineers	input arm	mechanical advantage	output gear
force	input force	mechanical systems	prototype
fulcrum	input gear	output	simple machine

4.1 Forces in Machines

How do you move something that is too heavy to carry? How do humans move mountains? How were the Great Pyramids built? The answer to these questions has to do with the use of simple machines. In this section, you will learn how simple machines manipulate forces to accomplish many tasks.

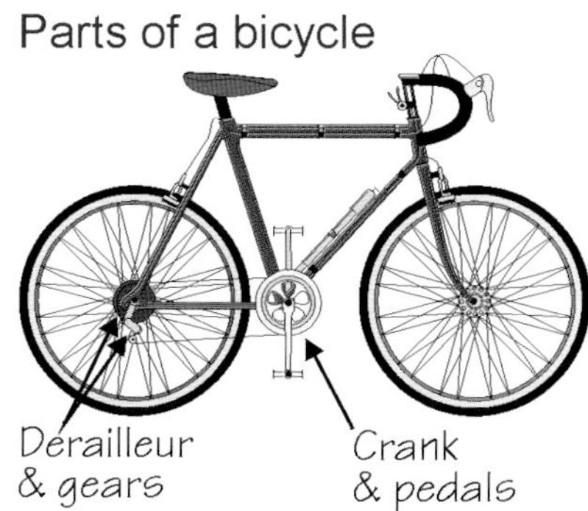

Figure 4.1: *A bicycle is a good example of a machine. A bicycle efficiently converts forces from your muscles into motion.*

Mechanical systems and machines

The world without machines Ten thousand years ago, people lived in a much different world. Their interactions were limited by what they could pick up and carry, how fast they could run, and what they could eat (or what could eat them!). It would be quite a problem for someone to bring a woolly mammoth back home without today's cars and trucks.

What technology allows us to do Today's technology allows us to do incredible things. Moving huge steel beams, digging tunnels that connect two islands, or building 1,000-foot skyscrapers are examples. What makes these accomplishments possible? Have we developed super powers since the days of our ancestors?

Figure 4.2: *Applying the ideas of input and output to a bicycle.*

What is a machine? In a way we *have* developed super powers. Our powers came from our clever invention of machines and mechanical systems. A machine is a device with moving parts that work together to accomplish a task. A bicycle is a good example. All the parts of a bicycle work together to transform forces from your muscles into speed and motion. In fact, a bicycle is one of the most efficient machines ever invented.

The concepts of input and output Machines are designed to do something useful. You can think of a machine as having an input and an output. The *input* includes everything you do to make the machine work, like pushing on the pedals. The *output* is what the machine does for you, like going fast.

Simple machines

The beginning of technology The development of the technology that created computers, cars, and the space shuttle begins with the invention of simple machines. A simple machine is an unpowered mechanical device, such as a lever. A lever allows you to move a rock that weighs 10 times as much as you do (or more). Some other important simple machines are the wheel and axle, the block and tackle, the gear, and the ramp.

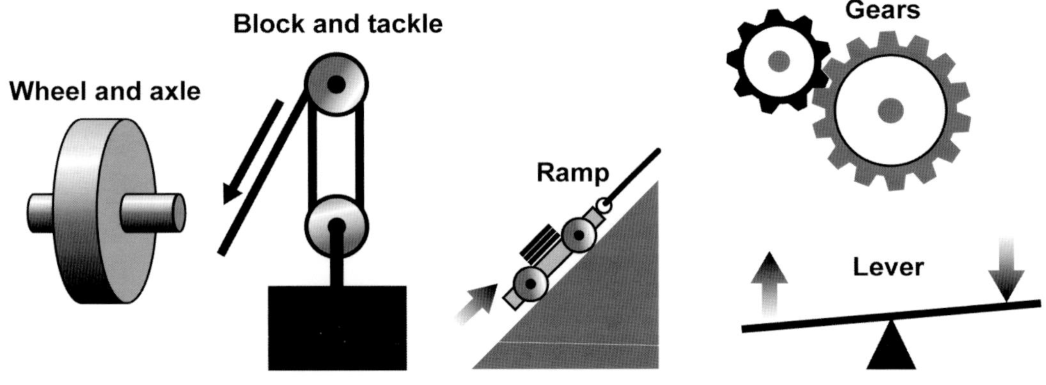

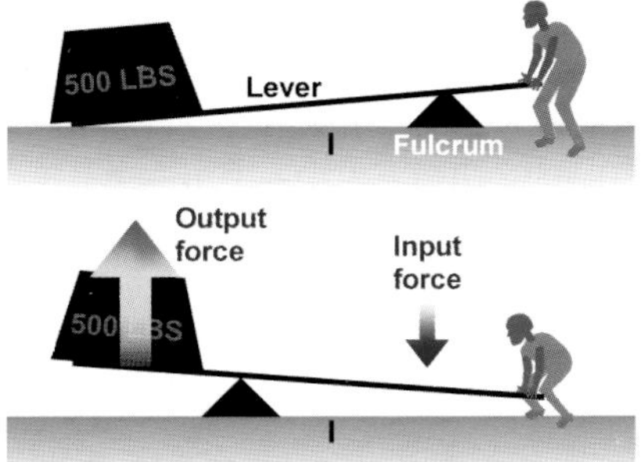

Figure 4.3: *With a properly designed lever, a person can move many times his own weight.*

Input force and output force Simple machines work by manipulating forces. It is useful to think in terms of an *input force* and an *output force*. With a lever the input force is what you apply. The output force is what the lever applies to what you are trying to move. Figure 4.3 shows an example of using a lever to move a heavy load.

The block and tackle The block and tackle is another simple machine that uses ropes and pulleys to multiply forces. The input force is what you apply to the rope. The output force is what gets applied to the load you are trying to lift. One person could easily lift an elephant with a properly designed block and tackle! (figure 4.4)

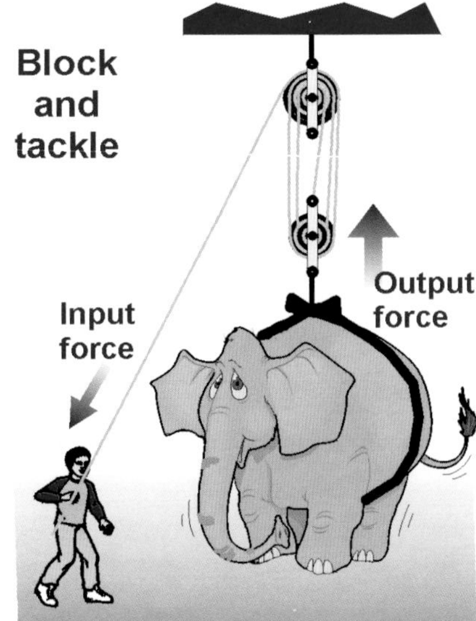

Figure 4.4: *A block and tackle machine made with ropes and pulleys allows one person to lift tremendous loads.*

Machines within machines Most of the machines we use today are made up of combinations of different types of simple machines. For example, the bicycle uses wheels and axles, levers (the pedals and a kickstand), and gears. If you take apart a VCR, a clock, or a car engine you will also find simple machines adapted to fit almost everywhere.

Mechanical advantage

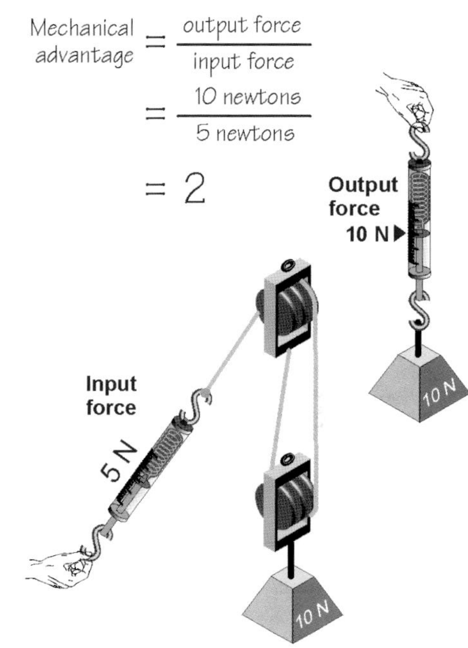

Figure 4.5: *A block and tackle with a mechanical advantage of two. The output force is two times stronger than the input force.*

Definition of force Simple machines work by changing force and motion. Remember that a **force** is an action that has the ability to change motion, like a push or a pull. Forces do not always result in a change in motion. For example, pushing on a solid wall does not make it move (at least not much). But, if the wall is not well built, pushing *could* make it move. Many things can create force: wind, muscles, springs, motion, gravity, and more. The action of a force is the same, regardless of its source.

Units of force Recall from the last unit that there are two units we use to measure force: the newton and the pound. The newton is a smaller unit than the pound. A quantity of 4.48 newtons is equal to 1 pound. A person weighing 100 pounds would weigh 448 newtons.

Simple machines and force As discussed, simple machines are best understood through the concepts of input and output forces. The input force is the force applied to the machine. The output force is the force the machine applies to accomplish a task.

Mechanical advantage **Mechanical advantage** is the ratio of output force to input force. If the mechanical advantage is bigger than one, the output force is bigger than the input force (figure 4.5). A mechanical advantage smaller than one means the output force is smaller than the input force.

Mechanical Advantage

$$MA = \frac{F_o}{F_i}$$

Mechanical advantage → MA; Output force (N) → F_o; Input force (N) → F_i

Mechanical engineers Today, we call the people who design machines *mechanical engineers.* Many of the machines they design involve the multiplication of forces to lift heavy loads; that is, the machines must have a greater output force than input force in order to accomplish the job.

How a block and tackle works

The forces in ropes and strings

Ropes and strings carry tension forces along their length. A tension force is a pulling force that always acts along the direction of the rope. Ropes or strings do *not* carry pushing forces. This would be obvious if you ever tried to push something with a rope. We will be using the term rope, but the strings used in your lab investigations behave just like ropes used in larger machines.

Every part of a rope has the same tension

If friction is very small, then the force in a rope is the same everywhere. This means that if you were to cut the rope and insert a force scale, the scale would measure the same tension force at any point.

The forces in a block and tackle

The diagram in (figure 4.6) shows three different configurations of block and tackle. Notice that the number of ropes attached directly to the load is different in each case. Think about pulling with an input force. This force appears everywhere in the rope. That means in case A the load feels two upward forces equal to your pull. In case B the load feels three times your pulling force, and in case C the load feels four times your pull.

Mechanical advantage

If there are four ropes directly supporting the load, each newton of force you apply produces 4 newtons of output force. Configuration C has a mechanical advantage of 4. The output force is four times bigger than the input force.

Multiplying force with the block and tackle

Because the mechanical advantage is 4, the input force for machine C is 1/4 the output force. If you need an output force of 20 N, you only need an input force of 5 N! The block and tackle is an extremely useful machine because it multiplies force so effectively.

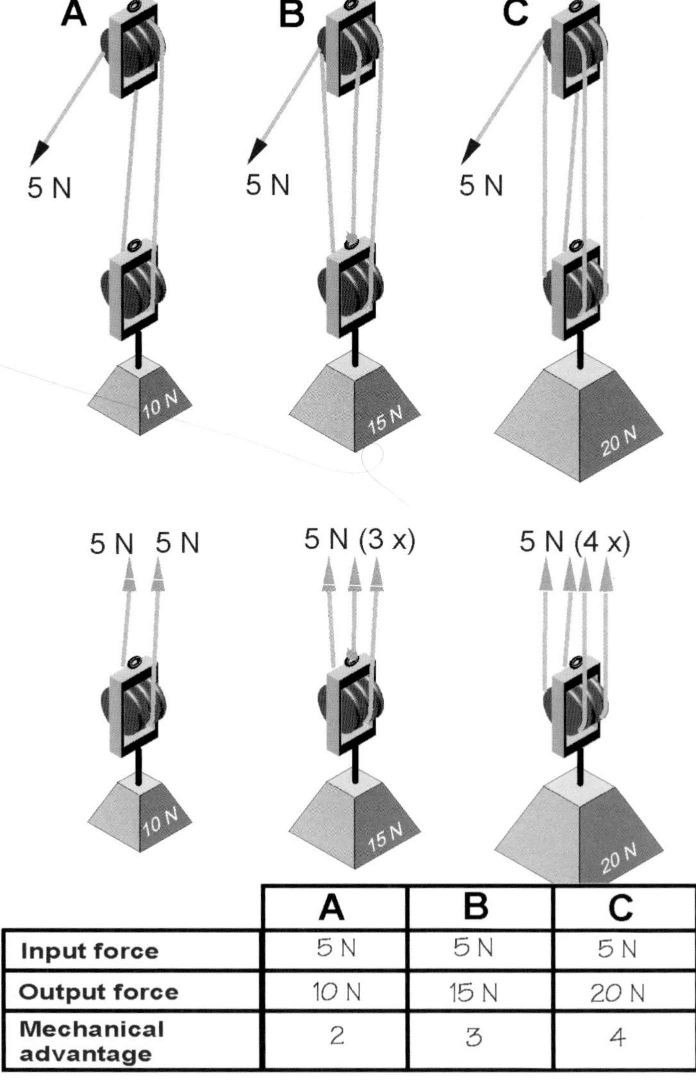

	A	B	C
Input force	5 N	5 N	5 N
Output force	10 N	15 N	20 N
Mechanical advantage	2	3	4

Figure 4.6: *How the block and tackle creates mechanical advantage using forces in ropes.*

4.2 The Lever

The lever is another example of a simple machine. In this section, you will learn about the relationships between force and motion that explain how a lever works. After reading this section and doing the Investigation, you should be able to design a lever to move almost anything!

What is a lever?

Levers are used everywhere The principle of the lever has been used since before humans had written language. Levers still form the operating principle behind many common machines. Examples of levers include: pliers, a wheelbarrow, and the human biceps and forearm (figure 4.7).

Your muscles and skeleton use levers You may have heard the human body described as a machine. In fact, it is: Your bones and muscles work as levers to perform everything from chewing to throwing a ball.

Parts of the lever A lever includes a stiff structure (the **lever**) that rotates around a fixed point called the **fulcrum**. The side of the lever where the input force is applied is called the **input arm**. The **output arm** is the end of the lever that moves the rock or lifts the heavy weight. Levers are useful because we can arrange the fulcrum and the lengths of the input and output arms to make almost any mechanical advantage we need.

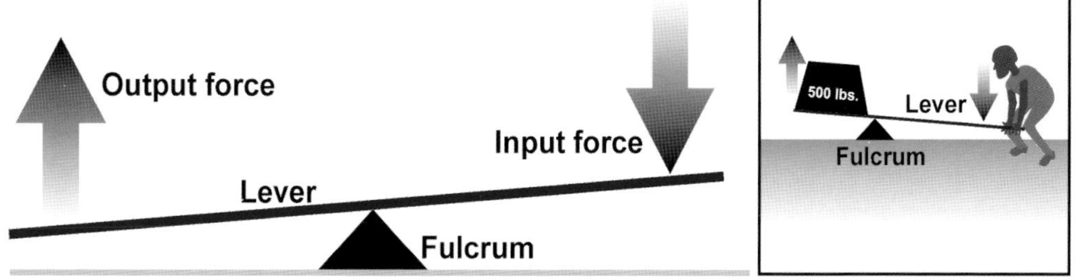

How it works If the fulcrum is placed in the middle of the lever, the input and output forces are the same. An input force of 100 pounds makes an output force of 100 pounds.

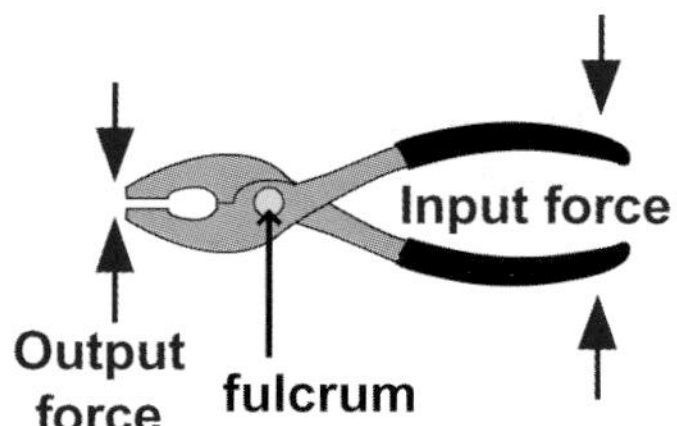

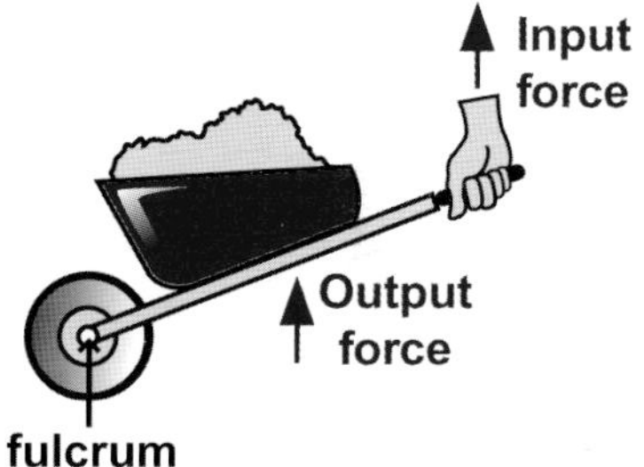

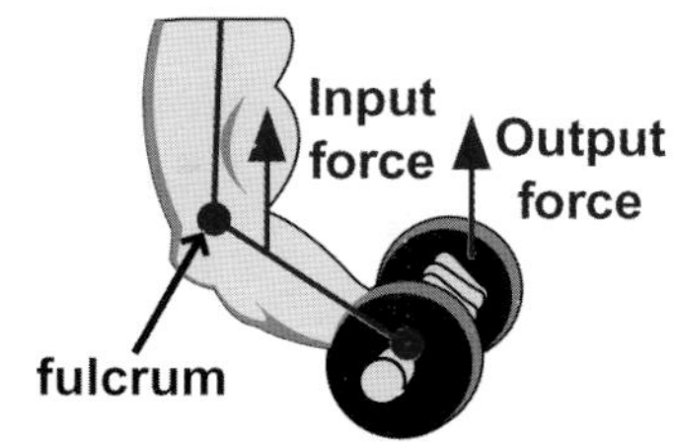

Figure 4.7: *Examples of three kinds of levers. The pair of pliers is a first class lever because the fulcrum is between the forces. The wheelbarrow is a second class lever because the output force is between the fulcrum and input force. Human arms and legs are all examples of third class levers because the input forces (muscles) are always between the fulcrum (a joint) and the output force (what you accomplish with your feet or hands).*

The mechanical advantage of a lever

Input and output forces for a lever

The input and output forces are related by the lengths on either side of the fulcrum. When the input arm is longer, the output force is larger than the input force. If the input arm is 10 times longer than the output arm, then the output force will be 10 times bigger than the input force (figure 4.8).

The mechanical advantage of a lever

Another way to say this is that the mechanical advantage of a lever is the ratio of lengths between the input arm and the output arm. If the input arm is 5 meters and the output arm is 1 meter, then the mechanical advantage will be 5. The output force will be five times as large as the input force.

The output force can be *less* than the input force

You can also make a lever where the output force is less than the input force. You would be right if you guessed that the input arm is shorter than the output arm on this kind of lever. You might design a lever this way if you needed the motion on the output side to be larger than the motion on the input side.

The three types of levers

There are three types of levers, as shown in figure 4.9. They are classified by the location of the input and output forces relative to the fulcrum. All three types are used in many machines and follow the same basic rules. The mechanical advantage is always the ratio of the lengths of the input arm over the output arm.

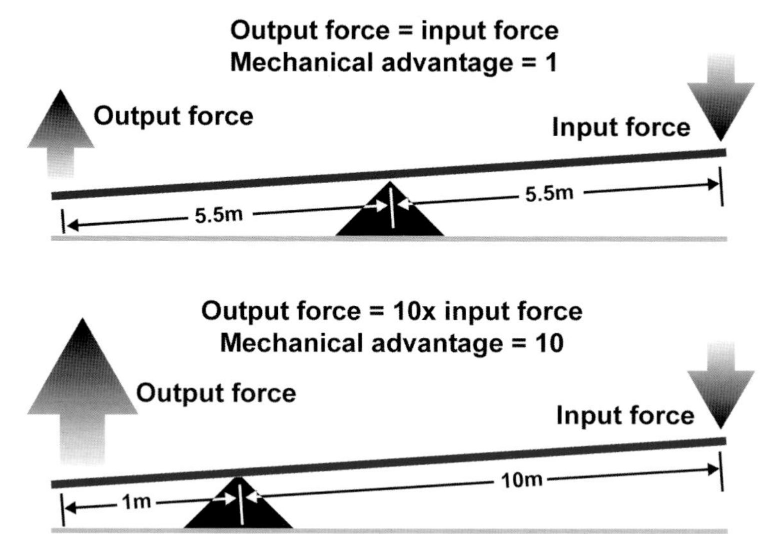

Figure 4.8: *The mechanical advantage of a lever is the ratio of the length of the input arm over the length of the output arm.*

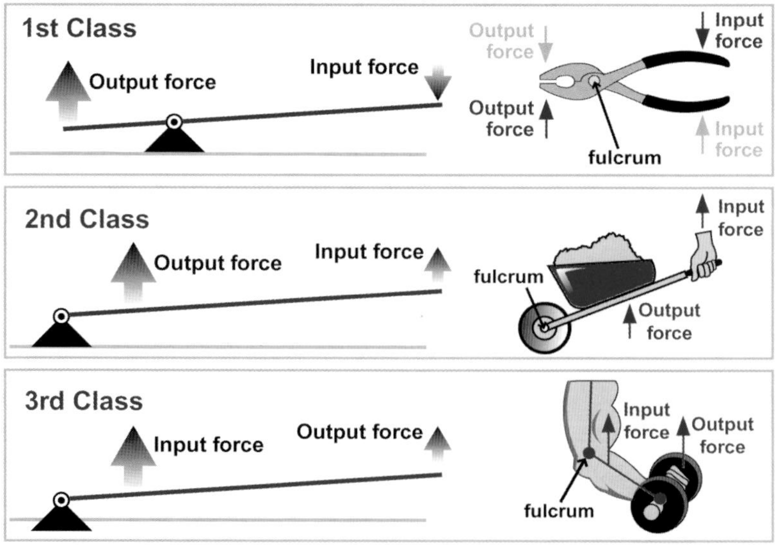

The 3 classes of levers

Figure 4.9: *The three classes of levers. For the third class, the input force is larger than the output force.*

4.3 Designing Gear Machines

In this section, you will learn how people design complex machines to solve real problems. You may have practiced designing machines with gears in your Investigation. The process of learning how gears work and then using that information to solve a problem is common to the invention of almost every kind of machine, from the wheel and axle to the space shuttle. This process is called the engineering cycle, which is how ideas for inventions become something real you can actually use.

Science and engineering

Inventions solve problems You are surrounded by inventions, from the toothbrush you use to clean your teeth to the computer you use to do your school projects (and play games). Where did the inventions come from? Most of them came from a practical application of science knowledge.

What is technology? The application of science to solve problems is called **engineering** or technology. From the invention of the plow to the microcomputer, all technologies arise from someone's perception of a need for things to be done better. Although technology is widely different in the details, there are some general principles that apply to all forms of technological design or innovation. People who design technology to solve problems are called **engineers**.

Science
Physics
Chemistry
Biology
Astronomy
Earth Science

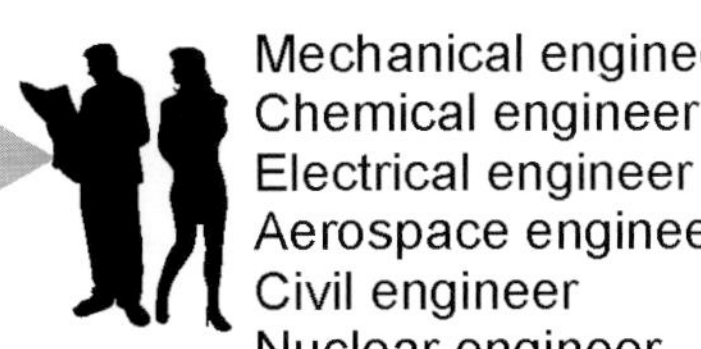

Engineering
Mechanical engineer
Chemical engineer
Electrical engineer
Aerospace engineer
Civil engineer
Nuclear engineer

Technology
Automobile
Plastics
Telephone
Airplane
Suspension bridge
MRI scanner

Science and technology Scientists study the world to learn the basic principles behind how things work. Engineers use scientific knowledge to create or improve inventions that solve problems.

Leonardo da Vinci

Leonardo da Vinci (1452-1519) was one of the greatest engineers ever. His inventions are remarkable for their creativity, imagination, and technical detail. He often described technologies that most people of his time thought were impossible

Da Vinci's mind was constantly looking for new ways to do things. For example, he was constantly developing ideas that he hoped would allow people to fly. His flying machines were so far ahead of the times that they could not be built. Many look remarkably like modern designs. The first helicopter and the hang glider are both similar to da Vinci's designs of 500 years ago.

A sample engineering problem

Suppose you are given a box of toothpicks and some glue, and are assigned to build a bridge that will hold a brick without breaking. After doing research, you come up with an idea for how to make the bridge. Your idea is to make the bridge from four structures connected together. Your structure is a truss because you have seen bridges that use trusses. Your idea is called a *conceptual design*.

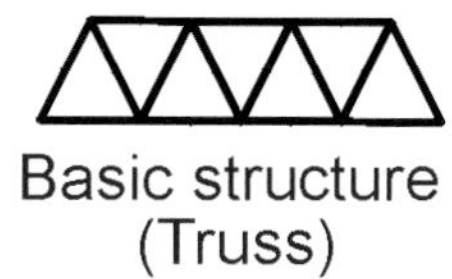

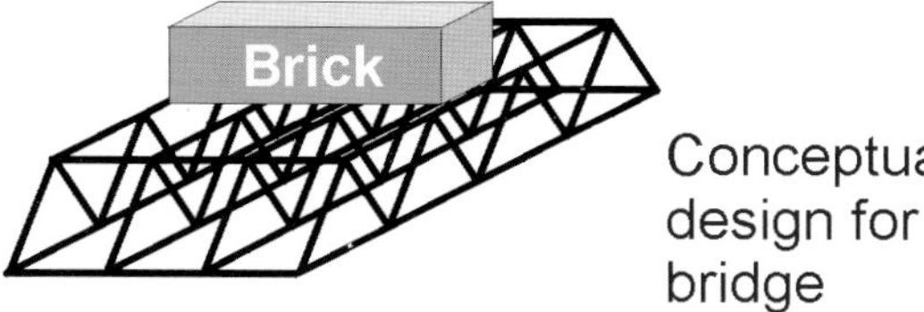

The importance of a prototype

You need to test your idea to see if it works. If you could figure out how much force it takes to break *one* structure, you would know if four structures will hold the brick. Your next step is to build a **prototype** and test it. Your prototype should be close enough to the real bridge that what you learn from testing can be applied to the final bridge. For example, if your final bridge is to be made with round toothpicks, your prototype also has to be made with round toothpicks.

Testing the prototype

You test the prototype truss by applying more and more force until it breaks. You learn that your truss breaks at a force of 5 newtons. The brick weighs 25 newtons. Four trusses are not going to be enough. You have two choices now. You can make each truss stronger, by using thread to tie the joints. Or, you could use more trusses in your bridge (figure 4.10). The *evaluation* of test results is a necessary part of any successful design. Testing identifies potential problems in the design in time to correct them. Adding more trusses should make the bridge strong enough to withstand additional newtons before breaking, which gives an extra margin of safety.

Changing the design and testing again

If you decide to build a stronger structure, you will need to make another prototype and test it again. Good engineers often build many prototypes and keep testing them until they are successful under a wide range of conditions. The process of design, prototype, test, and evaluate is the **engineering cycle** (figure 4.11). The best inventions go through the cycle many times, being improved each cycle until all the problems are worked out.

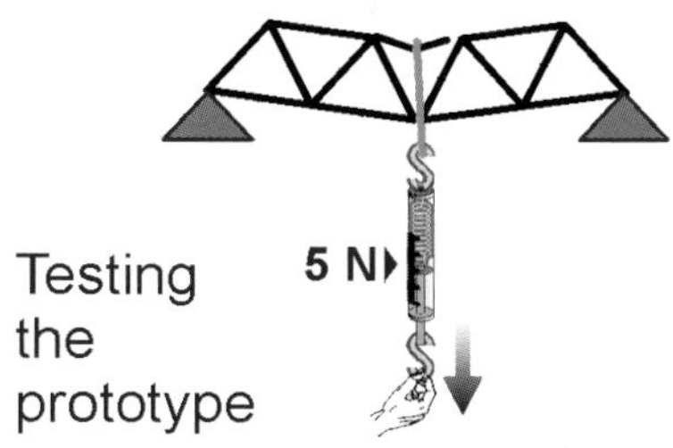

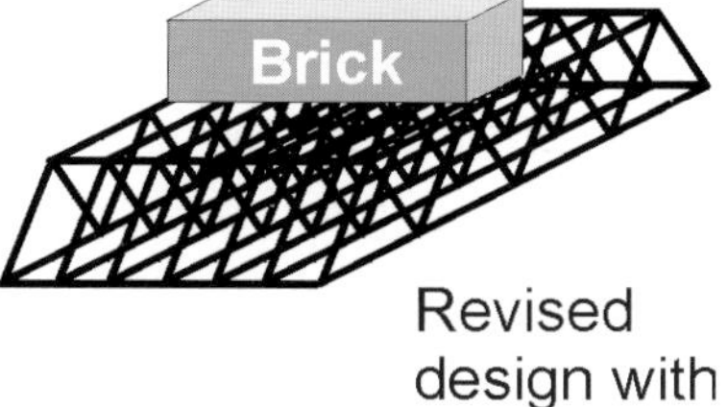

Figure 4.10: *Testing the prototype tells you if it is strong enough. Testing often leads to a revised design, for example, using more trusses.*

Engineering cycle

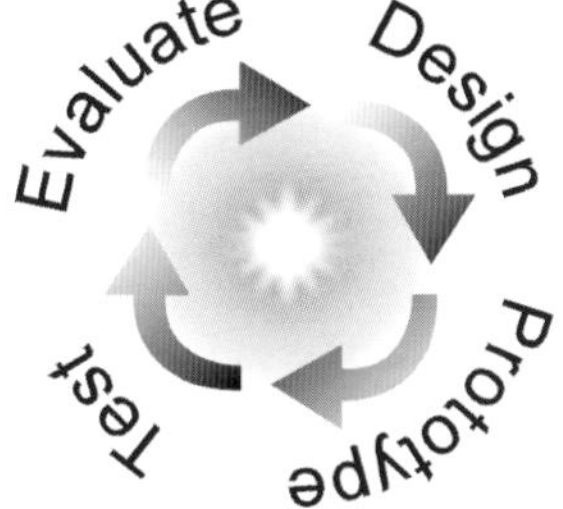

Figure 4.11: *The engineering design cycle is how we get an invention from concept to reality.*

Gears and rotating machines

Why are gears used? Many machines require that rotating motion be transmitted from one place to another. The transmission of rotating motion is often done with shafts and gears (figure 4.12). When one or more shafts are connected with gears, the shafts may turn at different speeds and in different directions.

Gears change force and speed Some machinery, such as small drills, require small forces at high speed. Other machinery, such as mill wheels, require large forces at low speed. Since they act like rotating levers, gears also allow the forces carried by different shafts to be changed with the speed.

The relationship between gears and wheels Gears are better than wheels because they have teeth and don't slip as they turn together. Two gears with their teeth engaged act like two touching wheels with the same diameters as the *pitch diameters* of the gears (Figure 4.13). You can transmit much more force (without slipping) between two gears than you could with smooth wheels. Gears find application in a wide range of machines, including everything from pocket watches to turbocharged engines.

How gears work The rule for how gears turn depends on the number of teeth in the gears. Because the teeth don't slip, moving 36 teeth on one gear means that 36 teeth have to move on any connected gear. If one gear has 36 teeth it turns once to move 36 teeth. If the connected gear has only 12 teeth, it has to turn 3 times to move 36 teeth ($3 \times 12 = 36$).

What is the gear ratio? Like all machines, gears have input and output. The *input gear* is the one you turn, or apply forces to. The *output gear* is the one that is connected to the output of the machine. The *gear ratio* is the ratio of output turns to input turns. Smaller gears turn faster, so the gear ratio is the inverse of the ratio of teeth in two gears.

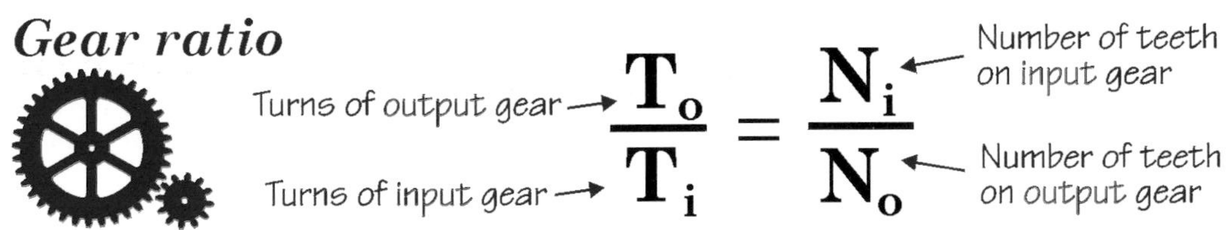

$$\frac{T_o}{T_i} = \frac{N_i}{N_o}$$

4 turns of rotating motion (small gear)
Gear
Shaft
2 turns of rotating motion (large gear)

Figure 4.12: *Gears are used to change the speeds of rotating shafts. By using gears of different sizes, the shafts can be made to turn at different rates.*

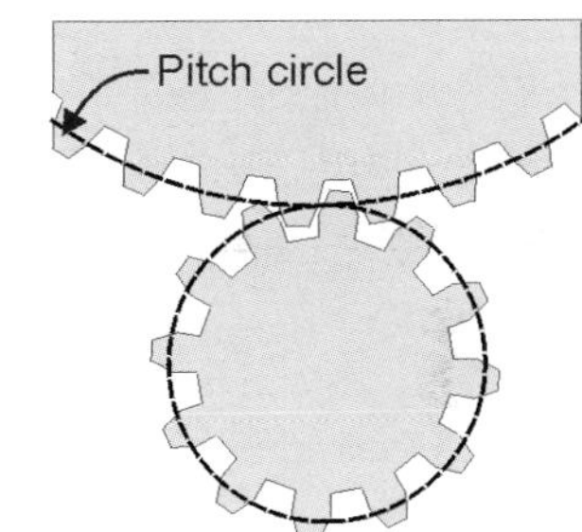

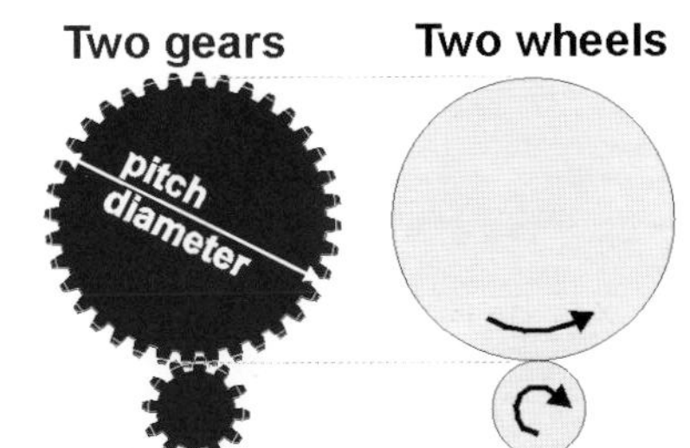

Figure 4.13: *Gears act like touching wheels, but with teeth to keep them from slipping as they turn together.*

Designing machines

How machines are designed

Machines are designed to do specific things, such as carry passengers or move earth around. To design a machine you need to know how each part works, and how the parts work together to create a machine that does what you want it to. You need the right parts and the right design to fit the job the machine has to accomplish. A machine designed to do one task may not be able to do another task effectively. A bus is a good machine for moving passengers, but a poor machine for moving earth around. A bulldozer is good for moving earth but poor for carrying passengers.

Simple and complex machines

Simple machines can be combined to solve more complex problems. You can use two pairs of gears with ratios of 2 to 1 to make a machine with a ratio of 4 to 1. Figure 4.14 shows an example of a how you could make a ratio of 4 to 1 with 12-tooth and 24-tooth gears.

How to combine simple machines into complex machines

To design complex machines from simpler machines, you need to know how each simple machine relates to the whole. For gears you need to know how the ratios from each pair of gears combine to make an overall ratio for the whole machine. For the example in figure 4.14, the two ratios of 2:1 multiply together to make the final ratio of 4:1. When combining two gear machines, the total ratio for the machine is found by multiplying together the ratios of turns for each pair of gears. This works because the two gears that are stacked on the middle axle are connected so they turn together.

Design involves tradeoffs

Combining gears to get higher speeds also affects the amount of force the machine creates. If you design a gear machine for higher output speed, you will get less output force. Design often involves trading off improvements in one area for costs in another area.

Even the best designs are always being improved

It is *very* rare that an invention works perfectly the first time. In fact, machines go through a long history of building, testing, analyzing, redesigning, building, and testing again. Most practical machines such as the automobile are never truly completed. There are always improvements that can be added as technology gets better (figure 4.15). The first cars had to be cranked by hand to start! Today's cars start with the touch of a key.

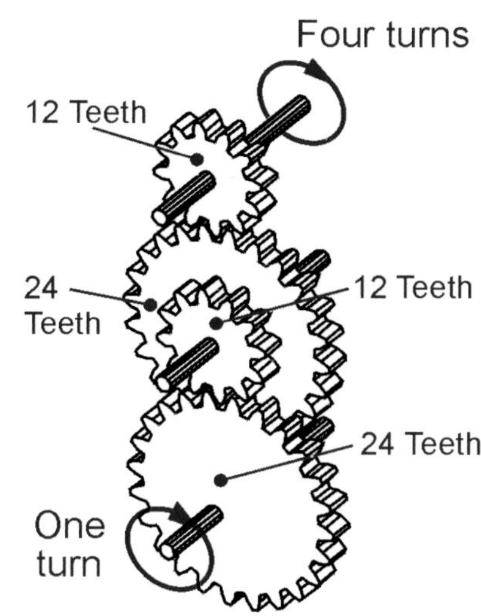

Figure 4.14: *A machine that uses two pairs of gears to make a larger ratio of turns.*

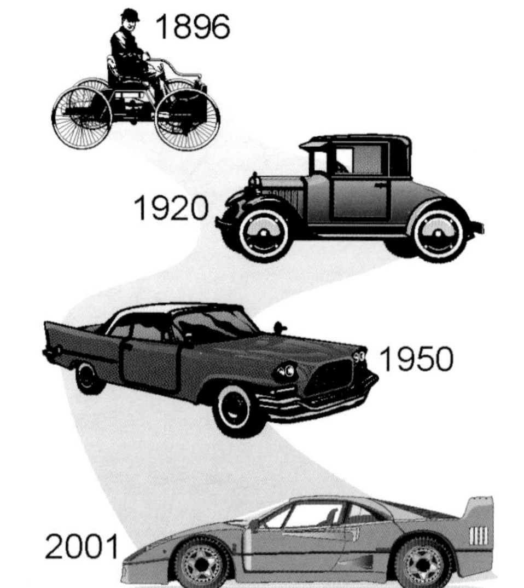

Figure 4.15: *Many inventions are continually being redesigned and improved.*

Chapter 4 Review

Vocabulary review

Match the following terms with the correct definition. There is one extra definition in the list that will not match any of the terms.

Set One

1. input force	a. The force applied by a machine to accomplish a task after an input force has been applied
2. machine	b. A device that multiplies force
3. mechanical system	c. An unpowered mechanical device, such as a lever, that has an input and output force
4. output force	d. The force applied to a machine
5. simple machine	e. A measurement used to describe changes in events, motion, or position
	f. An object with interrelated parts that work together to accomplish a task

Set Two

1. fulcrum	a. The force applied to a machine to produce a useful output force
2. input arm	b. The pivot point of a lever
3. lever	c. The distance from the fulcrum to the point of output force
4. output arm	d. The distance from the fulcrum to the point of input force
	e. A simple machine that pivots around a fulcrum

Set Three

1. engineering cycle	a. A working model of a design
2. engineering	b. A scientific field devoted to imagining what machines will be used in the future
3. prototype	c. Output force divided by input force
4. mechanical advantage	d. A wheel with teeth that is used to change direction and/or speed of rotating motion
5. gear	e. The process used by engineers to develop new technology
	f. The application of science to solve problems

Concept review

1. Why is a car a good example of a mechanical system? Write a short paragraph to explain your answer.
2. What does the phrase *multiply forces* mean? Include the terms machine, input force, and output force in your answer.
3. Compare and contrast the scientific method and the engineering cycle.
4. You are an inventor who wants to devise a new style of toothbrush. Describe what you would do at each phase of the engineering cycle to invent this new toothbrush.
5. Describe a problem that would have to be solved by an engineer. Try to think of example problems you see in your school, home, city, or state.
6. Describe an example of a new technology that you have seen recently advertised or sold in stores.
7. How would you set up a lever so that it has a mechanical advantage greater than 1? Include the terms input arm, output arm, and fulcrum in your answer.
8. Draw diagrams that show a seesaw at equilibrium and at nonequilibrium. Include captions that describe each of your diagrams. Be sure to discuss forces and motion in your captions.
9. Why are levers considered to be simple machines?
10. Which configuration is the best lever for lifting the rock?

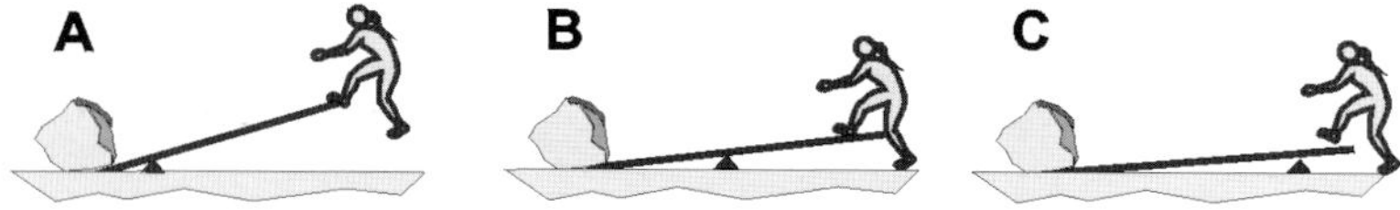

11. The lever in the picture will:

    a. stay balanced.

    b. rotate clockwise.

    c. rotate counterclockwise.

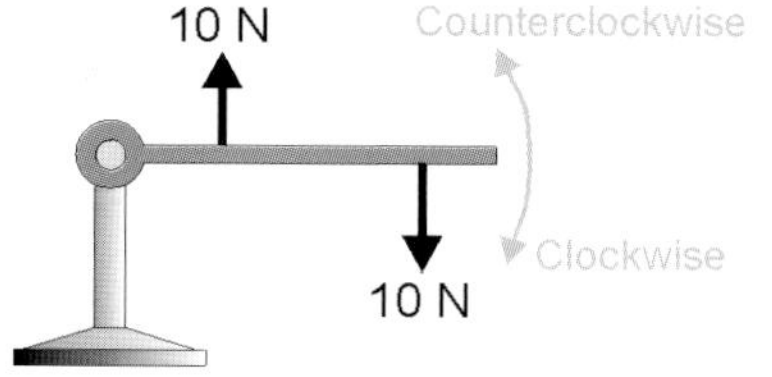

12. The lever has a mass of 3 kilograms at 30 centimeters on the left, and a mass of 2 kilograms at 30 centimeters on the right. What mass should be hung at 10 centimeters (on the right) for the lever to be in balance?

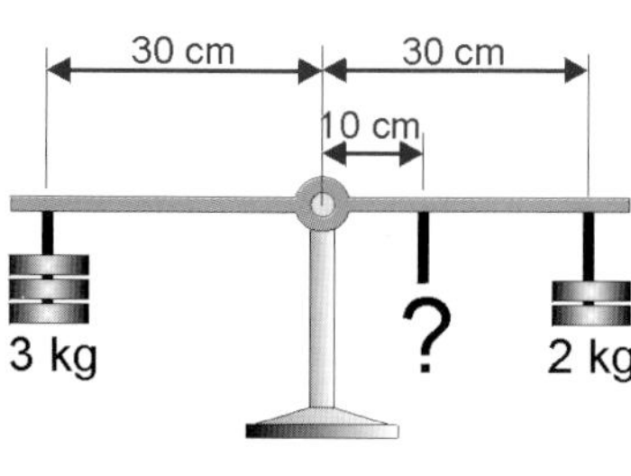

    a. 1 kg
    b. 2 kg
    c. 2.5 kg
    d. 3 kg
    e. 10 kg

13. How are force and distance related to how a lever works?
14. Would you rather use a machine that has a mechanical advantage of 1 or a machine that has a mechanical advantage of more than 1? Explain your reasoning in your answer.
15. You have a kit of gears, which contains many gears with 12, 24, and 36 teeth. Can you make a clock mechanism with a 12:1 gear ratio? Why or why not?

Problems

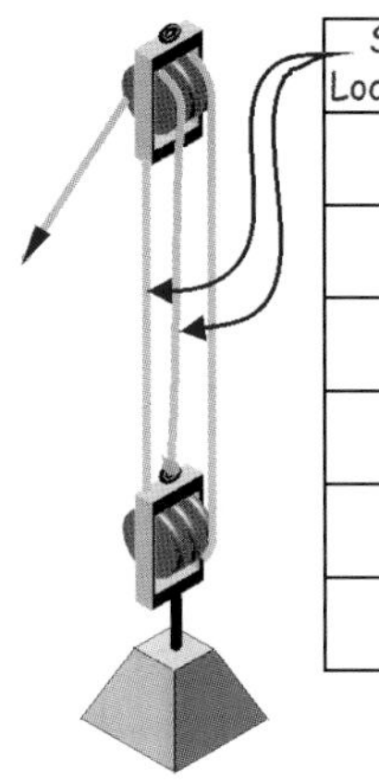

Supporting Loops of String	Input Force	Output Force	Mechanical Advantage
2	5 N	10 N	
4	2.5 N	10 N	
6	1.7 N	10 N	
1	10 N	10 N	
3	3.3 N	10 N	
5	2 N	10 N	

1. Above is a data table with sample data for lifting (input) force vs. the number of supporting strings in a block and tackle machine. Use the data to answer the following questions.
   a. Describe the relationship between the lifting (input) force and the number of supporting strings in the pulley.
   b. Make a graph that shows the relationship between lifting (input) force and number of supporting strings. Which variable is dependent and which is independent?
   c. Calculate the mechanical advantage for each number of supporting strings.
2. If you were going to use a pulley to lift a box that weighs 100 newtons, how much force would you need to use if the pulley had:
   a. 1 supporting string?
   b. 2 supporting strings?
   c. 5 supporting strings?
   d. 10 supporting strings?
3. Use the input and output forces listed in the table below to calculate the mechanical advantage.

Input Force	Output Force	Mechanical Advantage
10 newtons	100 newtons	
30 N	30 N	
500 N	1,350 N	
625 N	200 N	

4. One of the examples in the table in problem 3 has a very low mechanical advantage. Identify this example and explain why you might or might not want to use this machine to lift something that weighs 200 newtons.
5. Does mechanical advantage have units? Explain your answer.
6. If you lift a 200-newton box with a block and tackle machine and you apply 20 newtons to lift this box, what would be the mechanical advantage of the machine?
7. If a lever has an input arm that is 15 feet long and an output arm that is 25 feet long, does the lever have mechanical advantage? Why or why not?
8. Betsy wants to use her own weight to lift a 350-pound box. She weighs 120 pounds. Suggest input and output arm lengths that would allow Betsy to lift the box with a lever. Draw a lever and label the input and output arms with the lengths and forces.

Applying your knowledge

1. Why is a ramp a simple machine? Describe how a ramp works to multiply forces using your knowledge of simple machines.

2. You need a wheelbarrow to transport some soil for your garden. The one you have gives you a mechanical advantage of 3.5. If you use 65 newtons of force to lift the wheelbarrow so that you can roll it, how much soil can you carry with this wheelbarrow? Give the weight of the soil in newtons and be sure to show your work.

3. The block and tackle machine on a sailboat can help a sailor raise her mainsail. Without a machine, she needs 500 newtons of force to raise the sail. If the block and tackle gives her a mechanical advantage of 5, how much input force must be applied to raise the sail? Be sure to show your work.

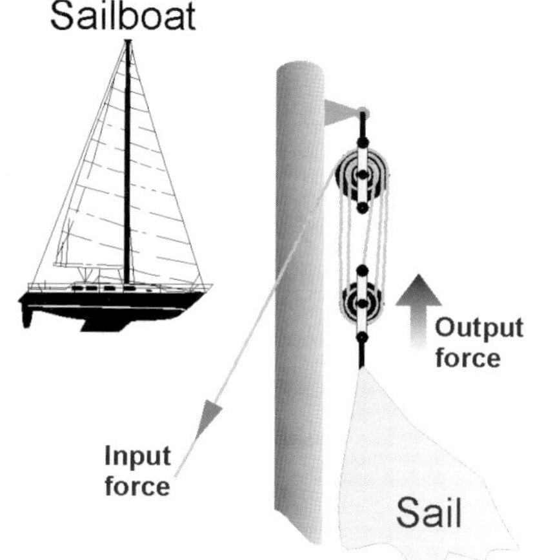

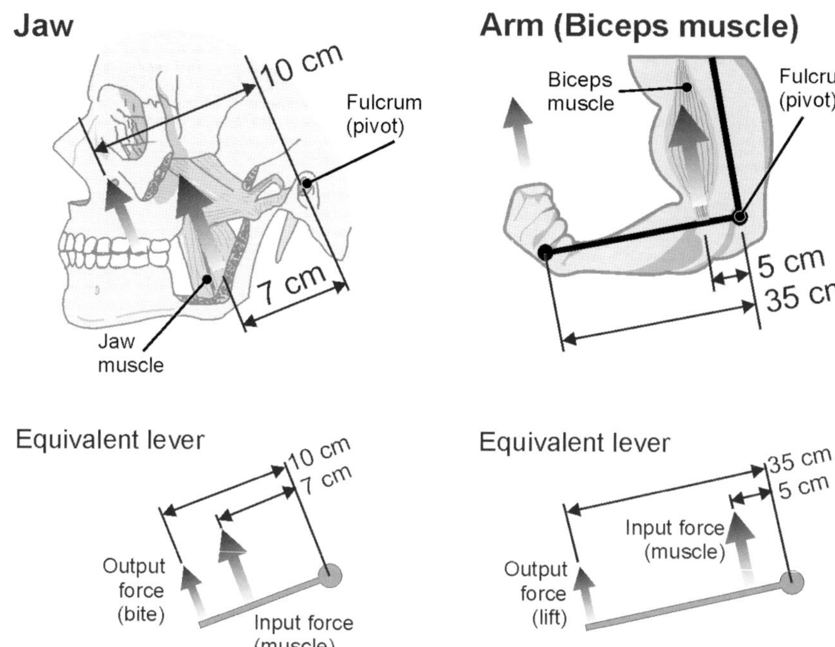

Your jaw works as a lever when you bite an apple. Your arm also works as a lever, as do many of the bones in your body. Using the diagrams above, answer the following questions by analyzing the changes in force and distance.

4. Using the distances shown, calculate and compare the mechanical advantage of the jaw and arm. Which is larger?

5. Suppose the jaw and biceps muscles produce equal input forces of 800N (178 lbs.). Calculate and compare the output forces in biting (jaw) and lifting (arm). Which is larger?

6. Suppose you need an output force of 500N (112 lbs). Calculate and compare the input forces of the jaw and biceps muscles required to produce 500 N of output force. Explain how your calculation relates to the relative size of the two muscles.

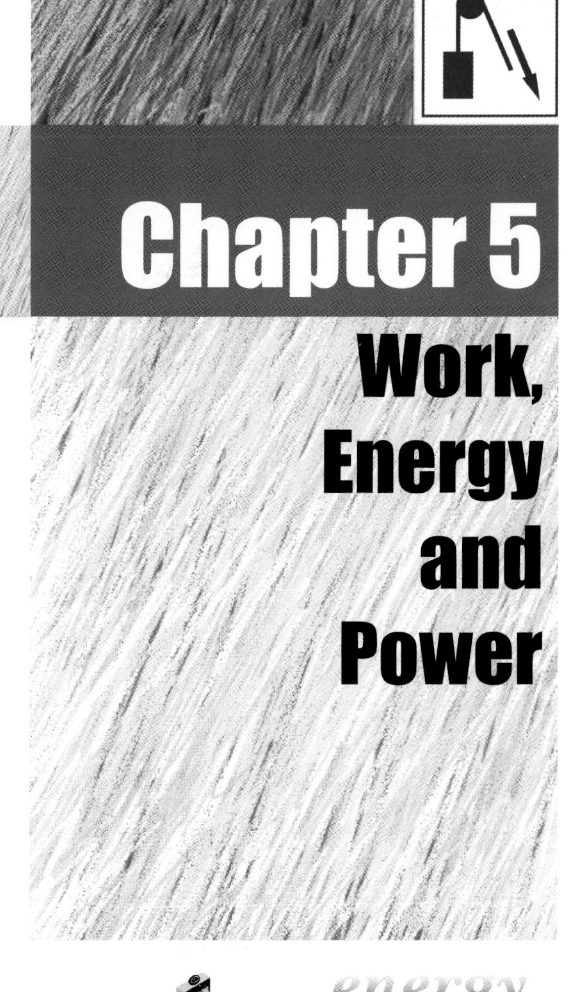

Introduction to Chapter 5

This chapter introduces the concept of work. Understanding the scientific meaning of work leads to an understanding of energy. Once we understand energy, we can look at both natural and human-made systems from the perspective of the flow and transformation of energy from one form to another.

Investigations for Chapter 5

5.1	Work	*What happens when you multiply forces in a machine?*

Nature gives nothing away for free. In this Investigation you will discover what you pay for making clever machines that multiply force. You will come to an interesting conclusion about work and energy that is true for all machines.

5.2	Energy Conservation	*What is energy and how does it behave?*

What happens to the speed of a marble as it rolls up and down hills? By making measurements of height and speed, you will investigate one of the most important laws in physics: the law of conservation of energy. By applying the concepts of potential and kinetic energy, you will develop a theory for how objects move.

5.3	Energy Transformations	*Where did the energy go?*

Our world runs on energy. Working with a group of students, you will analyze and identify the energy transformations that occur in real-life situations. By charting the flow of energy you will come to understand some of the interactions between humans and their environment. This Investigation requires you not only to apply what you have learned so far, but also to use your creativity and imagination.

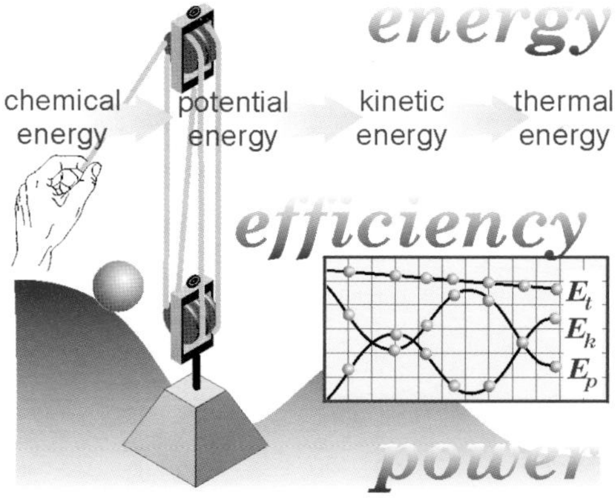

Learning Goals

In this chapter, you will:

- ✔ Calculate the amount of work done by a simple machine.
- ✔ Use units of joules to measure the amount of work done.
- ✔ Analyze the effects of changing force or distance in a simple machine.
- ✔ Calculate the efficiency of a machine.
- ✔ Calculate power in machines.
- ✔ Discuss perpetual motion machines.

Vocabulary

chemical energy	heat	nuclear energy	solar power
efficiency	horsepower	potential energy	watt
electrical energy	joule	power	work
energy	kinetic energy	radiant energy	
energy transformations	law of conservation of energy	radiation	

5.1 Work

When you arranged the string on the ropes and pulleys to pull with less force, you had to pull more string to raise the weight. When you built a lever with a large advantage, you had to move the input arm down a great distance while the output arm moved only a little. These details are clues to one of the most powerful laws of physics. In this chapter, you will learn about work and energy and about a fundamental rule that applies to all machines.

is the amount of work done by pushing with a force of 1 newton for a distance of 1 meter.

What is work?

The word work means many different things

The word *work* is used in many different ways.

- You *work* on science problems.
- You go to *work*.
- Your toaster doesn't *work*.
- Taking out the trash is too much *work*.

What *work* means in physics

In science, work has a very specific meaning. If you push a box with a force of one newton for a distance of one meter, you have done exactly one joule of work (figure 5.1). In physics, work is force times distance. When you see the word *work* in a physics problem, it means force times distance.

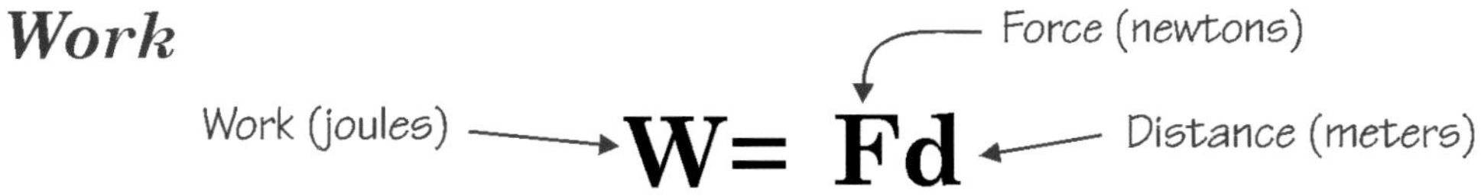

To be exact, work is force times the distance moved in the direction of the force. A force at an angle (figure 5.2) is not as effective at doing work. Only the part of the force in the direction of the motion does work in the physics sense.

Machines do work in the physics sense

When we apply force to machines we are doing work. For example, when a block and tackle machine lifts a heavy weight, force is applied. As a result of the force, the weight moves a distance. Work has been done by the machine because force was exerted over some distance.

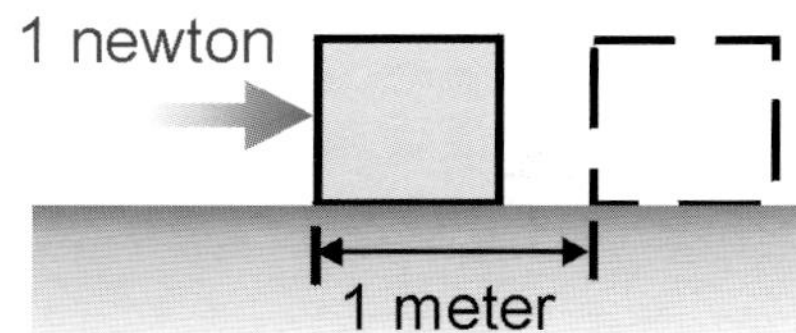

Figure 5.1: *One joule of work. One joule = 1 newton-meter.*

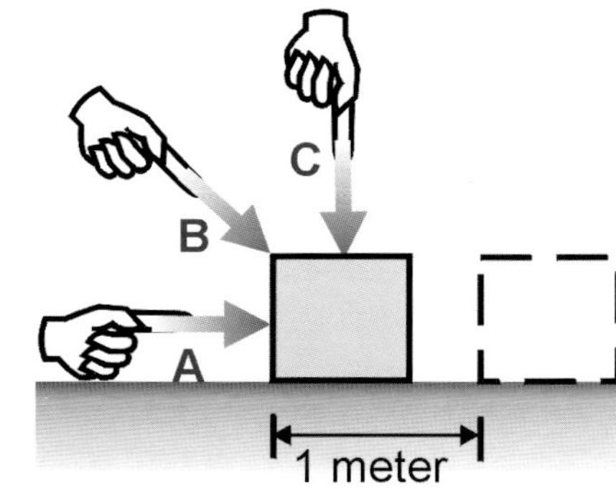

Figure 5.2: *Force (A) does 1 joule of work if it moves the box one meter. Only part of force (B) does work on the box since it is at an angle. None of force (C) does work on the box because it does not help move the box to the right at all.*

Work done by a machine

Work is done *by* forces *on* objects

In physics, work is done *by* forces. When thinking about work you should always be clear about which force is doing the work. Work is done *on* objects. If you push a block one meter with a force of one newton, you have done one joule of work *on the block*. We need to keep careful track of where the work goes because later we will see that it may be possible to get the work back.

Units of work

The unit of measurement for work is the joule. One joule is equal to one newton of force times one meter of distance. Joules are a combination unit made of force (newtons) and distance (meters).

Input work and output work

Just as we did for forces, we want to analyze machines in terms of work input and work output (figure 5.3). As an example, consider using the block and tackle machine to lift a load weighing 10 newtons. Suppose you lift the load a distance of 1/2 meter. Your machine has done five joules of work on the load (figure 5.4) so the work output is five joules.

What about the work input? You pulled on the string with a force of only five newtons because your machine gave you an advantage of two. But you had to pull the string twice as far as you lifted the block. The weight moved up 1/2 meter, but you pulled one whole meter of string. The work input is the force you apply times the distance you pulled the string. This is five newtons times one meter, or five joules. The work input is the same as the work output!

The work output of a simple machine can never exceed the work input.

The example illustrates a rule that is true *for all machines*. You can *never* get more work out of a machine than you put into it. Nature does not give something for nothing. When you design a machine that multiplies force, you pay by having to apply the force over a greater distance.

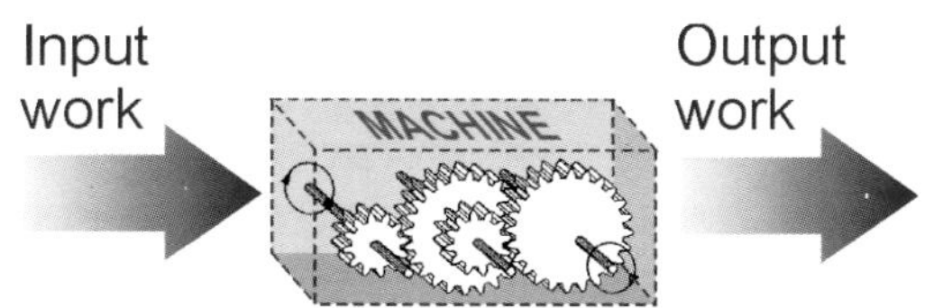

Figure 5.3: *You can think about any machine in terms of the work input and the work output.*

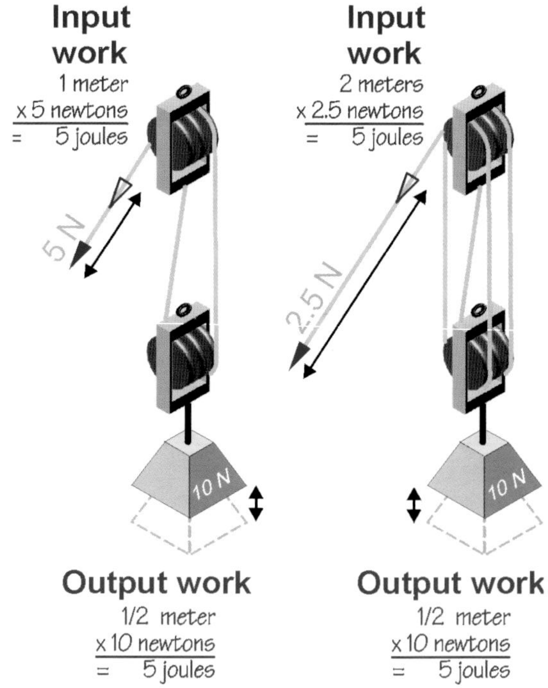

Figure 5.4: *The work input of the block and tackle is the same as the work output. You get mechanical advantage by trading force for distance.*

Efficiency

What is an efficient machine? In a very efficient machine, all (or most) of the work input becomes work output. In the block and tackle machine on the previous page, all five joules of input work were transformed to five joules of output work. An engineer would say the machine was 100 percent efficient, because all the input work became output work and none was lost.

How friction affects real machines In real machines, the work output is always less than the work input. Other forces, like friction, use up some of the input work before it reaches the output of the machine. For example, a wheel turning on an axle can get very hot. When the wheel gets hot, it means some of the input work is being converted to heat. The work output is reduced by the work that is converted to heat.

The definition of efficiency The efficiency of a machine is the ratio of work output to work input. Efficiency is usually expressed in percent. A machine that is 75 percent efficient can produce three joules of output work for every four joules of input work. One joule out of every four (25 percent) is lost to friction. You calculate efficiency by dividing the work output by the work input. You can convert the ratio into a percent by multiplying by 100.

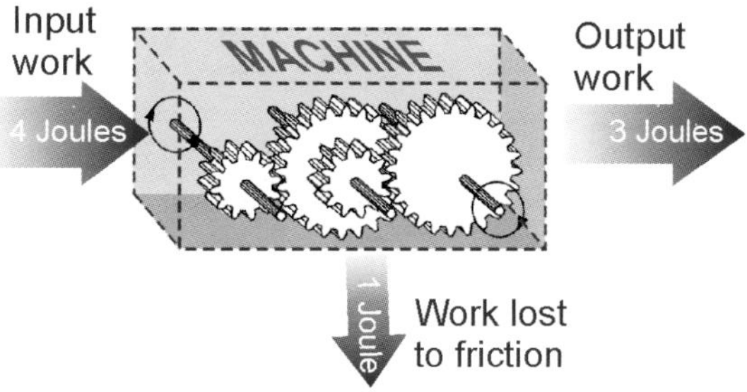

The ideal machine The ideal machine would be 100 percent efficient. Even though friction always lowers efficiency, engineers strive to make the efficiency as close to 100 percent as possible.

A most efficient machine

The bicycle is the most efficient machine ever invented for turning the work of human muscles into motion. Its efficiency is more than 95 percent.

The need for simple, efficient machines for traveling inspired many inventions that led to today's bicycle. In the mid-1800s, a very shaky ride could be achieved with the "bone shaker," which had a huge front wheel. The big wheel allowed the rider to travel farther with one push of the pedals, but it was not always safe!

James Starley (1830-1881) of the Coventry Sewing Machine Company in Britain is credited with building the first modern two-wheel bicycle in 1885. The derailleur, which is the heart of a modern multispeed bike, was invented by the Italian bicycle racer Tullio Campagnolo in 1933.

The bicycle also figured into another important invention: the airplane. Wilbur and Orville Wright were bicycle mechanics and inventors. They used their expertise in racing and building lightweight bicycles to create the first successful powered airplane in 1903.

Power

How fast the work is done

It makes a difference how fast you do work. Suppose you drag a box with a force of 100 newtons for 10 meters, and it takes you 10 seconds. You have done 1,000 joules of work. Suppose your friend drags a similar box but takes 60 seconds. You both do the same amount of work because the force and distance are the same. But something is different. You did the work in 10 seconds and your friend took six times longer.

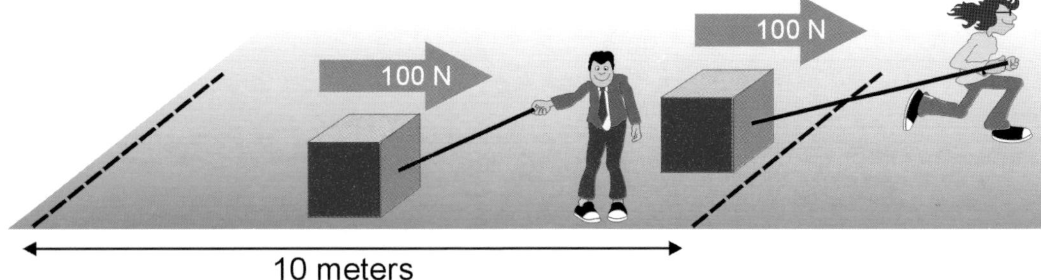

What is power?

The rate at which work is done is called **power**. You and your friend did the same amount of work, but you used six times more power because you did the work six times faster. You can determine the power of a machine by dividing the amount of work done by the time it takes in seconds. A more powerful machine does the same amount of work in less time than a less powerful machine.

Power

$$P = \frac{W}{t}$$

Power (watts) → P; Work (joules) → W; Time (seconds) → t

The units of power

The unit of power is called the **watt**, named after James Watt (1736-1819), the Scottish engineer and inventor of the steam engine. One watt is equal to one joule of work done in one second. Another unit of power commonly used is the **horsepower**. One horsepower is equal to 746 watts. As you might have guessed, one horsepower was originally the average power output of a horse.

Example:

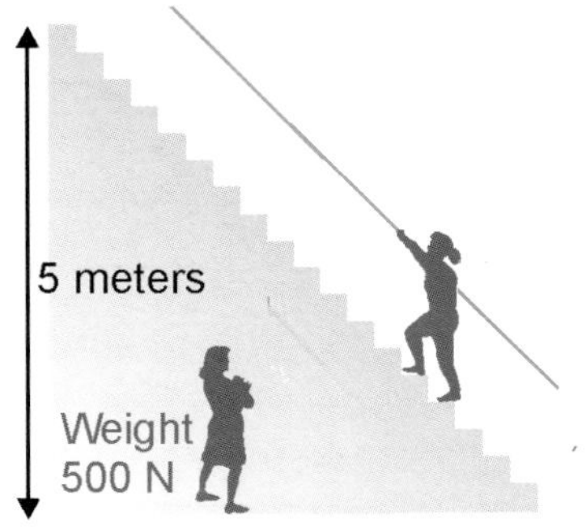

You can lift your own weight (500 newtons) up a staircase that is 5 meters high in 30 seconds.

a) How much power do you use?

b) How does your power compare with a 100-watt light bulb?

Solution:

(1) You are asked for power.

(2) You know force, distance, and time.

(3) Relationships that apply:
$W = Fd$ $P = W/t$

(4) Solve for power.
$P = FD/t$

(5) Plug in numbers. Remember:
1 joule = 1 N-m
1 watt = 1 N-m/sec
$P = (500\ N) \times (5\ m) / 30\ sec$

Answers:

(a) 2500 N-m/30 sec = 83 watts

(b) This is less power than a 100-watt light bulb. Most human activities use less power than a light bulb.

5.2 Energy Conservation

In this unit you will learn about energy. *Energy* is one of the fundamental building blocks of our universe. Energy appears in different forms, such as motion and heat. Energy can travel in different ways, such as light, sound, or electricity. The workings of the universe (including all of our technology) can be viewed from the perspective of energy flowing from one place to another and changing back and forth from one form to another.

What is energy?

The definition of energy

Energy is the ability to do work. That means anything with energy can produce a force that is capable of acting over a distance. The force can be any force, and it can come from many different sources, such as your hand, the wind, or a spring.

Energy is the ability to do work. Any object that has energy has the ability to create force.

- A moving ball has energy because it can create forces on whatever tries to stop it or slow it down.
- A sled at the top of a hill has energy because it can go down the hill and produce forces as it goes.
- The moving wind has energy because it can create forces on any object in its path.
- Electricity has energy because it can turn a motor to make forces.
- Gasoline has energy because it can be burned in an engine to make force to move a car.
- You have energy because you can create forces.

Units of energy

Energy is measured in joules, the same units as work. That is because energy is really stored work. Any object with energy has the ability to use its energy to do work, which means creating a force that acts over a distance.

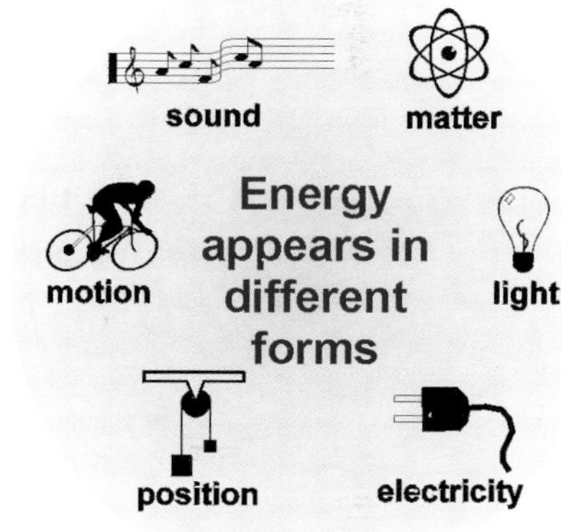

Figure 5.5: *Energy appears in many different forms.*

Potential energy

What is potential energy?

The first type of energy we will explore is called potential energy. Potential energy comes from the position of an object relative to the Earth. Consider a marble that is lifted off the table (figure 5.5). Since the Earth's gravity pulls the marble down, we must apply a force to lift it up. Applying a force over a distance requires doing work, which gets stored as the potential energy of the marble. Potential energy of this kind comes from the presence of gravity.

Where does potential energy come from?

How much energy does the marble have? The answer comes from our analysis of machines from the last section. It takes work to lift the marble up. Energy is stored work, so the amount of energy must be the same as the amount of work done to lift the marble up.

How to calculate potential energy

We can find an exact equation for the potential energy. The force required to lift the marble is the weight of the marble. From Newton's second law we know that the weight (the force) is equal to mass of the marble (m, in kilograms) times the acceleration of gravity (g, equal to 9.8 m/sec^2). We also know that work is equal to force times distance. Since force is the weight of the marble (mg) and the distance is how far we lift the marble (h), the work done equals weight times height.

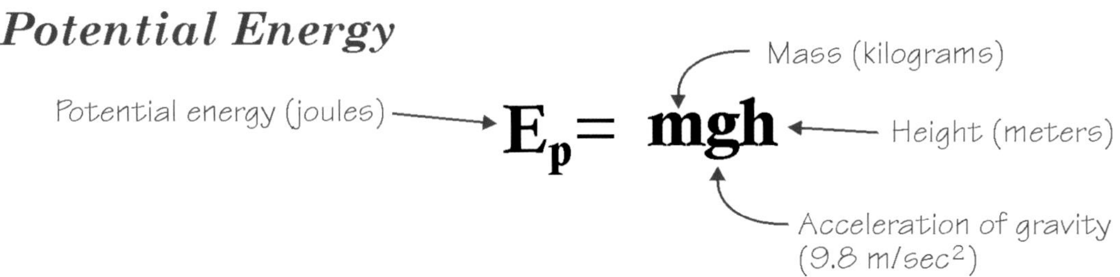

Why is it called potential energy?

Objects that have potential energy don't use their energy until they move. That's why it is called *potential* energy. Potential means that something is capable of becoming active. Any object that can move to a lower place has the potential to do work on the way down, such as a ball rolling down a hill.

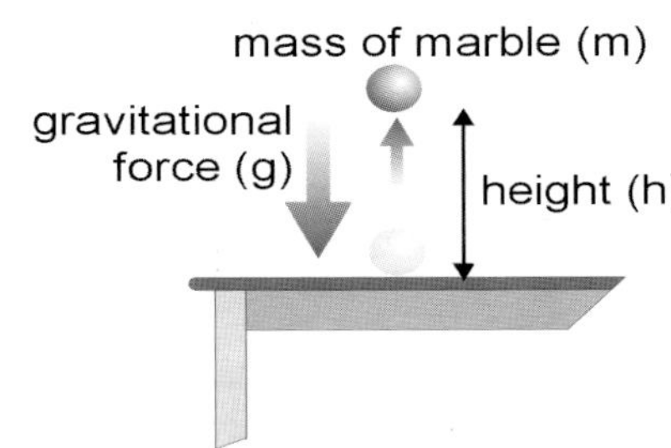

Figure 5.6: *The potential energy of a marble is equal to its mass times gravity (9.8 m/sec^2) times the height of the marble above the surface.*

Example:

You need to put a 1-kilogram mass that is on the floor, away on a shelf that is 3 meters high. How much energy does this use?

Solution:

(1) You are asked for the potential energy.

(2) You know the mass and height.

(3) The equation for potential energy is $E_p = mgh$.

(4) The equation is already in the right form.

(5) Plug in numbers. Remember: 1 N = 1 kg-m/sec^2, and 1 joule = 1 N-m.
$E_p = (1\text{ kg}) \times (9.8\text{ m/sec}^2) \times (3\text{ m})$
$= 29.4$ joules

Kinetic energy

Kinetic energy is energy of motion

Objects also store energy in motion. A moving mass can certainly exert forces, as you would quickly observe if someone ran into you in the hall. Energy of motion is called kinetic energy.

Kinetic energy increases with speed

We need to know how much kinetic energy a moving object has. Consider a shopping cart moving with a speed *v*. To make the cart move faster you need to apply a force to it (figure 5.7). Applying a force means you do some work, which is stored as energy. The higher the speed of the cart, the more energy it has because you have to do work to increase the speed.

Kinetic energy increases with mass

If you give the cart more mass, you have to push it with more force to reach the same speed. Again, more force means more work. Increasing the mass increases the amount of work you have to do to get the cart moving, so it also increases the energy. Kinetic energy depends on two things: mass and speed.

The formula for kinetic energy

To get an equation for kinetic energy, we would look at work, just like we did for potential energy. The energy is equal to the amount of work you have to do to get a mass (m) from rest up to speed (*v*). The amount of work you need can be calculated from the formula for kinetic energy.

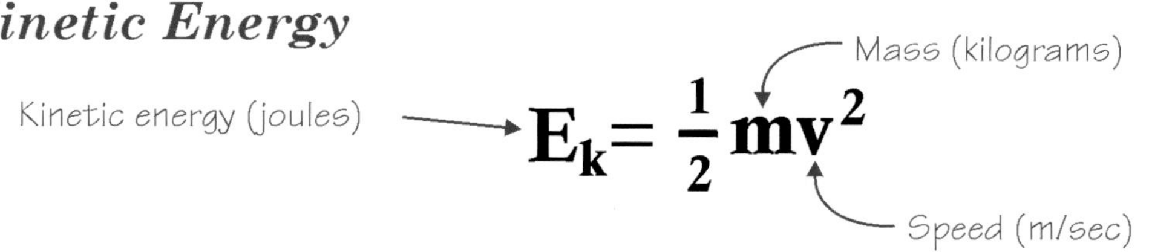

$$E_k = \frac{1}{2} m v^2$$

Kinetic energy increases as the square of the speed

The kinetic energy increases as the square of the speed. This means if you go twice as fast, your energy increases by four times ($2^2 = 4$). If your speed is three times higher, your energy is nine times bigger ($3^2 = 9$). More energy means more force is needed to stop, which is why driving fast is so dangerous. Going 60 mph, a car has four times as much kinetic energy as it does at 30 mph. At a speed of 90 mph you have *nine times* as much energy as you did at 30 mph.

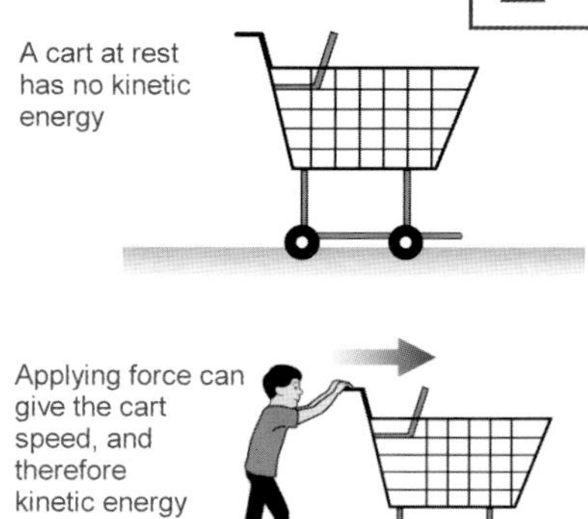

A cart at rest has no kinetic energy
Applying force can give the cart speed, and therefore kinetic energy

Applying more force increases the speed and the kinetic energy

Increasing the mass also increases the kinetic energy because it takes even more force.

Figure 5.7: *Kinetic energy depends on two things: mass and speed. The amount of kinetic energy the cart has is equal to the amount of work you do to get the cart moving.*

Conservation of energy

The law of conservation of energy

Nature never creates or destroys energy; energy only gets converted from one form to another. This concept is called the law of conservation of energy. The rule we found for the input and output work of a machine was an example of the law of conservation of energy.

Energy can never be created or destroyed, just transformed from one form into another

An example of energy transformation

What happens if you throw a ball straight up in the air? The ball leaves your hand with kinetic energy from the speed you give it when you let go. As the ball goes higher, it gains potential energy. The potential energy gained can only come from the kinetic energy the ball had at the start, so the ball slows down as it gets higher.

Eventually, all the kinetic energy has been converted to potential energy. At this point the ball has reached as high as it will go and its upward speed has been reduced to zero.

The ball falls back down again and gets faster and faster as it gets closer to the ground. The gain in speed comes from the potential energy being converted back to kinetic energy. If there were no friction the ball would return to your hand with exactly the same speed it started with—except in the opposite direction!

The total energy never exceeds the starting energy

At any moment in its flight, the ball has exactly the same energy it had at the start. The energy is divided between potential and kinetic, but the total is unchanged. In fact, we can calculate exactly how high the ball will go if we know the mass and speed we have at the beginning.

Friction can divert some energy

The law of conservation of energy still holds true, even when there is friction. Some of the energy is converted to heat or wearing away of material. The energy converted to heat or wear is no longer available to be potential energy or kinetic energy, but it was not destroyed.

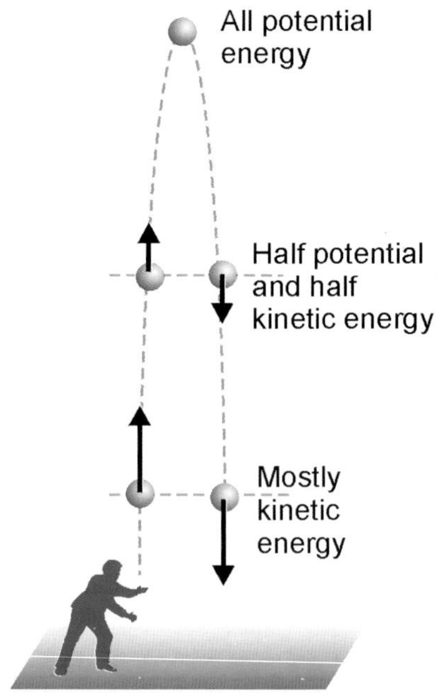

Figure 5.8: *When you throw a ball in the air, its energy transforms from kinetic to potential and back to kinetic.*

5.3 Energy Transformations

In the last section, you investigated how energy is changed from one form to another. You discovered that kinetic and potential energy change back and forth with the total amount of energy staying constant. In this section, you will apply what you learned to a wide variety of real-life situations involving other kinds of energy transformations.

Following an energy transformation

The different kinds of energy

Kinetic energy and potential energy are only two of the forms energy can take. Sometimes these two forms are called mechanical energy because they involve moving things. There are many other kinds of energy, including *radiant energy, electrical energy, chemical energy* and *nuclear energy*. Just as you saw with kinetic and potential, any of these forms of energy can be transformed into each other and back again. Every day of your life, you experience multiple energy transformations (figure 5.9) whether you know it or not!

An example of energy transformation

For example, suppose you are skating and come up to a steep hill. You know skating up the hill requires energy. From your mass and the height of the hill you can calculate how much more potential energy you will have on the top (figure 5.10). You need at least this much energy, plus some additional energy to overcome friction and inefficiency.

Chemical energy to potential energy

The energy you use to climb the hill comes from food. The chemical potential energy stored in the food you ate is converted into simple sugars. These sugars are burned as your muscles work against external forces to climb the hill—in this case, the external force is gravity. In climbing the hill you convert some chemical energy to potential energy.

Figure 5.9: *Anything you do involves transforming energy from one kind to another. Exercise transforms chemical energy from food into kinetic and potential energy.*

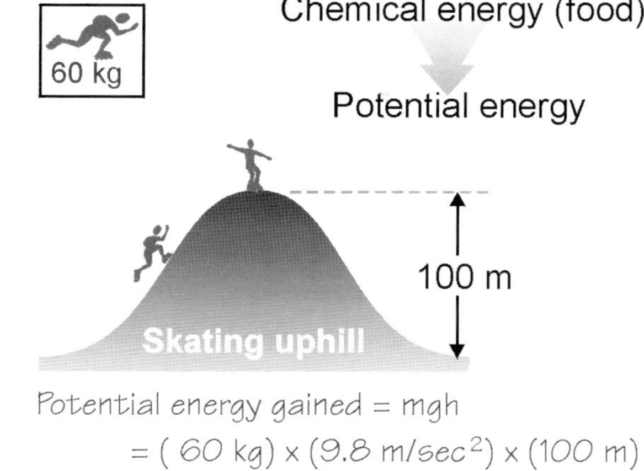

Potential energy gained = mgh

$= (60 \text{ kg}) \times (9.8 \text{ m/sec}^2) \times (100 \text{ m})$

$= 58{,}800$ joules

Figure 5.10: *At the top of the hill you have gained 58,800 joules of potential energy. This energy originally started as chemical energy in food.*

Where does "spent" energy go?

Upon reaching the top of the hill, you will probably feel like you "spent" a lot of energy. Where did the energy you spent climbing the steep hill go? Some of the energy you spent is now stored as potential energy because your position is higher than when you began. Some of the energy was also converted by your body into heat, chemical changes in muscles, and the evaporation of sweat from your skin. Can you think of any other places the energy might have gone?

How does potential energy get used?

Once you get over the top of the hill and start to coast down the other side, your speed increases, even if you just coast. An increase in speed implies an increase in kinetic energy. Where does all this kinetic energy come from? The answer is that it comes from the potential energy that was increased while you were climbing up the hill. Nature did not steal your energy. Instead, it was saved up and used to "purchase" greater speed as you descend down the other side of the hill.

Kinetic energy is used up in the brakes

If you are not careful, the stored up potential energy can generate too much speed! Assuming you want to make it down the hill with no injuries, some of the kinetic energy must change into some other form. That is what brakes do. Brakes convert kinetic energy into heat and the wearing away of the brake pads.

As you slow to a stop at the bottom of the hill, you should notice that your brakes are very hot, and some of the rubber is worn away. This means that some of the energy from the food you ate for lunch ended up heating your brake pads and wearing them away!

The flow of energy

During the trip up and down the hill, energy flowed through many forms. Starting with chemical energy, some energy appeared in the form of potential energy, kinetic energy, heat, air friction, sound, evaporation, and more. During all these transformations no energy was lost because energy can never be created or destroyed. All the energy you started with went somewhere.

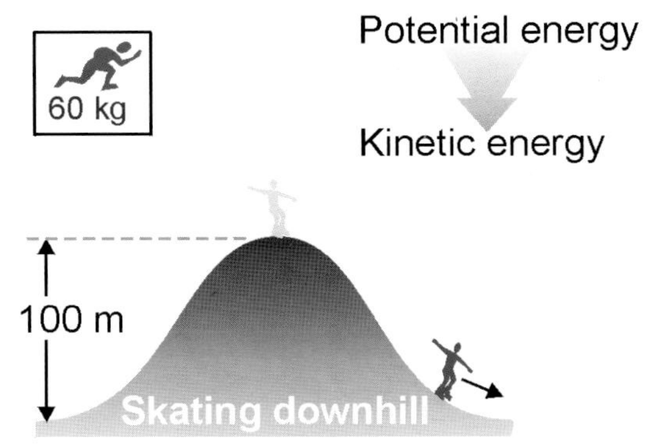

Potential energy at top = kinetic energy at bottom

58,800 joules = 1/2 mv ^{2}

assuming no friction

v = 44 m/sec

Figure 5.11: *On the way down, your potential energy is converted to kinetic energy and you pick up speed. In real life not all the potential energy would become kinetic energy. Air friction would use some and you would use your brakes*

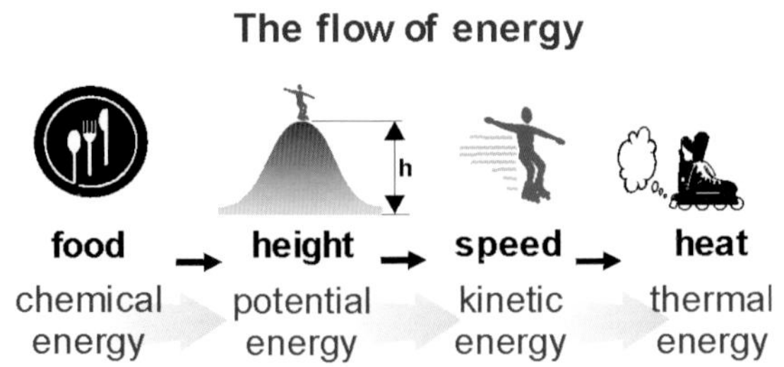

The flow of energy

food → height → speed → heat

chemical energy → potential energy → kinetic energy → thermal energy

Figure 5.12: *A few of the forms the energy goes through during the skating trip.*

Other forms of energy

Energy: nature's money

One way to understand energy is to think of it as nature's money. It is spent and saved in a number of different ways any time you want to do something. You can use energy to buy speed, height, temperature, mass, and other things. But you have to have some energy to start with, and what you spend diminishes what you have left.

Mechanical energy

Mechanical energy is the energy possessed by an object due to its *motion* or its stored energy of *position*. Mechanical energy can be either kinetic (energy of motion) or potential (energy of position). An object that possesses mechanical energy is able to do work. Mechanical energy is the form involved in the operation of the simple machines you have studied in this unit.

Radiant energy

Radiant (meaning light) energy is also known as electromagnetic energy. Light is made up of waves called electromagnetic waves (Unit 5). There are many different types of electromagnetic waves, including the light we see, ultraviolet light, X rays, infrared radiation (also known as heat – that's how you feel the heat from a fire), radio waves, microwaves, and radar.

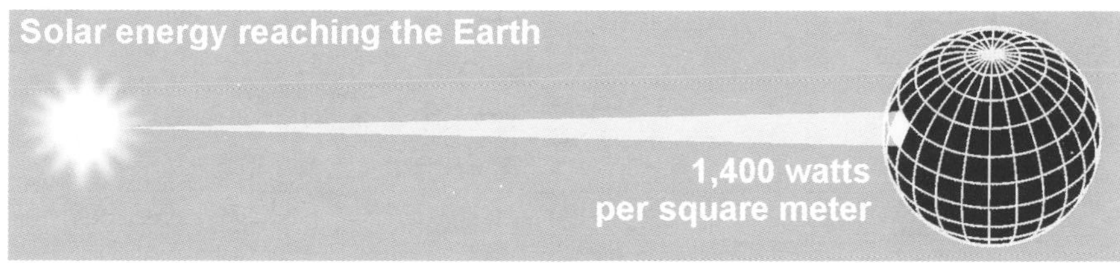

Energy from the sun

Radiant heat from the sun is what keeps the Earth warm. The sun's energy falls on the Earth at a rate of about 1,400 watts for each square meter of surface area. Not all of this energy reaches the Earth's surface though; even on a clear day, about one-fourth of the energy is absorbed by the Earth's atmosphere. When we harness the radiant energy from the sun, it is called solar power.

Example

A water-powered turbine makes electricity from the energy of falling water. The diagram shows a turbine where 100 kg of water falls every second from a height of 20 meters.

(a) 100 kg of water 20 meters high has how much potential energy?

(b) How much power in watts could you get out of the turbine if it was perfectly efficient?

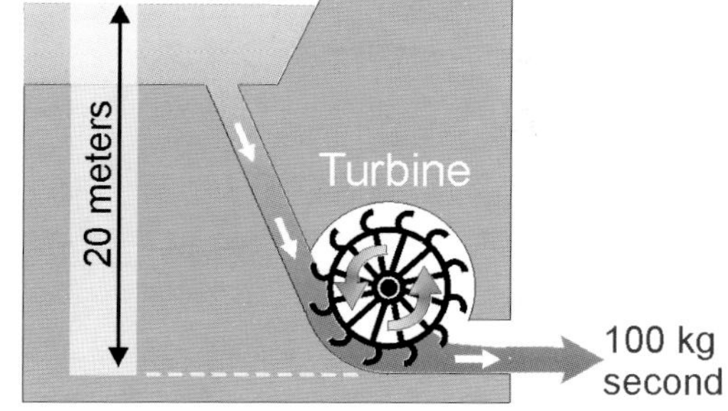

Solution: Part a

(1) You are asked for potential energy.
(2) You are given mass (100 kg) and height (20 m).
(3) The relationship you need is $E_p = mgh$.
(4) Plug in numbers:

$$E_p = (100 \text{ kg}) \times (9.8 \text{ m/sec}^2) \times (20 \text{ m})$$
$$= 19{,}600 \text{ joules}$$

Solution: Part b

(1) You are asked for power.
(2) You know energy (19,600 J) and time (1 sec).
(3) The relationship you need is $P = W/t$.
(4) Plug in numbers:

$$P = 19{,}600 \text{ J} / 1 \text{ sec}$$
$$= 19{,}600 \text{ watts}$$

This is enough energy for nearly 200 light bulbs if each bulb uses 100 watts.

Electrical energy

Electrical energy is something we take for granted whenever we plug an appliance into an outlet. The electrical energy we use in our daily lives is actually derived from other sources of energy. For example, in a natural gas power plant the energy starts as chemical energy in the gas. The gas is burned, releasing heat energy. The heat energy is used to make high-pressure steam. The steam turns a turbine which transforms the heat energy to mechanical energy. Finally, the turbine turns an electric generator, producing electrical energy.

Chemical energy

Chemical energy is the type of energy stored in molecules. Chemical reactions can either use or release chemical energy. One example of chemical energy is a battery. The chemical energy stored in batteries changes to electrical energy when you connect wires and a light bulb. Your body also uses chemical energy when it converts food into energy so that you can walk or run or think. All the fossil fuels we depend on (coal, oil, gas) are useful because they contain chemical energy we can easily release.

Nuclear energy

Nuclear energy comes from splitting an atom, or fusing two atoms together. When an atom is split or fused, a huge amount of energy is released. Nuclear energy is used to generate or make electricity in power plants. A new kind of environmentally safe nuclear power (fusion) is the focus of a worldwide research program. If we could extract the fusion energy from a single teaspoon of water, it would be the equivalent of 55 barrels of oil. Nuclear energy is really the basic source for all other energy forms because it is how the sun and stars make energy. The chemical energy in fossil fuels comes from sunlight that was absorbed by plants millions of years ago. Nuclear energy is also used in medicine to treat cancer and other diseases.

Thermal energy

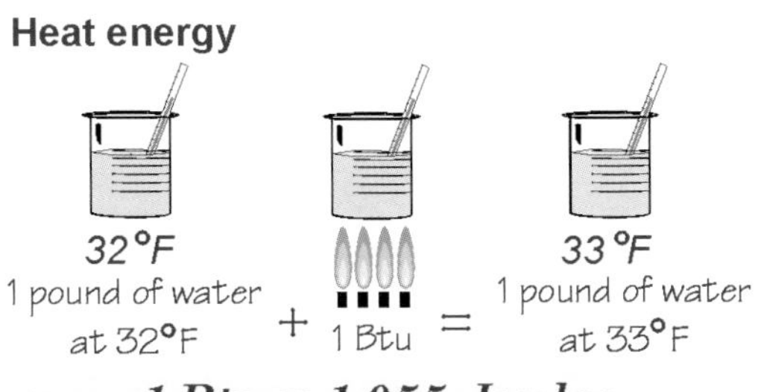

Heat is a form of thermal energy. When you design a heating system for a house, you need to specify how much heat energy you need. Heating contractors measure heat using the British thermal unit (Btu). One Btu is the same amount of energy as 1,055 joules.

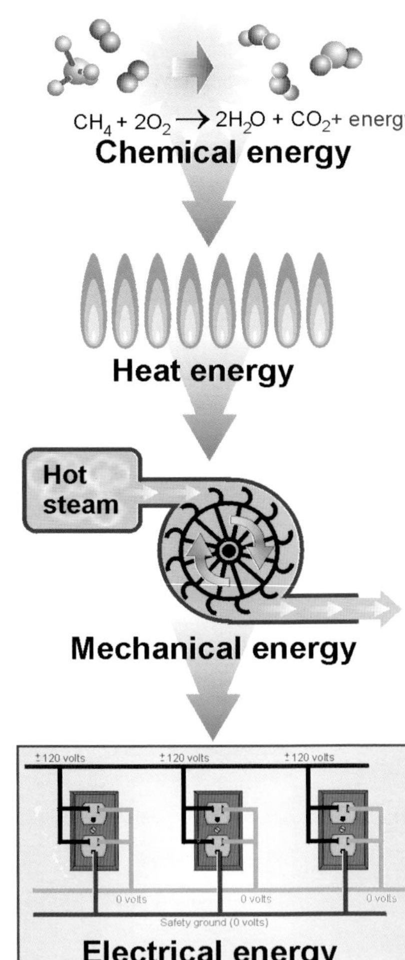

Figure 5.13: *Power plants convert chemical energy, mechanical energy and heat into electrical energy.*

Chapter 5 Review

Vocabulary review

Match the following terms with the correct definition. There is one extra definition in the list that will not match any of the terms.

Set One

1. energy
2. joule
3. law of conservation of energy
4. newton-meter
5. work

a. The ability to do work
b. The combined units of force and distance used to quantify work
c. One newton-meter is equal to one of these
d. Energy is never created or destroyed
e. The amount of work that can be done by an object is equal to the energy available in the object
f. Force times distance

Set Two

1. efficiency
2. perpetual motion machine
3. power
4. watt

a. Force times distance
b. The amount of work performed over time
c. One joule of work performed in 1 second
d. An imaginary machine that can be 100 percent efficient
e. The ratio of work output to work input

Concept review

1. Why is it correct to say that energy is *conserved* in a machine?
2. In your own words, explain the relationship between work and energy.
3. You want to prove the law of conservation of energy to a friend. For your demonstration you show that you can use a block and pulley machine to lift 100 newtons with only 20 newtons of input force. What would you say to your friend to explain how this is possible?
4. You have a machine that tells you exactly how much work in joules is put into a machine and how much work was produced. The readings that you just received from the machine state that the input work was 345 joules and the output work was 330 joules. The law of conservation of energy states that input should equal output. How can you explain the "lost" 15 joules?
5. The following diagram shows a cart rolling along a hilly road. Ignore the effect of friction. Arrange the five locations in order of increasing potential and kinetic energy.

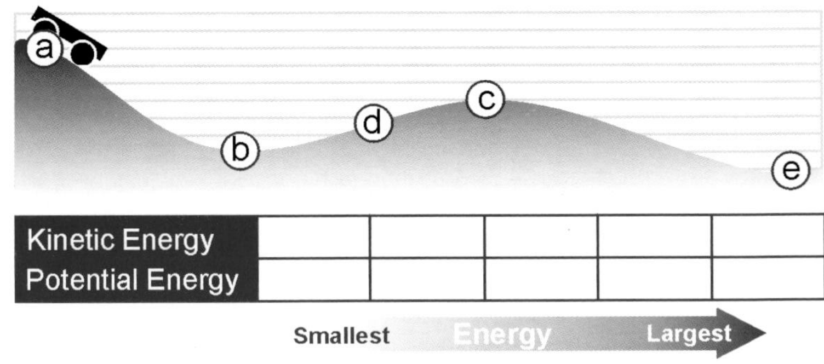

Problems

1. Calculate work using the following values for force and distance. Give your answers in joules.
   a. 12 newtons lifted 5 meters
   b. 3 newtons pushed 3 meters
   c. 400 newtons dragged 10 meters
   d. 7.5 newtons lifted 18.4 meters
2. How many joules of work are done if you carry a box that weighs 28 newtons up a ladder for a distance of 2 meters?
3. For each statement, write W if work is being done and NW if no work is being accomplished.
   a. I carried my books upstairs to my bedroom.
   b. The wind blew the lawn chair across the yard.
   c. The wall in my classroom won't budge no matter how much I push on it.
   d. I blew some dust off my paper.
   e. I stood very still and balanced a book on my head.

4. Which requires more work, lifting a 15-newton load a distance of 3 meters with a block and tackle, or lifting a 7-newton load a distance of 10 meters with the same block and tackle machine? Be sure to show your work and explain your answer clearly.

5. A block and tackle machine performed 30 joules of work on a 15-newton block. How high did the machine lift the block?

6. At the end of the ride up a steep hill, Ken was at an elevation of 1,600 meters above where he started. He figured out that he and his bicycle had accomplished 1,000,000 joules of work. If Ken has a mass of 54 kg, what is the mass of his bicycle? (Note: $g = 9.8\ m/sec^2$.)

7. If a block and tackle machine has a mechanical advantage of 2, you can use 20 newtons of force to lift a 40-newton load. If you lift the block 1 meter, what length of rope do you have to pull?

8. A machine has a work output of 45 joules. In order to accomplish the work, 48 joules of work was put into the machine. What is the efficiency of this machine? Be sure to give your answer as a percentage.

9. One machine can perform 280 joules of work in 40 seconds. Another machine can produce 420 joules of work in 2 minutes. Which machine is more powerful? Justify your answer by calculating the amount of power in watts each machine produces.

10. You attach a motor to a block and tackle machine. After using it, you find that you want a more powerful motor. You purchase one that has twice the power of the old motor.

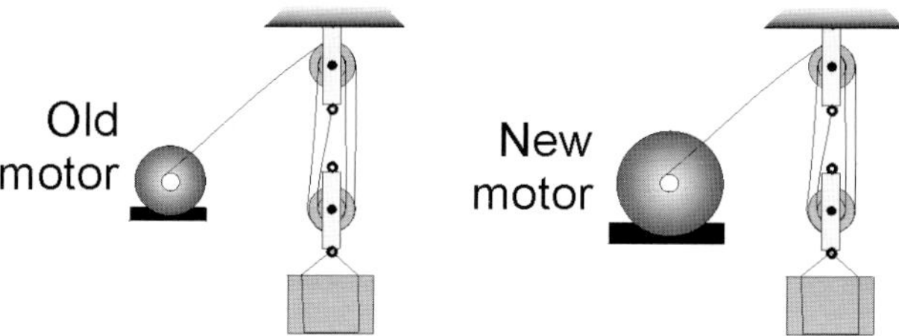

a. How much bigger a load can the new motor lift in the same amount of time?

b. If the new motor lifts the same load as the old motor, how much faster can it go?

11. A motor pushes a car with a force of 35 newtons for a distance of 350 meters in 6 seconds.

a. How much work has the motor accomplished?

b. How powerful is the motor in watts?

12. How much power is required to do 55 joules of work in 55 seconds?

13. The manufacturer of a machine said that it is 86 percent efficient. If you use 70 joules to run the machine (input work), how much output work will it produce?

14. A machine is 72 percent efficient. If it produces 150 joules of work output, how much work was put into the machine?

Applying your knowledge

1. A car is about 15 percent efficient at converting energy from gas to energy of motion. The average car today gets 25 miles for each gallon of gas.
   a. What would the gas mileage be if the car could be made 100 percent efficient?
   b. Name three things that contribute to lost energy and prevent a car from ever being 100 percent efficient.
2. Why, according to the laws of physics, is it impossible to build a perpetual motion machine?
3. Research question: Investigate light bulb wattage and describe what watts mean in terms of power and work.
4. Imagine we had to go back to using horses for power. One horse makes 746 watts (1 hp). How many horses would it take to light up all the light bulbs in your school?
   a. First, estimate how many light bulbs are in your school.
   b. Estimate the power of each light bulb, or get it from the bulb itself where it is written on the top.
   c. Calculate the total power used by all the bulbs.
   d. Calculate how many horses it would take to make this much power.
5. Make a chart that shows the flow of energy in the situation described below. In your chart, use some of the key concepts you learned, including potential energy and kinetic energy.

Martha wakes up at 5:30 am and eats a bowl of corn flakes. It's a nice day, so she decides to ride her bicycle to work, which is uphill from her house. It is still dark outside. Martha's bike has a small electric generator that runs from the front wheel. She flips on the generator so that her headlight comes on when she starts to pedal. She then rides her bike to work. Draw a diagram that shows the energy transformations that occur in this situation.

Chapter 6

Electricity and Electric Circuits

Introduction to Chapter 6

Electricity is everywhere around us. We use electricity to turn on lights, cool our homes, and run our TVs, radios, and portable phones. There is electricity in lightning and in our bodies. Even though electricity is everywhere, we can't easily see what it is or how it works. In this chapter, you will learn the basic ideas of electricity. You will learn about electric circuits and electric charge, the property of matter responsible for electricity.

Investigations for Chapter 6

6.1	**What Is a Circuit?**	*What is an electric circuit?*

Can you make a bulb light? In this Investigation, you will build and analyze a circuit with a bulb, battery, wires, and switch. You will also learn to draw and understand diagrams of electric circuits using standard electrical symbols.

6.2	**Charge**	*What is moving through a circuit?*

In this Investigation, you will create two kinds of static electricity and see what happens when the two charges come together. During the Investigation, you will also demonstrate that there only two kinds of charge.

Learning Goals

In this chapter, you will:

- ✔ Build simple circuits.
- ✔ Trace circuit paths.
- ✔ Interpret the electric symbols for battery, bulb, wire, and switch.
- ✔ Draw a circuit diagram of a real circuit.
- ✔ Explain why electrical symbols and circuit diagrams are useful.
- ✔ Explain how a switch works.
- ✔ Identify open and closed circuits.
- ✔ Charge pieces of tape and observe their interactions with an electroscope.
- ✔ Identify electric charge as the property of matter responsible for electricity.
- ✔ List the two forms of electric charge.
- ✔ Describe the forces electric charges exert on each other.
- ✔ Describe how lightning forms.

Vocabulary

circuit diagram
closed circuit
coulomb
electric charge
electric circuits
electrical symbols
electrically charged
electrically neutral
electroscope
natural world
negative charge
open circuit
positive charge
static electricity
versorium

6.1 What Is a Circuit?

There are lots of electrical devices and wires around us. What is inside those light bulbs, stereos, toasters, and other electrical devices? All these devices contain electric circuits. In this section, you will figure out how to build circuits with a bulb, batteries, wires, and a switch, and learn how to draw circuit diagrams using electrical symbols.

Electricity

Why learn about electricity? We use electricity every day. Our homes, stores, and workplaces all use many electrical appliances and devices such as electric ovens, TVs, stereos, toasters, motors that turn fans, air conditioners, heaters, light bulbs, etc. In fact, the use of electricity has become so routine that many of us don't stop to think about what happens when we switch on a light or turn on a motor. If we do stop to look, we find that most of what is "happening" is not visible. What exactly is electricity? How does it work?

What is electricity? *Electricity* usually means the flow of something called *electric current* in wires, motors, light bulbs, and other devices. Think about making a water wheel turn. Water flows over the wheel and as it falls, it gives up energy and the wheel turns. We build ponds, canals, and pipes to carry water from one place to another where we want to use it.

Electric current Electric current is like water, except it flows through solid metal so we can't usually see it. Just like water, electric current can carry energy over great distances. Look around you and you can probably see wires carrying electric current into houses and buildings.

Electricity can be powerful and dangerous Electric current can be very powerful. An electric saw can cut wood 30 times faster that a hand saw (figure 6.2). An electric motor the size of a basketball can do as much work as five big horses or 15 strong men. Electric current can also be dangerous. Touching a live electric wire can give you a very serious injury. The safe use and understanding of electricity is what this unit is about.

Figure 6.1: *A water wheel uses a current of water to turn a wheel and do useful work.*

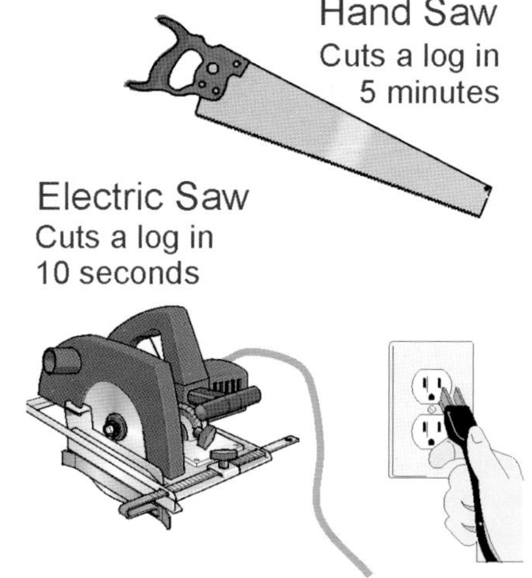

Figure 6.2: *Electricity uses an electric current to power light bulbs and electric motors.*

Electric circuits

What is an electric circuit?

To start to understand electricity, let's look inside a simple electrical appliance, like an electric blender. Inside are lots of wires and other electrical parts. The wires, switches, and motors are connected in electric circuits. An electric circuit is something that provides a path through which electricity travels.

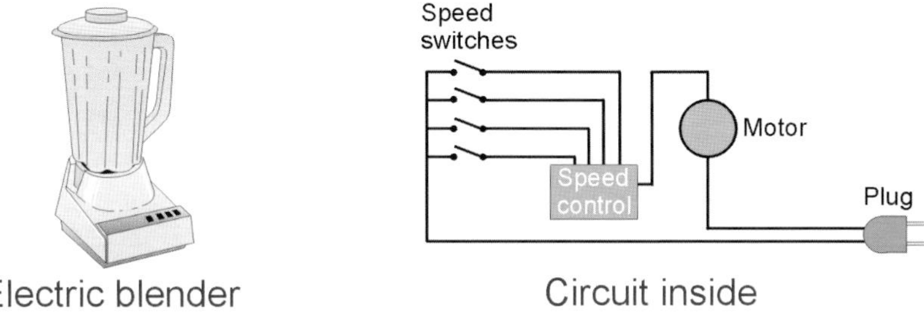

Circuits also exist in the natural world

Circuits are not confined to appliances, wires, and devices built by people. People's first experience with electricity was in the natural world. Some examples of circuits are:

- The wiring that lights your house is an electric circuit.
- The nerves in your body create electric circuits.
- Lightning, clouds, and the planet Earth form an electric circuit.
- The car battery, ignition switch, and starter form an electric circuit.

Electric circuits are like water pipes

Electric circuits are similar to pipes and hoses for water (figure 6.3). You can think of wires as pipes for electricity. The big difference is that you can't get the electricity to leave the wire. If you cut a water pipe, the water comes out. If you cut a wire, the electricity immediately stops flowing. Electric current cannot flow except in complete circuits.

Switches turn circuits on and off

Because a complete path through wire is need for electricity to work, a switch works by breaking or completing the circuit path. When a switch is on, the circuit path is complete. When a switch is off, the circuit path is broken (figure 6.4).

Figure 6.3: *We use pipes to carry the flow of water where we need it.*

Electric current only flows in closed circuits.

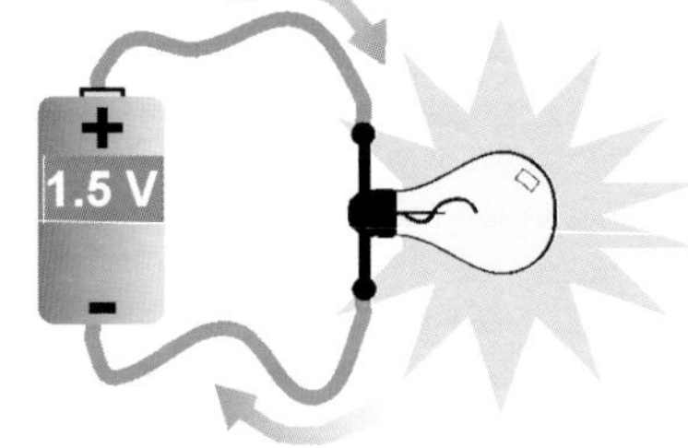

Electric current does not flow in open circuits.

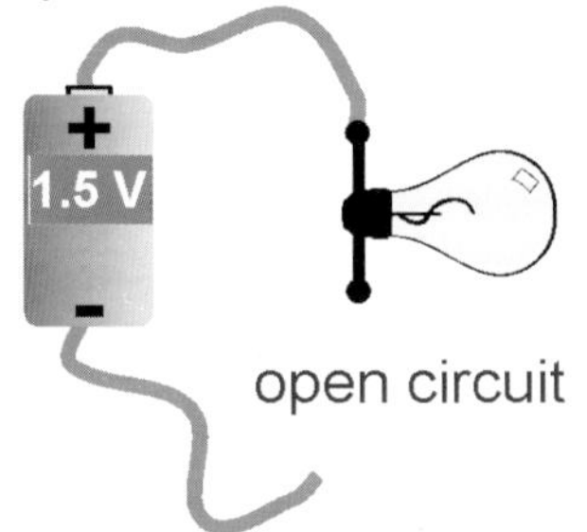

Figure 6.4: *We use electric circuits with wires to carry the flow of electricity where we need it.*

Circuit diagrams and electrical symbols

Circuit diagrams

Circuits are made up of wires and electrical parts, such as *batteries*, *light bulbs*, *motors*, or *switches*. When people build and design circuits to accomplish a task, they use a special kind of drawing called a circuit diagram. In a circuit diagram we use symbols to represent parts of the circuit. These electrical symbols are quicker to draw and can be read by anyone familiar with electricity.

A circuit diagram uses electrical symbols

A circuit diagram is a shorthand method of describing a real circuit. By using a diagram with standard symbols you don't have to draw a battery and bulb realistically every time you need to write down a circuit you have made. Figure 6.5 shows some common things you find in a circuit and their electrical symbols.

The graphic below shows a photograph of a simple circuit and two circuit diagrams. Each circuit diagram represents the simple circuit. See if you can match the symbols in the circuit diagrams with each part of the simple circuit.

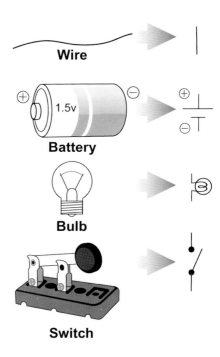

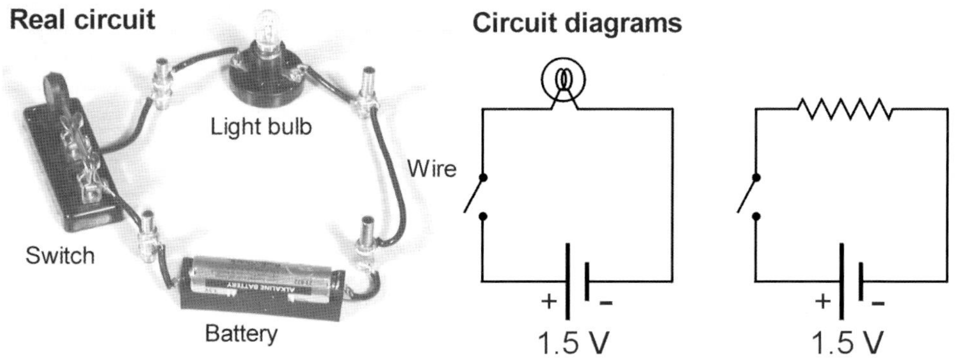

Resistors and what they represent

In many circuit diagrams any electrical device is shown as a *resistor*. A resistor is an electrical component that uses energy. In a few sections, you will see that when analyzing how a circuit works, we often treat things like light bulbs as if they were resistors.

Figure 6.5: *Commonly used electric parts and their symbols*

Open and closed circuits

Circuits are controlled by switches

You have just learned that we use switches to turn electricity on and off. Turning the switch off creates a break in the wire. The break stops the flow of current because electricity travels through the metal wire but can't normally travel through air.

Open and closed circuits

A circuit with a switch turned to the off position or a circuit with any break in it is called an **open circuit**. Electricity can't travel through an open circuit. When the switch is turned to the on position, there are no longer any breaks anywhere in the wire and the light goes on. This is called a **closed circuit**. Electricity can travel easily through a closed circuit.

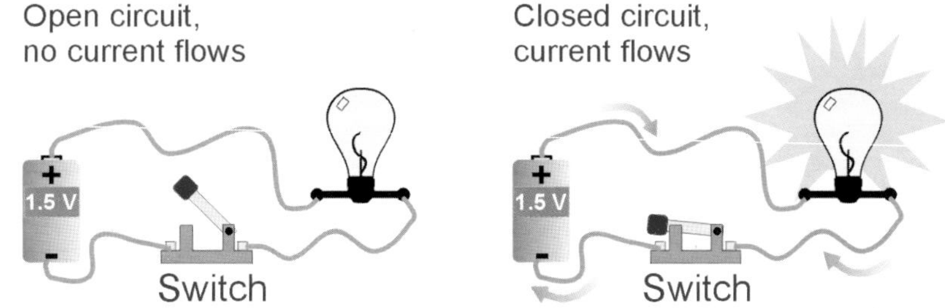

Trace circuits to test them

A common problem found in circuits is that an unintentional break occurs. When building circuits it is a good idea to trace your finger around the wires to tell if the circuit is open or closed. If there are any breaks, the circuit is open. If there is a complete loop then the circuit is closed.

Short circuits

A *short circuit* is not the same as either open or closed circuits. A short circuit is usually an accidental extra path for current to flow. Short circuits are covered in more detail in a later section when we talk about *parallel* and *series* circuits.

Spinal cord injuries

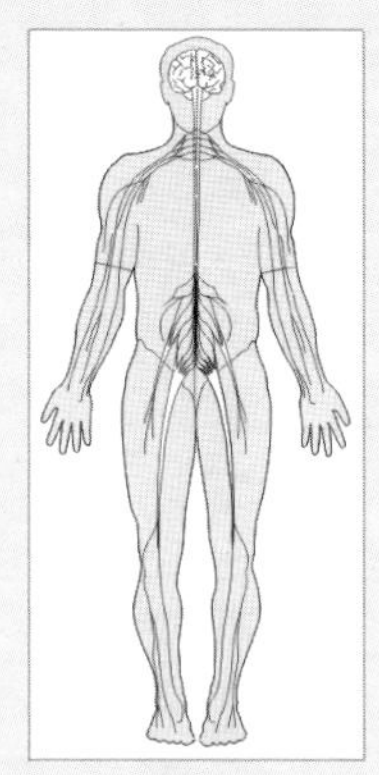

Our nervous system is a network of electric circuits including the brain, spinal cord, and many nerves. Motor nerves branch out from the spinal cord and send electrical messages to muscles, telling them to contract so that you can move. If a motor nerve is injured, an open circuit is created. The message from the brain can no longer reach the muscle, so the muscle no longer works.

Although a surgeon can sew the two ends of a broken nerve back together, scar tissue forms that blocks the circuit. If a person injures a small nerve (a motor nerve in the thumb, for example), they may regain movement after a period of time as other nerves create alternate paths for the signal. However, injury to a large bundle of nerves, like the spinal cord, is irreparable. That is why spinal cord injuries can cause paralysis.

6.2 Charge

You have built circuits and made light bulbs glow. Now we will find out exactly what is moving through those wires. In this section, you will learn about electric charge and build a simple electroscope to observe the electrical forces exerted by electric charges on each other.

Electricity

Use of electricity is relatively new

The understanding and use of electricity is relatively recent history. Michael Faraday discovered the principles of the electric motor in 1830. The electric light was invented by Thomas Edison in 1879. Two lifetimes later we now see light bulbs and motors everywhere.

Faraday and Edison were only two of the many people who observed, investigated, and thought about electricity. Today's technology results from an accumulation of knowledge about electricity over a long period of time.

First experiments in electricity

To understand electricity, people first studied events like lightning and the sparks that can occur when certain materials are rubbed together. We observe the same effect when we rub our feet on a carpet and then feel a shock or see a spark when we touch a metal doorknob. *Something* in ordinary materials "electrifies" our body. What is it?

Electric charge

The source of the shock and the sparks is *electric charge*. **Electric charge**, like mass, is a fundamental property of matter. An important difference between mass and charge is that charge comes in two kinds, called **positive charge** and **negative charge**.

History of the terms positive and negative charge

The terms *positive* and *negative* to describe the opposite kinds of charge were first used by Benjamin Franklin (1706-1790). He and other scientists were seeking to describe their new observations about electricity. In 1733, French scientist Charles DuFay had published a book describing how like charges repel and unlike charges attract. He theorized that two fluids caused electricity: vitreous (positive) fluid and resinous (negative) fluid.

Later that century, Franklin invented his own theory that argued that electricity is a result of the presence of a single fluid in different amounts. Franklin claimed that when there was too much fluid in an object, it would exhibit positive charge behavior, and if there were not enough, the object would exhibit negative charge behavior. Although scientists no longer believe that electricity is caused by different kinds of fluids, the words positive and negative are still used to describe the two types of charge.

Electric charge

Static electricity

When we acquire a static charge from walking across a carpet, our bodies gain a tiny amount of excess negative charge. In general, if materials or objects carry excess positive or negative charge we say they are electrically charged. When charge builds up on an object or material it is sometimes referred to as static electricity.

The explanation of static cling

What happens when there is a buildup of excess charge? We observe that clothes fresh out of a dryer stick together. This is because all the tumbling and rubbing makes some clothes positive and others negative. Do you notice what happens when you brush your hair on a dry day? Each hair gets the same kind of charge and they repel each other, making your hair appear fuller.

Like charges attract, unlike charges repel

These scenarios show us how charges affect each other. A positive and a negative charge will pull each other closer. Two positive charges will push each other away. The same is true of two negative charges. The rule for the force between two charges is: Unlike charges attract each other and like charges repel each other.

Like charges repel

Unlike charges attract

Electrical forces

These forces between positive and negative charges are called electrical forces or electrostatic forces. If you increase the amount of one kind of charge on an object, it exerts a greater electrical force. This kind of force is very strong! Suppose you could separate the positive and negative charges in a bowling ball. The force between the separated charges would be 10 times the weight of the entire Earth!

Most matter is neutral

It is very difficult to separate the positive and negative charges in a bowling ball or in anything else. Most matter has the exact same amount of positive and negative charges. Total charge is zero, since the positives cancel the negatives. An object with zero charge is electrically neutral. The electrical events we observe are the result of the separation of relatively small amounts of charge.

This object is neutral

positive charge +8
negative charge -8
total 0

This object is charged

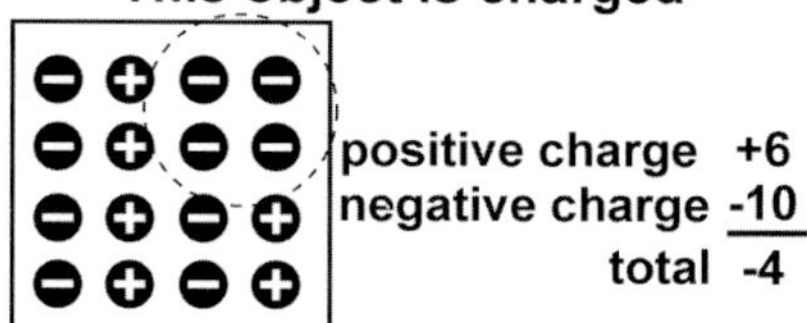

Figure 6.6: *Most matter is neutral, with equal amounts of positive and negative charge. If an object gains or loses one kind of charge, it is said to be charged.*

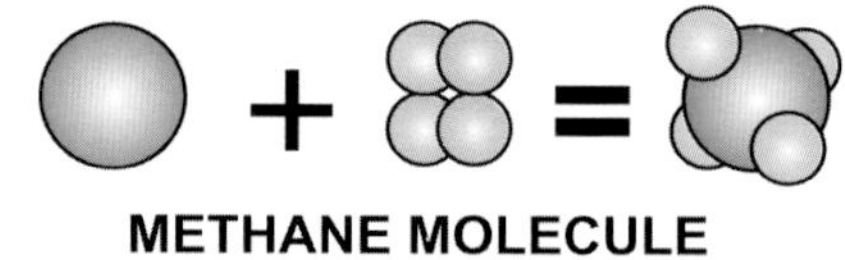

Figure 6.7: *You will study chemical reactions like the one shown above later in this book. Electrical forces are the cause of many properties of matter and all reactions.*

The coulomb and the atom

Electric charge is measured in coulombs

The unit of electric charge is the coulomb (C). The name is chosen in honor of Charles-Augustin de Coulomb (1736-1806), a French physicist who succeeded in making the first accurate measurements of the forces between charges in 1783.

The charge of protons and electrons

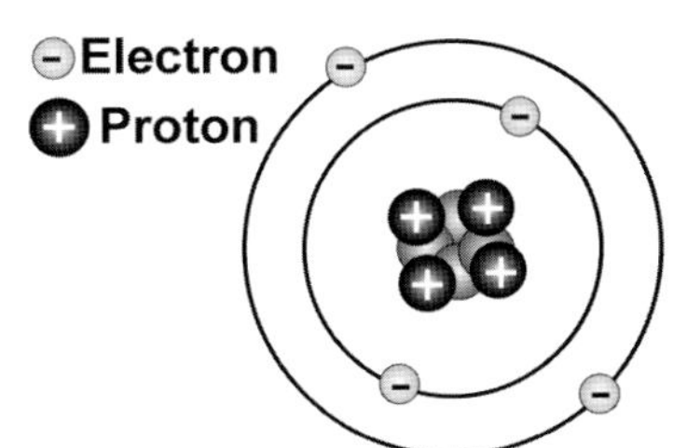

Since Coulomb's time, people have discovered that different parts of the atom carry electric charge. The protons in the nucleus are positive and the electrons in the outer part of the atom are negative.

Electrical forces in atoms

Electrons in atoms stay close to the protons because they are attracted to each other. If you could put 1 coulomb of positive charge a meter away from the same amount of negative charge, the electrical force between them would be 9,000,000,000 (9 billion) newtons!

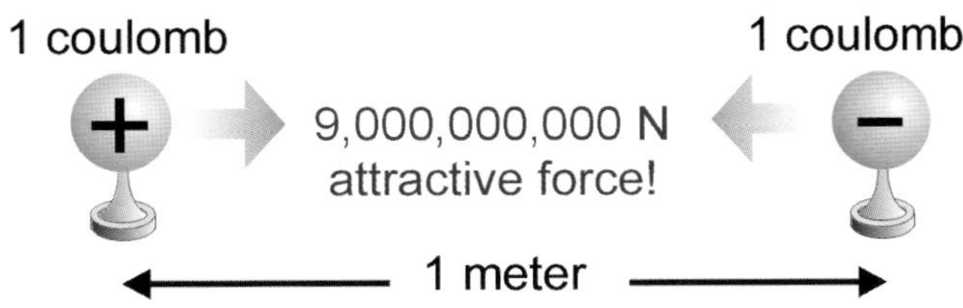

Lightning and charged particles

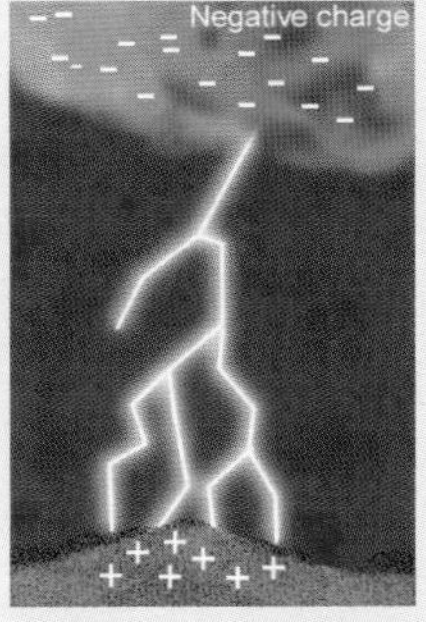

Lightning is caused by a giant buildup of static charge. Before a lightning strike, particles in a cloud collide and charges are transferred from one particle to another. Positive charges tend to build up on smaller particles and negative charges on bigger ones.

The forces of gravity and wind cause the particles to separate. Positively charged particles accumulate near the top of the cloud and negatively charged particles fall toward the bottom. Scientists from the National Aeronautics and Space Administration (NASA) have measured enormous buildups of negative charge in storm clouds. These negatively charged cloud particles repulse negative charges in the ground, causing the ground to become positively charged. This positive charge is why people who have been struck by lightning sometimes say they first felt their hair stand on end.

The negative charges in the cloud are attracted to the positively charged ground. When enough charges have been separated by the storm, the cloud, air, and ground act like a giant circuit. All the accumulated negative charges flow from the cloud to the ground, heating the air along the path (to as much as 20,000°C!) so that it glows like a bright streak of light.

The electroscope

Detecting charge with an electroscope

We can detect charged objects by using an electroscope. The electroscope has two very light leaves that hang down. The leaves attract or repel each other depending on the charge nearby. By watching the leaves you can tell what kinds of electric charges are near, and roughly how strong they are. A more complex electroscope can measure the exact amount of charge present on an object.

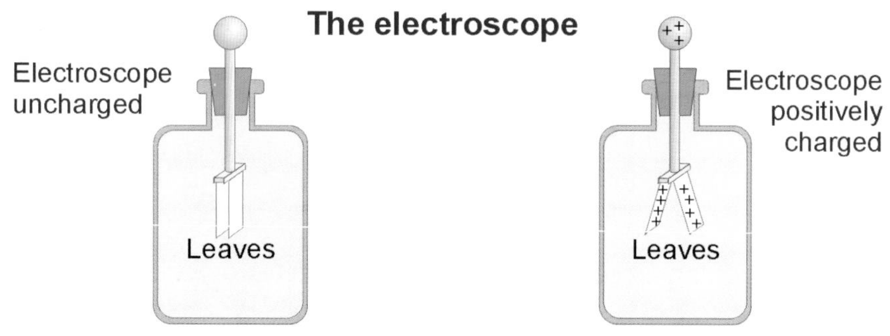

Using a charged electroscope to test an unknown charge.

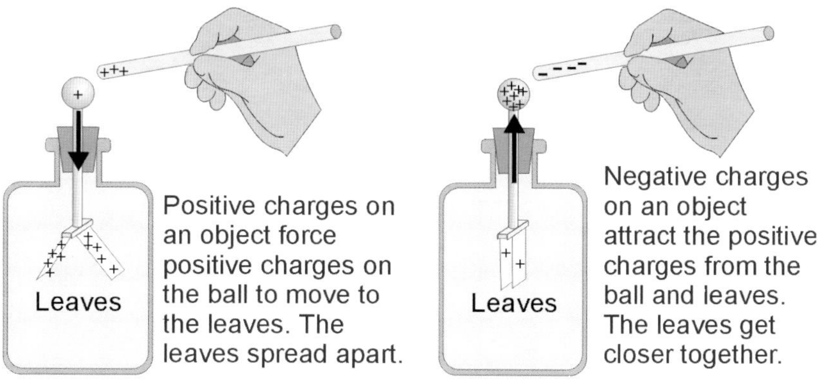

Leaves
Positive charges on an object force positive charges on the ball to move to the leaves. The leaves spread apart.
Leaves
Negative charges on an object attract the positive charges from the ball and leaves. The leaves get closer together.

History of the electroscope

In sixteenth-century England, Queen Elizabeth I had a physician named William Gilbert who was very interested in magnetism because he thought that it might help his patients. Gilbert discovered that rubbing semiprecious stones would cause them to attract light objects. Like others of his time, Gilbert thought that static attraction was caused by magnetism. In his experiments, he found that some stones attracted better than others. To measure just how well these objects worked, he invented the first electrical instrument, the versorium. Like a compass needle, the thin, balanced pointer would swing to show a very small attraction. The versorium was the earliest version of today's electroscope.

Objects like paper and straw that were attracted to the versorium Gilbert called electrics. Those that were not attracted, he called non-electrics. From these two words, Gilbert gets credit for making up the word ***electricity***.

Chapter 6 Review

Vocabulary Review

Match the following terms with the correct definition. There is one extra definition in the list that will not match any of the terms.

Set One

1. electrical circuits	a. A shorthand method of drawing an electrical part
2. open circuit	b. A device that turns a circuit on and off by causing a break in a circuit
3. closed circuit	c. A circuit with no breaks in it
4. circuit diagram	d. Structures that provide paths through which electricity travels
5. electrical symbol	e. A shorthand method of drawing the physical arrangement of a circuit
	f. A circuit with one or more breaks in it

Set Two

1. electric charge	a. A unit used in measuring the amount of charge
2. static electricity	b. The pushes and pulls that electric charges exert on each other
3. electrical force	c. Property of matter responsible for electrical events; it has two forms, positive and negative
4. electroscope	d. An instrument that can detect, and sometimes measure the amount of, electric charges
5. coulomb	e. An object that has equal amounts of positive and negative charges
	f. A buildup of charge on an object or material

Concept review

1. How are electrical circuits and systems of carrying water (such as the pipes that bring water to your house) alike? List at least two ways
2. List three examples of circuits from the reading.
3. Describe how a switch turns a circuit on and off.
4. Why do people use electrical symbols and circuit diagrams to describe a circuit?
5. What happens to the electrical connection of a nerve in the human body if the nerve is cut? Does the nerve ever fully heal?
6. List the kinds of electric charge and where they are found in an atom.
7. Objects can be charged or neutral. Explain what these two terms mean.
8. State the rules of attraction and repulsion between electric charges.
9. If you brush your hair for a long time, your hair may look fuller. Explain what is happening in terms of electric charges.
10. Use your own words to describe how lightning forms.
11. What is the name of the earliest electroscope?

Problems

1. Circle each diagram that shows a closed circuit that will light the bulb.

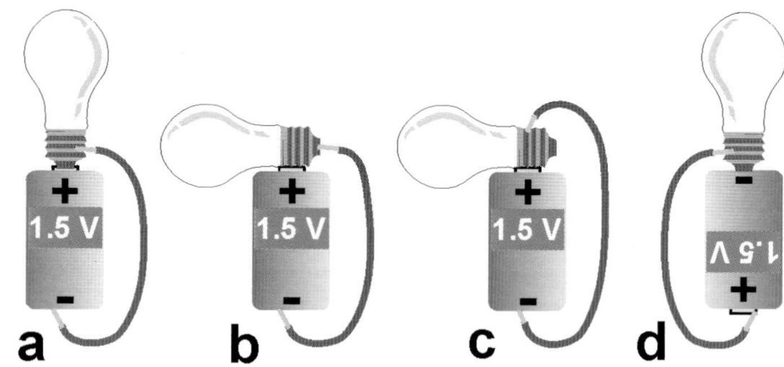

2. If any of the diagrams are not closed circuits, explain what you would do to close the circuit. You may, if you wish, draw your own picture to support your answer.
3. Build a circuit that has a battery, three wires, a bulb, and a switch. Draw a circuit diagram of this circuit.
4. In the electric charge Investigation, you used pieces of Scotch tape. If you simply took two pieces of tape off the roll and put them on the electroscope, you would see no interaction. If you put two pieces of tape together and then tear them apart quickly the two pieces of tape now attract each other. Explain what happened to the two pieces of tape that caused the attraction to occur.
5. A lightning rod is a safety device that is meant to be hit by lightning. Charges tend to concentrate on the pointed end of the lightning rod. Explain why the lightning rod would draw the lightning to itself.
6. In general, excess negative charge can move within a material, or be transferred from material to material. If you rub a balloon on your hair on a dry day, negative charge is transferred from your hair to the balloon. You bring the balloon close to a wall. The excess negative charge on the balloon repels the negative charges in the wall and the charges move to another part of the wall. The surface of the wall near the balloon is now positively charged. Will the balloon stick to the wall? Why or why not?

Applying your knowledge

1. Write a paragraph describing on what a typical day at home or school would be like if we had no electricity.
2. Examine the labels or instructions that come with home appliances and see if you can find examples of circuit diagrams. What parts of the diagrams do you recognize?
3. Research Benjamin Franklin's experiments in electricity. Draw and label a picture showing one of his experiments.
4. Static cling causes clothes to stick together when they come out of the dryer. What kinds of material seem to stick together?

UNIT 3

Electricity and Magnetism

Chapter 7

Measuring Electricity

Introduction to Chapter 7

Have you ever thought about how electricity is measured? If you look at the back of many appliances you will see electrical units that are most likely unfamiliar to you, such as volts and amperes. Like all units, electrical units are measurements of useful quantities. In this chapter you will learn about voltage, the energy of charges, current, the rate of travel of charges, and resistance, the ability of objects to carry charges.

Investigations for Chapter 7

7.1	Voltage	*Why do charges move through a circuit?*

In this Investigation, you will learn how to use an electrical meter to measure voltage, and you will observe how a change in voltage affects a light bulb.

7.2	Current	*How do charges move through a circuit?*

In this Investigation, you will learn how to use an electrical meter to measure current, and you will observe how a change in current affects a light bulb.

7.3	Resistance	*How well does current travel through different materials and objects?*

In this Investigation, you will learn how to use an electrical meter to measure resistance, and you will observe how differences in materials and size affect current.

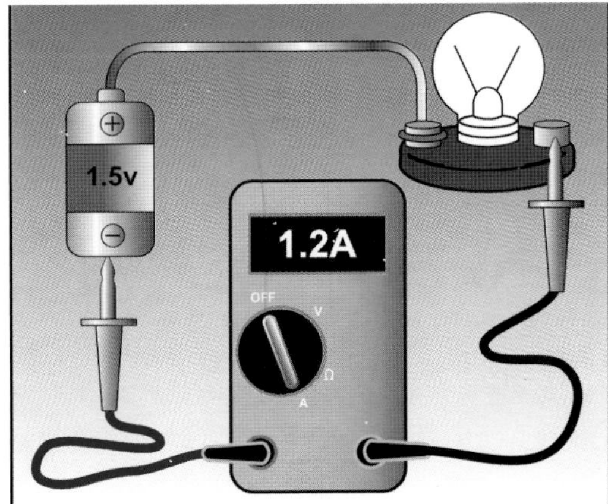

Learning Goals

In this chapter, you will:

- ✔ Measure volts with an electrical meter.
- ✔ Describe the role of a battery in a circuit.
- ✔ Describe the transfer of energy in a circuit.
- ✔ Explain the relationship between voltage and energy in a circuit.
- ✔ Describe current as a flow of electric charge.
- ✔ Measure amperes with an electrical meter.
- ✔ Classify materials as conductors, semiconductors, or insulators.
- ✔ Differentiate between electrical conductivity and resistance.
- ✔ Explain why metals are good electrical conductors.
- ✔ Measure ohms with an electrical meter.

Vocabulary

alternating current
ampere
battery
current
direct current
electrical conductivity
electrical conductor
electrical insulator
ohm
resistance
semiconductor
volt
voltage

7.1 Voltage

Atoms are in everything and are made up of equal amounts of positive and negative charges. How is this useful in an electric circuit? In this section, you will learn that a battery adds energy to charge and makes it flow through circuits to do work for us.

Voltage

What does a battery do? A **battery** uses chemical energy to move charges. If you connect a circuit with a battery the charges flow out of the battery carrying energy. They can give up their energy to electrical devices, like a light bulb. When a bulb is lit, the energy is taken from the charges which return to the battery to get more energy. A battery is an energy source for charges that flow in circuits.

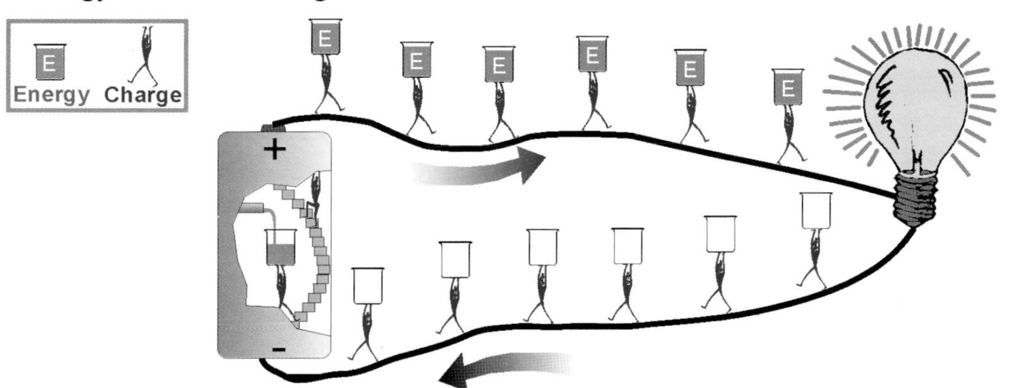

Making higher voltage by stacking batteries

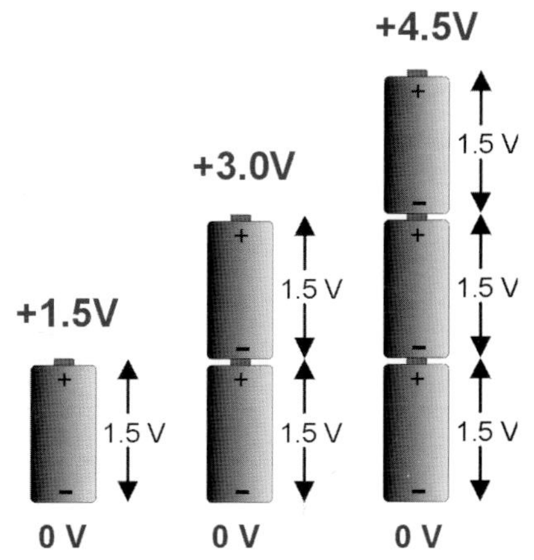

Figure 7.1: *The positive end of a 1.5 volt battery is 1.5 volts higher than the negative end. If you connect batteries positive-to-negative, each battery adds 1.5 volts to the total. Three batteries make 4.5 volts. Each charge coming out of the positive end of the 3-battery stack has 4.5 volts of energy.*

Volts measure the energy level in a circuit We measure the energy level of any place in a circuit in **volts**. Charges gain and lose energy by changing their voltage. If a charge goes up from 1 volt to 3 volts, it *gains* 2 joules of energy. If the charge goes down from 3 volts to 1 volt, it *loses* 2 joules of energy.

Batteries add energy A fully charged battery adds energy proportional to its voltage. The positive end of a 1.5 volt battery is 1.5 volts higher in energy than the negative end. That means every charge that leaves the positive end has 1.5 joules more energy than it had going in. This energy is what lights the light bulb. When the battery is dead, there is almost no energy to give to charges flowing through.

Voltage is related to potential energy

Voltage is related to *potential energy,* just like height is related to pressure in water flow. Imagine you have two tanks of water. One is higher than the other (figure 7.2). The water in the higher tank has more energy than water in the lower tank. The water flows downhill, from high energy to low energy. A greater difference in height means that the water has more potential energy.

Differences in electrical energy are measured in volts. If there is a difference in volts, current will flow from the higher voltage to the lower voltage, just like water flows from higher energy to lower energy.

A battery is like a water tower

A water tower and pump make a good analogy for a battery. The pump lifts water up to the tower by giving it energy. The water can flow out and give the energy back. In a battery, chemical reactions provide energy to pump charges from low voltage to high voltage. The charges can then flow back to low voltage and give their energy back to turn motors and light bulbs.

Wires are like water pipes

The water tower is connected by a pipe to a faucet in a house that is lower than the tower. If you open the faucet, the difference in energy makes the water flow. In a circuit, the wires act like pipes to carry the charges from high voltage to low voltage. If you connect the switch, the current will flow.

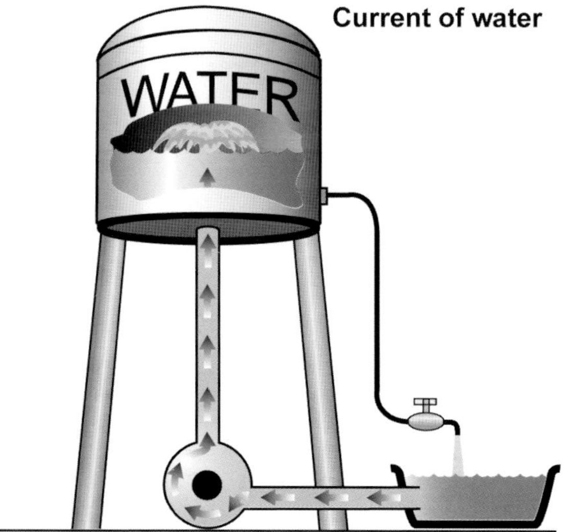

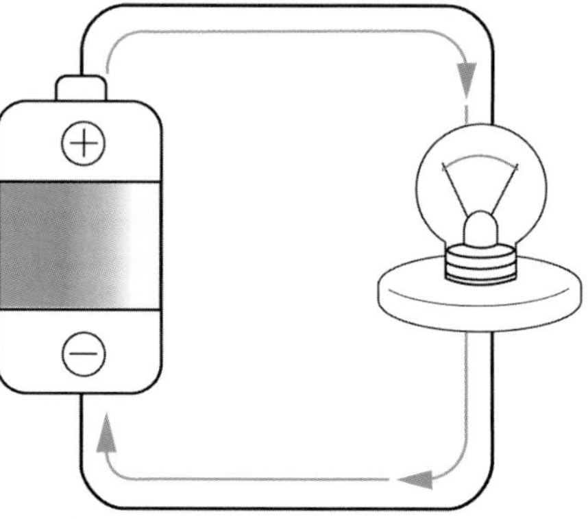

Water flows from high energy (height) to lower energy.

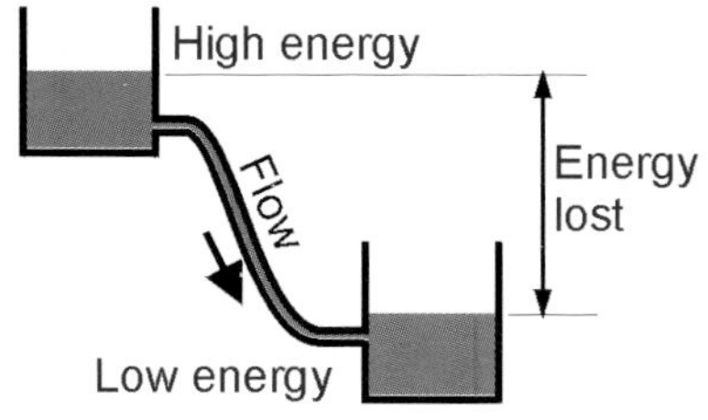

Electric charge flows from high energy (voltage) to lower energy.

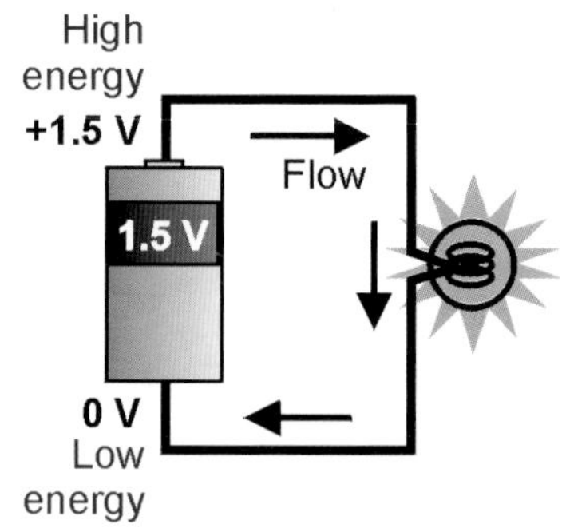

Figure 7.2: *Water flows from high energy to low energy. The energy difference is related to the difference in height. Electric charge also flows from high energy to low energy, but the energy difference is related to the difference in volts.*

Measuring voltage

Connecting a meter to measure volts

Volts measure the energy difference between two places in a circuit. To measure volts you have to connect a meter to two places. The meter measures the voltage difference between the two. If you connect a meter to the two ends of a battery you should read at least 1.5 volts from the negative end to the positive end. A fresh battery might even give you more than 1.5 volts.

Measuring the voltage of a battery

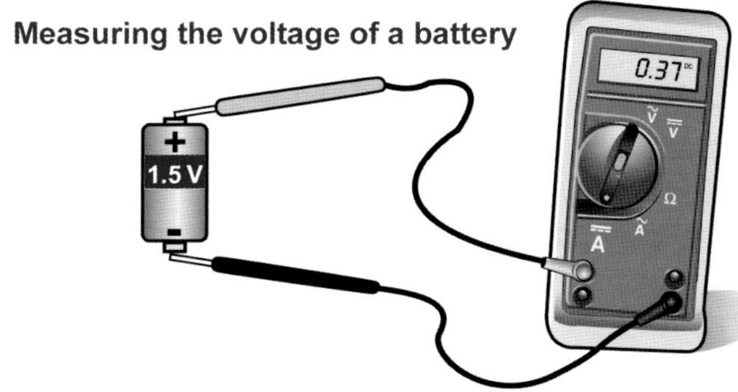

Choosing a voltage reference

Since voltage is measured from one point to another, we usually assign the negative terminal of a battery to be zero volts (0 V). This makes the voltage of every other place in the circuit relative to the negative end of the battery.

All points on a wire are the same voltage

Every point in a circuit connected to the same wire is at the same voltage. Charges move easily through copper so they do not lose much energy. That is why we make electrical wires out of copper. Since the charges all have the same energy, the voltage is the same everywhere along the wire.

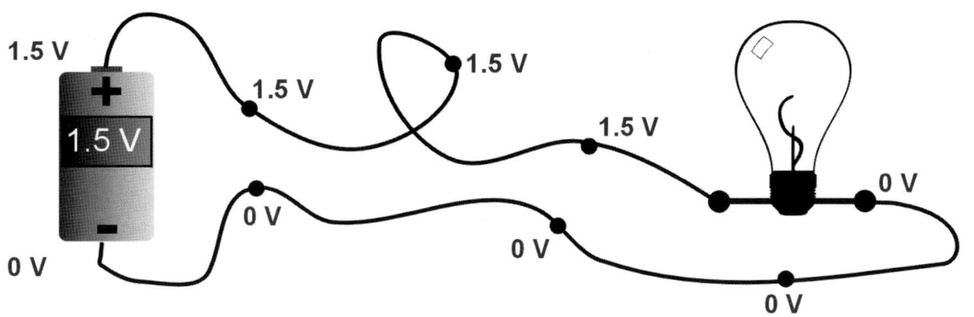

The volt

Voltage is measured in volts (V). The volt is named for the Italian physicist Alessandro Volta (1745-1827), who invented the first battery in 1800. Volta's batteries used pans of different chemicals connected by metal strips. Today's batteries are very similar except the chemicals are contained in convenient, safe packages of useful sizes.

One volt is equal to 1 joule of energy for each coulomb of charge.

Voltage drops when energy is used

Voltage is reduced when energy is used

If we connect anything that uses energy, like a light bulb, we reduce the voltage. This should make sense since voltage is a measure of energy. Anything that uses energy (motors, bulbs, resistors) lowers the voltage since it takes energy away from any moving charges in the circuit.

Two examples of circuits

Suppose you connect two circuits as shown in figure 7.3. Both circuits have 1.5 volts as the highest voltage and zero volts as the lowest voltage. One circuit has a single light bulb and the other circuit has two bulbs.

The single-bulb circuit is much brighter. This is because all the energy is used up in one bulb. The voltage goes from 1.5 V to 0 V across the bulb.

In the two-bulb circuit, the voltage drops from 1.5 volts to 0 across *two* bulbs. The voltage starts at 1.5 volts. After the first light bulb the voltage is reduced to 0.75 volts because the first bulb used half the energy. The second light bulb reduces the voltage another 0.75 volts, to get down to zero. Each bulb only "sees" a voltage difference of 0.75 volts so each of the two bulbs gets less energy, and is dimmer.

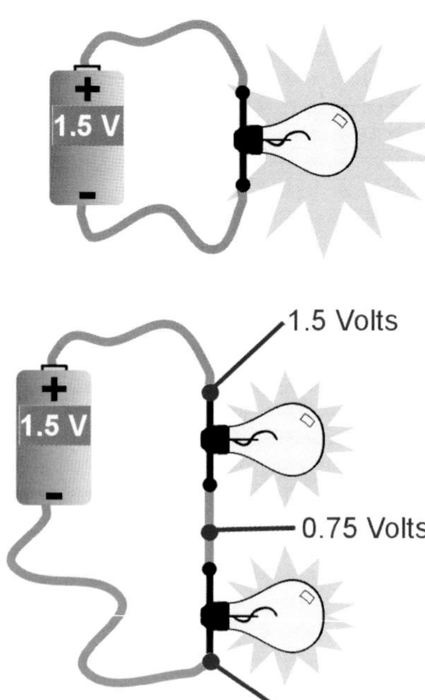

Figure 7.3: *Every time you connect something that uses energy, like a light bulb, some of the voltage is reduced. One bulb is bright because it gets all the energy. Two bulbs are dimmer because each one gets only half the energy. The voltage is lower between the two bulbs because the first bulb uses up half the energy.*

Batteries, energy, and voltage

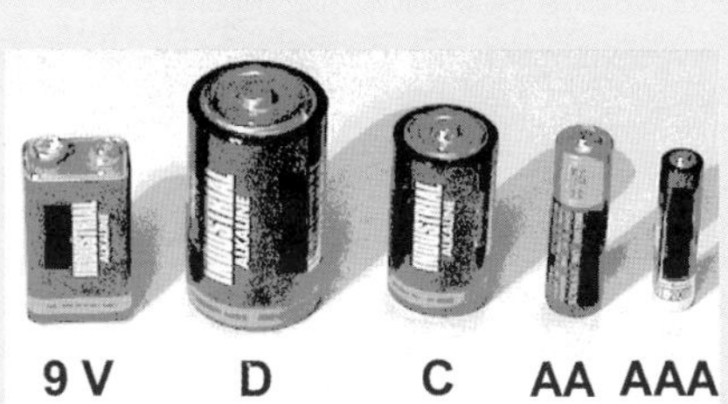

What is the difference between AA, AAA, C, and D batteries? If you measure the voltage of each, you will see that it is the same. The main difference between them is that the AAA battery is small, and does not store as much energy. AAA batteries will not last as long as D batteries. Think of two identical cars, one with an extra-big gas tank and one with a regular gas tank. Both cars go the same speed, but the one with the big gas tank will keep going longer.

If you need charge that has more energy, you must increase the voltage. Radio batteries have 9 volts and car batteries have 12 volts. In a 12-volt battery each charge that flows carries 12 joules of energy.

Some kinds of batteries can be recharged. Batteries made with nickel and cadmium (NiCad) are used in cell phones and power tools because they can be recharged many times.

7.2 Current

In the last section, you learned that charges move from places of high voltage in a circuit to places of lower voltage. Electrical current is how we describe the flow of charges. Current is what flows through wires and does work, like making light or turning a motor.

Current

Current is flow of charge

Current is the flow of electric charges. You can think of electrical current much as you would think of a current of water. If a faucet is on, you can measure the rate of water flow by finding out how much water comes out in one minute. You might find that the current (or flow) is 10 gallons per minute. In a circuit, you can measure the current, but it is measured in amperes. One ampere is a flow of one coulomb per second. A current of 10 amperes means that 10 coulombs of charge flow through the wire every second.

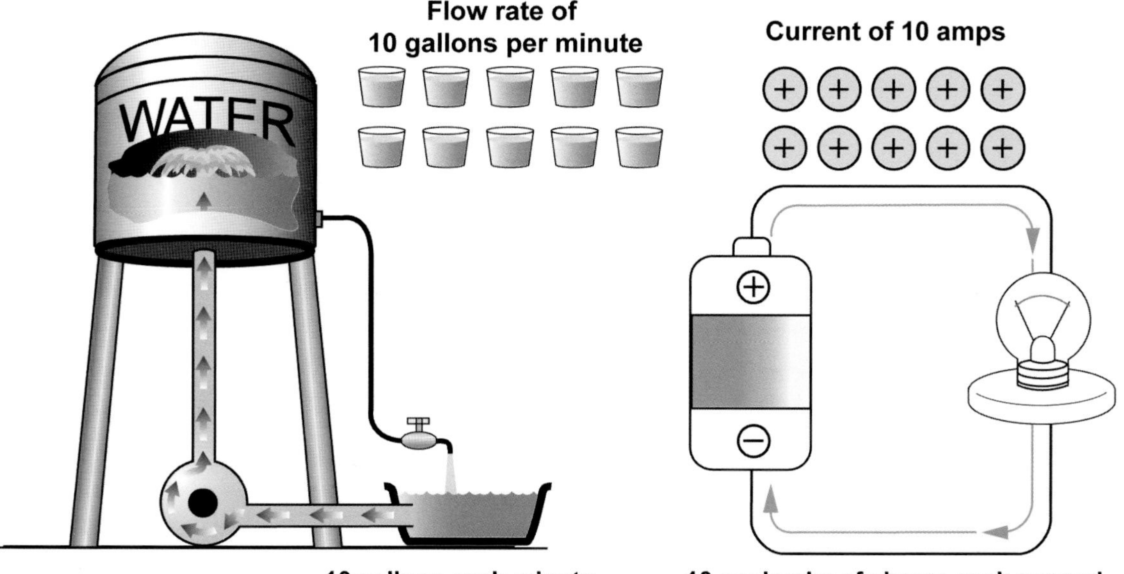

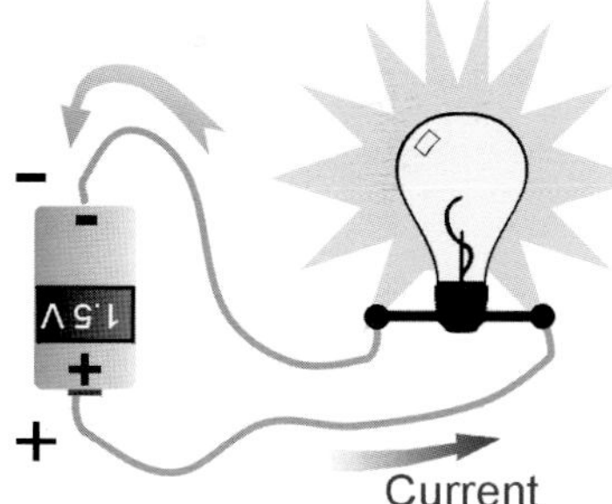

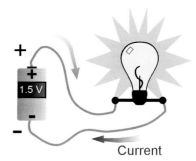

Figure 7.4: *Current flows from plus to minus, or from high voltage to low voltage.*

Where does electrical current come from?

Charges are very small

When you look at a wire, you can't see current. The particles that carry charge are electrons. Electrons are parts of atoms, and they are so small that they can flow in the spaces between atoms. That is why we can't see any movement in a wire.

The charges are already in the wire

Batteries do not provide most of the charges that flow in a circuit. Current occurs because electrons in the battery repel electrons in the wire, which repel other electrons in the wire, and so on. This is why a light goes on as soon as you connect your circuit together. Since the wire is made of copper atoms, there are plenty of electrons. When there is no voltage, electrons in the wire do not flow in a current.

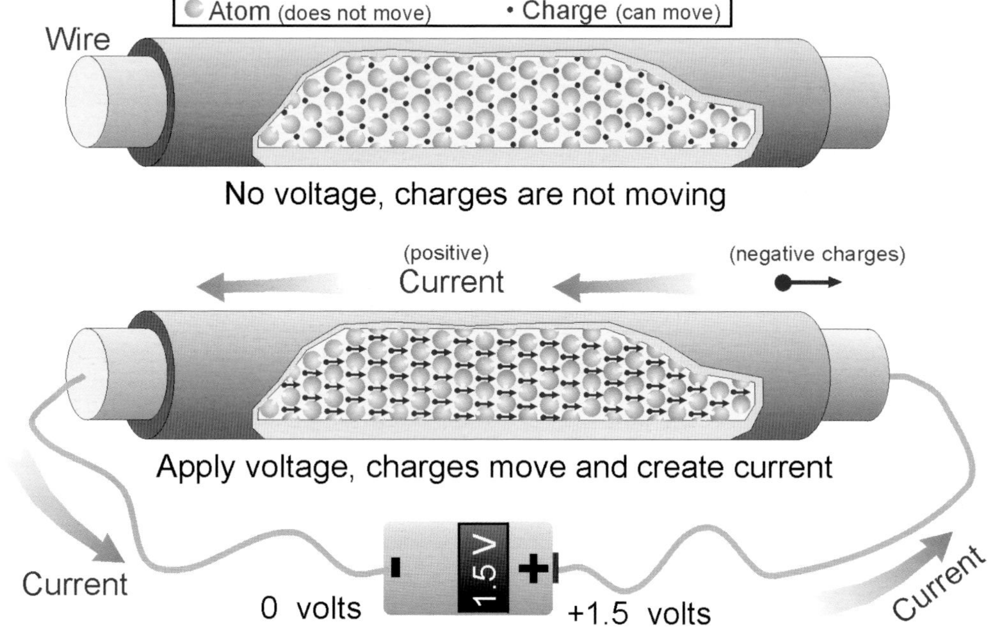

Things to remember:

A voltage difference supplies energy to make charges flow.

Current carries energy and does work.

What really flows?

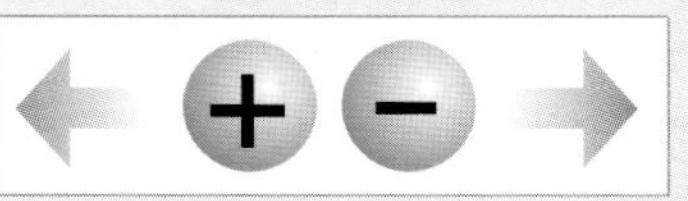

Either positive charges or negative charges can move to make an electric current. The type of charge depends upon the materials that make up the circuit. For example, in the human body, current is the movement of both positive and negative charges in nerves.

Electric current was first thought to be positive charge moving from plus to minus.

In reality, most charge flow in circuits is the movement of *negative* charge from minus to plus.

In practical electricity, we still say current flows from plus to minus or from high voltage to low voltage. The fact that it is actually negative charge moving does not matter when working with most electric circuits.

Measuring current

The ampere or amp Current is measured in units called amperes (A), or amps for short. The unit is named in honor of Andre-Marie Ampere (1775-1836), a French physicist who studied electromagnetism.

Definition of 1 amp One amp is a flow of 1 coulomb of charge per second. A 100-watt light bulb uses a little more than 1 amp of current. A single D battery can supply a few amps of current for about a half hour before being completely drained.

Measuring current To measure current you have to make it flow through the meter. The moving charges can't be counted unless they pass through the meter. That means you must connect the meter into your circuit so the current is forced to flow through it.

Setting up the meter Most meters have settings for both voltage and current. You will need to set your meter to measure current. Meters can also measure alternating current (AC) and direct current (DC). We will discuss AC and DC in a later section. For circuits with light bulbs and batteries you want to use the DC settings.

Be careful measuring current The last important thing about measuring current is that the meter itself can be damaged by too much current. Your meter may contain a *circuit breaker* or *fuse*. Circuit breakers and fuses are two kinds of devices that protect circuits from too much current. If your meter does not work the circuit breaker or fuse may have acted. A circuit breaker can be reset but a fuse must be replaced.

Circuit breakers

Electrical circuits in your house have a *circuit breaker* that stops too much current from flowing. Many wires in your house can carry 15 or 20 amps of current. Wires can get dangerously hot if they carry more current than they are designed for.

One of the things that can overload a circuit is using too many electrical appliances at once, such as an air conditioner and an iron on the same circuit. If many appliances try to draw too much current, the circuit breaker trips and breaks the circuit before the wires get hot enough to cause a fire.

A circuit breaker uses temperature-sensitive metal that expands with heat. When the current gets too high, the expanded metal bends and breaks the circuit. You have to unplug some appliances and reset the circuit breaker.

Electricity in your house

Circuits in your house You use electric current in your house every day. When you plug in an electrical appliance, you connect it to a circuit created by wires in the walls. The wires eventually connect to power lines outside your house that bring the current from a power station.

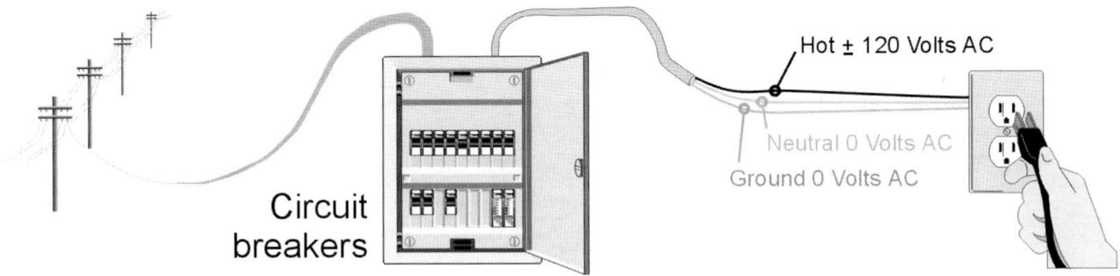

AC current The electricity in your house uses **alternating current**, also called **AC** current. This means the direction of the current goes back and forth. In the electrical system used in the United States, the current reverses direction 60 times per second. Each wall socket has three wires feeding it. The hot wire carries 120 volts AC. The neutral wire stays at zero volts. When you plug something in, current flows in and out of the hot wire, through your appliance (doing work) and back through the neutral wire. The ground wire is for safety and is connected to the ground near your house. If there is a short circuit in your appliance, the current flows through the ground wire rather than through you!

DC current The current from a battery does not alternate. A battery only makes current that flows in one direction. This is called **direct current**, or **DC**. Most of the experiments you will do in the lab use DC current.

Household electricity is AC For large amounts of electricity, we use AC current because it is easier to transmit and generate. All the power lines you see overhead carry AC current. Other countries also use AC current. However, in Europe, the current reverses itself 50 times per second rather than 60, and wall sockets are at a different voltage. When traveling in Europe, you need special adapters to use electrical appliances you bring from home.

What is a ground fault circuit interrupter?

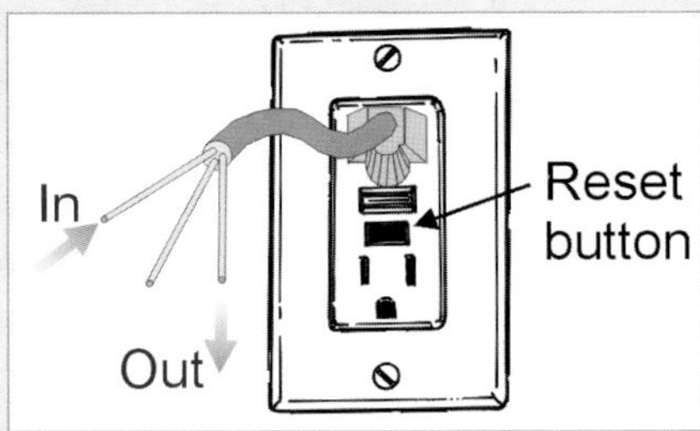

Circuits in wet or damp locations are wired with a ground fault circuit interrupter (GFCI). You may have seen this device, with its red button, in a bathroom, or near the kitchen sink.

Plugs usually have two or three wires. Electricity goes in one wire of a plug and out another wire. The same current should go in and out. If there is a difference, then some of the electricity could be going through YOU instead of back through the plug. Current flowing through the human body is dangerous.

The GFCI senses differences and breaks the circuit if the current coming out of the plug is different from the current going back in. The GFCI disconnects the circuit in 0.03 seconds if it detects a leak as small as a few thousandths of an amp. A GFCI protects you from being electrocuted.

7.3 Resistance

Parts of electrical devices are made up of metals but often have plastic coverings. Why are these materials chosen? How well does current move through these materials? In this section, you will learn about the ability of materials and objects to carry electrical current.

Conductors and insulators

What is a conductor? Charge flows very easily through some kinds of materials, like copper. We call a material like copper an **electrical conductor** because it can *conduct*, or carry, electrical current. Most metals are good conductors.

What is an insulator? Other materials, like glass or plastic, do not allow charge to flow. We call these materials **electrical insulators** because they insulate (or block) the flow of current.

What is a semiconductor? The third category of materials are not as easy-flowing as conductors, but not quite insulators either. These materials are named **semiconductors** because they are between conductors and insulators in their ability to carry current. Computer chips, LED's and some kinds of lasers are made from semiconductors.

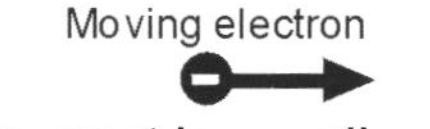

Electrical current is usually carried by moving electrons, atoms stay fixed in place.

In an *insulator*, the electrons are tightly bound to atoms and cannot move.

In a *conductor,* the electrons come free and can move to create electrical current. Since electrons are negative, they move in the opposite direction as the (positive) current.

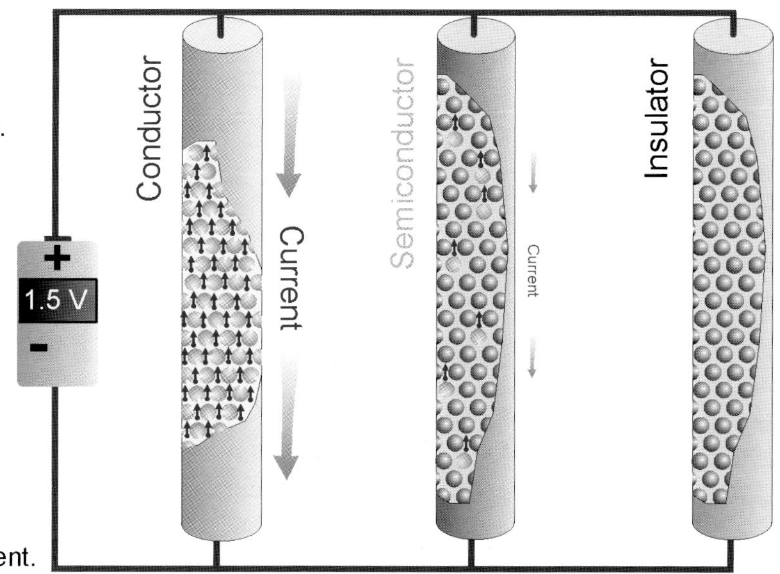

Why are some materials conductors and some insulators?

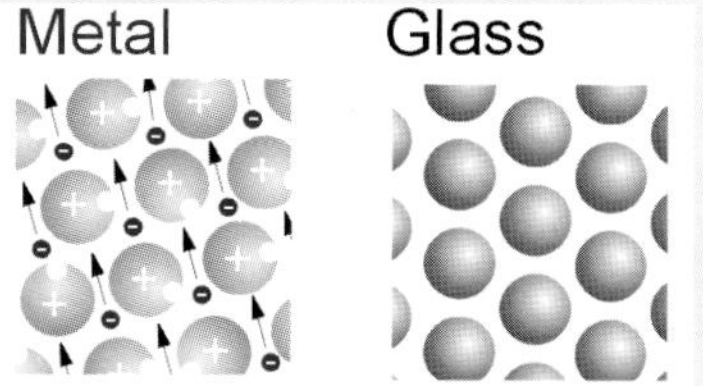

Metals are good conductors. To understand why, we have to understand how metal atoms behave. When many metal atoms are together, like in a wire, they each lose one or more electrons. These "free" electrons can move around in a sea of atoms. Metals are good conductors because there are lots of "free" electrons to carry charge.

Glass is a good insulator. Glass does not have free electrons. When atoms of glass are together they keep their electrons tightly bound. Since no electrons can move free of their atoms, glass is a good insulator.

Conductivity

What makes a material a conductor or insulator?

Materials are not pure conductors or insulators. A little charge flows through all materials if you connect them to a battery. The difference is in how much current flows. If you do the experiments you find that the amount of current varies from very small to very large. The property of a material to allow charge to flow is called its **electrical conductivity**. Materials with high conductivity (like metals) allow charge to flow easily and are conductors. Materials with low conductivity block charge from flowing and are insulators.

Electrical conductivity	Category	Material
High	conductors	silver
		copper
		gold
		aluminum
		tungsten
		iron
	semiconductors	carbon
		silicon
		germanium
	insulators	air
		rubber
		paper
		Teflon
		plastics (varies by type)
		glass
Low		mica

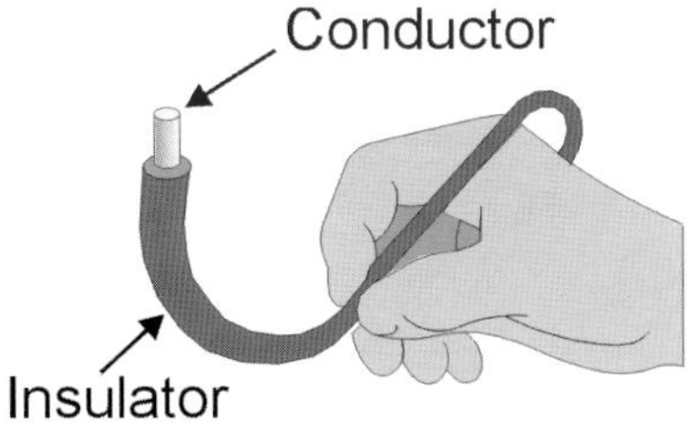

Figure 7.5: *A wire uses both conductors and insulators. The conductor carries the current through the center. The insulator keeps the current from reaching you when you touch the wire.*

Resistance

Current and resistance The resistance of an object measures how easily charges flow through. High resistance means it is difficult for current to flow. Low resistance means it is easy for current to flow.

Resistance of water flow Emptying a jar of water through a narrow opening is a good example of resistance. If the opening of the jar is large, there is low resistance. Lots of water flows out quickly. If the opening of the jar is small, there is a lot of resistance. Water does not flow out as fast.

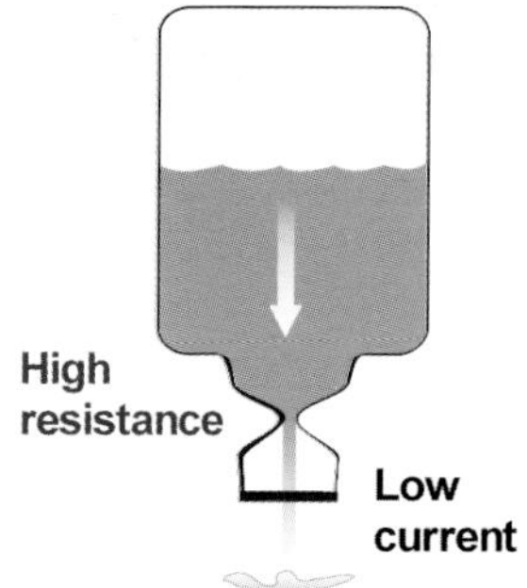

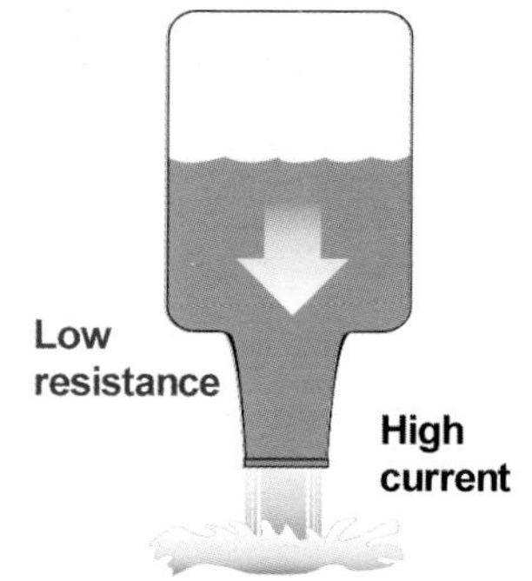

Electrical resistance Electrical resistance restricts the flow of current. If the resistance is high, not much current flows. If the resistance is low, a lot of current flows.

Devices that use electrical energy have resistance. For example, light bulbs have resistance. If you string more light bulbs together the resistance adds up and the current goes down.

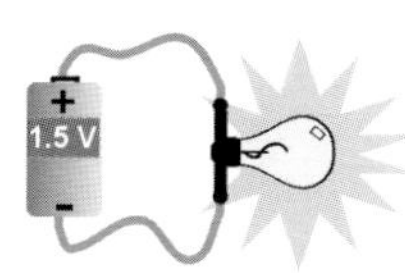

One bulb
Single resistance
Full current

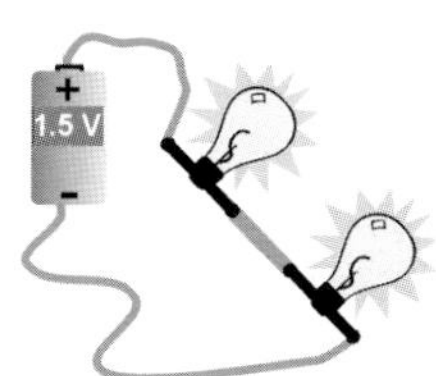

Two bulbs
Twice the resistance
1/2 the current

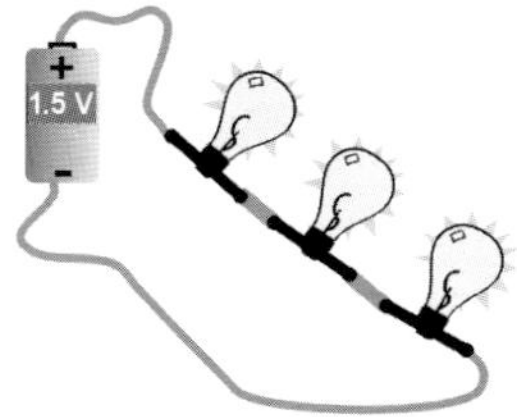

Three bulbs
Three times the resistance
1/3 the current

Breakdown voltage

You previously learned that lightning is caused by electric charge. In a thunderstorm, positive and negative charges become separated. The voltage difference becomes huge, reaching 10,000 volts per centimeter.

Air, usually a good insulator, breaks down under these conditions. The high voltage created by the storm rips the electrons away from atoms of air. The air conducts, and we see lightning.

The lowest voltage at which an insulator turns into a conductor is called its breakdown voltage. The breakdown of air occurs when 8,000 volts or more is applied across a centimeter of air.

The ohm

Units of resistance

Electrical resistance is measured in units called ohms. This unit is abbreviated with the Greek letter omega (Ω). When you see Ω in a sentence, think or read "ohms." The ohm is named for the German physicist Georg S. Ohm (1787-1854). Ohm spent many years studying how circuits work.

How much current flows in a circuit?

We can now answer the question of how much current flows in a circuit. If the voltage goes up, the current goes up too. If the resistance goes up, the current goes *down*. Voltage and resistance determine how much current flows in a circuit. If a circuit has a resistance of 1 ohm (1 Ω), then a current of 1 amp flows when a voltage of 1 volt is applied.

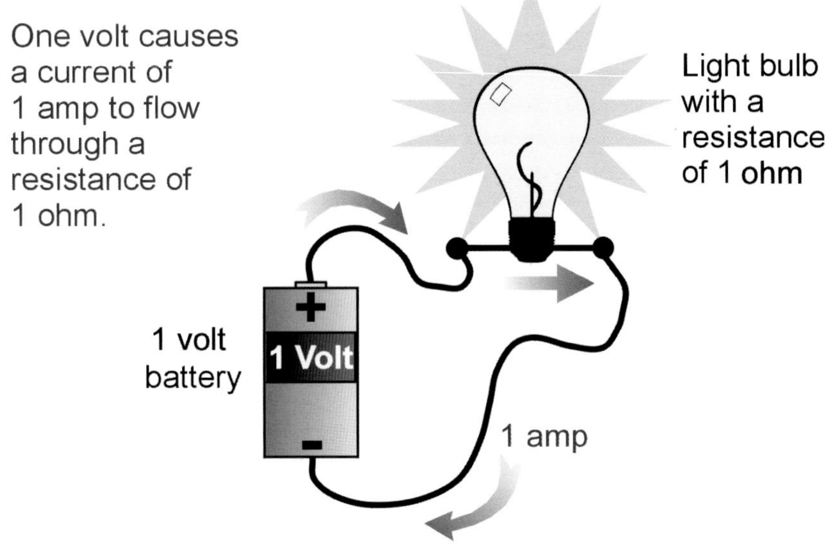

How a photocopier works

A photocopier has a plate coated with a thin layer of a special material (like selenium, arsenic, or tellurium) that acts as an insulator in the dark but as a conductor when exposed to light.

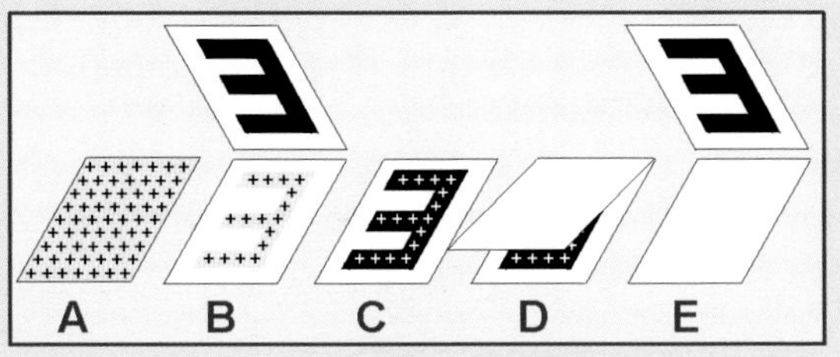

(**A**) The plate starts with a positive charge. Light creates an image on the plate (**B**). The white areas of the image become conductive and let the charge flow away. The dark areas stay insulating and keep their positive charge.

Next, a negatively charged powdered ink (called toner) is brushed over the plate. Because opposite charges attract, the toner sticks to the positively charged areas of the plate (**C**).

A piece of paper is given a positive charge, and held on the plate (**D**). The paper attracts the ink and now has a perfect image made of powder (**E**). To prevent the image from rubbing off, the paper is heated, which melts the toner onto the paper.

Why does a bulb light?

What's in a light bulb? Electricity would not be so useful if it flowed equally through every material. Let's look at some of the materials in a light bulb. A light bulb contains a copper wire and a thin tungsten filament in a glass bulb filled with argon gas (figure 7.6). Why are these materials chosen?

Copper wire We use copper wire to conduct current to a light bulb filament because copper is a good conductor.

Tungsten filament We use a thin tungsten filament for several reasons. Just as a narrow pipe resists water flow more than a wide pipe, the very thin filament resists the flow of current. Because of the high resistance of the tungsten filament, the current going through it generates a lot of heat. The filament continues to heat up until it reaches 2,500°C (4,500°F). The filament glows white as it heats up, creating the light that we see.

Most substances would melt under these circumstances. Tungsten is chosen because it does not melt until it reaches an even higher temperature. Tungsten also doesn't corrode easily.

Argon gas We use argon inside the bulb because it is an inert gas. An inert gas will not interact with the hot tungsten. If the hot tungsten filament were in air, it would interact with the oxygen in air and burn up quickly like a match. The argon protects the tungsten so that it can heat up many, many times before breaking down.

Other kinds of light bulbs Much of the electrical power going into a light bulb becomes heat, and not light. Fluorescent bulbs are more efficient because they convert more of the electrical energy to light than does a regular (incandescent) bulb. Researchers are trying to make lights from many new materials that are even more efficient. In the laboratory, tiny light emitting diodes (LED's) have been made that produce more light from less electricity than any other type of light source.

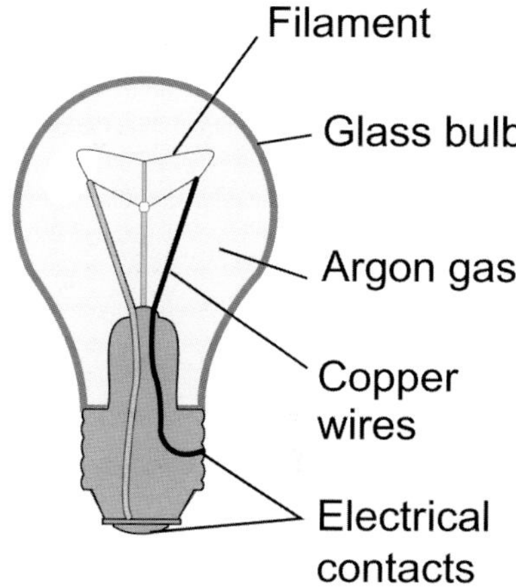

Figure 7.6: *Some parts of a light bulb. There are two electrical contacts in the base of the light bulb. Both of these must come in contact with an electrical circuit for the light bulb to work.*

Chapter 7 Review

Vocabulary Review

Match the following terms with the correct definition. There is one extra definition in the list that will not match any of the terms.

Set One

1. battery
2. voltage
3. volt
4. current
5. ampere

a. Flow rate of electric charges
b. The representation of circuit current as the flow of positive charges
c. The commonly used unit of measurement for current, equal to coulombs/second
d. A device that uses energy of chemical reactions to separate positive and negative charges
e. The amount of potential energy per unit of charge
f. The commonly used unit of measurement for voltage, equal to joules/coulomb

Set Two

1. amp
2. alternating current
3. direct current
4. conductor
5. insulator

a. Current that moves in only one direction through a wire
b. A material that conducts current easily
c. A material that conducts current poorly
d. The abbreviation often used for ampere
e. Current that reverses direction through a wire
f. The representation of circuit current as the flow of negative charges

Set Three

1. semiconductor
2. electrical conductivity
3. resistance
4. ohm

a. A material that conducts current when exposed to light
b. The ability of an object to resist current
c. The ability of a material to conduct current
d. The commonly used unit of measurement for resistance
e. A material that conducts current at a medium rate

Concept review

1. Explain in two or three sentences how a battery creates potential energy.
2. Explain how a water pump and battery are similar in terms of creating potential energy.
3. Explain the difference between a AA alkaline battery and a D alkaline battery. Discuss both voltage and life span.
4. The measurement of current in a circuit is similar to the measurement of the flow of water out of a faucet. Explain why this is so.
5. A circuit breaker is a safety device that shuts down a circuit when the current is too high. Describe how a circuit breaker works.
6. The electrical system in the United States runs on __________ current.
7. A battery circuit runs on __________ current.
8. A ground fault circuit interrupter is usually wired into circuits that are in wet or damp locations. What is the main purpose of this device?
9. Explain why a circuit contains a copper wire with a plastic cover over the wire.
10. List one example of each of the following.
    a. electrical conductor
    b. electrical insulator
    c. semiconductor
11. A light bulb uses a very thin tungsten filament to provide light.
    a. Why is the filament thinner than the copper wire used in circuit wiring?
    b. Why is tungsten a good material for the filament?

Problems

1. When two batteries are connected together correctly, their voltage adds together. If a circuit has two AA alkaline batteries (connected correctly!), how many joules of energy does each coulomb of charge have at the battery terminals?
2. When you use a meter to measure battery voltage, you place one probe on one battery terminal and one probe on the other battery terminal. Why do you measure voltage in this way?
3. When measuring the voltage of a D alkaline battery, which is usually at 1.5 volts, you accidentally reverse the probes. The probe that is set at zero volts is placed at the positive terminal and the other probe is placed at the negative terminal. What will the meter read now?
4. A toaster oven uses a current of 650 coulombs each minute. What is the current in amps?

5. You build a circuit with one battery and a bulb. You remove the wire from the positive terminal of the battery, insert the meter in the circuit, and measure the current. The meter reads 0.5 amps. You remove the meter and rebuild your circuit. Now you remove the wire from the negative terminal of the battery, insert the meter, and measure the current at this new point in the circuit. What will the meter read now?
6. When you measure current of a circuit with an electrical meter you keep the circuit on and insert the meter at one point in the circuit. Explain why.
7. List these materials in order from least to greatest resistance: light bulbs, clip leads, air, and pencil lead.
8. You have two pieces of wire of the same size, one made of copper and the other made of iron. Which wire is the better conductor?
9. An electrical meter measures resistance of an object by applying a voltage through the material and then measuring how much current the object will carry. Do you measure resistance of an object when it is in a working circuit, or do you turn the circuit off first? Explain your answer.

Applying your knowledge

1. With an adult, inspect all cords and plugs in your home. Make sure that the insulation cover on them is in good condition, without breaks or cracks. With help, replace any damaged cords or plugs.
2. Brain and nerve cells communicate by the movement of charged chemicals, which is a type of current. Some diseases, like epilepsy, occur because of currents that occur when they shouldn't. Research electrical currents in the brain and problems that occur when the system doesn't work correctly.
3. With an adult, find out the location of the circuit breakers for your home. If the circuit breakers aren't labeled, determine which outlets are connected to which fuse or circuit breaker, and then label them.

Electricity and Magnetism

Chapter 8

Electrical Relationships

Introduction to Chapter 8

You have learned that mathematical models are used to describe the exact relationships between physical quantities. What relationships exist among voltage, current and resistance? How can we use these relationships to analyze circuits? What are practical applications of these relationships?

Investigations for Chapter 8

8.1	Ohm's Law	*How are voltage, current, and resistance related?*

In this Investigation, you will use a step-by-step method to determine the mathematical relationship between voltage, current, and resistance in a circuit.

8.2	Work, Energy, and Power	*How much does it cost to use the electrical appliances in your home?*

You previously studied power in a mechanical system. What does power mean in an electric circuit? How much power do everyday appliances need? In this Investigation, you will learn how to read power ratings on electrical appliances and use this information to estimate electrical costs in your home.

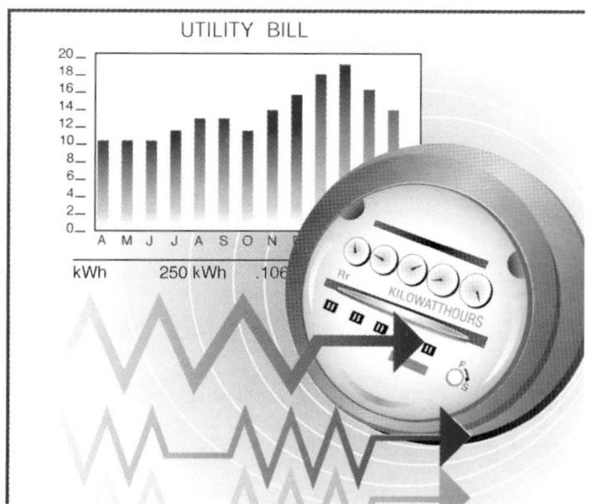

Learning Goals

In this chapter, you will:

- ✔ Measure how current changes when voltage is increased.
- ✔ Measure how current changes when resistance is increased.
- ✔ Describe how voltage, current, and resistance are related.
- ✔ Use Ohm's law to solve circuit problems.
- ✔ Explain why resistors are used in a circuit.
- ✔ Define power as the rate at which energy flows.
- ✔ Describe relationships between work, energy, and power.
- ✔ Calculate power use in a circuit.
- ✔ Rank the amount of power used by various household appliances.
- ✔ Estimate the cost per month of using a common household appliance.
- ✔ Use dimensional analysis to find out what we buy from electric utility companies.
- ✔ Explain how to choose a safe extension cord.

Vocabulary

horsepower	kilowatt-hour	potentiometer	resistor
kilowatt	Ohm's law	power	watt

8.1 Ohm's Law

You know about three important electrical quantities: voltage, current, and resistance. Of the three, current is the one that carries energy through a circuit. How does the current depend on the voltage and resistance? In this section you will learn the fundamental relationship for circuits known as Ohm's law.

One volt causes a current of 1 amp to flow through a resistance of 1 ohm.

What is Ohm's law?

The relationship between amps, volts, and ohms If you have been working with circuits, you probably have an idea of how voltage, current, and resistance are related. You know that if you increase the voltage, the current goes up. You know that if you increase the resistance by adding a second light bulb, the current goes down.

Ohm's law German physicist Georg S. Ohm (1787-1854) experimented with circuits to find the exact mathematical relationship present in most circuits. The relationship that he discovered is called Ohm's law.

Ohm's law

$$I = \frac{V}{R}$$

Current (amps) → I

Voltage (volts) → V

Resistance (ohms, Ω) → R

Equation	Gives you...	If you know...
I = V/R	current (I)	voltage and resistance
V = IR	voltage (V)	current and resistance
R = V/I	resistance (R)	voltage and current

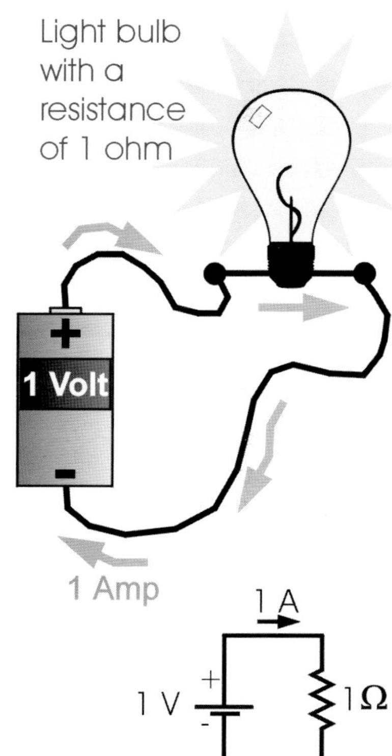

Figure 8.1: *Ohm's law in a circuit.*

Using Ohm's law to analyze circuits

Ohm's law can be used to predict any of the three variables given the other two. Sometimes you want to know the current in the circuit. Sometimes you want to know voltage or resistance. Use the problem-solving steps to help set up and work through problems.

Example A light bulb with a resistance of 2 ohms is connected to a 1.5 volt battery as shown. Calculate the current that will flow.

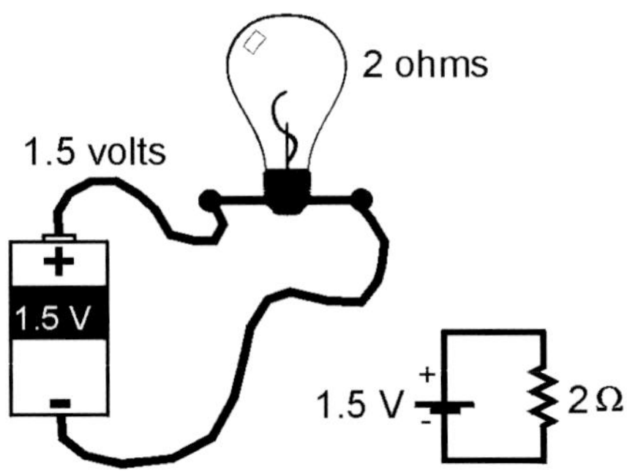

Solution:

(1) We are asked for the current, I.

(2) We know V and R.

(3) Use the formula $I = V \div R$.

(4) Plug in numbers.
$I = 1.5\ V \div 2\ \Omega = 0.75\ A$

Answer: 0.75 amps will flow in the circuit.

Example A light bulb requires 3 amps to produce light. The resistance of the bulb is 1.5 ohms. How many batteries do you need if each battery is 1.5 volts?

(1) We are asked for the number of batteries, which means we need to know the voltage since each battery is 1.5 volts.

(2) We know current and resistance.

(3) Use the formula $V = IR$.

(4) Plug in numbers.
$V = 3\ A \times 1.5\ \Omega = 4.5\ V$

Answer: Each battery can produce 1.5 volts so we need three batteries to get the required 4.5 volts.

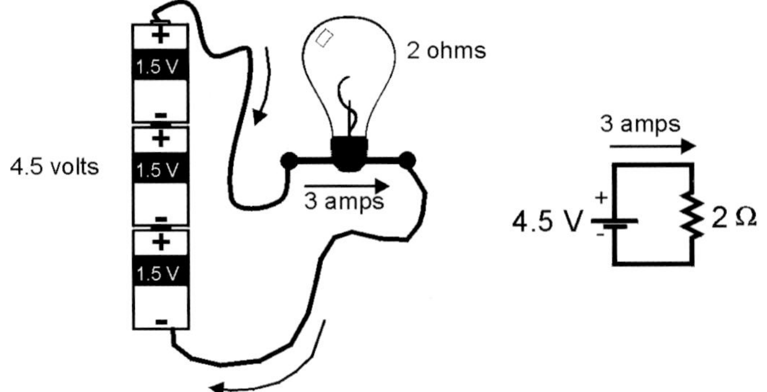

Graphing and Ohm's law

Devices and Ohm's law Ohm's law tells us how much current flows for different amounts of voltage. If a device has the same resistance under different conditions we say that it obeys Ohm's law. We can predict current flow at different voltages. Not all electrical devices obey Ohm's law! If resistance changes, a device does *not* obey Ohm's law. For example, a light bulb's resistance increases when voltage and current increase.

The current vs. voltage graph A current vs. voltage graph shows us if resistance changes. Often, these graphs have both positive and negative values of current and voltage. These positive and negative values are just a way to refer to the direction of current in a wire. You can apply voltage two ways across a wire (figure 8.2). How you apply voltage determines current direction. One direction is positive and the other negative.

I vs. V for a diode A simple resistor obeys Ohm's law—its current vs. voltage graph is a straight line. Resistance is the same at all values of voltage and current. For a *diode*, the graph is not a straight line. A diode only allows charge to flow in one direction! This is why current is zero when voltage is negative. Diodes do not obey Ohm's law. Diodes, like computer chips, are made from semiconductors.

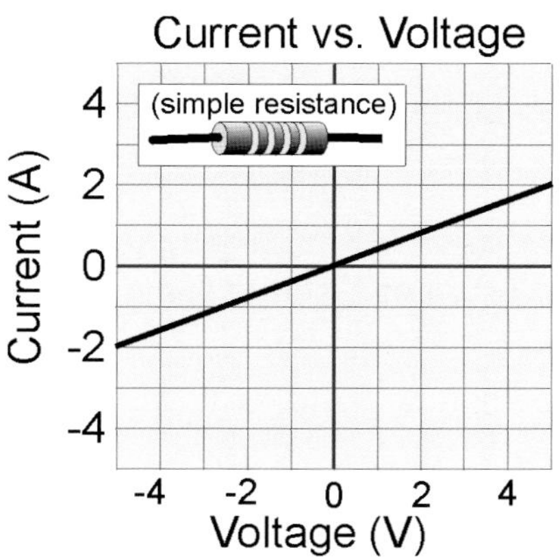

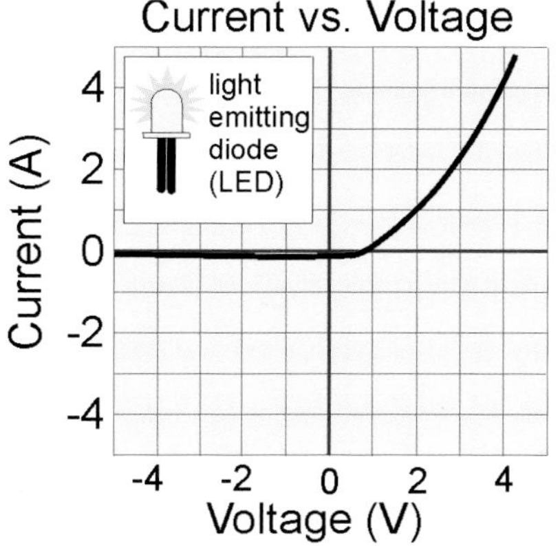

Finding resistance from a graph You can find resistance from a current vs. voltage graph. If the graph is a straight line (obeying Ohm's law), pick a point on the line. Read voltage and current (figure 8.3) from the graph. Calculate resistance using the R = V/I form of Ohm's law.

Positive and negative

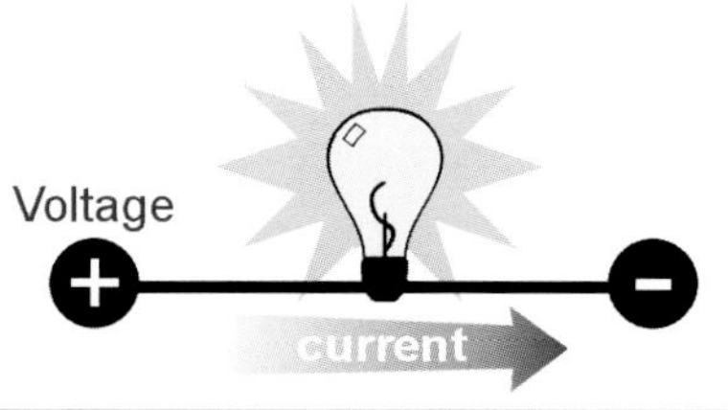

You choose that ...

Current is positive when it flows from left to right.

Voltage is positive when + is on the left and - on the right.

That means IF current goes the other way you call it NEGATIVE current.

Figure 8.2: *How to interpret positive and negative voltage. You have to choose which direction to call positive. After you choose, the other direction is negative!*

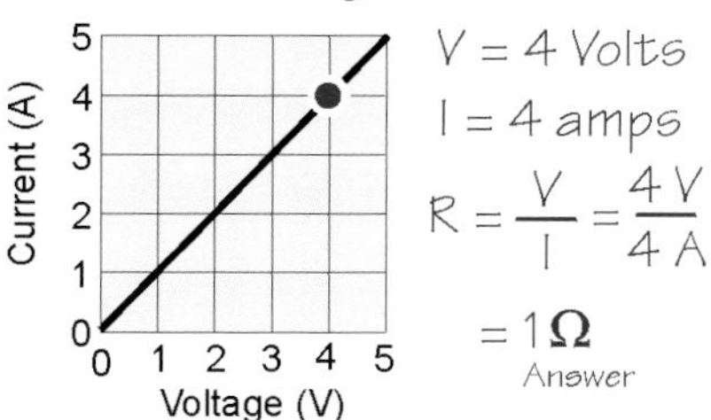

Figure 8.3: *Using a graph of current vs. voltage to determine resistance.*

Temperature and Ohm's law

The cause of resistance

Resistance happens because the charges bounce into and around atoms as they weave their way through a material. If the voltage goes up, the charges move a little faster between atoms and we get more current. Think about a highway. On a stretch of road there may be the same number of cars whether they are going 30 or 60 miles per hour. But, at 60 mph, twice as many cars flow past you per minute compared with 30 mph. Materials obey Ohm's law because the speed of moving charges increases proportionally with voltage.

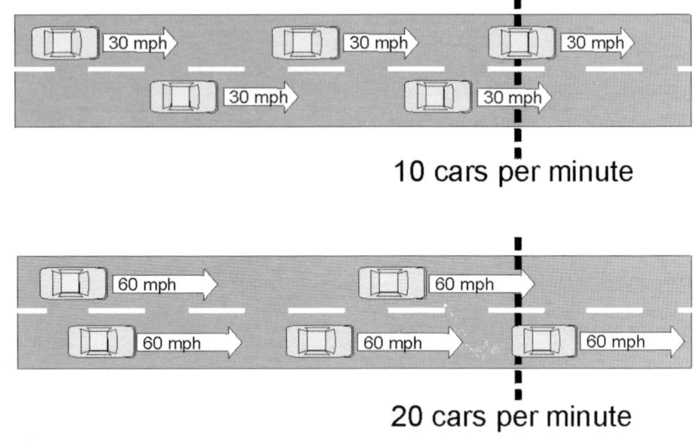

Resistance of metals increases with temperature

Even if a material obeys Ohm's law, its resistance can change when it is cooler or warmer. Atoms gain energy when they are heated up. With extra energy, the atoms move around more. They collide more often with moving charges that make up the current. The extra collisions mean that hot metal has more resistance than cold metal.

Superconductivity

The LDX experiment at MIT uses a superconducting coil to explore fusion energy.

What happens to the resistance of a material as its temperature is lowered? This question intrigued Dutch physicist Heike Kamerlingh Onnes (1853-1926). In 1911, he discovered that when mercury is cooled to 269 degrees below zero (-269°C), its resistance suddenly drops to zero. He called this property "superconductivity." A ***superconductor*** allows current to flow without losing *any* energy as heat or light.

Until the 1960s, superconductivity remained of little practical value because it was very hard and expensive to cool wires down to such extremely low temperatures. A few practical uses were invented, such as the magnetic resonance imaging machines found in many hospitals. In the 1980s, scientists made another big discovery. They discovered special ceramic materials that become superconductors at higher temperatures. Although they still must be cooled to -70°C, the new superconductors work at temperatures 200 degrees warmer than mercury. Engineers are working with these "high temperature" superconductors to see if they can be used to make more efficient motors, generators, power cables, and magnetically levitated trains.

Resistors

What is a resistor?

Using Ohm's law, if the voltage is prescribed, then the only way we can change the current is by changing the resistance. Components called **resistors** are used to control current in many circuits. Resistors are made from materials that keep the same resistance over a wide range of temperatures and currents.

Fixed and variable resistors

There are many kinds of resistors. The two basic kinds are fixed and variable. A fixed resistor always has the same value. An application of fixed resistors is a three-way light switch. Each setting connects the circuit to a different resistor. The three values of resistance determine three levels of current. The three levels of current control the brightness of the bulb.

If you look inside a stereo or telephone you will find a circuit board. The circuit board has wires printed on it and is covered with little parts. The little parts are called **electronic components** and are soldered to the circuit board. Many of the components are resistors, which look like small skinny cylinders with colored stripes on them. Because they are so tiny, it is impossible to write how much resistance each one has. The colored stripes are a code that tells you the resistance.

Example:

Figure out the value of this resistor.

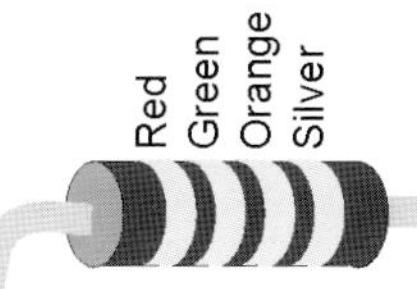

(1) The first two stripes are a number. Red (2) and green (5) make 25.

(2) The third stripe is the multiplier. Orange is 1,000.

(3) The fourth stripe is the accuracy tolerance. Silver is +/- 10%.

The example resistor is 25,000 ohms.

Resistor Color Codes

Color	Digit	Multiplier
Black	0	1
Brown	1	10
Red	2	100
Orange	3	1,000
Yellow	4	10,000
Green	5	100,000
Blue	6	1,000,000
Violet	7	10,000,000
Gray	8	not a multiplier
White	9	not a multiplier

Electrical controls

What are controls? Every time you turn a knob or push a switch you are using an electrical control. We use controls for lights, motors, air conditioners, and almost every electrical device you can think of. Many controls use variable resistors.

Making a dimmer switch An application of variable resistors is a dimmer switch. As you turn the dimmer switch from low to high, it changes the resistance, which also changes the current. Current is increased as the resistance goes down, and the bulb glows brighter in response.

The potentiometer A **potentiometer** is a variable resistor. Inside the potentiometer is a circular resistor and a little sliding contact called a wiper. As shown in the diagram below, the wiper moves when you turn the knob and is connected to a wire (B). You choose the resistance by turning the knob.

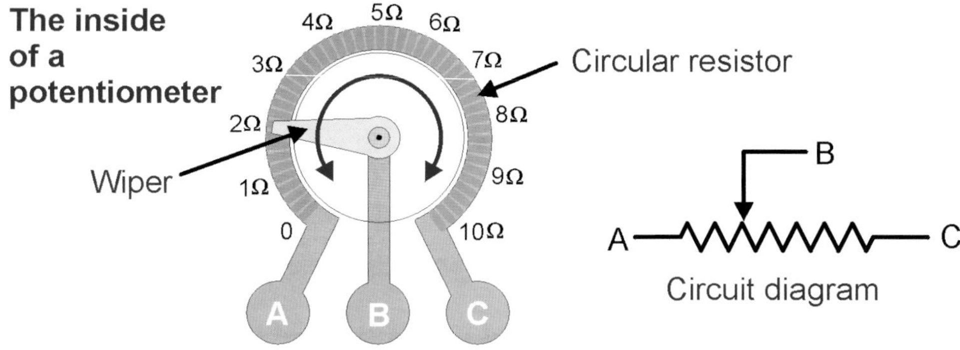

How the potentiometer works Potentiometers (or *pots* for short) have three wires. The resistance between A and C always stays the same. As you turn the knob the resistance between A and B changes. The resistance between B and C also changes. With the wiper rotated like the diagram above, the resistance between A and B is 2 ohms. The resistance between B and C is 8 ohms (10 minus 2).

You can choose how to connect a potentiometer into your circuit to change the resistance from zero to the maximum value of the potentiometer. For the potentiometer in the diagram the resistance can vary between zero and 10 ohms.

8.2 Work, Energy, and Power

If you look carefully at a stereo, hair dryer, or other household appliance, you find that most devices list a "power rating" that tells how many watts the appliance uses. In this section you will learn what these power ratings mean, and how to figure out the electricity costs of using various appliances.

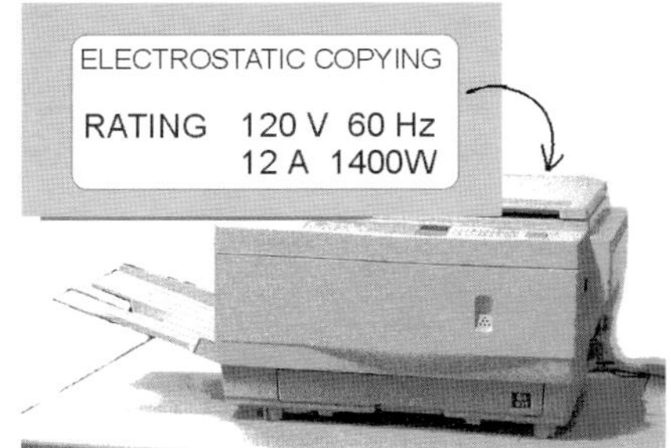

Figure 8.4: *The back of an electrical device often tells you how many watts it uses.*

Electric power

The three electrical quantities

We have now learned three important electrical quantities:

Amps	Current is what flows in a circuit. Current is measured in amps.
Volts	Voltage measures the potential energy difference between two places in a circuit. Voltage differences make current flow.
Ohms	Resistance measures the ability to resist the flow of current.

Paying for electricity

Electric bills sent out by utility companies don't charge by the volt, the amp, or the ohm. You may have noticed that electrical appliances in your home usually include another unit – the *watt*. Most appliances have a label that lists the number of watts or kilowatts. You may have purchased 60-watt light bulbs, or a 900-watt hair dryer, or a 1500-watt toaster oven. Electric companies charge for the energy you use, which depends on how many watts each appliance consumes in a given month.

A watt is a unit of power

The watt (W) is a unit of power. Power, in the scientific sense, has a precise meaning. Power is the rate at which energy is flowing. Energy is measured in joules. Power is measured in joules per second. One joule per second is equal to one watt. A 100-watt light bulb uses 100 joules of energy *every second.*

Where does the electrical power go?

Electrical power can be easily transformed into many different forms. An electric motor takes electrical power and makes mechanical power. A light bulb turns electrical power into light and a toaster oven turns the power into heat. The same unit (watts) applies to all forms of energy flow, including light, motion, electrical, thermal, or many others.

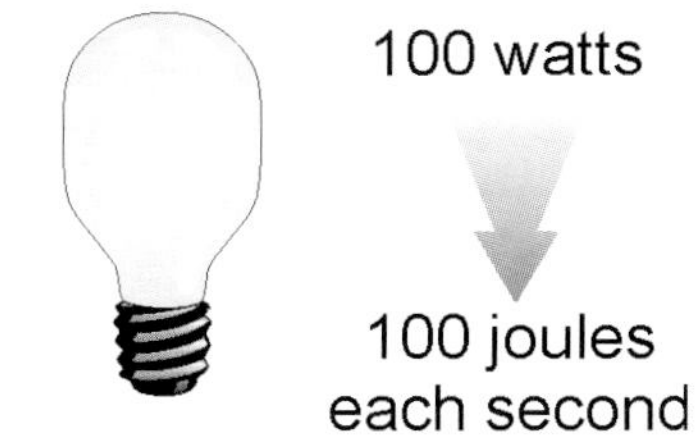

Figure 8.5: *One watt is an energy flow of one joule per second. A 100-watt light bulb uses 100 joules every second. A person running uses about 300 watts, or 300 joules every second.*

How can we measure power in a circuit?

Power in a circuit

Power in a circuit can be measured using the tools we already have. Remember that one watt equals an energy flow of one joule per second.

Amps	One amp is a flow of one coulomb of charge per second
Volts	One volt is an energy of one joule per coulomb of charge

If these two quantities are multiplied together, you will find that the units of coulombs cancel out, leaving the equation we want for power.

Voltage x Current = Power

$$\frac{\text{Joules}}{\cancel{\text{Coulomb}}} \times \frac{\cancel{\text{Coulomb}}}{\text{Second}} = \frac{\text{Joules}}{\text{Second}}$$

Power = voltage × current

Watts equal joules/second, so we can calculate electrical power in a circuit by multiplying voltage times current.

Electrical Power

$$P = VI$$

Power (watts) → P; Voltage (volts) → V; Current (amps) → I

Watts and kilowatts

A larger unit of power is sometimes needed. The 1500-watt toaster oven may instead be labeled "1.5 kW." A kilowatt (kW) is equal to 1000 watts or 1000 joules per second.

Horsepower

The other common unit of power often seen on electric motors is the horsepower. One horsepower is 746 watts. Electric motors you find around the house range in size from 1/25th of a horsepower (30 watts) for a small electric fan to 2 horsepower (1492 watts) for an electric saw.

Electric cars

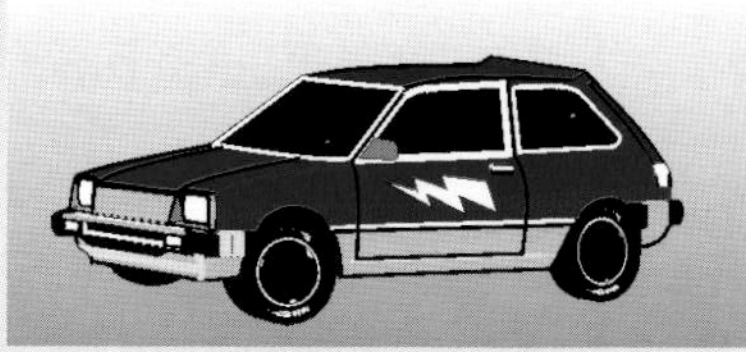

Many people believe that all cars will eventually be electric because electric cars give off little or no pollution. Electric cars are challenging to build because of the power you need. A gas engine for a car makes 100 horsepower, or about 75,000 watts.

Suppose you want to use 12-volt batteries, like the ones used to *start* cars today. To make 75 kilowatts of power at 12 volts, you need a current of 6,250 amps! By comparison, most people's homes use less than 100 amps.

The solution is to use more efficient motors and higher voltages. Research into electric cars is being done all over the world.

You buy electricity by the kilowatt-hour

Kilowatt-hours What do we buy from the electric utility company? Let's look at a utility bill. Utility companies charge customers for a unit called the kilowatt-hour (abbreviated kWh). One kilowatt-hour means that a kilowatt of power has been used for one hour.

You pay for kilowatt-hours Electric companies charge for kilowatt-hours over a set period of time, often a month. Your home is connected to a meter that counts up total number of kilowatt-hours used and a person comes to read the meter once a month.

Estimating your electric bill If you know the cost per kilowatt-hour that your utility company charges, you can estimate the cost of running an appliance for a period of time.

Example: Your electric company charges 14 cents per kilowatt-hour. Your coffee-maker has a power rating of 1,050 watts. The coffeemaker is on for about 1 hour each day. What does this cost you each month in electricity?

Solution: Find the number of kilowatts of power that the coffeemaker uses.
1,050 W × 1 kW/1,000 W = 1.05 kW

Find the kilowatt-hours used by the coffeemaker each day.
1.05 kW × 1 hr/day = 1.05 kWh per day

Find the kilowatt-hours of electricity used by the coffeemaker each month. Assume there are 30 days in a month.
1.05 kWh/day × 30 days/month = 31.5 kWh per month

Find the cost of using the coffeemaker for one month.
31.5 kWh/month × $0.14/kWh = $4.41 per month

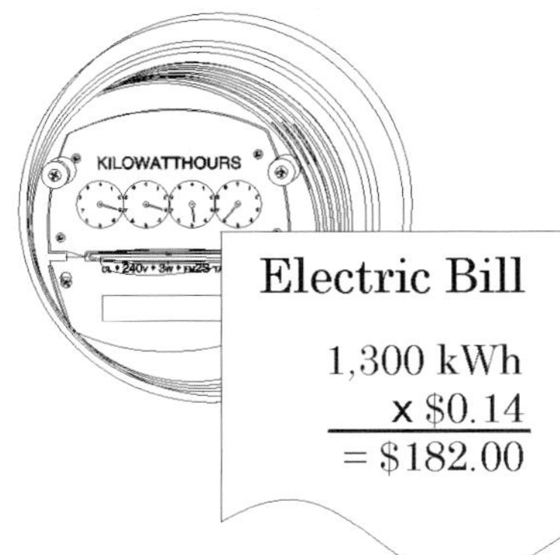

Figure 8.6: *Every month most people pay an electric bill that charges for the kilowatt-hours of energy used.*

Typical power ratings

Appliance	Power (watts)
Electric stove	5,000
Electric heater	1,500
Hair dryer	1,200
Iron	800
Washing machine	750
Light	100
Small fan	50
Clock radio	10

Electricity, power, and heat

How do you get more power?

How do you get more power when you need it? From the power formula we can see that increasing voltage or current will increase power. The disadvantage of raising voltage is that the electricity in your standard outlets is at 120 volts, and it is hard to change. Some appliances use 240 volts, but they have special plugs because 240 volts is more dangerous than 120 volts.

Higher power usually means more current

The more usual way to get higher power is to use more current. However, when current flows through a wire, part of the energy is transformed into heat. More current means more heat. If too much power goes into heat, the wire could melt or start a fire.

Reducing heat in electrical wires

Fortunately, there is a way to let more current flow through a wire without making more heat. Remember (from Ohm's law) that voltage is current times resistance. If we make the resistance smaller, more current can flow with less voltage change along the wire. Since power is voltage times current, less voltage means less power is lost as heat.

Different size wires have different resistance

Lower resistance is the reason wires come in different sizes. Thick wire has lower resistance and can safely carry more current than thin wire (figure 8.7). Often we use extension cords to plug in electric tools or appliances. Extension cords come with many thicknesses, or *gauges*, of wire. Typical kinds of extension cords you can buy have 18 gauge wire, 16 gauge wire, 14 gauge wire, and 12 gauge wire (figure 8.8). The bigger the gauge, the higher the resistance. To carry a lot of current, you want low resistance, so you need lower gauge (fatter) wires.

Length and resistance

The length of a wire also affects its resistance. The longer a wire is, the more resistance it has. Think about moving around your school and how you can get through a short, crowded hallway quickly. But, it takes a long time to get down a long, crowded hallway.

Check your extension cords for safety

If you look at an extension cord, it will tell you how many amps of current it can safely carry. The length and wire thickness are both important. *Always* check to see if the extension cord can carry *at least* as much current as the device you plug in will require. Many fires have been caused by using the wrong extension cord!

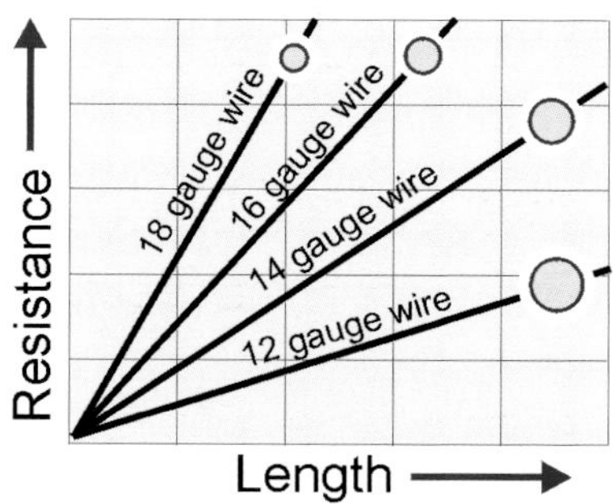

Figure 8.7: *The resistance of a wire depends on the length and size. Longer length means greater resistance. Bigger diameter means lower resistance.*

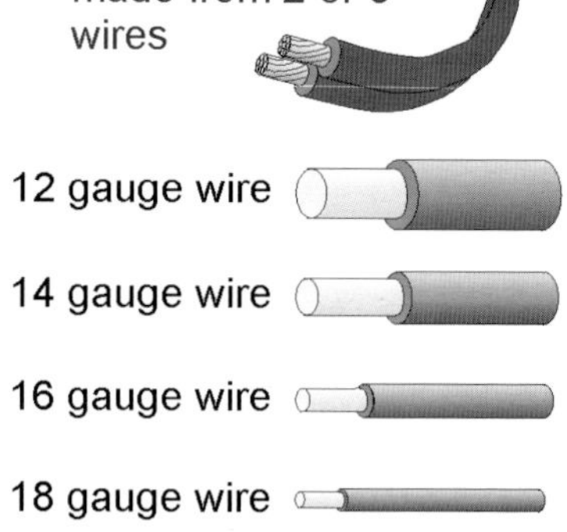

Wire Gauge	Current (amps)
12	20
14	15
16	10
18	7

Figure 8.8: *The safe amount of current for different gauges of wire.*

Chapter 8 Review

Vocabulary review

Match the following terms with the correct definition. There is one extra definition in the list that will not match any of the terms.

Set One

1. Ohm's law	a. A semiconductor component that allows current to flow in one direction only
2. diode	b. A shorthand method of describing the resistance of a resistor
3. superconductor	c. A component used to control current in circuits because it has a relatively constant resistance
4. resistor	d. A part soldered onto a circuit board
5. electronic component	e. An equation relating voltage, current and resistance in a circuit
	f. A material that has zero resistance at low temperatures

Set Two

1. potentiometer	a. A unit equal to 100 watts
2. watt	b. The use of a kilowatt of power for one hour
3. power	c. The unit commonly used to measure power, equal to joules/second
4. kilowatt	d. A unit equal to 1000 watts
5. kilowatt-hour	e. The rate at which work is being performed
	f. A variable resistor

Concept review

1. Explain what will happen to the value of current in a circuit if the voltage is increased.
2. Explain what will happen to the value of current in a circuit if the resistance is increased.
3. High resistance leads to an increase in heat. A person repaired a broken light in a house and replaced the copper wire with a thin piece of aluminum. Explain why this replacement is a fire hazard.
4. Explain why the amps rating on an extension cord should be the same as, or larger than, the current drawn by the device plugged into the extension cord.
5. What is the scientific definition of power?
6. What type of work is done by an electric fan? (In other words, electrical energy is changed into what other form(s) when the fan is running?)
7. What is the metric unit used to measure power?
8. List three appliances and their power ratings.

9. Express the metric unit of power in fundamental units.

10. Power companies charge us for kilowatt-hours. What type of quantity is being measured by a kilowatt-hour?

Problems

1. A hair dryer draws a current of 10 amps. If it is plugged into a 120-volt circuit, what is the resistance of the hair dryer?
2. A child's toy robot draws a current of 2.0 amps. The robot's circuit has a total resistance of 4.5 ohms. What is the total voltage of the battery or batteries required by the toy?
3. A flashlight bulb has a resistance of approximately 6 ohms. It works in a flashlight with two AA alkaline batteries. About how much current does the bulb draw?
4. Household circuits in the United States commonly run on 120 volts of electricity. Frequently, circuit breakers are installed that open a circuit if it is drawing more than 15 amps of current. What is the minimum amount of resistance that must be present in the circuit to prevent the circuit breaker from activating?
5. A 2,500-watt room air conditioner could also be called a ________ kilowatt appliance.
6. If you bake potatoes in a 900-watt microwave oven for 15 minutes, how many kilowatt-hours of electrical energy have you consumed?
7. If a toaster oven draws 6 amps of current when plugged into a 120-volt outlet, what is the power rating of the appliance?
8. A student uses three appliances in her dormitory room: a 1,200-watt iron, which she uses 3.5 hours per month; a lamp with a 100-watt bulb which she uses 125 hours per month; and a 700-watt coffee maker, which she uses 15 hours per month
   a. How many kilowatt-hours of electrical energy are consumed in one month by each of these appliances?
   b. If the local utility company charges 15 cents per kilowatt-hour of electrical energy consumed, how much does it cost per month to operate each appliance?
9. Calculate the current through each of the following bulbs if they are connected to a 120-volt circuit in your house.
   a. 40 W b. 60 W c. 100 W d. 150 W

Applying your knowledge

1. Using power ratings, analyze how much your family spends to run every appliance in your home. Enact a plan to reduce electricity use and see if your family saves money.
2. With an adult, check the safety of appliances that are plugged into extension cords, in your home or school. Make sure that the current ratings of the extension cord meet or exceed the current ratings of the appliance.
3. Find out what programs are available through your local utility company to reduce electricity use (discounted low-wattage bulbs, home energy checks, etc.). Prepare a pamphlet on the programs.
4. Research superconductivity. Find out what it is and what applications it may have.

UNIT 3

Electricity and Magnetism

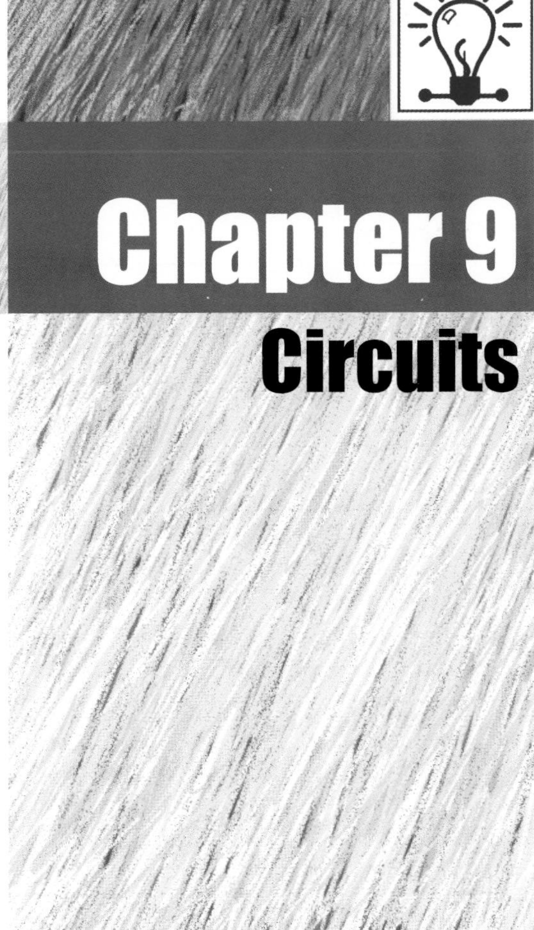

Chapter 9

Circuits

Introduction to Chapter 9

In our homes, you can have many electrical devices on at any one time. How is this possible? What do circuits in our homes look like? In this chapter, you will learn about the two kinds of circuits, called *series circuits* and *parallel circuits*. In series circuits, all the current flows through one path. In parallel circuits, current can flow through two or more paths.

Investigations for Chapter 9

9.1	**More Electric Circuits**	*What kinds of electric circuits can you build?*

In this Investigation, you will compare how two kinds of circuits work by building and observing series and parallel circuits. You will explore an application of these circuits by wiring two switches in series and in parallel.

9.2	**Series Circuits**	*How do you use Ohm's law in series circuits?*

In this Investigation, you will find out how to add resistance in a series circuit. You will also build a light bulb circuit with a dimmer switch and use this circuit to graph the resistance of a light bulb at different levels of current.

9.3	**Parallel Circuits**	*How do parallel circuits work?*

In this Investigation, you will analyze how a parallel circuit works by measuring voltage and current in different parts of the circuit. You will use your understanding of parallel circuits to design a battery voltage tester circuit.

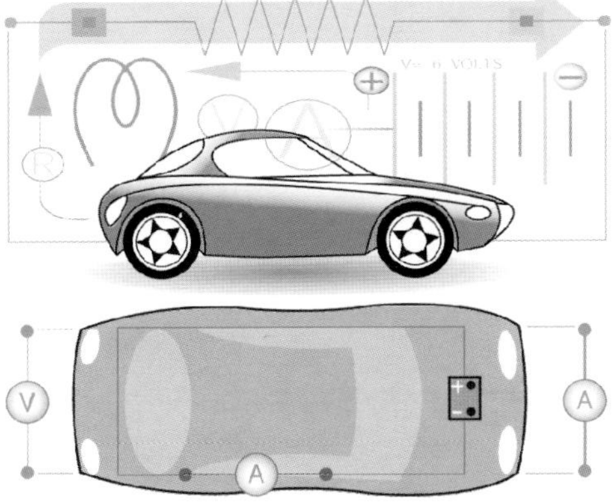

Learning Goals

In this chapter, you will:

- ✔ Identify a series circuit.
- ✔ Identify a parallel circuit.
- ✔ Describe how our houses are wired.
- ✔ Build series and parallel circuits.
- ✔ Calculate total resistance in series circuits.
- ✔ Build circuits with fixed and variable resistors.
- ✔ Analyze series circuits using Ohm's law.
- ✔ Use Kirchhoff's voltage law to find the voltage drop across a circuit component.
- ✔ Compare current in series and parallel circuits.
- ✔ Compare voltage in series and parallel circuits.
- ✔ Use Kirchhoff's current law to find an unknown current in a parallel circuit.
- ✔ Identify a short circuit.
- ✔ Explain why a short circuit is dangerous.

Vocabulary

Kirchhoff's current law
Kirchhoff's voltage law
parallel circuit
series circuit
short circuit

9.1 More Electric Circuits

We use electric circuits for thousands of different things from cars to computers. In this section you will learn about two basic ways to put circuits together. These two types of circuits are called *series* and *parallel*. Series circuits have only one path; the flow of charge has only one place to go. Parallel circuits have branching points and multiple paths for current to flow.

Series circuits

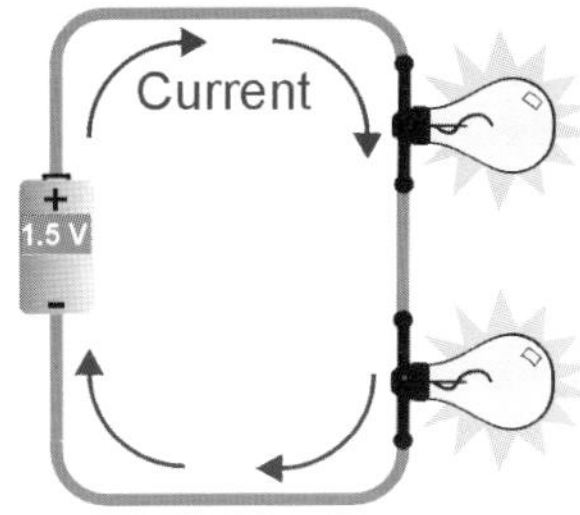

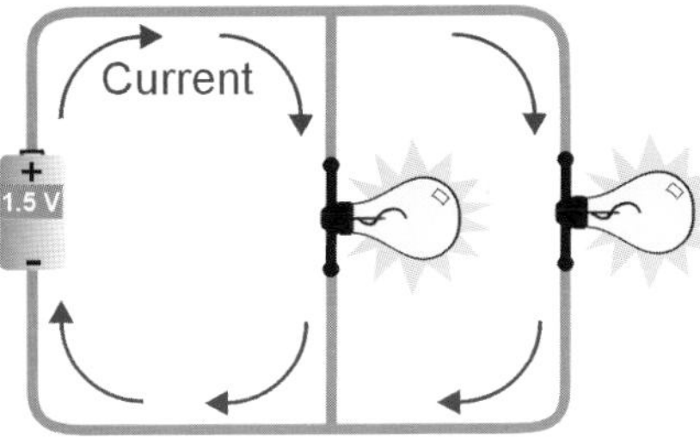

What is a series circuit? In a **series circuit** the current can only take one path. All the current flows through every part of the circuit. All the circuits you have studied so far have been series circuits. For example, if you have a battery, a light bulb, and one switch, everything is connected in series because there is only one path through the circuit.

What is a parallel circuit? In a **parallel circuit** the current can take more than one path. Parallel circuits have at least one branch where the current can split up.

Combinations It is possible to create circuits with both series and parallel wiring. You need at least three light bulbs. Can you think of a way to wire three bulbs using both series and parallel connections?

Holiday lights

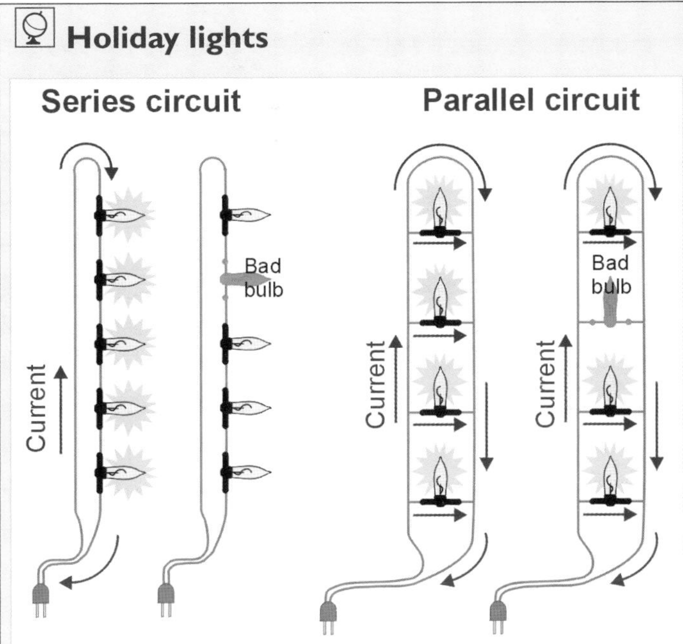

Many people use strings of lights to decorate their houses, especially at holiday time. Inexpensive versions of lights are wired in series, while better ones are wired in parallel.

In the series circuit, if one bulb goes bad the whole circuit is broken and no bulbs light. It is very difficult to find the bad bulb to replace it because all the lights are out.

In the parallel circuit, each bulb has its own path for current, independent of the others. If one bulb fails, the others will still light. The bad bulb is easy to spot and replace.

Household wiring

Parallel circuits for homes and buildings

The electrical circuits in homes and buildings are parallel circuits. There are two great advantages of parallel circuits that make them a better choice than series circuits.

1. Each outlet has its own current path. This means one outlet can have something connected and turned on (with current flowing), while another outlet has nothing connected or something turned off (no current flowing).
2. Every outlet sees the same voltage because one side of each outlet is connected to the same wire.

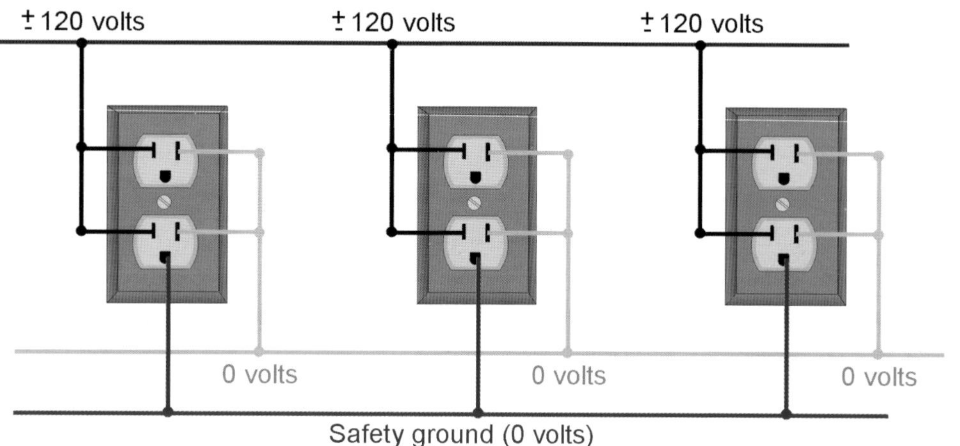

Why series circuits would not work

Parallel circuits mean that a light in your home can be on at the same time that the TV is off. If our homes were wired in series, turning off *anything* electrical in the house would break the whole circuit. This is not practical; we would have to keep everything on all the time just to keep the refrigerator running! Also, in a series circuit, everything you plugged in would use some energy and would lower the voltage available to the next outlet.

What happens if you plug in too many things?

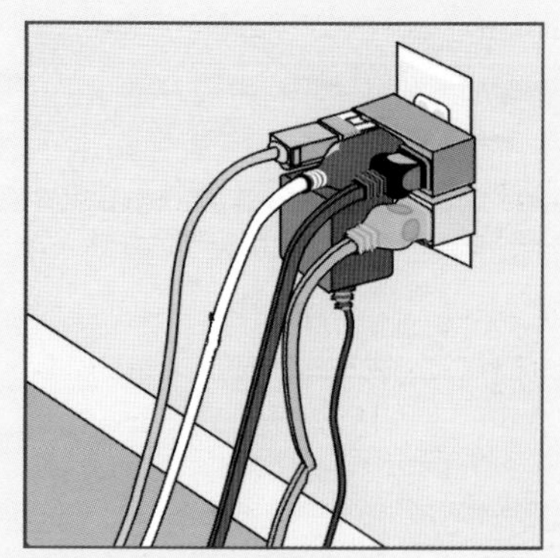

In a parallel circuit, each connection uses as much current as it needs. If you plug in a coffeemaker that uses 10 amps and a toaster oven that uses 10 amps, a total of 20 amps needs to come through the wire.

If you plug too many appliances into the same outlet, you will eventually use more current than the wires can carry without overheating. Your circuit breaker will click open and stop the current. You should unplug things to reduce the current in the circuit before resetting the circuit breaker.

9.2 Series Circuits

Ohm's law is a powerful tool for analyzing circuits. You have studied Ohm's law in a series circuit with one resistor. In this section you will learn how to analyze more complex series circuits with more than one resistance.

Current and voltage in a series circuit

In a series circuit, current is the same at all points

In a series circuit, all current flows through a single path. What goes into one end of the wire must come out the other end of the wire. The value of current is the same at all points in the circuit. The amount of current is determined by the voltage and resistance in the circuit, using Ohm's law.

Voltage is reduced by each resistance

The law of conservation of energy helps us to understand what happens to energy in a series circuit. Consider a circuit with three bulbs. Using two batteries, every charge starts at 3 volts. As each charge moves through the circuit, some energy is transformed into light by each bulb. That means that after every bulb, the energy must be lower. We see the lower energy as a drop in voltage from 3 volts, to 2 volts, to 1 volt and finally down to zero volts after the last bulb.

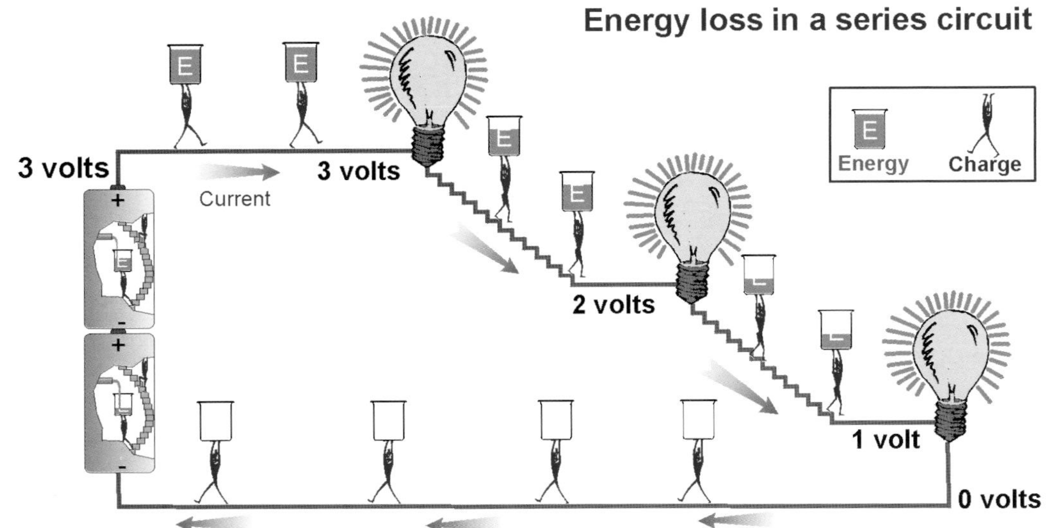

Drills, saws, and extension cords

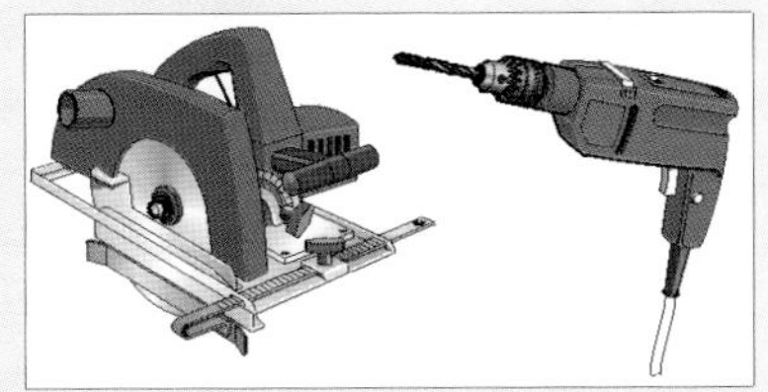

If you know people who work with power tools, you may have noticed that they use a heavy extension cord when the regular cord can't reach. One reason to use a heavy cord is that it can safely carry the amps used by power tools.

There is a second reason as well. If a thin extension cord is used, the motor in a power tool can overheat and burn out. This happens because the voltage available for the motor is lower than it should be.

The motor gets lower voltage when energy is lost along the cord. This energy loss is called a voltage drop, and is related to resistance. Heavy extension cords have lower resistance and use less energy than thin cords of the same length.

How to find the current in a series circuit

Start with resistance and voltage

You need to know how much resistance the circuit has to find the current. In many cases you know the voltage, such as from a battery. If you know the resistance, Ohm's law can be used to find the current.

Each resistance in a series circuit adds to the total. You can think of it like adding pinches to a hose (figure 9.1). Each pinch adds some resistance. The total resistance is the sum of the resistances from each pinch.

Two ways to find the current

How would you find the exact amount of total resistance in a series circuit? You could use several methods:

- You could measure total voltage and current through the circuit, and use Ohm's law to calculate the total resistance of the circuit (R = V/I).
- You could add together the resistance of each component in the circuit.

Add up resistances to get the total

If you know the resistance of each component, you can simply add them up to get the total for the circuit. Once you know the total resistance, use Ohm's law to calculate the current.

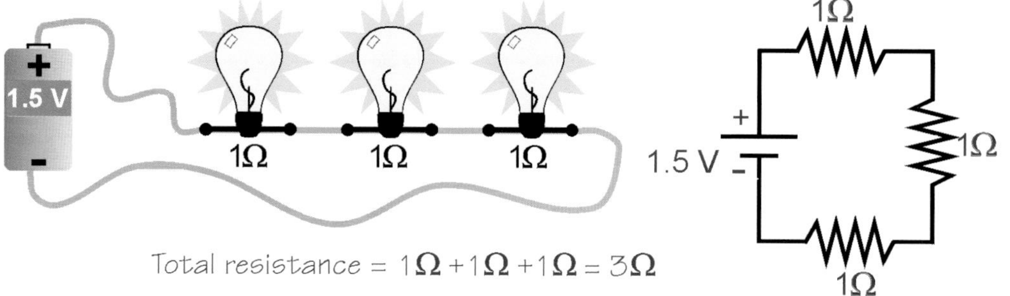

Ignore resistance of wires and batteries

Every part in a circuit has some resistance, even the wires and batteries. However, light bulbs, resistors, motors and heaters usually have much greater resistance than wires and batteries. Therefore, when adding resistances up, we can almost always leave out the resistance of wires and batteries.

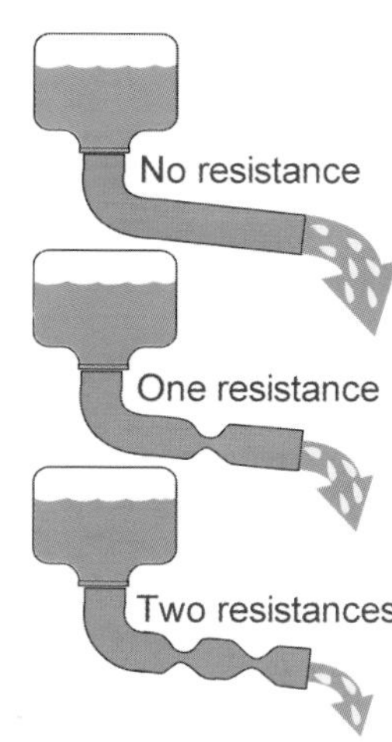

Figure 9.1: *Each time a hose is pinched, the flow of water slows more.*

Example

How much current is in a circuit with a 1.5 volt battery and three 1 ohm resistances (bulbs) in series?

Solution

Add the resistance of each component:

1 ohm + 1 ohm + 1 ohm = 3 ohms

Use Ohm's law to calculate the current from the voltage and the total resistance.

I = V/R = 1.5 volts ÷ 3 ohms = 0.5 amps

Answer: 0.5 amps

Voltage in a series circuit

Each resistance drops the voltage You have learned that energy is not created or destroyed. This rule is known as the law of conservation of energy. However, energy is constantly being transformed from one form to another. As current flows along a series circuit, each resistance uses up some of the energy. As a result, the voltage gets lower after each resistance.

The voltage drop We often say each separate resistor creates a *voltage drop*. If you know the current and resistance, Ohm's law can be used to calculate the voltage drop across each resistor. For example, in the three-bulb series circuit, the voltage drop across each bulb is 0.5 volts (figure 9.2).

Each resistance drops the voltage

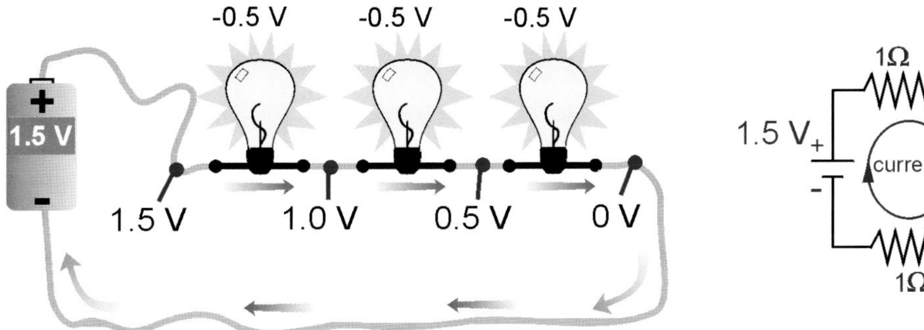

Voltage drop across a resistor (bulb)

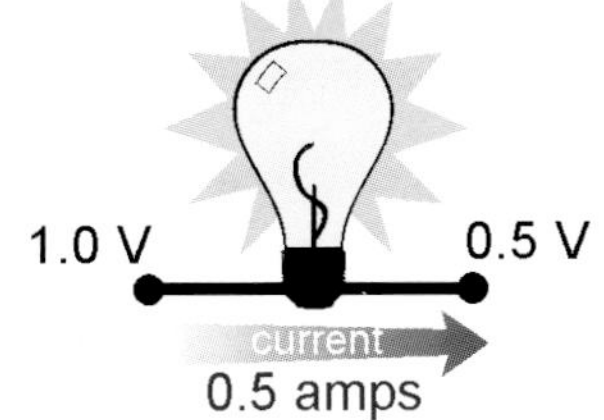

Calculating the voltage drop

Ohm's law

$V = IR$

$= (0.5 \text{ amps}) \times (1 \text{ ohm})$

$= 0.5 \text{ volts}$

Figure 9.2: *When current flows through any resistance the voltage drops because some of the energy is used up. The amount of the voltage drop is given by Ohm's law.*

Kirchhoff's law Over the entire circuit, the energy taken out must equal the energy supplied by the battery. This means the total of all the voltage drops must add up to the total voltage supplied by the battery (energy in). This rule is known as Kirchhoff's voltage law, after German physicist Gustav Robert Kirchhoff (1824-87):

Kirchhoff's voltage law

Around any closed circuit, all the voltage changes must add up to zero.

Batteries raise voltage, resistances lower voltage.

For the example circuit above, the total of all voltage changes is:

$$\text{Voltage changes} = \underset{\text{Battery}}{+1.5\text{ V}} - \underset{\text{Bulb}}{0.5\text{ V}} - \underset{\text{Bulb}}{0.5\text{ V}} - \underset{\text{Bulb}}{0.5\text{ V}} = 0$$

9.3 Parallel Circuits

In the last section, you learned how to analyze series circuits. In this section, you will take a closer look at parallel circuits. You previously learned that parallel circuits are used for almost all electrical wiring in houses and buildings.

Current in a parallel circuit

Separate paths are parallel branches A parallel circuit has at least one point where the circuit divides, creating more than one path for current to flow. Each path in the circuit is sometimes called a *branch*. The current through a branch is also called the *branch current*.

Kirchhoff's current law When analyzing a parallel circuit, remember that the current always has to go somewhere. If current flows into a branching point in a circuit, the same total current must flow out again. This rule is known as Kirchhoff's current law.

Example, three bulbs in parallel For example, suppose you have three light bulbs connected in parallel, and each has a current of 1 amp. The battery must supply 3 amps since each bulb draws 1 amp and there are 3 bulbs. At the first branch, 3 amps flow in, 1 amp flows down to the first bulb, and 2 amps flow on to the remaining 2 bulbs.

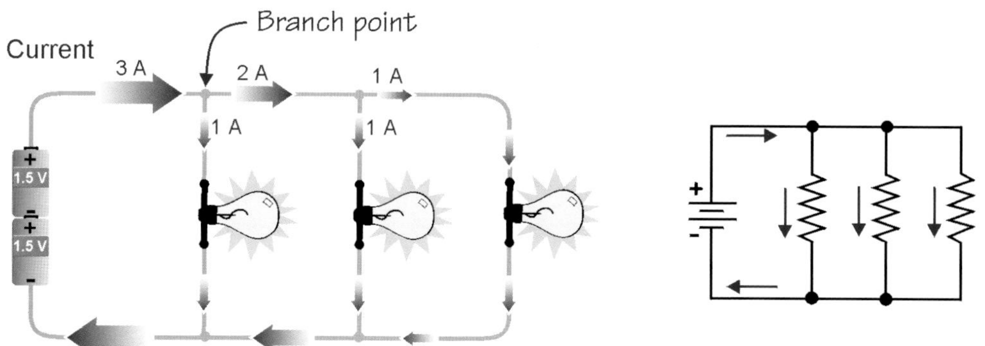

Kirchhoff's current law

All the current flowing into a branch point in a circuit has to flow out again.

Why aren't birds electrocuted?

If high-voltage wires are so dangerous, how do birds sit on them without being instantly electrocuted? First, the bird's body has a higher resistance than the electrical wire. The current tends to stay in the wire because the wire is an easier path.

The most important reason, however, is that the bird has both feet on the same wire. That means the voltage is the same on both feet and no current flows through the bird.

If a bird had one foot on the wire and the other foot touching the electric pole, then there would be a voltage difference. A lot of electricity would pass through the bird.

Voltage and resistance in a parallel circuit

Each branch sees the same voltage

In a parallel circuit the voltage is the same across each branch because all the branch points are on the same wire. One way to think of a parallel circuit is to imagine several series circuits connected to the same battery. Each branch has a path back to the battery without any other resistance in the way.

Branches don't always have the same current

The amount of current in each branch in a parallel circuit depends on how much resistance is in the branch. When you plug a desk lamp and a power saw into an outlet, they each use very different amounts of current (figure 9.3).

Lower resistance means more current flows

You can calculate current through the lamp and saw with Ohm's law (figure 9.4). The 100-watt bulb has a resistance of 145 ohms. Since the outlet has 120 volts across it, the bulb draws about 0.8 amps. A power saw has a much lower resistance, 12 ohms. Consequently, the power saw draws a much higher current of 10 amps when connected to the 120-volt outlet.

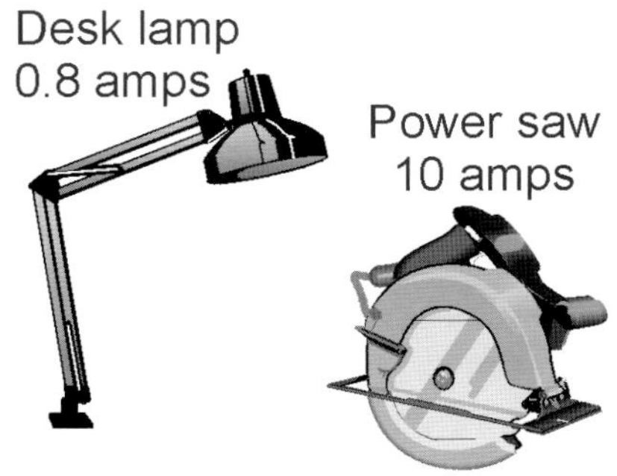

Figure 9.3: *Different appliances use different amounts of currrent.*

Example: Calculating currents in a parallel circuit

For the circuit and its diagram shown below, a student was able to calculate the currents from the information given about the circuit. Can you duplicate her work?

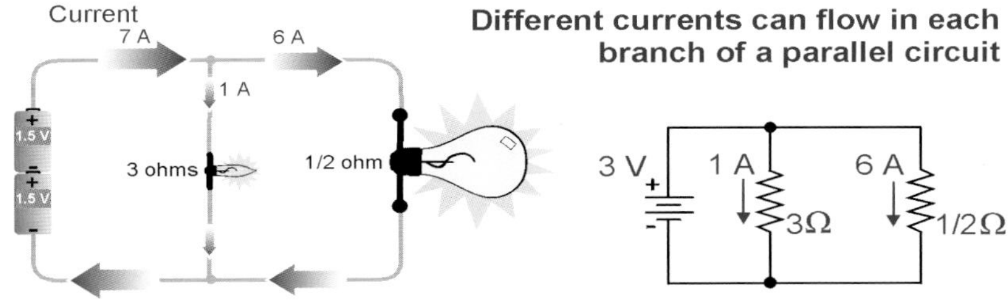

Step 1: Calculate current through each part of the circuit.

Step 2: You are given total voltage and the resistance of each bulb.

Step 3: Useful equations are: Ohm's law, $V = IR$, and Kirchhoff's current law, $I_t = I_1 + I_2$

Step 4: Branch 1 current: $I_1 = V/R_1$ Branch 2 current: $I_2 = V/R_2$ Total current: $I_t = I_1 + I_2$

Step 5: $I_1 = 3\ V / 3\ \Omega = 1$ $I_2 = 3\ V / 0.5\ \Omega = 6\ A$ $I_t = 1\ A + 6\ A = 7\ A$

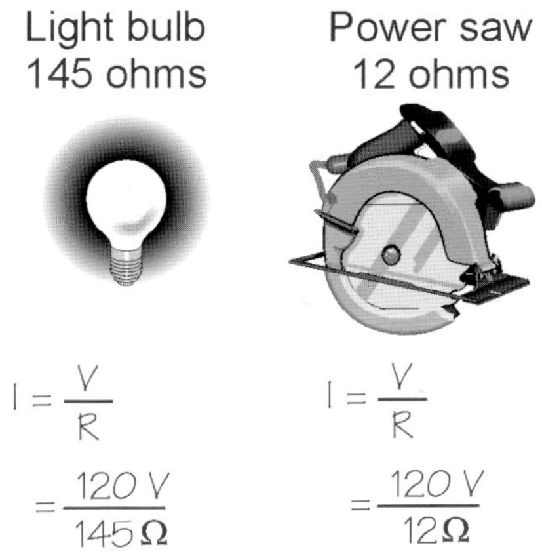

$$I = \frac{V}{R} = \frac{120\ V}{145\ \Omega} = 0.83\ \text{amps}$$

$$I = \frac{V}{R} = \frac{120\ V}{12\ \Omega} = 10\ \text{amps}$$

Figure 9.4: *Calculating the current from the resistance and voltage. Household electric circuits are wired in parallel at 120 volts.*

Open circuits and short circuits

What is a short circuit? A short circuit is a circuit path with zero or very low resistance. You can create a short circuit by connecting a wire directly between two ends of a battery. Often, short circuits are accidentally caused by connecting a wire between two other wires at different voltages. This creates a parallel path with very low resistance. In a parallel circuit, the branch with the lowest resistance draws the most current (figure 9.5).

Why short circuits are dangerous Short circuits are dangerous because they can cause huge amounts of current. For example, suppose you connect a length of wire across a circuit creating a second current path as shown below. The resistance of the wire could be as low as 0.001 ohms. That means the current through your wire could be as high as 1,500 amps! This much current would melt the wire in an instant and probably burn you as well. Short circuits should always be a concern when working around electricity. Fuses or circuit breakers are protection from the high current of a short circuit.

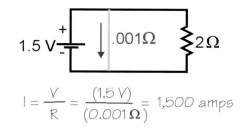

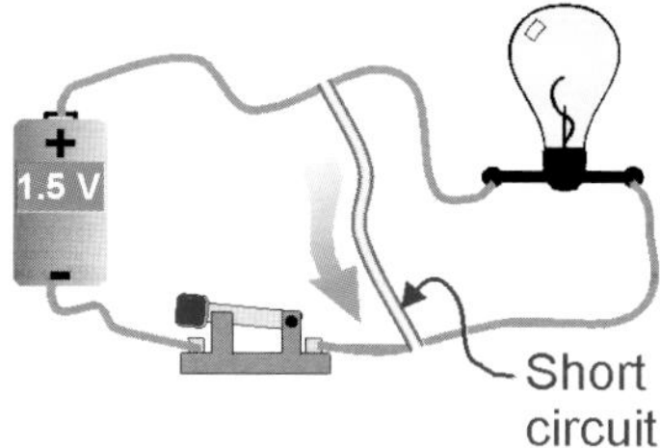

1.5 V + - .001Ω 2Ω

$$I = \frac{V}{R} = \frac{(1.5\ V)}{(0.001\ \Omega)} = 1{,}500 \text{ amps}$$

Open and closed circuits Open and closed circuits are not the same as short circuits. An open circuit means the current path has been broken, possibly by a switch (figure 9.5). Current cannot flow in an open circuit. A closed circuit is a circuit that is complete and allows current to flow.

Protecting against short circuits Every electrical outlet in your house or apartment is connected to a circuit breaker that allows a maximum of 15 or 20 amps to flow. If something electrical breaks and causes a short circuit, the breaker will open before the current has time to cause a fire. If a circuit breaker always trips when you plug in an appliance, that appliance probably has a short circuit.

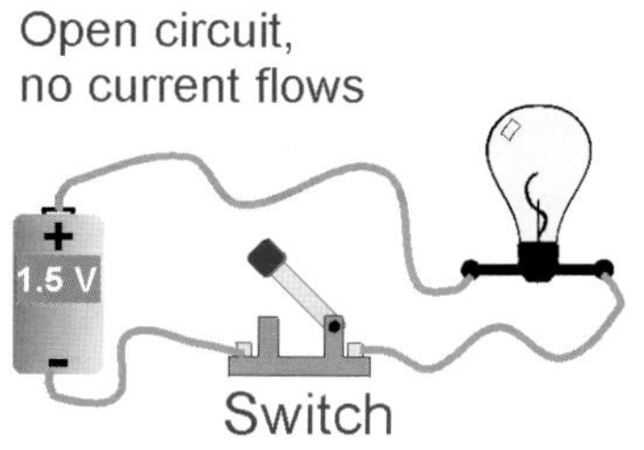

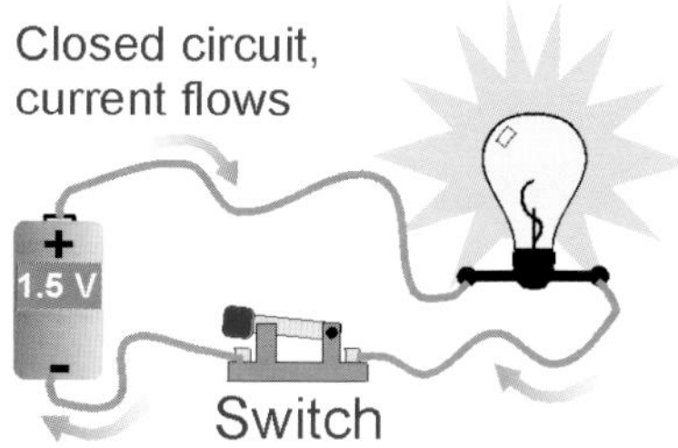

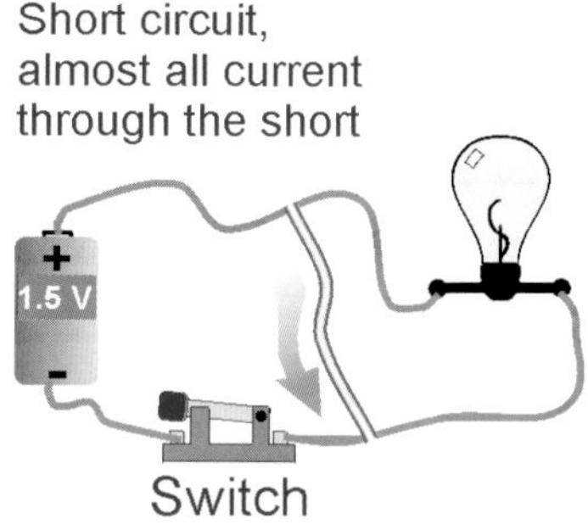

Figure 9.5: *A short circuit is a very low resistance path that can draw huge amounts of current. An open circuit is a break in the circuit that shuts off the flow of current. Switches are used to open and close circuits.*

Chapter 9 Review

Vocabulary review

Match the following terms with the correct definition. There is one extra definition in the list that will not match any of the terms.

Set One

1. series circuit	a. In a circuit, all the voltage drops must add up to the total voltage supplied by the battery
2. parallel circuit	b. A circuit that has only one path for the flow of charge
3. Kirchhoff's voltage law	c. A circuit that has more than one path for the flow of charge
4. Kirchhoff's current law	d. Two switches wired in parallel
5. short circuit	e. A circuit path with very low resistance
	f. If current flows into a branch in the circuit, the same amount of current must flow out again

Concept review

1. Explain the advantage of using a parallel circuit if you have more than one device in the circuit.
2. Imagine that an electrician wired the kitchen in your house so that all the outlets were connected in a single series circuit. Describe what you would have to do to keep the refrigerator running constantly.
3. If you have a light, and one switch that controls it, the light and the switch are wired in ________.
4. Is the current at every point in a series circuit the same?
5. What happens to the total resistance of a series circuit as you add more resistance? Does total resistance of the circuit decrease, increase, or stay the same?
6. Explain why Kirchhoff's voltage law is an application of the law of conservation of energy.
7. Describe what happens to the potential energy of charges in a circuit as they move through a bulb.
8. What happens to the total current of a parallel circuit as you add more branches with current through them? Does total current of the circuit decrease, increase, or stay the same?

9. The voltage across each branch of a parallel circuit is equal to the ________.
10. If a parallel circuit has two branches with equal resistance, what is the total resistance of the circuit?
11. For each diagram below, label the circuit *series*, *parallel*, or *short circuit*. The arrows indicate the flow of current.

   a.

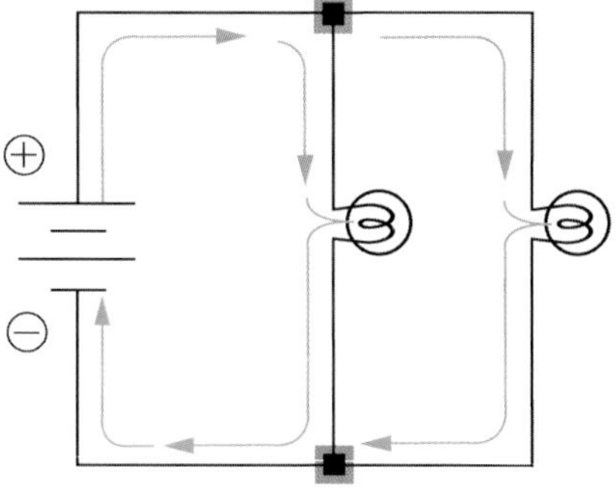

   b.

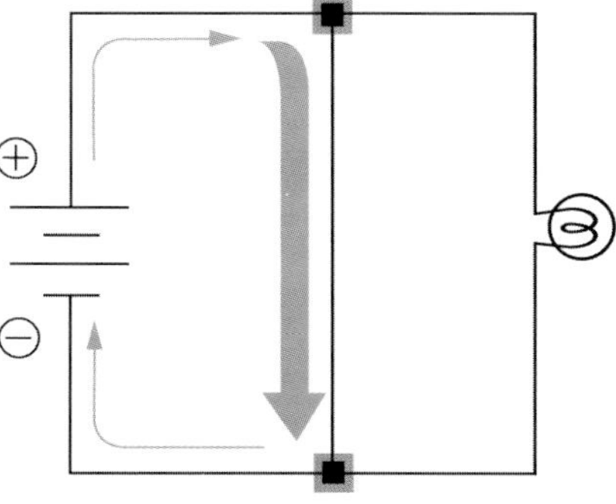

   c.

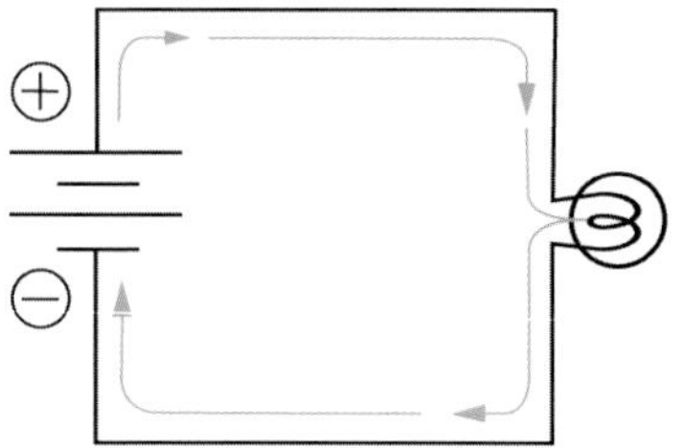

Problems

1. Answer the following:

   a. A circuit with three 1.5-volt batteries has two matching light bulbs. What is the voltage drop across each light bulb?

   b. Explain how you figured out your answer.

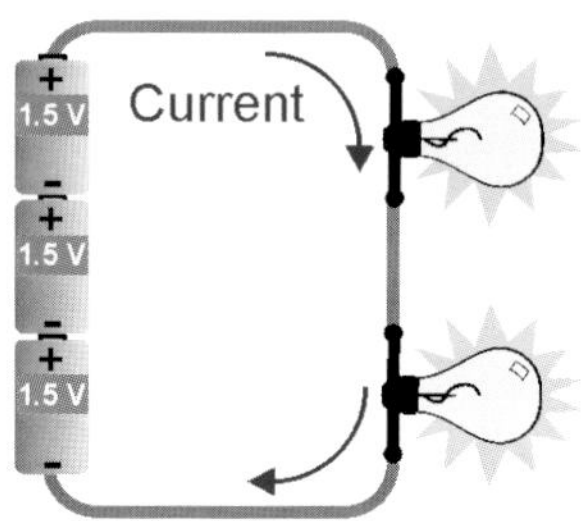

2. A student builds a circuit using three 1-ohm resistors in series. The current in the circuit is 1.5 amps. Use Ohm's law to determine the voltage of the circuit. (Hint: Draw the circuit described in the question.)

3. A student sets up a series circuit with four 1.5-volt batteries, a 5-ohm resistor, and two 1-ohm resistors. (Hint: Draw the circuit described in the question.)

   a. What is the total resistance in her circuit?

   b. Use Ohm's law to determine the value of current for the circuit.

4. A lab group was given a kit containing four 1.5-volt batteries, eight wires, and a resistor set containing three 1-ohm resistors and two 5-ohm resistors. They use all the batteries to build a series circuit. They use a meter to find that the current is 0.857 amps. What resistors did they use and what was the total resistance in the circuit?

5. A lab group was asked to create two circuits with two 1.5-volt batteries. They are given three 1-ohm resistors and two 5-ohm resistors.
   a. The first circuit should have the highest possible current without creating a short circuit. Which resistor(s) should they use and what will the current in the circuit be?
   b. The second circuit should have a current of exactly 1 amp. Which resistor(s) should they use?
6. A circuit breaker in your house is set for 15 amps. You have plugged in a coffeemaker that uses 10 amps. You want to plug in four more things. Which of the four items will cause the circuit breaker to trip because the current is too high?
   a. A light that uses 1 amp.
   b. A can opener that uses 2 amps.
   c. A mixer that uses 6 amps.
   d. An electric knife that uses 1.5 amps.
7. Which of the following statements are **true** about the circuit drawn?

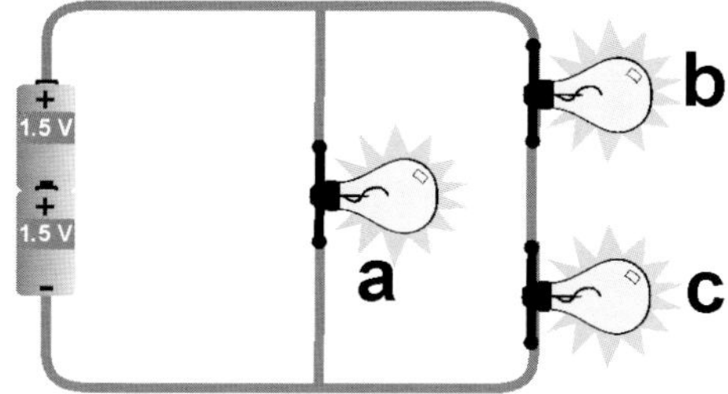

   a. Bulb **a** is brighter than bulb **b** or bulb **c**.
   b. Bulb **a** is dimmer than bulb **b** or bulb **c**.
   c. Bulb **b** is the same brightness as bulb **c**.
   d. Bulb **c** is brighter than bulb **b**.
8. Shown below is a parallel circuit with three branches. Branch 1 contains a 1-ohm resistor, branch 2 contains a 2-ohm resistor, and branch 3 contains a 3-ohm resistor. The circuit is powered by one 9-volt battery.

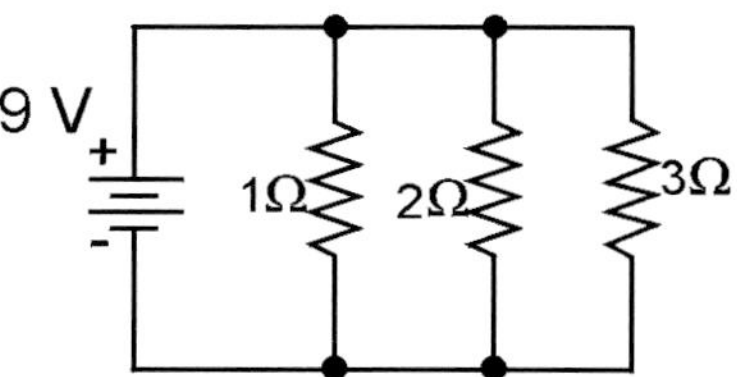

   a. Use Ohm's law to calculate the current in each branch of the circuit.
   b. Use Kirchhoff's current law to calculate the total current in the circuit.
   c. It is possible to replace all three resistors with a single resistor and have the total current in the circuit be the same. Use Ohm's law to calculate what the value of the single resistor should be to keep the total current the same.
   d. If someone were to add a fourth branch (containing a 4-ohm resistor) to the circuit, would the total current of the circuit decrease, increase, or stay the same?
9. Two 1.5-volt batteries are used to connect the circuit below.

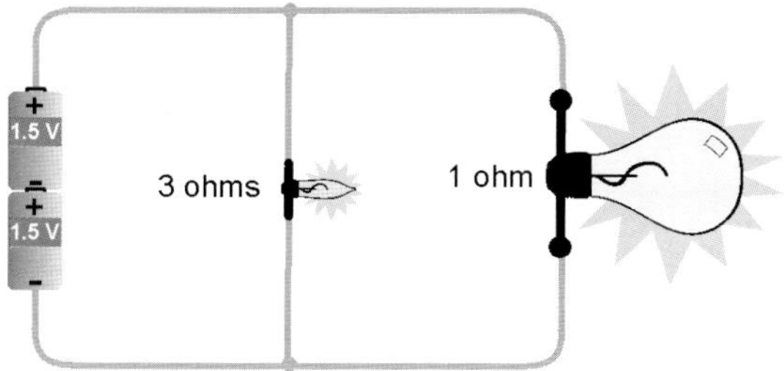

   a. What is the total current in the circuit?
   b. Which bulb uses more current?

10. If one bulb is removed from the circuit below, the other bulbs will:

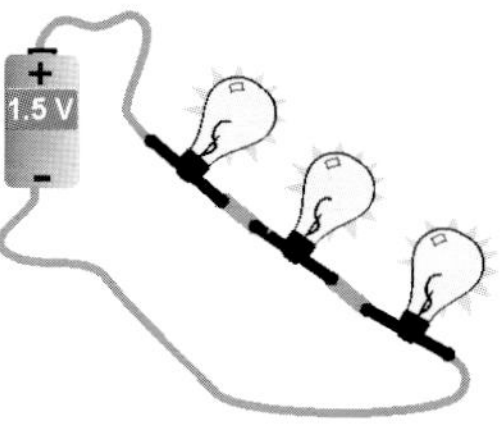

a. get brighter.

b. go out.

c. get dimmer.

d. stay at the same brightness.

11. The resistance of each of the three bulbs in the circuit below is:

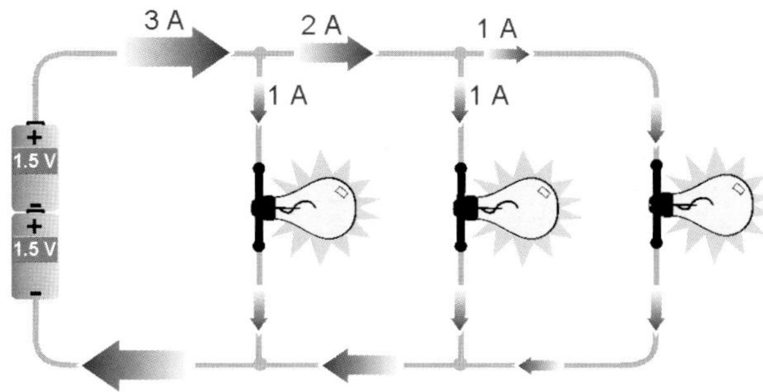

a. 1 ohm.

b. 2 ohms.

c. 6 ohms.

d. 3 ohms.

Applying your knowledge

1. In an automobile, the warning bell turns on if you open the door while the key is in the ignition. The bell also turns on if you open the door while the headlights are on. A single circuit with three switches and a bell can be built to ring in both cases. One switch is attached to the door, one switch is attached to the ignition, and one switch is attached to the headlights. Figure out what circuit would make the bell ring at the right times and build or draw your circuit.
2. A burglar alarm system has switches in each door and window. If the door or window is opened, the switch opens a circuit. Draw a circuit that uses one battery and one light bulb to check five doors and windows. The bulb should go out if any of the five doors or windows is opened.

UNIT 3

Electricity and Magnetism

Chapter 10

Magnets and Motors

Introduction to Chapter 10

Electricity and magnetism are related to each other. As you will learn in this chapter, the interactions between electricity and magnetism are the core of many important technologies, from the generation of electricity to recording data on computer disks.

Investigations for Chapter 10

10.1	**Permanent Magnets**	*What effects do magnets have?*

Like charges, magnets exert forces on each other. Every magnet has two distinct ends, called the north pole and the south pole. In this Investigation, you will explore how magnets affect each other, and discover which materials are attracted to magnets.

10.2	**Electromagnets**	*Can electric current create a magnet?*

In this Investigation, you will build an electromagnet and measure the electromagnet's strength as the current is varied.

10.3	**Electric Motors and Generators**	*How does an electric motor or generator work?*

In this Investigation, you will design and build different electric motors and evaluate them for speed and electric power. You will also build and test several designs of an electric generator.

Learning Goals

In this chapter, you will:

- ✔ Describe the properties of a permanent magnet.
- ✔ Describe the forces that magnets exert on other.
- ✔ Explain why materials like iron and steel are attracted to magnets.
- ✔ Explain why a compass points north.
- ✔ Build an electromagnet.
- ✔ Analyze how electric current affects the strength of the magnetic field in an electromagnet.
- ✔ List three ways that the strength of an electromagnet can be increased.
- ✔ Compare permanent magnets and electromagnets.
- ✔ List several applications of electromagnets.
- ✔ Explain electromagnetic induction.
- ✔ Describe how electric motors and generators work.

Vocabulary

electromagnet	magnetic field	magnetic north pole
electromagnetic induction	magnetic field intensity	magnetic south pole
generator	magnetic force	permanent magnet

10.1 Permanent Magnets

What effects do magnets have, both on each other and on other materials? What is magnetic force? What is a magnetic field? In this section you will learn about magnets, magnetic forces, and the magnetic field.

What is a magnet?

A magnet is a material that is magnetic

Magnetism has fascinated people since the earliest times. Up until the Renaissance, many people thought magnetism was a form of life-force since it could make rocks move. We know that magnets stick to refrigerators and pick up paper clips or pins. They are also part of electric motors, computer disc drives, burglar alarm systems, and many other common devices.

What does magnetic mean?

Magnetic means the ability to make forces on magnets or other magnetic materials. Some materials are actively magnetic, and we call them magnets. Other materials are attracted to nearby magnets but do not show magnetism otherwise. Iron and steel are in the second category because they are attracted by magnets but are not themselves magnetic.

Permanent magnets

A **permanent magnet** is a material that keeps its magnetic properties, even when it is not close to other magnets. Bar magnets, refrigerator magnets, and horseshoe magnets are good examples of permanent magnets.

Bar magnet

Horseshoe magnet

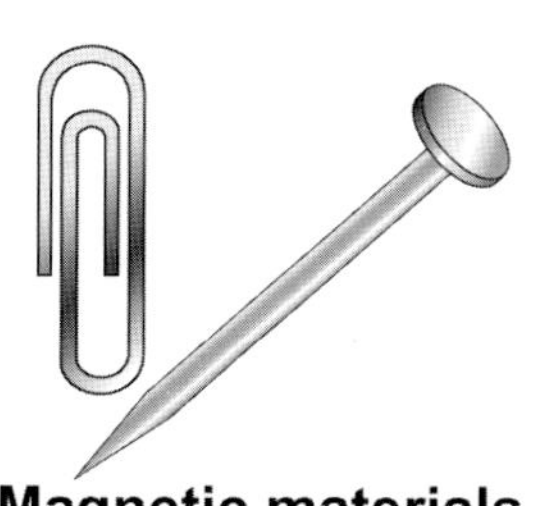

Magnetic materials

How a computer disc works

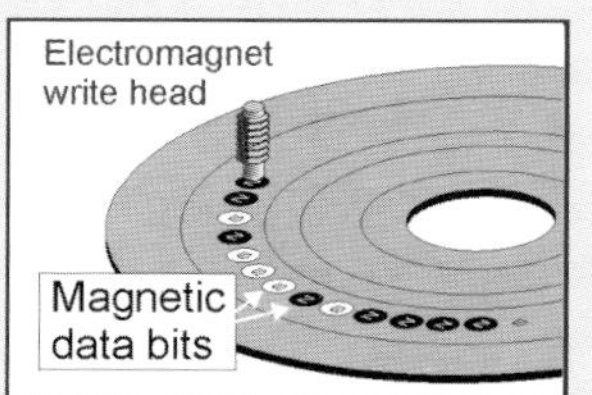

Computer discs are coated with a material that can become magnetized by tiny electromagnets. By pulsing on and off, an *electromagnet* writes data by creating tiny north and south poles in the surface of the disc.

When reading data, a second electromagnet senses the north and south poles from the spinning disc. When a north pole changes to a south pole, these changes are converted to binary numbers used in programs and data.

A strong magnet can change the north and south poles on a disc surface. This removes the data just like an eraser removes pencil marks.

Properties of magnets

Magnets have common properties

All magnets have the following common properties:

- Magnets always have two opposite "poles," called north and south.
- If divided, each part of a magnet has both north and south poles; we never see an unpaired north or south pole.
- When near each other, magnets exert magnetic forces on each other.
- The forces between magnets depend on the alignment of the poles; two unlike poles will attract each other and two like poles will repel each other.

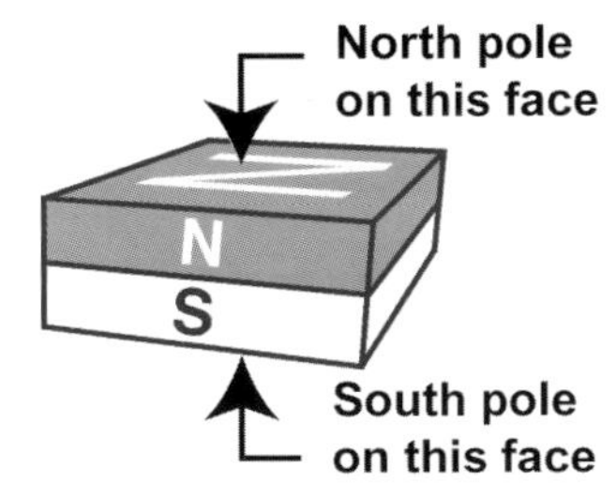

Figure 10.1: *The north and south poles of a small rectangular magnet.*

Why magnets attract a paperclip

The fact that magnets exert forces on each other explains why a permanent bar magnet is able to pick up a paperclip. When near the magnet, the paperclip becomes a temporary magnet. The two magnets are then attracted to each other. This magnetic force is so strong it easily overcomes the gravitational force that would otherwise cause the paperclip to fall down.

Exceptional scientists: Michael Faraday

Michael Faraday was born in London in 1791. After basic schooling, Faraday worked as a bookbinder and became very good at it. In fact, some of the books he bound are still in existence today!

Faraday often read the books he bound. From these books, he became interested in science and began to repeat the experiments that he read about. He was particularly interested in electricity and chemistry. At age 21, he decided to pursue further education in science.

At the age of 30, Faraday made his first electrical discovery. He then went on to became one of the great scientists of his time. He invented early motors using *electromagnets* (you will study these in the next section) and made many other discoveries in physics and chemistry.

Faraday loved to show children demonstrations of the exciting experiments of his day. He gave his demonstrations during an annual Christmas lecture at the Royal Institution where he worked. This tradition is still carried on today, and is televised. If you ever go to London you can still see Faraday's laboratory at the Royal Institution's museum.

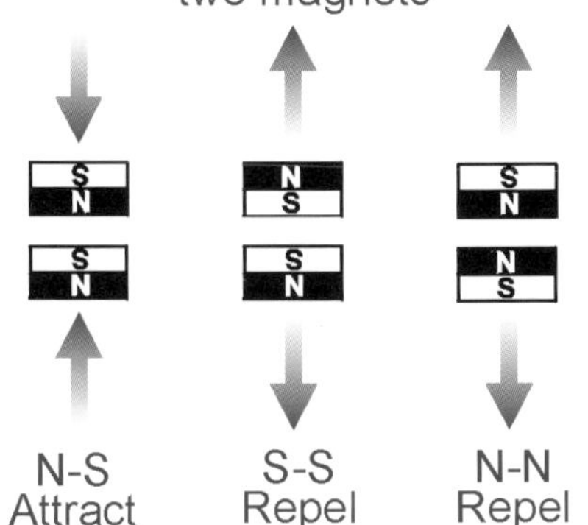

Figure 10.2: *Depending on their position, two magnets can either attract each other or repel each other.*

Discovering and using magnetism

Natural materials are magnetic

As early as 500 B.C. people discovered that some naturally occurring materials have magnetic properties. These materials include *lodestone* and *magnetite.* Ptolemy Philadelphos (367-283 B.C.) plated the entire surface of a temple in Egypt with magnetite, a magnetic mineral capable of attracting iron. He was hoping to suspend a statue of himself in midair!

Lodestone

In about 500 B.C., the Greeks discovered that a stone called lodestone had special properties. They observed that one end of a suspended piece of lodestone pointed north and the other end pointed south, helping sailors and travelers to find their way. This discovery was the first important application of magnetism, the *compass*.

The Chinese "south pointer"

The invention of the compass is also recorded in China, in 220 B.C. Writings from the Zheng dynasty tell stories of how people would use a "south pointer" when they went out to search for jade, so that they wouldn't lose their way home. The pointer was made of lodestone. It looked like a large spoon with a short, skinny handle. When balanced on a plate, the "handle" was aligned with magnetic south.

The first iron needle compass

By 1088 A.D., iron refining had developed to the point where the Chinese were making a small needle-like compass. Shen Kua recorded that a needle-shaped magnet was placed on a reed floating in a bowl of water. Chinese inventors also suspended a long, thin magnet in the air, realizing in both cases that the magnet ends were aligned with geographic north and south. Explorers from the Sung dynasty sailed their trading ships all the way to Saudi Arabia using compasses among their navigational tools. About 100 years later a similar design appeared in Europe and soon spread to the rest of the region.

The compass allows explorers to sail away from land

By 1200, explorers from Italy were using a compass to guide ocean voyages beyond the sight of land. The Chinese also continued exploring with compasses, and by the 1400s, they were traveling to the eastern coast of Africa. The compass, and the voyages that it made possible, led to many interactions among cultures.

1820 A.D. Principle of electromagnetism discovered
1200 A.D. Italian explorers use compass to sail open ocean
1183 A.D. Modern compass appears
1088 A.D. Iron compass needle made in China
220 B.C. South pointing lodestone compass made in China
500 B.C. Lodestone discovered in Greece

Figure 10.3: *Timeline of the discovery of lodestone and the development of the modern compass.*

How does a compass work?

The north pole of a magnet points north

A compass needle is a magnet that is free to spin until it lines up in the north-south direction. The origin of the terms "north pole" and "south pole" of a magnet come from the direction that a magnetized compass needle points. The end of the magnet that pointed north was called the north pole of the magnet and the end that pointed south was called the south pole.

Remember that two unlike poles of a magnet attract each other. So the north pole of the compass needle must point north because it is attracted by the south pole of another magnet. Where is this other magnet?

Figure 10.4: *A Chinese compass dating from 220 B.C., made of lodestone. The "handle" of the spoon points south.*

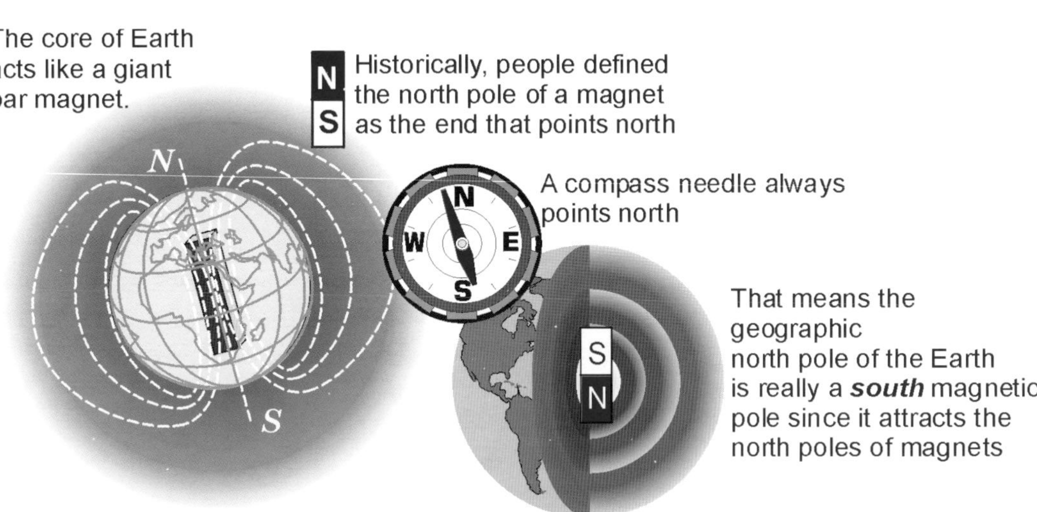

The core of Earth acts like a giant bar magnet.
N
S
Historically, people defined the north pole of a magnet as the end that points north
A compass needle always points north
N
W
E
S
That means the geographic north pole of the Earth is really a ***south*** magnetic pole since it attracts the north poles of magnets
N
S
S
N

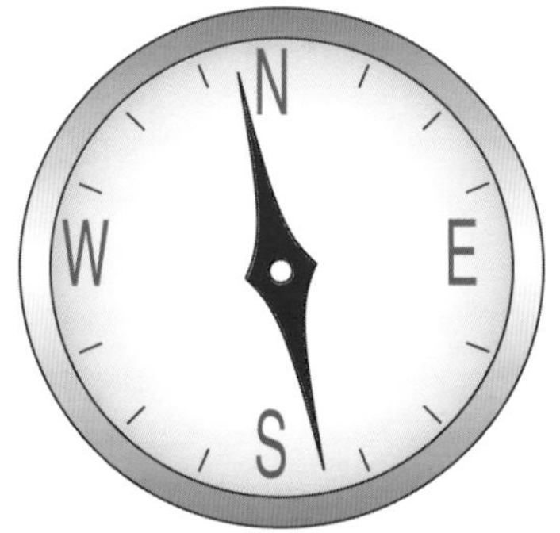

Figure 10.5: *A modern compass.*

The center of the Earth is a large magnet

It turns out that the core of our planet acts like a large magnet made of molten iron ores. This giant magnet is roughly aligned in the north-south direction. When the compass needle's north pole swings towards the *geographic north pole*, it is actually attracted by the *magnetic south pole* of Earth. The Earth's magnetic south pole is within a few degrees of geographic north!

The magnetic field

Why the magnetic field is a useful concept People investigating magnetism needed a way to describe the forces between two magnets. They knew that the force depended on the direction and orientation of the two magnets and also on the distance between them. The model of a magnetic field was developed to describe how a magnet exerts magnetic force.

Imagine testing one magnet with another Imagine you have a small test magnet (figure 10.6) that you are moving around another magnet (the source magnet). The north pole of your test magnet feels a force everywhere in the space around the source magnet. To keep track of the force, imagine drawing an arrow in the direction your test magnet is pulled as you move it around.

What is a field? The arrows that you draw show you the magnetic field. If you connect all the arrows from north to south, you get lines called *magnetic field lines*. In physics, the word "field" means that there is a quantity (such as force) that is associated with every point in space. There can be many other kinds of fields. For example, the "odor field" near a sewer would be strongest nearest the sewer and get weaker farther away!

The magnetic field How do you interpret a drawing of a magnetic field? The number of field lines in a certain area indicates the relative strength of the source magnet in that area. The arrows on the field lines show where the north pole of a test magnet will point. Figure 10.7 shows the magnetic field lines around a small rectangular magnet.

Magnets interact through their fields It is useful to think about the interactions between two magnets in two steps.

- First, every magnet creates an energy field, called the magnetic field, in the space around it.
- Second, the field (not the magnet directly) exerts forces on any other magnet that is within its range.

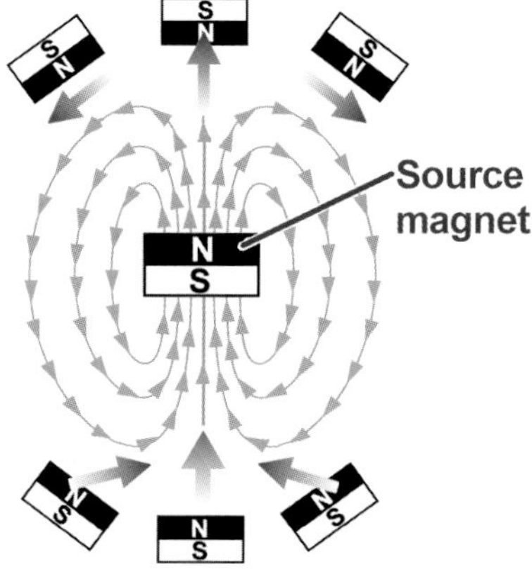

Figure 10.6: *The magnetic field is defined in terms of the force exerted on the north pole of another magnet.*

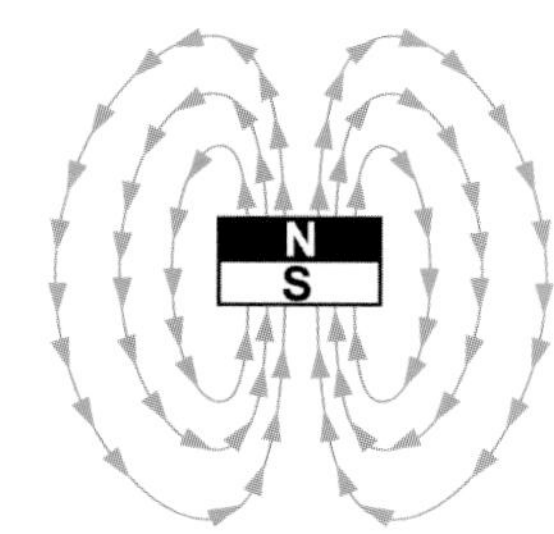

Figure 10.7: *Magnetic field lines around a magnet.*

10.2 Electromagnets

In the last section you learned about permanent magnets and magnetism. There is another type of magnet, one that is created by electric current. This type of magnet is called an electromagnet. What is an electromagnet? Why do magnets and electromagnets act the same way? In this section, you learn about electromagnets and how they helped scientists explain all magnetism.

What is an electromagnet?

Searching for a connection For a long time, people thought about electricity and magnetism as different and unrelated effects. Starting about the 18th century, scientists suspected that the two were related. As scientists began to understand electricity better, they searched for relationships between electricity and magnetism.

The principle of an electromagnet In 1819, Hans Christian Øersted, the Danish physicist and chemist (1777-1851), noticed that a current in a wire caused a compass needle to deflect. He had discovered that moving electric charges create a magnetic field! A dedicated teacher, he made this discovery while teaching his students at the University of Copenhagen. He suspected there might be an effect and did the experiment for the very first time in front of his class. With his discovery, Øersted was the first to identify the principle of an electromagnet.

How to make an electromagnet Electromagnets are magnets that are created when there is electric current flowing in a wire. The simplest electromagnet uses a coil of wire, often wrapped around some iron (figure 10.8). Because iron is magnetic, it concentrates the magnetic field created by the current in the coil.

The north and south poles of an electromagnet The north and south poles of an electromagnet are located at each end of the coil (figure 10.8). Which end is the north pole depends on the direction of the electric current. When your fingers curl in the direction of current, your thumb points toward the magnet's north pole. This method of finding the magnetic poles is called the *right hand rule* (figure 10.9). You can switch north and south by reversing the direction of the current. This is a great advantage over permanent magnets. You can't easily change the poles of a permanent magnet.

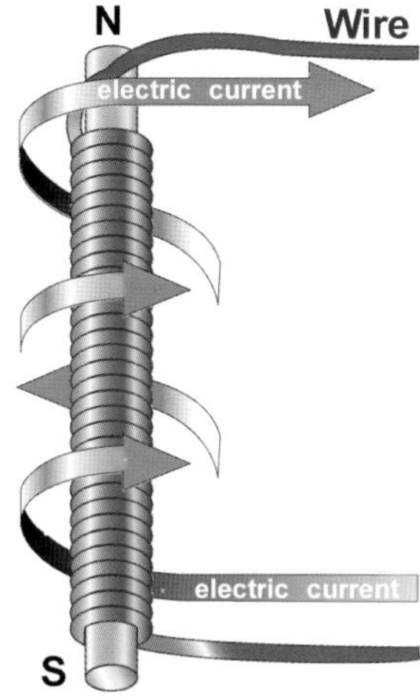

Figure 10.8: *The simplest electromagnet uses a coil of wire, often wrapped around some iron or steel. In the picture, the arrows indicate the direction of current.*

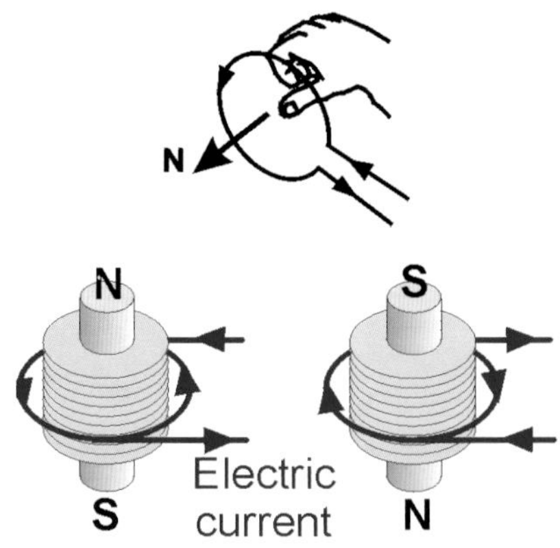

Figure 10.9: *The right hand rule: When your fingers curl in the direction of current, your thumb points toward the magnet's north pole.*

Applications of electromagnets

Current controls an electromagnet

By changing the amount of current, you can easily change the strength of an electromagnet or even turn its magnetism on and off. Electromagnets can also be much stronger than permanent magnets because the electric current can be large. For these reasons, electromagnets are used in many applications.

Magnetically levitated trains

Magnetically levitated (abbreviated to maglev) train technology uses electromagnetic force to lift a train a few inches above its track (figure 10.10). By "floating" the train on a powerful magnetic field, the friction between wheels and rails is eliminated. Maglev trains achieve high speeds using less power than a normal train. In 1999, in Japan, a prototype five-car maglev train carrying 15 passengers reached a world-record speed of 552 kilometers (343 miles) per hour. Maglev trains are now being developed and tested in Germany, Japan, and the United States.

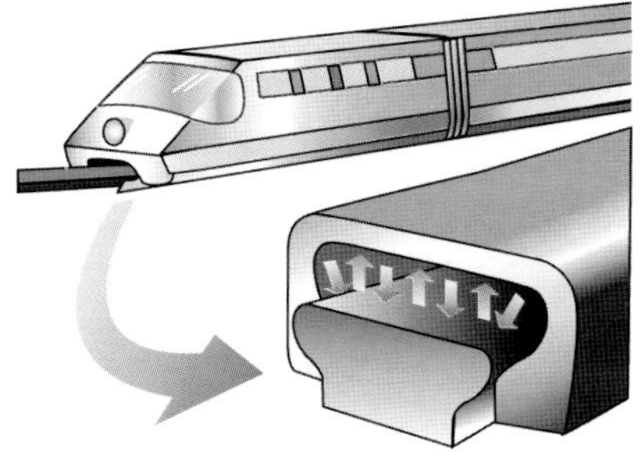

Figure 10.10: *A maglev train track has electromagnets in it that both lift the train and pull it forward.*

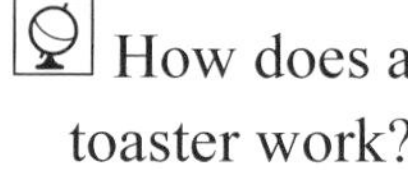

How does a toaster work?

The sliding switch on a toaster does several things: First, it turns the heating circuit on. Secondly, it activates an electromagnet that then attracts a spring-loaded metal tray to the bottom of the toaster. When a timing device signals that the bread has been toasting long enough, current to the electromagnet is cut off. This releases the spring-loaded tray that then pushes up on the bread so that it pops out of the toaster.

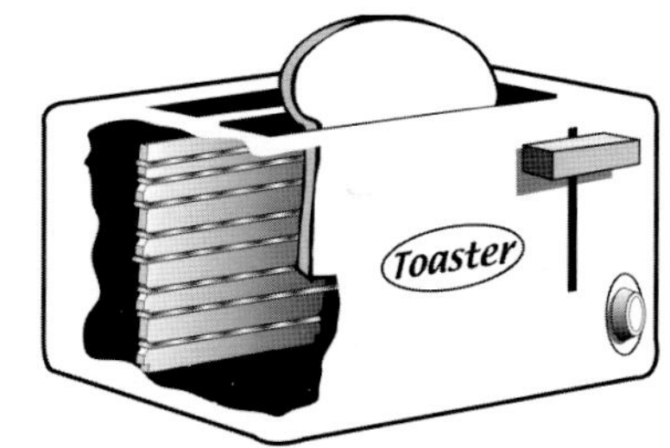

Figure 10.11: *A toaster tray is pulled down by an electromagnet while bread is toasting. When the toast is done, current is cut off and the tray pops up. The cutaway shows the heating element -- nichrome wires wrapped around a sheet of mica.*

How does an electric doorbell work?

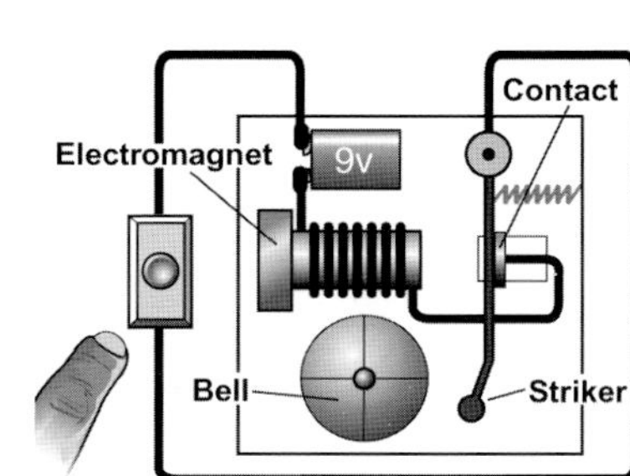

A doorbell contains an electromagnet. When the button of the bell is pushed, it sends current through the electromagnet. The electromagnet attracts a piece of metal called the striker. The striker moves towards the electromagnet but hits a bell that is in the way. The movement of the striker away from the contact also breaks the circuit after it hits the bell. A spring pulls the striker back and reconnects the circuit. If your finger is still on the button, the cycle starts over again and the bell keeps ringing.

Building an electromagnet

Make an electromagnet from wire and a nail

You can easily build an electromagnet from wire and a piece of iron, such as a nail. Wrap the wire in many turns around the nail and connect a battery as shown in figure 10.12. When current flows in the wire, the nail becomes a magnet. Use the right hand rule to figure out which end of the nail is the north pole and which is the south pole. To reverse north and south, reverse the connection to the battery, making the current flow the opposite way.

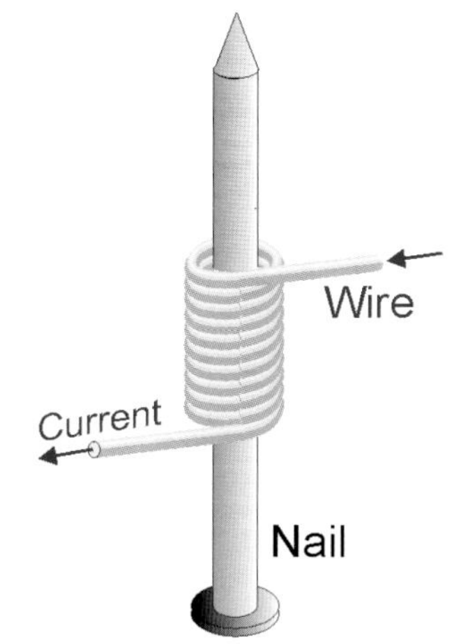

Figure 10.12: *Making an electromagnet from a nail and wire.*

Increase the strength of an electromagnet

You might expect that more current would make an electromagnet stronger. You would be right, but there are two ways to increase the current.

1 You can apply more voltage by adding a second battery.

2 You can add more turns of wire around the nail.

Why adding turns works

The second method works because the magnetism in your electromagnet comes from the *total* amount of current flowing *around* the nail. If there is 1 amp of current in the wire, each loop of wire adds 1 amp to the total amount that flows around the nail. Ten loops of 1 amp each make 10 total amps flowing around. By adding more turns, you use the same current over and over to get stronger magnetism.

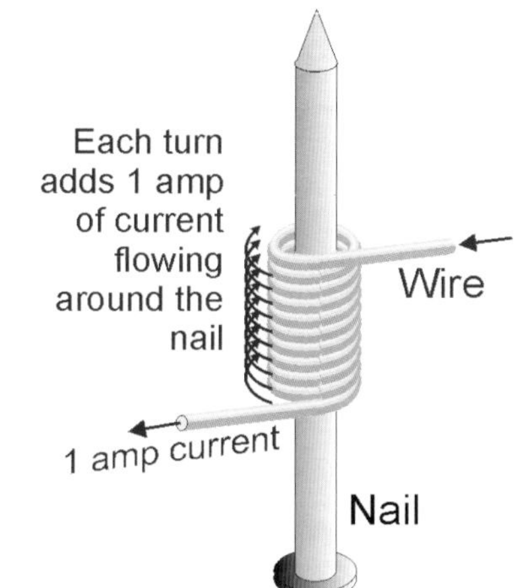

Figure 10.13: *Adding turns of wire increases the total current flowing around the electromagnet. The total current in all the turns is what determines the strength of the electromagnet.*

More turns also means more resistance

Of course, nothing comes for free. By adding more turns you also increase the resistance of your coil. Increasing the resistance makes the current a little lower and generates more heat. A good electromagnet is a balance between too much resistance and having enough turns to get a strong enough magnet.

Factors affecting the force

The magnetic force exerted by a simple electromagnet depends on three factors:

- The amount of electric current in the wire
- The amount of iron or steel in the electromagnet's core
- The number of turns in the coil

In more sophisticated electromagnets, the shape, size, material in the core and winding pattern of the coil also have an effect on the strength of the magnetic field produced.

The relationship between permanent magnets and electromagnets

Electric currents cause all magnetism

Why do permanent magnets and electromagnets act the same way? The discovery of electromagnets helped scientists to determine why magnetism exists. Electric current through loops of wire creates an electromagnet. Atomic-scale electric currents create a permanent magnet.

Electrons move, creating small loops of current

Remember, atoms contain two types of charged particles, protons (positive) and electrons (negative). The charged electrons in atoms behave like small loops of current. These small loops of current mean that atoms themselves act like tiny electromagnets with north and south poles!

We don't usually see the magnetism from atoms for two reasons.

1 Atoms are very tiny and the magnetism from a single atom is far too small to detect without very sensitive instruments.

2 The alignment of the atomic north and south poles changes from one atom to the next. On average the atomic magnets cancel each other out (figure 10.14).

How permanent magnets work

If all the atomic magnets are lined up in a similar direction, the magnetism of each atom adds to that of its neighbors and we observe magnetic properties on a large scale. This is what makes a permanent magnet. On average, permanent magnets have the magnetic fields of individual atoms aligned in a similar direction.

Why iron always attracts magnets and never repels them

In magnetic materials (like iron) the atoms are free to rotate and align their individual north and south poles. If you bring the north pole of a magnet near iron, the south poles of all the iron atoms are attracted. Because they are free to move, the iron near your magnet becomes a south pole and it attracts your magnet.

If you bring a south pole near iron, the opposite happens. The iron atoms nearest your magnet align themselves to make a north pole, which also attracts your magnet. This is why magnetic materials like iron always attract your magnet, and never repel, regardless of whether your test magnet approaches with its north or south pole.

Non-magnetic materials

The atoms in non-magnetic materials, like plastic, are not free to move and change their magnetic orientation. That is why most objects are not affected by magnets.

Nonmagnetic material

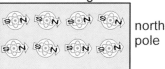

Permanent magnet

south pole

north pole

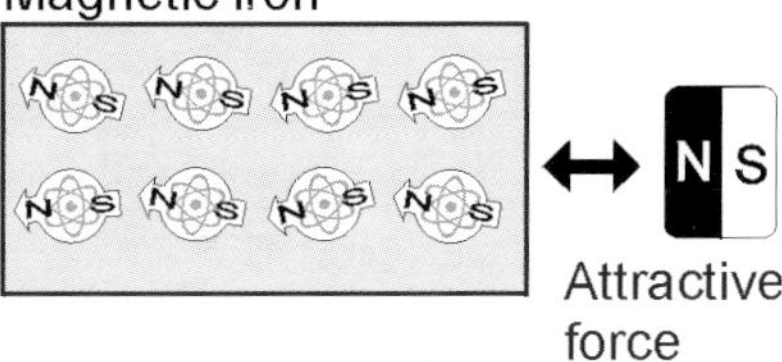

Figure 10.14: *Atoms act like tiny magnets. Permanent magnets have their atoms partially aligned, creating the magnetic forces we observe.*

The magnetic properties of iron occur because iron atoms can easily adjust their orientation in response to an outside magnetic field.

10.3 Electric Motors and Generators

Permanent magnets and electromagnets work together to make electric motors and generators. In this section you will learn about how a real electric motor works. The secret is in the ability of an electromagnet to reverse form north to south. By changing the direction of electric current, the electromagnet changes from attract to repel, and spins the motor! Electric motors convert electrical energy into mechanical energy.

Using magnets to spin a disk

Imagine a spinning disk with magnets

Imagine you have a disk that can spin. Around the edge of the disk are magnets. You have cleverly arranged the magnets so they alternate north and south. Figure 10.15 shows a picture of your rotating disk.

How to make the disk spin

To make your disk spin, you bring a magnet near the edge. The magnet attracts one of the magnets in the disk and repels the next one. These forces make the disk spin a little way (figure 10.15)

Reversing the magnet is the key

To keep the disk spinning, you need to reverse the magnet in your fingers as soon as each magnet comes by. This way you first attract a magnet, then reverse your magnet to repel it away again. You make the disk spin by using your magnet to alternately attract and repel the magnets on the disk.

Knowing when to reverse the magnet

The disk is called the *rotor* because it can rotate. The key to making the rotor spin smoothly is to reverse your magnet when the disk is at the right place. You want the reversal to happen just as a magnet passes by. If you reverse too early, you will repel the magnet in the rotor backwards before it reaches your magnet. If you reverse too late, you attract the magnet backwards after it has passed. For it to work best, you need to change your magnet from north to south just as the magnet on the rotor passes by.

First you repel magnet A and attract magnet B

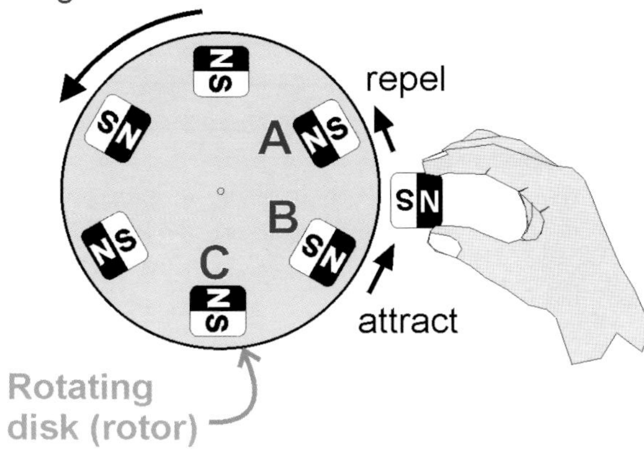

Reverse your magnet to repel magnet B and attract magnet C.

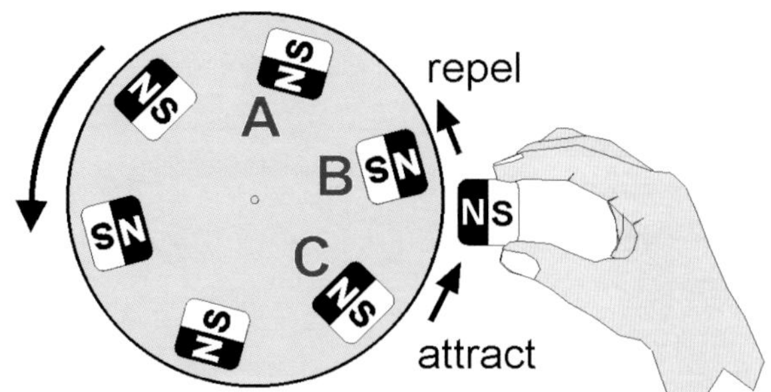

Figure 10.15: *Using a single magnet to spin a disk of magnets. Reversing the magnet in your fingers attracts and repels the magnets in the rotor, making it spin.*

Using electricity to reverse the magnet

How electromagnets are used in electric motors

The spinning disk of magnets is like the rotor of a real electric motor. In a real electric motor, the magnet you reversed with your fingers becomes an electromagnet. The switch from north to south is done by reversing the electric current in a coil. The sketch below shows how the electromagnets switch to make the rotor keep turning.

First the electromagnet repels magnet A and attracts magnet B

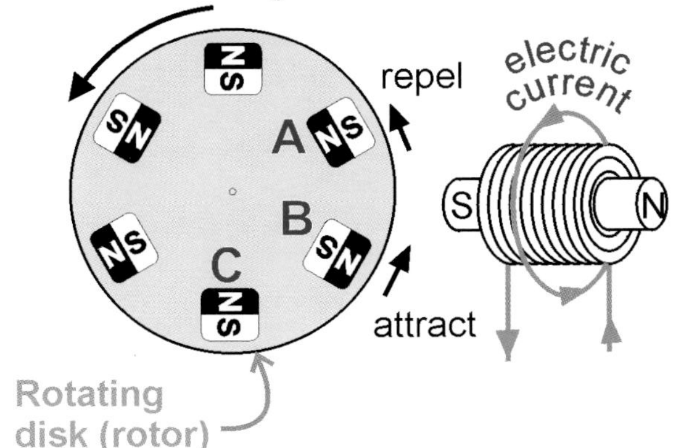

Then the electromagnet switches so it repels magnet B and attracts magnet C.

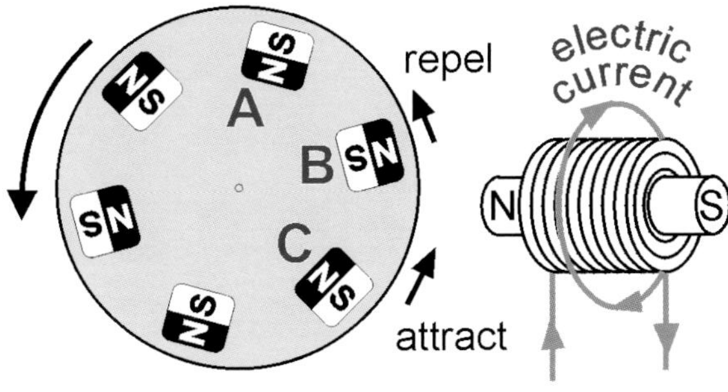

Figure 10.16: *There are electric motors all around you, even where you don't see them. The heating system in your house or school uses electric motors to move hot air or water to heat rooms.*

The commutator is a kind of switch

Just as with the finger magnet, the electromagnet must switch from north to south as each rotor magnet passes by to keep the rotor turning. The switch that makes this happen is called a *commutator*. As the rotor spins, the commutator switches the direction of current in the electromagnet. This makes the electromagnet change from north to south, and back again. The electromagnet attracts and repels the magnets in the rotor, and the motor turns.

The three things you need to make a motor

All types of electric motors must have three things to work. The three things are:

1. A rotating element (rotor) with magnets.
2. A stationary magnet that surrounds the rotor.
3. A commutator that switches the electromagnets from north to south at the right place to keep the rotor spinning.

How a battery-powered electric motor works

Inside a small electric motor

If you take apart an electric motor that runs from batteries, it doesn't look like the motor you built in the lab. But the same three mechanisms are still there. The difference is in the arrangement of the electromagnets and permanent magnets. The picture below shows a small battery-powered electric motor and what it looks like inside with one end of the motor case removed. The permanent magnets are on the outside, and they stay fixed in place.

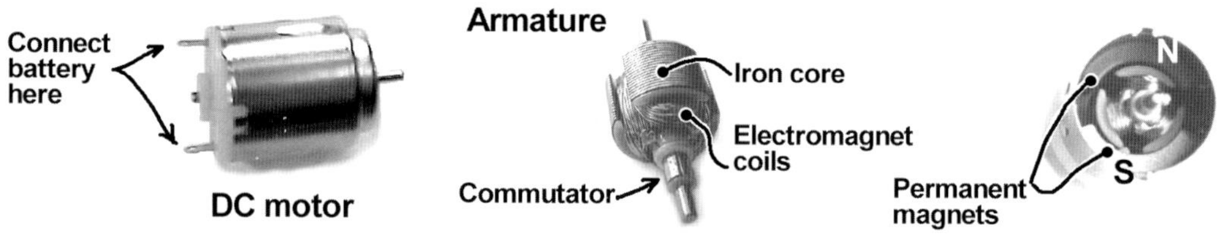

Electromagnets and the armature

The electromagnets are in the rotor, and they turn. The rotating part of the motor, including the electromagnets, is called the *armature*. The armature in the picture has three electromagnets, corresponding to the three coils (A, B, and C) in the sketch below.

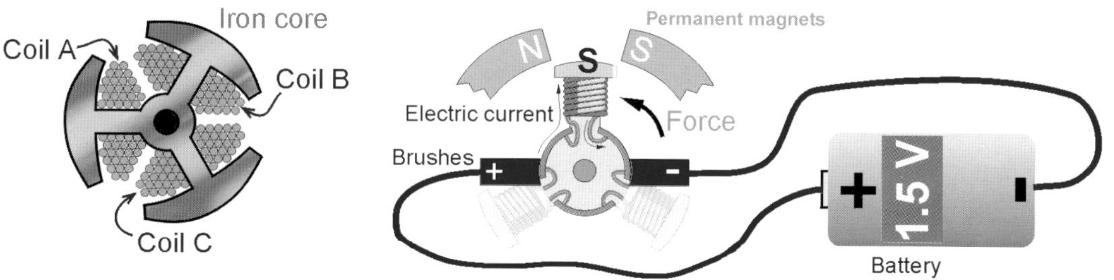

How the switching happens

The wires from each of the three coils are attached to three metal plates (commutator) at the end of the armature. As the rotor spins, the three plates come into contact with the positive and negative *brushes*. Electric current flows through the brushes into the coils. As the motor turns, the plates rotate past the brushes, switching the electromagnets from north to south by reversing the positive and negative connections to the coils. The turning electromagnets are attracted and repelled by the permanent magnets and the motor turns.

AC and DC motors

Almost all the electric motors you find around your house use AC electricity. Remember, AC means alternating current, so the current switches back and forth as it comes out of the wall socket. This makes it easier to build motors.

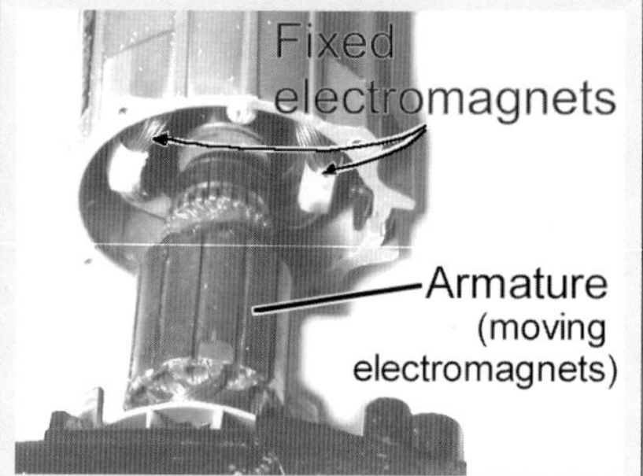

Most AC motors use electromagnets for the rotating magnets on the armature, and also for the stationary magnets around the outside. The attract-repel switching happens in both sets of electromagnets.

Electromagnetic force and electromagnetic induction

Electromagnetic force Both electrical force and magnetic force exist between electric charges. Scientists now believe both forces are two aspects of one force, the electromagnetic force.

Electromagnetic induction Many laws in physics display an elegant kind of symmetry. This symmetry is seen in the interactions between magnetism and electricity. A current through a wire creates a magnet. The reverse is also true: If you move a magnet through a coil of wire, then electric current is created. This process is called electromagnetic induction (figure 10.17) because a moving magnet *induces* electric current to flow.

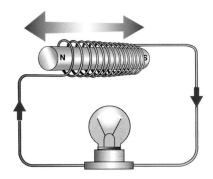

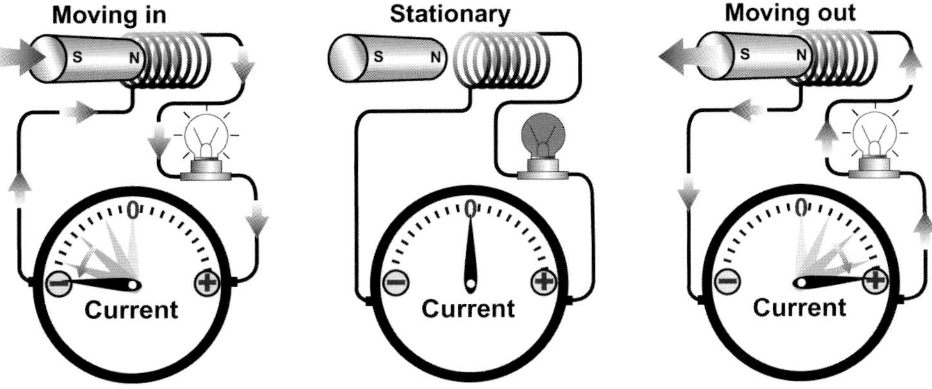

Moving magnets make current flow When a magnet moves into a coil of wire, it induces electric current to flow in the coil (diagram above). The current stops if the magnet stops moving. If you pull the magnet back out again, the current flows in the opposite direction. A changing magnetic field is what makes the electricity flow. If the magnetic field does not change, no electricity flows. As you might expect, the faster we make the magnetic field change, the greater the amount of electric current we generate.

Induction and energy transformations Electromagnetic induction enables us to transform mechanical energy (moving magnets) into electrical energy. Any machine that causes magnets to move past wire coils generates electric currents. These machines include giant electric power plants and computer disk drives. Tiny sensors on the disk drive read data on a magnetic disk by looking at the pulses of current that are generated as a high-speed disk spins past the coil of wire in the drive's sensor head (figure 10.18).

Figure 10.17: *Electromagnetic induction: Moving a magnet in loops of wire generates current in the wire.*

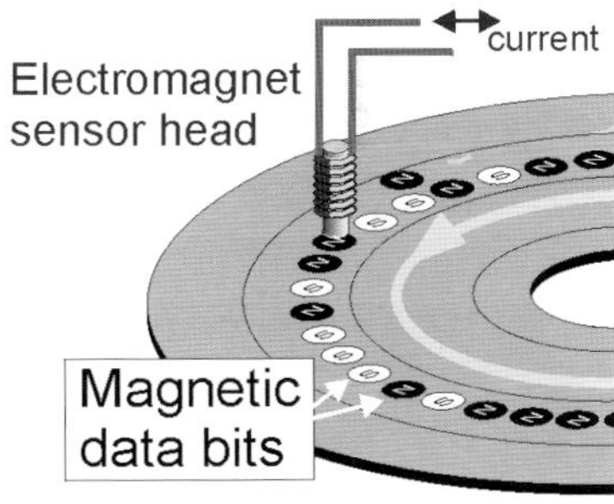

Figure 10.18: *A computer hard drive uses induction to read data from the magnetic writing on a spinning disk.*

Generating electricity

What is a generator? Power plants use electromagnetic induction to create electricity. A generator is a combination of mechanical and electrical systems that converts kinetic energy into electrical energy (figure 10.19).

Batteries are not powerful enough Although batteries can convert energy from chemical reactions into electrical energy, batteries are not practical for creating large amounts of electric current. Power plants, which supply current to homes and businesses, use generators.

How a generator works As an example of how the electricity is made, consider a disk with magnets in it (figure 10.20). As the disk rotates, first a north pole and then a south pole passes the coil. When the north pole is approaching, the current flows one way. When the north pole passes and a south pole approaches, the current flows the other way. As long as the disk is spinning, there is a changing magnetic field near the coil and electric current is induced to flow.

Generators make alternating current Because the magnetic field alternates from north to south as the disk spins, generators produce *alternating current* (AC). Alternating current is used in the electrical system in your home and school.

Energy is conserved The electrical energy created from a generator isn't free. You have to do work to turn the disk and make the electric current flow. Power plants contain a rotating machine called a *turbine*. The turbine is kept turning by a flow of air heated by gas, oil, coal, or nuclear energy. One kind of energy is transformed into another and energy is conserved. The energy stored in the gas, oil, coal, or nuclear fuel is transformed into the movement of the turning turbine, which is then transformed into electrical energy.

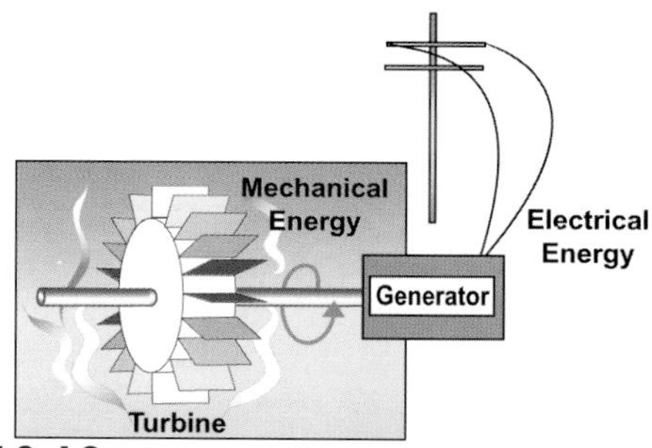

Figure 10.19: *A power plant generator contains a turbine that turns magnets inside loops of wire, generating electricity.*

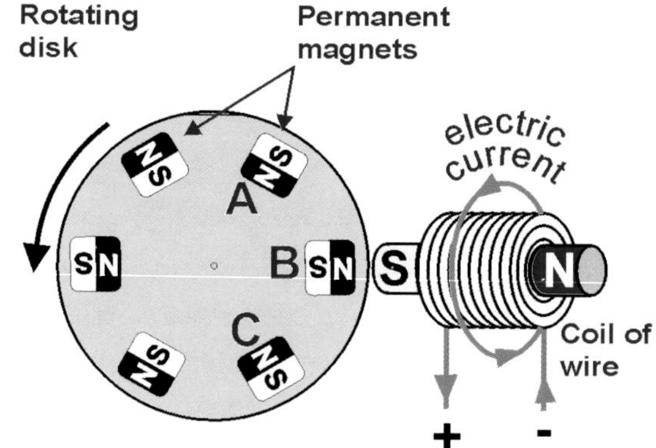

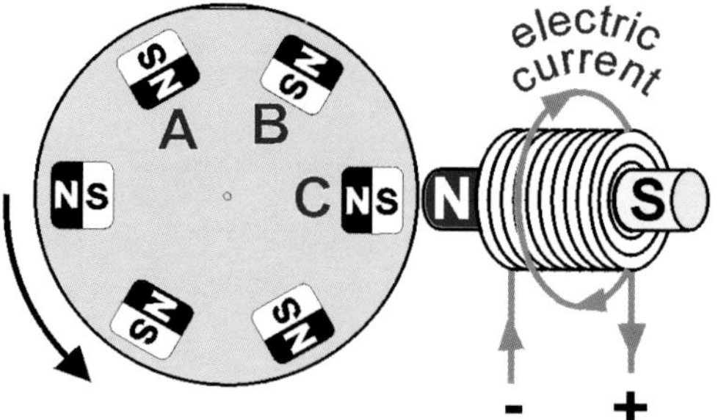

Figure 10.20: *How a generator works. In the top sketch the north pole on the disk induces a south pole in the electromagnet, causing current to flow one way. When the disk rotates, the magnetism in the coil is reversed, and the electric current generated also reverses.*

Chapter 10 Review

Vocabulary review

Match the following terms with the correct definition. There is one extra definition in the list that will not match any of the terms.

Set One	
1. permanent magnet	a. A naturally occurring magnetic material
2. magnetic north pole	b. A material that is magnetic; it has a north and a south pole, and interacts with other magnets
3. magnetic south pole	c. The large magnet located inside the Earth
4. magnetic forces	d. The end of a magnet that will point north if suspended in air near the surface of the Earth
5. lodestone	e. The end of a magnet that will point south if suspended in air near the surface of the Earth
	f. The forces that magnets exert on each other

Set Two	
1. compass	a. A device that uses electricity and magnets to turn electrical energy into rotating mechanical energy
2. magnetic field	b. The movement of electrons that causes them to act like tiny atomic magnets
3. electromagnet	c. A magnet that is created from current through a wire
4. electric motor	d. The part of an electric motor that switches the electromagnets from north to south
5. commutator	e. Magnets create this in the space around them and it exerts forces on other magnets
	f. A device that uses magnets to tell direction

Set Three	
1. generator	a. The process by which a moving magnet creates voltage and current in a loop of wire
2. electromagnetic force	b. A device to float a train above the track
3. electromagnetic induction	c. A mechanical wheel that might work with steam or water to turn a generator
4. alternating current	d. The force that exists between electric charges; often described as electrical force or magnetic force depending on how charges interact
5. turbine	e. Electrical current flowing back and forth
	f. A device that uses electromagnetic induction to make electricity

Concept review

1. Name two examples of naturally occurring magnetic materials.
2. What is the first known application of magnetism?
3. Explain the origin of the terms "north pole" and "south pole" used to describe the two ends of a magnet.
4. Explain why a compass points north.
5. Describe the types of forces that magnetic poles exert on each other.
6. What are three ways you can increase the strength of an electromagnet?
7. Explain why an electromagnet usually has a core of iron or steel.
8. Name two examples of machines that use electromagnets. Explain the purpose of the electromagnet in each machine.
9. In your own words, explain how atoms give rise to magnetic properties in certain materials.
10. Which picture shows the correct location of the north and south poles of the electromagnet? Choose A or B and explain how you arrived at your choice.

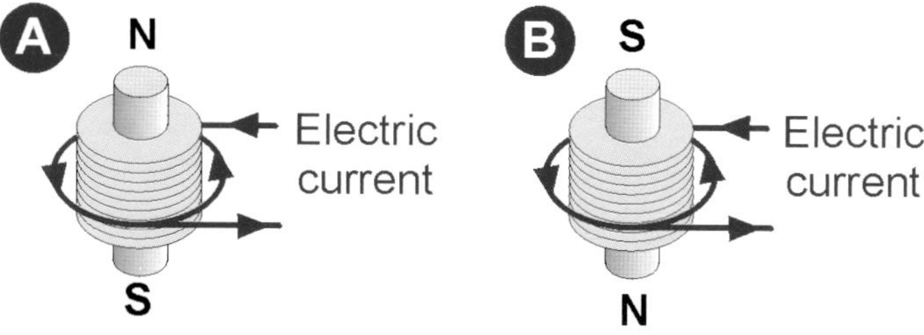

11. An electric generator is constructed that uses a rotating disk of magnets that spin past a coil of wire as shown in the diagram. Which of the following statements are TRUE?

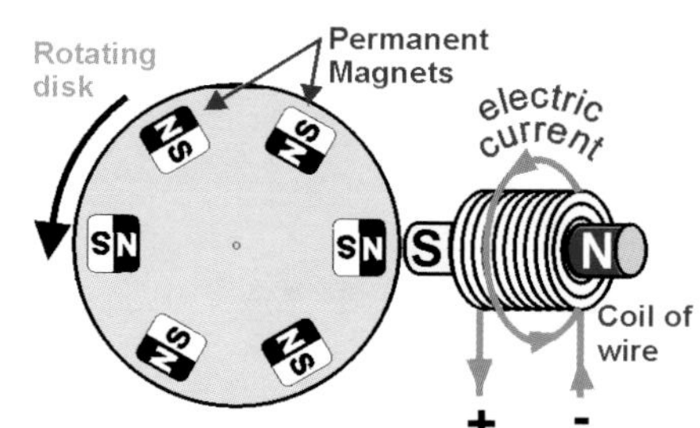

    a. Turning the disk 2 times faster generates 4 times as much electricity.
    b. Turning the disk 2 times faster generates 2 times as much electricity.
    c. Doubling the number of magnets generates 2 times as much electricity.
    d. Doubling the number of magnets and spinning twice as fast generates 4 times as much electricity.

12. The amount of electricity generated by a magnet moving through a coil of wire can be INCREASED by:
    a. Using a stronger magnet and holding the magnet stationary in the coil.
    b. Moving the magnet through the coil faster.
    c. Adding more turns of wire to the coil.
    d. Moving the magnet more slowly through the coil so the coil has time to feel the effects of the magnetic force.

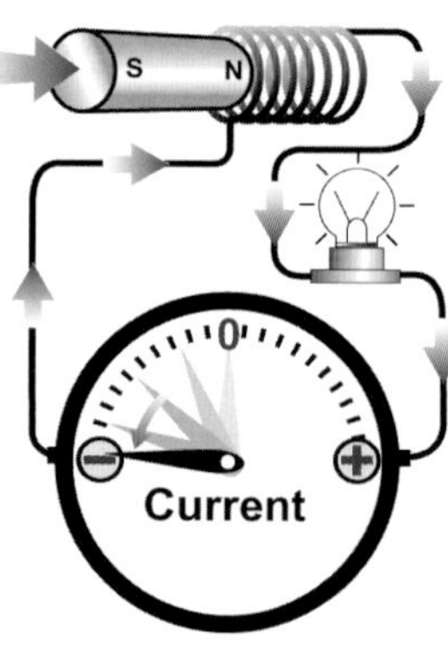

Problems

1. A student knocked a ceramic magnet off her desk and it shattered when it hit the floor. Copy the broken pieces and label the north and south poles on each one.

2. A student placed two magnets with opposite poles facing each other. He slowly brought the two magnets closer and observed the distance at they first interacted with each other. The student observed that one magnet could move the other at a distance of 33 millimeters.

    a. Next, he placed the two north poles facing one another. Predict the distance at which he would observe one magnet moving the other through repelling forces.

    b. The student put one of his magnets on his wooden desk with the north pole down. If the desk top is 2.5 centimeters thick, do you think he could move the top magnet by sliding another magnet under the desk? Explain how the observed data supports your answer.

3. The atoms of a permanent magnet can't move, and the electrons in the atoms are lined up so that a magnetic field is created around the magnet. The atoms in iron or steel can move. Describe what you think happens to the atoms of a steel paperclip when the paperclip is near a permanent magnet.

4. A magnet attracts a pin, as shown in the picture. The pin has become a temporary magnet. Copy the picture and then, using what you know about magnetic forces, label the north and south poles of the pin.

5. A horseshoe magnet is shown at right. Copy the picture and then draw the magnetic field lines between the north and south poles of the magnet.

6. Draw an electromagnet. Label all parts including the magnetic poles.

7. What property of matter gives rise to both electricity and magnetism?

8. A working electric motor needs to have three things. Which of the following are the three?

    a. A device to switch the electromagnets at the right time.

    b. A moving element with magnets.

    c. An even number of magnets.

    d. A stationary element with magnets.

9. An electric motor running from a single 1.5-volt battery draws a current of 1 amp. How much electric power does the motor use in watts?

10. Describe the function of the commutator in an electric motor.

Applying your knowledge

1. You read that Ptolemy Philadelphos (367-283 BC) covered the entire surface of a temple in Egypt with magnetite, a magnetic stone capable of attracting iron. He was hoping to suspend a statue of himself in midair. Ptolemy's experiment did not work, but you can suspend something using magnets. Build a device like the diagram below and see if you can make the lower magnet float. See how much weight you can hang from the lower magnet by changing the distance between the upper and lower magnets.

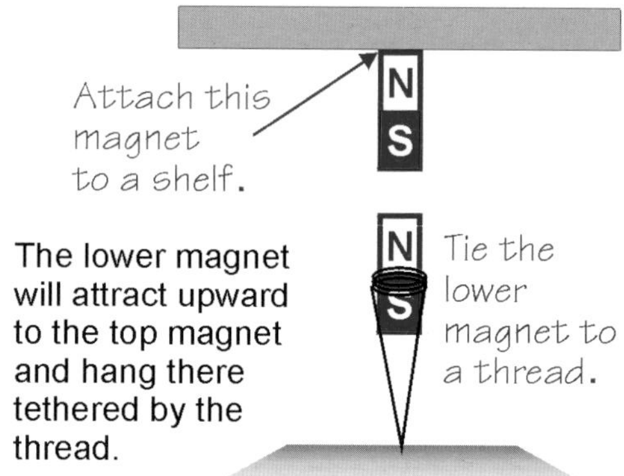
Attach this magnet to a shelf.
N
S
N
S
The lower magnet will attract upward to the top magnet and hang there tethered by the thread.
Tie the lower magnet to a thread.

2. Speakers and microphones use electromagnets to turn electric currents into sound, and vice versa. Research how electromagnets are used in sound systems. Draw a diagram that shows the location of permanent magnets and eletromagnets in a speaker. How does the electromagnet produce vibrations that create sound?

3. A bicycle light generator is a device that you place on the wheel of your bike. When you turn the wheel, the generator powers a light. When you stop, the light goes out. Explain how you think the bike generator makes electricity.

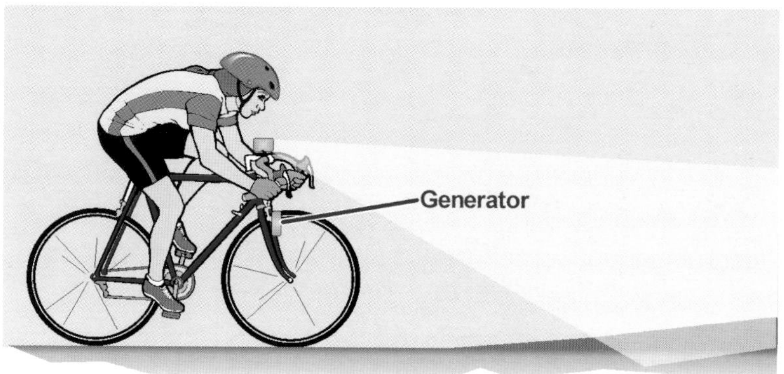
Generator

4. A clever inventor claims to be able to make an electric car that makes its own electricity and never needs gas or recharging. The inventor claims that as the car moves, the wind created by its motion spins a propeller that turns a generator to make electricity and power the wheels. Do you believe the car can work, and why (or why not)? (Hint: Think about conservation of energy.)

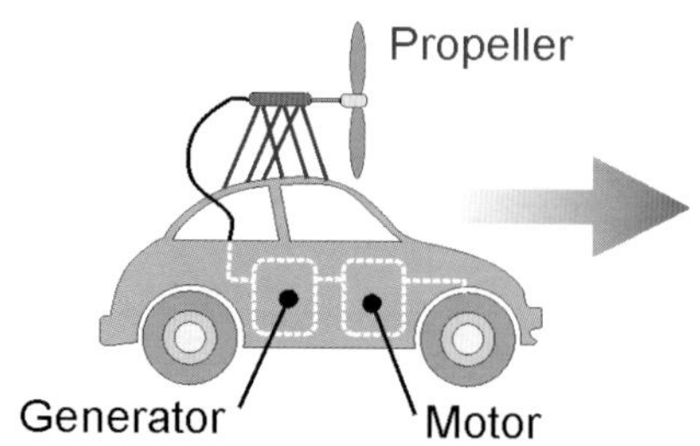
Propeller
Generator
Motor

UNIT 4

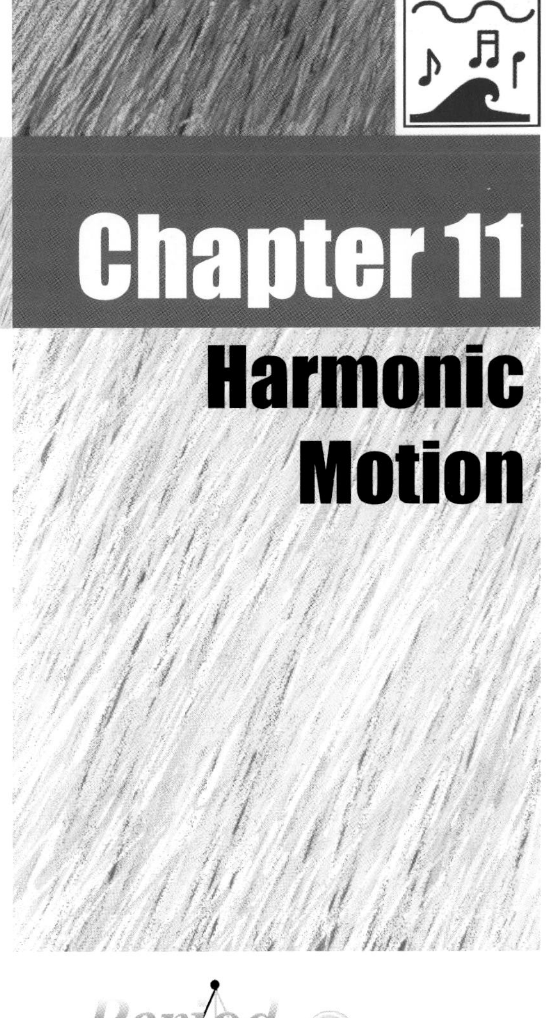

Introduction to Chapter 11

The motion we have studied so far has been from one place to another. In this chapter we will investigate harmonic motion, which is motion that repeats in cycles. From the orbit of the Earth to the rhythmic beating of your heart, harmonic motion is fundamental to our understanding of nature.

Investigations for Chapter 11

11.1	**Harmonic Motion**	*How do we describe the back and forth motion of a pendulum?*

The pendulum is an ideal start for investigating harmonic motion. The objective for this Investigation is to design a clock that can keep accurate time using a pendulum.

11.2	**Graphs of Harmonic Motion**	*How do we make graphs of harmonic motion?*

Graphs tell us much about straight-line motion. This Investigation will apply graphing techniques to oscillators. Learn how to read a heartbeat from an EKG and how to read the seismogram of a powerful earthquake!

11.3	**Simple Mechanical Oscillators**	*What kinds of systems oscillate?*

Many things in nature oscillate. Guitar strings, trees in the wind, and stretched rubber bands are all examples of oscillators. In this Investigation we will construct several simple oscillators and learn how to adjust their frequency and period.

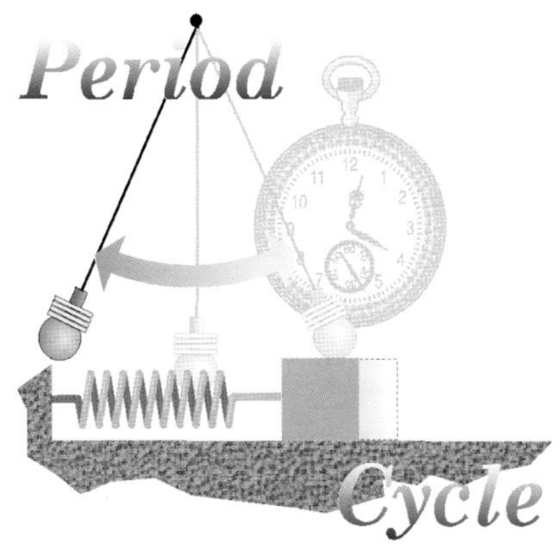

Learning Goals

In this chapter, you will:

- ✔ Learn about harmonic motion and how it is fundamental to understanding natural processes.
- ✔ Use harmonic motion to keep accurate time using a pendulum.
- ✔ Learn how to interpret and make graphs of harmonic motion.
- ✔ Construct simple oscillators.
- ✔ Learn how to adjust the frequency and period of simple oscillators.
- ✔ Learn to identify simple oscillators.

Vocabulary

amplitude	harmonic motion	period	system
cycle	hertz	periodic motion	
frequency	oscillator	phase	

11.1 Harmonic Motion

As you watch moving things, you see two different kinds of motion. One kind of motion goes from one place to another. This is called *linear motion*. The concepts of distance, time, speed, and acceleration come from thinking about this kind of motion.

The second kind of motion is motion that repeats itself over and over. We call motion that repeats over and over harmonic motion and that is what you will learn about in this section. The word comes from *harmony* which means "multiples of." Swinging back and forth on a swing is a good example of harmonic motion (figure 11.1). Many moving things have both kinds of motion. A bicycle moves forward but the wheels and pedals go around and around in harmonic motion (figure 11.2).

Harmonic Motion

Linear Motion

Figure 11.1: *Linear motion goes from one place to another without repeating. Harmonic motion repeats over and over the same way.*

Cycles, systems, and oscillators

What is a cycle? The cycle is the building block of harmonic motion. A cycle is a unit of motion that repeats over and over. All harmonic motion is a repeated sequence of cycles. The cycle of the pendulum is shown below.

The cycle of the pendulum

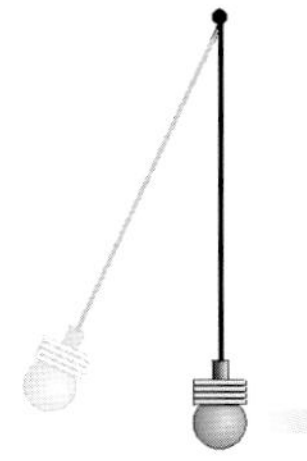

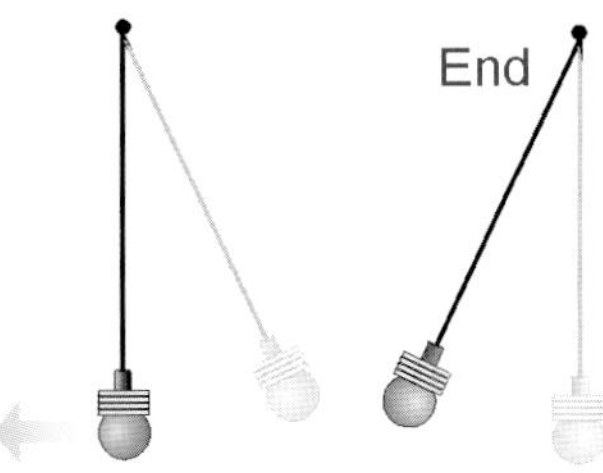

Figure 11.2: *Real-life situations can include both linear motion and harmonic motion.*

Finding the cycle When investigating harmonic motion we start by identifying the basic cycle. A cycle has a beginning and ending. Between beginning and end, the cycle has to include all the motion that repeats. The cycle of the pendulum is defined by where we choose the beginning. If we start the cycle when the pendulum is all the way to the left, the cycle ends when the pendulum has returned all the way to the left again. If we choose the cycle correctly, the motion of the pendulum is one cycle after the next with no gaps between cycles.

Harmonic motion in nature

Choosing a system

In science we often refer to a system. A system is a group we choose that includes all the things we are interested in. Choosing the system helps us concentrate on what is important and exclude what is not important. For the pendulum, the system is the hanger, string, and weight. We don't need to include the floor or the table, since these are not directly important to the motion.

We might choose the system differently depending on what we want to investigate. If we wanted to see how gravity affected the pendulum, we would have to include Earth's gravity as part of the system.

An oscillator is a system with harmonic motion

A system that shows harmonic motion is called an oscillator. The pendulum is an example of an oscillator. So is your heart and its surrounding muscles (figure11.3). Oscillators can be very small. The electrons in the atom make harmonic motion, so an atom is an oscillator. Oscillators can also be very large. The solar system is an oscillator with each of the planets in harmonic motion around the sun. We are going to study oscillators using simple models, but what we learn will also apply to more complex systems, like a microwave communications satellite.

Earth is part of several systems in harmonic motion

Earth is a part of several oscillating systems. The Earth/sun system has a cycle of one year, which means Earth completes one orbit around the sun in a year. The Earth/moon system has a cycle of approximately one month. Earth itself has several different cycles (figure 11.4). It rotates around its axis once a day making the 24-hour cycle of day and night. There is also a wobble of Earth's axis that cycles every 22,000 years, moving the north and south poles around by hundreds of miles. There are cycles in weather, such as the El Nino and La Nina oscillations in ocean currents that produce fierce storms every decade or so. Much of the planet's ecology depends on cycles.

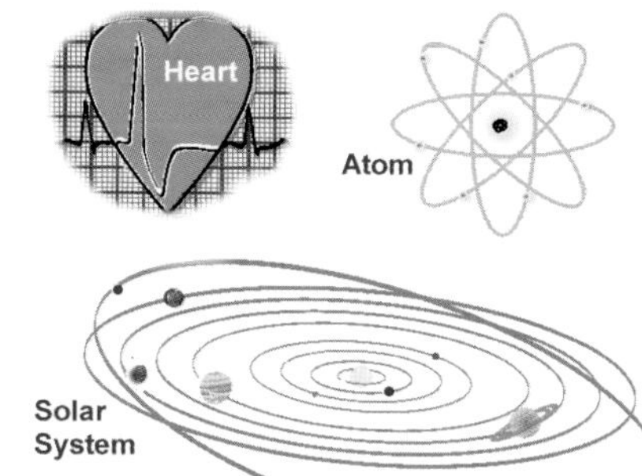

Figure 11.3: *The pendulum is an oscillator. Other examples of oscillators are an atom, your beating heart, and the solar system.*

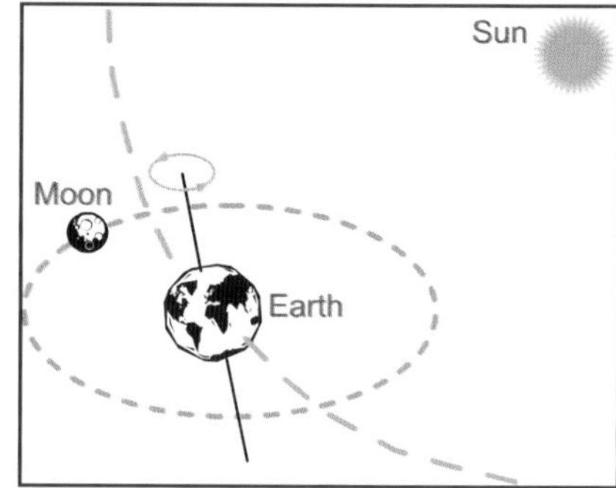

Figure 11.4: *The Earth/sun/moon system has many different cycles. The year, month, and day are the result of orbital cycles.*

Harmonic motion in art and music

Music comes from oscillations

Both light and sound come from oscillations. Music and musical instruments are oscillators that we design to create sounds with specific cycles that we enjoy hearing. Sound is an oscillation of the air. A moving speaker pushes and pulls on the air creating a small oscillation in pressure (figure 11.5). The oscillation travels to where it hits your eardrum. Your vibrating eardrum moves tiny bones in the ear setting up more oscillations that are transmitted by nerves to the brain. There is harmonic motion at every step of the way, from the musical instrument to the perception of sound by your brain.

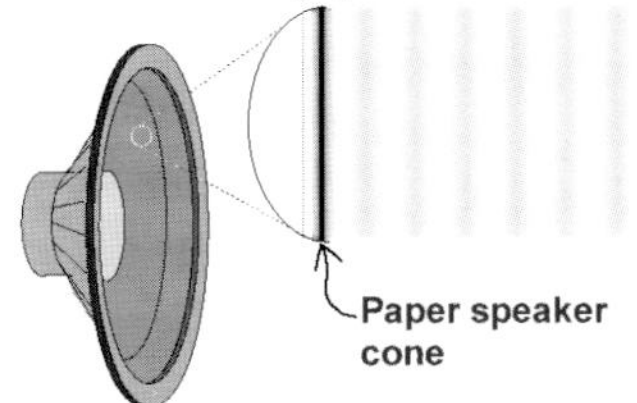

Figure 11.5: *A moving speaker oscillates back and forth, making sound that you can hear.*

Color comes from oscillations

We see colors in light waves, which are oscillations of electricity and magnetism. Faster oscillations make blue light while slower oscillations make red light. When painting a picture, each color of paint contains different molecules that absorb and reflect different colors of light. The colors you see come from the interaction between the oscillations of light and the oscillations of the electrons in the pigment molecules.

Figure 11.6: *The cordless phone you use has an electronic oscillator at millions of cycles per second.*

Harmonic motion in technology

Oscillators are used in communications

Almost all modern communication technology relies on fast electronic oscillators. Cell phones use oscillators that make more than 100 million cycles each second (figure 11.6). FM radio uses oscillators between 95 million and 107 million cycles per second. When you tune a radio you are selecting the frequency of the oscillator you want to listen to. Each station sets up an oscillator at a different frequency. Sometimes, you can get two stations at once when you are traveling between two radio towers with nearly the same frequency.

Oscillators are used to measure time

The cycles of many oscillators always repeat in the same amount of time. This makes harmonic motion a good way to keep time. If you have a pendulum that has a cycle one second long, you can count time in seconds by counting cycles of the pendulum. Grandfather clocks and mechanical watches actually count cycles of oscillators to tell time (figure 11.7). Even today, the world's most accurate clocks keep time by counting cycles of light from a cesium atom oscillator. Modern atomic clocks are so accurate they lose only one second in 1,400,000 years!

Figure 11.7: *Clocks and watches use oscillators to keep time. This works because many oscillators have precisely stable cycles.*

Investigating harmonic motion

Period is the time for one cycle

What makes harmonic motion useful for clocks is that each cycle takes the same amount of time. The time for one cycle is called the period. Some clocks have a pendulum with a period of exactly two seconds. The gears in the clock cause the minute hand to move 1/60 of a turn for every 30 swings of the pendulum. The period is one of the important characteristics of all harmonic motion (figure 11.8).

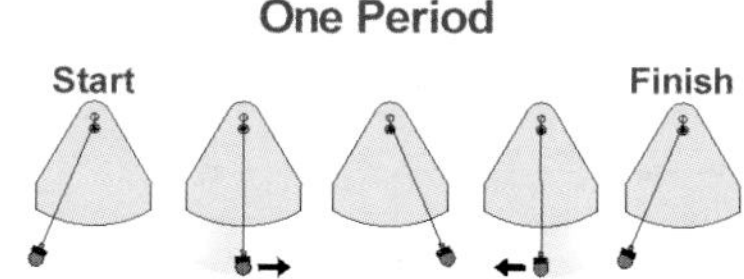

Figure 11.8: *The period is the time it takes to complete one cycle.*

Frequency is the number of cycles per second

Frequency is closely related to period. The frequency of an oscillator is the number of cycles it makes per second. Every day, we experience a wide range of frequencies. FM radio uses frequencies between 95 million and 107 million cycles per second (the FM standing for frequency modulation) (figure 11.9). Your heartbeat probably has a frequency between one-half and two cycles per second. The musical note "A" has a frequency of 440 cycles per second. The human voice contains frequencies mainly between 100 and 2,000 cycles per second.

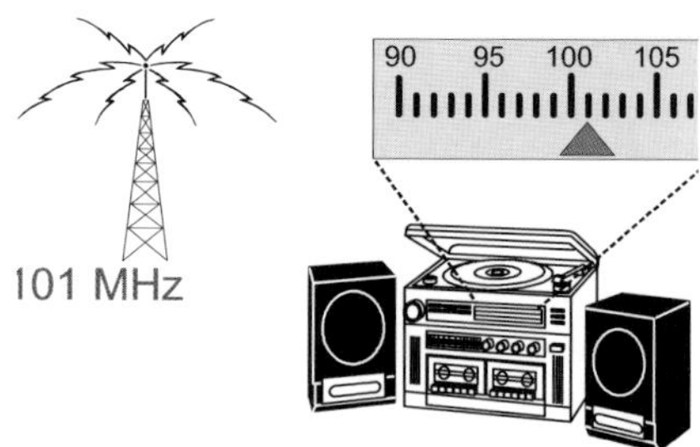

Figure 11.9: *When you tune a radio to receive a station, you are matching frequencies between receiver and transmitter.*

Frequency is measured in hertz

The unit of one cycle per second is called a hertz. A frequency of 440 cycles per second is usually written as 440 hertz, or abbreviated 440 Hz. The Hz is a unit that is the same in English and metric. When you tune into a station at 101 on the FM dial, you are actually setting the oscillator in your radio to a frequency of 101 megahertz, or 101,000,000 Hz. You hear music when the oscillator in your radio is exactly matched to the frequency of the oscillator in the transmission tower connected to the radio station.

Period and frequency

$$T = \frac{1}{f} \qquad f = \frac{1}{T}$$

Period (seconds) → T; Frequency (hertz) → f; Frequency (hertz) → f; Period (seconds) → T

Frequency and period are inversely related. The period is the time per cycle. The frequency is the number of cycles per time. If the period of a pendulum is 1.25 seconds, its frequency is 0.8 cycles per second (0.8 Hz). If you know one, you can calculate the other.

Example:

Calculate the frequency of a pendulum that has a period of 1/4 second.

Solution:

(1) You are asked for frequency.

(2) You are given the period.

(3) The relationship you need is F=1/T.

(4) Plug in numbers.

F = 1 / (0.25 sec)

= 4 Hz

Amplitude

Amplitude describes the size of a cycle

Another important characteristic of a cycle is its size. The period tells how long the cycle lasts. The **amplitude** describes how big the cycle is. The diagram below shows a pendulum with small amplitude and large amplitude. With mechanical systems (such as a pendulum), the amplitude is often a distance or angle. With other kinds of oscillators, the amplitude might be voltage or pressure. The amplitude is measured in units appropriate to the kind of oscillation you are describing.

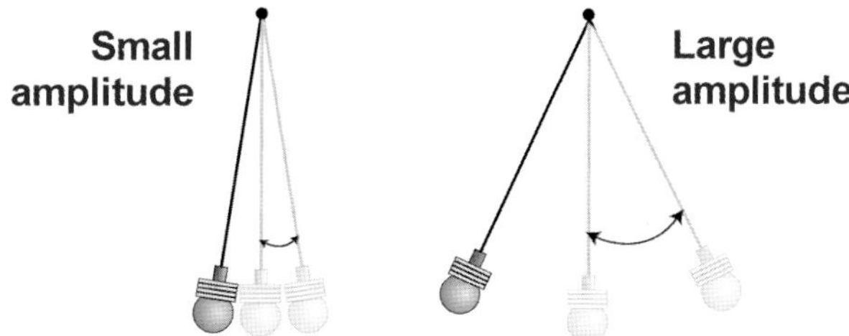

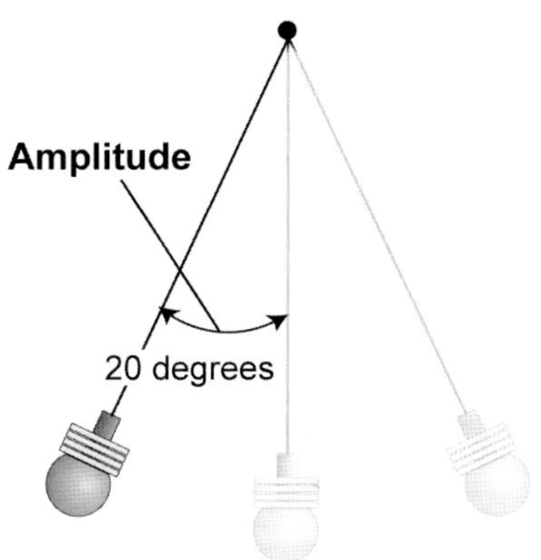

Figure 11.10: *A pendulum with an amplitude of 20 degrees swings 20 degrees away from the center.*

How do you measure amplitude?

The amplitude is the maximum distance the motion moves away from the average. For a pendulum, the average is at the center. The pendulum spends as much time to the right of center as it does to the left. For the pendulum in figure 11.10, the amplitude is 20 degrees, because the pendulum moves 20 degrees away from center in either direction.

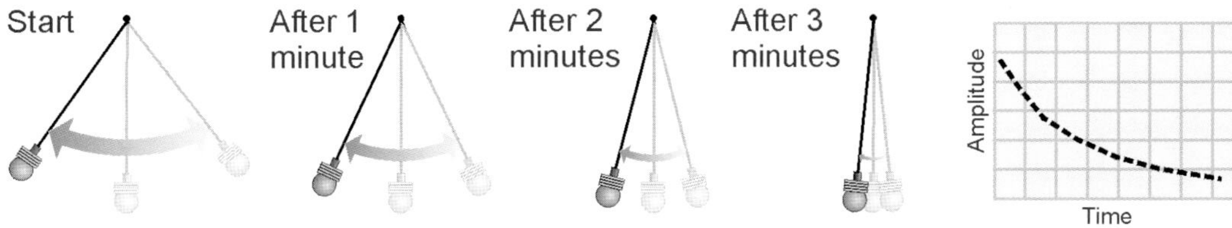

Damping

Friction slows a pendulum down, as it does all oscillators. That means the amplitude slowly gets reduced until the pendulum is hanging straight down, motionless. We use the word **damping** to describe the gradual loss of amplitude of an oscillator. If you wanted to make a clock with a pendulum, you would have to find a way to keep adding energy to counteract the damping of friction.

11.2 Graphs of Harmonic Motion

Harmonic motion graphs show cycles. This is what makes them different from linear motion graphs (figure 11.11). The values of the period and amplitude can be read from the graphs. If you know the period and amplitude, you can quickly sketch a harmonic motion graph.

Typical Linear Motion Graphs

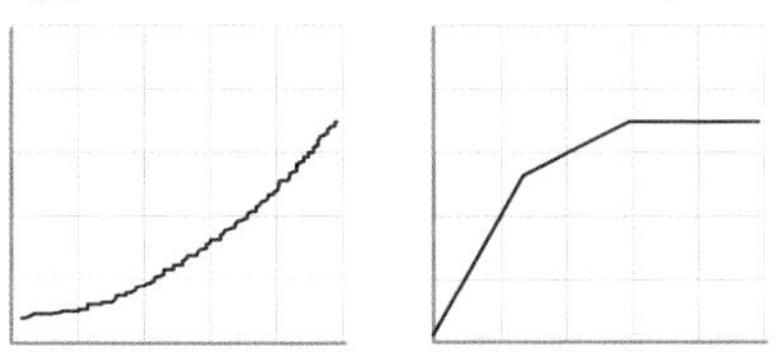

Typical Harmonic Motion Graphs

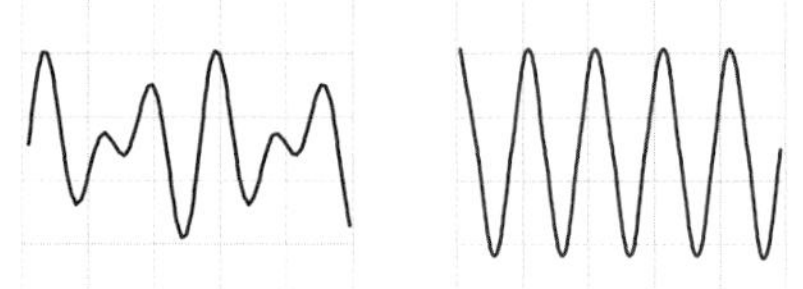

Figure 11.11: *Typical graphs for linear motion (top) and harmonic motion (bottom). Harmonic motion graphs show cycles.*

Reading harmonic motion graphs

Cycles and time Most graphs of harmonic motion show how things change with time. The pendulum is a good example. The diagram below shows a graph of position vs. time for a pendulum. The graph shows repeating cycles just like the motion. Seeing a pattern of cycles on a graph is an indication that harmonic motion is present.

Using positive and negative numbers Harmonic motion graphs often use positive and negative values to represent motion on either side of center. We usually choose zero to be at the equilibrium point of the motion. Zero is placed halfway up the *y*-axis so there is room for both positive and negative values. The graph alternates from plus to minus and back. The example graph below shows a pendulum swinging from +20 centimeters to -20 centimeters and back. The amplitude is the maximum distance away from center, or 20 centimeters.

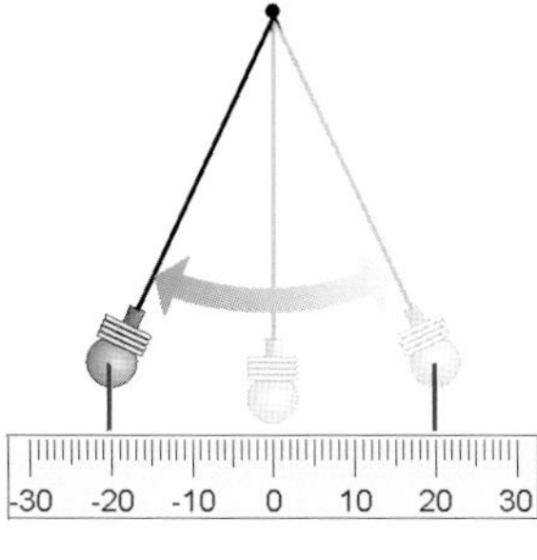

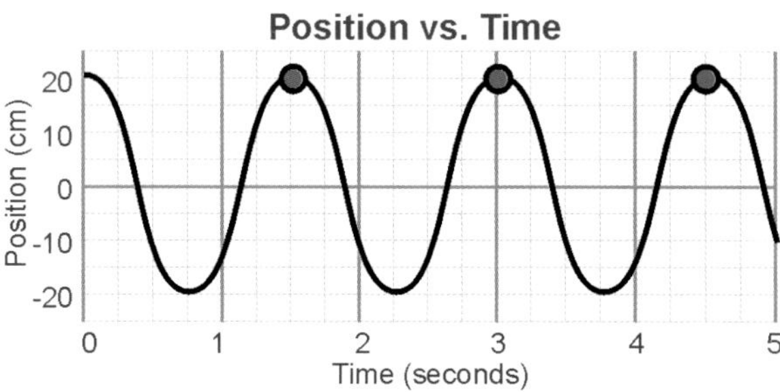

Harmonic graphs repeat every period Notice that the graph (above) returns to the same place every 1.5 seconds. No matter where you start, you come back to the same value 1.5 seconds later. Graphs of harmonic motion repeat every period, just as the motion repeats every cycle. Harmonic motion is sometimes called periodic motion for this reason.

Determining amplitude and period from a graph

Calculating amplitude from a graph The amplitude is half the distance between the highest and lowest points on the graph. For the example in figure 11.12, the amplitude is 20 centimeters, as illustrated by the calculation below. The difference between the highest and lowest value of the graph is the *peak-to-peak* value.

$$\text{Amplitude} = \frac{1}{2}(\text{high} - \text{low}) = \frac{1}{2}(20 - (-20))$$
$$= 20 \text{ cm}$$

Calculating period from a graph To get the period from a graph, start by identifying one complete cycle. The cycle must begin and end in the same place on the graph. Figure 11.13 shows how to choose the cycle for a simple harmonic motion graph and for a more complex one. Once you have identified a cycle, you use the time axis of the graph to determine the period. The period is the time difference between the beginning of the cycle and the end. Subtract the beginning time from the ending time, as shown in the example below.

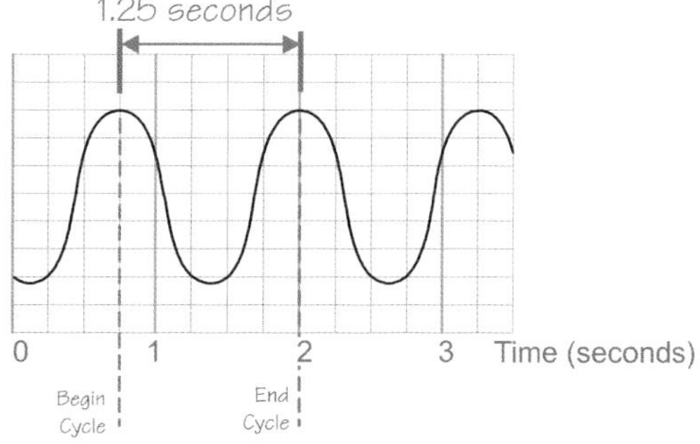

$$\text{Period} = (\text{ending time} - \text{beginning time})$$
$$= (2.0 \text{ sec} - 0.75 \text{ sec})$$
$$= 1.25 \text{ seconds}$$

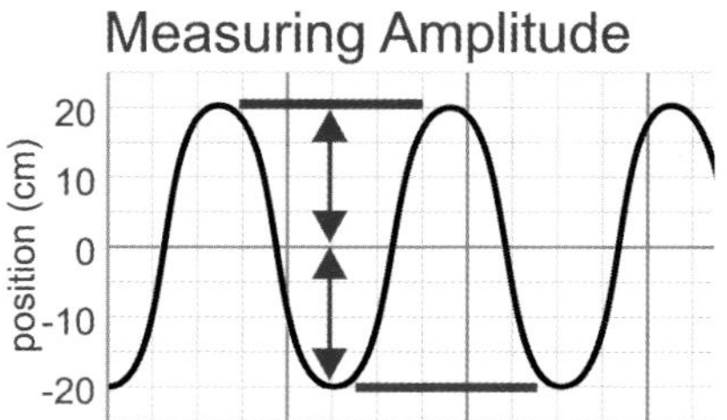

Figure 11.12: *The amplitude of a wave is one-half the peak-to-peak distance. In this graph of harmonic motion, the amplitude of the wave is 20 centimeters.*

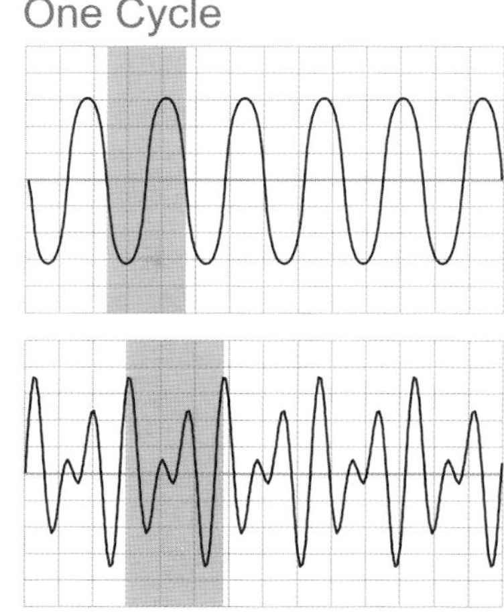

Figure 11.13: *The cycle is the part of the graph that repeats over and over. The gray shading shows one cycle for each of the graphs above. Before you can find the period, you need to identify the cycle.*

Circles and harmonic motion

Circular motion

Circular motion is very similar to harmonic motion. For example, a turning wheel returns to the same position every 360 degrees. Rotation is a cycle, just like harmonic motion. One key difference is that cycles of circular motion *always* have a length of 360 degrees. It does not matter how big the wheel is, each full turn is 360 degrees.

Figure 11.14 shows a shadow of a peg on a rotating wheel. As the wheel rotates, the shadow of the peg goes back and forth on the wall. If we make a graph of the position of the shadow, we get a harmonic motion graph. The period of the cycle is exactly the time it takes the wheel to turn 360 degrees.

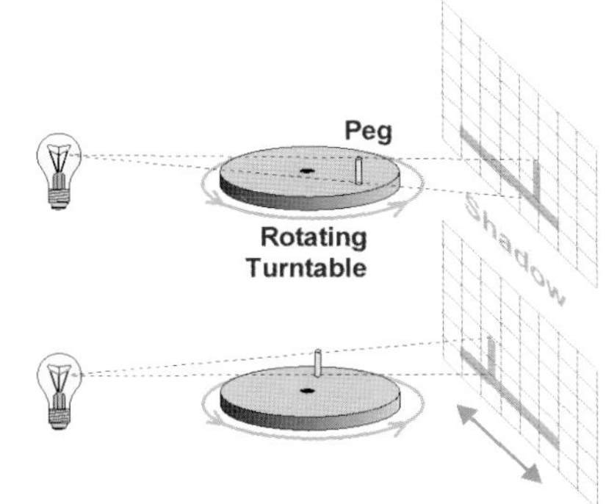

Figure 11.14: *The shadow of a peg moves back and forth on the wall as the turntable rotates. The shadow itself appears to be in harmonic motion.*

The phase of an oscillator

We often use degrees to tell us where we are within the cycle of an oscillator. For example, how would you identify the moment when the pendulum was one-tenth of the way through its cycle? If we let one cycle be 360 degrees, then one-tenth of that cycle is 36 degrees. Thirty-six degrees is a measure of the phase of the oscillator. The word "phase" means where the oscillator is in the cycle.

What do we mean by "in phase"?

The concept of phase is important when comparing one oscillator with another. Suppose we have two identical pendulums, with exactly the same period. If we start them together, their graphs would look like the picture below. We describe the two pendulums as being *in phase* because cycles are aligned. Each oscillator is always at the same place at the same time.

Both pendulums in phase

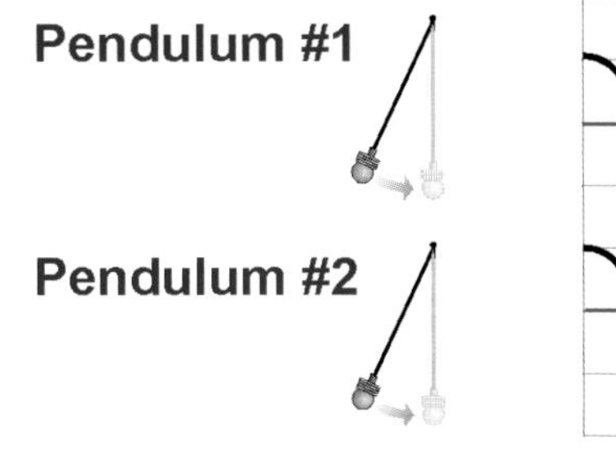

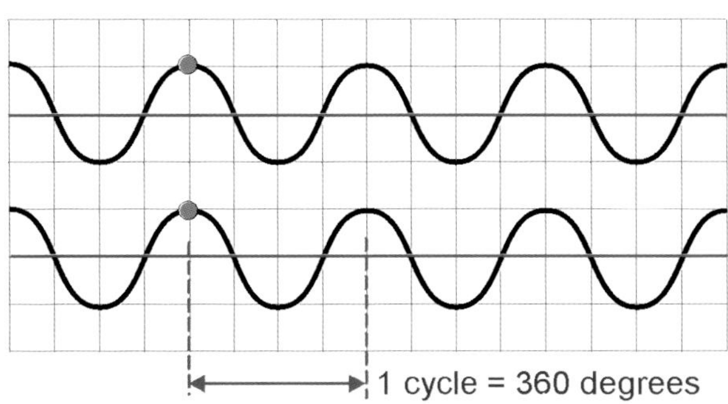

Out of phase by 90 degrees

If we start the first pendulum swinging a little before the second one, the graphs look like the diagram below. Although, they have the same cycle, the first pendulum is always a little ahead of the second. The graph shows the lead of the first pendulum as a phase difference. Notice that the top graph reaches its maximum 90 degrees *before* the bottom graph. We say the two pendulums are *out of phase* by 90 degrees, or one-fourth of a cycle.

90 degrees out of phase

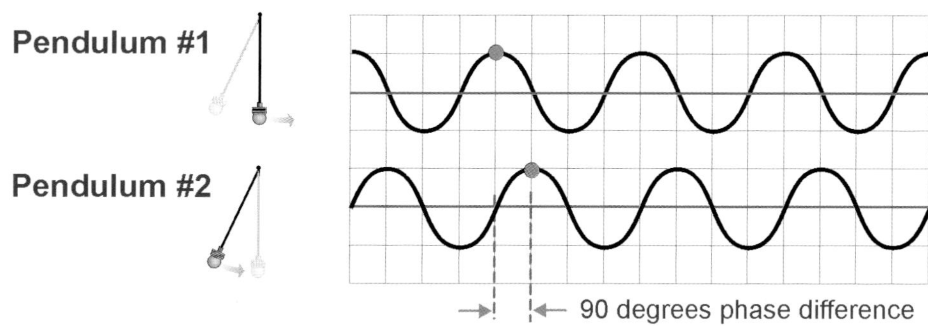

Out of phase by 180 degrees

When they are out of phase, the relative motion of the oscillators may differ by a little or by as much as half a cycle. Two oscillators 180 degrees out of phase are one-half cycle apart. The next diagram (below) shows that the two pendulums are always on opposite sides of the cycle from each other. The concepts of in phase and out of phase will be very important to our Investigations with waves and sound.

180 degrees out of phase

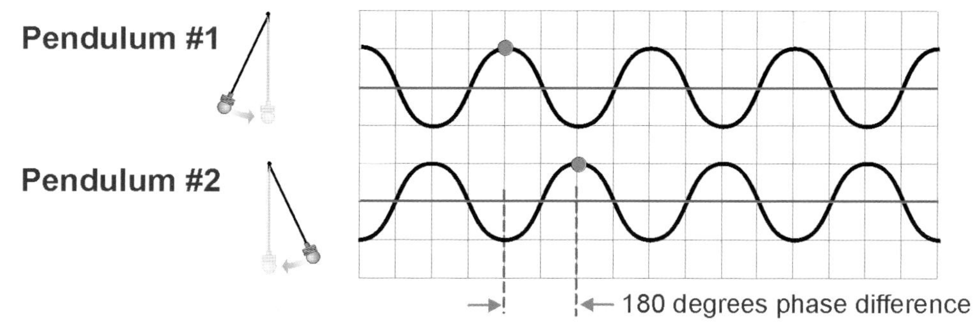

11.3 Simple Mechanical Oscillators

Harmonic motion is so common that it would be impossible to list all the different kinds of oscillators you might find. Fortunately, we can learn much about harmonic motion by looking at just a few examples. Once we understand some basic oscillators, we will have the experience needed to figure out more complex ones.

Examples of oscillators

The pendulum The simplest pendulum is a weight hanging from a string. The weight swings back and forth once it is pulled away and released. The force that always pulls the pendulum back to center comes from its weight (figure 11.15). If you swing a pendulum to one side, the string causes it to lift slightly.

The period of a pendulum does not change much, even when its amplitude is changed. This is because two opposite effects occur. First, if you make the amplitude large, the pendulum has a greater distance to travel, which increases the period. But remember that by releasing it from a high position, it also starts with more energy. More energy means the pendulum goes faster and higher speed decreases the period. The effect of higher speed almost exactly cancels the effect of longer swing distance.

A mass on a spring If you have ever been in a car with worn-out shock absorbers, you have experienced another common oscillator. The system of a car and shock absorbers is an example of a mass on a spring. Springs resist being extended or compressed. Figure 11.16 shows how the force from a spring always acts to return to equilibrium. A mass attached to a spring adds inertia to the system. If the mass is given an initial push, the mass/spring system oscillates.

A vibrating string Vibrating strings are used in many musical instruments. A stretched rubber band is a good example. If you pull the rubber band to one side, it stretches a bit. The stretching creates a restoring force that tries to pull the rubber band back straight again. Inertia carries it past being straight and it vibrates. Vibrating strings tend to move much faster than springs and pendulums. The period of a vibrating string can easily be one-hundredth of a second (0.01) or shorter.

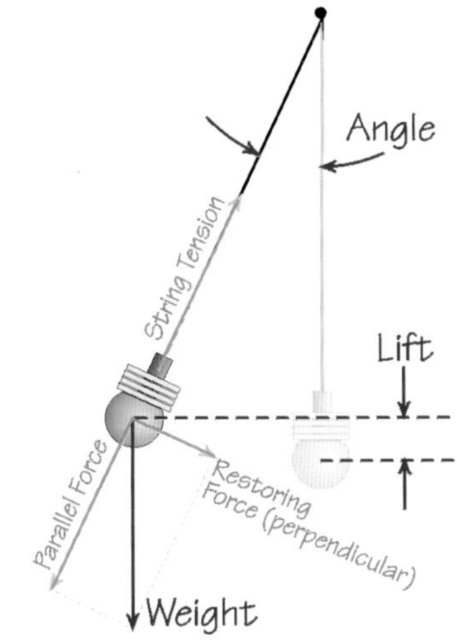

Figure 11.15: *The forces acting on the pendulum. The weight (gravity) points straight down.*

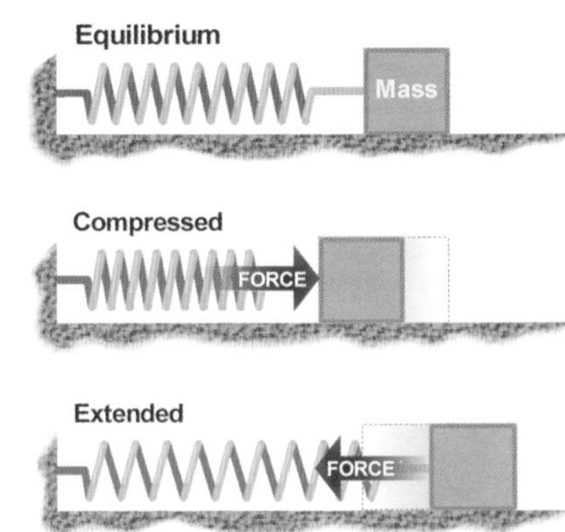

Figure 11.16: *A mass on a spring oscillator. When the spring is compressed or extended, it pushes the mass back toward equilibrium.*

Chapter 11 Review

Vocabulary review

Match the following terms with the correct definition. There is one extra definition in the list that will not match any of the terms.

Set One

1. harmonic motion	a. A system in harmonic motion
2. cycle	b. A unit of one cycle per second
3. system	c. Back and forth or repeating motion
4. oscillator	d. A part of motion that repeats over and over
5. hertz	e. A group of things we think are important to consider when analyzing something
	f. Motion that goes from one point to another without repeating

Set Two

1. period	a. The number of cycles per second
2. frequency	b. The size of a cycle
3. amplitude	c. A way to identify where an oscillator is in its cycle
4. damping	d. The time it takes to complete one cycle
5. phase	e. Any process that causes cycles to get smaller and smaller in amplitude
	f. A unit of one cycle per second

Concept review

1. Name three objects or systems around you that have cycles.

2. What is the relationship between frequency and period?

3. Which pictures show only periodic motion?

   a. A girl running a race.

   b. The swinging pendulum of a clock.

   c. An ocean wave rising and falling.

   d. A boy swinging.

   e. A car moving down the street.

4. If the length of the rope on a swing gets longer, the period of the swing will:

   a. Get longer.

   b. Get shorter.

   c. Stay the same.

   d. I need more information to answer.

5. In a pendulum experiment, the ____________ is the maximum angle that the pendulum swings away from center. (Pick one.)
   a. cycle
   b. amplitude
   c. period
   d. speed

6. Oscillations have something to do with the answers to which of the following questions? (You can pick more than one.)
   a. What color is it?
   b. How much mass does it have?
   c. How long is it?
   d. How loud is that noise?
   e. What radio station is this?

7. A clock is made using a pendulum to count the time. The weight at the bottom of the pendulum can be adjusted to make the length of the pendulum longer or shorter. The clock runs too fast, meaning it counts 50 minutes as one full hour. What should you do to correct the clock?
   a. Move the weight upward, making the pendulum shorter.
   b. Move the weight downward, making the pendulum longer.
   c. Add more weight to make the pendulum heavier.

8. Which of the graphs clearly shows harmonic motion? You may choose more than one.

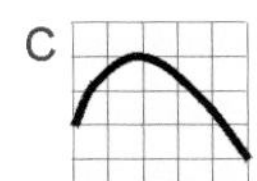

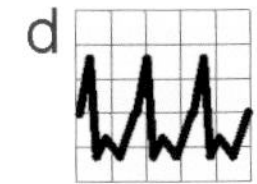

9. The measurement of 2.5 seconds could be:
   a. The frequency of an oscillator.
   b. The period of an oscillator.
   c. The mass of an oscillator.
   d. The system where we find an oscillator.

10. A measurement of 1 meter could be:
   a. The frequency of an oscillator.
   b. The amplitude of an oscillator.
   c. The mass of an oscillator.
   d. The system where we find an oscillator.

11. An oscillator is made with a rubber band and a block of wood, as shown in the diagram. What happens to the oscillator if we make the block of wood heavier?
   a. The frequency increases.
   b. The period increases.
   c. The frequency stays the same.
   d. The period stays the same.

Rubber band
Block

12. If the amplitude of a pendulum is doubled, which of the following will be true?
   a. It will swing twice as far away from center.
   b. Its period will be twice as long.
   c. Its frequency will be twice as high.
   d. It must have twice the mass.

Problems

1. A person's heartbeat is measured to be 65 beats per minute. What is the period between heartbeats in seconds?
    a. 65 seconds
    b. 65 Hertz
    c. 0.92 seconds
    d. 1.08 seconds
2. A pendulum has a period of 1.5 seconds. How many cycles do you have to count to make one minute?
3. A string vibrates back and forth 30 times per second. What is the period of the motion of the string?
4. The graph shows the motion of an oscillator that is a weight hanging from a rubber band. The weight moves up and down. Answer the following questions using the graph.

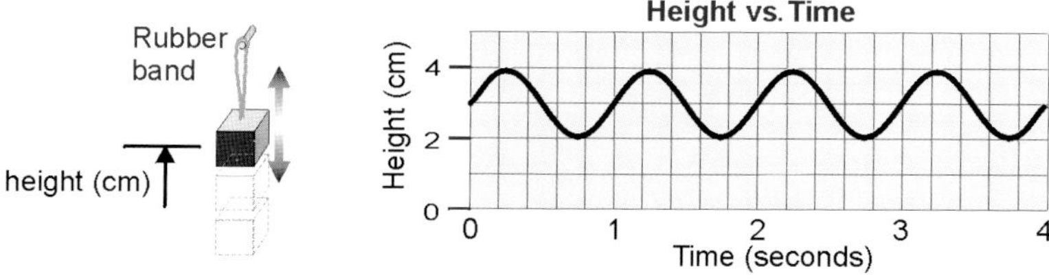

    a. What is the period?
    b. What is the amplitude?
    c. If you counted for 5 seconds, how many cycles would you count?

5. Four different groups of students make measurements of the period of a pendulum. Each group hands in a lab with no names on it. Can you tell which lab group was working with which pendulum? Match the letter of the pendulum to the number of the lab group.

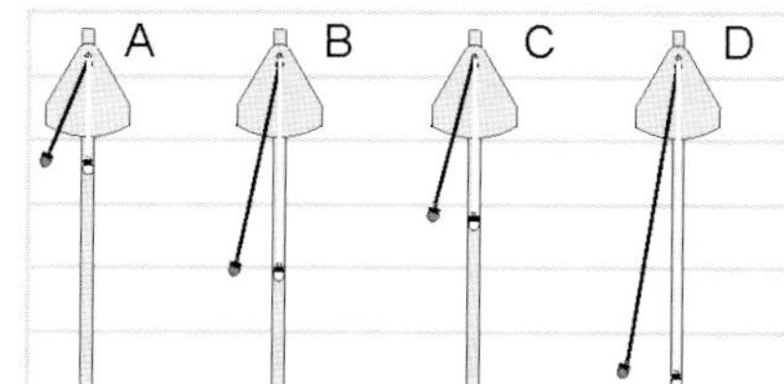

Group	Period	Pendulum
1	1.0 sec	
2	1.2 sec	
3	1.4 sec	
4	1.7 sec	

Questions 6, 7, and 8 refer to the three graphs below. Distance in these graphs means displacement of the oscillator.

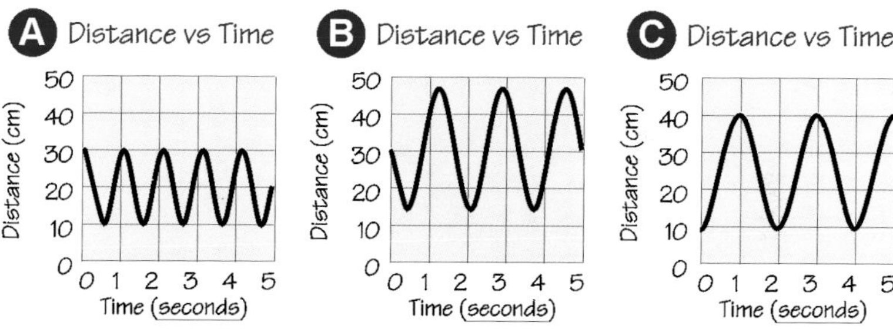

6. Which graph shows exactly 3 cycles?
7. Which graph has a period of 2 seconds?
8. Which graph has an amplitude of 10 centimeters?

Applying your knowledge

1. What is the period of the rotation of the Earth that gives us day and night?
2. An animal research scientist films a small bird and counts 240 beats of the bird's wings in 2 minutes. What is the frequency of the motion of the bird's wings?
3. The Earth, moon, and sun make a system with many cycles. Give at least two examples of cycles that relate to the Earth, moon, or sun and also give the period of each example you find.

4. You invent a bicycle speedometer that counts how many spokes of the wheel pass by each second. You ride your bicycle to test the speedometer and measure 2,160 spokes pass in one minute.
   a. What is the frequency of spokes passing your sensor in hertz?
   b. The wheel has 36 spokes. How many turns per minute does the wheel make?
5. The human heart is both strong and reliable. As a demonstration of how reliable the heart is, calculate how many times your heart beats in one day. Start by measuring the frequency of your pulse in beats per minute and use the result for your calculation.

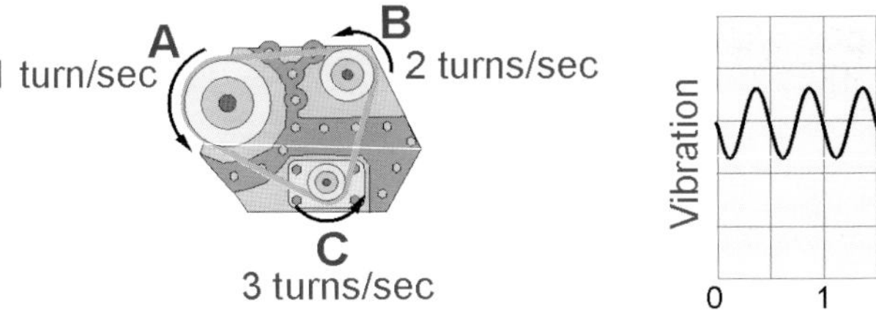

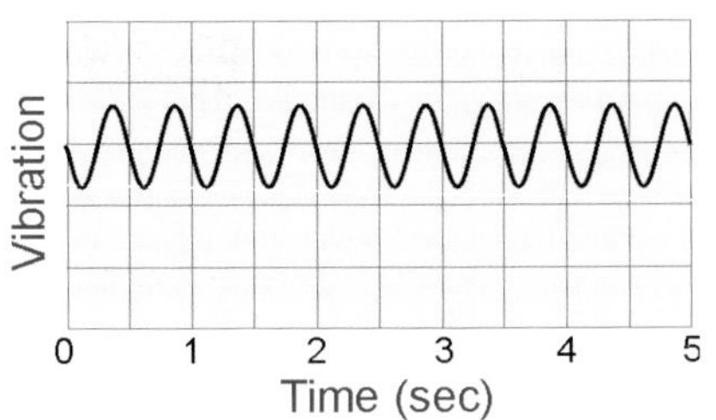

6. Frequency can be a clue to finding problems in engines before they cause serious damage. Suppose the engine has three spinning parts (A, B, C), each turning at a different speed. Since the speed of each part is different, the frequency of each is also different. If one part starts to wear out, it will vibrate more than it should. By looking at the frequency of vibration for the whole engine, you can spot which part is the problem by looking for vibrations at its characteristic frequency.
The graph shows the vibration of the whole engine, including all three spinning parts. From the graph, can you tell which part is making too much vibration, and is therefore likely to fail?

UNIT 4 Sound and Waves

Introduction to Chapter 12

Waves carry energy and information over great distances. A cell phone conversation is carried on waves that travel for thousands of miles. Waves on the ocean also travel thousands of miles before they splash at your feet on the beach. In this chapter, you will learn how to measure and control waves so that you can use them for music, communication, and many other useful things.

Investigations for Chapter 12

12.1	Waves	*How do we make and describe waves?*

A stretched string seems simple but it gets very interesting when you use it to make a wave! For this Investigation you will make wave pulses on springs and strings to see how they move and what they do at boundaries.

12.2	Waves in Motion	*How do waves move and interact with things?*

Waves in water are a familiar sight. In this Investigation we will use water waves to explore reflection, diffraction, and other things waves do.

12.3	Natural Frequency and Resonance	*What is resonance and why is it important?*

Everything has a natural frequency, and most things have more than one. When you force something to vibrate at its natural frequency you can make very large waves. In this Investigation we will use a fascinating electronic synthesizer to make waves on a vibrating string so that we can explore resonance and harmony. We will learn the foundation upon which all musical instruments are built.

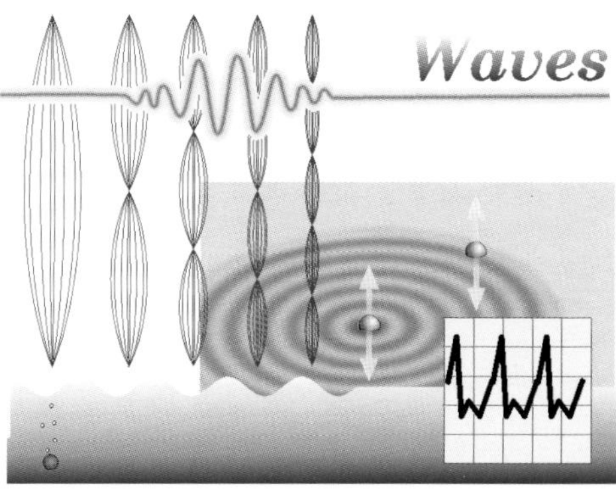

Learning Goals

In this chapter, you will:

- ✔ Learn the role waves play in our daily lives, including our effort to communicate.
- ✔ Learn the parts and shapes of waves.
- ✔ Model transverse and longitudinal waves and their characteristics with a stretched string.
- ✔ Explore the properties of waves (like reflection and diffraction) with water.
- ✔ Investigate resonance and harmony using an electronic synthesizer.
- ✔ Learn how natural frequency and resonance are involved in making music.

Vocabulary

circular waves	diffraction	natural frequency	response
constructive interference	fundamental	plane waves	standing wave
continuous	harmonics	reflection	transverse wave
crest	hertz	refraction	trough
destructive interference	longitudinal wave	resonance	wave fronts

12.1 Waves

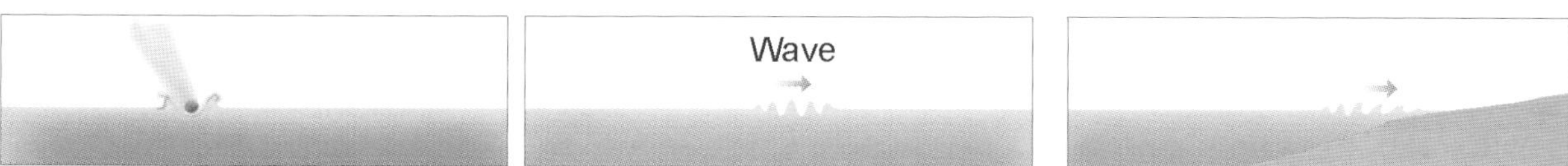

Suppose a big meteor falls into the ocean. The energy of the falling meteor creates a wave that carries the energy to distant shores. You watch a great musician on stage. The voice or instrument creates waves that carry the sound to your ears. You dial a cell phone to call a friend. A microwave comes from the antenna and carries a signal to your friend.

In this section you will learn about waves. What you learn will apply to the water waves, sound waves, and light waves you see around you all the time. What you learn will also apply to the radio waves and microwaves that are also around even though you can't feel them or see them. Even gravity has waves that astronomers believe are created when black holes crash into each other.

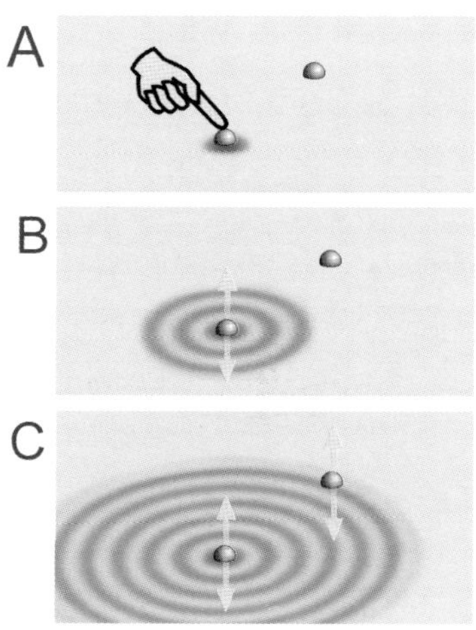

Figure 12.1: *If we poke a floating ball, it moves up and down in harmonic motion (A). The oscillating ball creates a wave (B) that travels on the surface of the water. The wave can cause oscillation of a second ball (C) placed far away from the first.*

Why learn about waves?

Waves carry oscillations from one place to another

A ball floating on the water is a good example of the difference between a wave and ordinary harmonic motion. If you poke the ball, it moves up and down. The oscillating ball creates a wave on the surface of the water that spreads outward, carrying the oscillation to other places (figure 12.1). A second ball floating farther away also starts oscillating as soon as the wave reaches it. The wave started by an earthquake can travel around the world, reaching places far away from where it began.

Waves carry information and energy

We use waves to carry information and energy over great distances. The sound wave that travels through the air carries information about the vibration of the string from the instrument to your ear. Your ear hears the vibration as music. In a similar way, a radio wave carries sounds from a transmitter to your stereo. Another kind of radio wave carries television signals. A microwave carries cell phone conversations. Waves carry energy and information from one place to another. The information could be sound, color, pictures, commands, or many other useful things.

Waves are all around us.

Waves are part of everyday experience. We might not recognize all the waves we see, but they are there. Consider standing on the corner of a busy street. How are you affected by waves?

- The stoplight that you see with your eyes is a wave.
- The sounds that you hear are waves.
- The ripples in a puddle of water are waves.
- The electricity flowing in the wires attached to the street lights is a wave.
- Waves carry radio and TV and cell phone transmissions through the air around you.

There are waves *inside* the atoms that make up everything we see. By understanding how waves work we can learn about nature and also about technology (figure 12.2).

Figure 12.2: *The same system can support more than one kind of wave at the same time. Sound waves and light waves travel through water so dolphins can hear and see. At the same time, a boundary wave travels on the surface. Three of our five senses (sight, hearing, touch) respond to waves.*

How do you recognize a wave?

All waves have things in common. When you see the things in this list, you should suspect that there is some kind of wave involved.

Evidence for suspecting there are waves:

- Anytime you see a vibration that moves, there is a wave.
- Anything that makes or responds to sound uses waves.
- Anything that makes or responds to light uses waves.
- Anything that transmits information through the air (or space) without wires uses waves. This includes cell phones, radio, and television.
- Anything that allows you to "see through" objects uses waves. This includes ultrasound, CAT scans, MRI scans, and X rays (figure 12.3).

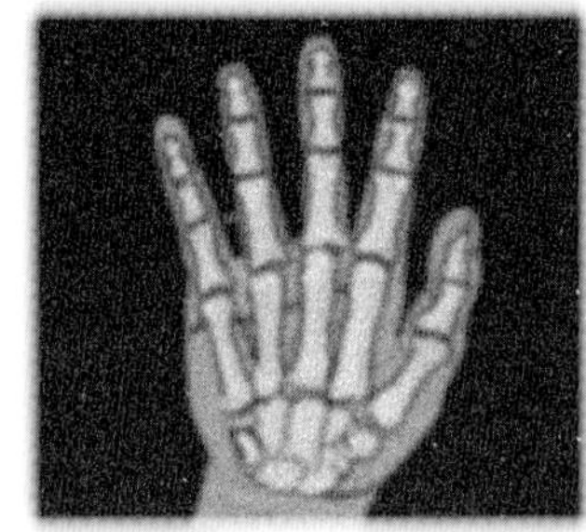

Figure 12.3: *X rays use light waves to make images that show bones under the skin.*

Where can we find waves?

We will usually find waves whenever information, energy, or motion is transmitted over a distance without anything obviously moving. The remote control on a TV is an example. To change the channel you can use the remote or get up and push the buttons with your finger. Both actions carry information (the channel selected) to the TV. One uses physical motion and the other uses a wave that goes from the remote control to the television. Your knowledge of physics and waves tells you there must be some kind of wave because information traveled from one place to another, and nothing appeared to move. The wave is actually an infrared light wave, which is invisible to the eye.

Transverse and longitudinal waves

Waves spread through connections

A wave moves along a string because the string is continuous. By continuous we mean it is connected to itself. Waves spread through connections. If we were to break the string in the middle, the wave would not spread across the break. Whenever you have an extended body that is all connected to itself, you get waves. The ocean is an example: Waves can travel all the way across because the water is continuous from one shore to another.

Transverse waves

A transverse wave has its oscillations perpendicular to the direction the wave moves. The wave moves from left to right. The oscillation is up and down. Water waves are also transverse waves because the up and down oscillation is perpendicular to the motion of the wave.

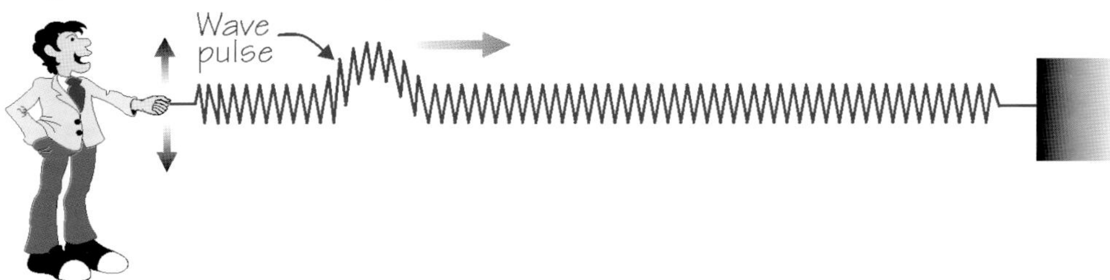

Longitudinal waves

A longitudinal wave has oscillations in the same direction as the wave moves. Stretch a fat Slinky with one end fastened to the wall. Give the free end a sharp push toward the wall and pull it back again. You see a compression wave of the Slinky that moves toward the wall. The compression wave on the Slinky is a longitudinal wave because the compression is in the direction the wave moves.

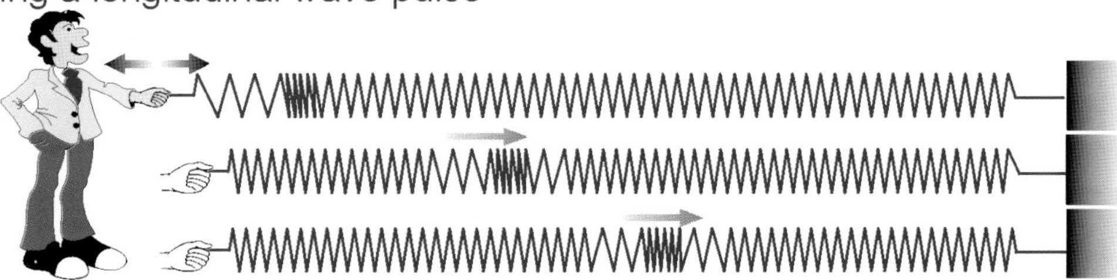

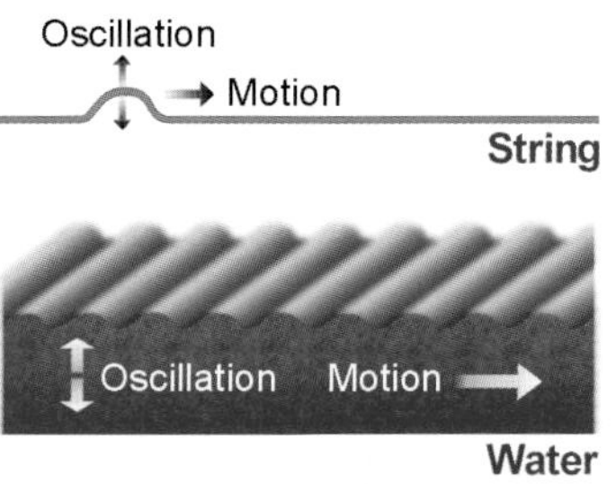

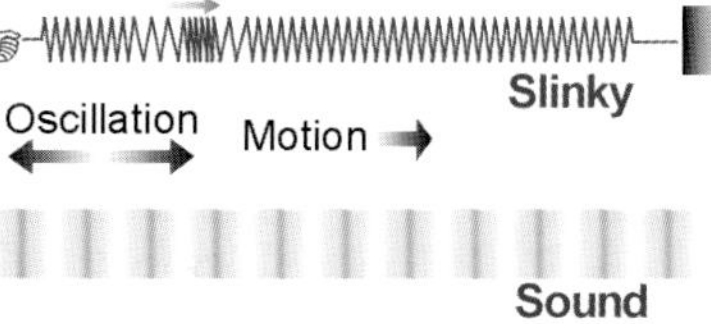

Figure 12.4: *Transverse waves oscillate perpendicular to the direction the wave moves. Strings and water are examples.*

Longitudinal waves oscillate in the same direction the wave moves. The Slinky and sound waves are examples.

Frequency, amplitude and wavelength

Basic properties

Waves have cycles, frequency, and amplitude, just like oscillations. Because waves are spread out and move, they have new properties of wavelength and speed. Also, because waves are spread out, we have to be careful how we define and measure frequency and amplitude.

Frequency

The frequency of a wave is a measure of how often it goes up and down (figure 12.5). To measure the frequency, we look at one place as the wave passes through. The frequency of the oscillating motion of one point is the frequency of the wave. The wave also causes distant points to oscillate up and down *with the same frequency.* A wave carries its frequency to every area it reaches.

Frequency is measured in Hz

Wave frequency is measured in **hertz** (Hz), just like any oscillation. A frequency of one hertz (1 Hz) describes a wave that makes everything it touches go through a complete cycle once every second. Your laboratory-size water waves typically have low frequencies, between 0.1 and 10 hertz.

Amplitude

The amplitude of a wave is the largest amount that goes above or below average (figure 12.6). You can also think of the amplitude as one-half of the distance between the highest and lowest places.

Wavelength

Wavelength is the length of one complete cycle of a wave (figure 12.7). For a water wave, this would be the distance from a point on one wave to the same point on the next wave. You could measure the wavelength from crest-to-crest or from trough-to-trough. For the vibrating string, the wavelength is the length of one complete "S" shape. We use the Greek letter "lambda" to represent wavelength. You write a lambda like an upside down "y."

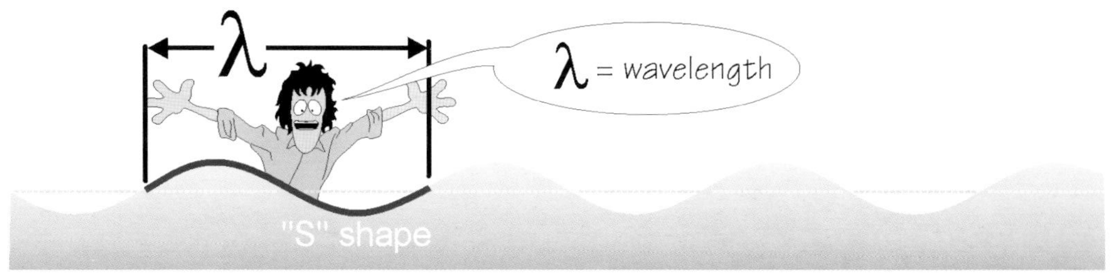

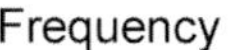

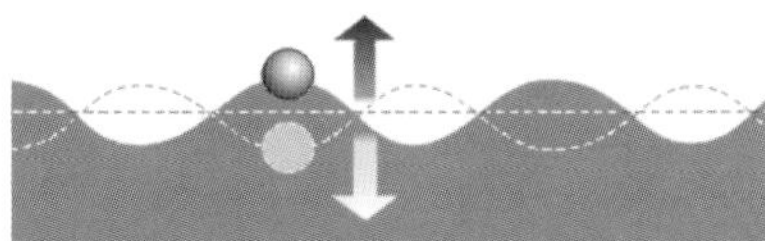

Figure 12.5: *The frequency of a wave is the frequency at which every point on the wave oscillates. The floating ball oscillates up and down at the frequency of the wave.*

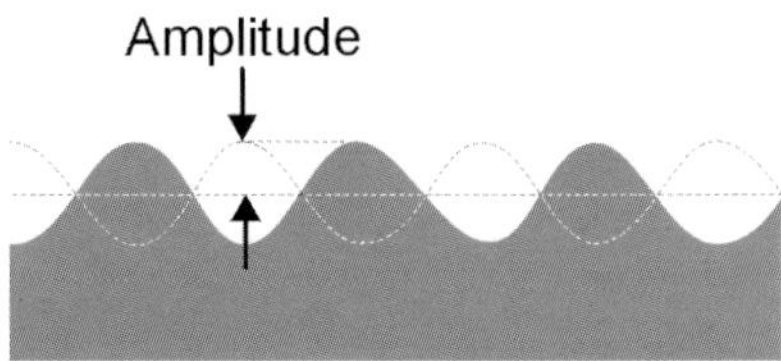

Figure 12.6: *The amplitude of a water wave is the maximum distance above the level surface. This is the same as half the distance between the lowest and highest places.*

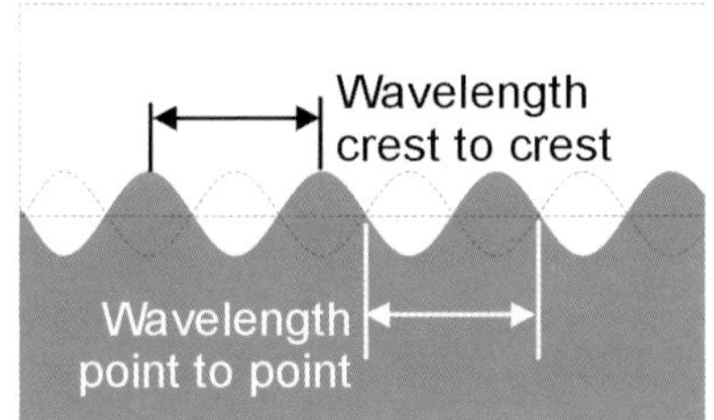

Figure 12.7: *The wavelength of a water wave can be measured from crest to crest. This is the same as the distance from one point on a wave to the same point on the next wave.*

Speed The speed of a wave describes how fast the wave can transmit an oscillation from one place to another. Waves can have a wide range of speeds. Most water waves are slow; a few miles per hour is typical. Light waves are extremely fast—186,000 miles per *second*. Sound waves travel at about 660 miles per hour, faster than water waves and much slower than light waves.

The speed of a wave measures how fast the wave spreads

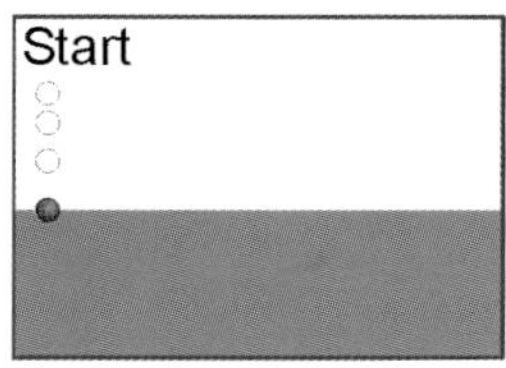

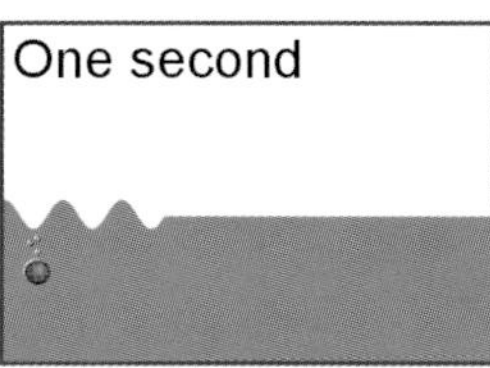

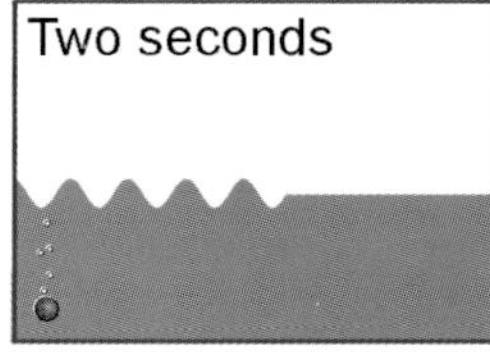

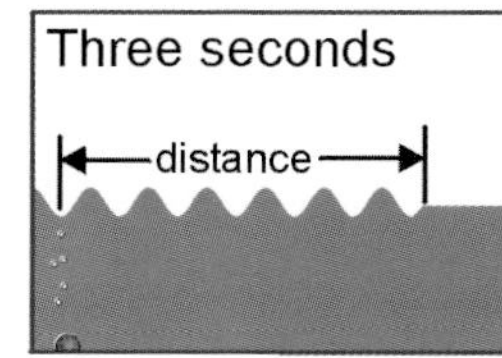

What is the speed of a wave? The speed of a wave is different from the speed of whatever the wave is causing to move. In a water wave, the surface of the water moves up and down. You could measure the up-down speed of the water surface, but that would NOT be the speed of the wave. The speed of the wave describes how quickly a movement of one part of the water surface is transmitted to another place. To measure the speed of the wave, you would have to start a ripple in one place and measure how long it takes the ripple to affect a place some distance away.

Speed is frequency times wavelength In one complete cycle, a wave moves forward one wavelength (figure 12.8). The speed of a wave is the distance traveled (one wavelength) divided by the time it takes (one period). Since the frequency is the inverse of the period, it is usually easier to calculate the speed of the wave by multiplying wavelength and frequency. The result is true for sound waves, light waves, and even gravity waves. Frequency times wavelength is the speed of the wave.

$$\text{Speed} = \frac{\text{Distance Traveled}}{\text{Time Taken}} = \frac{\text{Wavelength}}{\text{Period}} = \text{Wavelength} \times \left(\frac{1}{\text{Period}}\right)$$

$$\text{Speed} = \text{Wavelength} \times \text{Frequency}$$

The speed of a wave

$$v = f\lambda$$

Speed (m/sec) → v; Frequency (hertz) → f; Wavelength (meters) → λ

A wave moves one wavelength in one cycle.

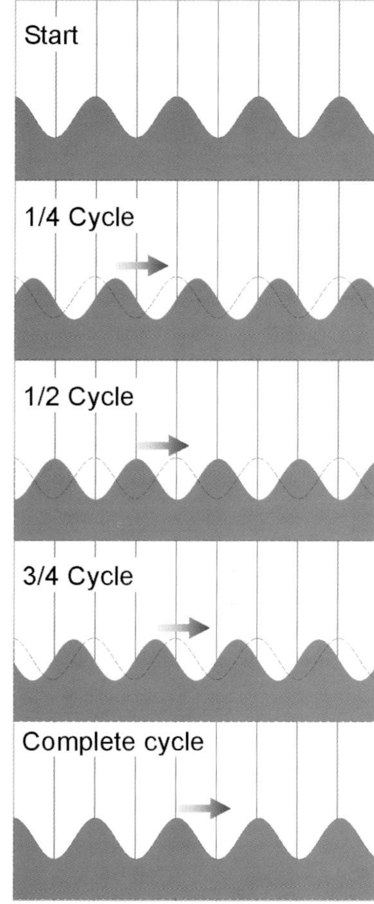

Figure 12.8: *A wave moves a distance equal to one wavelength in one cycle. Since a cycle takes one period, the speed of the wave is the wavelength divided by the period.*

12.2 Waves in Motion

In what shapes do we find waves?

What happens when a wave hits something?

You will learn the answers to these questions in this section. We start with waves in water, because these are easy to make and observe. The shape of wave fronts, and the explanation for reflection, diffraction, and other interesting things, can be seen in the lab. Almost every process we see with water waves also occurs with sound and light waves. Water waves are convenient because they are big and slow, so we can see the details of what happens. Light waves, on the other hand, are small and fast, and sound waves are invisible.

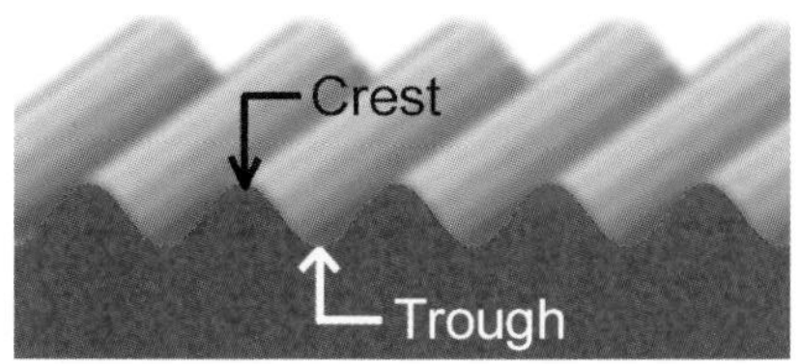

Figure 12.9: *The crest is the highest point on the wave. The trough is the low point.*

Wave shapes

Crests, troughs, and wave fronts Since a wave extends over a large area, to talk about the motion of a wave we need to pick a reference point. You can think of a wave as a series of high points and low points. A **crest** is the shape of the high points of the wave, a **trough** is the low points. When we describe the shape and motion of wave, it is useful to think in terms of the crests. As the wave moves, the crests move. The crests of a wave are sometimes called **wave fronts**. You can think of the crest as the front of a wave if it helps you to remember the definition of a wave front (figure 12.9).

Plane waves and circular waves The shape of a wave is determined by the shape of the wave fronts. You can make waves in all shapes but **plane waves** and **circular waves** are easiest to create and study (figure 12.10). The crests of a plane wave look like straight lines. The crests of a circular wave are circles. A plane wave is started by disturbing the water in a line. A circular wave is started by disturbing the water at a single point. A fingertip touched to the surface will start a circular wave.

Determining the direction the wave moves The shape of the wave front determines the direction the wave moves. Circular waves have circular wave fronts that move outward from the center. Plane waves have straight wave fronts that move in a line perpendicular to the wave fronts. To change the direction the wave moves, you have to change the shape of the wave front. In later chapters, we will see that this is exactly how lenses work.

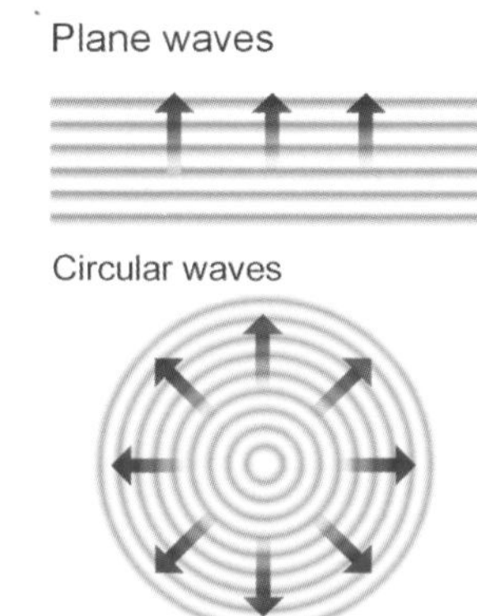

Figure 12.10: *Plane waves and circular waves. Plane waves move perpendicular to the wave fronts. Circular waves radiate outward from the center.*

What happens when a wave hits something?

The four wave interactions

Waves can do different things when they hit an obstacle (figure 12.11).

Reflection	The wave can bounce off and go in a new direction.
Refraction	The wave can pass straight into and through the obstacle.
Diffraction	The wave can bend around or through holes in the obstacle.
Absorption	The wave can be absorbed and disappear.

Sometimes, the wave can do all those things at once, partly bouncing off, partly passing through, partly being absorbed, and partly going around. You may have noticed the radio in a car sometimes loses the station as you enter a tunnel. Part of the wave that carries the signal bends around the entrance to the tunnel and follows you in. Part is absorbed by the ground. The deeper in the tunnel you go, the weaker the wave gets until the radio cannot pick up the signal at all and you hear static. Simple things like mirrors and complex things like ultrasound or X rays all depend on how waves act when they encounter objects.

Boundaries

Waves are affected by boundaries where conditions change. The first three interactions (reflection, refraction, diffraction) usually occur when a wave crosses a boundary. Absorption can also occur at a boundary, but often happens within the body of a material.

Reflection

When a wave bounces off an obstacle we call it **reflection**. If you make water waves travel toward a wall they will be reflected. The wave that reflects is like the original wave but moving in a new direction. The wavelength and frequency are usually unchanged. The reflection of a wave happens at a boundary (or edge) where the wave has to pass from one condition to another. Mirrored sunglasses are a good example. The lenses reflect some light so they look like mirrors. The boundary is the surface of the lens where the light wave crosses from air to glass. Abrupt changes in material will almost always cause reflections.

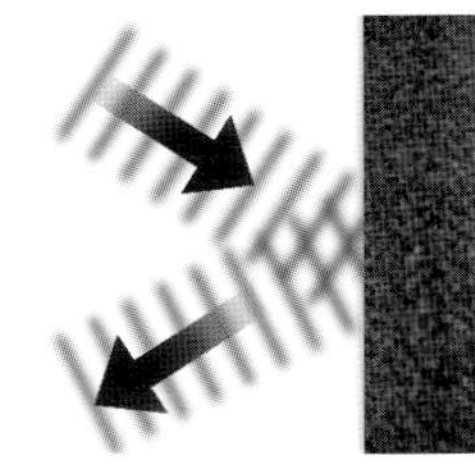

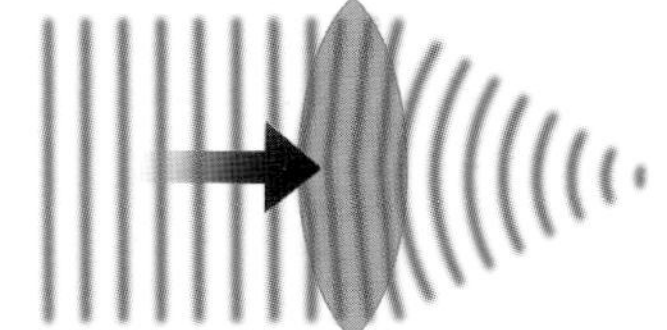

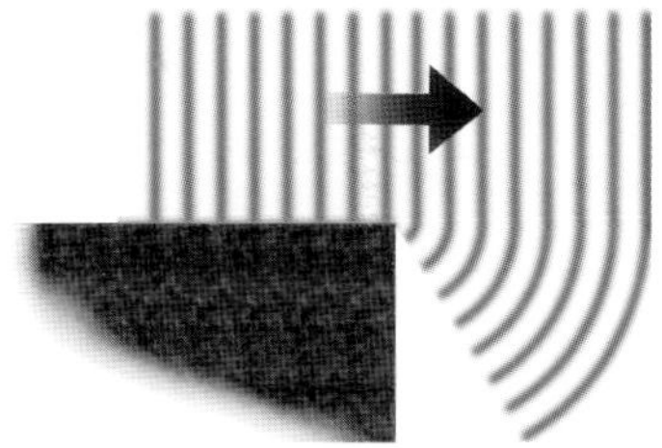

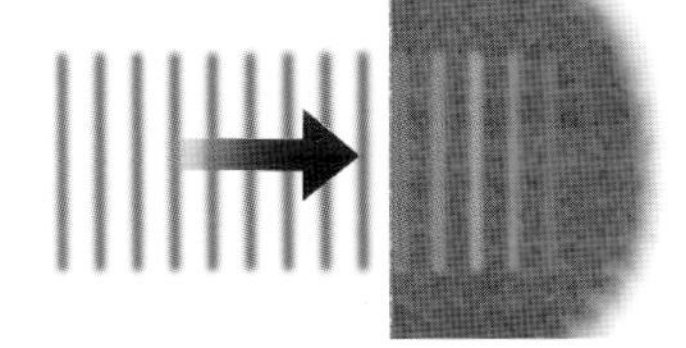

Figure 12.11: *The four processes for waves interacting with boundaries.*

Refraction Waves can cross boundaries and pass into or through objects. Placing a thin plate on the bottom of ripple tank creates a boundary where the depth of the water changes. If you look carefully, you see that waves are bent as they cross the boundary. The wave starts in one direction and changes direction as it crosses. We call it **refraction** when a wave bends as it crosses a boundary. We say the wave is *refracted* as it passes through the boundary. Refraction is useful because it allows us to shape and control waves. Eyeglasses are a very good example where refraction is used to change light waves. Glasses help people to see by bending the light waves into an easier shape for some people's eyes to focus.

Absorption Waves can be absorbed as they pass through objects. Absorption is what happens when the amplitude of a wave gets smaller and smaller as it passes through a material. Some objects and materials have properties that absorb certain kinds of waves. A sponge can absorb a water wave while letting the water pass. A heavy curtain absorbs sound waves. Theaters often use heavy curtains so the audience cannot hear backstage noise. Dark glass absorbs light waves, which is how some kinds of sunglasses work.

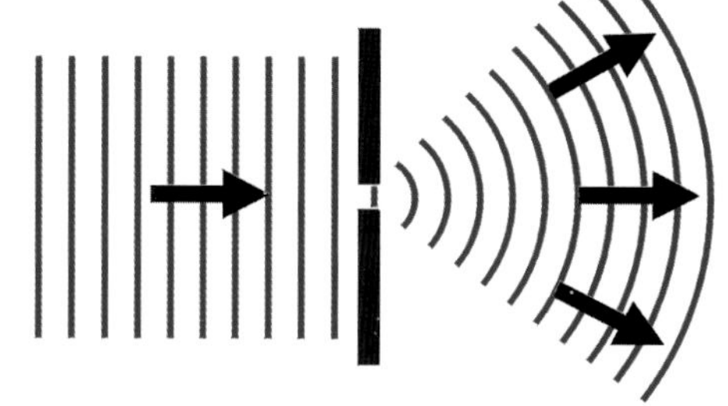

Diffraction through a small opening turns plane waves into circular waves.

Diffraction Waves can bend around obstacles and go through openings. The process of bending around corners or passing through openings is called **diffraction**. We say a wave is *diffracted* when it is changed by passing through a hole or around an edge. Diffraction usually changes the direction and shape of the wave. Diffraction turns a plane wave into a circular wave when the wave passes through a narrow opening. Diffraction explains why you can hear someone even though a door is only open a tiny crack. Diffraction causes the sound wave to spread out from the crack.

 **Seismic waves**

Seismic waves are generated when Earth's crust slips in an earthquake. Two kinds of seismic waves travel through Earth: primary waves (P-waves) and secondary waves (S-waves).

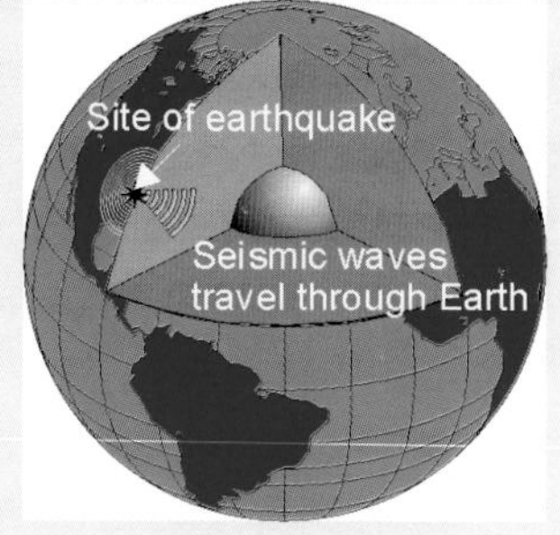

P-waves are longitudinal. S-waves are transverse and cause powerful, sideways shaking of the ground. As the P-waves and S-waves encounter layers in the Earth, they refract and reflect. By studying the patterns of waves that are recorded after an earthquake, geologists have identified the parts of Earth's internal structure.

12.3 Natural Frequency and Resonance

Theoretically, waves can extend forever. Realistically, they are limited by the size of the system. Boundaries create conditions that favor special frequencies or wavelengths. Just as the length of the string set the period of the pendulum, the boundaries and properties of the system make certain waves much more powerful than others. The concepts of *resonance* and *natural frequency* apply to a huge range of natural and human-made systems. These two powerful ideas are the key to understanding the tides of the ocean, the way our ears separate sound, and even how a microwave oven works.

Natural frequency

The natural frequency is the frequency at which a system oscillates when it is disturbed.

Natural frequency

What is natural frequency? If you pluck a guitar string in the middle it vibrates back and forth. If you pluck the same string 10 times in a row and measure the frequency of vibration you find that it is always the same. When plucked, the string vibrates at its **natural frequency**. The pendulum also had a natural frequency.

Why natural frequency is important The natural frequency is important for many reasons:

1 All things in the universe have a natural frequency, and many things have more than one.

2 If you know an object's natural frequency, you know how it will vibrate.

3 If you know how an object vibrates, you know what kinds of waves it will create.

4 If you want to make specific kinds of waves, you need to create objects with natural frequencies that match the waves you want.

Microwave ovens, musical instruments, and cell phones all use the natural frequency of an oscillator to create and control waves. Musical instruments work by adjusting the natural frequency of vibrating strings or air to match musical notes. The A string on a guitar has a natural frequency of 440 hertz.

Figure 12.12: *A guitar uses the natural frequency of the strings to make the correct notes. Once it is tuned, the A string, when plucked, will always vibrate at 440 hertz.*

Changing the natural frequency The natural frequency depends on many factors, such as the tightness, length, or weight of a string. We can change the natural frequency of a system by changing any of the factors that affect the size, inertia, or forces in the system. For example, tuning a guitar changes the natural frequency of a string by changing its tension.

Resonance

The response of an oscillator

To keep a system oscillating, we apply an oscillating force. For example, if you want to get a jump rope going, you shake the end up and down. What you are really doing is applying an oscillating force to the rope. The response of the rope is to oscillate up and down with the same frequency of your applied force.

If you try this, you notice that at certain frequencies your force is noticeably more effective at making the rope oscillate. For example, shaking the end up and down twice per second (1.6 Hz) results in an amplitude of a few centimeters. Slowing down to once per second (1 Hz) makes an amplitude of more than a meter! Slowing even more, to once every two seconds (0.5 Hz), causes the amplitude to drop back down again. Your experiment shows that the frequency of 1 hertz is *many times* more effective than any other frequency.

Resonance

The extra-strong response at 1 hertz is an example of resonance. You can think of resonance as having the natural frequency of the system exactly in tune with your force. Each cycle of your force exactly matches each cycle of the system. As a result, each push adds to the next one and the amplitude of the oscillation grows (figure 12.13). Resonance happens when something is vibrated at its natural frequency (or a multiple of the natural frequency). Resonance is an important idea because it is used to transfer power into all kinds of waves from lasers to microwave ovens to musical instruments.

A swing is a good example of resonance

The example of a swing (that you might sit on at the park) is one of the best ways to describe resonance. With a swing, small pushes applied over time build up a large amplitude of motion. This happens because each push is synchronized to the natural motion of the swing. A forward push is always given when the swing is as far back as it can go. The swing is like a pendulum, which has a natural frequency. By applying small pushes at a frequency matched to the natural frequency, we are able to create a large motion. The interaction of the repeating pushes and the natural motion of the swing is what creates resonance. The effect of the resonance is that the swing's motion gets large even though the pushes are small. Resonance is not a single thing. Resonance is an interaction between a wave, a driving force, and the boundaries of the system.

An example of resonance

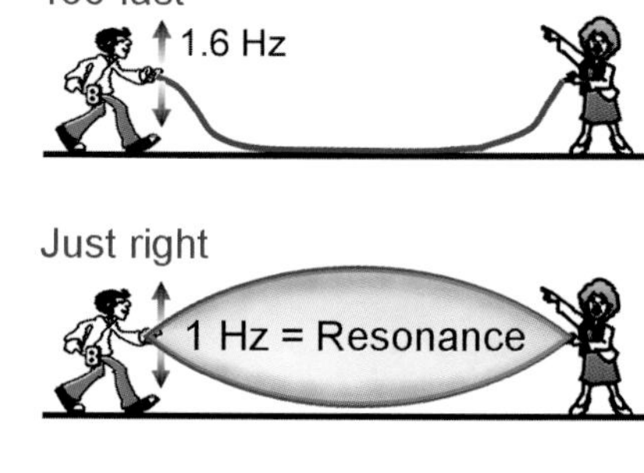

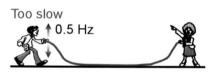

Figure 12.13: *A jump rope is a good experiment for resonance. If you shake it at the right frequency, it makes a big wave motion. If your frequency is not just right, the rope will not make the wave pattern at all.*

Standing waves on a string

What is a standing wave?

Although waves usually travel, it is possible to make a wave stay in one place. A wave that is trapped in one spot is called a **standing wave**. It is possible to make standing waves of almost any kind, including sound, water, and even light. A vibrating string is a great example for doing experiments with standing waves. Vibrating strings are what make music on a guitar or piano.

Harmonics are multiples of the natural frequency of a standing wave

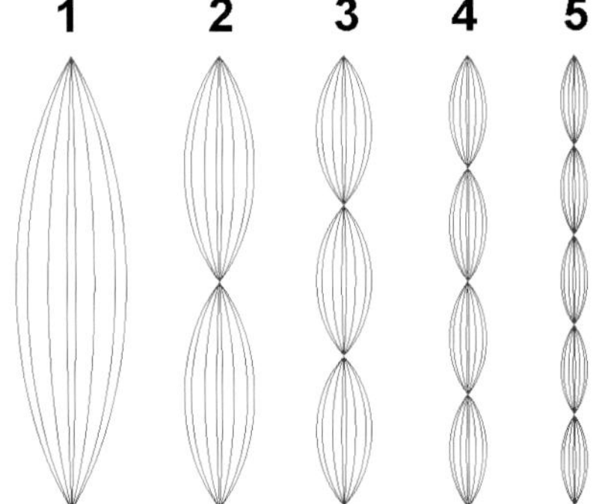

The first five harmonics of the vibrating string

Standing waves occur at frequencies that are multiples of the **fundamental**, which is the natural frequency of the string. The fundamental and multiples of its frequency are called **harmonics**. The diagram to the left shows the first five harmonics. You can tell the harmonic number by counting the number of "bumps" on the wave. The first harmonic has one bump, the second has two bumps, the third has three, and so on. If the frequency of the first harmonic is 10 hertz, then the second will be at a frequency of 20 hertz, the third will be at 30 hertz, and so on.

Wavelength

A vibrating string moves so fast that your eye averages out the image and you see a wave-shaped blur (figure 12.14). At any one moment the string is really in only one place within the blur. The wavelength is the length of one complete "S" shape on the string. Higher frequency waves have shorter wavelengths.

Why are standing waves useful?

Standing waves are useful because we can control their frequency and wavelength. Because the wave is trapped, it is easy to put power into it and make large amplitudes. In your microwave oven, there is a device called a magnetron. Inside the magnetron is a standing wave driven by electricity. A small hole in the boundary lets some of the wave's energy out to cook food. The shape of the magnetron forces the standing wave to oscillate at exactly 2.4 billion cycles per second (2.4 gigahertz). Energy that leaks out at the same frequency is perfectly matched to heat water molecules in food.

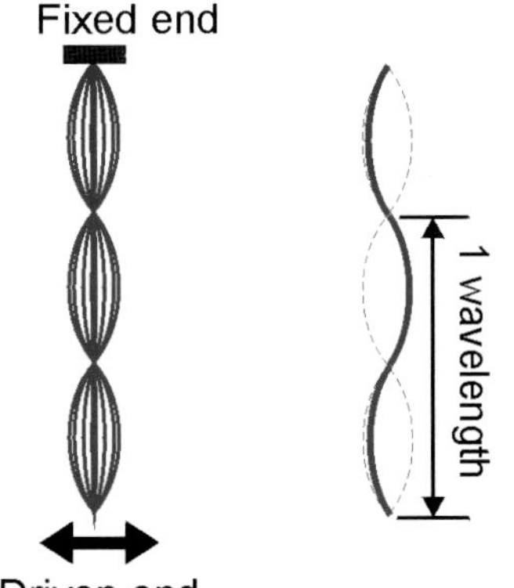

Figure 12.14: *A standing wave on a vibrating string. The wavelength is the length of one complete **S** shape of the wave.*

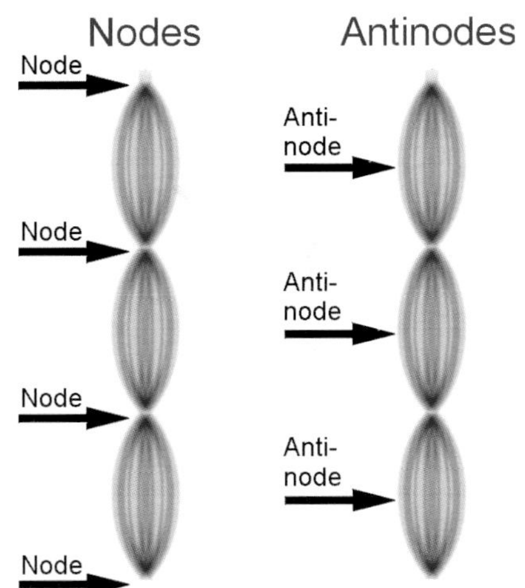

Figure 12.15: *Nodes and antinodes for the third harmonic of the vibrating string. Nodes are points where the string does not move. Antinodes are points of the greatest amplitude.*

Interference

What is interference? Interference happens when two or more waves come together. Because there are so many waves around us, they often interfere with each other. In fact, radio and television use the interference of two waves to carry music and video. The resonance of a vibrating string can be understood using the interference of waves. Sometimes on the ocean, two big waves add up to make a gigantic wave that may only last a few moments but is taller than ships, and can have a terrible impact.

Constructive interference Suppose you make two wave pulses on the stretched spring. One comes from the left and the other comes from the right. When they meet in the middle, they combine to make a single large pulse. This is called constructive interference. Constructive interference occurs when waves add up to make a larger amplitude (figure 12.16).

Destructive interference There is another way to launch the two pulses. If we make pulses on opposite sides of the cord, something different happens. When the pulses meet in the middle they cancel each other out! One wants to pull the string up and the other wants to pull it down. The result is that the string is flat and both pulses vanish for a moment. This is called destructive interference. In destructive interference waves add up to make a smaller amplitude (figure 12.17).

After they interfere, both wave pulses separate again and travel on their own. This is surprising if you think about it. For a moment, the middle of the cord is flat in the example of destructive interference. A moment later, two wave pulses come out of the flat part and race away from each other. Waves still store energy, even when they interfere.

Waves at the atomic level Down at the scale of atoms, there are many extremely strong waves. Because there are so many and they are tiny and random, they interfere destructively on average. We don't see the wavelike nature of atoms because of large-scale destructive interference. In special cases, like with a magnetic resonance imaging (or MRI) machine, or a laser, we create constructive interference of atomic waves. The result is very powerful and useful technology.

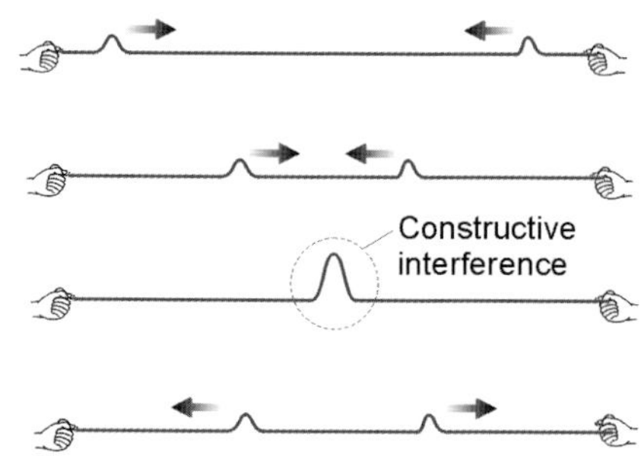

Figure 12.16: *Two wave pulses on the same side add up to make a single, bigger pulse when they meet. This is an example of constructive interference.*

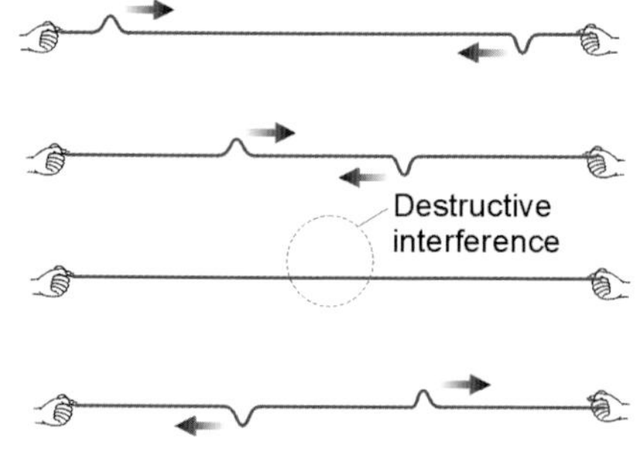

Figure 12.17: *Two equal wave pulses on opposite sides subtract when they meet. The upward movement of one pulse exactly cancels with the downward movement of the other. For a moment there is no pulse at all. This is an example of destructive interference.*

Chapter 12 Review

Vocabulary review

Match the following terms with the correct definition. There is one extra definition in the list that will not match any of the terms.

Set One

1. wave
2. vibration
3. wave pulse
4. transverse
5. longitudinal

a. A short length of wave that travels
b. A wave where the oscillation is perpendicular to the direction of motion
c. An oscillation that travels
d. A wave where the oscillation is in the same direction as the direction of motion
e. A word that means the same as oscillation
f. The time it takes to complete one cycle

Set Two

1. wavelength
2. natural frequency
3. resonance
4. interference
5. boundary

a. A place where a wave changes suddenly
b. The interaction of two or more waves with each other
c. A special frequency (or frequencies) at which objects vibrate if they are disturbed
d. A special condition where the frequency you push matches the natural frequency of the system, resulting in large amplitude waves
e. The length of one complete wave
f. A unit of one cycle per second

Set Three

1. reflection
2. refraction
3. diffraction
4. absorption

a. The process where a wave gets smaller and smaller
b. The process of bouncing a wave off a boundary
c. The process of bending a wave as it crosses a boundary
d. What happens when a wave bends around obstacles or through holes
e. A word that means the same as oscillation

Set Four

1. node
2. antinode
3. harmonic
4. standing wave

a. A wave whose frequency is a multiple of another wave
b. A point on a wave where there is no motion
c. A wave that is trapped between boundaries
d. The place on a wave where the amplitude is largest
e. The length of one complete wave

Concept review

1. A wave which vibrates at 60 Hz has a higher ______ than a wave that vibrates at 30 Hz.

   a. wavelength
   b. frequency
   c. amplitude
   d. transverse

2. Which of the following things must involve a wave? You may choose more than one. Explain each of your choices.

   a. A bulldozer is moving the dirt for a highway.
   b. A person is talking to someone on a cell phone.
   c. An earthquake in the Pacific Ocean causes the floor of a house to shake in Texas.
   d. A car is going 70 miles per hour on a highway.
   e. Two people stop to listen to a jet plane passing overhead.
   f. A doctor makes an X ray to check for broken bones.
   g. An explorer shines a flashlight to see a passage in a cave deep underground.

3. Which of the following pictures shows a correct measure of the wavelength? You may choose more than one.

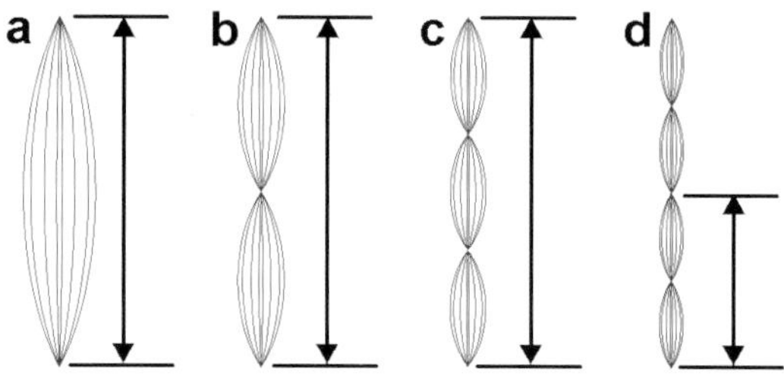

4. A wave is moving toward a hole in a wall. What will the wave look like as it passes through the wall?

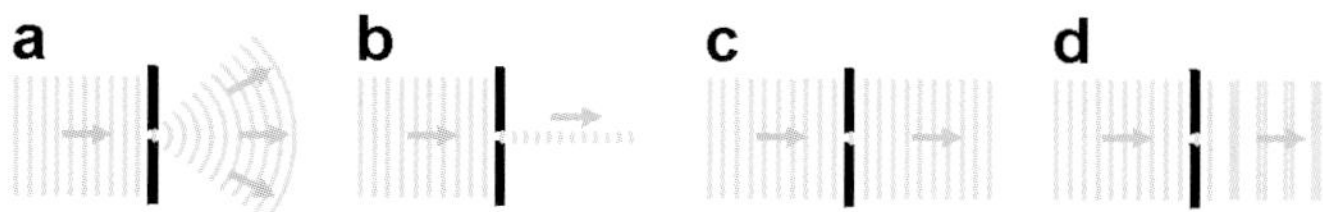

5. Which of the following best describes what happens when a water wave hits a solid wall?

   a. reflection
   b. refraction
   c. diffraction
   d. absorption

6. An elastic string is attached to a wall on one end. A wave pulse traveling on the string reflects off the wall and comes back:

   a. On the same side of the string as it started.
   b. On the opposite side of the string from where it started.
   c. Split equally between both sides of the string.

7. A transverse wave is:

   a. A wave with a very high frequency, like light.
   b. A wave that oscillates perpendicular to the direction it moves.
   c. A wave that oscillates along the direction it moves.
   d. A wave with a frequency that is a multiple of another frequency.

8. A string with natural frequency of 15 Hz will likely show resonance when wiggled at which frequency.

   a. 20 Hz
   b. 40 Hz
   c. 30 Hz
   d. 50 Hz

Problems

1. You find the pattern in the picture at a frequency of 40 Hz. Answer the following questions.
   a. What is the period?
   b. At what frequency will you find the third harmonic?
   c. At what frequency will you find the eighth harmonic?
   d. How many antinodes are in the wave in the picture?

40 Hz

2. A group of students shows you sketches in their lab book of four patterns they found on a vibrating string. You suspect that one of the pictures is either a fake, or a mistake. Which picture is the fake (or mistake) and how did you know?

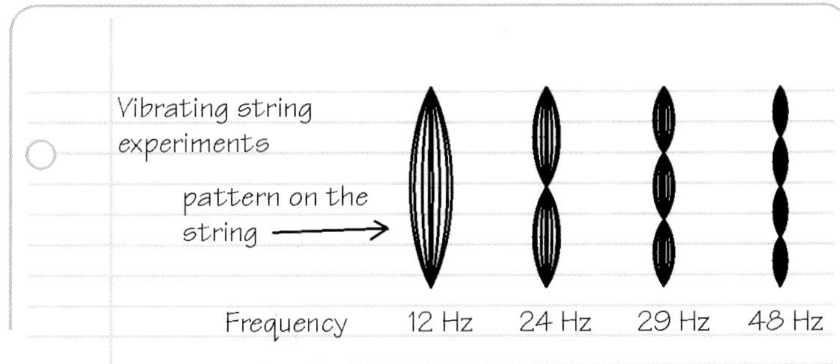

3. The wave in the picture has how many nodes?

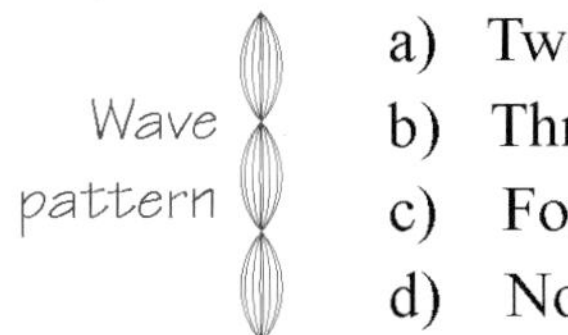

a) Two
b) Three
c) Four
d) None

4. The wavelength of a wave on a string is 25 centimeters and the frequency is 20 Hz. Calculate the speed of the wave.

5. A wave has a frequency of 5 Hz and a wavelength of 2 meters. What is the speed of the wave?

   a. 10 m/sec
   b. 0.4 m.sec
   c. 2.5 m/sec
   d. 7 m/sec

6. You are doing a vibrating string experiment and observe the seventh harmonic at a frequency of 63 Hz. At what frequency will you find the third harmonic?

   a. 21 Hz
   b. 27 Hz
   c. 189 Hz m/sec
   d. 9 Hz

7. You are doing a vibrating string experiment and observe a resonance that looks like the picture below. You measure a frequency of 22 Hz. Fill in the rest of the data table with the frequency and wavelengths you would expect to find in an experiment. Note: Harmonics 6 and 8 are not included on the table.

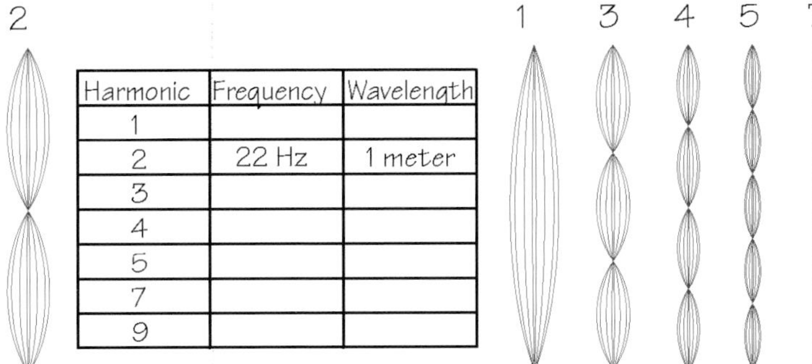

Harmonic	Frequency	Wavelength
1		
2	22 Hz	1 meter
3		
4		
5		
7		
9		

Applying your knowledge

1. A guitar string is divided by frets. When you hold your finger on each fret, you make the length of the string shorter. This makes the wavelength shorter. If the wavelength gets shorter, the frequency must get higher to compensate.

   You know that multiplying frequency and wavelength for a vibrating string always gives you the same number. Suppose your guitar string is 68 centimeters long and vibrates with a natural frequency of 120 Hz. What length of string would you need to make it vibrate at 180 Hz, which is 1.5 times higher?

2. Marching is when many people walk exactly in step with each other. Tromp, tromp, tromp, every foot falls at exactly the same moment with a steady frequency. It has been known since early times that troops should never march across a bridge. When soldiers cross a bridge they all walk with a different pace. Discuss why marching across a bridge is a bad idea, knowing what you learned in this chapter.

3. Waves in the ocean are created by the wind acting on the surface of the water. It is suspected that many ships have been wrecked by the interference of two waves. Discuss how the meeting of two waves might sink a ship that could easily ride over a single wave.

4. Earthquakes make vibrations of the ground that can literally shake buildings to pieces. Buildings are not completely stiff, and tall buildings sway quite a bit. Swaying is a form of oscillation, and all buildings have at least one natural frequency. What do you think happens if the natural frequency of a building matches the frequency of an earthquake? How might you change the natural frequency of a building?

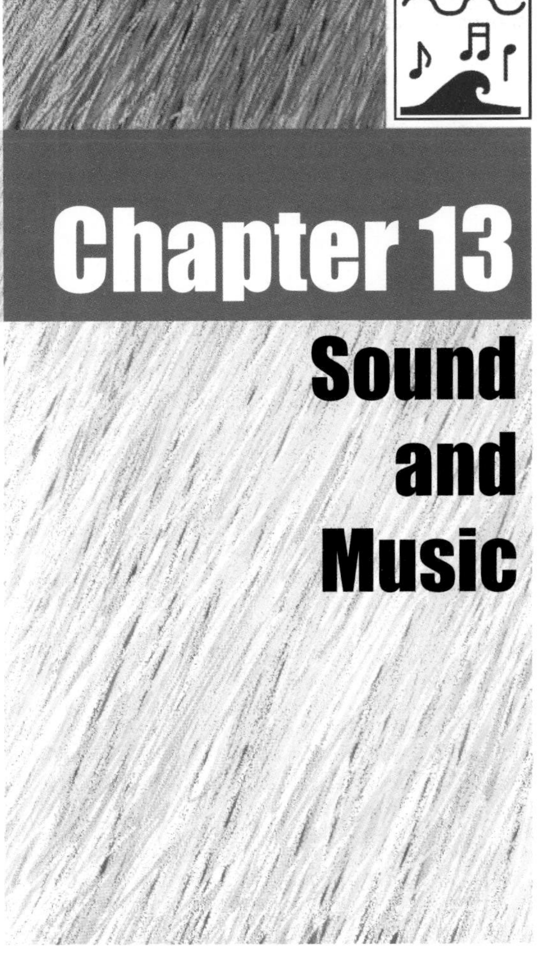

Introduction to Chapter 13

Sound is one of the richest of our five senses. In this chapter you will explore a field of study that includes everything from making computers that can understand speech to building concert halls and speaker boxes. The end of the chapter provides an introduction to music, truly a universal language that humans have always enjoyed.

Investigations for Chapter 13

13.1	**Sound**	*What is sound and how do we hear it?*

The first investigation explores the perception of sound. Humans hear frequencies between 20 Hz and 20,000 Hz, a range that varies widely with people. You will measure the sensitivity of your own ears as well as those of your classmates.

13.2	**Properties of Sound**	*Does sound behave like other waves?*

Using an electronic synthesizer, you will create resonance, beats, and interference of sound waves. The evidence you collect will dramatically demonstrate that sound is a wave, and show you how to control sound waves for useful purposes.

13.3	**Music**	*What is music and how do we make music?*

The musical scale was known to humans 20,000 years before anyone invented writing. Musical sounds are derived from an elegant mathematical foundation of simple fractions and ratios. Once you know the ratios, you can design and build your own musical instruments.

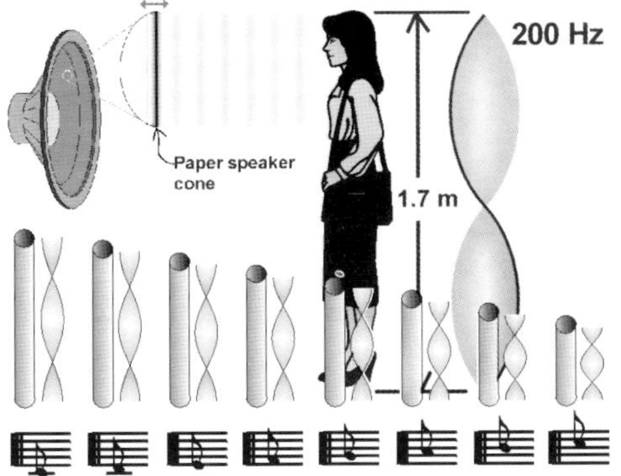

Learning Goals

In this chapter, you will:

- ✔ Learn how we hear sound.
- ✔ Learn how your brain interprets sound to understand words and music.
- ✔ Learn what kinds of sounds we can hear, and what kinds we cannot hear.
- ✔ Learn what a sound wave is and how it travels.
- ✔ Learn how the loudness of sound is measured.
- ✔ Learn the basics of acoustics as applied to the design of buildings and musical instruments.
- ✔ Learn to read a sonogram and how a computer recognizes spoken words.
- ✔ Learn what *supersonic* means.
- ✔ Learn why a musical scale sounds good, or why it sounds bad.
- ✔ Learn how we tell voices and instruments apart from each other.

Vocabulary

acoustics	dissonance	pitch	sonogram
beat	harmonics	pressure	supersonic
cochlea	musical scale	reverberation	white noise
consonance	beats	ultrasound	decibel
pitch	harmony	sound	rhythm

13.1 Sound

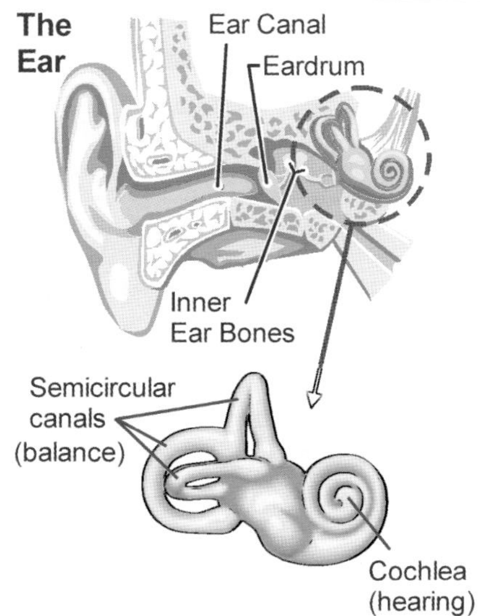

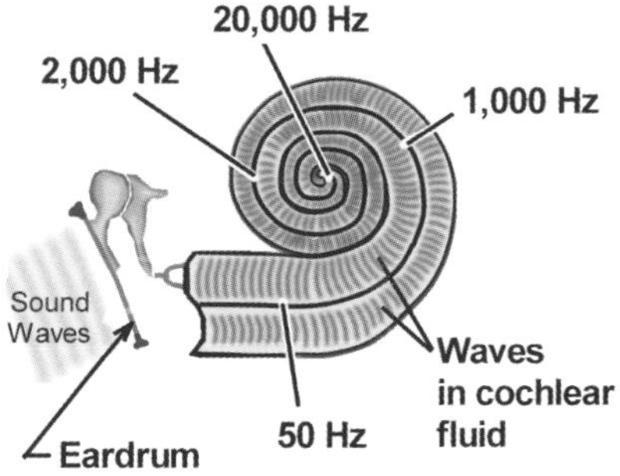

Figure 13.1: *The structure of the inner ear. When the eardrum vibrates, three small bones transmit the vibration to the cochlea. The vibrations make waves inside the cochlea, which vibrates nerves in the spiral. Each part of the spiral is sensitive to a different frequency.*

Sound is one of the most important of our senses. We use sound to express the whole range of human emotion. In this section you will learn about sound and sound waves. Scientifically, sound is one of the simplest and most common kinds of waves. But what a huge influence it has on our everyday experience! Sound is a rich and beautiful palette from which musicians create works of joy, excitement, and drama. We know sound is a wave because:

1. Sound has a frequency that we hear as higher or lower pitch.
2. Sound has a wavelength that we can construct experiments to show.
3. The speed of sound is frequency times wavelength.
4. Resonance happens with sound.
5. Sound can be reflected, refracted, and absorbed.
6. Sound shows evidence of interference and diffraction.

How do we hear a sound wave?

Hearing sound

We get our sense of hearing from the cochlea, a tiny fluid-filled organ in the inner ear (figure 13.1). The inner ear actually has two important functions: providing our sense of hearing and our sense of balance. The three semicircular canals near the cochlea are also filled with fluid. Fluid moving in each of the three canals tells the brain whether the body is moving left-right, up-down, or forward-backward.

How the cochlea works

The perception of sound starts with the eardrum. The eardrum vibrates in response to sound waves in the ear canal. The three delicate bones of the inner ear transmit the vibration of the eardrum to the side of the cochlea. The fluid in the spiral of the cochlea vibrates and creates waves that travel up the spiral. The spiral channel of the cochlea starts out large and gets narrower near the end. The nerves near the beginning see a relatively large channel and respond to longer wavelength, low-frequency sound. The nerves at the small end of the channel respond to shorter wavelength, higher-frequency sound.

The range of human hearing

The range of human hearing is between 20 Hz and 20,000 Hz (20 kHz). The combination of the eardrum, bones, and the cochlea all contribute to the limited range of hearing. You could not hear a sound at 50,000 Hz, even at 100 decibels (loud). Animals such as cats and dogs can hear much higher frequencies because they have more sensitive structures in their inner ears.

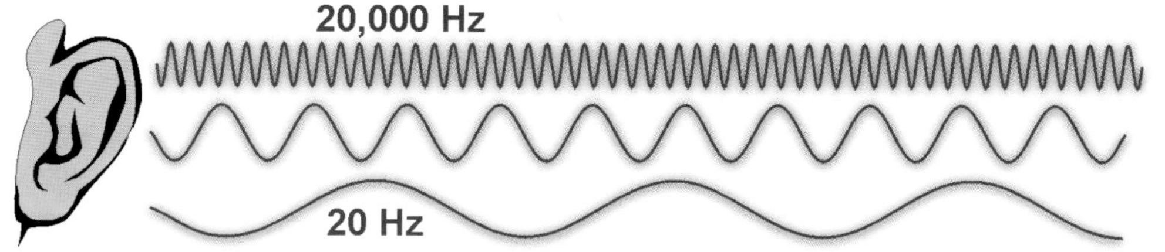

Figure 13.2: *Hearing protection is recommended when working in loud environments.*

Hearing ability changes with time

Hearing varies greatly with people and changes with age. Some people can hear very high frequency sounds and other people cannot. People gradually lose high frequency hearing with age. Most adults cannot hear frequencies above 15,000 Hz, while children can often hear to 20,000 Hz.

Hearing can be damaged by loud noise

Hearing is affected by exposure to loud or high-frequency noise. The nerve signals that carry sensation of sound to the brain are created by tiny hairs that shake when the fluid in the cochlea is vibrated. Listening to loud sounds for a long time can cause the hairs to weaken or break off. Before there were safety rules about noise, people who worked in mines or other noisy places often became partly deaf by the time they retired. It is smart to protect your ears by keeping the volume reasonable and wearing ear protection if you have to stay in a loud place (figure 13.2). Many musicians wear earplugs to protect their hearing when playing in concerts!

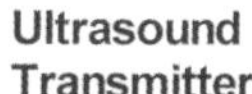

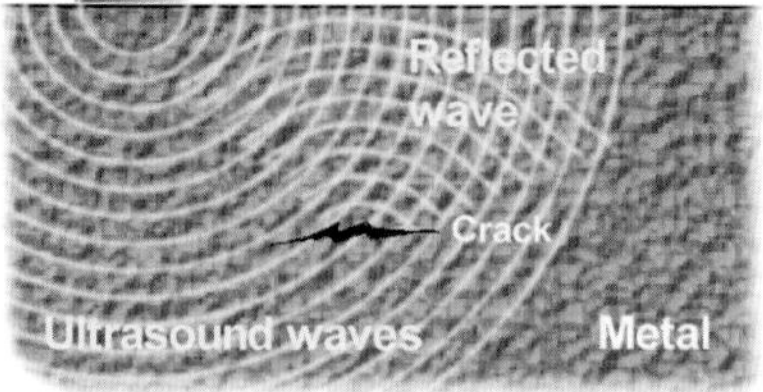

Figure 13.3: *Ultrasound can be used to find tiny cracks in metal. The crack reflects the sound wave. The reflection can tell the engineer the depth and size of the crack.*

Ultrasound

It is possible to make sound of much higher frequency than the human ear can hear. Ultrasound is sound that has very high frequency, often 100,000 Hz or more. We cannot hear ultrasound, but it can pass through the human body easily. Medical ultrasound instruments use the refraction and reflection of sound waves inside the body to create images. Doctors often take ultrasound pictures of a beating heart or a baby in the womb. Ultrasound is also used to find cracks in materials (figure 13.3). If you pass ultrasound through a solid material, any small cracks create reflections that can be detected by instruments. Ultrasound examinations are routinely done on the structural frames of aircraft.

13.2 Properties of Sound

Like other waves, sound has the fundamental properties of frequency, wavelength, amplitude, and speed. Because sound is such a part of human experience, you probably already know its properties, but you know them by different names. For example, you will rarely hear someone complain about the high amplitude of sound. What you hear instead is that the sound is too *loud*.

What is sound?

Air pressure

Air, like any other gas, is made of free molecules whizzing around and bumping into each other (figure 13.4). The molecules in a gas have lots of space around them. Because of the extra space it is easy to squeeze molecules together to fit more in a given volume. Squeezing more into the same volume makes the pressure of the gas go up (figure 13.5). Pressure is a measure of the force felt by the walls of the container holding the gas. If there are more molecules bouncing off the walls, there is more pressure.

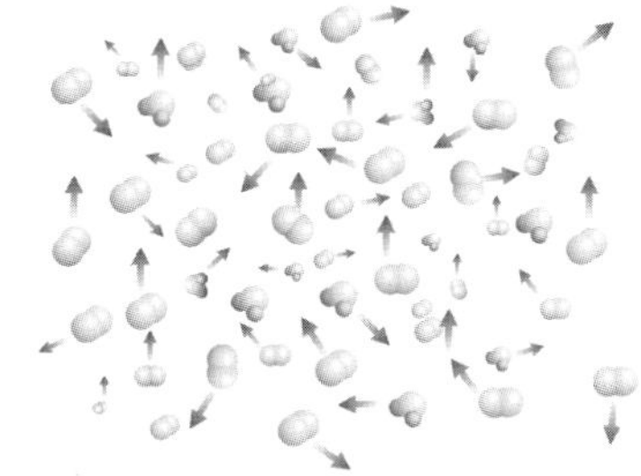

Figure 13.4: *Air is made of molecules in constant random motion, zooming around, bumping off each other and the walls of their container. There is a great deal of empty space between molecules.*

We can also lower the pressure. If we expand the volume, but don't let any molecules in or out, the pressure will go down. The pressure goes down because for every unit of area of our container there are fewer molecules bouncing off the walls.

We can also heat the gas up so the molecules move a little faster. Faster means they bang into the walls faster and bounce off with more force. Raising the temperature is a second way to increase pressure. For sound waves, however, we are mostly concerned with changes in density, or number of molecules per unit of volume.

Pressure is a restoring force

The pressure of a gas is a type of restoring force. If we increase the pressure in one place, the natural tendency is for the atoms to spread back out again, lowering the pressure. Conversely, if we reduce the pressure in one spot, other atoms nearby rush in to fill in the extra open space and raise the pressure. Atoms have mass, and therefore inertia. Pressure provides a restoring force. The combination of inertia and restoring force results in harmonic motion and waves. The harmonic motion is an oscillation in pressure and the wave is a sound wave.

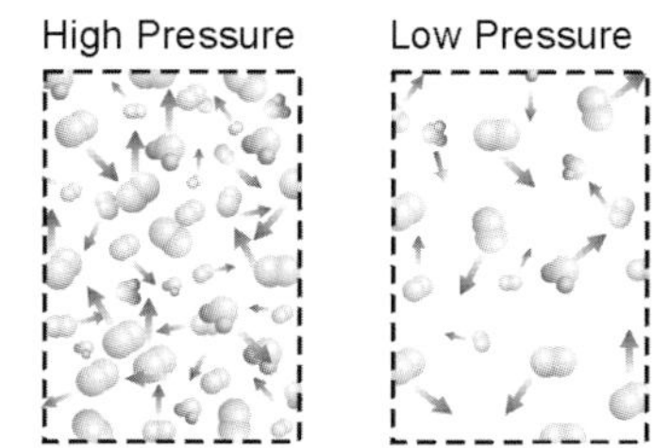

Figure 13.5: *More molecules per unit volume makes pressure go up. Fewer molecules makes pressure go down.*

Close-up look at a sound wave

Figure 13.6 shows a greatly magnified illustration of a speaker, a sound wave and the oscillation of pressure. If you touch the speaker surface you can feel the vibration. Imagine looking at the air very close to the speaker. The surface of the speaker is going back and forth. When the surface moves forward it pushes on the air touching the surface, compressing it and raising the pressure. The speaker then moves back and lowers the pressure. The back and forth motion of the speaker creates alternating layers of high and low pressure. The pressure waves travel away from the speaker as a sound wave.

A sound wave is a wave of alternating high pressure and low pressure regions of air. Anything that vibrates in air creates a sound wave. The wave travels away from the source and eventually reaches our ear, where it vibrates the eardrum and we hear the sound.

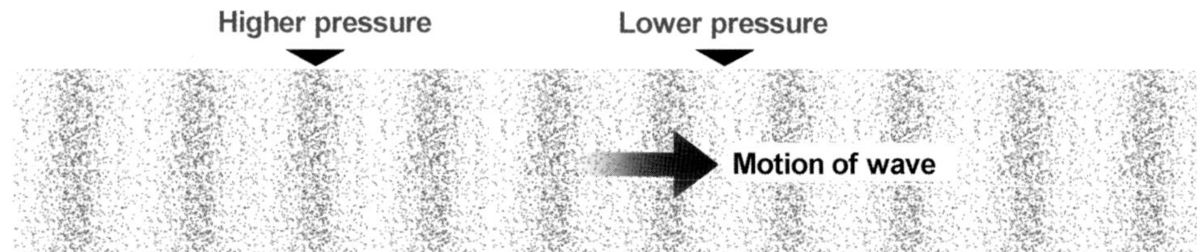

The pressure waves are small

It is hard to feel the pressure directly because the amplitude of the pressure wave is very small for most ordinary sounds. The vibrations of most sounds are also too fast for nerves in the skin to react. However, for very low frequency sounds you can feel the vibration with your skin. If you put your fingertips very close (but not touching) a speaker, you can feel the vibrating air for frequencies lower than about 100 Hz. Anyone who has listened to a loud bass guitar will confirm that sound is a vibration that you can feel at low frequencies!

Sound is a longitudinal wave

Sound waves are longitudinal because the air is compressed in the direction of travel. You can think of a sound wave like the compression wave on the Slinky. Anything that vibrates creates sound waves as long as there is air or some other material. Sound does *not* travel in space. Science fiction movies always add sound to scenes of space ships exploding. If the scenes were real, there would be total silence because there is no air in space to carry the sound waves.

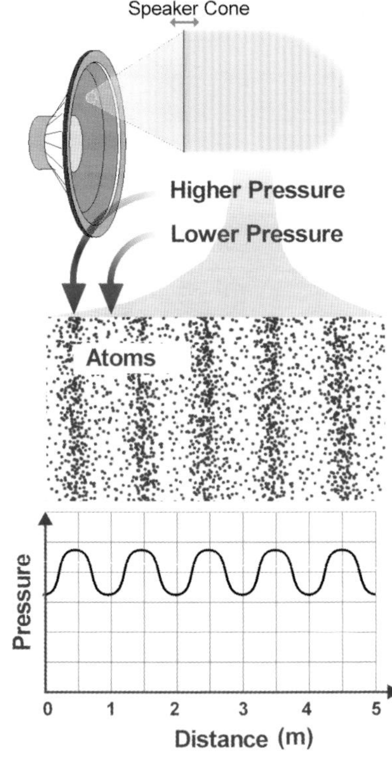

Figure 13.6: *What a sound wave might look like if you could see the atoms. The effect is greatly exaggerated to show the variation. In an actual sound wave, the difference in pressure between the highest and lowest is much smaller, less than one part in a million. From the graph you can tell the wavelength of this sound is about a meter.*

The loudness of sound

The decibel scale

The loudness of sound is measured in decibels (dB). As you might expect, loudness is related to the amplitude of the sound wave. The amplitude of a sound wave is one half of the difference between the highest pressure and the lowest pressure in the wave. Because the pressure change in a sound wave is very small, almost no one uses pressure to measure loudness. Instead we use the decibel scale. Most sounds fall between 0 and 100 on the decibel scale, making it a very convenient number to understand and use.

Table 13.1: ***Some common sounds and their loudness in decibels***

10 - 15 dB	A quiet whisper, 3 feet away
30 dB	A house in the country
40 dB	A house in the city
45 - 55 dB	The noise level in an average restaurant
65 dB	Ordinary conversation, 3 feet away
70 dB	City traffic
90 dB	A jackhammer cutting up the street, 10 feet away
110 dB	A hammer striking a steel plate 2 feet from your ear. This would be a very loud sound.
120 dB	The threshold of physical pain from loudness

What is a decibel?

The decibel scale is a *logarithmic* measure of sound pressure. This is different from linear measures you are familiar with. Every increase of 20 dB means the pressure wave has 10 times greater amplitude.

Logarithmic scale	Linear Scale
Decibels (dB)	Amplitude
0	1
20	10
40	100
60	1,000
80	10,000
100	100,000
120	1,000,000

We use the decibel scale because our ears can hear such a wide range of amplitudes. Our ears also hear changes in loudness proportional to dB and not to amplitude. Every 20 dB increase sounds about twice as loud.

The sensitivity of the ear

The actual oscillations in pressure from a sound wave are very small (figure 13.7). Table 13.2 gives some examples of the amplitude for different decibel levels. As you can see, the human ear is very sensitive. We can easily hear a pressure wave that is only 2 parts different out of 100 million! If you were looking at a pile of a million coins, you could never notice one missing. Yet our ears can detect a change in pressure of less than one part in a 100 million! This exquisite sensitivity is why hearing can be damaged by listening to very loud noises for a long time.

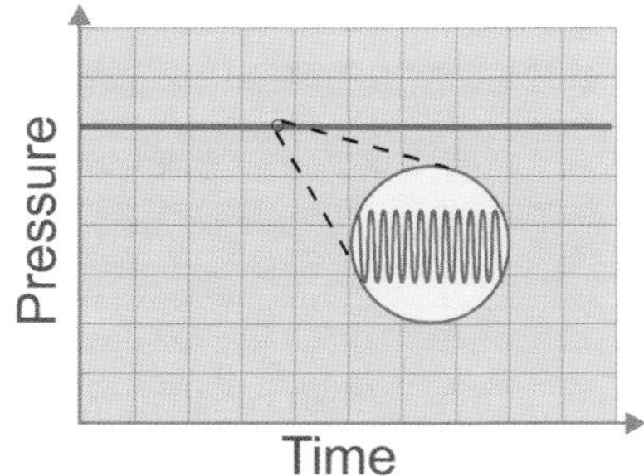

Figure 13.7: *The amplitude of a sound wave is very small. Even an 80 dB noise (quite loud) creates a pressure variation of only a few millionths of an atmosphere.*

Table 13.2: *Loudness and amplitude of sound waves in air*

Loudness in Decibels	Amplitude of Pressure Wave (fraction of 1 atmosphere)
20 dB	2 / 1,000,000,000
40 dB	2 / 100,000,000
80 dB	2 / 1,000,000
120 dB	2 / 10,000

Acoustics

Reducing the loudness of sound is important in many applications. For example, a library might want to absorb all sound to maintain quiet. A recording studio might want to block sound from the outside from mixing with sound from the inside. Acoustics is the science and technology of sound. Knowledge of acoustics is important to many careers, from the people who design stereo speakers to the architects who designed your school.

Soundproofing

Because the ear is so sensitive, it is difficult to block sound. Sound can be transmitted through materials or through gaps in walls and around doors (figure 13.8). Sound can also be reflected from hard surfaces. A good soundproofing design addresses all ways that sound can travel. To stop transmitted sound, we use dense, thick wall materials such as concrete or brick. Careful sealing around doors and openings stops sound from leaking through cracks. Thick curtains and carpets help absorb reflected sound on floors and walls. Acoustic tiles are used to reduce the loudness of sound reflected off the ceiling. Music is often recorded in studios with good soundproofing so only music inside the studio is recorded and not sounds from outside.

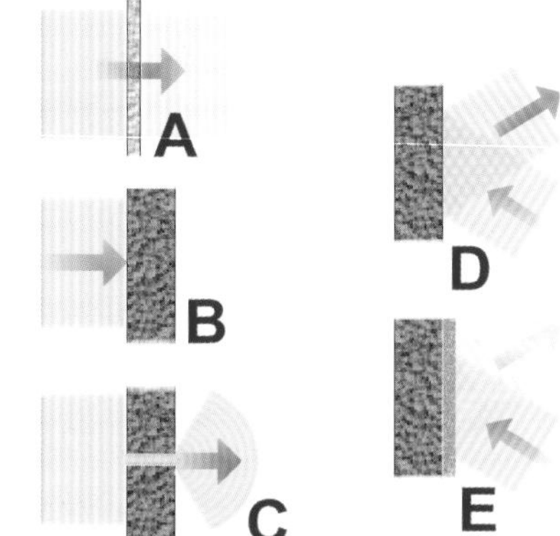

Figure 13.8: *Soundproofing requires careful attention to the way sound behaves.*
(A) It can pass through thin walls.
(B) It is stopped by dense walls.
(C) It goes through cracks.
(D) It reflects from hard surfaces.
(E) Carpet reduces reflection of sound.

The frequency of sound

Frequency and pitch We hear the different frequencies of sound as having different pitch. A low-frequency sound has a low pitch, like the rumble of a big truck. A high-frequency sound has a high pitch, like a whistle or siren. The range of frequencies that humans can hear varies from about 20 Hz to 20,000 Hz.

The sensitivity of the ear How we respond to the loudness of sound is affected by the frequency of the sound as well as by the amplitude (figure 13.9). High-frequency sounds seem louder than low-frequency sounds, even if the decibel level is the same. This is because our ears are more sensitive to sounds between 100 and 2,000 Hz than to sounds outside this range. Most of the frequencies that make up speech are between 100 and 2,000 Hz.

Sound can have more than one frequency Most sound that we hear contains many frequencies, not just one. A good analogy is to think of sound as having a recipe. The different frequencies are like different ingredients. To make the sound of a guitar you add a bunch of one frequency, a bit of a few different frequencies, and a pinch of a few others (figure 13.10). The opposite process also works. You can take a complex sound and break it down into different amounts of pure frequencies.

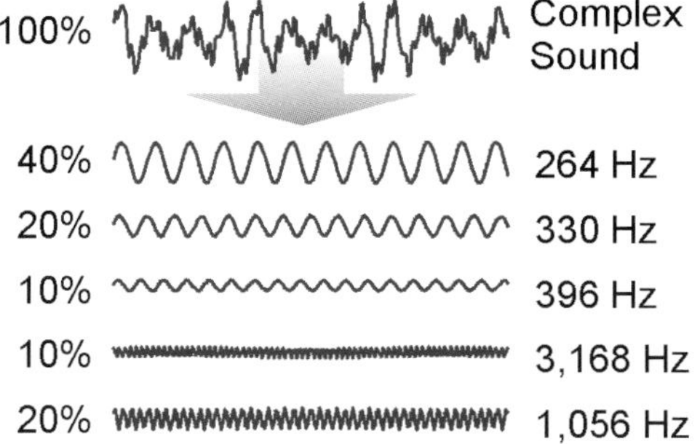

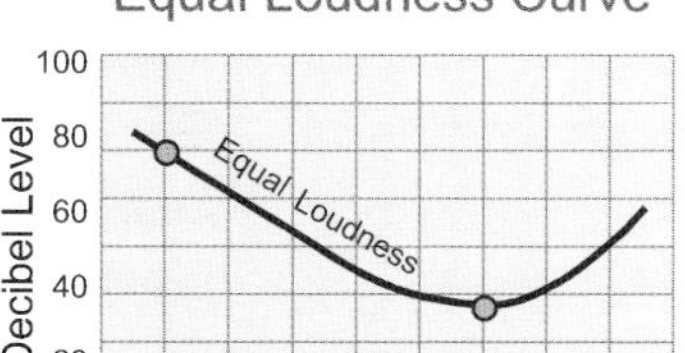

Figure 13.9: *How loud we perceive sound to be depends on the frequency as well as the amplitude. The ear is most sensitive to sounds around 2,000 Hz. The solid line on the graph represents sounds that are heard as equally loud. From the graph you can tell that an 80 dB sound at 50 Hz seems just as loud as a 38 dB sound at 2,000 Hz.*

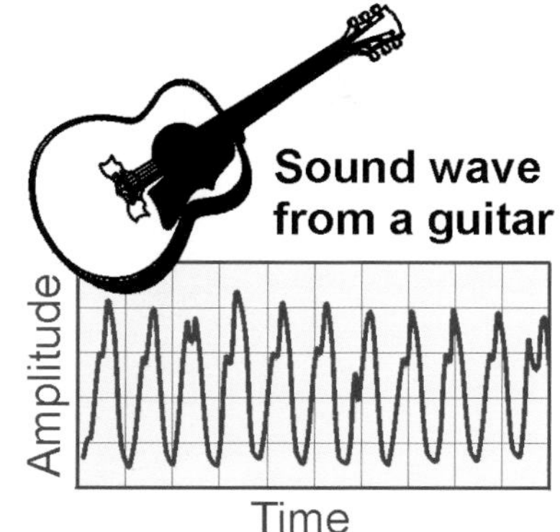

Figure 13.10: *The sound wave from a guitar playing the note E. Several frequencies are present because the graph is not a simple wave.*

Finding meaning in sound

Each nerve in the ear responds to a different range of frequency. One nerve might hear 330 Hz while another hears 800 Hz. Our brain has learned to assemble all the different frequencies and attach meanings to different patterns. The spoken word "hello" has a characteristic sound that contains a pattern of frequencies. We are taught to recognize the pattern and interpret the sound to be a word with meaning.

Think about reading one single word from a story. You recognize the word, but it does not tell you much about the story. When you read the whole story you put all the words together to get the meaning. The brain does a similar thing with different frequencies of sound. A single frequency by itself does not have much meaning. The meaning comes from patterns in many frequencies together.

Reading a sonogram

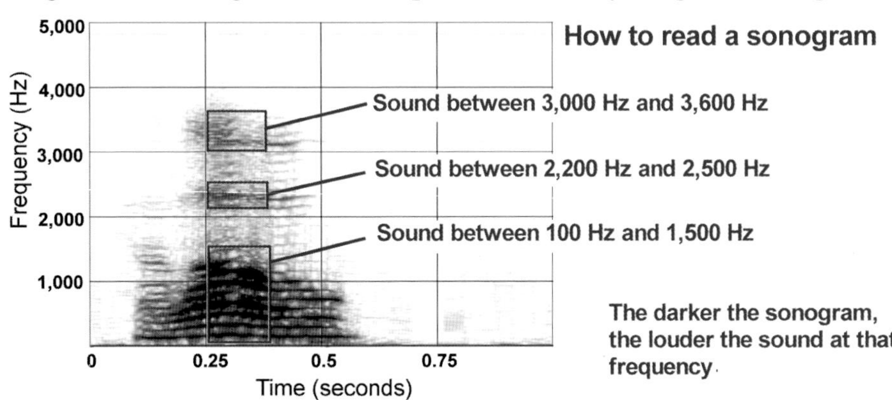

Sonograms

A **sonogram** is a special kind of graph that shows how loud "sound" is at different frequencies. The sonogram above is for a male voice saying "hello." The word lasts from 0.1 seconds to about 0.6 seconds. You can see lots of sound below 1,500 Hz and two bands of sound near 2,350 Hz and 3,300 Hz. Every person's sonogram is different, even when saying the same word.

White noise

Sometimes you do not want to hear meaning in sound, like when you want to go to sleep. Many people find **white noise** to be a relaxing sound. White noise is an equal mixture of all frequencies, like white light is a mixture of all colors. Because all frequencies are at the same level there is no pattern the brain can recognize. The lack of pattern is helpful for relaxing because it can drown out more distracting noises, like people talking or a television.

Talking to computers

Today there are programs that allow you to speak while the computer types what you say. Many people see a day when we talk to our computers rather than type at a keyboard.

Voice recognition programs have to be trained. The program gives you a story to read. The program knows every word in the story. You read the story into the microphone and the computer learns to recognize words from the frequency patterns of your voice.

Since everyone's voice is different, voice programs work only for the person who trained them! The computer types nonsense if you talk into a program trained to someone else's voice.

The wavelength of sound

Bass and treble speakers

Speakers that have great bass (low frequency) are large. Speakers that have good treble (high frequency) are usually much smaller. This is because of the wavelength and energy of the different frequencies of sound (figure 13.11). The chart below gives some typical frequencies and wavelengths for sound in air.

Table 13.3: ***Frequency and wavelength for some typical sounds***

Frequency (Hz)	Wavelength	Typical Source
20	17 meters	rumble of thunder
100	3.4 meters	bass guitar
500	70 cm (27")	average male voice
1,000	34 cm (13")	female soprano singer
2,000	17 cm (6.7")	fire truck siren
5,000	7 cm (2.7")	highest note on a piano
10,000	3.4 cm (1.3")	whine of a jet turbine
20,000	1.7 cm (2/3")	highest pitched sound you can hear

Why the wavelength of sound is important

Although we usually think about different sounds in terms of frequency, the wavelength can also be important. If there are boundaries or objects similar in size to the wavelength we will get resonance. Resonance makes certain sounds much louder. If you want to make sound of a certain wavelength, you often need to have a vibrating object that is similar in size to the wavelength (figure 13.12). This is the reason organ pipes are made in all different sizes. Each pipe is designed for a specific wavelength of sound.

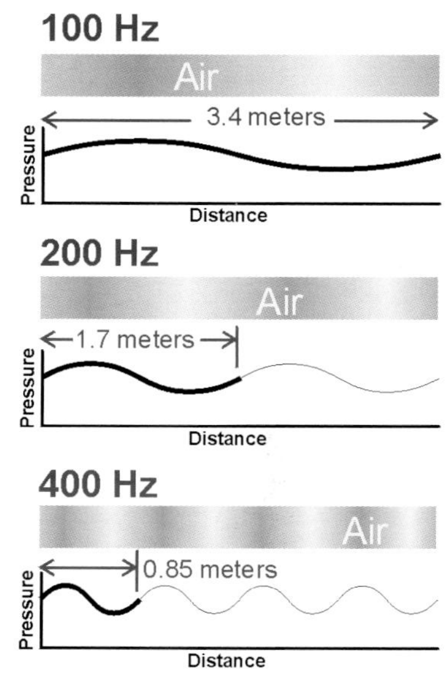

Figure 13.11: *The frequency and wavelength of sound are inversely related. When the frequency goes up, the wavelength goes down proportionally.*

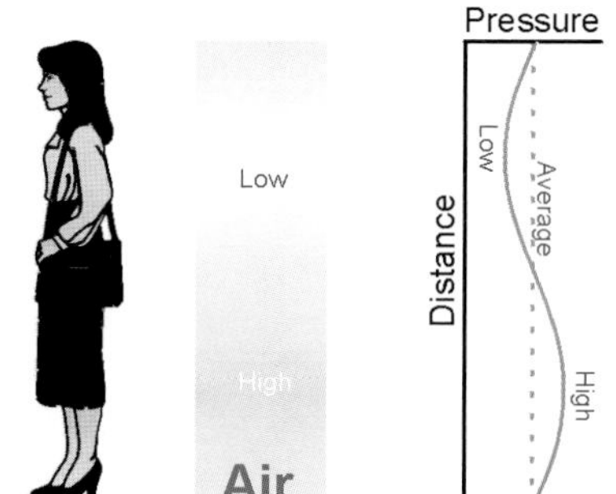

Figure 13.12: *A 200 Hz sound has a wavelength about equal to the height of a person*

The speed of sound

Sound is fast, about 340 meters per second

Sound moves faster than most motion you are familiar with. Under average conditions the speed of sound is about 340 meters per second (660 mph). Ordinary passenger jets fly slower than sound, usually around 400 to 500 miles per hour. We use the term supersonic to describe motion that is faster than sound. Only one kind of passenger jet (the Concorde) is supersonic (figure 13.13). If you were on the ground watching the Concorde flying toward you, there would be silence. The sound would be *behind* the plane, racing to catch up. You would hear the sound after the plane passed overhead. You would also hear a deafening sonic boom when the sound finally reached your ears.

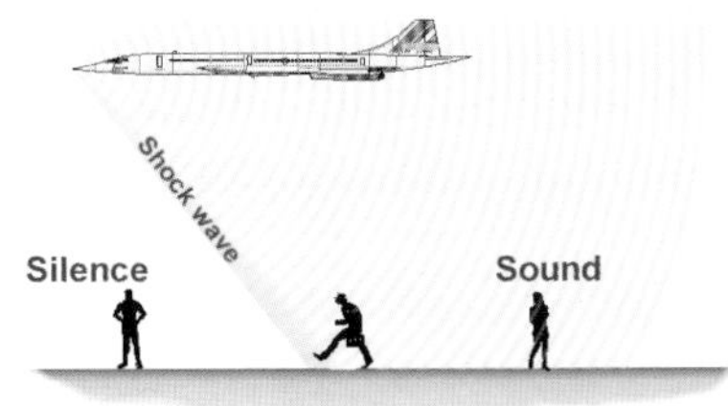

Figure 13.13: *The Concorde is a supersonic jet. If one flew overhead, you would not hear the sound until the plane was far beyond you. The boundary between sound and silence is called a shock wave. It is almost as if all the sound were compressed into a thin layer of air. The person in the middle hears a sonic boom as the shock wave passes over him. Because the sonic boom can shatter windows, planes are not allowed to fly over cities at supersonic speeds.*

The speed depends on pressure and temperature

The speed a sound wave travels in air depends on how fast the molecules in the air are moving. If the molecules are moving slowly (cold), sound does not travel as fast as when they are moving fast (hot). The kind of molecules also affects the speed of sound. Air is made up of mostly of oxygen (O_2) molecules and nitrogen (N_2) molecules. Lighter molecules, like hydrogen (H_2), move faster for a given temperature. Because of the speed difference, sound travels faster in hydrogen than in air.

Like other waves, the speed of sound also depends on the strength of the restoring force. High pressure creates larger restoring forces and increases the speed of sound. Lower pressure decreases the restoring force and decreases the speed of sound.

Sound in liquids and solids

Sound can also travel through liquid and solid materials, like water and steel (figure 13.14). The speed of sound in other materials is often faster than in air. The restoring forces in solid steel (for example) are much stronger than in a gas. Stronger restoring forces tend to raise the speed of sound. People used to listen for an approaching train by putting an ear to the rails. The sound of the approaching train travels much faster through the steel rails than through the air.

Material	Sound speed (m/sec)
Air	330
Helium	965
Water	1530
Wood (average)	2000
Gold	3240
Steel	5940

Figure 13.14: *The speed of sound in various materials (helium and air at 0°C and 1 atmospheric pressure).*

How sound waves are affected by surfaces

Reverberation

Sound waves reflect from hard surfaces. In a good concert hall the reflected sound adds to the direct sound. You hear a multiple echo celled reverberation. The right amount of reverberation makes the sound seem livelier and richer. Too much reverberation and the sound gets muddy from too many reflections. Concert hall designers work hard on the shape and surface of the walls and ceiling to provide the best reverberation. Some concert halls even have movable panels that can be raised or lowered from the ceiling to help with the sound.

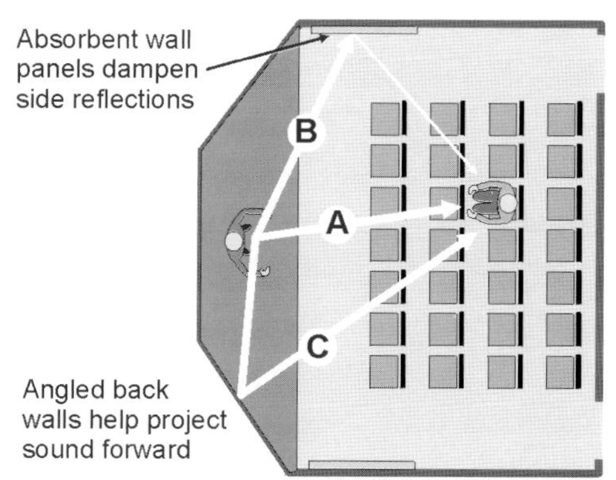
Absorbent wall panels dampen side reflections
B
A
C
Angled back walls help project sound forward

Making a good concert hall

Direct sound (**A**) reaches the listener along with reflected sound (**B, C**) from the walls. The shape of the room and the surfaces of the walls must be designed so that there is some reflected sound, but not too much.

Interference can also affect sound quality

Reverberation also causes interference of sound waves. When two waves interfere, the total can be louder or softer than either wave alone. The diagram above shows a musician and an audience of one person. The sound reflected from the walls interferes as it reaches the listener. If the distances are just right, one reflected wave might be out of phase with the other. The result is that the sound is quieter at that spot. An acoustic engineer would call it a *dead spot* in the hall. Dead spots are areas where destructive interference causes some of the sound to cancel with its own reflections. It is also possible to make very loud spots where sound interferes constructively. Good concert halls are designed to have even sound, not too lively, but not too quiet, either.

Diffraction

Because sound is a wave, it can be diffracted. This means that sound can bend around objects and pass through openings of any size.

Avery Fisher Hall

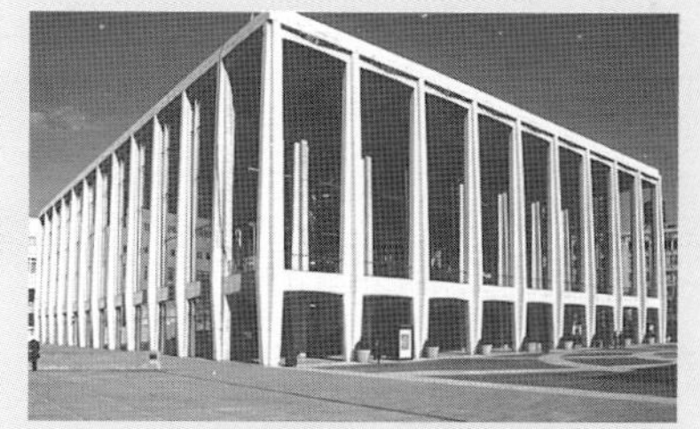

New York's Philharmonic Hall opened in 1962, and it was an acoustic disaster. The building was beautiful but the sound quality in the hall was awful, with loud spots, dead spots, and muddy reflections. How did some of the best architects and acoustic experts go wrong?

The hall was redesigned in 1976 by Cyril Harris, an acoustical specialist from Columbia University. Professor Harris altered almost all of the interior, changing wall shapes, and adding or moving many absorbing and reflecting panels. The sound quality was greatly improved and the building was renamed Avery Fisher Hall.

13.3 Music

Music is a combination of sound and rhythm that we find pleasant. The kinds of sounds and rhythms can be very different for different styles of music. Some people like music with a heavy beat and strong rhythm. Other people like music where the notes rise and fall in beautiful melodies. Music can be slow or fast, loud or soft, happy or sad, comforting or scary. In this chapter we will learn what kinds of sounds music is made from.

Pitch and rhythm

Pitch The pitch of a sound is how high or low we hear its frequency. Pitch and frequency usually mean the same thing. However, because pitch depends on the human ear and brain, sometimes pitch and frequency can be different. The way we hear a pitch can be affected by the sounds we heard before and after.

Rhythm Rhythm is a regular time pattern in a sound. Rhythm can be loud and soft, tap-tap-TAP-tap-tap-TAP-tap-tap-TAP. Rhythm can be made with sound and silence or with different pitches. People respond naturally to rhythm. Cultures of people are distinguished by their music and the special rhythms used in the music.

The musical scale Most of the music you listen to is made from a set of frequencies called a musical scale. The scale that starts on the note C is show in the diagram below.

C major scale								
Note	C	D	E	F	G	A	B	C
Frequency (Hz)	264	297	330	352	396	440	495	528
Ratio to C-264	$^1/_1$ $\left(\frac{264}{264}\right)$	$^9/_8$ $\left(\frac{297}{264}\right)$	$^5/_4$ $\left(\frac{330}{264}\right)$	$^4/_3$ $\left(\frac{352}{264}\right)$	$^3/_2$ $\left(\frac{396}{264}\right)$	$^5/_3$ $\left(\frac{440}{264}\right)$	$^{15}/_8$ $\left(\frac{495}{264}\right)$	$^2/_1$ $\left(\frac{528}{264}\right)$

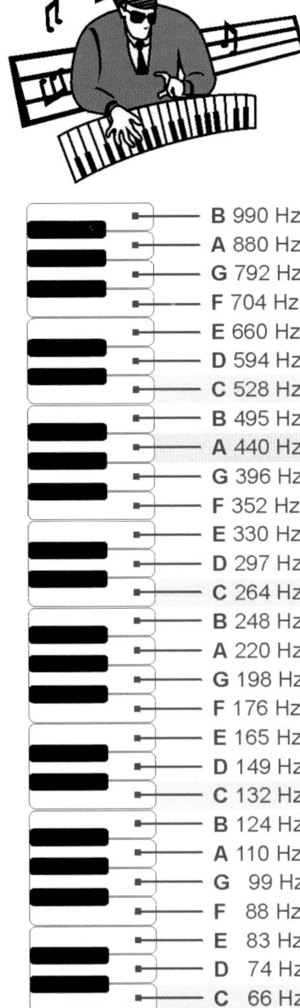

Figure 13.15: *A portion of a piano keyboard showing the frequencies of the notes*. Four octaves are shown. A grand piano has 88 keys and covers seven octaves. (*tuned to perfect C major scale)*

Consonance, dissonance, and beats

Harmony Music can have a profound effect on people's mood. The tense, dramatic soundtrack of a horror movie is a vital part of the audience's experience. Harmony is the study of how sounds work together to create effects desired by the composer. Harmony is based on the frequency relationships of the musical scale.

Beats An interesting thing happens when two frequencies of sound are close, but not exactly the same. The phase of the two waves changes in a way that makes the loudness of the sound seem to oscillate or beat. Sometimes the two waves are in phase, and the total is louder than either wave separately. Other times the waves are out of phase and they cancel each other out, leaving periods of silence. The rapid alternations between loudness and silence are referred to as beats. Most people find beats very unpleasant to listen to. Out-of-tune instruments make beats. The frequencies in the musical scale are chosen to reduce the occurrence of beats.

Beats come from adding two waves that are only slightly different in frequency

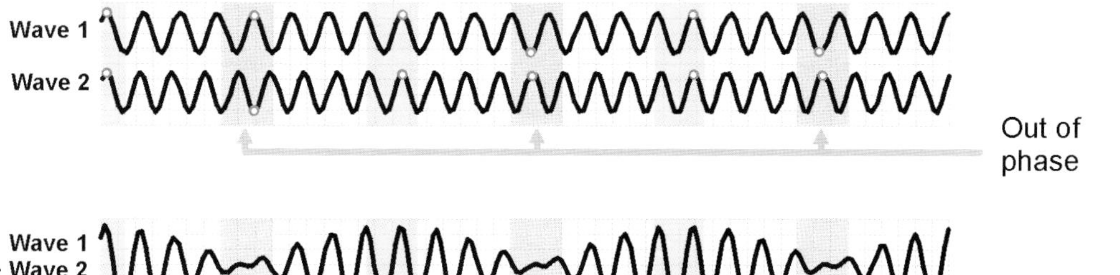

Consonance and dissonance When we hear more than one frequency of sound and the combination sounds good, we call it consonance. When the combination sounds bad or unsettling, we call it dissonance. Consonance and dissonance are related to beats. When frequencies are far enough apart that there are no beats, we get consonance. When frequencies are too close together, we hear beats that are the cause of dissonance. Dissonance is often used to create tension or drama. Consonance can be used to create feelings of balance and comfort.

Echolocation and beats

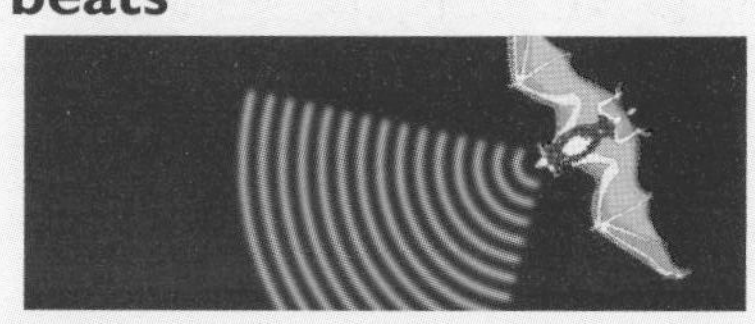

Bats "see" at night using ultrasound waves instead of light. A bat's voice is like a "sonic flashlight" shining a beam of sound. A bat emits bursts of sound that rise in frequency, called "chirps." When the sound reflects from a bug, the bat's ears receive the echo. Since the frequency of the chirp is always changing, the echo comes back with a slightly different frequency. The difference between the echo and the chirp makes *beats* that the bat can hear. The beat frequency is proportional to how far the bug is from the bat. A bat triangulates the bug's position by comparing the echo from the left ear with that of the right ear.

Harmonics and the "color" of sound

The same note can sound different

The same note sounds different when played on different instruments. As an example, suppose you listen to the note C-264 Hz played on a guitar and the same C-264 Hz played on a piano. A musician would recognize both notes as being C because they have the same frequency and pitch. But the guitar sounds like a guitar and the piano sounds like a piano. If the frequency of the note is the same, what gives each instrument its characteristic sound?

Instruments make mixtures of frequencies

The answer is that the sound we hear is not a single pure frequency. If the piano and the guitar both made a pure 264 Hz sound, we could not tell the difference. We can tell because real instruments make sounds with many frequencies. The most important one is still the fundamental note (for example, C-264 Hz). The variation comes from the **harmonics**. Remember, harmonics are frequencies that are multiples of the fundamental note. We have already learned that a string can vibrate at many harmonics. The same is true for all instruments. A single C from a grand piano might include 20 or more different harmonics.

Frequencies in a Guitar's E

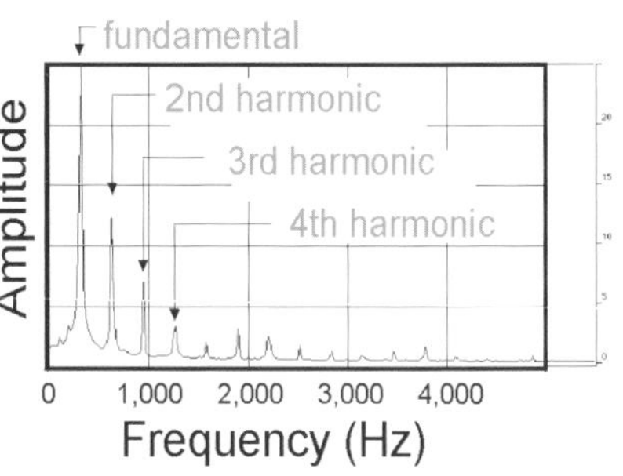

Figure 13.16: *This graph shows the frequencies in a guitar playing an E note. Notice how many harmonics there are!*

Recipes for sound

A good analogy is that each instrument has its own *recipe* for sound. The "guitar" sound shown in figure 13.16 has a mix of many harmonics. For this guitar, the fundamental is twice as big as the 2nd harmonic. There are strong 3rd, 4th and 5th harmonics. The piano recipe would have a different mix.

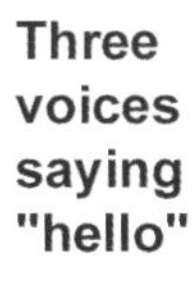

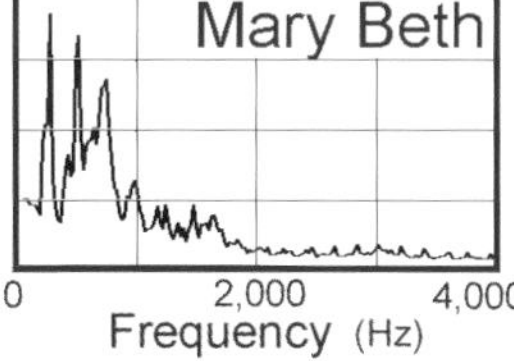

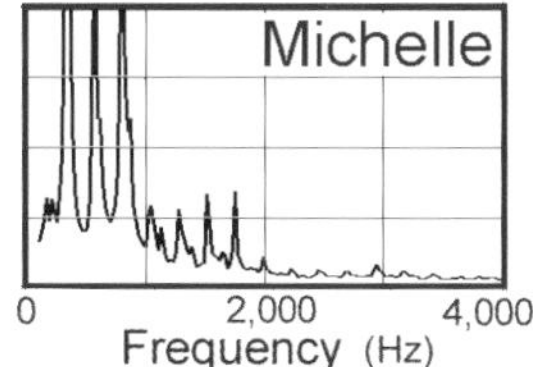

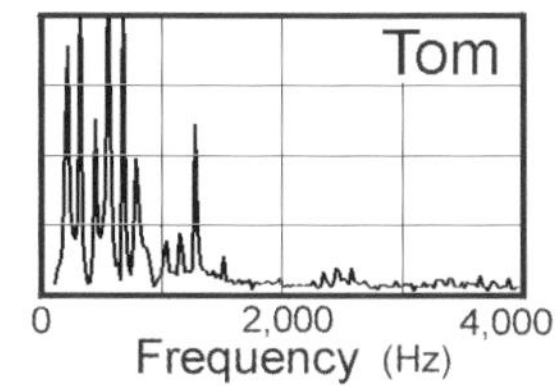

Human voices

The human voice also has harmonics. We recognize different people's voices by the patterns in frequency. The diagrams above show the frequencies of male and female voices saying the word "hello." The frequencies range from 100 Hz to about 4,000 Hz. The peaks in the diagrams indicate the harmonics in the voices. Each voice has a unique set of harmonics. This is why it is possible to identify someone by their voice even if you only hear that person say "hello."

Chapter 13 Review

Vocabulary review

Match the following terms with the correct definition. There is one extra definition in the list that will not match any of the terms.

Set One

1. sound	a. The force of molecules colliding with each other and the walls of a container
2. pressure	b. A scale to measure the loudness of sound
3. soundproofing	c. A pressure wave we hear with our ears
4. cochlea	d. Building and designing ways to control sound
5. decibel	e. The highest frequency of sound
	f. The part of the ear that senses sound

Set Two

1. ultrasound	a. The technology of making and using sound
2. acoustics	b. How we hear different frequencies of sound
3. pitch	c. A graph showing frequency, loudness, and time
4. sonogram	d. An equal mixture of all frequencies of sound
5. white noise	e. Sound of frequencies too high for the human ear to hear
	f. The speed of sound

Set Three

1. supersonic	a. The time pattern in sound
2. reverberation	b. A set of frequencies that we find pleasant to listen to
3. rhythm	c. The effect of multiple echoes in a room
4. musical scale	d. A speed faster than the speed of sound
5. octave	e. A nerve in the ear that is sensitive to sound
	f. The interval between a frequency and double the frequency

Set Four

1. note	a. The artistic mixing of sounds of many different frequencies
2. beats	b. When two or more sounds are pleasant to hear together
3. consonance	c. When two or more sounds are unpleasant to hear together
4. dissonance	d. The loudness of sound
5. harmony	e. A frequency of sound that is part of a musical scale
	f. An oscillation in loudness that occurs when two frequencies of sound are close but not equal

Concept review

1. A string that vibrates at 150 Hz creates a sound wave of:

   a. 150 cycles/sec
   b. 150 decibels
   c. 150 m/sec
   d. 150 meters

2. Which of the following is evidence that sound is a wave? You may choose more than one.

   a. Sound has a frequency we hear as differences in pitch.
   b. Some sounds are represented by special symbols.
   c. The speed of sound is the product of frequency times wavelength.
   d. We observe interference and diffraction of sound.

3. Which frequencies can most people hear? You may choose more than one.

   a. 300 Hz
   b. 10,000 Hz
   c. 2,500 Hz
   d. 100,000 Hz
   e. 5 Hz
   f. 50,000 Hz

4. Ultrasound is used for:

   a. Making images of the body for medical purposes.
   b. Extremely loud music.
   c. Making digital recordings for music CDs.
   d. Creating scary soundtracks for horror movies.

5. Air pressure is affected by (you may choose more than one):

   a. The movement of atoms and molecules.
   b. The temperature of a gas.
   c. Sound waves.
   d. Light waves.

6. The decibel scale is a measure of the ______ of a sound wave?

   a. frequency
   b. wavelength
   c. amplitude
   d. speed

7. The human voice contains only one frequency of sound at a time. True or false?

8. We recognize people's voices by patterns in the frequency of sound. True or false?

9. The frequency of sound has no effect on how loud we hear the sound. True or false?

10. A sonogram is a graph that shows how patterns of frequency change over time, as when someone is speaking. True or false?

11. If you wanted to create a very quiet room, you would do what (you may choose more than one):

    a. Cover the walls and ceilings with a hard surface like paneling.
    b. Cover surfaces with materials like carpet and foam.
    c. Seal doors and windows to eliminate cracks.

12. Arrange the following in order of the speed of sound in the material: air, wood, steel, water, helium.

Fastest				Slowest

13. Beats are caused by:

    a. Two frequencies of sound that are close but not identical.
    b. Two frequencies of sound that are consonant.
    c. Two frequencies of sound that are exactly one octave apart.
    d. Two frequencies of sound that are exactly the same.

14. Choose *all* the following that are true of the human voice:

    a. The frequencies of female voices are usually lower than male voices.
    b. The frequencies of female voices are usually higher than male voices.
    c. Voices mostly contain frequencies between 100 Hz and 2,000 Hz.
    d. Voices mostly contain frequencies between 2,000 Hz and 10,000 Hz.

Problems

1. The speed of sound is approximately 340 m/sec. What is the wavelength of a sound wave with a frequency of 1,000 Hz?

    a. 3.4 meters
    b. 34 centimeters
    c. 340 meters
    d. 2.9 meters

2. If a sound is 20 decibels louder than another sound, the amplitude of the louder sound is:

    a. 20 times the amplitude of the softer sound.
    b. 10 times the amplitude of the softer sound.
    c. 20 pounds per square inch more than the softer sound.
    d. 2 times the amplitude of the softer sound.

3. What is the loudest frequency shown in the graph?

    a. The fundamental.
    b. The second harmonic.
    c. The third harmonic.
    d. The fourth harmonic.

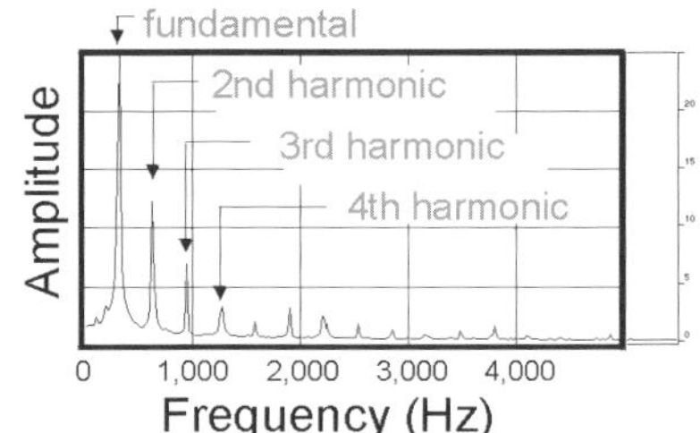

170 m

4. Suppose you stand in front of a wall that is 170 meters away. If you yell, how long does it take for the echo to get back to you if the speed of sound is 340 m/sec?

5. The sonogram shows:

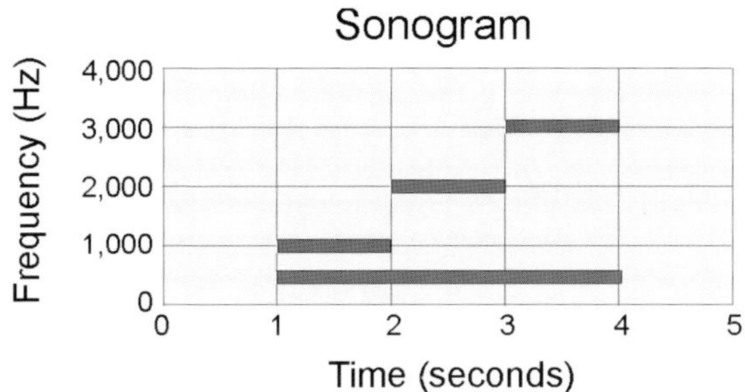

    a. A frequency of 1,000 Hz that lasts for 1 second.
    b. A frequency of 1,000 Hz that lasts for 2 seconds.
    c. A frequency of 1,500 Hz that lasts for 1 second.
    d. A frequency of 1,500 Hz that lasts for 2 seconds.

Applying your knowledge

1. Resonance applies to sound waves in boxes just like it does to strings. However, in a box there are three dimensions: length, width, and height. Each dimension can support a wave, so there can be three different wavelengths (a, b, c) that are resonant in a box.

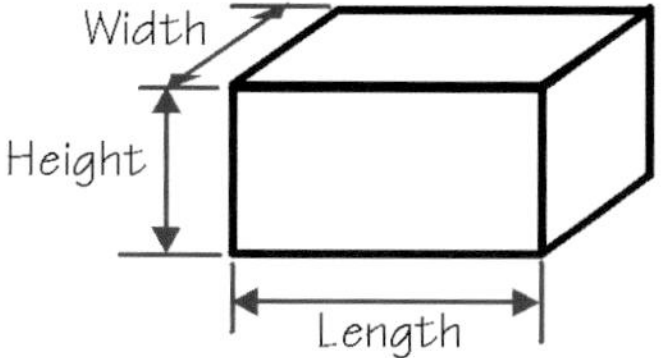

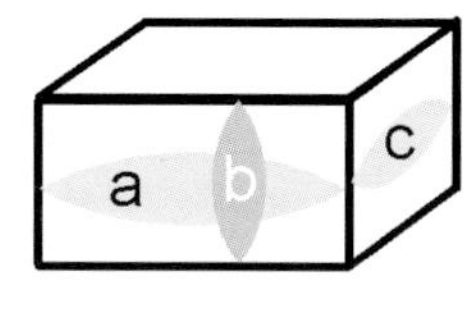

Suppose you are designing stereo speakers and you don't want resonance. Resonance would make some wavelengths (frequencies) of sound always be louder than others. This is usually bad for music. You want speakers to reproduce sound as it was recorded, and not make some sounds louder than others.

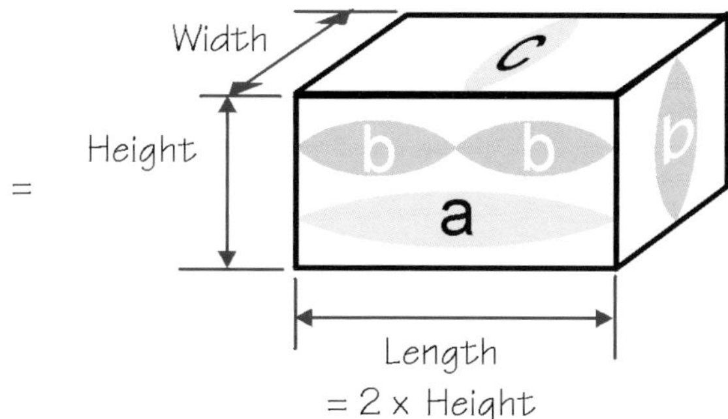

You can't escape some resonance. But suppose one side of your box was exactly twice another side. Then the second harmonic of one resonance (a) would be the same as the first harmonic of another resonance (b) and your sound problem would be twice as bad. Can you think of a rule for the three dimensions of a speaker box that would make sure that none of the three resonances, or their lower harmonics, would ever overlap?

2. Railroad engineers could always tell when a train was coming long before they could hear it. They would put their ear to the track and listen to the steel rails. Compare the speed of sound in steel to the speed of sound in air and explain why listening to the rails was a smart thing to do.

3. When it was first invented, the telephone was a marvel. The electronics of Alexander Graham Bell's days were much less sophisticated than we have today. Today, stereo makers claim they can reproduce frequencies over the whole range of human hearing from 20 Hz to 20,000 Hz. The early telephones could not deliver such a range. Look back at the graphs of frequencies of voices in the chapter. What is the minimum range of frequencies that telephones had to cover to make people's voices understandable? Have you ever noticed that a voice on the telephone never sounds like a real person's voice? Why do you think that is?

UNIT 5
Light and Optics

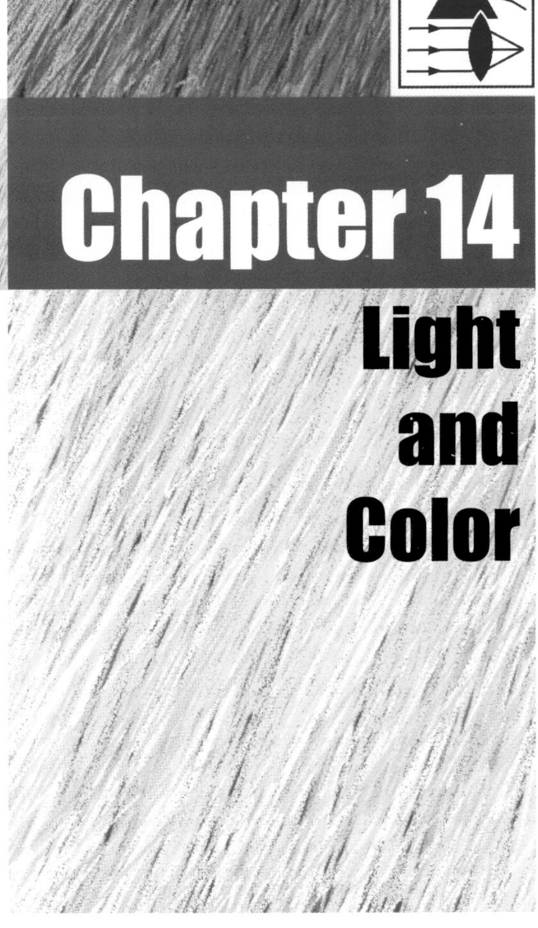

Chapter 14
Light and Color

Introduction to Chapter 14

We live in a world where light and color play a pivotal role in the very survival of life on this planet. Plants use sunlight to make sugar. Our ability to see helps us gather food. These processes and many others hinge on the unique properties of light. This chapter will introduce you to some of light's unique characteristics.

Investigations for Chapter 14

14.1	**Introduction to Light**	*How can you make light and how can you study it?*

In this Investigation you will look through a diffraction grating at a light source to see all the different colors that make up light. This leads us to the question "What makes different colors?" The different colors of light will be explained in terms of the energy of electrons falling from high energy to lower energy inside atoms. Different atoms have different energy levels and produce different colors.

14.2	**Color**	*What happens when you mix different colors of light?*

All of the colors of light that you see are really a combination of three primary colors: red, blue and green. In this Investigation, you will discover how to make all colors of light by mixing the three primary colors. You will also use a tool called a spectrometer to analyze light. This instrument allows you to break light into its "fingerprint" wavelengths.

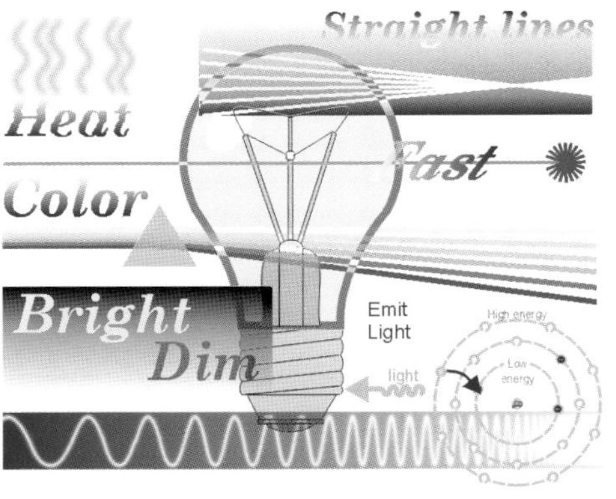

Learning Goals

By the end of this chapter, you will be able to:

- ✔ Describe the atomic origin of light.
- ✔ Explain the difference between incandescence and fluorescence.
- ✔ Identify uses for the other categories of electromagnetic energy.
- ✔ Compare the speed of sound to the speed of light.
- ✔ Identify the parts of the eye that see black and white, and color.
- ✔ Describe the physical reason for different colors in terms of the wavelength and energy of light.
- ✔ Identify and explain the RGB color model.
- ✔ Identify and explain the CMYK color model.
- ✔ Understand the mixing of light and pigment.
- ✔ Compare how a color printer makes color and how a color monitor makes color.

Vocabulary

chemical reaction	fluorescent	photoluminescence	subtractive primary colors
cone cells	incandescence	pixel	terahertz
cyan	magenta	polarizer	visible light
electromagnetic spectrum	nanometers	rod cells	yellow

14.1 Introduction to Light

What is light? How do we see? These questions intrigue us because, from infancy through adulthood, we are drawn to bright, flashing lights and brilliant, sparkling colors. "Bright and shiny" is a common phrase that refers to this attraction. Although light is only a small part of the sensory energy around us, many people would say sight is the most important of our five senses.

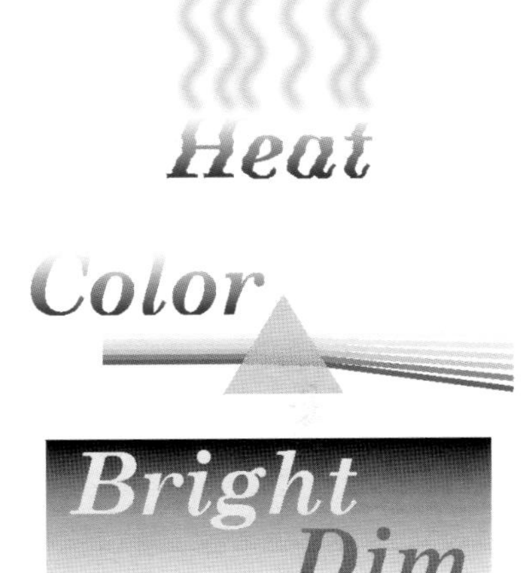

Figure 14.1: *Some words that are associated with the properties of light. What words do you use to describe light?*

What is light?

Light is a wave that we see Light is a wave that we can see with our eyes. Besides helping us to see the world around us, light has many other qualities that we use.

- Light can carry heat and warmth.
- Light has color.
- Light can be bright or dim.
- Light travels almost unimaginably fast and far.
- Light travels in straight lines, but can be bent by lenses or reflected by mirrors.

How do we see? What happens when you see a car? Sunlight bounces off the car and into your eyes. Your eyes send signals to your brain, which creates an *image* of the car. Because the brain is so important in forming images, different people see things differently. This is one reason why paintings and drawings of a landscape or person are not the same when created by different people.

There are forms of "light" we cannot see The light we see, visible light, is only one part of the *electromagnetic spectrum*. Radio waves, microwaves, and X rays are also *electromagnetic waves*. Although we can't see them, these waves are widely used in food preparation (microwaves), communication (radio waves and microwaves), and medicine (X rays).

What makes light?

Atoms make light

We know of many things that throw off light: the sun, fireflies, lightning, fire, incandescent and fluorescent bulbs are a few examples. But what actually makes the light? The thing that is common to all these different sources of light is that they are made up of atoms. Almost everything that creates light is made of atoms.

Atoms, electrons, and energy levels

You may remember that each atom contains smaller particles within it: a nucleus made up of protons and neutrons at the center of the atom and electrons at the outside edge of the atom. The electrons are always arranged in *levels*, like layers of onion skin. The electrons in each level have a different amount of energy. The farther away the electrons are from the nucleus, the more energy they have. Electrons can gain energy and rise to a higher level in the atom. When this happens, they can also fall back to a lower level in the atom and release energy.

Glow-in-the-dark stuff

Consider an amazing but very common material, glow-in-the-dark plastic. If this material is exposed to light, it soon gives off its own light. What is happening?

An example of making light

Embedded in glow-in-the-dark plastic are atoms of the element *phosphorus*. When light hits phosphorus atoms, some of the electrons absorb the light, rise to a higher energy level and then stay up there. Slowly, the electrons fall back down and give off their stored light. Because the electrons fall back over a long period of time, glow-in-the-dark stuff gives off light for many minutes. When all the electrons have finally fallen to the lowest levels, no more light comes out. To "recharge" your glow-in-the-dark material, you have to expose it to light again.

When phosphorus gives off light the process is called photoluminescence. The word "photo" means light and the word "luminescence" means glowing. Light energy has led to the production of light by something else.

Energy is required to raise electrons to higher levels.

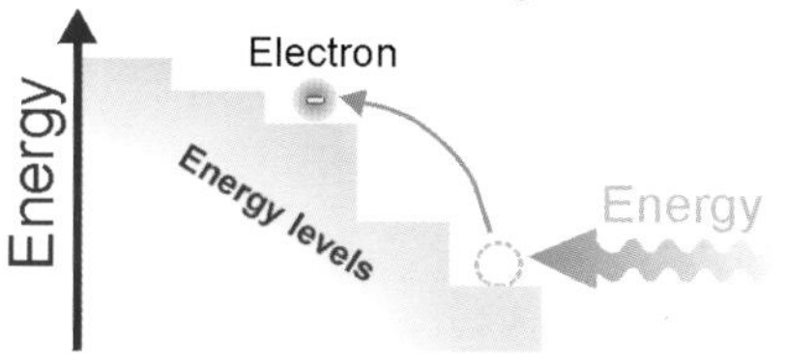

Energy is given off when electrons drop levels.

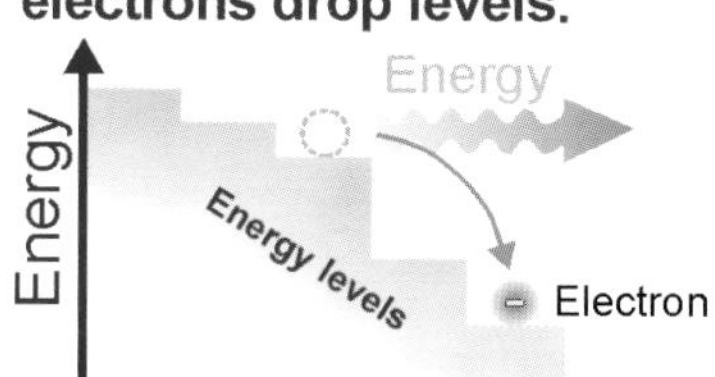

Glow sticks

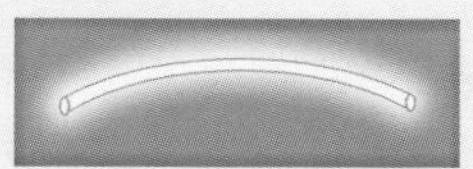

Glow sticks are a great example of atoms emitting light. When you bend a glow stick, two chemicals are mixed. The active chemical is called Luminal. When Luminal mixes with the other chemicals in the glow stick, a reaction takes place, causing electrons to fall from high energy levels to lower levels.

The energy released is almost completely in the form of light. After all the electrons have fallen to their lowest energy levels, the light stick stops glowing. You can slow the reaction down by cooling the chemicals in cold water or the freezer.

If you activate two glow sticks and put one in hot water and the other in ice water, you can graphically see how reaction rate is linked to temperature.

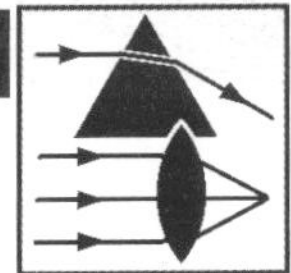

More about energy levels and light

What is an energy level? Think about Earth orbiting the sun. Earth is attracted to the sun by the force of gravity, but it is not pulled into the sun because it has kinetic energy from moving in its orbit. Electrons in atoms also have kinetic energy. The energy of electrons keeps them in stable energy levels, like orbits (figure 14.2). That is why they don't fall into the nucleus.

Why are there energy levels? The question "Why are there energy levels?" is hard to answer. When we look at nature and study atoms, we find energy levels. Niels Bohr built a model of the atom to help us understand how energy levels work. He used something called quantum mechanics to explain his model. We know that the energy of electrons in atoms comes in levels. We can use quantum mechanics to calculate what the energy levels are. We know how to use our knowledge of energy levels to make lasers and TV screens. But, fundamentally, we don't know *why* quantum mechanics works or why there are energy levels. Maybe someday you will find out and win the Nobel Prize!

Light from chemical reactions If an atom has some electrons in a high energy level and they somehow fall into a lower energy level, the atom will give off energy that our eyes might see. This happens all the time. When wood is burning, a chemical reaction takes place between the atoms in the wood and the atoms of oxygen in the air. Chemical reactions move electrons around. If any electrons move to lower levels, light can come out. The warm flickering light from a candle comes from trillions of tiny electrons falling down energy levels as the wick combines with oxygen and burns.

Light from lightning and the sun When electricity moves through the air, it can cause the atoms in the air to rearrange their electrons. This can also produce light, which we call lightning. We cannot see the electricity (although we could certainly feel it), but we can see the light that is created. The light from the sun comes from moving electrons in the sun's very hot outer layers. Because reactions inside the sun release a lot of energy, the sun makes several kinds of electromagnetic waves, including infrared light, visible light, and ultraviolet (UV) light. These waves move through space and reach the Earth, sustaining life by bringing heat and light.

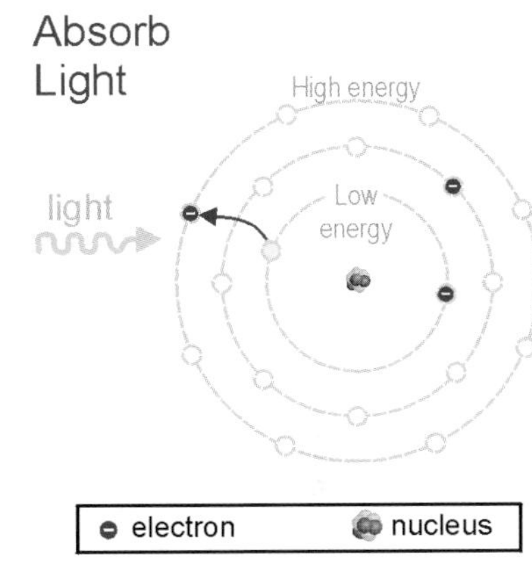

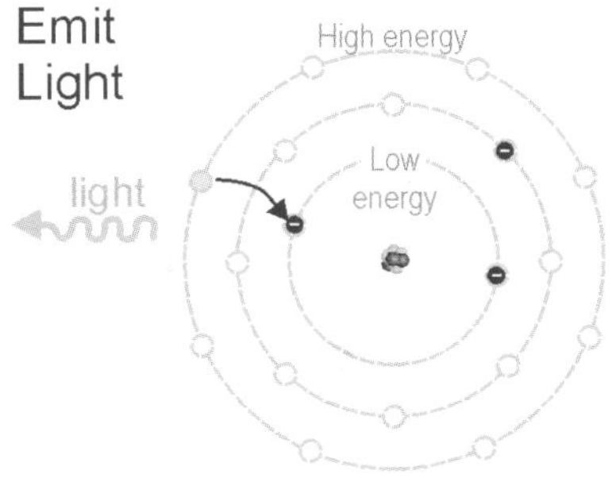

Figure 14.2: *If we want an atom to give off light, we need at least one electron that can fall back down to an empty spot at lower energy.*

1) We can have an atom absorb some light and move an electron to high energy.

2) We can let the electron fall back down and the atom emits light.

Electric lights

Incandescent light bulbs

The light we use at night or indoors is usually made with electricity. When electricity passes through materials, it heats them up. If the atoms get hot enough, some of the energy moves electrons from low energy levels to higher ones. The electrons fall back down immediately and give off energy as light. The process of making light with heat is called **incandescence**. This is how incandescent light bulbs work. The filament in the light bulb is heated white-hot by electricity. The hot filament emits light. These bulbs actually produce more heat energy than light energy. (Heat, not light, is why these bulbs are used to help chicken eggs hatch!)

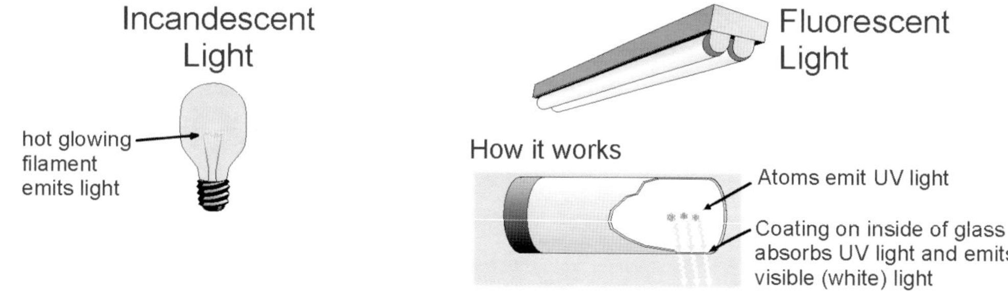
Incandescent Light
hot glowing filament emits light
Fluorescent Light
How it works
Atoms emit UV light
Coating on inside of glass absorbs UV light and emits visible (white) light

Fluorescent light bulbs

The other common kind of electric light bulb is the **fluorescent** bulb. We are seeing many more fluorescent bulbs today because they are much more efficient. Compared with a standard (incandescent) bulb, you get four times as much light from a fluorescent bulb for the same amount of electricity! The reason is that not as much energy is lost as heat. In a fluorescent bulb, high-voltage electricity energizes atoms in a gas with a diffuse spark, much like lightning. Much more of the electrical energy is used to raise electrons and less is used to heat the atoms.

Getting useful light from a fluorescent bulb is actually a two-step process. The light emitted by the electrons in the gas is mostly ultraviolet, which we cannot see. In a fluorescent bulb the ultraviolet light hits a white coating on the inside surface of the bulb. The coating absorbs the UV light and emits it again as white light. You can buy fluorescent bulbs with different coatings to make the light more blue or more yellow, like natural sunlight.

Please turn out the lights when you leave!

There are about 285,000,000 people living in the United States. If an average house has four light bulbs per person, it adds up to 1,140,000,000 light bulbs. The average bulb uses 100 watts of electricity. Multiplying it out gives an estimate of 114,000,000,000 watts, just for light bulbs.

A big electric power-plant puts out 2,000,000,000 watts. That means 67 big power plants are burning up resources just to run your light bulbs. If everyone were to switch their incandescent bulbs to fluorescent lights we would save 75 percent of this electricity. That means we could save 50 big power plants' worth of pollution and wasted resources!

Light waves and the electromagnetic spectrum

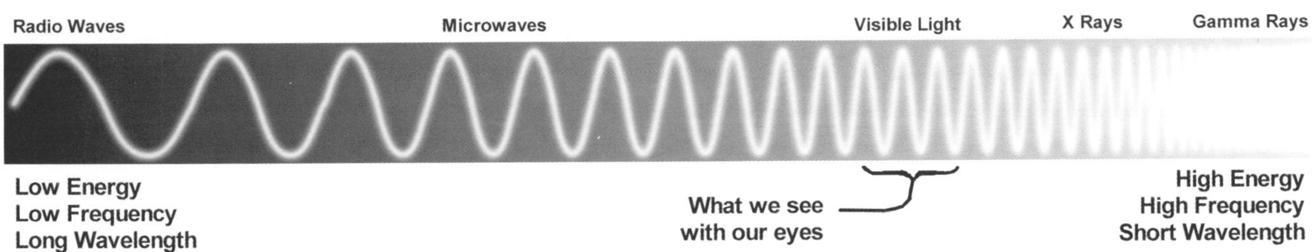

The amount of energy given off by atomic electrons can be tiny or huge. The light we can see, visible light, is only a small part of the possible energy range. The whole range is called the electromagnetic spectrum and visible light is in the middle of it. On the low energy end of the spectrum are radio waves with wavelengths billions of times longer than those of visible light. On the high energy end are gamma rays. These have wavelengths millions of times smaller than those of visible light. We will see that visible light, with a medium energy range, is perfectly suited for sustaining life. That is why our eyes are so well adapted to this part of the spectrum.

Figure 14.3: *The 140-foot-diameter radio telescope at Green Bank, West Virginia. The giant reflecting mirror is so large because the wavelength is large. Mirrors for optical telescopes can be smaller because the wavelength of visible light is smaller.*

Uses of different waves

Radio waves — Radio waves are used to transmit radio and television signals. Radio waves have wavelengths that range from hundreds of meters down to less than a centimeter. Radio broadcast towers are so tall because they have to be at least 1/4 wavelength long. Your clock radio uses the length of wire that plugs into the wall socket as its antenna. If your station doesn't come in properly, you should untangle that wire. FM radio waves are shorter than AM radio waves so a radio must have two antennas; one is a coil of wire inside the unit, and the other is the expanding metal rod that you pull out when you want to use FM.

Microwaves — Microwave wavelengths range from approximately 30 centimeters (about 12 inches) to about one millimeter (the thickness of a pencil lead). In a microwave oven, the waves are tuned to frequencies that can be absorbed by the water in food. The food absorbs the energy and gets warmer. Microwaves are also used for cell phone transmissions.

Figure 14.4: *Cell phones use microwaves to transmit signals.*

Infrared waves Infrared is the region of the spectrum with a wavelength of about one millimeter to approximately 700-billionths of a meter. Infrared waves include thermal radiation. For example, burning charcoal may not give off very much light, but it does emit infrared radiation which is felt as heat. Infrared images obtained by sensors in satellites and airplanes can yield important information on the health of crops and can help us see forest fires even when they are covered by clouds of smoke.

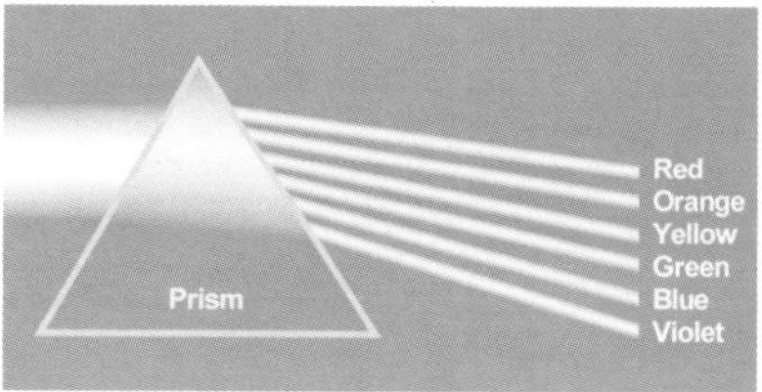

Figure 14.5: *Light carries information about color.*

Visible light The rainbow of colors we know as visible light is the part of the spectrum with wavelengths between 700-billionths and 400-billionths of a meter (700 to 400 nanometers). When people talk about "light" in ordinary conversation, they are usually talking about visible light. When scientists talk about "light" they could be referring to any part of the electromagnetic spectrum from microwaves to X rays.

Ultraviolet waves Ultraviolet radiation has a range of wavelengths from 400-billionths of a meter to about 10-billionths of a meter. Sunlight contains ultraviolet waves that can burn your skin. A small amount of ultraviolet radiation is beneficial to humans, but larger amounts cause sunburn, skin cancer, and cataracts. Most ultraviolet light is blocked by ozone in the Earth's upper atmosphere. Scientists are concerned that damage to the Earth's ozone layer could allow more ultraviolet light to reach the surface of the planet, creating problems for humans, plants, and animals.

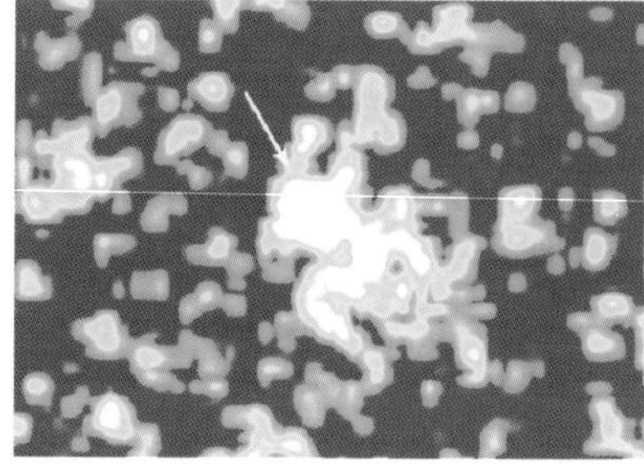

Figure 14.6: *Gamma rays are given off in nuclear reactions on Earth and also in stars. Astronomers are searching for explanations for unusually strong gamma rays that appear and disappear in space. The bright spots show regions of the sky with strong gamma ray emissions.*

X rays X rays are high-energy waves which have great penetrating power and are used extensively in medical applications and for inspecting metal welds. Their wavelength range is from about 10-billionths of a meter to about 10-trillionths of a meter.

Gamma rays Gamma rays have wavelengths of less than about 10-trillionths of a meter. Gamma rays are generated by radioactive atoms, in nuclear reactions, and are used in many medical applications. Gamma rays have even higher energy than X rays. The energy is so high that it can push electrons right out of the atom and break chemical bonds, including the chemical bonds holding the molecules in your body together. You do not want to be around strong gamma rays without a heavy shield!

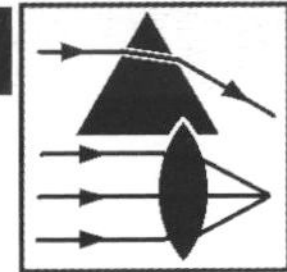

The speed of light

Seeing lightning and hearing thunder

How does light get from one place to another? This is a question that has intrigued people for many hundreds of years. Lightning and thunder actually happen at the same time. You see a bolt of lightning and then hear the thunder a few seconds later because light travels much faster than sound.

Measuring the speed of sound

Sound (the thunder) travels so slowly that you could almost time it yourself with a stopwatch. If you stood 170 meters from a large building and shouted at the building, you would hear your own echo about one second later. The sound traveled the 170 meters to the wall, bounced and traveled the 170 meters back to you in one second (figure 14.7). The speed of sound is about 340 meters per second.

Measuring the speed of light

Trying this trick with light is much more difficult. Suppose you shine a light at a mirror 170 meters away (figure 14.8). You wouldn't even begin to push down on the stopwatch before you saw the reflected light. It only takes light about a millionth of a second to get to your mirror and back. When scientists did eventually come up with a way to measure the speed of light, they used mirrors more than 20 miles apart. Even with such a long distance they needed a fancy spinning mirror to measure the speed of light.

Using this spinning mirror, scientists discovered that the speed of light is about 300 million (300,000,000) meters *per second*. The widest part of the Earth is 11 million (11,000,000) meters. Light is so fast that a beam can circle the Earth 27 times in 1 second!

The universal speed limit

The speed of light is special because nothing in the universe travels faster than light. This idea forms part of Albert Einstein's theory of relativity. This brilliant theory explains that space and time are tied together. One of the ways that Einstein developed his theory was by asking himself about how light behaves. He wondered what light would look like if it were to stop and stand still (he imagined himself observing a beam of light while traveling as fast as light himself). Using what he knew about light, Einstein showed that it was impossible to stop light or even to observe a stationary beam of light.

Sound echo

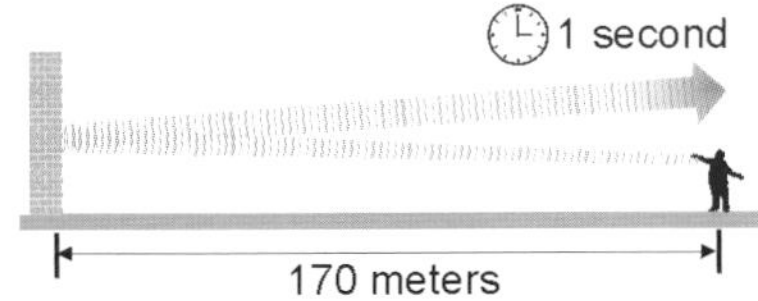

Figure 14.7: *A sound echo takes about one second from a wall that is 170 meters away.*

Light echo

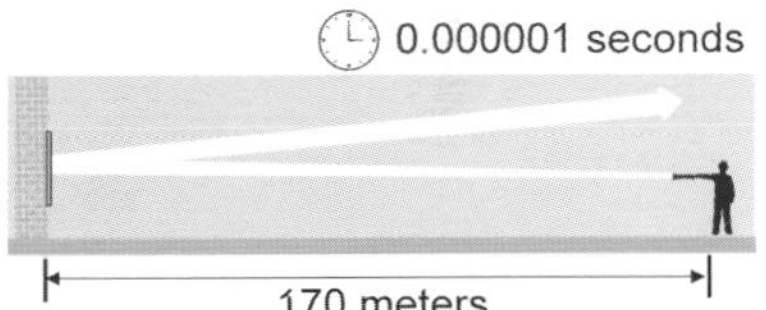

Figure 14.8: *The reflection of light from a mirror 170 meters away reaches you in 0.000001 seconds. Light travels much faster than sound.*

Polarization

Polarization

Polarization is a useful property of light waves. Light is a transverse wave of electricity and magnetism. To understand polarization, think about shaking a taut string up and down to make a vertical wave. We say a light wave with an up-down electrical pattern is "polarized" in the vertical axis. If you vibrate the string side to side, you create a horizontal wave. A light wave with a side-to-side electrical pattern is "polarized" in the horizontal axis. Polarization at an angle between vertical and horizontal can be understood as being part vertical and part horizontal, like the sides of a triangle. Each atom usually emits light at a different polarization; therefore, most of the light you see is a mixture of polarizations. We call this light "unpolarized" since no single polarization dominates the mixture.

How we use polarization of light

A polarizer is a partially transparent material that lets only one polarization of light through. Microscopically, polarizers behave like a grid of tiny wires. Light that is electrically aligned with the wires can pass through. A vertical polarizer only lets light with vertical polarization pass through. Horizontally polarized light is blocked. At different angles, a polarizer allows different polarizations of light to pass through (figure 14.9).

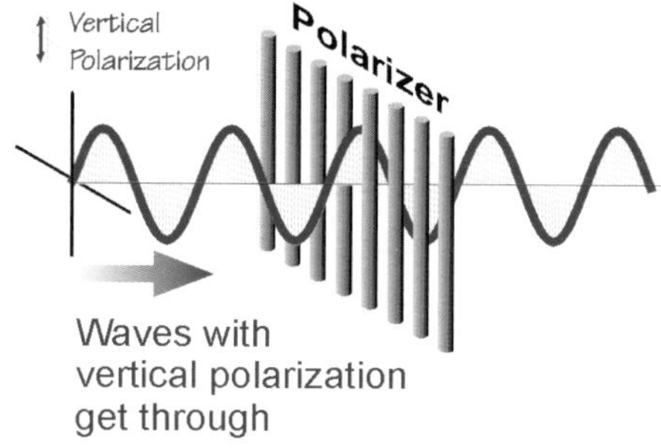

Horizontal
Polarization
Polarizer
Waves with
horizontal polarization
get stopped by the polarizer

Using two polarizers

If you use two polarizers, you can control the flow of light (figure 14.9). Light coming through the first one is polarized in a known direction. If the axis of the second polarizer is in the same direction, the light gets through. If the second polarizer is not in the same direction, some or all of the light cannot get through. You can control how much light gets through by adjusting the angle of the second polarizer relative to the first one.

A vertical polarizer polarizes the light by letting through only the light that is vertically oriented (about 50%).

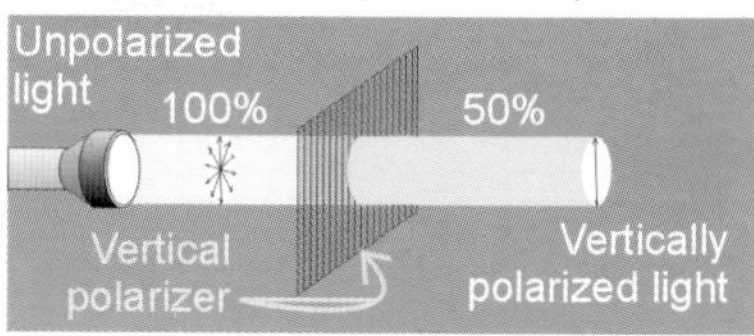

The vertically polarized light gets through a second vertical polarizer.

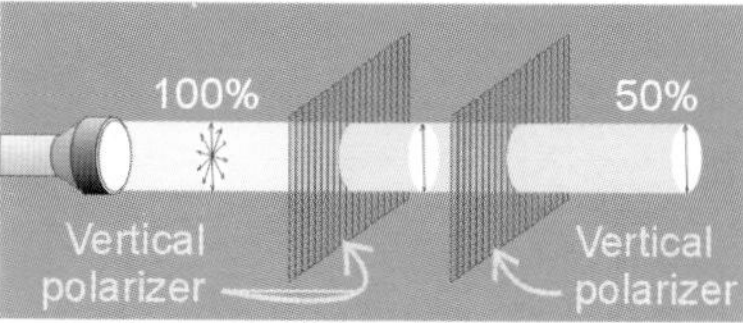

A second polarizer at 45 degrees cuts out half of the vertically polarized light.

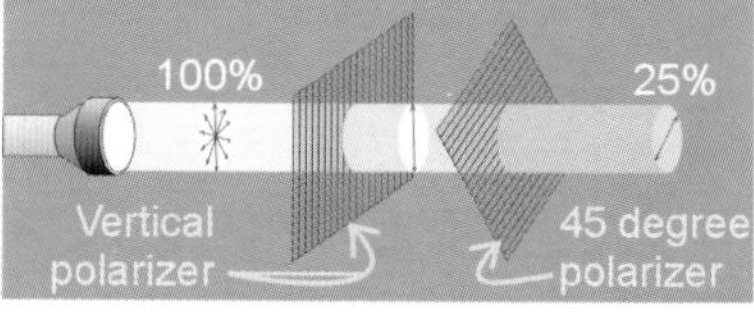

A second polarizer that is horizontal (90°) stops all vertically polarized light.

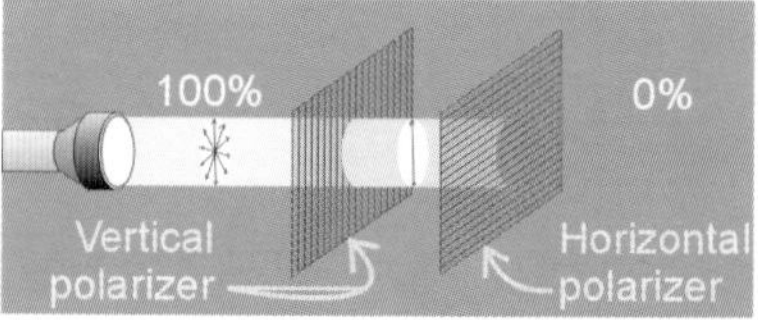

Figure 14.9: *A single polarizer polarizes light by letting through only the portion of the original light that has the right polarization. You can use two polarizers to filter some or all of the light.*

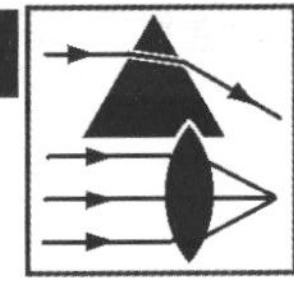

How polarizing sunglasses work

Polarizing sunglasses are used to reduce the glare of reflected light. Light that reflects at low angles from horizontal surfaces is polarized mostly horizontal. Polarizing sunglasses are made from a vertical polarizer. The glasses block light waves with horizontal polarization. Because glare is horizontally polarized, it gets blocked much more than other light which is unpolarized.

Polarizing filters for cameras

Photographers often use polarizing filters on camera lenses. The filters allow them to photograph a river bed or ocean bottom without the interfering glare of reflected light. Polarizing filters are used in landscape photography to make the sky appear a deeper blue color. Can you explain why a polarizer has this effect?

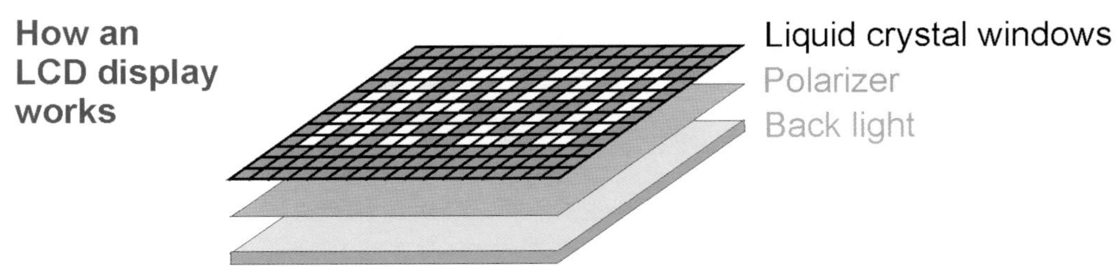

Glare reflected from the water

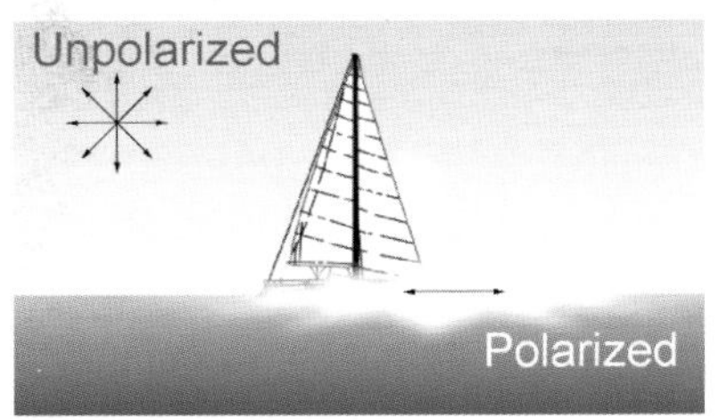

Regular sunglasses

Polarizing sunglasses

Figure 14.10: *Reflected glare is partly polarized, while the rest of the light you see is usually unpolarized. Regular sunglasses block all the light equally. Polarizing sunglasses block the polarized glare more than other light, enhancing what you see.*

How an LCD computer screen works

The LCD (liquid crystal diode) screen on a laptop computer uses polarized light to make pictures. The light you see starts with a lamp that makes unpolarized light. A polarizer then polarizes all the light. The polarized light passes through thousands of tiny pixels of liquid crystal that act like windows. Each liquid crystal window can be electronically controlled to act like a polarizer, or not. When a pixel is NOT a polarizer, the light comes through, like an open window and you see a bright dot. The polarization direction of the liquid crystal is at right angles to the first polarization direction. When a pixel becomes a polarizer, the light is blocked and you see a dark dot. The picture is made of light and dark dots.

Because the first polarizer blocks half the light, LCD displays are not very efficient, and are the biggest drain on a computer's batteries. New technologies are being developed to make more efficient flat-panel displays. Many companies are doing research aimed at developing flat-panel televisions that can hang on the wall like pictures!

14.2 Color

Color adds much richness to the world. The rainbow of colors our eyes can see ranges from deep red, through the yellows and greens, up to blue and violet. Just as we hear different frequencies of sound as different notes, we see different frequencies of light as different colors. Artists through the ages have sought recipes for paints and dyes to make vivid colors for paintings and clothing. In this section we will explore some of the ways we make and use colors.

Where does color come from?

Frequency and wavelength

To understand color we need to look at light as a wave. Like other waves, light has frequency and wavelength.

Frequency 4.6 x 10^{14} to 7.5 x 10^{14} Hz

Wavelength 4 x 10^{-7} to 6.5 x 10^{-7} meters wavelength

The frequency of light waves is incredibly high: 10^{14} is a 10 with 14 zeros after it! Red light has a frequency of 460 trillion, or 460,000,000,000,000 cycles per second. Because the frequency is so high, the wavelength is tiny. Waves of red light have a wavelength of only 0.00000065 meters (6.5 x 10^{-7}m). More than 200 wavelengths of red light fit in the thickness of a human hair! Because of the high frequency and small wavelength, we do not normally see the true wavelike nature of light (table 14.1). Instead, we see reflection, refraction, and color.

Table 14.1: ***Wavelength and frequency of light***

Color		Wavelength (nanometers)	Frequency (THz)
Red		650	462
Orange		600	500
Yellow		580	517
Green		530	566
Blue		470	638
Violet		400	750

Figure 14.11: *The wavelength of visible light is much smaller than the thickness of a hair! The drawing is greatly exaggerated. In reality more than 200 wavelengths of red light would fit in the thickness of a single hair.*

Big and small numbers

The wavelength of light is so small that we use nanometers to describe it. One nanometer is one-billionth of a meter.

The frequency is so large we need units of terahertz (THz). One terahertz is equal to one trillion cycles per second.

How does the human eye see color?

Energy Scientists discovered something rather interesting near the turn of the 20th century. A German physicist, Max Planck, thought that color had something to do with the energy of light. Red light was low energy and violet light was high energy. Albert Einstein was awarded the 1921 Nobel Prize for proving the exact relationship between energy and color. When light hits some metals, electrons are ejected. If more light is used, more electrons come out, but the energy of each electron does not change. Einstein showed that the energy of an ejected electron depends on the frequency of the light, not the amount of light. His observation proved that the energy of light is related to its frequency, or color.

Energy and color All of the colors in the rainbow are really light of different energies. Red light has low energy compared with blue light. The closer to violet, the higher the energy. Low energy means lower frequency so waves of red light oscillate more slowly than waves of blue light. We see the different energies of light as different colors.

How we see color Scientists have discovered cells in the retina of the eye that contain **photoreceptors** (figure 14.12). That fancy phrase means that they receive light and release a chemical. When light hits a photoreceptor cell, the cell releases a chemical signal that travels down the optic nerve to the brain. In the brain, the signal is translated into a perception of color.

Rods and cones Our eyes have two different types of photoreceptors, called **rod cells** and **cone cells**. Cone cells respond to color, and there are three kinds. One kind only gives off a signal for red light. Another kind only works with green light and the last kind only works for blue light. Each kind of cone cell is tuned to respond only to a certain energy range of light (figure 14.13). We get millions of different colors from just three primary colors: red, green, and blue.

Rod cells see black and white The rod cells respond only to differences in brightness. Rod cells essentially see in black, white, and shades of gray. The advantage is that rod cells are much more sensitive and work at very low light levels. At night, colors seem washed out because there is not enough light for your cone cells to work. When the overall light level is very dim, you are actually seeing "black and white" images from your rod cells.

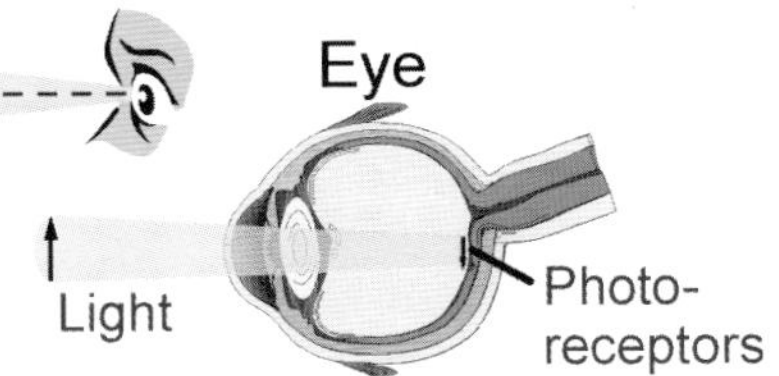

Figure 14.12: *The photoreceptors that send color signals to the brain are at the back of the eye.*

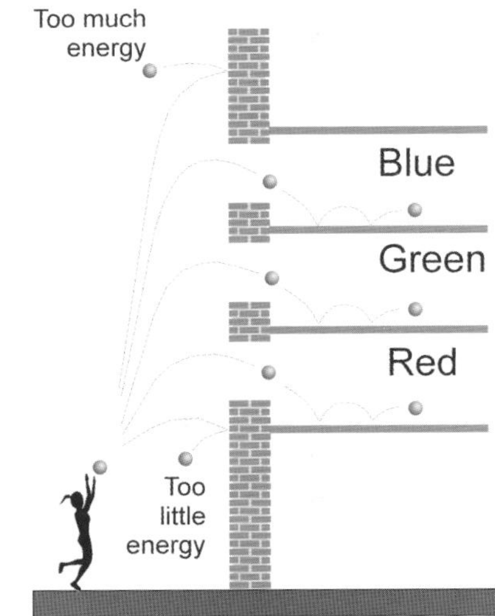

Figure 14.13: *Imagine trying to throw a basketball up into a window. If you get the energy right, it will go in. The three photoreceptors are like windows of different heights. If the light has a certain energy, it lands in the RED window. Higher energy and you get the GREEN window. Even higher energy falls into the BLUE window. If the energy is too low or too high, we don't see the light at all.*

How do we see colors other than red, green, and blue?

How we perceive color

The human eye allows us to see millions of different colors. When the brain receives a signal *only* from the red cone cells, it thinks *red*. If there is a signal from the green cone cells (figure 14.14) and neither blue nor red, the brain thinks *green*. This seems simple enough.

The additive color process

Now consider what happens if the brain gets a signal from both the red and the green cone cells *at the same time*? These energies add together and the sensation created is different from either red or green. It is what we have learned to call *yellow*. If all three cone cells are sending a signal to the brain at once, we think *white*. This is called an *additive* process because new colors are formed by the addition of more than one color signal from cone cells to the brain.

The additive primary colors

The **additive primary colors** are red, green, and blue. In reality, our brains are receiving all three color signals just about all of the time. If so, then why aren't we seeing everything in white? Two reasons: There are lots of different places in our field of vision, such as top, bottom, left, and right. The other reason is that the *strength* of the signal matters too. It's too simple to say that red and green make yellow. What if there's a lot of red and only a little green, like in figure 14.15 (strong red signal, weak green signal)? As you might guess, you will see a color that is quite orange (maybe like the color of orange juice.) There are an unlimited number of adjustments you can make to the strengths of the signals by changing the proportions of red, green, and blue. Thus, you can get millions of different colors.

Color blindness

Some people don't have all three types of cone cells. The condition of color blindness is caused by one or more missing types of cone cells. The most common type of color blindness is the one in which the person lacks the red cone cells. This would imply that everything they see would be in shades of blue, green, cyan, and black, of course. We have to be very careful not to assume too much. Perhaps a person who has this form of color blindness can look at *cyan* (blue-green) and have the same sensation or experience that a person who has normal color vision has when they see white. But then, perhaps not. We really don't know. The *sensation* of color is quite subjective.

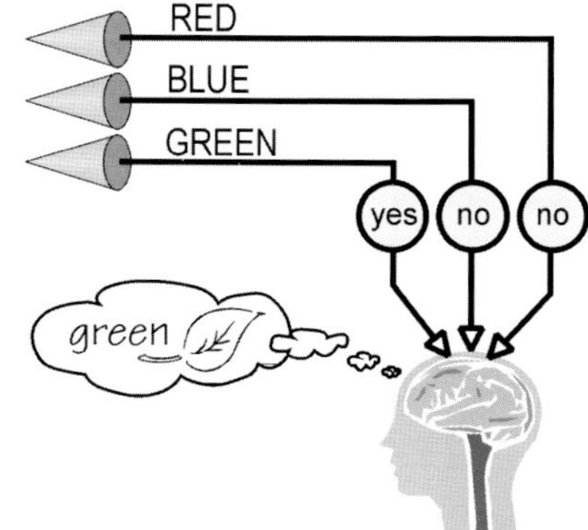

Figure 14.14: *If the brain gets a signal ONLY from the GREEN cone cells, we see "green."*

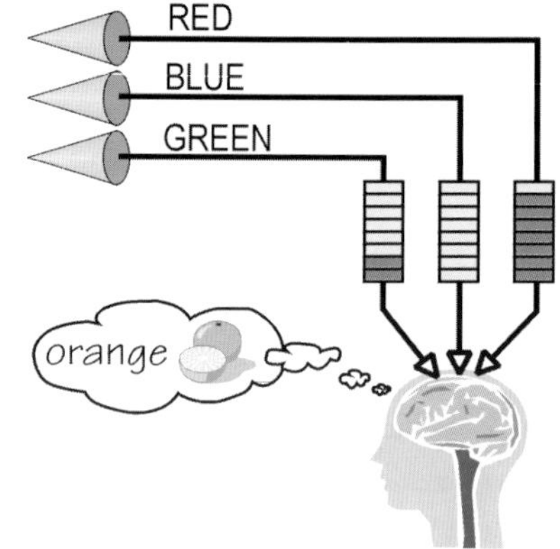

Figure 14.15: *If there is a strong RED signal and a weak GREEN signal, we see orange. All the range of colors can be made from combinations of red, green, and blue at different strengths.*

Do animals see in color?

Not all animals see the same colors

To the best of our knowledge, only humans and other primates (such as chimpanzees and gorillas) have all three kinds of red, green, and blue color sensors. Dogs and cats lack any color sensors at all. They have only rod cells that sense black, white, and shades of gray. Other creatures, like the honeybee, have three sensors but not the same three that we do. The primary colors for a honeybee's vision are two shades of blue-green and ultraviolet. So how do we know this? It has to do with the color of flowers and the bee's habit of collecting nectar and pollen from them.

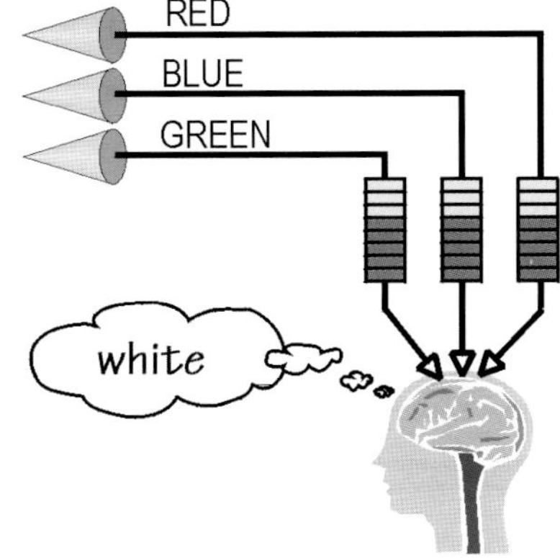

Figure 14.16: *White light is a mixture of all colors. When the red, green, and blue cone cells are all equally stimulated, we see white light.*

How do you see the colors of things?

We see mostly reflected light

When we see an object, the light that reaches our eyes can come from two different processes.

1 The light can be emitted directly from the object, like a light bulb or glow stick.

2 The light can come from somewhere else, like the sun, and we only see objects by their reflected light.

Most of what we see is actually from reflected light. When you look around you, you are seeing light originally from the sun (or electric lights) that has been reflected from people and objects around you. To convince yourself of this, turn off the lights in a room with no windows. You don't see anything. If you remove the source of light, there isn't any light to reflect, so you see nothing.

What gives objects their color?

When we look at a blue piece of cloth, we believe that the quality of blue is in the cloth, which is not actually true. The reason the cloth looks blue is because the pigments in the cloth have taken away (absorbed) all the frequencies of light for colors *other than blue* (figure 14.17). Since blue vibrations are all that is left, they are the ones that are reflected to our eyes. The blue was never *in the cloth*. The blue was hidden or mixed in with the other colors in white light even before it first hit the piece of cloth. The cloth unmasked the blue by taking away all the other colors and sending only the blue to our eyes.

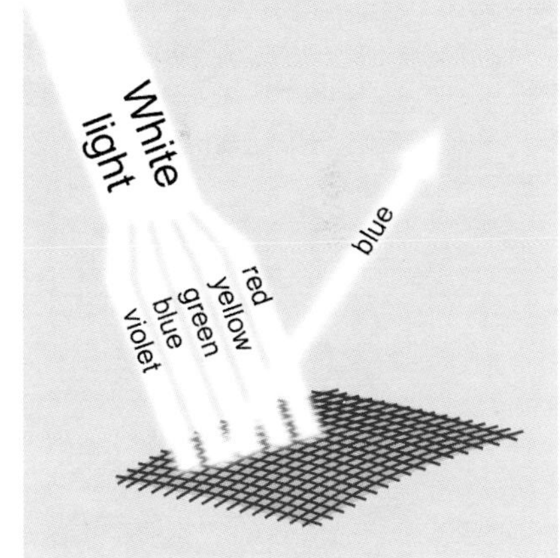

Figure 14.17: *You see blue cloth because the dyes in the fabric absorb all colors EXCEPT blue. The blue is what gets reflected to your eyes so you see the cloth as blue.*

The subtractive color process

Colored fabric gets color from a *subtractive* process. The dyes subtract out colors by *absorption* and *reflect* the colors you actually see. It works because white light is a mixture of red, orange, yellow, green, blue, indigo, and violet. But actually, you need just three primary colors—red, green, and blue—to make white light. How, then, does this work?

The subtractive primary colors

To make all colors by subtraction we also need three primary dyes. We need one that absorbs blue, and reflects red and green. This color is called yellow. We need another dye that absorbs only green, and reflects red and blue. This is a kind of pink-purple color called magenta. The last one absorbs red and reflects green and blue. The third color is called cyan, and is a greenish kind of light blue. Magenta, yellow, and cyan are the three subtractive primary colors. By using different combinations of the three we can make paper look any color because we can vary the amount of red, green, and blue reflected back to your eyes.

Black

You see black when no light is reflected. If you add magenta, cyan, and yellow you have a mixture that absorbs all light so it looks black. Some electronic printers actually make black by printing cyan, magenta, and yellow together. Because the dyes are not perfect, you rarely get a good black this way. Better printers have a black ink to make black separately.

Table 14.1: ***The three subtractive primary colors***

Color	Absorbs	Reflects
Cyan	Red	Blue and green
Magenta	Green	Red and blue
Yellow	Blue	Red and green

How to mix green paint

Suppose you want to make green paint. White light falling on your paint has equal parts red, green, and blue. To reflect only the green you need to get rid of the red and blue light. Starting from white paint, you need to add cyan and yellow. The cyan absorbs red, leaving blue and green. The yellow absorbs the blue, leaving only the green, just as you wanted.

Color printers

Color printers work by putting tiny dots on paper. The dots use four colors, cyan, magenta, yellow, and black. Printers refer to these as CMYK where the letter K stands for black.

The dots are so tiny that you see them as a single color. By using only the three subtractive primary colors, printers can reproduce a very wide range of reflected colors. The smaller the dots, the sharper the overall image. Newspapers print about 150 dots per inch, resulting in photographs being a little blurry. Good color printers print as many as 1,200 dots per inch.

Why are plants green?

Light is necessary for photosynthesis

Plants are green because of how they use visible light. In a very unique way, plants absorb physical energy in the form of light and convert it to chemical energy in the form of sugar. The process is called photosynthesis. The graph in figure 14.18 shows the wavelengths of visible light that plants absorb. The x-axis on the graph represents the wavelengths of visible light. The y-axis on the graph represents the amount of light absorbed by plant pigments for photosynthesis.

Chlorophyll

The green pigment, chlorophyll *a*, is the most important light-absorbing pigment. You can see on the graph that chlorophyll *a* absorbs light at each end of the spectrum. In other words, it reflects most of the green light and uses blue and red light. Plants are green because they reflect green light. In fact, plants will not grow well if they are placed under pure green light!

Why leaves change color

Notice that chlorophyll *b* and carotenoids (orange pigments) absorb light where chlorophyll *a* does not. These extra pigments help plants catch more light. Leaves change color in the fall when chlorophyll *a* breaks down and these pigments become visible. They are the cause of the beautiful bright reds and oranges that you see when leaves change color in the fall.

Plants reflect some light to keep cool

Why don't plant pigments absorb all wavelengths of visible light? The reason for this has to do with why you might want to wear light colored clothes when it is really hot outside. Like you, plants must reflect some light to avoid getting too hot!

Visible light has just the right energy for life

Visible light is just a small part of the electromagnetic spectrum. Why do living things see and use this part the most? In other words, why can't plants grow in dark places? Why can't we see ultraviolet or infrared light?

Visible light, it turns out, is just right for living things to use. The other parts of the electromagnetic radiation spectrum are not as useful. Ultraviolet light, for example, has too much energy. It can break bonds in important molecules. Infrared radiation is mostly absorbed by water vapor and carbon dioxide in the atmosphere. Therefore, this longer wavelength light is not as available as visible light for living things to use.

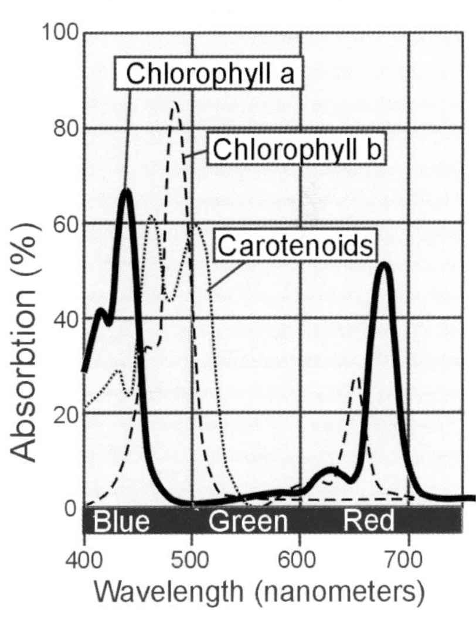

Figure 14.18: *The lines in the graph show which colors of light are absorbed by plant pigments for photosynthesis. Chlorophyll a is used in photosynthesis. Chlorophyll b and carotenoids help absorb light for photosynthesis. The graph shows that blue light and red light are absorbed (two peaks) and green light is not absorbed (flat center). Plants are green because green light is reflected by the pigments in the leaves and other green parts of the plant.*

How does a color TV work?

TV makes its own light

Televisions give off light. They do not rely on reflected light to make color. You can prove this by watching a TV in a dark room. You can see light from the TV even if there are no other sources of light in the room. Computer monitors and movie projectors are similar. All these devices make their own light.

Figure 14.19: *Television makes color using tiny glowing dots of red, green, and blue. All devices that make their own light (like TV) use the RGB color model to make color.*

The RGB color process

To make color with a TV you can use red, green, and blue (RGB) directly. You do not need to use the subtractive colors. Take a magnifying glass and look closely at a television screen while it is running. You will notice something interesting. The screen is made of tiny red dots, green dots, and blue dots! Each of the dots gives off light. The colored dots are separated by very thin black lines. The black lines help give intensity to the resultant colors and help make the darker colors darker. By turning on the different dots at different intensities TV sets can mix the three colors to get millions of different colors. From far away, you can't see the small dots. What you see is a nice smooth color picture.

If you see a big screen at a sporting event it looks just like a color television. Looking closer, you see that image is actually made up of small colored light bulbs. The bulbs are red, green, and blue, just like the dots in the television screen.

Two complementary color processes

All devices that make their own light use the RGB (red, green, blue) color model. They create millions of colors by varying the strengths of each of the three primaries. Anything that relies on reflected light to make color uses the CMYK (cyan, magenta, yellow, black) color process. This includes printing inks, fabric dyes, and even the color of your skin.

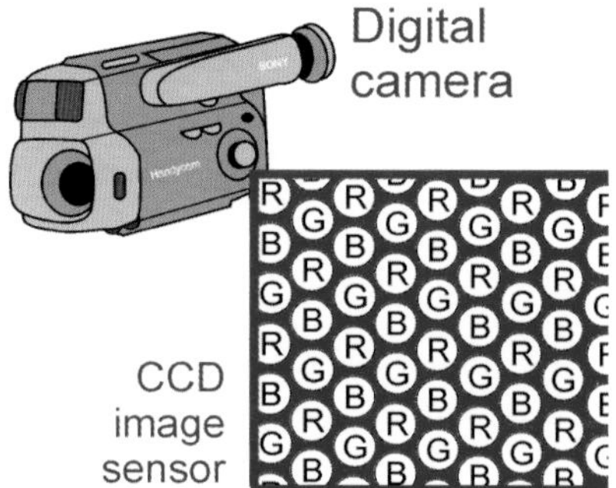

Figure 14.20: *Digital cameras have a device called a CCD that is an array of tiny light sensors, just like the human eye. A 1-megapixel camera has a million of each red, green, and blue sensors on a chip smaller than a dime.*

How computers make color

Computers use numbers to represent the values for red, green, and blue. Every pixel, or dot, on your computer screen has three numbers that tell it what color to make. Each color can go from 0 to 256, with 256 being the brightest. The value RGB = (0,0,0) is pure black, no color. Setting RGB = (255, 255, 255) gives pure white, or equal red, green, blue. Using this model, computers can represent 256 x 256 x 256 or 16,777,216 different colors. More than 16 million colors can be made from just three numbers!

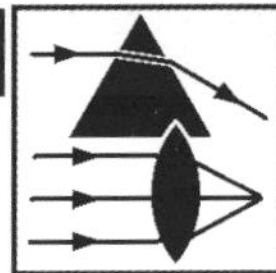

Chapter 14 Review

Vocabulary review

Match the following terms with the correct definition. There is one extra definition in the list that will not match any of the terms.

Set One

1. light
2. electromagnetic spectrum
3. energy level
4. incandescence
5. fluorescence

a. A property of electrons inside atoms
b. A wave we see with our eyes
c. Heating something up so hot it gives off light
d. Stimulating atoms to emit light using light of another energy
e. The range of waves that includes radio waves, light, and X rays
f. The interaction of two or more waves with each other

Set Two

1. radio waves
2. infrared
3. ultraviolet
4. X rays
5. gamma rays

a. Electromagnetic waves that we feel as heat
b. Electromagnetic waves that have very high energy and come from nuclear reactions
c. Electromagnetic waves that have very low energy and wavelengths of many meters
d. Electromagnetic waves that can pass through skin and make images of the body
e. Electromagnetic waves with more energy than visible light and that cause sunburns
f. Electromagnetic waves that we see with our eyes

Set Three

1. polarization
2. color
3. photoreceptors
4. primary colors
5. RGB model

a. How we perceive different frequencies of light within the visible range
b. Making all colors as mixtures of red, green, and blue light
c. Red, green, and blue
d. A way of aligning the direction of light wave vibration by blocking some of the waves
e. Nerves in the eye that are sensitive to light
f. The wavelength of X rays

Set Four

1. magenta
2. yellow
3. cyan
4. photosynthesis
5. CMYK model

a. A dye that absorbs red light
b. A dye that absorbs green light
c. Making all colors with cyan, magenta, yellow, and black pigments
d. The process plants use to get energy from light
e. A dye that absorbs blue light
f. A wavelength absorbed by the ozone layer

Concept review

1. What does photoluminescence mean?
2. What does incandescence mean?
3. What must happen to the electron in order for an atom to emit light?
   a. Move from a low energy level to a high energy level.
   b. Stay in a high energy level.
   c. Move from a high energy level to a low energy level.
   d. Stay in a low energy level.
4. Identify which of the following produces electromagnetic waves in the gamma ray part of the spectrum.
   a. A nuclear reaction
   b. A cell phone
   c. A radio transmitter
   d. A flashlight
5. Identify which of the following devices uses microwaves. You may choose more than one.
   a. an oven for heating food
   b. a cell phone
   c. a satellite transmitter
   d. a small flashlight
6. A polarizer is:
   a. A filter that separates light.
   b. An ink that absorbs green light.
   c. A sensor in the eye that detects blue light.
   d. A device for creating diffraction.
7. Infrared radiation belongs where in the electromagnetic spectrum diagram below? (Choose a, b, c, or d)

Radio waves

Microwaves

Visible light

X rays

Gamma rays

a b c d

8. Which of the following would produce the sensation of white light?

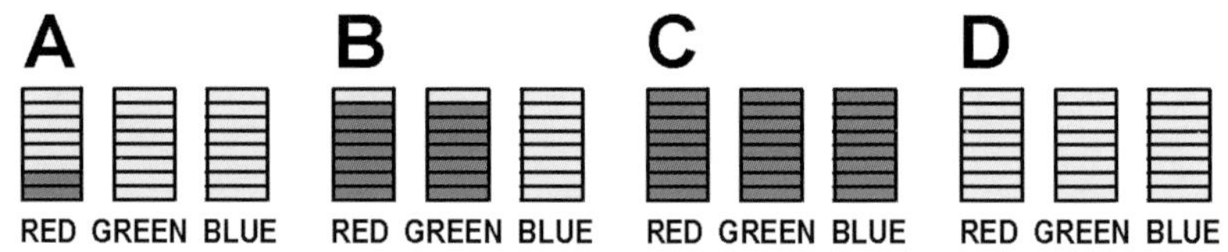

9. Which of the following would produce the sensation of yellow light?

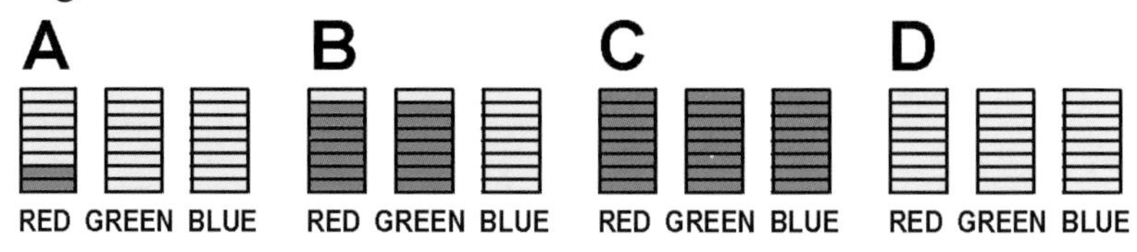

10. What are the three primary colors of light?
    a. red, green, and blue
    b. red, yellow, and blue
    c. magenta, cyan, and yellow
    d. orange, green, and violet
11. What are the three primary colors of pigments?
    a. red, green, and blue
    b. red, yellow, and blue
    c. magenta, cyan, and yellow
    d. orange, green, and violet

Problems

1. Arrange the following in order of speed from fastest to slowest:

   a. Sound waves b. Light waves c. Water waves

2. What color is obtained when the three primary colors of light are combined in equal strengths?

3. Which photochemical receptors in our eyes are stimulated when we see the color yellow?

4. If you wanted to make green paint, you would use which combination of dyes?

   a. cyan and magenta
   b. cyan and yellow
   c. magenta and yellow
   d. magenta only

5. What does a piece of blue cloth do to the colors in white light that falls upon it?

   a. It absorbs blue light and reflects all the rest of the colors to our eyes.
   b. It absorbs all the colors except blue and reflects only blue light to our eyes.
   c. It absorbs all of the colors in the white light.
   d. It absorbs none of the colors in the white light.

6. What happens to the light energy that is shined upon a black object?

7. Name the four colors used by color computer printers?

8. What are the primary colors used to construct the image on a color TV monitor?

9. When a store clerk adds more colorants (pigments) to a can of white paint, what will be the result?

   a. More colors are taken away from the light we use to view the paint.
   b. More colors are added to the light we use to view the paint.
   c. Fewer colors are taken away from the light we use to view the paint.
   d. No change occurs in the light we use to view the paint.

10. Describe wavelength and frequency of green light and why using only green light would not allow plants to grow.

11. Arrange the following in order from LOWEST energy to HIGHEST energy: Gamma rays, visible light, X rays, microwaves, radio waves, infrared light, ultraviolet light.

12. Calculate how much money you would save in one year by changing from an incandescent bulb to a fluorescent bulb. Assume electricity costs 10 cents per kilowatt hour and that the bulb is on all the time for the whole year. The two bulbs in the picture produce the same amount of light.

Incandescent Bulb
100 watts

Compact Fluorescent Bulb
23 watts

Applying your knowledge

1. Why does fire give off light?
2. Why would putting out a fire with water stop it from giving off light?
3. How many different kinds of photochemical receptors are found in the eyes of most people? What colors of light do these photochemical receptors respond to? To what location does a photochemical receptor send its signal?
4. What is different about the photochemical receptors in the eyes of people with color blindness?
5. What may be different about the photochemical receptors in the eyes of other animals?
6. Research color blindness using your library or the Internet. How many different kinds of color blindness are there? Find out what kinds of receptors are missing in the eyes of people with the various kinds of color blindness. Find out which tasks are more difficult for them and which ones are actually easier.
7. Design an improvement to a common product to make it easier for color blind people to use. Suggest ways that people with normal color vision can avoid making life unnecessarily difficult for people with color blindness.
8. How do we know anything about the color vision of animals? Look up the studies done on honeybees and report on the experimental methods. Design your own study to find out if dogs or cats can tell one color from another.
9. What makes the colors on a computer screen different from the colors in paint? How can you get red, green, and blue from both?
10. Computer graphic artists use two different color models to represent color. The RGB model has three numbers that represent the strengths of red, green, and blue. The CMYK model uses four numbers that represent the strength of cyan, magenta, yellow, and black.
    a. What are the maximum and minimum values for the numbers that determine color on a computer?
    b. Find a table of colors and identify the numbers you need to make orange in both RGB and CMYK systems.
    RBG: R = _____ B = _____ G = _____
    CMYK: C = _____ M = _____ Y = _____ K = _____
    c. If a picture contains 1,000 pixels, or dots, how much computer memory is needed to store the picture in RGB and CMYK models? Assume that each number takes 8 bits of memory to store.
11. Why is ice sometimes clear and sometimes cloudy white? Experiment with freezing ice in your home freezer. Find out how you can control the transparency of ice.

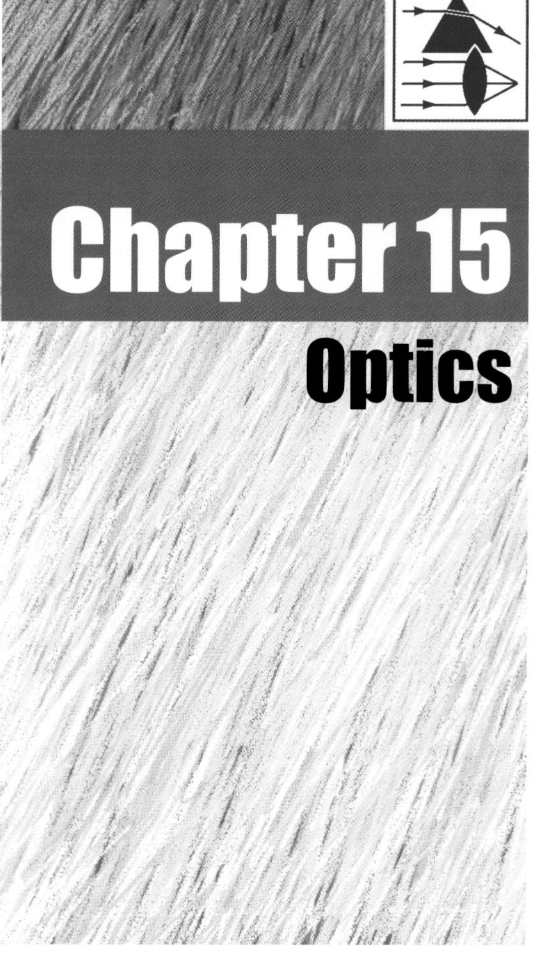

Introduction to Chapter 15

Cameras, telescopes, and our eyes are all optic devices. Rays of light are everywhere and optic devices bend and bounce these rays to produce all the colors and images that you can see. This chapter will introduce you to the science of optics.

Investigations for Chapter 15

15.1	Seeing an Image	*What does magnification really mean and how do you plot a reflected image?*

We see images based on what happens to light. In this Investigation you will discover how light can be bent by a lens to magnify an image, or bounced by a mirror to produce a reflected image. Plotting the rays of light from an object will allow you to understand what a mirror or lens is doing.

15.2	The Human Eye	*How does a lens form an image?*

A lens can bend light to create amazing images. The actual bending of the light in our eye is caused by a clear lens that can change shape slightly. The shape-changing lens in the eye allows us to see close up or far away. In this Investigation, you will work with lenses to focus light and create images

15.3	Optical Technology	*How are optics used in everyday life?*

Fiber optics are becoming one of the most important and versatile aspects of optical technology. Fiber optics work on a simple principle. If light is traveling in a material like glass or water, and enters into air, it can become trapped in the material. In this Investigation you will explore total internal reflection, the process that makes fiber optics possible.

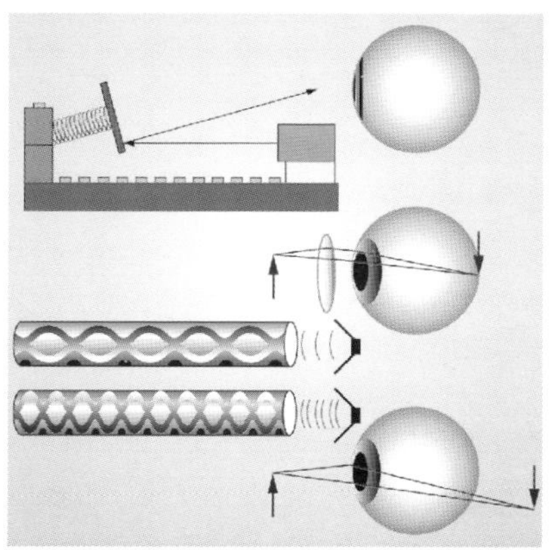

Learning Goals

By the end of the lesson, you will be able to:

- ✔ Describe the function of the human eye.
- ✔ Describe the difference between objects and images.
- ✔ Describe and demonstrate the formation of an image.
- ✔ Draw a ray diagram for a lens.
- ✔ Calculate the magnification of a lens.
- ✔ Describe the index of refraction and explain how it is applied in the making of lenses.
- ✔ Identify the characteristics of reflection.
- ✔ Draw a reflected ray.
- ✔ Predict how light will bend when its speed changes.
- ✔ Understand internal reflection.
- ✔ Identify uses of fiber optics.

Vocabulary

angle of incidence	focal length	index of refraction	reflected ray
angle of refraction	focal point	lens	refraction
converging	focus	normal	total internal reflection
critical angle	image	ray diagrams	virtual image
diverging	incident ray	real image	

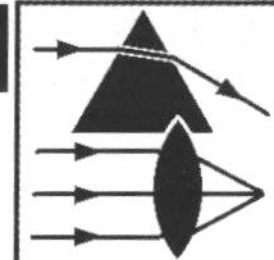

15.1 Seeing an Image

Try this quick experiment: Take a magnifying lens and look through it at your thumb. You can adjust the distance until the thumb is big. You are actually seeing a big thumb. You are bending the light that is coming from your thumb, so that you *see* a huge thumb. Imagine how big your hand would be if your thumb really was that big. It would be a giant hand!

Now imagine that a few cells of your thumb were under a microscope. You can see the individual cells of your skin. You can see parts of the cell and they look big. Now imagine how big your thumb would be if all the cells were actually that big. Wow! You have the hand of super giant! Of course, your hand is actually the same size it always was, though what you see is a super giant hand. One branch of optics is the study of how to manipulate light to create images that are different from the original object.

Figure 15.1: *A magnifying glass makes your thumb look as big as if you were a giant!*

What is optics?

Definition of optics

The study of how light behaves is called optics. Optics deals with the collection and use of light to create images. The category of optics covers devices that direct light like lenses, mirrors, cameras, telescopes, and microscopes. It includes events of light like rainbows, sunsets, and eclipses. Ultimately, all of the light from these sources gets to your eye. We will see that the eye itself is an optical instrument.

Lenses, mirrors, and prisms

Your eye contains a lens. A lens is one kind of optical device that is used to bend light. By bending the light so that it comes together (converging), you can magnify an image and by bending the light so that it spreads apart (diverging), you can get a smaller image.

A mirror is a familiar optic device; you probably used one this morning. Mirrors reflect light and allow us to see ourselves. Flat mirrors show a true-size image. Curved mirrors cause light to come together or spread apart. A fun house at the circus uses curved mirrors to make you look thin, wide, or upside down. Curved mirrors distort images. The curved side-view mirror on a car, for example, makes the cars behind you look farther away than they really are.

A prism is another optic device that can cause light to change directions. Traditionally, a prism is used to separate the colors of light and to demonstrate how light bends (refracts) as it travels through different media (figure 15.2).

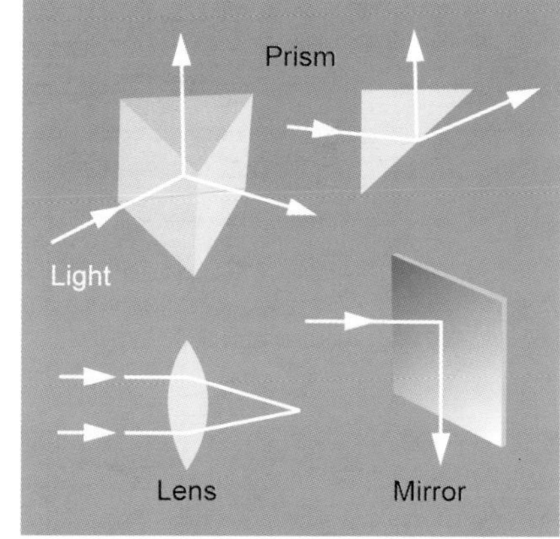

Figure 15.2: *Lenses, mirrors, and prisms are part of the study of optics.*

Light rays

What is a light ray? It is convenient to think about light in terms of rays. A ray of light can be considered an imaginary arrow that follows a single beam of light. This simplification allows us to analyze where the light travels. We only need to follow the rays. Very often we will need to follow several rays of light to determine what will happen.

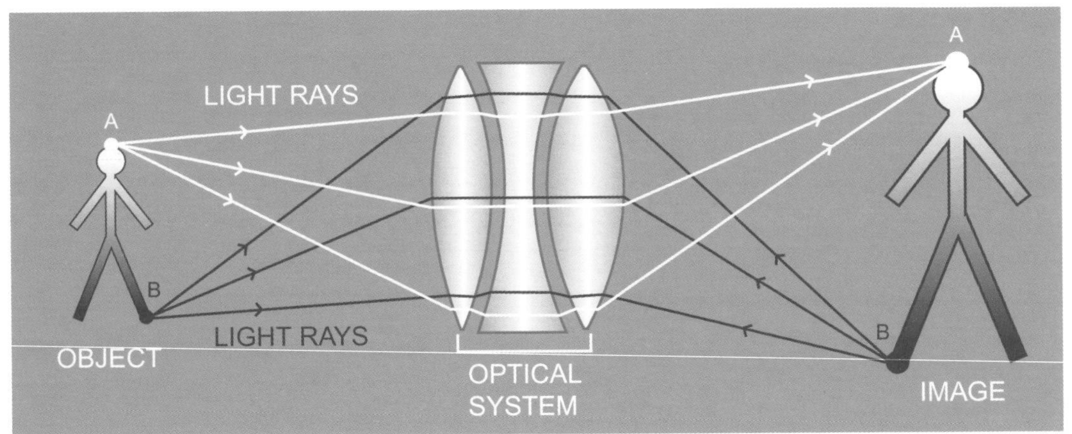

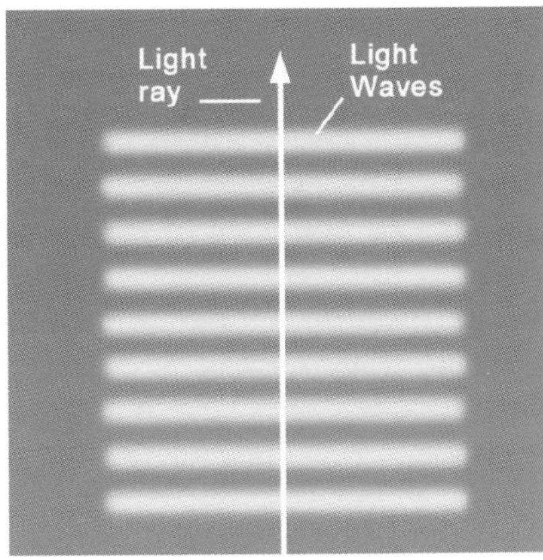

Figure 15.3: *The relationship between rays and wave fronts. The ray is the path of the wave.*

Drawing light rays in diagrams Light waves are like the waves you see in the ocean as they move continually toward the beach. Rays are represented by lines that are perpendicular to the wave fronts. The lines have arrows that show you which way the light is moving. When you see a ray drawn on a diagram, you should know that technically, the ray isn't really one ray of light but a series of light waves. Figure 15.3 uses an arrow to represent which way the light waves are moving.

Figure 15.4: *Every point on an object is the source of many light rays that come at all angles to the viewer.*

Rays come from objects When we see an object, every point on the object reflects many rays of light. Let's consider an example to demonstrate what this means. Look at the clock in your classroom, and focus on the number seven. If you walk around the room, you will find that you can still see the number seven. This demonstrates how light from a single point (in this case, the number seven) can be seen from different angles. This is true because light is reflected to all angles in the room. Figure 15.4 is an illustration of how light rays are reflected off a vase.

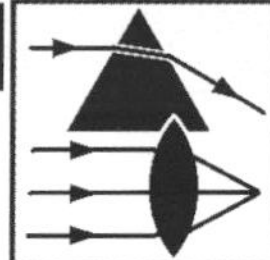

Images

Rays come together in an image

Suppose you could collect all the rays from one point on an object, bringing them all together again. You would have created an image. An image is a place where many rays from the same point on an object meet together again in a point. A camera works by collecting the rays from an object and bending them so they form an image on the film.

Objects and images

It is helpful to think about optics in terms of objects and images. Objects are any real physical things that give off or reflect light rays. Images are "pictures" of objects that are formed in places where light rays from the object meet. The focus is the place where all the light rays from the object meet to form the image.

Light travels in straight lines

Normally, light travels in straight lines. Most of the time, when you see some object, it is because the light traveled in a straight line from the object to your eye. As long as nothing is in the way, you can be sure the object is precisely where you perceived it to be. This is because the light rays did not bend.

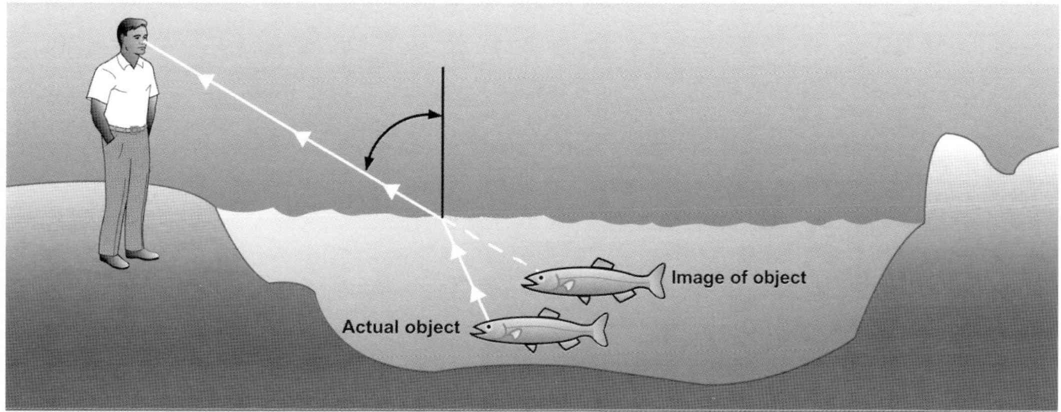

Light rays can be bent

To make images, we often need to bend light rays. Light is sometimes bent *between* an object and your eye. This bending will usually make the image appear different from the object in size or location. A good example is seeing a fish under water. The light waves from the fish bend as they travel from the water to the air. Due to the bending rays, the *image* of the fish appears in a different place from where the fish is actually swimming.

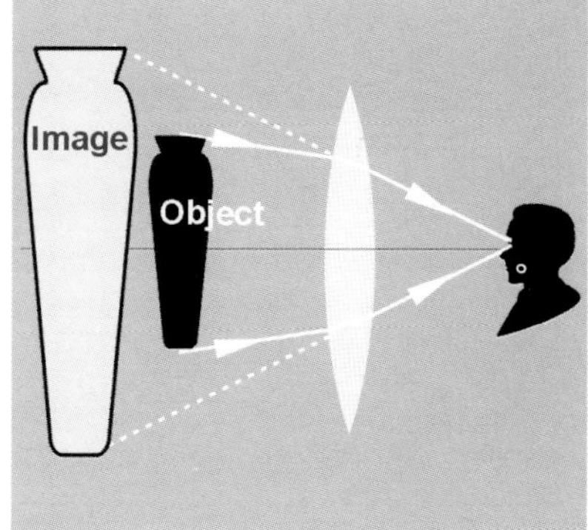

Figure 15.5: *The difference between objects and images.*

The light rays from the object are bent when they go through the lens. Our brain does not know the rays were bent. We "see" the rays as having traveled in straight lines.

The image appears larger because the lens has bent the light rays so they appear to come from a larger object. This is the principle of the magnifying glass.

Figure 15.6: *A magnifying glass makes a virtual image that appears larger than the object.*

Optical systems

What is an optical system? An optical system collects light and uses refraction and reflection to form an image. When we use an optical system, we do not see the actual object. What we really see is an image. When light is bent through an optical system before it gets to our eyes, the image we see might not represent the actual object as it truly is.

Refraction Refraction is the bending of light that occurs when light crosses a boundary between two different substances. Usually one is air and the other is a clear material such as glass, plastic, or even water. A lens is a special shape of clear solid material that uses refraction to cause light to come together or spread apart. A magnifying glass on a sunny day can be used to illustrate how one type of lens works (figure 15.7).

Reflection A mirror reflects rays of light so that they change their path. Reflection happens when objects or waves can "bounce" off a surface. Whenever a wave strikes a surface, part of the energy is reflected. By changing the shape of a mirror you can also cause light to come to a focus, just like with a lens (figure 15.8).

The telescope A telescope is a collection of lenses that can magnify an image. When you look through a telescope, the rays of light are bent and appear as if they were coming from an image much closer than the actual object. A telescope is an optical system that makes objects appear larger than they are, and sometimes upside down!

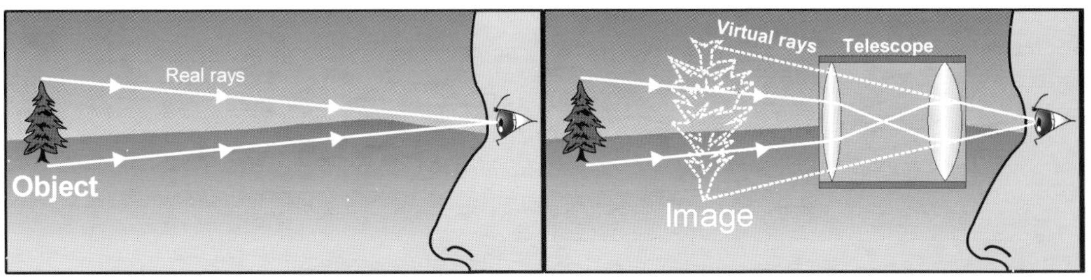

Why we see magnified images The illusion created by a telescope happens because we perceive that light travels in a straight line. If the device bends light so that it appears to have come straight from a large object, then we see a magnified image.

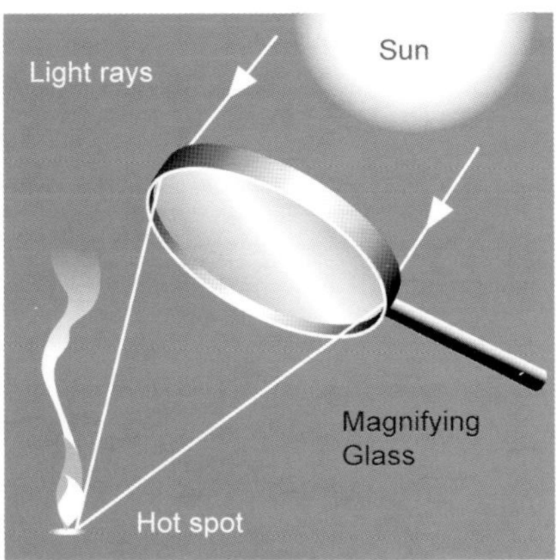

Figure 15.7: *A magnifying glass can bend many rays to come together at a focus. On a sunny day the focus can be quite hot!*

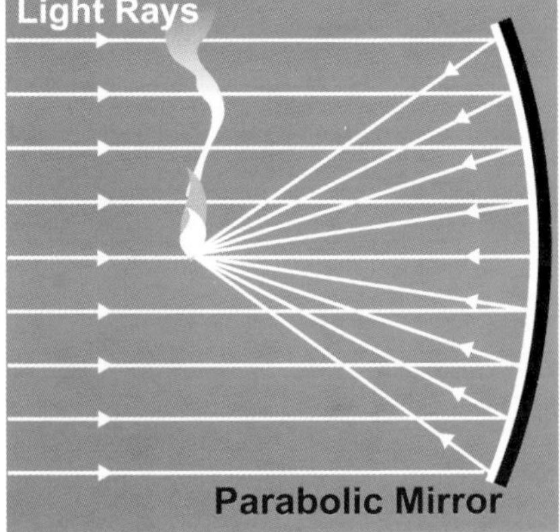

Figure 15.8: *Mirrors also change the direction of light rays. A curved mirror can make light rays from the sun change direction and meet at a focus, just like a lens. This is how solar ovens work.*

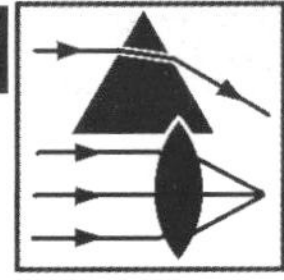

The functions of an optical system

Most optical devices have two important functions.

1 They collect light rays.

2 They bend the collected light rays to form an image.

Both functions are important. If you are interested in astronomy, for example, most of the things in the night sky don't produce enough light for our eyes to see. Not only does a telescope make things appear larger, it also collects more light so we can see fainter objects.

The ray diagram

To figure out how an optical system works we often draw ray diagrams. Ray diagrams trace how several light rays behave as they go through the system. The rays come straight from an object and are bent or bounced as they encounter a lens or mirror. By tracing the rays through the system we are usually looking to find what kind of image will be produced.

Some typical questions that we use ray diagrams to answer are:

1 Where is the focus (or is there a focus)?

2 Will the image be magnified or reduced in size?

3 Will the image be upside down or right side up?

4 Will the image be inverted left to right?

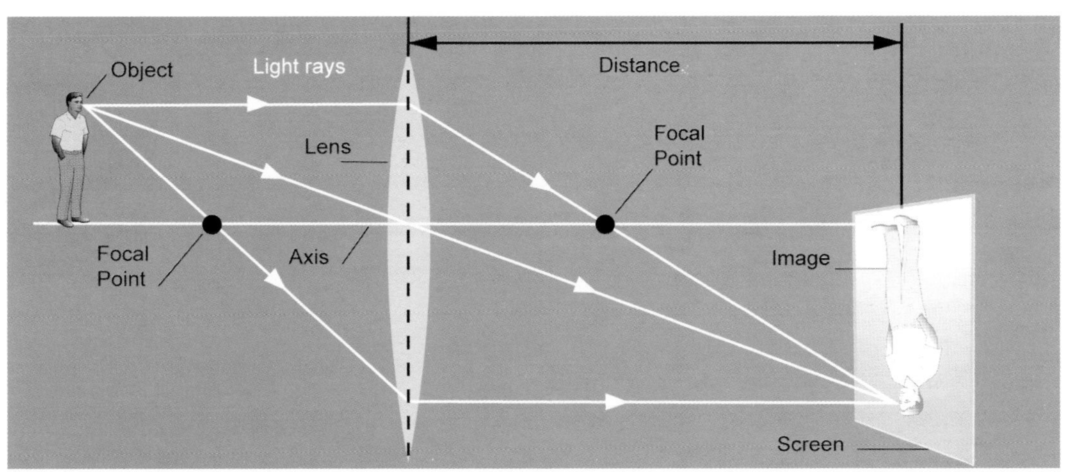

A plastic bag lens

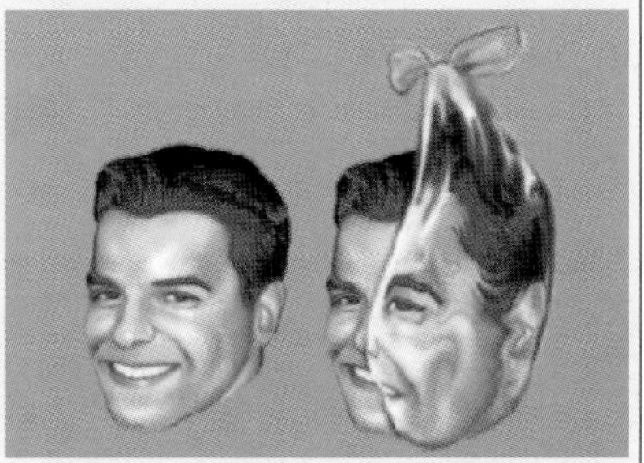

Water is capable of bending light. Take a clear plastic bag and fill it with water. Now look through it. What you see is called an image. The shape of the optic device determines the shape of the image. Squeeze the bag in different places and see how the image changes.

Reflection and mirrors

Mirrors create a virtual image

When you look in a mirror, you see an image. The image appears to be behind the mirror and is reversed from left to right. For example, if you hold a stop sign in front of a mirror, the letters appear backward. Why does this occur?

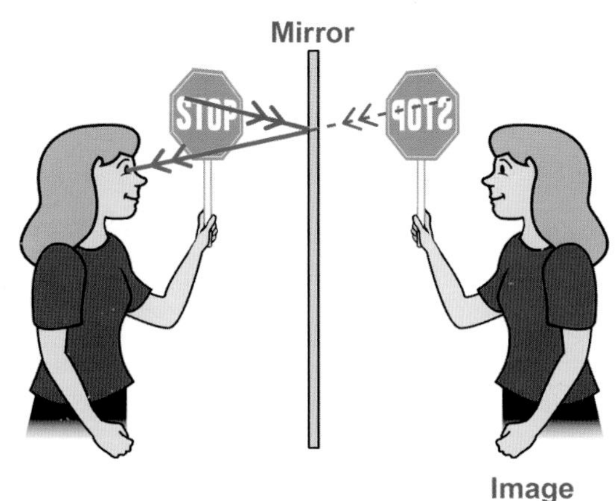

The light rays that travel from the "S" in the stop sign hit the mirror at an angle and are reflected back to your eye at an equal but opposite angle.

Your brain assumes that this reflected ray traveled to your eye in a straight line from an "object" behind the mirror. As a result, the image of the "S" appears to have come from the opposite direction as the actual letter on the stop sign.

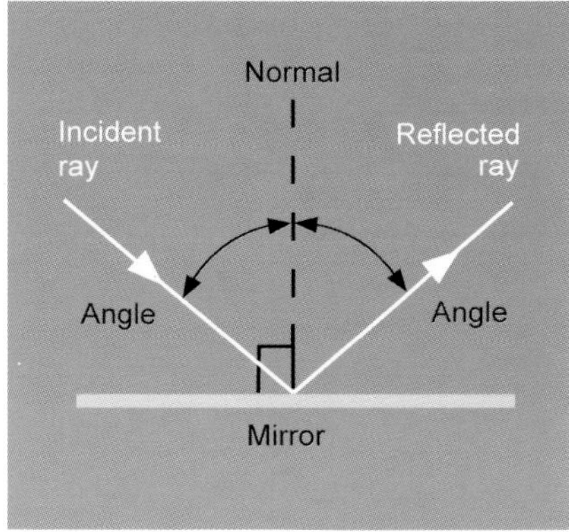

Figure 15.9: *The normal is a line perpendicular to the mirror. The incident ray is the ray that comes in to the mirror. The reflected ray is the ray that bounces off the mirror.*

Incident and reflected rays

To investigate mirrors further, we will talk about incident and reflected rays. The incident ray is the ray that comes from the object and hits the mirror. The reflected ray is the ray that bounces off the mirror (figure 15.9). There is a rule that tells us how to predict the direction of the reflected ray once we know the incident ray's direction.

The law of reflection

The rule that determines the reflected ray is called the *law of reflection*. This law is very simple: Light rays bounce off a mirror at the same angle at which they arrive. The only tricky part is defining the angles. To keep things clear we always define angles relative to the normal. In optics, the normal is a line perpendicular to the mirror (figure 15.9).

If a light ray comes in at an angle of 30 degrees from the normal, it bounces off at the same angle, 30 degrees. If a ray comes in at zero degrees (straight on) it also bounces back at zero degrees. In other words, the light comes in and reflects out on the same normal.

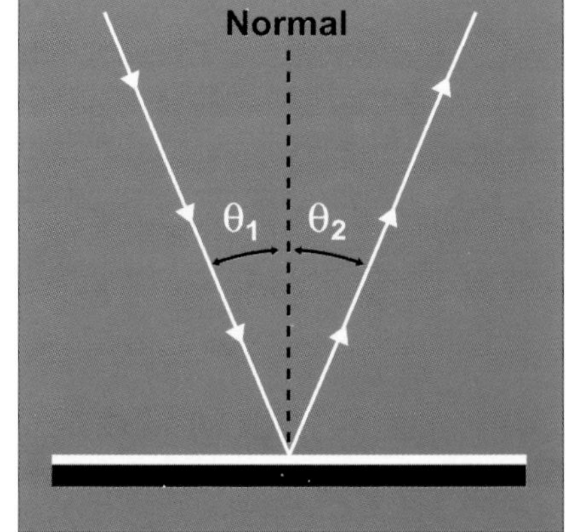

Figure 15.10: *The law of reflection states that the angle of incidence (θ_1) is equal to the angle of reflection (θ_2). By throwing a ball against a wall, how could you demonstrate that $\theta_1 = \theta_2$?*

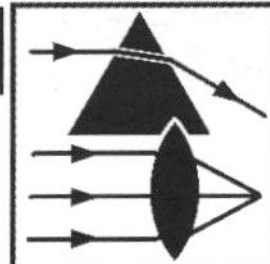

Refraction and lenses

Refraction When light crosses the boundary between two different (transparent) materials the rays may bend. We call the bending refraction. Refraction happens because the wave fronts move more slowly in materials other than air (figure 15.11). As we already learned, if we change the shape of wave fronts we can turn a wave.

What is a lens? A lens is a shape of transparent material, like glass, that is used to bend the light rays. Figure 15.12 shows how the curved surface of a lens works. We choose the shape of the lens depending on how strongly we want to bend the light. Lenses come in many different shapes and strengths.

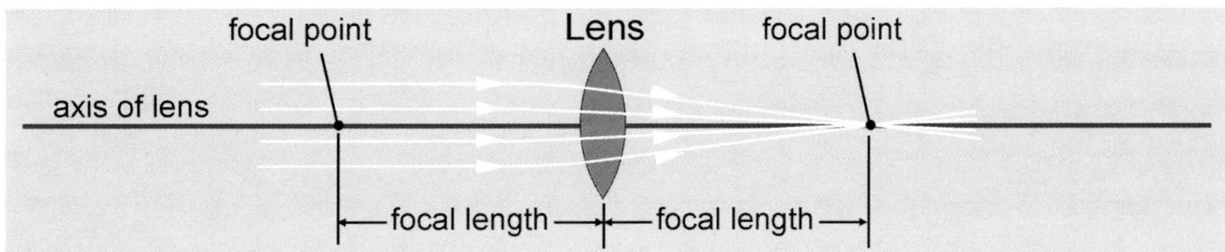

Focal point and focal length Almost all lenses are shaped to have a very useful property. Light rays that enter a lens parallel to its axis will bend to meet at a point called the focal point. The distance from the center of the lens to the focal point is called the focal length. The focal length of a lens determines how powerful the lens is and how it can be used to focus light.

Converging and diverging lenses There are two kinds of lenses we will examine. Converging lenses bend the parallel light rays passing through them inward toward the focal point. Diverging lenses bend the parallel light rays passing through them outward away from the focal point. A parallel beam coming into a diverging lens is bent away from the focal point.

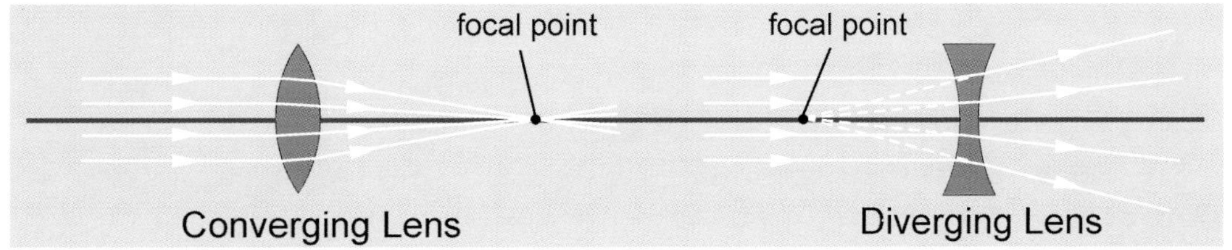

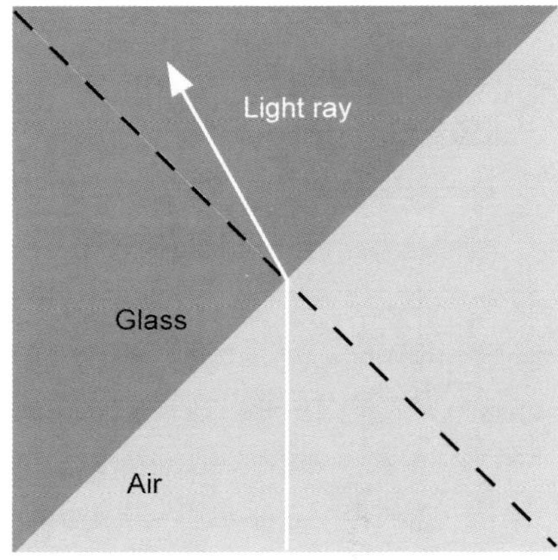

Figure 15.11: *A ray of light is refracted (bent) when it crosses from one material into another.*

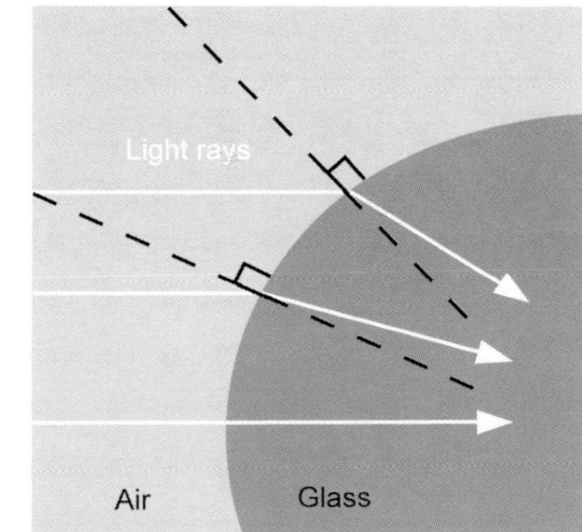

Figure 15.12: *For a curved surface, the amount the ray bends depends on where it hits the surface. Rays farther out are bent the most. If the surface is curved just right, all the rays that hit the lens are bent so they meet at the focus.*

Forming images with lenses

Why are lenses useful? Lenses are used in eyeglasses, microscopes, telescopes, and other devices to form images. An image, as you have learned, forms when light rays emitted or reflected from one point on an object meet at a point again. Ray diagrams can be used to show where the image will form, how large the image will appear, and whether it is upside down or right side up.

What kinds of images are formed? If an object is placed to the left of a converging lens at a distance greater than the focal length, an inverted image is formed on the right-hand side of the lens. We call this image a **real image**. Real images can be projected on a smooth surface, like photographic slides onto a wall. Since real images are inverted, slides must be loaded into the carousel upside down, so that the picture appears right side up!

Example: A lens has a focal length of 10 centimeters. An object is placed 15 centimeters to the left of the lens. Trace the rays and predict where the image will be. Is the image bigger, smaller, or inverted?

Step 1: Draw the axis and focal points.

Step 2: Draw three rays from the object's tip.

Step 3: The image of the object's tip is found where the three rays meet.

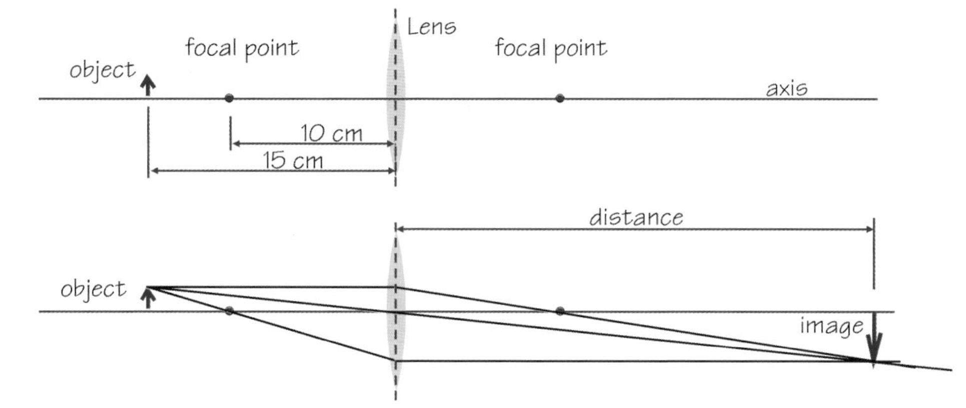

The image is formed 30 cm to the right of the lens. It is magnified and inverted.

If an object is placed to the left of a converging lens at a distance less than the focal length, the lens acts as a magnifying glass. The lens bends the rays so that they appear to be coming from an object larger and farther away than the real object. These rays appear to come from an image, but don't actually meet, so the images are called **virtual images**. Mirrors create virtual images.

Galileo and the telescope

Lenses were being made as early as the 13th century to help people see. Galileo did not invent the telescope, but he learned of it around 1608. He was the first to use it as a tool for astronomy, and by 1609 he had created an improved telescope of far better magnification than any in existence.

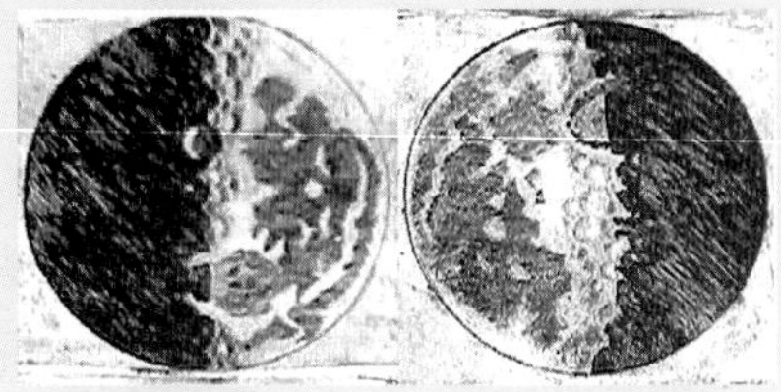

One of the first things Galileo saw was that the line between dark and light on the Moon was not smooth, but jagged. Galileo correctly recognized that the jagged line was due to tall mountains on the moon casting shadows onto the lighter side. His 400-year- old sketches show incredible detail including craters and the lunar maria (seas).

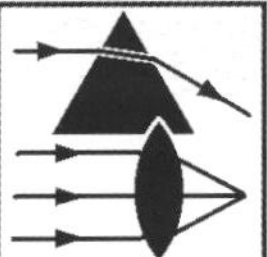

The index of refraction

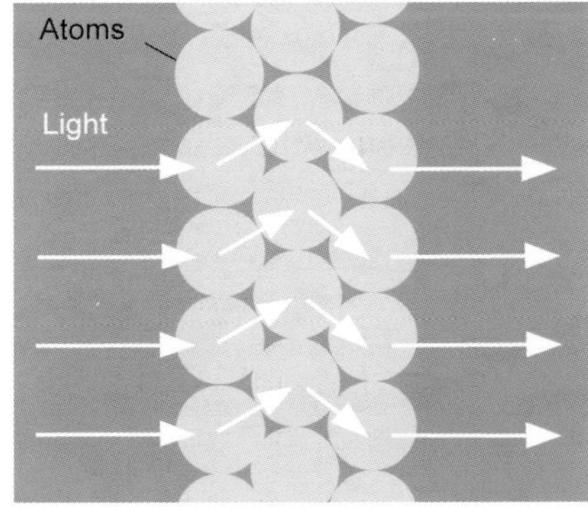

Figure 15.13: *Light travels slower through glass because it is continually absorbed and reemitted by each atom it passes through.*

The index of refraction (n)

$$n = \frac{\text{speed of light in air}}{\text{speed in material}}$$

Material	Index (n)
Air	1.00
Ice	1.31
Water	1.33
Ethyl alcohol	1.36
Fused quartz	1.46
Crown glass	1.52
Cubic zirconia	2.20
Diamond	2.41

Figure 15.14: *Index of refraction (n) for some common materials.*

The index of refraction Light waves travel at a slower rate through glass and other transparent materials than through air. This is because the wave has to constantly be absorbed and reemitted by all the atoms in a material (figure 15.13). Since not all atoms are alike, you might expect different materials to slow the light by different amounts. This is indeed true, and we have a ratio called the index of refraction that tells how much the speed of light is reduced when it passes through a material.

The index of refraction is a ratio of the speed of light in a vacuum (or air) compared with its speed in a material. The number is always greater than one because light travels fastest in a vacuum. We use the letter n to represent the index of refraction.

Higher index means more bending The higher the index of refraction, the more a light wave bends when crossing in or out of the material. Figure 15.14 gives some typical values of n for common materials. Light waves are strongly bent by a diamond. It is the high index of refraction that gives diamonds their sparkle and beautiful rainbows of color.

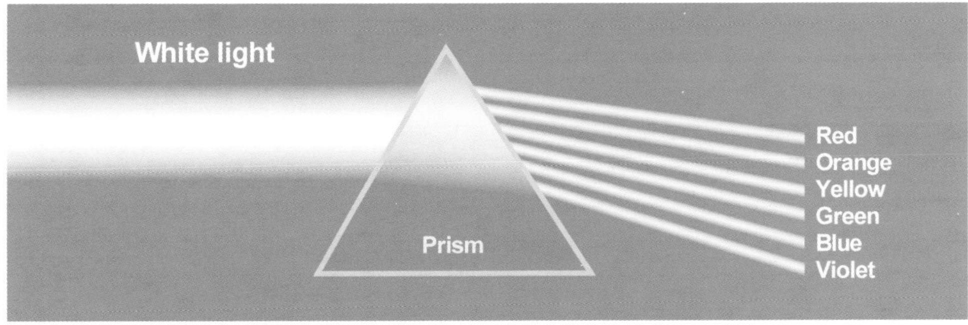

The prism A prism is a polished shape of glass that you can use to investigate refraction. A common shape for a prism is a triangle. Light coming into any face of the prism is bent by refraction. The light is bent again when it comes out of the prism.

Splitting colors with a prism The index of refraction varies slightly depending on the color of the light. Blue light is bent more strongly than red light. Because of this you can use a prism to split white light up into different colors. Blue light is on one end of our visible spectrum. Red light is on the other end.

15.2 The Human Eye

Your eye is an entire optical system that works together with the optic nerve and your brain to help you see images. Some scientists even consider the eye to be part of the brain itself. Everything we have learned about refraction and images applies to the eye.

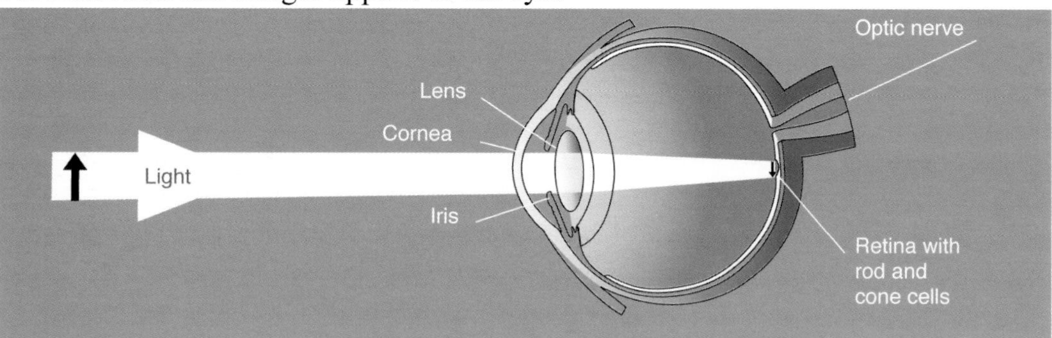

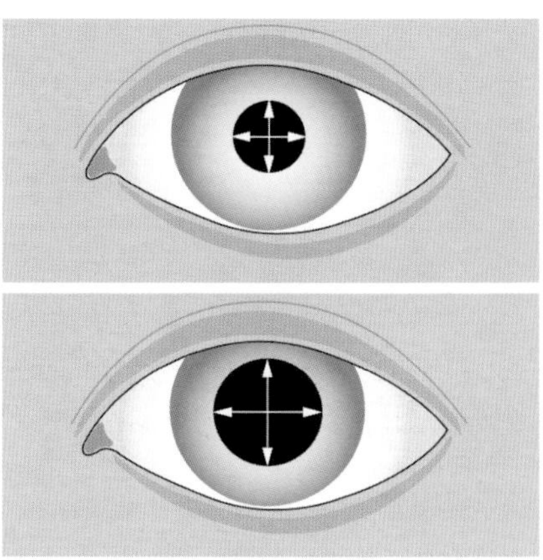

Figure 15.15: *The pupil of the eye is really the opening created by the iris. When there is a lot of light the iris constricts and the pupil gets smaller. When the light level is dim, the iris opens up and the pupil gets larger.*

The parts of your eye work together to help you see objects. The cornea and lens focus light so that an image forms on a special membrane at the back of the eye called the retina. The iris is a circular opening in front of the lens that can change to let more or less light into the eye (figure 15.15). The rod and cone cells that make up the retina sense the images and transmit them via the optic nerve to the brain.

Nerves

What is a nerve?

Nerves are the body's sensors and wires. Some nerves respond to sensation like pressure, heat, cold, pain, or light, and others transmit signals to and from the brain. When you touch something, nerves in your finger link to other nerves and send a message to your brain. You have more nerves in your fingertips than you do on the back of your arm. That is why you will notice that something is hot much faster if you touch it with your fingertip than if you brush against it with your arm. In your ear you have nerves that can detect sound.

Your eye also has nerve cells

The rod and cone cells in your eye are also nerves. Rod cells respond to light intensity only, so they see black, white, and shades of gray. Cone cells are sensitive to color but need brighter light. Your cones are located closer to the center of your eye. If somebody were to bring an object from the side of your vision slowly into your line of sight, you could detect the object but not the color.

Forming an image

The image on the retina

The lens focuses light on the retina at the back of the eyeball. Since it is a single lens, ray tracing tells you that the image is upside down! Of course, our brains have learned to flip the image right side up, so we don't notice.

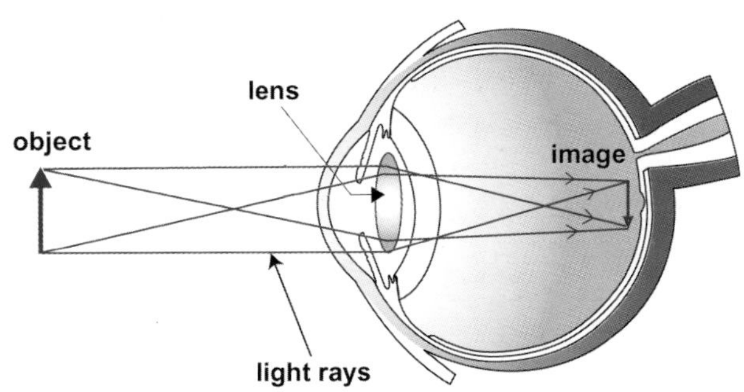

The lens can change focal length

The lens in your eye also has a unique feature which makes it different from the lenses you used in the lab. The lens of your eye is flexible. Small muscles around the edge can stretch it and change its shape. This allows you to focus on objects close by and also focus on objects far away (figure 15.16). As you get older the lens loses some of its flexibility. Many people wear contact lenses or glasses that adjust the light before it gets to their eye. Bifocal glasses have two regions; one to help you see close and the other to help you see far.

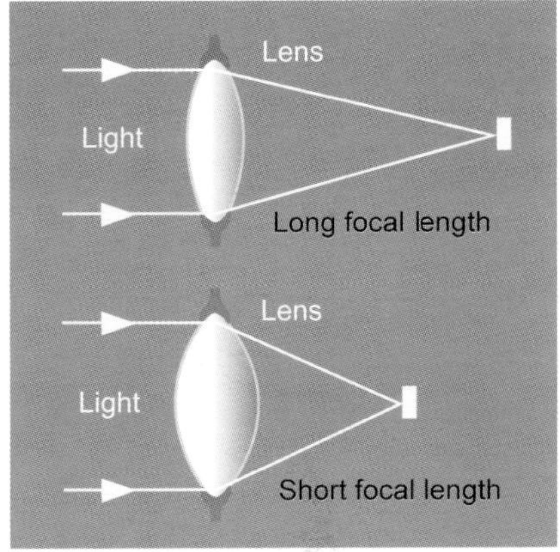

Figure 15.16: *The lens of the eye can change its shape to focus at different distances. The lens is quite tiny, about 4 millimeters thick and 9 millimeters in diameter.*

How the eye makes an image

The spot on the retina where an image forms is called the fovea. For the average human eye, the fovea has about 120 million rod cells and another 5 million cone cells. Each of these cells contributes one dot, or pixel, to the image received by the brain. The brain puts all the pixels together to perceive an image. This is much like a computer monitor creates images from pixels.

Comparing the eye to a computer monitor

Let's examine a computer monitor that is 1,600 pixels wide and 1,200 pixels high. Multiplying 1,600 times 1,200 gives a total of 1.9 million pixels. By comparison, the image created by the eye is equivalent to a computer screen 8 times bigger, 13,000 pixels wide, and 9,600 pixels high! The optic nerve carries 64 times more data than a high-resolution computer graphics display.

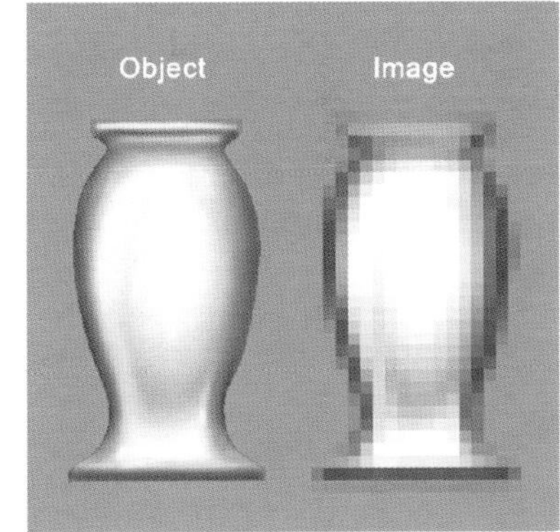

Figure 15.17: *The eye senses images in pixels. Each of the 125 million rod and cone cells sends one dot. The brain assembles the dots into the perception of an image.*

Stereoscopic vision and depth perception

Stereoscopic vision means that the brain receives two images of the same object, one from each eye. The brain interprets small differences between the images. We use this information to determine distances between objects and how far they are from us. Our ability to judge distances is called depth perception.

Optical illusions

The brain interprets the image

No matter what has actually happened to the light entering our eyes, our brains produce a single image. The image produced is always based on the assumption that light travels in a straight line. It doesn't matter if you use funny mirrors to bend light in all different directions or use a lens to make rays of light appear to come from places they weren't really coming from. The brain always creates an image of an object that would have existed if the rays had come straight to your eye.

Figure 15.18: *Objects that are smaller are often interpreted by the brain as being farther away. A perspective grid uses this visual cue to create the illusion of depth.*

The virtual image in a mirror

This is why a virtual image in a mirror works. The rays that reach your eye after bouncing off the mirror travel along lines that seem to come from the virtual image. Your brain places the image where the rays appear to come from. If you are standing three feet in front of a mirror, you see a virtual image standing three feet behind the mirror (six feet from you).

Optical illusions

There are many well-known optical illusions where the brain interprets an image to be something that it is not. Such illusions trick the brain by using cues such as light and shadow. For example, how is your brain tricked by the drawing in figure 15.19? The elephant may look normal at first glance. However, clever shading and lines create an image that cannot exist in reality. The artist M.C. Escher was famous for creating "impossible" images that trick the brain into seeing a three-dimensional object that is physically impossible.

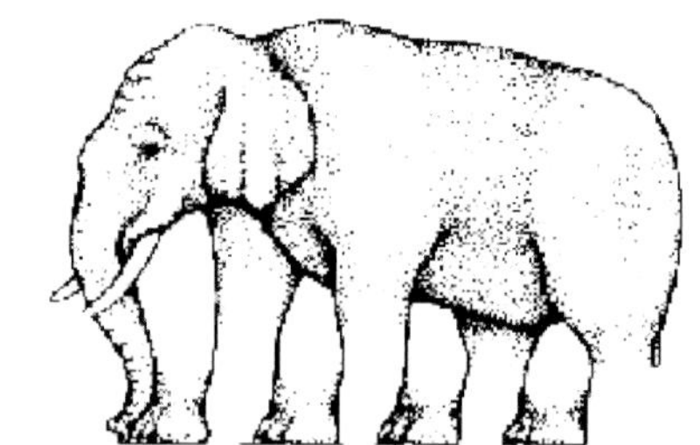

Figure 15.19: *What has the artist done to make this normal-looking elephant an optical illusion?*

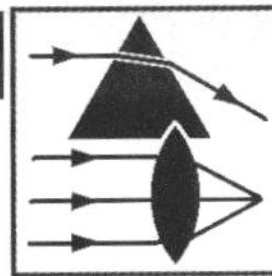

15.3 Optical Technology

We use a wide range of optical technology every day. Glasses and contact lenses are obvious examples. Light-emitting diode (LED) lights and remote controls are other examples. Internet and telephone signals are transmitted using optical fibers and lasers. Your compact disc player uses a laser and a sophisticated miniature optical system. People are even trying to build optical computers that use light rather than electricity. It is very likely that your future will keep you in daily contact with optical technology.

Fiber optics

Bouncing a rock off the water

Have you skipped a stone on a pond? First, you need to find a flat stone. Now you hold the stone between your thumb and forefinger. Pull your arm back and throw the stone. If you throw it just right, the stone will bounce off the surface of the water! To be successful, you have to throw the stone at a very large angle of incidence. It's amazing that you can throw a rock at water and have the water bounce the rock back into the air. You don't usually think of water being able to bounce a rock but, if the angle is right, the rock bounces instead of sinks.

When light enters glass, it bends toward the normal

Light, which would normally go through glass, can also be made to bounce off. The key is to get the angle of incidence large enough. If light is traveling in a material with a low index of refraction (air: $n = 1.00$), and it goes into a material with a higher index of refraction (glass: $n = 1.50$), it will bend so that the angle of refraction is less than the angle of incidence. Figure 15.20 shows how a light ray bends toward the normal when going into a material with a higher index of refraction.

When light exits glass, it bends away from the normal

On the other hand, if the light is already in the glass and it is going into air, it will bend so that the angle of refraction is greater than the angle of incidence. This means the light bends away from the normal. In a window, both conditions occur. The light bends toward the normal when it enters and away from the normal when it leaves. That is why light going through a flat sheet of glass comes out in the same direction it went in. We see images through windows almost perfectly clearly because the surfaces are flat.

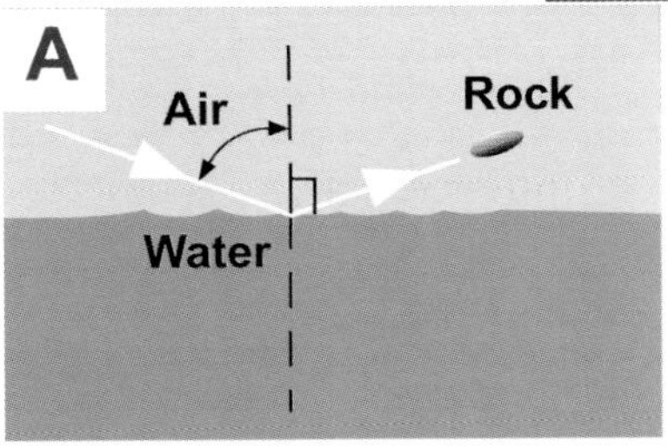

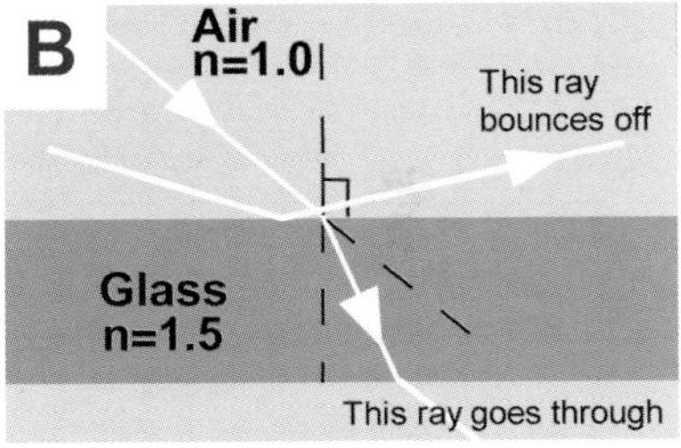

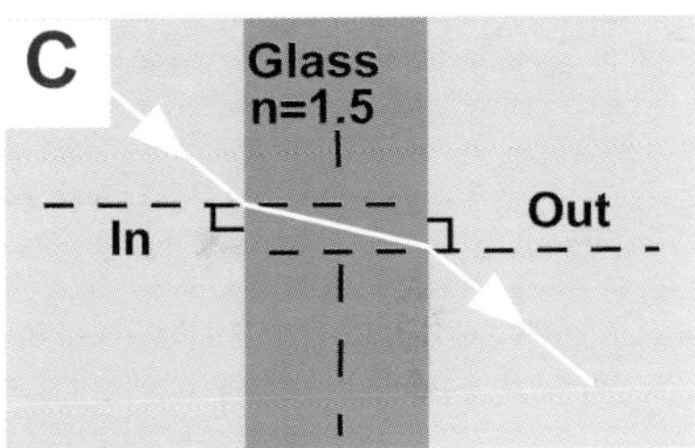

Figure 15.20:
A *You can skip a rock off the surface of water if you throw it at a large angle of incidence.*
B *A light ray bounces off glass if it encounters the surface at a large angle of incidence. A light ray will enter glass if it encounters the surface at a small angle of incidence.*
C *With a flat sheet of glass, the refraction going in exactly cancels the refraction going out and the light comes out in the same direction.*

Total internal reflection If the angle of incidence is great enough, light enters but does not leave a material because all the light is reflected back into the material. This angle is called the **critical angle**, and it depends on the index of refraction. If light approaches the surface at greater than the critical angle, it reflects back. This is called **total internal reflection**. The critical angle for glass is about 41 degrees.

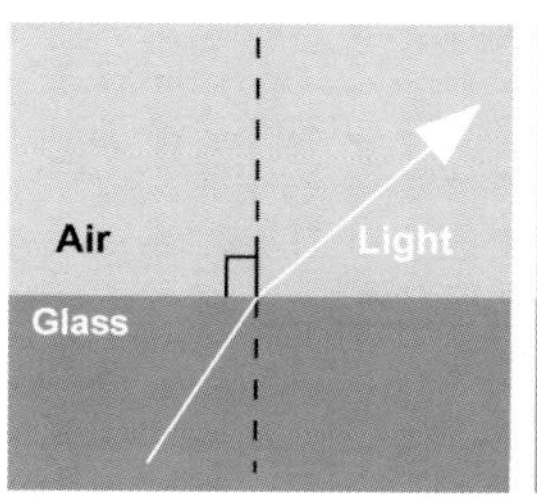

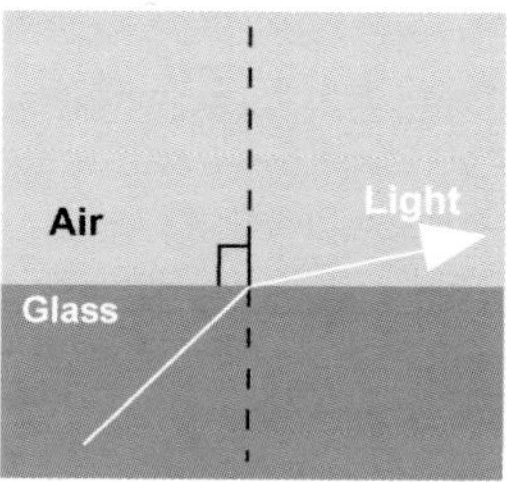

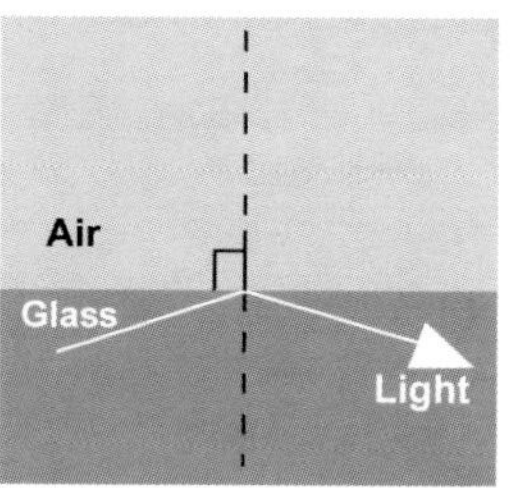

Past a certain angle, light is reflected from the surface instead of being transmitted

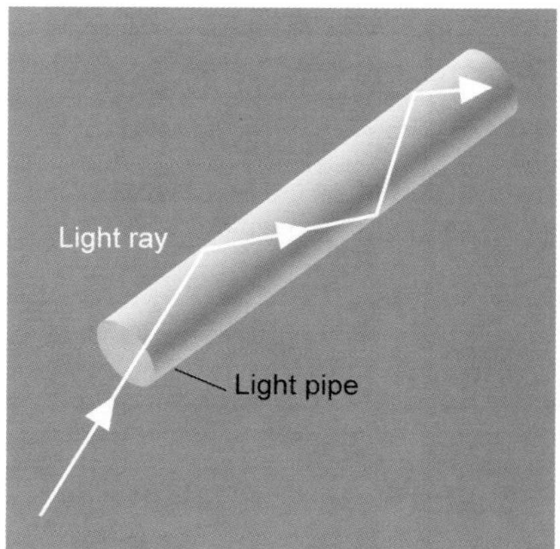

Figure 15.21: *A light pipe traps light by total internal reflection. The light always approaches the wall at greater than the critical angle.*

A pipe for light Suppose you have a tube of glass and you send light into the end at greater than the critical angle. The light reflects off the wall and bounces back. It then reflects off the opposite wall as well. In fact, the light always approaches the wall at greater than the critical angle so it always bounces back into the tube. You have constructed a light pipe! Light goes in one end and comes out the other. Fiber optics use total internal reflection to trap light into a flexible glass fiber. To connect a fiber optic, you must be careful to feed light in along a cone of the right angle (figure 15.23). Any light outside the cone will leak out the edges because it will not be internally reflected.

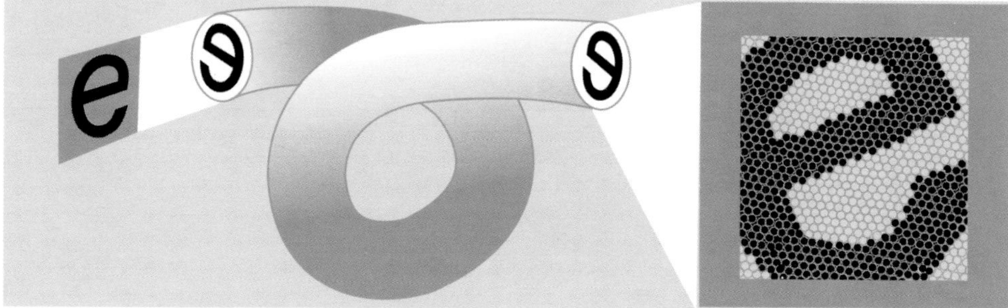

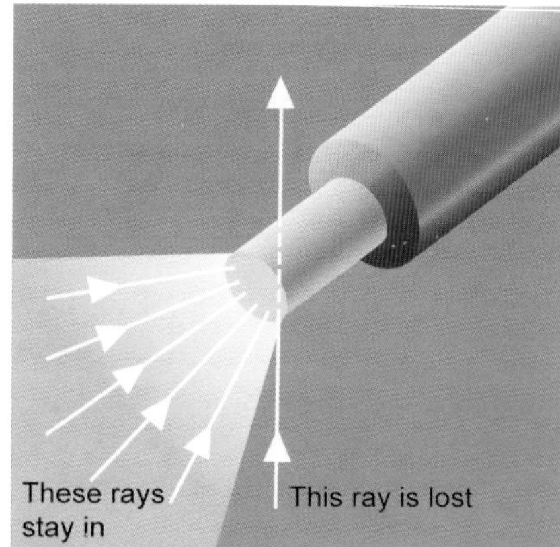

Figure 15.22: *A fiber optic is a thin light pipe that is flexible. Any light that enters the fiber outside a certain angle will be lost since internal reflection of this light will not occur.*

Carrying images on a fiber Bundles of fiber optics can transmit an image without lenses. If all the fibers at one end of a bundle are perfectly aligned at the other end, then they will send an image through the fiber, even if the fiber is tied in a knot!

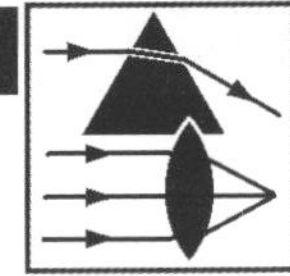

Fiber optics technology speeds up the exchange of information between telephones and computers

Imagine you invented a code to signal a far-off friend with a flashlight. You tell your friend to look for a light pulse every second. Two "on" pulses followed by an "off" might mean the letter "a" for example. You could invent a different code for every letter. This is essentially how light wave communications work. The light pulses are carried through very thin, glass fibers and can travel great distances. Most long-distance telephone calls today are carried on these fibers. This kind of technology is called *fiber optics*. Computers that communicate over fiber optic links can exchange data much faster than using any other means.

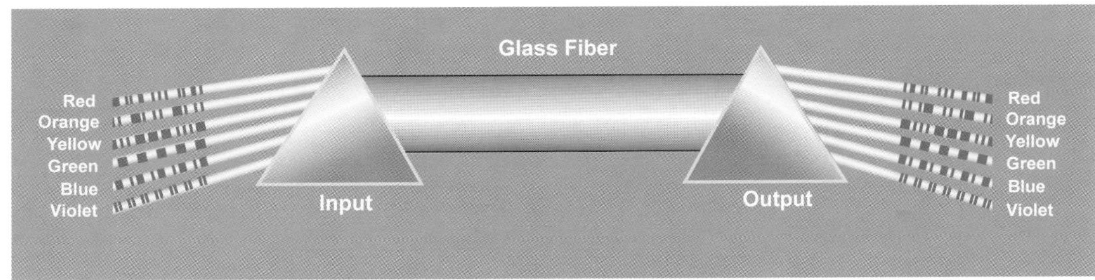

Each color carries a signal

Many different colors of light can go through a glass fiber without interfering with each other. In the graphic above, colors of light are shown. The dark bands represent the pulses of each color. A single glass fiber can carry as many as 64 different signals. Each signal is given its own frequency (color) of light. The light from all signals is first combined using a prism and sent through the fiber. At the other end of the fiber, the signal is split into different colors, also using a prism. Each color is then decoded separately.

The Internet

Almost all Internet data communication is over fiber optic networks that stretch between cities and between important buildings. Most long-distance telephone is also carried over fiber optics. The only part that is still carried on copper wires is the link from your home or desk to the main telephone company station near where you live. Once the signal reaches the telephone station, it is converted to light using lasers. When you make a long distance call, your voice makes a journey thousands of miles over fiber optics.

Fiber optics and the future

Someday, a fiber optic cable will come right to your house or apartment. Your telephone, computer, radio, and TV stations will all ride the light waves down the fiber. This is possible because light has such a high frequency. The higher the frequency, the more information you can send. One fiber optic cable can carry more information than used to be carried by a thousand copper wires.

Lasers

What is a laser? A *laser* is a special type of flashlight. Lasers typically have a special material. When energized in a specific way, electrons in a laser material move into a higher energy level. Like electrons in the "glow-in-the-dark stuff," electrons in a laser material do not fall to a lower energy level right away. The operator of a laser can cause electrons in the laser material to be energized or to fall at the same time. If all the electrons fall at the same time, then the light waves that are created are very unique. All the waves will be aligned in phase. The resulting light is one color because all the waves are the same frequency. This light is also very bright because the aligned waves do not spread out quickly. (The term LASER is an acronym; it stands for Light Amplification by Stimulated Emission of Radiation.)

The first laser The first laser was made using a short rod made out of synthetic ruby. The ruby rod was surrounded by a special flash bulb that was shaped like a coil. Mirrors were placed at each end of the ruby rod. The light from the flash caused electrons in the ruby to rise to an excited orbit. Any energy that was traveling straight down the ruby rod would cause other electrons to fall and add to the energy that was moving. When this light hit the mirror it reflected straight back to continue collecting more and more energy from falling electrons. One mirror was slightly less reflective than the other. When the light was bright enough it would escape.

Helium neon lasers The lasers you may see at school look like long narrow boxes. They have a gas tube inside of them instead of a ruby rod. The tube is filled with helium and neon gases. These helium neon lasers produce red light and use high voltage electricity to energize the electrons instead of a flash lamp.

Diode lasers *Diode lasers* are becoming the laser of choice because of their low cost, reliability, low voltage, and safety. If you have ever played with a laser pointer, you have used a diode laser. Supermarket scanners also use diode lasers. A diode laser can be smaller than a pinhead and can make light from a tiny amount of electricity. There are diode lasers that make red, green, and blue light. Researchers are trying to put red, green, and blue lasers together to make a "laser TV" that could project bright color images.

How bar-code readers work

The bar-code reader at the grocery checkout uses a laser light source and photo diode reader. The laser light is "scanned" across the bar-code label on the items you buy. The photo diode is used to measure the intensity of the light as it reflects back from the label. The black stripes absorb light and white stripes reflect it. The width of each stripe determines its number. The reader is tuned to receive only the specific frequency of light that the laser emits.

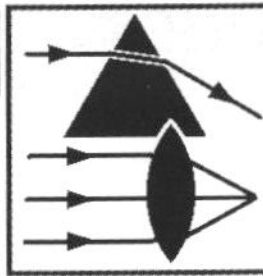

Chapter 15 Review

Vocabulary review

Match the following terms with the correct definition.

Set One

1. optics
2. lens
3. mirror
4. prism
5. light ray

a. A device that uses reflection to bend light to form an image
b. A device that bends different frequencies of light to separate colors
c. The study of how light behaves
d. An imaginary arrow used to show the path of a single beam of light
e. A device that uses refraction to bend light to form an image

Set Two

1. refraction
2. reflection
3. telescope
4. real image
5. virtual image

a. An image formed by rays of light coming together on a surface like the retina of the eye
b. The bouncing of light rays from a surface
c. Bending of light rays that results as light crosses a boundary between two different substances
d. An image formed when light rays seem to come from a point other than where the object exists
e. A device (used by Galileo) that uses a collection of lenses to magnify an image

Set Three

1. normal
2. incident ray
3. reflected ray
4. angle of incidence
5. angle of reflection

a. The ray of light that bounces off a mirror
b. The angle measured from the normal to the incident ray
c. A line drawn perpendicular to the surface of a mirror or any surface
d. The angle measured between the normal and the reflected ray
e. The ray of light that strikes a mirror
f. The ray of light that passes through a mirror

Set Four

1. retina
2. lens
3. stereoscopic vision
4. total internal reflection
5. fiber optics

a. A device that uses the stimulation of electrons to create an amplified emission of radiation
b. The back of a human eyeball where an image is formed
c. A light pipe that uses total internal reflection to carry light and signals from one point to another
d. This part of the human eye bends the light that comes into it
e. This process happens when light inside a glass of water tries to get out but is reflected back into the material
f. The process by which humans use two eyes to see things with depth

Concept review

1. A ray of light falls on a lens made of glass. Which of the following (a, b, or c) best describes the path of the light ray leaving the lens?

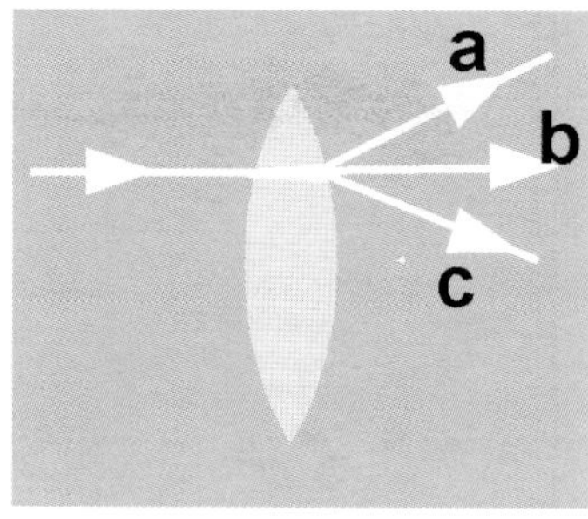

2. An image is best described as:
   a. A place where light rays leaving one point on an object come together again.
   b. A light source that creates objects.
   c. The splitting of white light into different colors.
   d. A group of light rays leaving from the same point on an object.

3. A ray of light falls on a mirror. Which of the following (a, b, c, or d) best describes the path of the light ray leaving the mirror?

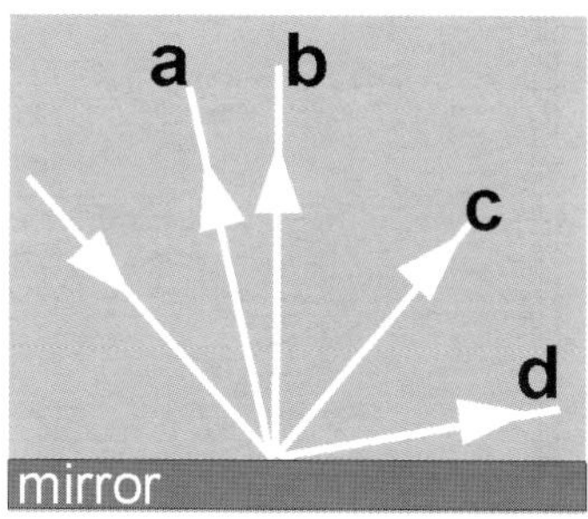

4. Total internal reflection happens when light comes from air and strikes the surface of water.
   a. True b. False

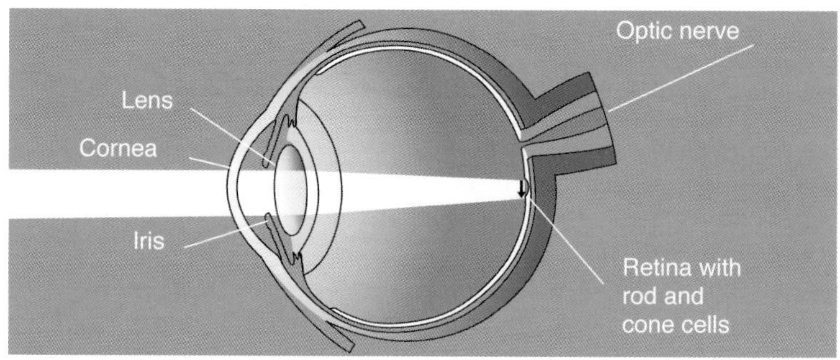

5. What is the purpose of the iris in the eye?
6. What is the purpose of the optic nerve?
7. What is the purpose of a rod or cone cell?
8. What is the purpose of the lens?
9. Identify which of the following kinds of electromagnetic waves are used by the bar-code scanner at a grocery store.
   a. microwaves
   b. visible light
   c. radio waves
   d. X rays
10. Identify which of the following kinds of electromagnetic waves are transmitted through fiber optics.
    a. microwaves
    b. visible light
    c. radio waves
    d. X rays
11. Which creature must take total internal reflection and refraction into account when hunting in its natural environment?
    a. An eagle
    b. A tiger
    c. An alligator
    d. A wolf

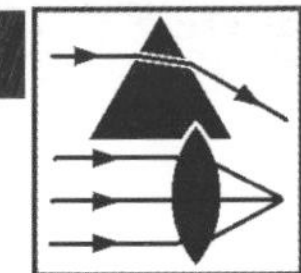

12. Why do you use a ruler to draw rays of light?
    a. The ruler makes the picture look more professional.
    b. The ruler has light that comes out of it.
    c. The ray of light has marks every centimeter like a ruler.
    d. The ray of light travels in a perfectly straight line.

13. How many rays of light do you need to draw to find where an image is located?
    a. Only one ray is needed.
    b. One ray is needed but it must be flashing.
    c. A minimum of two rays is needed to find an image.

Problems

1. What does the term ***normal*** mean?
    a. Average
    b. The middle
    c. Perpendicular
    d. All of these are correct

2. The angle between the incident ray and the reflected ray is 60°. What is the angle of reflection?
    a. 10°
    b. 20°
    c. 30°
    d. 40°

3. How do you measure the incident angle?
    a. The angle between the incident ray and the normal.
    b. The angle between the incident ray and the surface of the mirror.
    c. The angle between the surface of the mirror and the normal.
    d. The angle between the reflected ray and the surface of the mirror.

4. Which of the arrows in the diagram shows the path taken by a light ray as it travels through the lens?

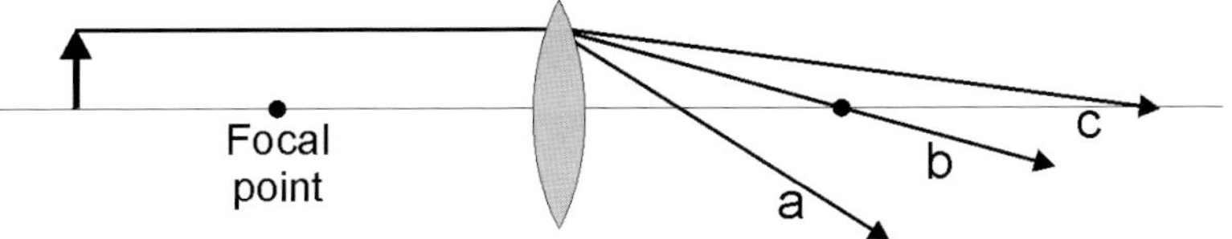

5. As light goes from air into glass the angle of refraction is:
    a. The same as the angle of incidence.
    b. Less than the angle of incidence.
    c. Greater than the angle of incidence.
    d. Is not related to the angle of incidence.

6. As light goes from glass into air the angle of refraction is:
    a. The same as the angle of incidence.
    b. Less than the angle of incidence.
    c. Greater than the angle of incidence.
    d. Not related to the angle of incidence.

Applying your knowledge

1. Sketch an eyeball. Draw and label all the major parts of the eye.
2. A microscope is a tool scientists use to magnify cells and very small objects. Find a drawing of a microscope and make a sketch of how many lenses there are. What do the following words mean when talking about a microscope?
   a. Eyepiece
   b. Objective
   c. Magnification
3. A telescope can be used for looking at objects on Earth as well as in the sky. What do the following words mean when used to describe the working of a telescope?
   a. Aperture
   b. Magnification
   c. Reflector
   d. Refractor
4. Explain how glow-in-the-dark material works.
5. Explain the things that happen to an atom that cause it to give off light.
6. The rear view mirror on some cars has a message, “Objects may be closer than they appear,” painted on the mirror surface. Explain why car manufacturers thought it was necessary to put this message there.

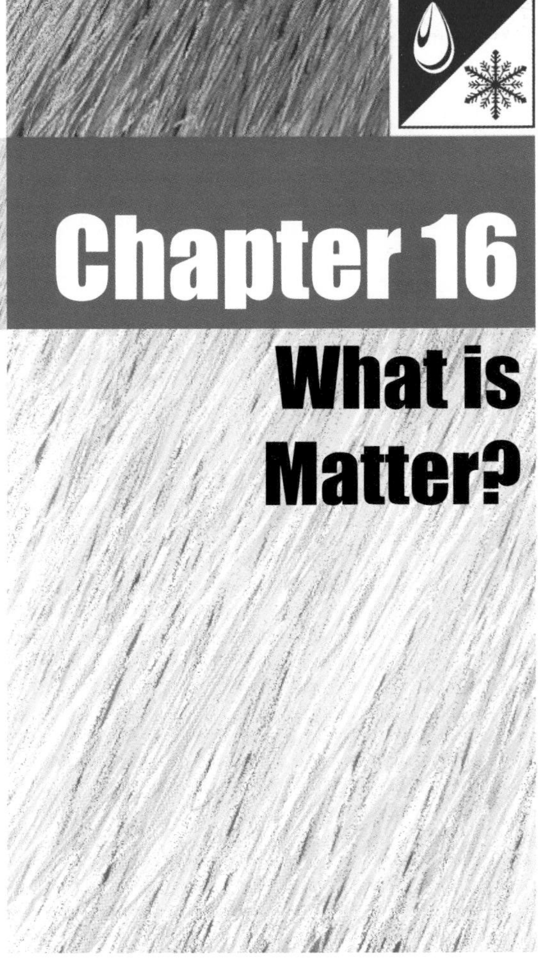

Introduction to Chapter 16

What do a silver necklace, a glass of orange juice, a helium-filled balloon, and a star have in common? All of these objects are made of matter. In this chapter, you will learn how matter is classified and how it undergoes changes of state. All matter can exist as a solid, liquid, or gas. Changes in temperature and atmospheric pressure can cause changes in state.

Investigations for Chapter 16

16.1	Classifying Matter	*How can a homogeneous mixture be separated?*

In this Investigation, you will use a technique called paper chromatography to separate water-soluble ink (a homogeneous mixture) into its components.

16.2	Measuring Matter	*How is matter measured?*

In this Investigation, you will demonstrate your ability to measure the mass and volume of liquids, and of regular and irregular solids using a variety of techniques.

16.3	States of Matter	*How fast can you melt an ice cube?*

In this Investigation, you will attempt to influence the rate at which 15 milliliters of water changes from solid to liquid. Next, you will measure the average kinetic energy of water molecules as they undergo a change of state and analyze the transfer of energy that occurred.

Learning Goals

In this chapter, you will:

- ✔ Classify samples of matter from everyday life as heterogeneous mixtures, homogeneous mixtures, compounds, or elements.
- ✔ Measure volume using the displacement technique.
- ✔ Measure mass with scales and balances.
- ✔ Use an indirect technique to infer mass from density measurements.
- ✔ Identify the states of matter.
- ✔ Classify the states of matter in order of energy.
- ✔ Recognize changes in state as a physical change in matter.
- ✔ Explain the states of matter in terms of molecular motion.
- ✔ Identify and investigate the law of conservation of mass.

Vocabulary

atom	heterogeneous mixture	matter	substances
compounds	homogeneous mixture	mixtures	
elements	law of conservation of mass	molecule	

16.1 Classifying Matter

What is matter? Matter is easier to describe than to define. Your book, your desk, your lunch, the air that you breathe and the water you drink are all made of matter. **Matter** is a term used to describe anything that has mass and takes up space. Different kinds of matter have different characteristics, such as boiling and melting temperatures, hardness, and elasticity. In this section, you will learn how matter is classified. By the end of the section, you should be able to define mixture, homogeneous mixture, heterogeneous mixture, substance, element, and compound.

Figure 16.1: *Carbonated soft drinks are homogeneous mixtures.*

How do scientists classify matter?

Mixtures contain more than one kind of matter

Matter can be divided into two categories: mixtures and substances. **Mixtures** contain more than one kind of matter. For example, cola is a mixture that can be separated into carbonated water, corn syrup, caramel color, phosphoric acid, natural flavors, and caffeine.

Homogeneous mixture is the same throughout

A **homogeneous mixture** is the same throughout. In other words, all samples of a homogeneous mixture are the same. For example, an unopened can of cola is a homogeneous mixture. The cola in the top of the unopened bottle is the same as the cola at the bottom. Once you open the can, however, carbon dioxide will escape from the cola making the first sip a little different from your last sip. Brass is another example of a homogeneous mixture. It is made of 70 percent copper and 30 percent zinc. If you cut a brass candlestick into ten pieces, each piece would contain the same percentage of copper and zinc.

Two samples of a heterogeneous mixture could be different

A **heterogeneous mixture** is one in which different samples are not necessarily made up of exactly the same proportions of matter. One common heterogeneous mixture is chicken noodle soup: One spoonful might contain broth, noodles, and chicken, while another contains only broth.

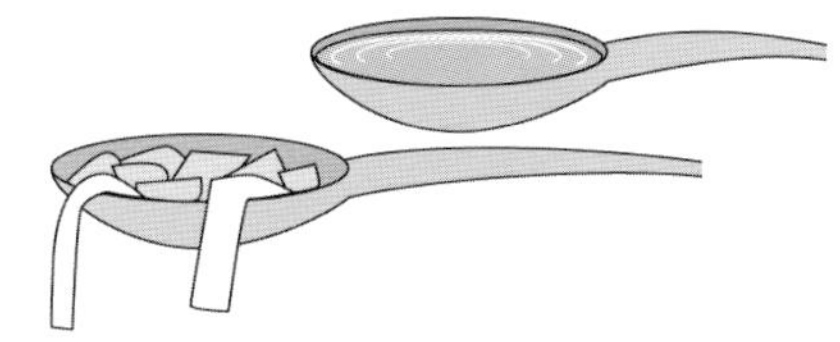

Figure 16.2: *Chicken noodle soup is a heterogeneous mixture.*

Mixtures can be separated by physical means

All mixtures, whether homogeneous or heterogeneous, share one common property: They can be separated into different types of matter by physical means such as sorting, filtering, heating, or cooling. Chicken noodle soup, for example, could be separated into its components by using strainers and filters of different sizes. The separation process does not change the characteristics of each component. You still have broth, noodles, and chicken.

Substances cannot be separated by physical means

Substances, on the other hand, cannot be separated into different kinds of matter by physical means such as sorting, filtering, heating, or cooling. Some substances, like silver, contain only one kind of matter. These substances are called **elements**. Other substances contain more than one kind of matter, but the different kinds cannot be separated without changing the substance. For example, table salt is made up of two elements, sodium and chlorine. If you could separate table salt into its two elements, you would no longer have a crystallized substance that you sprinkle onto french fries and other foods. Instead, you would have sodium, a soft metal that can cause an explosion if dropped into water, and chlorine, a yellowish, poisonous gas.

All substances are either elements or compounds

Table salt and other substances that are made of two or more elements that cannot be separated by physical means are called **compounds**.

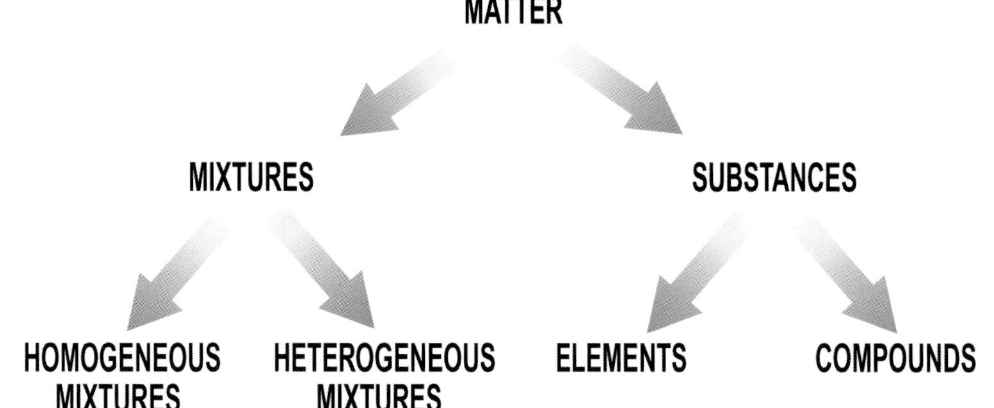

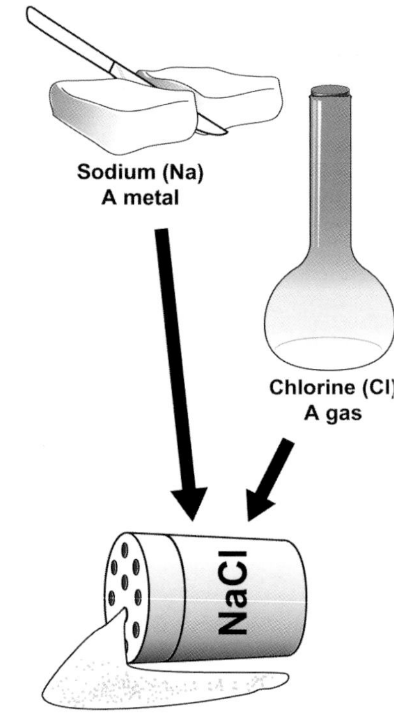

Figure 16.3: *Sodium, a soft metal, and chlorine, a toxic gas, react to form the very edible and useful compound table salt (NaCl).*

How can you separate mixtures into substances?

Separating mixtures into substances is a very important part of scientific work. Medical researchers try to isolate the substances in plants that may help heal diseases. Forensic scientists try to match evidence from the scene of a crime with substances found with a suspect. Nutritionists evaluate the amount of carbohydrates, fats, proteins, vitamins, and minerals in various foods.

Separating mixtures is not always an easy task. In this unit you will learn about a variety of physical properties that can be used to identify substances in a mixture. Later, you will learn how chemists work to break down substances even further, so that they can separate compounds into elements.

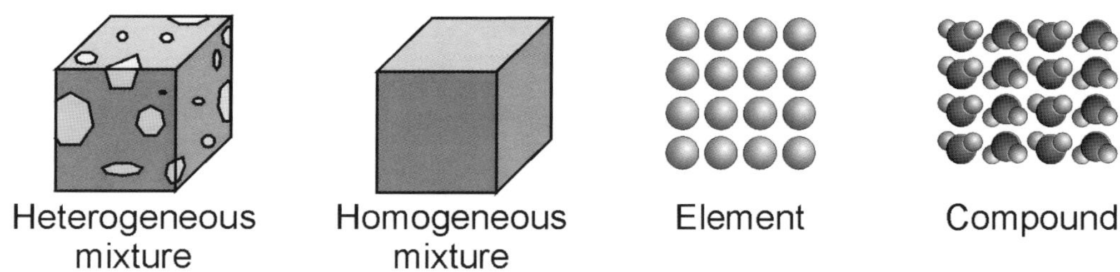

Table 16.1: ***Summary of the types of matter***

Type of matter	Definition	Examples
Homogeneous mixture	A mixture that contains more than one type of matter and is the same throughout.	soda pop, air, chocolate ice cream
Heterogeneous mixture	A mixture that contains more than one type of matter and is not the same throughout.	chicken soup, soil, fudge ripple ice cream
Element	A substance that contains only one type of atom.	copper metal, oxygen gas, liquid nitrogen
Compound	A substance that contains more than one type of atom.	table salt, rust (iron oxide), carbon dioxide gas

Petroleum is a heterogeneous mixture

Petroleum is a very old and complex mixture that we extract from the Earth. Formed millions of years ago, petroleum contains 100,000 to 1,000,000 different molecules! A use has been found for just about every component of this heterogeneous mixture. Important petroleum products include fuel, oils, asphalt, and waxes. Refining petroleum is a process that is used to separate the specific components to make each product. Refining includes physical processes (like distillation) and chemical reactions to isolate the components of petroleum.

16.2 Measuring Matter

How many gallons of gasoline do I need to fill the tank of this car? Do I have enough sugar to make a batch of brownies? Will this suitcase fit in the airplane's overhead compartment? Every day, people need to measure various amounts of matter. In this section, you will review how to measure the mass and volume of matter, and become proficient at using the displacement method to find the volume of irregular objects.

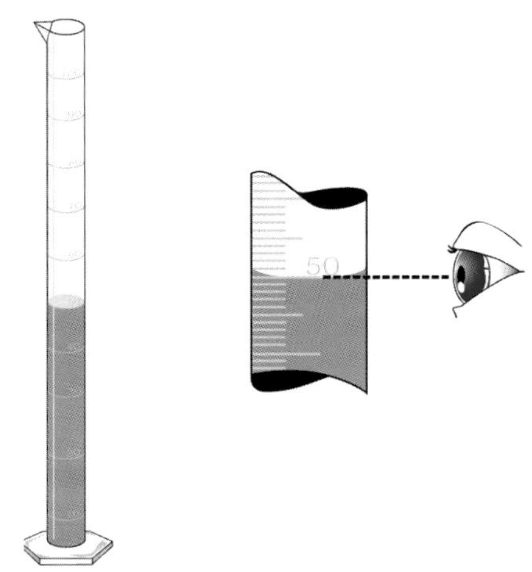

Figure 16.4: *The meniscus of water curves downward. Read the mark at the bottom of the curve.*

Measuring volume and mass

Read volume marks at eye level for accuracy

Measuring the volume of liquid matter is easy. You simply pour it into a marked container such as a measuring cup, graduated cylinder, or beaker, and read the volume mark. To get the greatest accuracy, there are two things to keep in mind. First, read the mark at eye level. Second, you may notice that the surface of the liquid forms a curve (like a hill or a valley), rather than a straight line. This curve is called the meniscus. If the surface curves downward, (liquid water does this) read the volume at the bottom of the curve. A few liquids, like mercury, will form an upward curve. In this case, read the volume mark at the top of the curve.

You can calculate the volume of solids using a formula

You have probably already learned to measure the volume of some solid shapes. The volume of a rectangular solid (a shoebox shape), for example, is found by multiplying length times width times height. Some common volume formulas are shown in table 16.2.

Table 16.2: *Volume Formulas*

Shape	Formula in words	Formula in symbols
rectangular solid and cube	length × width × height	$l \times w \times h$
cylinder	pi ×radius^2 × height	$\pi r^2 \times h$
cone	1/3 × pi × radius^2 × height	$1/3 \times \pi r^2 \times h$
sphere	4/3 × pi × radius^3	$4/3 \times \pi r^3$

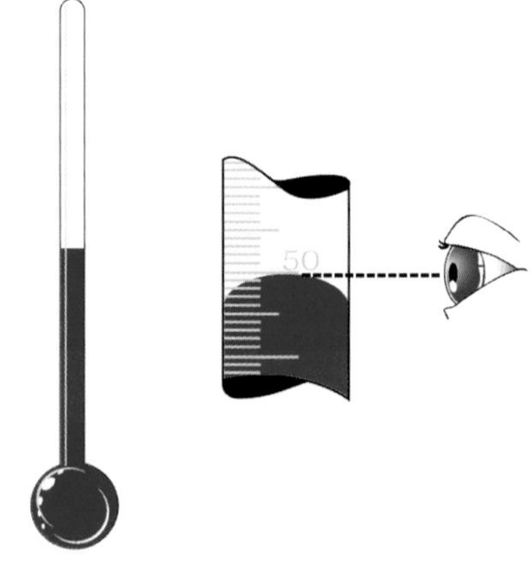

Figure 16.5: *The meniscus of mercury curves upward. Read the mark at the top of the curve.*

The displacement method

We can find the volume of an irregular shape using a technique called displacement. To displace means to "take the place of" or to "push aside." You can find the volume of an irregularly shaped object by submerging it in water and measuring how much water the object displaces or pushes aside.

How you make the measurement

You can use this method to find the volume of an ordinary item like a house key. Fill a 100-milliliter graduated cylinder with 50 milliliters of water (figure 16.6). Gently slide the key into the water. The water level in the container will rise, because the key displaced, or pushed aside, some water. If the level now reads 53.0 milliliters, you know that the key displaced 3.0 milliliters of water. The volume of the key, or of any object you measured in this way, is equal to the volume of the water it displaced. The key has a volume of 3.0 milliliters, or 3.0 cubic centimeters (cm^3).

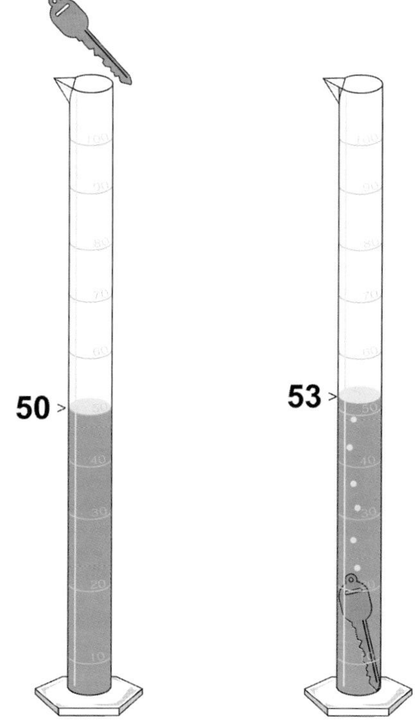

Figure 16.6: *The key displaced 3.0 milliliters of water.*

Mass is the amount of matter in an object

Sometimes we are more concerned about the quantity of matter we have, rather than the space it takes up. Breakfast cereal, for example, isn't sold by volume. As boxes of cereal are shipped from plant to warehouse to store, the contents "settle." By the time the cereal is purchased by the consumer, the container may appear only three-fourths full. For this reason, cereal is measured in grams. An equal mass of cereal is placed into each container at the factory.

How does a scale work?

A scale measures the gravitational force between an object and Earth. This means that a scale that reads in grams or kilograms has actually measured *weight* and calculated the mass from the weight.

How does a balance work?

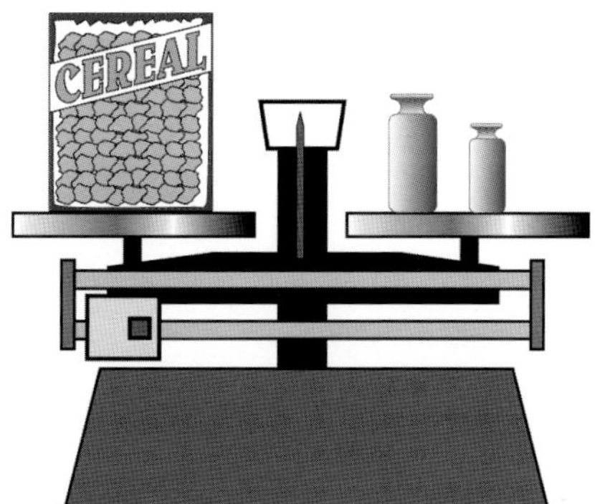

A balance measures the mass of an object (like a quantity of cereal) by comparing it with objects whose masses are known. Since a balance measures by comparing standard masses, it is not affected by changes in gravity.

Would a balance function correctly on the moon? Why or why not?

Measuring very large or very small quantities of matter

How could you measure a quantity of matter that is too large for a balance or displacement tank? Read on to find out how a citizen's group solved this problem.

How could you measure the mass of an asphalt tennis court?

After years of watching a tennis court fall into disrepair at a local park, a group of neighbors got together to discuss what could be done with the site. They voted to approach the town council to see if a children's play structure could be built there.

The town council asked the group to provide a budget for the renovation. It was easy for the group to find prices for new play structures; but first, the tennis court would have to be taken down and the asphalt removed. The group learned that the fee for disposing of construction or demolition debris was 5 cents per kilogram. How did they figure out the cost of asphalt disposal?

Indirect measurement

The group used a technique called *indirect measurement* to estimate the disposal cost. First, they picked up a palm-sized chunk of loose asphalt from the tennis court. They used displacement to find its volume: 1,687 cubic centimeters. Using a balance, they found that the chunk had a mass of 1.94 kilograms.

Next, they measured the tennis court: 36.51 meters by 18.29 meters. They estimated the asphalt to be 0.075 meters thick. By multiplying length × width × depth, they found that the court contained 50.08 cubic meters of asphalt.

Set up a proportion

Now they could set up a proportion:

$$\frac{\text{mass of chunk}}{\text{volume of chunk}} = \frac{\text{mass of court}}{\text{volume of court}}$$

The volume of the chunk was converted to cubic meters so that the units would match. The group solved their equation for the mass of the court, and found that the asphalt had a mass of 57,590.5 kilograms.

At 5 cents per kilogram, the disposal fee came to $2,879.52.

How to measure very small objects

Indirect measurement can also be used to measure very small quantities. If you put one sunflower seed on a balance, the balance still reads 0.0 grams. This means that the mass of the seed is less than 0.1 gram! It might be 0.04 grams or 0.00964 grams, but how could you find out? Use indirect measurement by finding the mass of 100 sunflower seeds and then dividing it by 100.

Figure 16.7: *When the old tennis court asphalt is removed, a child's playground can be built in its place.*

1. equation

$$\frac{\text{mass of chunk}}{\text{volume of chunk}} = \frac{\text{mass of court}}{\text{volume of court}}$$

2. rearrange variables

$$\text{mass of court} = \frac{(\text{mass of chunk}) \times (\text{volume of court})}{(\text{volume of chunk})}$$

3. plug in data and cancel units

$$\text{mass of court} = \frac{(1.94\ \text{kg}) \times (50.08\ \cancel{\text{m}}^3)}{(0.001687\ \cancel{\text{m}}^3)}$$

4. solve

mass of court = 57,590.5 kg

16.3 States of Matter

Suppose your teacher gave each student a teaspoon of salt and offered a reward to the person who could separate out the smallest piece. How would you do it? You might start by sprinkling a few grains onto a piece of dark paper. Perhaps you could isolate one grain. Next, you might try to smash that grain into smaller particles with a hammer. If you were able finally to divide the grain of salt into particles as small as a speck of dust, you might have won the contest, but your bit of salt would still be about 100 trillion times as large as the smallest possible piece! In this section, you will learn about the smallest whole particles of matter, atoms and molecules. By the end of the section, you should be able to describe how those particles move in solids, liquids, and gases.

Atoms and molecules

Molecules and atoms Scientists call the smallest possible particle of a compound that retains the properties of the compound a molecule. The smallest possible particle of an element is called an atom. Atoms and molecules are more than a trillion times smaller than a human cell, a bacterium, and everything else that can be seen with an optical microscope. We know they exist because we can describe and predict how they will act in various substances and mixtures.

Movement of molecules Let's examine a very common compound, water. Water is one of the most important substances on the planet. It covers more than 70 percent of the Earth's surface. Without it, life would not be possible. We need water for our bodies to function properly and for plants to grow. We use ice to preserve food. Steam-powered turbines and hydroelectric dams provide electricity for homes and businesses.

Atoms and molecules are always in motion Each tiny water molecule contains one oxygen atom and two hydrogen atoms. A single drop of water is made up of more than 3×10^{21} molecules. These molecules are always in motion. At higher temperatures, they move faster and bump into one another with more force. At lower temperatures, they move with less energy.

Figure 16.8: *A single crystal of sodium chloride (table salt) is a cube. The molecules are arranged in the crystal so that each sodium atom is surrounded by six chlorine atoms, and six sodium atoms surround each chlorine atom.*

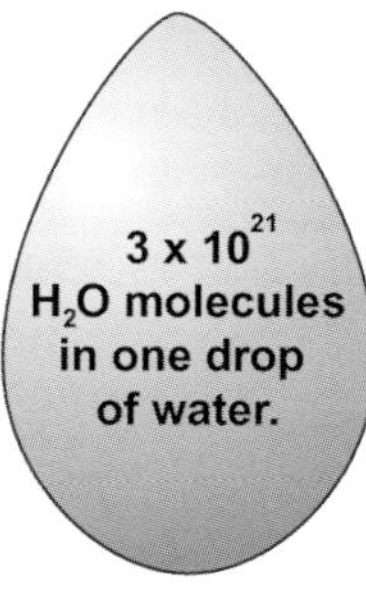

Changes of state

Molecules in solids, liquids and gases vibrate differently

At temperatures below 0°C, water is a solid called ice. In the solid state, molecules constantly vibrate, but cannot switch places with other molecules. Between zero and 100°C, water is a liquid. Molecules in a liquid move faster and slip out of position. Liquids flow because the molecules can move. At temperatures above 100°C, water becomes a gas. At this high temperature molecules move so fast that they bounce out of the liquid state and become a gas. In the gaseous state, molecules are widely separated.

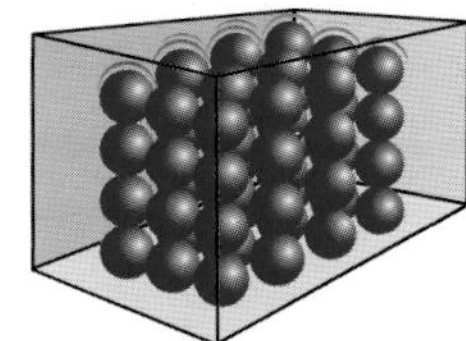

Frozen water molecules vibrate, but can't switch places.

What is temperature?

Temperature influences changes of state. Temperature measures the average energy of a certain amount of molecules, and is related to the average velocity of the molecules. The higher the temperature, the faster (on average) the molecules move.

Water molecules in the liquid state move over and around one another.

Melting and boiling

The temperature at which the water changed from solid to liquid is called its melting point. The temperature at which it changed from liquid to gas is called the boiling point. Different substances change from solid to liquid and from liquid to gas at different temperatures. Iron, for example, melts at 1538°C (2800°F) and boils at 2861°C (5182 °F). These changes are called changes of state.

What is evaporation?

Fast-moving molecules in a liquid can escape to become a gas. The word *evaporation* describes the transformation from the liquid to gas. Evaporation is a cooling process. For example, when you step out of a shower, you often feel cold. The reason is that when water evaporates from the surface of your skin, the highest energy molecules are the ones that jump from liquid to gas. Lower energy molecules are left behind. The high energy molecules that leave take away energy so your body feels cooler!

Water molecules in the gaseous state move randomly throughout their container.

What is condensation?

The evaporation of water is an important part of the Earth's water cycle (also called the hydrologic cycle). Water in the oceans, lakes, ponds, and rivers becomes part of the Earth's atmosphere when it evaporates. Once water vapor is part of the atmosphere, some molecules will collect to form small droplets. Clouds are large formations of water droplets. The process of transforming from a gas to a liquid is called condensation. When water droplets in a cloud get too big, they fall back to the Earth as rain.

A solid can sometimes change directly into a gas

Have you ever noticed that ice cubes sometimes seem to shrink when they have been in the freezer for a long period of time? Sometimes a solid can change directly to a gas when heat energy is added. This process is called *sublimation*. Solid iodine is a substance that readily undergoes sublimation at room temperature. This is evident by a the formation of a purple cloud above the crystals.

States of matter

All substances can exist as a solid, liquid, or gas

On Earth, elements and compounds are usually found as solids, liquids, or gases. These are called states of matter. Each substance can exist in each of the three states, and each substance has a characteristic temperature and pressure at which it will undergo a change of state.

Table 16.3: ***Changes of state at 1 atm (normal atmospheric pressure)***

Substance	Melting/freezing point	Boiling/condensing point
helium	-272°C	-269°C
oxygen	-218°C	-183°C
mercury	-39°C	357°C
water	0°C	100°C
lead	327°C	1749°C
aluminum	660°C	2519°C

A solid retains its shape and size

Although we cannot easily see the molecules of a substance moving around, we can describe the resulting characteristics of the matter in each state. When a substance is in a solid state, the molecules vibrate, but they cannot change position. As a result, a solid retains its shape and size. For example, steel nails do not change shape so that you can fit more in a jar (figure 16.9).

A liquid has definite size, but not shape

In the liquid state, molecules of a substance can move over and around each other. Therefore, the liquid has a definite volume, but no definite shape. Instead, it will take on the shape of whatever container it is poured into (figure 16.10).

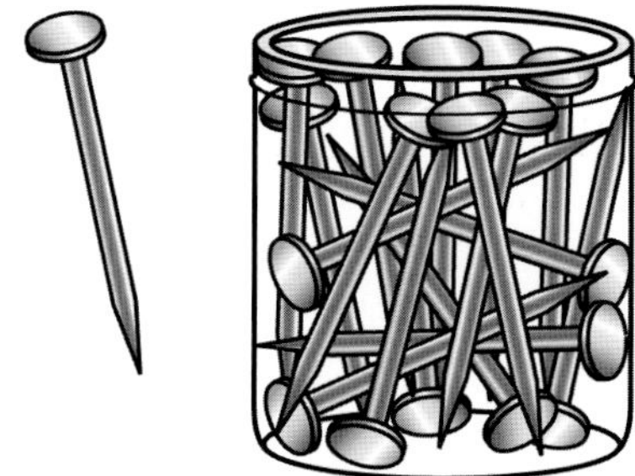

Figure 16.9: *Steel nails are an example of a solid.*

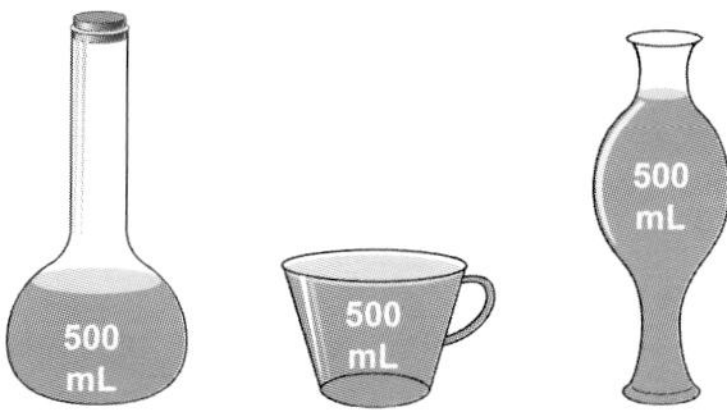

Figure 16.10: *Liquids flow to take the shape of the container but keep their volume.*

Figure 16.11: *A gas expands to fill its container, such as a balloon.*

A gas has no definite shape or size In the gas state, molecules move around freely and separate from one another. In this state, a substance has neither a definite size nor shape. It will spread out evenly throughout its container.

Change of state and mass When a substance undergoes a change of state, only the movement of the molecules changes. The number of molecules does not change. The mass of the substance remains the same whether it is in the solid, liquid, or gas state.

Plasma is a fourth state of matter The most common state of matter in the universe is a state rarely found on Earth: plasma. Matter enters the plasma state when it is heated to such a high temperature that some of the atoms actually begin to break apart. They lose their outer layer of electrons. For most materials this requires temperatures of more than 10,000 degrees.

Where do you find plasma? Our sun and other stars are made of plasma. Scientists believe the core of the sun has a temperature of about 15 million degrees. The surface of the sun is about 5,000 degrees. A type of plasma is used on Earth to make neon and fluorescent lights. Instead of heating the gases to an extremely high temperature, an electrical current is passed through them. The current strips the electrons off the atoms, producing plasma. You also see a plasma every time you see lighting.

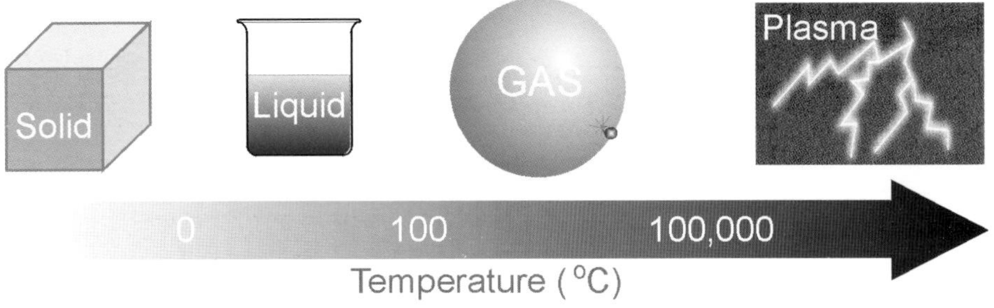

The four familiar states of matter Matter has four states that we experience. In order of increasing energy they are: solid, liquid, gas, and plasma. Since temperature is a measure of energy, matter changes from one phase to another as its temperature is increased.

Exotic super-hot states of matter If an atom of a substance keeps getting hotter, eventually even the nucleus of the atom comes apart. Some very exotic states of matter exist in particle accelerators that heat matter up to trillions of degrees and more.

High-altitude cooking

Did you know that the freezing and boiling points of a substance change as the air pressure changes? At a lower air pressure, it is easier for water molecules to escape from liquid into the air. Therefore, water will boil at a lower temperature. This is why cake mixes often have high-altitude directions. The lower air pressure at high altitudes allows the water in the mix to begin to turn to gas at a lower temperature, so it leaves the mix earlier. To prevent the cake from drying out, extra water is added to the mix.

Chapter 16 Review

Vocabulary Review

Match the following terms with the correct definition. There is one extra definition in the list that will not match any of the terms.

Set One	
1. matter	a. Two samples of this material might contain different kinds of matter
2. homogeneous mixture	b. A pure substance which contains only one kind of matter
3. heterogeneous mixture	c. Any material that contains at least two kinds of matter
4. element	d. Anything that has mass and takes up space
5. compound	e. Contains two or more kinds of matter that cannot be separated by physical means
	f. Every sample of this material is the same

Set Two	
1. substance	a. Very tiny; microscopic
2. mixture	b. Calculating size of very large or small objects through use of proportional relationships
3. meniscus	c. Measuring volume by placing an object in water and recording the change in water level
4. displacement	d. The curve formed by the surface of a liquid
5. indirect measurement	e. A sample of matter that cannot be separated by physical means; may contain only one or several kinds of matter
	f. A sample of matter that contains two or more kinds of particles that can be separated by physical means

Concept review

1. What are the two major categories of matter?
2. Name three foods that would be classified as heterogeneous mixtures, and three foods that are homogeneous mixtures.
3. Explain the difference between the two kinds of substances.
4. Explain the difference between an atom and a molecule.
5. Describe the movement of atoms or molecules in solid form.
6. Describe the movement of atoms or molecules in liquid form.
7. Describe the movement of atoms or molecules in gas form.
8. A liquid takes the shape of its container, but why doesn't a liquid expand to fill the container completely?
9. List at least two similarities between mass and volume and at least two differences.
10. Evaporation and boiling can be referred to at the same time as vaporization. Describe the difference between vaporization and sublimation.

Problems

1. How could you use indirect measurement to find the mass of a large boulder?
2. How could you use indirect measurement to calculate the thickness of one index card?
3. As you know, the Earth is a watery planet. About 70 percent of the Earth's surface is covered by water. There is water underground, and even in the atomosphere. What is water's state at each of the following temperatures?
   a. temperatures below zero degrees Celsius
   b. temperatures between zero and 100 degrees Celsius
   c. temperatures above 100 degrees Celsius

Applying your knowledge

1. Design a poster to illustrate the classification of matter. Provide examples of everyday objects that belong in each category.
2. Construct a three-dimensional model that could be used in a fourth-grade classroom to explain how molecules move in the solid, liquid, and gaseous states.
3. Land surveyors measure and map land. One of their jobs is to figure out the dimensions of land features and formations. Interview a surveyor to learn how indirect measurement is used to calculate precise distances. Prepare a five-minute report for your class.
4. Look around your classroom or home and name an object that has a relatively large mass, but has a relatively small volume. Name an object that has a relatively small mass, but has a relatively large volume.
5. Write a brief procedure for determining:
   a. the volume of a rock; and
   b. the mass of a small amount of orange juice.
6. How could you determine the percentage of empty space in a square cleaning sponge?
7. Design a poster or model to summarize for your classmates the difference between a solid, liquid, gas, and plasma.
8. Create a chart that illustrates the state changes: melting, boiling, freezing, evaporation, condensation, and sublimation.
9. Plasmas, or ionized gases as they are sometimes called, are of great interest both physically and technologically. Do some research to find out why plasmas are of great interest to scientists and manufacturers. Describe at least two current uses of plasmas, and describe one way scientists and engineers hope to use plasmas in the future.

UNIT 6 Properties of Matter

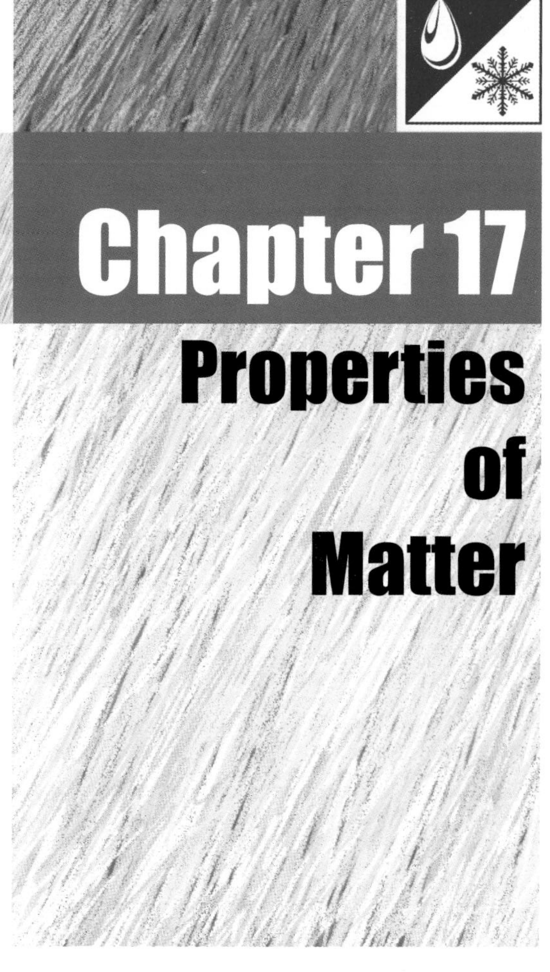

Introduction to Chapter 17

In this chapter, you learn how to describe matter—both solids and fluids. Solids are characterized by their hardness or malleability, for example. Terms that apply to fluids include buoyancy and viscosity. Density is a property of matter that can change with temperature.

Investigations for Chapter 17

17.1	Properties of Solids	*How can you find the density of a solid?*

In this Investigation, you will be measuring the mass and volume as a means to determine the density of a set of objects. Using your understanding of density, you will solve a historical problem—whether or not the U.S. Congress passed a law to change the metal composition of a penny.

17.2	Density of Fluids	*Can you create a stack of liquids?*

In this Investigation, you will use a density column to estimate the density of a few solids. You then will use this estimate to predict the density of rubber.

17.3	Buoyancy of Fluids	*Can you make a clay boat float?*

In this Investigation, you will discover how the shape of an object influences whether it sinks or floats. You will explore the relationship between the weight of an object and the weight of the water the object displaces.

17.4	Viscosity of Fluids	*How can viscosity be measured?*

In this Investigation, you will learn how to measure the viscosity of fluids. You will set up a "viscometer" to measure the velocity of a marble as it travels through fluids of different viscosities.

Learning Goals

In this chapter, you will:

- ✔ Learn the definitions of terms used to describe properties of matter.
- ✔ Learn how to calculate the density of solids.
- ✔ Learn how to find the density of liquids and use your understanding to make a density column.
- ✔ Use a density column to predict the density of a solid.
- ✔ Investigate how the shape of an object can determine whether it floats or sinks.
- ✔ Compare the weight of an object with the weight of the water it displaces.
- ✔ Learn why certain fluids are more viscous than others.
- ✔ Measure the viscosity of fluids using a viscometer.
- ✔ Compare the properties of viscosity and the density of fluids.

Vocabulary

Archimedes' principle	density	hardness	tensile strength
brittleness	elasticity	malleability	viscosity
buoyancy			

17.1 Properties of Solids

Different types of matter have different characteristics. They melt and boil at different temperatures. They might be different colors or have different odors. Some can stretch without breaking, while others shatter easily. These and other properties help us distinguish one kind of matter from another. They also help us choose which kind of material to use for a specific purpose. In this section, we will concentrate on the properties of matter in its solid form. By the end of this section, you should be able to understand and explain these terms: density, hardness, elasticity, brittleness, and malleability.

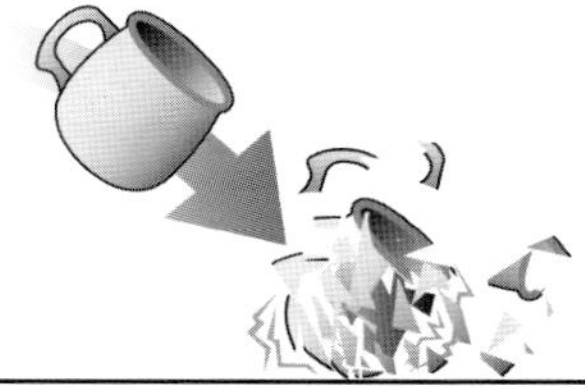

Figure 17.1: *Elasticity and brittleness are properties of solids*

Density

What is density?

Earlier in this unit, you learned two different ways to measure matter: You can find its mass or its volume. Density is a property that describes the relationship between these two measurements. If the matter is a homogeneous mixture or a substance, each cubic centimeter (cm^3) or milliliter will have the same mass. For example, one cubic centimeter of silver has a mass of 10.5 grams. Three cubic centimeters of silver have a mass of 10.5 + 10.5 + 10.5 grams, or 31.5 grams. Ten cubic centimeters of silver have a mass of 105 grams.

Density

$$D = \frac{m}{V}$$

Density (g/cm^3) — D; Mass (g) — m; Volume (cm^3) — V

Density can be found by dividing mass by volume

The density of a homogeneous material or substance is expressed as a ratio of grams per cubic centimeter. The density will stay the same no matter how large or small the sample of material. For example, a steel paper clip and a steel bicycle brake cable have the same density.

	Mass	Volume	Density
paper clip	0.36 grams	0.046 cm^3	7.8 g/cm^3
bicycle brake cable	19.8 grams	2.53 cm^3	7.8 g/cm^3

What is a cubic centimeter?

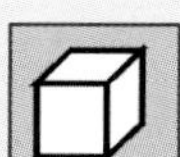

The formula for the volume of a rectangular solid or a cube is length times width times height. If all the sides were measured in centimeters, the unit for this volume would be in cubic centimeters. A shorthand way of writing cubic centimeters is "cm^3." One cubic centimeter will hold 1 milliliter of liquid. In other words, one cubic centimeter = 1 cm^3 = 1 milliliter.

Samples of heterogeneous mixtures will not always have the same density. Suppose you divide a chocolate chip cookie into three pieces and find the density of each. Why might one piece have a greater density than the others?

Density describes how tightly packed the atoms or molecules are in a substance

Density gives us information about how tightly the atoms or molecules of a particular material are "packed." Lead, for example, has many atoms squeezed very close together in one cubic centimeter of space. This gives it a relatively high density of 11.3 grams/cm^3. Paraffin, or wax, doesn't have nearly as many molecules packed into each cubic centimeter. Its density is a much lower: 0.87 grams/ cm^3.

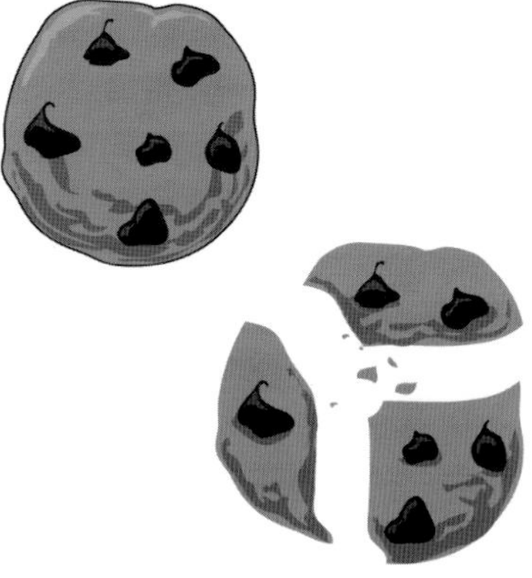

Figure 17.2: *Why do pieces of a chocolate chip cookie have different densities?*

Hardness

What is hardness?

Hardness measures a solid's resistance to scratching. Diamond is the hardest natural substance found on Earth. Geologists sometimes classify rocks based on hardness. Given six different kinds of rock, how could you line them up in order of increasing hardness?

Elasticity

What is elasticity?

If you pull on a rubber band, its shape changes. If you let it go, the rubber band returns to its original shape. The ability of rubber bands to stretch around things and hold them together is due to the property of elasticity. Elasticity is the measure of a solid's ability to be stretched and then return to its original size. This property also gives objects the ability to bounce and to withstand impact without breaking. Based on the property of elasticity, which would you rather play basketball with: a bowling ball or a volleyball?

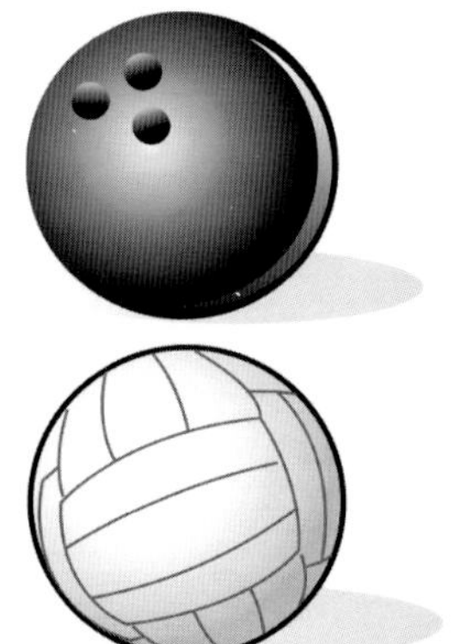

Figure 17.3: *Which ball would you rather play basketball with?*

Brittleness

What is brittleness? Brittleness measures a material's tendency to shatter upon impact. Brittleness is considered a hazardous property in the automobile industry, where, for instance, shattering glass can cause serious injuries.

Safety glass The first "safety glass," designed to reduce the brittle tendencies of regular glass, was discovered by accident. In 1903, a French chemist named Edouard Benedictus dropped a glass flask in the lab. The flask was full of cracks, but surprisingly, the pieces did not scatter across the floor. The shape of the flask remained intact.

The glass had been used to store a chemical called cellulose nitrate. Although the chemical had evaporated, it left a plastic film on the inside of the glass.

Initially, Benedictus had a hard time selling his shatter-resistant glass to automobile manufacturers. During World War I, he did sell it for use in gas mask lenses. Soon after the war, the auto industry began using his glass.

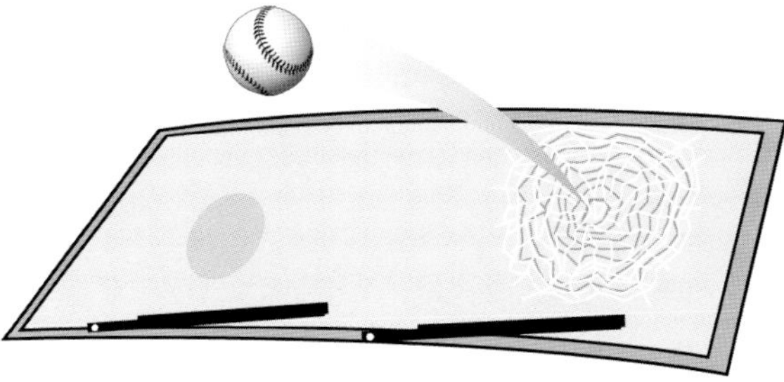

Enhanced Protective Glass is shatter-resistant Materials scientists have continued to seek better materials for safety glass. Solutia Inc. of St. Louis, Missouri, recently began marketing a new glass product called enhanced protective glass (EPG) with Saflex. It consists of a sheet of a material called polyvinyl butyral (PVB) sandwiched between two pieces of glass under high heat and pressure. EPG with Saflex is so shatter-resistant that it can prevent occupants from being ejected from a vehicle in a collision. Because it is so hard to shatter, it is marketed as a deterrent to thieves as well. The material has another significant benefit: It is a sound insulator, reducing highway noise by about six decibels, resulting in a noticeably quieter ride.

Cellulose nitrate

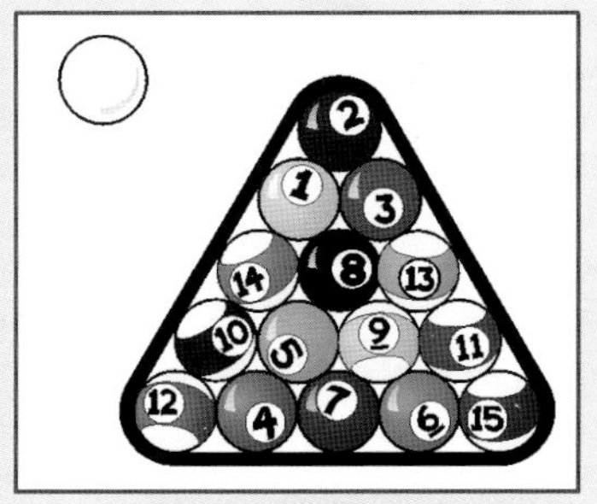

Cellulose is a polymer made by plants. Wood, paper, cotton, and plant fibers are all made of cellulose. When cellulose reacts with nitric acid, cellulose nitrate is produced.

In addition to being used to make safety glass, cellulose nitrate has been used to make billiard balls. Billiard balls used to be made of ivory from African elephants' tusks. The invention of cellulose nitrate created an excellent substitute for ivory. Elephants are now a protected species. Ivory is rare and it is no longer used to make billiard balls.

Malleability

What is malleability?

Malleability measures a solid's ability to be pounded into thin sheets. Aluminum is a highly malleable metal. Aluminum foil and beverage cans are two good examples of how manufacturers take advantage of the malleability of aluminum.

Tensile strength

What is tensile strength?

Tensile strength is a measure of how much pulling, or tension, a material can withstand before breaking. It is an important property of fibers, as it determines the strength of ropes and fabrics. It is also crucial to the manufacture of cables and girders used to support bridges.

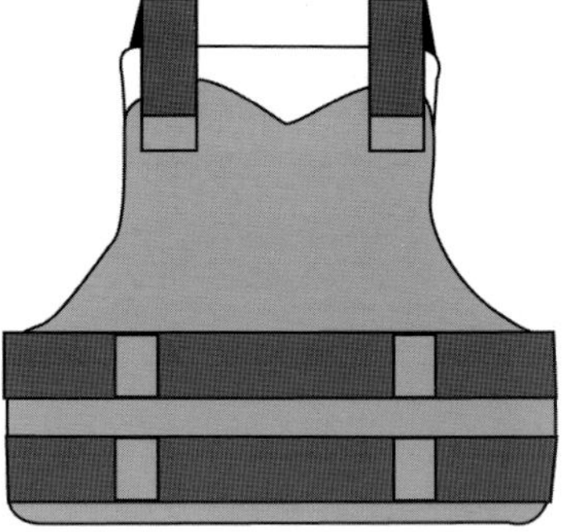

Figure 17.4: *Bullet-resistant vests and tennis racquets are often made from KEVLAR®. This product is used when manufactured goods need to be strong, lightweight, and long-lasting.*

KEVLAR® is a registered trademark of E.I. du Pont de Nemours and Company.

Inventing new materials: DuPont KEVLAR® brand fiber

What has five times the tensile strength of steel on an equal weight basis, and can be used to make canoe hulls, windsurfer sails, tennis racquets, and, of a lifesaving nature, motorcycle helmets, cut-resistant gloves, and bullet-resistant vests?

It's KEVLAR® brand fiber, a synthetic fiber manufactured by the DuPont Company. It was invented in 1964 by Stephanie Kwolek, a chemist who was trying to dissolve polymers, which are chains of molecules that are hooked together like the boxcars of a train. Kwolek found that when the polymers were placed in certain solvents, they formed liquid crystal fluids. This means that the chains of polymers were lined up in neat, repeating patterns.

She decided to spin one of her solutions to see if a fiber would form—and it did! She tested the tensile strength and stiffness of her new fiber and found that, although the fiber was very lightweight, it was extremely strong.

Kwolek and a team of researchers studied the properties of this new fiber, enabling them to modify the chains of molecules in order to make them even stronger. Kwolek has been the author or coauthor of 17 U.S. patents on polymers, polycondensation processes, liquid crystalline solutions, and fibers.

17.2 Density of Fluids

What is a fluid? A fluid is defined as any matter that is able to flow. Liquids, as you know, can be poured from one container to another. They flow. Gases exhibit this property as well. You may have noticed cool air flow into a room when a window was opened, or a waft of perfume drifting your way. In this section, we will investigate the first of three important properties of fluids: density.

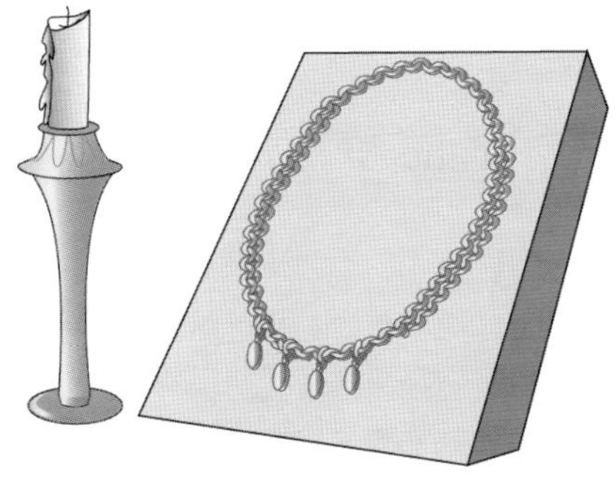

Figure 17.5: *The density of pure silver is the same, whether in the form of a necklace or a candlestick. Decorative "silver" items are often made of sterling silver, which is a mixture of 93 percent silver and 7 percent copper. Adding the copper creates a harder, more durable metal.*

Density

How could you find the density of *liquid* silver? A piece of pure silver in the shape of a candlestick has the same density as a pure silver necklace. Size and shape do not change a material's density. But what if you heated the silver until it completely melted? Could you measure its density in liquid form? Would the density change?

Measuring mass You could find the mass of your liquid silver using a balance. The amount of silver would not change when the candlestick melted. Therefore, the mass should not have changed.

Atoms in liquid form tend to take up more space The volume of the liquid silver, however, is greater than the volume of the solid silver! The atoms or molecules in a solid, as you remember, are fixed in position. Although the silver atoms in the candlestick were constantly vibrating, they could not switch places with another atom. They were neatly stacked in a repeating pattern. The atoms in the liquid silver are less rigidly organized. They can slide over and around each other. Because they are not as neatly stacked, they tend to take up more space.

Why liquids are less dense than solids The silver atoms in solid form could be compared to a brand-new box of children's wooden blocks. When you open the box, the blocks are tightly packed in an organized, repeating pattern. Now imagine that you empty the box of blocks into a large container, and then try to pour them back into their original box. Although the blocks would still be touching one another, they would not fit entirely inside the box. The blocks would now resemble the arrangement of silver atoms in liquid form.

Figure 17.6: *Toy blocks arranged in a tight, repeating pattern take up less space than those in a random arrangement.*

The density of liquid silver

How does the density of the silver in liquid form compare with its density in solid form? Remember, the mass stayed the same but the volume increased. The same mass divided by a larger volume results in a smaller value for density. Therefore, liquid silver is less dense than solid silver.

Table 17.1: ***Density of solid and liquid silver***

	Mass	Volume	Density
Candle holder (at 20°C)	1313 g	125 cm^3	10.5 g/ cm^3
Melted candle holder (962°C)	1313 g	141 ml	9.31 g/ml

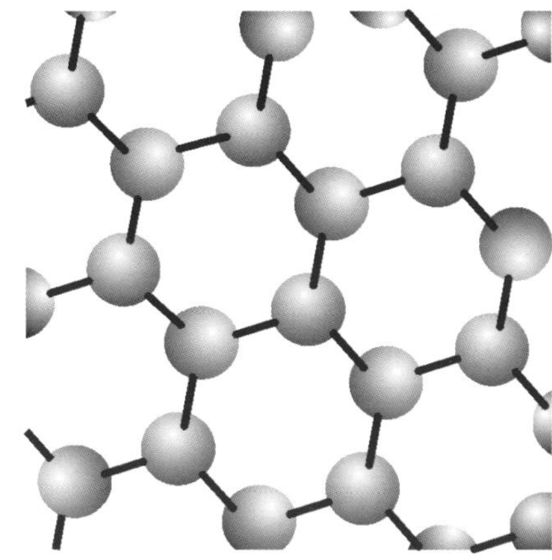

Figure 17.7: *Water molecules in solid form are arranged in a pattern with an unusually large amount of empty space. Water molecules in liquid form are more tightly packed with much less empty space!*

Temperature and solid density

The density of solids usually decreases slightly as temperature increases because solids expand when heated. As the temperature of the solid silver increases, the volume increases slightly, even before the silver melts. This is due to the increased vibration of the silver molecules.

Water is less dense in solid form

Most materials are more dense in their solid phase than in their liquid phase. Water is a notable exception. Ice is less dense than liquid water! When water molecules freeze into ice crystals, they form a pattern that has an unusually large amount of empty space. The molecules are more tightly packed in water's liquid form!

Because ice is less dense than liquid water, it floats on the surface in winter. If the ice were denser than the liquid, it would sink to the bottom. If you woke up one morning, and ice were denser than water, there would be serious consequences for life on Earth.

Ice crystals and snowflakes

Figure 17.8: *Because of the spacing, ice forms hexagonal crystals which give us the beautiful six-pointed shapes of snowflakes.*

What would happen if solid water was more dense?

For example, each winter, more ice would sink to the bottom of rivers, lakes, or oceans. In some places, the water would be too deep for the sun's rays to reach the ice. Consequently, the ice would not melt in the summer. Many aquatic plants could no longer grow. Frogs and turtles that burrow in the mud at the bottom of ponds could not complete their life cycles. The climate of cities along the Mississippi River, the Great Lakes, and other large bodies of water would become much cooler.

17.3 Buoyancy of Fluids

Have you ever noticed how easy it is to do a push-up to lift yourself up and out of a swimming pool? It's much easier than doing push-ups on land. That's because the water is exerting an upward force on you. In this section, you will learn more about the force that fluids exert on an object. By the end of the section, you should be able to define buoyancy and explain Archimedes' principle. You should also be able to explain how gases exert forces when they are confined in a container.

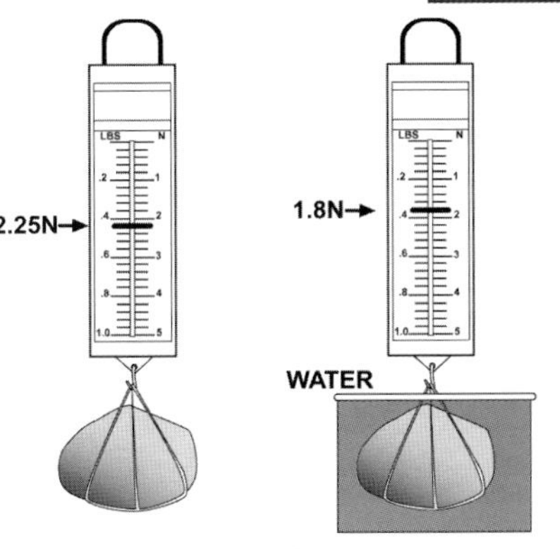

Figure 17.9: *Measuring the weight of a rock in newtons (N). When the rock is suspended in air, it weighs 2.25 N. In water, it weighs 1.8 N.*

What is buoyancy?

A simple experiment can be used to demonstrate the upward force of water you can feel in a swimming pool. A piece of string is tied to a rock, and its weight is measured with a spring scale. The rock weighs 2.25 newtons. Next, the rock is immersed in water, but not allowed to touch the bottom or sides of the container. Now the spring scale measures 1.8 newtons. The water has exerted a force of 0.45 newtons on the rock. We call this force *buoyancy*. Buoyancy is a measure of the upward pressure a fluid exerts on an object.

What is Archimedes' principle?

In the third century BC, a Greek mathematician named Archimedes made an important discovery about the buoyant force. He realized that the force exerted on an object in a liquid is equal to the weight of the fluid displaced by the object. We call this relationship Archimedes' principle.

Archimedes' principle tells us that the water displaced by the rock in the experiment above had a weight of 0.45 newtons.

Do all fluids exert the same buoyant force on an object?

Archimedes' principle can be used to find the buoyant force of liquids other than water. For example, we could immerse the rock from the previous experiment in glycerin, which has a density of 1.26 grams/cm^3.

The rock will always displace the same volume of liquid, in this case, about 43 milliliters. Forty-three milliliters of glycerin weigh 0.53 newtons. Therefore, the glycerin exerts a buoyant force of 0.53 newtons on the rock.

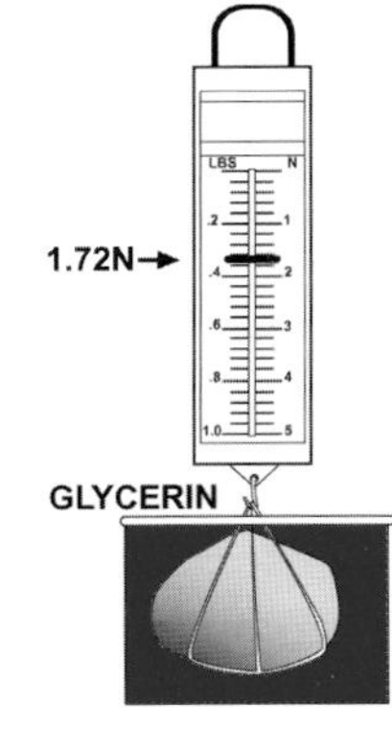

Figure 17.10: *When the rock is suspended in glycerin, it weighs 1.72 N.*

Why objects sink and float

Buoyancy helps explain why some objects sink and others float. If the buoyant force is greater than its weight, the object floats. In the example above, we would need a buoyant force greater than 2.25 newtons to make our rock float.

If the buoyant force is less than its weight, then the object will sink. Neutral buoyancy occurs when the buoyant force is equal to the weight of the object. When an object is neutrally buoyant, it will stay immersed in the liquid at the level where it was placed. Scuba divers use weights and a buoyancy control device (BCD) to help them maintain neutral buoyancy. When a scuba diver is neutrally buoyant he or she can swim and move underwater without rising to the top or sinking.

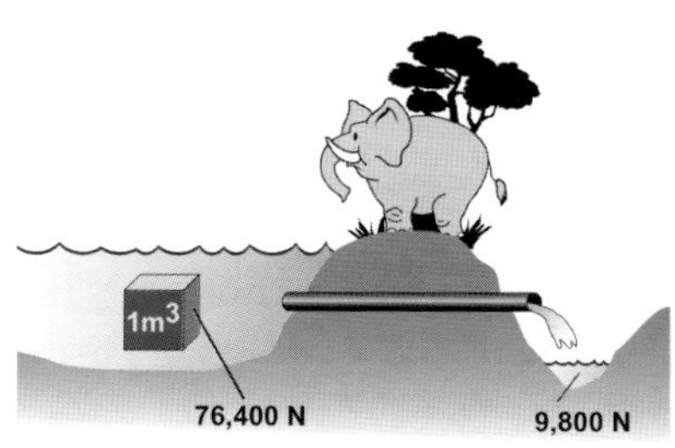

Figure 17.11: *A solid cubic meter of steel weighs 76,400 N. It displaces 9,800 N of water.*

Why does a block of steel sink, but a steel boat float?

Archimedes' principle explains why a substance in one shape will float and in another shape will sink. A cubic meter of steel has a weight of 76,400 newtons. When placed in water, the block would displace one cubic meter of water. The water would have a weight of 9,800 newtons. The weight of the steel block is much greater than the weight of the displaced water. As expected, the block sinks.

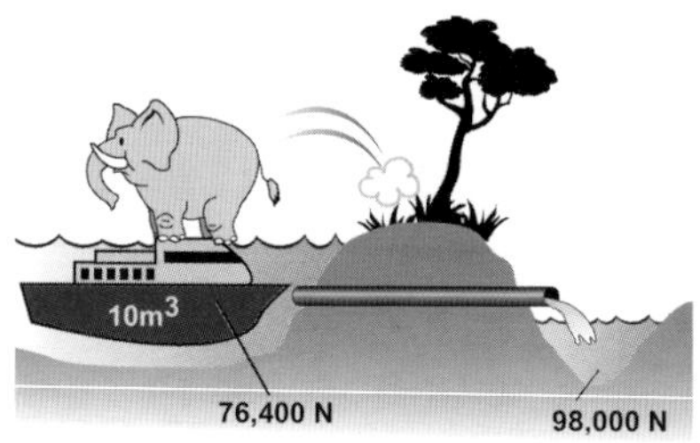

Figure 17.12: *The same amount of steel, shaped into a 10-cubic-meter boat, is pushed under water. Now it displaces 98,000 N of water.*

Why a steel boat floats

Imagine the same block of steel flattened into a thin sheet, its sides bent up into the shape of a boat. That original block of steel, now shaped to be hollow inside, might occupy 10 cubic meters of space instead of one. Ten cubic meters of displaced water has a weight of 98,000 newtons. Now the displaced water weighs *more* than the steel, which still weighs 76,400 newtons.

When placed in the water, your steel boat would settle in the water until it reached a level where it displaced 76,400 newtons of water. Then the upward force exerted by the water would equal the downward force exerted by the boat.

You can try a similar experiment with a stick of clay and a bucket of water. Drop the stick of modeling clay into the bucket and observe what happens. Now mold the clay into a boat shape. Can you make a clay boat float?

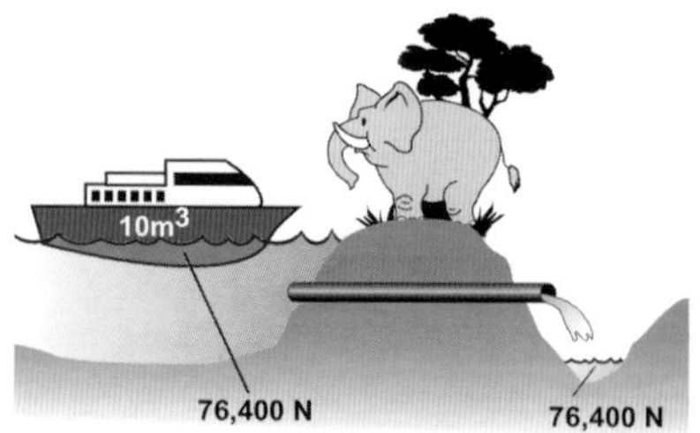

Figure 17.13: *When the boat floats, it displaces 76,400 N of water—which is equal to the boat's own weight.*

Buoyancy and gases

Figure 17.14: *A balloon uses the buoyancy of hot air to lift off.*

Why do hot air balloons float?

Buoyancy is a property of gases as well as liquids. A helium balloon floats because it displaces a very large volume of air. This volume of air weighs *more* than the total weight of the balloon, the gondola (the basket that the balloon carries), and the people in the gondola. The hot-air balloon floats because it weighs *less* than the volume of air displaced.

The relationship between the temperature and volume of a gas

So how can you get a hot-air balloon to take up a lot of space? You probably know the answer to this question. "Hot air" is important. To get their balloons to take flight, balloonists use a torch to heat the air molecules inside the balloon. Heated molecules move with greater energy. As they collide with each other and the sides of the balloon, they take up more space. In effect, the air in the balloon expands. This illustrates an important relationship, known as Charles' law, which was discovered by Jacques Charles in 1787. According to Charles' law, the volume of a gas increases with increasing temperature. The volume of a gas shrinks with decreasing temperature.

Charles' law

The volume of a gas increases with increasing temperature.
The volume of a gas decreases with decreasing temperature.

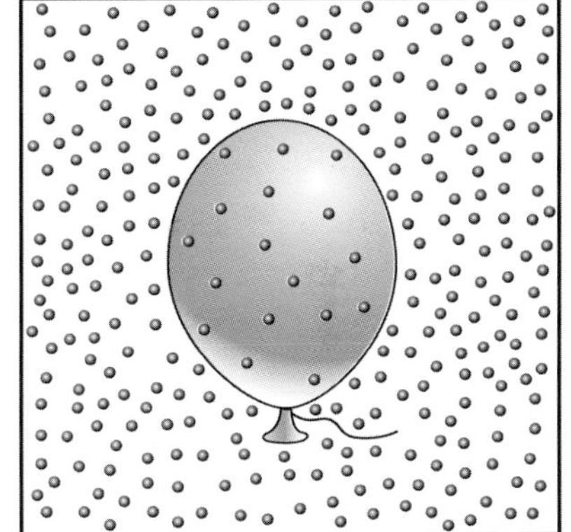

Figure 17.15: *A balloon will float when the volume of air displaced weighs more than the balloon weighs. To help objects like hot-air balloons take up a lot of space, air is heated to make it much less dense than the surrounding air. Helium is a low-density gas that is used to make party balloons and blimps float.*

The buoyancy of hot air

Charles law helps explain why the air inside the balloon becomes much less dense than the air outside the balloon. Because it is less dense, a hot-air balloon will rise in the atmosphere until the density of the air displaced by the balloon matches the average density of the air inside the balloon and the matter of the balloon itself. Stated another way, the weight of the air displaced by the balloon provides buoyant force to keep the balloon in flight.

Gases and pressure

What is pressure? Have you ever pumped up a bicycle tire? What is happening inside of the tire? As you pump more air into the tire, more and more particles of air are pushed into the tire, increasing the **pressure** inside. On a microscopic level, each particle of air collides with the inside walls of the tire, exerting a force which pushes the inner surface of the tire outward. As you pump more air into the tire, there are more particles that can exert forces on the inside walls of the tire. The forces of all of the particles of air inside the tire add together to create pressure.

Units of pressure Pressure is the force acting on a unit area of surface. You may have noticed that tire pressure is usually measured in units of pound per square inch (psi). A typical bicycle tire should be inflated to about 60 psi. The SI unit for pressure is called a **pascal** (Pa). One pascal is equal to one newton of force acting on one square meter of surface area.

What is atmospheric pressure? The air you breathe is made of many different gases including carbon dioxide, oxygen, and nitrogen. The Earth's air, known as the atmosphere, is held in place by the force of gravity on the air particles. Without the force of gravity, the air you breathe would escape into space. At the Earth's surface, the atmosphere exerts a pressure of 101,300 pascals, or 101,300 newtons of force per square meter—about the weight of an elephant! Atmospheric pressure decreases with altitude. This is why the atmospheric pressure on top of a mountain is less than the atmospheric pressure at sea level. Does this explain why your ears pop when you fly in a plane?

How are pressure and volume related? Suppose you pump five liters of air into a beach ball. If you pump the same amount of air into a basketball *half* the size of the beach ball, which has a greater amount of pressure? Assuming that the temperature remains constant, the basketball has *twice* as much pressure as the beach ball. This is because if you squeeze the same amount of gas into a smaller container, the gas particles collide with the walls of the container *more* often, increasing the pressure. On the other hand, the gas particles inside of the beach ball occupy *twice* as much volume so they collide with the walls *less* often. This property of gases, called **Boyle's law**, was discovered by Robert Boyle in 1662.

Figure 17.16: *The forces of all of the particles inside the tire add together to create pressure. As you add more particles, the pressure increases.*

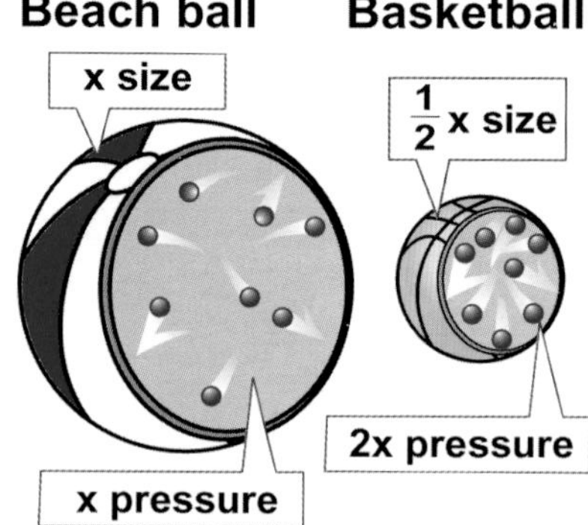

Figure 17.17: *The beach ball and basketball each contain the same amount of air. The basketball has greater pressure than the beach ball because the air particles are squeezed into a smaller space and collide with the walls more often.*

Boyle's law

As the pressure of a gas increases, its volume decreases proportionately.
As the pressure of a gas decreases, its volume increases proportionately.

Boyle's law equation

The relationship between pressure and volume for a gas, when temperature remains constant, is evident in the graph in figure 17.18. This relationship can also be expressed by the following equation:

Boyle's law

$$P_1 V_1 = P_2 V_2$$

Initial pressure → P_1; Initial volume → V_1; New pressure → P_2; New volume → V_2

This equation shows that the product of the *initial* pressure and volume of a gas is equal to the product of the *final* pressure and volume of a gas when either pressure or volume is changed. The example below shows how to solve a problem using the equation.

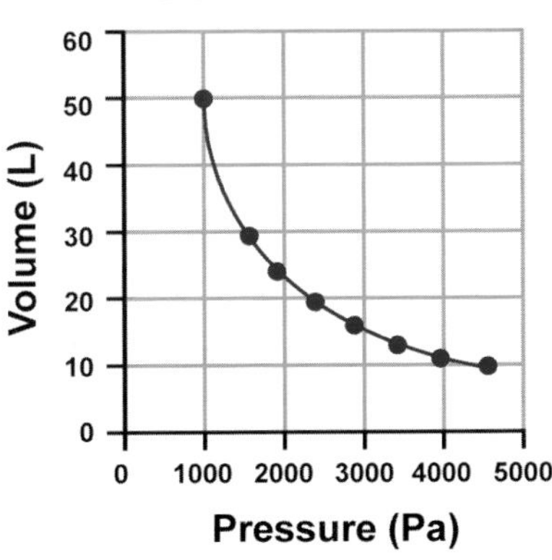

Figure 17.18: *The graph shows the relationship between the pressure and volume of a gas when the temperature does not change.*

Example problem

A kit used to fix flat tires consists of an aerosol can containing compressed air and a patch to seal the hole in the tire. Suppose 5 liters of air at atmospheric pressure (101.3 kilopascals) is compressed into a 0.5 liter aerosol can. What is the pressure of the compressed air in the can?

What do you know? The equation for Boyle's law is: $P_1V_1 = P_2V_2$
$P_1 = 101.3$ kPa; $V_1 = 5$ L; $P_2 =$ unknown; $V_2 = 0.5$ L

Rearrange the variables I am solving for P_2 and the equation is: $P_2 = \frac{P_1 \cdot V_1}{V_2}$

Plug in the numbers $P_2 = \frac{101.3 \text{ pKa} \times 5.0 \text{ L}}{0.5 \text{ L}}$

Solve the problem The pressure inside the aerosol can is 1,013 kPa.

Atmospheric pressure

The pressure exerted by the Earth's atmosphere at sea level is 101,300 pascals (Pa). Since pascals are very small, other units of pressure are often used. The pressure of the Earth's atmosphere at sea level is also equal to:

- 101.3 kilopascals (kPa)
- 1.00 atmosphere (atm)
- 14.7 pounds per inch^2 (psi)
- 760 millimeters of mercury (mm Hg)

17.4 Viscosity of Fluids

Viscosity is another important property of fluids. It is a measure of the material's resistance to flow. High-viscosity fluids take longer to pour from their containers than low-viscosity fluids. Catsup, for example, has a higher viscosity than tomato juice. Tomato juice has a higher viscosity than water. In this section, you will learn how the size and shape of a molecule influences a liquid's viscosity, and how an increase in temperature changes the viscosity of a fluid.

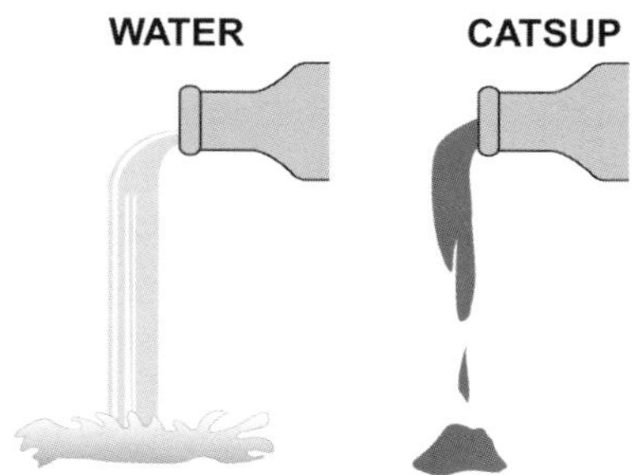

Figure 17.19: *Water is less viscous than catsup.*

Why does viscosity matter?

Thick substances are very viscous

Viscosity is an important consideration in food production. Fast-food restaurants advertise that their chocolate shakes are thicker than the competitor's. Special ingredients such as carrageenan, which is made from seaweed, are used to bring yogurts, puddings, and pasta sauces to the viscosity that consumers prefer. One company even based a large advertising campaign on the fact that its brand of catsup was so viscous, a spoon would stand up in a cupful.

Substances like motor oil need to have the right viscosity to work effectively

Viscosity is also an important property of motor oils. If an oil is too thick, it may not flow quickly to the parts of an engine, leaving them vulnerable to excess wear. However, if the oil is too thin, it may not provide enough "cushion" to protect any part of the engine from the effects of friction. A motor oil must function properly when the engine is started on a very cold day, and when the engine is operating at high temperatures. As a result, manufacturers make very careful choices about which types of molecules will be included in their formulas for motor oil.

Figure 17.20: *Numbers on the side of a quart of motor oil are based on a scale established by the Society of Automotive Engineers (SAE). The first number indicates the lowest temperature at which the oil will work well (-10°F in this case). The "W" means the oil works well in cold weather. The second number is a grade for the oil: "50" is best for summer driving, "30" for winter driving, and "40" for mild weather temperatures.*

Why are some liquids more viscous than others?

Large, bumpy molecules create more friction than small, smooth molecules

Viscosity is determined in large part by the shape of the molecules in a liquid. If the molecules are large and have bumpy surfaces, a great deal of friction will be created as they slide past each other. The liquid will flow at a slower rate than liquids made up of small molecules with a smoother surface.

How does temperature effect viscosity?

As a liquid gets warmer, its viscosity decreases

As the temperature of a liquid is raised, the viscosity of the liquid decreases. In other words, warm liquids have less viscosity than cold liquids. Warmed maple syrup or hot fudge, for example, is much easier to pour than the same syrup chilled. Why does this happen? Remember from your study of states of matter that when energy is added to a liquid, the movement of the molecules increases. The increasing speed allows the molecules to slide past each other with greater ease. As a result, the viscosity decreases.

The viscosity of a liquid is related to its temperature

The viscosity of some liquids changes a great deal as the temperature increases. Olive oil, for example, is more viscous at 20°C than 60°C. The oleic acid molecules that are in olive oil are made up of carbon, hydrogen, and oxygen atoms. At lower temperatures, the hydrogen atoms in the oleic acid molecules tend to form loose connections called "hydrogen bonds" with oxygen atoms in other oleic molecules. These connections make it hard for the individual oleic acid molecules to slide around. However, as molecular speed increases with an increase in temperature, some of the hydrogen-oxygen connections between neighboring molecules break apart. As a result, the oil's viscosity decreases significantly.

As a gas gets warmer, its viscosity *increases*

It is interesting to note that gases exhibit the opposite property. As you raise the temperature of a gas, it becomes *more* resistant to flow. This is due to the fact that gas molecules are spaced far apart, so they do not have to slide over one another very often in order to flow. Increasing the temperature increases the number of collisions between the molecules. Therefore, the net effect is an increase in friction and a corresponding increase in viscosity.

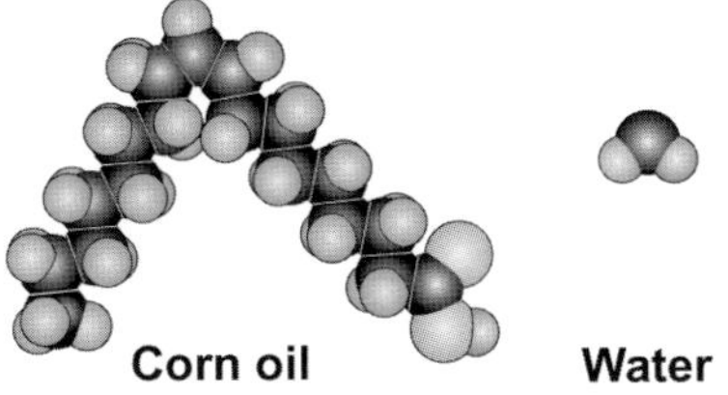

Figure 17.21: *Here are diagrams of two molecules. Which liquid is likely to have a higher viscosity?*

Substance (Temp)	Viscosity value
Water (25°C)	0.89
Acetic acid (18°C)	1.3
Oleic acid (30°C)	25.6
Olive oil (20°C)	84
Glycerin (20°C)	1490

Figure 17.22: *Viscosity depends on temperature. Viscosity values are usually in units of (force × time)/area. The unit that represents this fraction is the "poise." The viscosity values above are given in "centipoise." One centipoise is 1/100 of a poise. The viscosity of water, shown above as 0.89 centipoise, can also be written as 0.0089 poise.*

Physical science in action: Student research provides new hope for whales

Although many people in the United States and elsewhere become familiar with the plight of great whales through the classic Herman Melville novel, *Moby Dick*, they may not realize that the hazards faced by both Atlantic and Pacific whales have changed. They are no longer threatened by commercial hunting, which is now forbidden by law, but by collisions with ships.

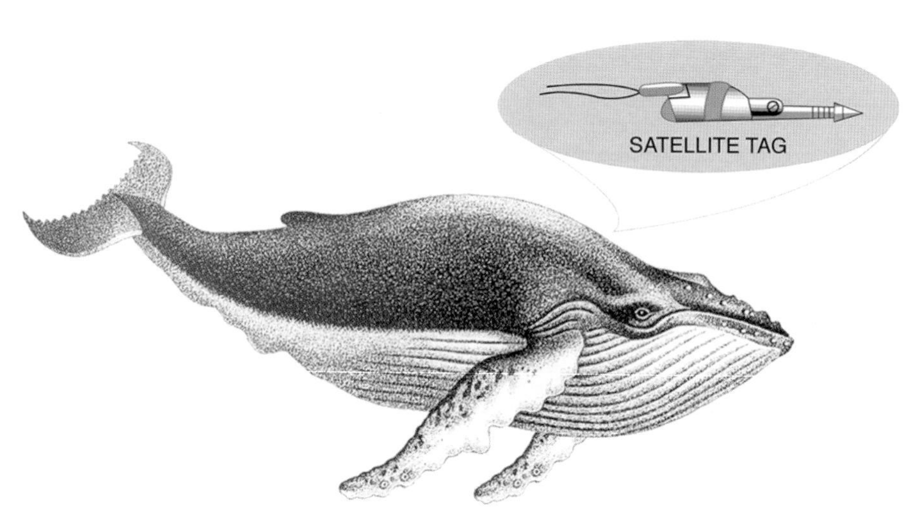

Whale researchers such as J. Michael Williamson, principal investigator with the Boston, Massachusetts, organization WhaleNet (http://whale.wheelock.edu), have used satellite tracking to follow the paths of migrating whales. This research has enabled scientists to better predict where the whales are at a given time during the year, so that ships can be warned of their presence and avert accidental contact.

The satellite tracking program works like this: Researchers (in a somewhat risky maneuver!) travel in a small, rigid, inflatable boat to within 3 to 7.5 meters (10 to 25 feet) of a whale. They use a crossbow to implant a radio tag in the whale's blubber, behind the blowhole. The whale's blubber does not contain many nerve endings, so the whale feels very little, if any, discomfort. The tag records the geographical location of the whale at regular intervals, and transmits this information to a satellite when the whale surfaces to breathe.

Williamson said that the greatest difficulty with satellite tagging is that the tags don't always stay in the blubber. "Just as our bodies will push out a foreign object like a splinter, the whale's body sometimes ejects the tag. And at a cost of $3,500 to $5,000 per tag, that is a significant loss."

In 1999, Williamson teamed up with John Vesalo at the University of Akron (Ohio) polymer research lab in hopes of finding a type of adhesive that would help keep the tag in the blubber.

Vesalo put some of his best researchers to work: high school students chosen through a program called Upward Bound Math/Science, which gives teenagers from nontraditional situations an opportunity to spend a summer exploring their interest in science, with the help of college professors in a modern, well-equipped lab. Six students participated in 1999, and another four in 2000.

The students used their knowledge of properties of matter to design their own investigations. First, they searched for a material with surface texture, elasticity, and tensile strength similar to whale skin. Squares of vinyl worked best. They designed an apparatus using pulleys, clamps, string, and 50-gram masses to test the strength of glue bonds in a way that would simulate the pushing and pulling forces the satellite tag would encounter when the whale swam at various depths and speeds.

Next, the students chose commercial glues to test. They considered the physical environment in which the glue must be effective: an oily substance immersed in salt water for long periods of time. For inspiration, they examined the "glue" that blue mussels secrete to affix themselves to rocks. One student chose denture adhesive, because it works in a moist environment. Another studied "superglue," while a third investigated a new type of glue designed to replace the stitches that doctors and veterinarians have traditionally used to sew up cuts.

Whitni Milton, 16, of Cincinnati, Ohio, explained, "I'm learning that science takes a lot of creativity. You couldn't have done this project without ingenuity."

After eliminating some glues based on their performance on vinyl, the students tested the best adhesives on blubber provided by WhaleNet. They experimented with three glue mixtures, but discovered that the viscosity of each was too great to penetrate the whale skin.

At the end of each summer, the participants shared their methods and results in a scientific paper. Their conclusions will provide a starting point for the next group of researchers. For example, through interviews with veterinarians at SeaWorld in Cleveland, Ohio, they learned that living whale skin is not as oily as their samples. Therefore, the students suggested that attempts should be made to attach the tag to the underside of the skin, which provided a much better bonding surface than the oily blubber.

Even though the project remains a work in progress, the 1999 and 2000 participants say they have already gained valuable insights. They know what it takes to do real research: time, patience, and, above all, creativity.

Chapter 17 Review

Vocabulary Review

Match the following terms with the correct definition. There is one extra definition in the list that will not match any of the terms.

Set One	
1. density	a. A measurement of how easily a solid can be pounded into thin sheets
2. hardness	b. A measurement of the "compactness" of a substance; the ratio of its mass to volume
3. brittleness	c. A measure of a solid's ability to return to its original shape after it is stretched or squeezed
4. elasticity	d. A measurement of how easily a solid will shatter
5. malleability	e. A measurement of how easily a solid can be scratched
	f. A measurement of how well a solid resists breaking when it is under tension

Set Two	
1. tensile strength	a. The upward force of a liquid or gas upon an object immersed in it
2. fluid	b. Any material that flows; commonly refers to matter in the liquid or gas state
3. buoyancy	c. A measure of a fluid's resistance to flow
4. Archimedes' principle	d. A measurement of how well a solid resists breaking when it is pulled on
5. viscosity	e. The force exerted on an object in a fluid is equal to the volume of the displaced fluid
	f. The force exerted on an object in a fluid is equal to the weight of the displaced fluid

Concept review

1. A wooden baseball bat and an aluminum bat have the exact same shape, size and mass. Aluminum is much denser than wood. Explain how the two bats could be the same size and mass.

2. At 20°C, the density of copper is 8.9 g/cm^3. The density of platinum is 21.4 g/cm^3. What does this tell you about how the atoms are "packed" in each material?

3. You are an engineer who must choose a type of plastic to use for the infant car seat that you are designing. Name two properties of solids that would help you decide, and explain why each is important.

4. Would a cube of solid silver sink or float in liquid silver? How do you know?

5. The Dead Sea is a body of water that lies between Israel and Jordan. It is so salty that almost no organisms other than a few types of bacteria can survive in it. The density of its surface water is 1.166 g/ml. Would you find it easier to float in the Dead Sea or in a freshwater lake? Give a reason for your answer.

6. You pump your soccer ball up with a certain volume of air the night before a game. The next morning, you wake up and go outside to get your ball. You notice that it is much colder outside than the night before. When you pick up the ball, you notice that it appears to need more air. Assuming that the ball does not have a leak, can you explain why it appears that the volume of air in the ball may have decreased?

Problems

1. The density of gasoline at 20°C is 0.7 g/ml. What is the mass of 4 liters of gasoline?

2. Your teacher gives you 2 stainless steel ball bearings. The larger has a mass of 25 g and a volume of 3.2 cm^3. The smaller has a mass of 10 g. Calculate the volume of the smaller ball bearing.

3. Ice has a density of 0.92 g/cm^3. What is the volume of 100 grams of ice? If the ice completely melted, what would the volume of the water be? (The density of water is 1.00g/ml).

4. A chunk of pure gold weighs 2.00 N. Its volume is 10.6 cm^3.
   a. If the gold is immersed in water at 20°C, find the weight of the displaced water. Hints: 1 cm^3 of water = 1 g; 1 g = 0.0098 N.
   b. If the gold were attached to a spring scale and suspended in the water, how much would it appear to weigh?

5. Six liters of helium gas held at 2,500 kilopascals are pumped into a balloon that holds 1 liter. What is the pressure inside the balloon? Assume that the temperature does not change.

Applying your knowledge

1. Ancient peoples learned to make tools out of bronze before they learned to make iron. Bronze is harder than copper, but not as hard as iron.
   Bronze is a homogeneous mixture made up of 90 percent copper and 10 percent tin. At 20°C, the density of pure copper is 8.9 g/cm^3 and the density of tin is 7.3 g/cm^3. What is the density of bronze at 20°C?

2. Scientists believe that if the density of ice were greater than that of water, the states of Michigan, Wisconsin, Ohio, and New York would be much colder in the summer than they currently are. Why? Research this phenomenon and create a poster presentation to explain your findings.

3. In the reading, you learned that the Earth's atomosphere exerts a pressure of about 101,300 newtons per square meter of surface—about the weight of an elephant. Why doesn't this pressure crush you? What conditions need to exist so that atmospheric pressure does not crush you?
   a. Research how humans (and other organisms that live on land) are adapted to live in this atmospheric pressure. Make a list of these adaptations and an explanation of each.
   b. Some organisms are adapted to life in the depths of the ocean. Research the amount of pressure these organisms need to be able to withstand. Make a list of their adaptations to life under tremendous pressure, and explain your findings.
4. Hardness is a property of matter that is easy to confuse with toughness or durability. Look around your classroom, your home, or outside, and name one object that has high hardness but low durability and one object that has low hardness but high durability.
5. Observe the world around you and find different objects or materials that fit each of the following descriptions:
   a. has both high elasticity and high tensile strength
   b. has both high hardness and low malleability
   c. has both high hardness and high brittleness
   d. has some elasticity but low tensile strength
6. JAN FEB MAR In the first century BC, the Roman architect Vitruvius related a story of how Archimedes uncovered a fraud in the manufacture of a golden crown commissioned by Hiero II, the king of Syracuse. The crown (*corona* in Latin) would have been in the form of a wreath, like the picture. Hiero would have placed such a wreath on an important statue. Suspecting that the goldsmith might have replaced some of the gold given to him by an equal weight of silver, Hiero asked Archimedes to determine whether the wreath was pure gold. Because the wreath was precious, he could not disturb the wreath in any way. (In modern terms, he was to perform nondestructive testing.)

   The solution occurred to Archimedes when he stepped into his bath and caused it to overflow. He decided to put a weight of gold equal to the crown and known to be pure into a bowl that was filled with water to the brim. Then the gold would be removed and the king's crown put in its place. An alloy of lighter silver would increase the bulk of the crown and cause the bowl to overflow.

   Explain whether you think Archimedes' method was correct and would have spotted the fake crown.
7. Quite a number of studies have been done on the viscosity of lava from various volcanic eruptions around the world. Do some research to find out how scientists determine the viscosity of lava, and discover if there is much variation in the viscosity of different lava flows.

Chapter 18
Atoms and Elements

Introduction to Chapter 18

What does matter look like at its most basic level? This question has intrigued people for thousands of years. In this chapter, you will learn about atoms, how they are put together, how many kinds of atoms exist, and how people keep track of the different kinds of atoms.

Investigations for Chapter 18

18.1	Atomic Structure	*How was the size of an atom's nucleus determined?*

You will use indirect measurement to find the radius of a circle, and compare your work with the classic experiment used to find the radius of an atomic nucleus.

18.2	Comparing Atoms	*What are atoms and how are they put together?*

You will construct models of several kinds of atoms using the atom-building game.

18.3	The Periodic Table of Elements	*What does atomic structure have to do with the periodic table?*

You will learn how different kinds of atoms (the elements) are arranged in the periodic table of elements. You will play Atomic Challenge, a game that will test your skills in reading the periodic table.

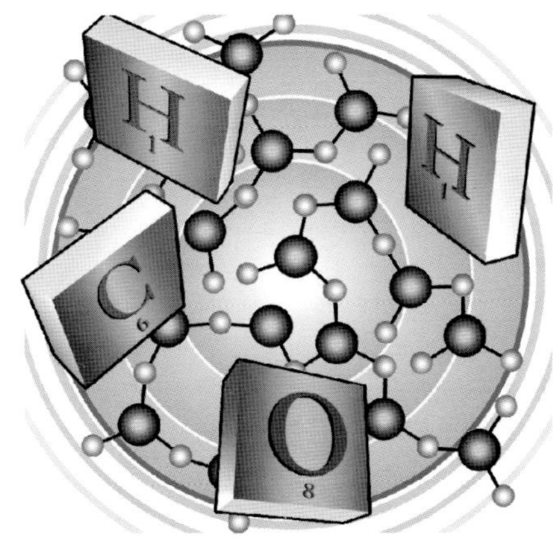

Learning Goals

In this chapter, you will:

- ✔ Use indirect measurement to determine the radius of a circle.
- ✔ Build models of atoms.
- ✔ Research one of the historical atomic models.
- ✔ Understand how atoms of each element differ.
- ✔ Describe the forces that hold an atom together.
- ✔ Use the concept of electron shells to arrange electrons in atomic models.
- ✔ Understand how elements are organized in the periodic table.
- ✔ Use the periodic table to identify the atomic number and mass numbers of each element.
- ✔ Calculate the numbers of protons and neutrons in each stable isotope of an element.

Vocabulary

atomic mass
atomic mass units
atomic number
atomic theory
chemical symbol
electrons
energy levels
group of elements
isotopes
mass number
neutrons
nucleus
periodic table of elements
protons
strong nuclear force
subatomic particles
valence electrons

18.1 Atomic Structure

All matter is formed from atoms. Atoms, by themselves or combined with other atoms in molecules, make up everything that we see, hear, feel, smell, and touch. An individual atom is so small that one cell in your body contains 100 trillion atoms, and a speck of dust contains many more atoms than that.

As small as they are, atoms and molecules are the building blocks of every type of matter. A few hundred incredibly tiny atoms of gold have the same density as a bar of gold. A few hundred very tiny molecules of water have the same density as a cup of water. (We would not, of course, be able to see or notice in any way those atomic clumps of gold nor those molecular masses of water!)

Why are atoms the smallest piece that is still recognizably matter? What do you find when you break apart an atom? How big is it? In this section you will find out what an atom looks like, and learn about the historical experiments that helped scientists understand atomic structure.

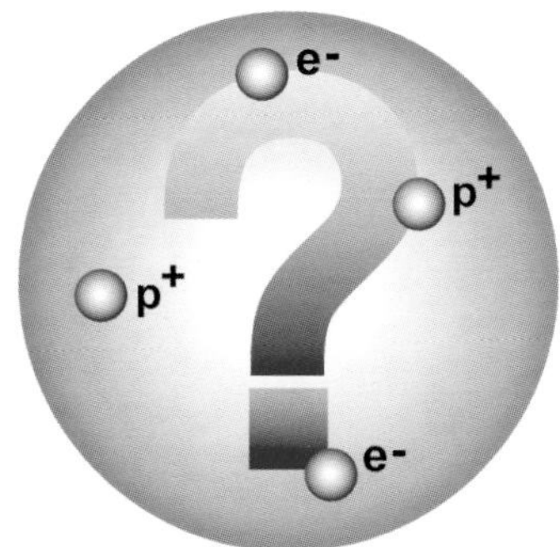

Figure 18.1: *What do atoms look like? What are they made out of? These questions have been asked by scientists ever since 400 BC, when Democritus proposed the existence of atoms.*

Inside an atom

Protons, neutrons, and electrons

Atoms and molecules are called the building blocks of matter because if you attempt to break down an atom, you no longer have gold or water or any other recognizable substance. If broken apart, almost all atoms contain three smaller particles called protons, neutrons, and electrons. Because these particles are even smaller than an atom, they are called subatomic particles. These three types of particles are arranged in an atom as shown in figure 18.2.

How are protons, neutrons, and electrons arranged within an atom?

Protons and neutrons cluster together in the atom's center, called the nucleus. The electrons move in the space around the nucleus. No one is able to say exactly where an electron is at any one time. A useful analogy is that electrons buzz around the nucleus much like bees around a hive. Some people describe each electron as a wave; just as the vibration of a guitar string exists all along the string, the electrons exist at all the shaded points in figure 18.2.

Subatomic particles have charge and mass

Subatomic particles have *charge* and *mass*. The proton is positive, the electron is negative, and the neutron is electrically neutral. Protons and neutrons have about the same mass. Each is about 2,000 times the mass of an electron. Since protons and neutrons exist in the nucleus, almost all the mass of an atom is concentrated there. These properties helped scientists figure out the atomic structure.

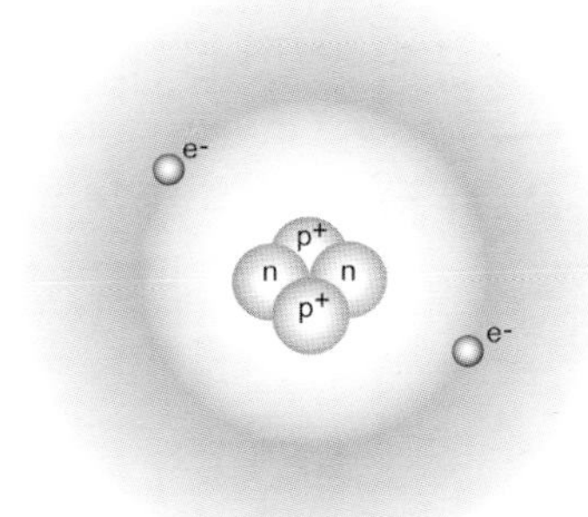

Figure 18.2: *An atom has a nucleus with one or more protons and neutrons and one or more energy levels occupied by electrons. The shaded area around the outside of the atom represents the places the electrons might be. A good analogy is that electrons "buzz" around the nucleus in energy levels like bees around a hive.*

How big are atoms?

Atoms are very small An atom and its parts are much smaller than a meter. The diameter of an atom is 10^{-10} (0.0000000001) meter, whereas an electron is smaller than 10^{-18} (0.000000000000000001) meter. Comparatively, this means that an electron is 10 million times smaller than an atom! The diameter of a nucleon (a proton or neutron) is a distance that is equal to one fermi. This unit (equal to 10^{-15} meter) is named for Enrico Fermi, an Italian-born physicist who studied the nucleus of the atom. For his work with neutrons, he received the Nobel Prize for physics in 1938.

Most of the atom is empty space You may be surprised to learn that most of the atom is actually empty space: If the atom was the size of your classroom, then the nucleus would be the size of a grain of sand in the center of the room.

Particle	Diameter (meters)
atom	10^{-10}
nucleus	10^{-14}
proton	10^{-15}
neutron	10^{-15}
electron	10^{-18}

Figure 18.3: *Diameters of an atom and its subatomic particles.*

John Dalton and the atomic theory

As early as 400 BC, Greek philosophers proposed the atomic theory. This theory states that all matter is composed of tiny particles called atoms. Many centuries later, English chemist and physicist John Dalton (1766-1844) was one of the first scientists to set out to gather evidence for the idea. Dalton was a remarkable person. Born into a family too poor to send him to school, young John educated himself and, at age 12, became a schoolteacher. He grew to be one of the leading scientists of his time.

In 1808, Dalton published a detailed atomic theory that contained the following important points:

1. Each element is composed of extremely small particles called atoms.
2. All atoms of a given element are identical.
3. Atoms of different elements have different properties, including mass and chemical reactivity.
4. Atoms are not changed by chemical reactions, but merely rearranged into different compounds.
5. Compounds are formed when atoms of more than one element combine.
6. A compound is defined by the number, type (element), and proportion of the constituent atoms.

Dalton's atomic theory laid the groundwork for later atomic models, and over time, his original theory has been expanded and updated.

Weather & atomic theory

One of John Dalton's interests was weather (he kept detailed records for 57 years), and that led him to study gases. He studied the evaporation of water into the air and was able to understand that the process increased gas pressure. From these observations of pressure, and from other experiments, he gathered evidence about the structure of matter.

The changing model of the atom

The current model of the atom represents our current understanding of atomic structure. This model is one of a series of models constructed by people as they learned new information about atoms. New information enabled people to update and change their ideas about how the atom is constructed.

The name *atom* comes from Democritus, a Greek philosopher (circa 460-370 BC) who proposed that matter is made up of small particles, which he called atoms, from the Greek word *atomos,* or indivisible. His model describes atoms as small particles that differ in size and shape, that combine in different configurations, and that are constantly in motion. Many of Democritus' ideas were based on logical thinking.

The idea that theories need to be supported by evidence—often gathered in carefully controlled experiments—became important in the 1600s. Then scientists began to design experiments to support or disprove ideas proposed by earlier thinkers such as Democritus. John Dalton (see previous page) was a chemist who experimented with different gases. His careful measurements gave him repeatable evidence that matter is made up of atoms. His model of the atom is a tiny hard sphere (figure 18.4).

Figure 18.4: *Dalton's model of the atom. He thought atoms were tiny, hard spheres.*

The idea that atoms might contain smaller particles came about through a series of observations of cathode ray tubes, devices that were early versions of fluorescent and neon lights. Julius Plucker (1801-1868) and William Crooks, an English physicist and chemist (1832-1919), and his countryman and fellow physicist Joseph John Thomson (1856-1940) conducted many of these experiments. They showed that different gases placed in the tubes generated streams of particles and conducted current.

From these experiments Thomson identified the electron, which carries a negative charge. Thomson knew that atoms were electrically neutral, so he proposed that the atom was a positive sphere with negative electrons embedded in it like raisins in a roll or bun (figure 18.5). The positive sphere and the negative electrons had an equal and opposite amount of charge, so the atom was neutral.

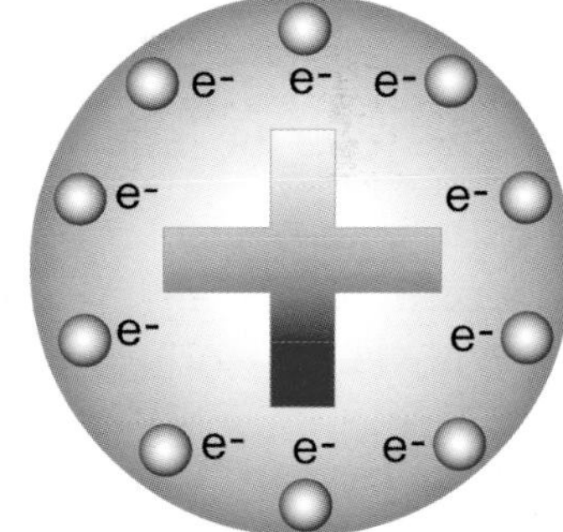

Figure 18.5: *The Thomson model of the atom. The atom is a positive sphere with negative electrons embedded in it. Thomson discovered the electron.*

In 1911 in England, physicists Ernest Rutherford (1871-1937), Hans Geiger (1882-1945), and Ernest Marsden (1889-1970), used high-speed, lightweight atoms called alpha particles (generated by radioactive material), to bombard very thin pieces of gold foil. Most of the alpha particles passed through the foil and hit a screen behind it. But surprisingly, some of them bounced back. They must have hit areas of the foil with greater density!

Rutherford hypothesized that an atom must be made up of mostly empty space, allowing most of the alpha particles to pass through the foil. In the center of the atom, he suggested, was a tiny core called a nucleus, which contained positively-charged protons. This is where most of the mass must be found. The lighter electrons occupied the area between the nucleus and the edge of the atom. However, Rutherford did not have enough information to describe the electrons' location more fully.

Danish physicist Niels Bohr (1885-1962) used information about the nature of the emission of light by heated objects to update Rutherford's model. He described electrons as moving around the nucleus in fixed orbits that have a set amount of energy (figure 18.6). Bohr's model of the electron orbits is still used in many analyses of the atom. However, other 20th century experiments have shown that radiating waves can behave like particles in motion, and particles in motion can behave like waves.

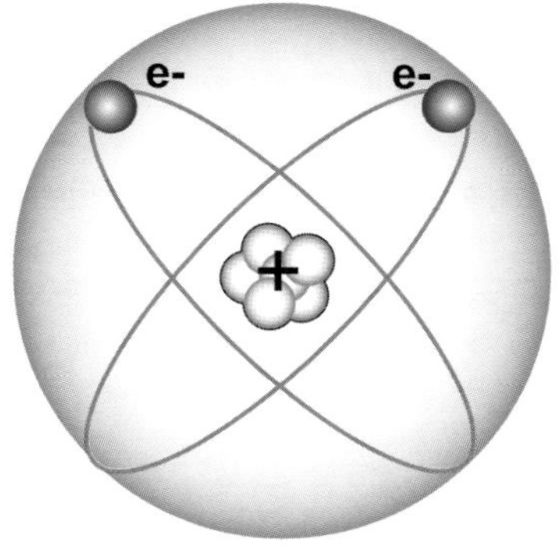

Figure 18.6: *The Bohr model of the atom. Electrons move around the nucleus in fixed orbits.*

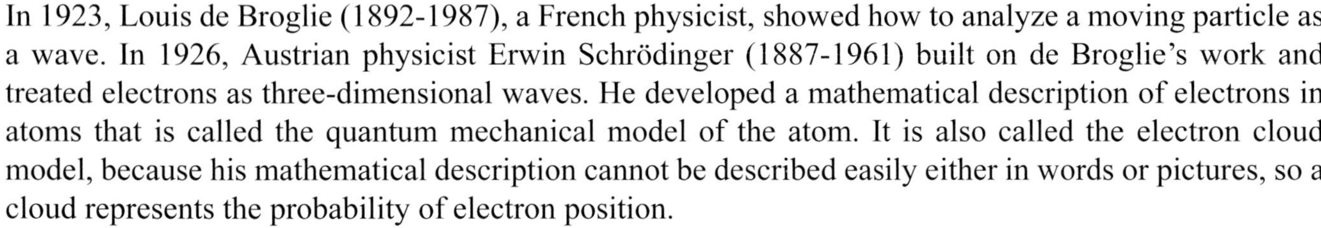

In 1923, Louis de Broglie (1892-1987), a French physicist, showed how to analyze a moving particle as a wave. In 1926, Austrian physicist Erwin Schrödinger (1887-1961) built on de Broglie's work and treated electrons as three-dimensional waves. He developed a mathematical description of electrons in atoms that is called the quantum mechanical model of the atom. It is also called the electron cloud model, because his mathematical description cannot be described easily either in words or pictures, so a cloud represents the probability of electron position.

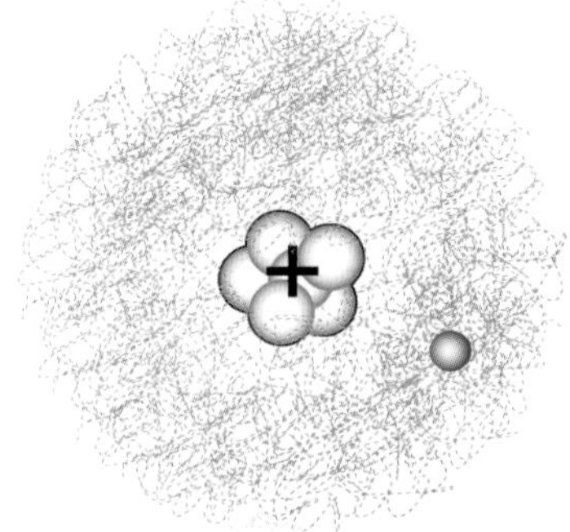

Figure 18.7: *Electrons in the Schrödinger model of the atom. This model is also called the electron cloud model. The cloud represents the probable locations of an electron.*

There still remained a serious problem with the atomic model, a problem Rutherford had identified so many years earlier: missing mass. In 1932, James Chadwick, an English physicist working in Rutherford's laboratory, finally solved the problem. He identified the third important subatomic particle, the neutron. Chadwick (1891-1974) based his work on earlier experiments by French physicists Irene and Frederic Joliot-Curie.

Understanding what is inside an atom has motivated many thousands of scientists and thinkers. What some of them discovered along the way changed the world, influencing not only theoretical spheres such as many of the sciences, philosophy, logic, and other areas, but also those subjects' practical applications. So many new technological developments of the late 20th century have been made possible by atomic research that the present era is often referred to as the "atomic age."

18.2 Comparing Atoms

As you know, some substances are made up of only one kind of atom and these substances are called elements. You already know something about a number of elements—you've heard of hydrogen, helium, silver, gold, aluminum, copper, lead, and carbon, for example.

Exactly how does one element differ from another? This information is important. Over the centuries chemists, physicians, technologists, and inventors have used this knowledge to create everything from better medicines to beautiful jewelry.

How people figured out *why* the elements are different from each other is one of the most fascinating stories in science. It brings together the work of physicists, who studied the structure of the atom, and chemists, who studied how elements react and combine.

Figure 18.8: *How does one kind of atom differ from another?*

Atomic number

The number of protons determines an element

Remember that atoms are themselves composed of protons, electrons, and neutrons. Through intense study of the structure of the atom, people discovered that it is the *number of protons* that distinguishes an atom of one element from the atom of another element.

Can you change the number of protons?

All atoms of the same element will have the same number of protons, and atoms of different elements will have different numbers of protons. Adding or removing a proton from an atom usually takes (or releases) huge amounts of energy. Therefore, most atoms are very stable. Even if atoms bond or break apart during chemical reactions, the number of protons in each atom always remains the same. The atoms themselves are only rearranged in different combinations.

What is the atomic number?

Because the number of protons in an atom remains the same during physical and chemical changes, we can refer to each element by the number of protons its atoms contain. This unique number is called the atomic number.

Atomic numbers start at 1, with the element hydrogen, and go up by ones until 111, the element unununium. The heaviest elements have been created in a laboratory and have not been seen in nature.

Figure 18.9: *Look at the periodic table in the back cover of this book. The atomic number tells you the number of protons in an atom.*

Atomic mass, mass number, and isotopes

In addition to the atomic number, every atomic nucleus can be described by its mass number. The mass number is equal to the total number of protons plus neutrons in the nucleus of an atom. Recall that atoms of the same element have the same number of protons. Atoms of the same element *can* have different numbers of neutrons.

What does the atomic mass tell you?

Chemists arrange the elements in a table called the periodic table of elements. If you look at the periodic table in the back cover of this book, you will notice that the atomic number increases by one whole number at a time. This is because you add one proton at a time for each element. The atomic masses however, increase by amounts greater than one (figure 18.10). This difference is due to the neutrons in the nucleus. Neutrons add mass to the atom, but do not change its charge.

Mass number and neutrons

The total number of protons and neutrons in the nucleus of an atom is called the mass number. Sometimes, the mass number of an element is included in the symbol. By convention, the mass number is written as a superscript above the symbol and the atomic number as a subscript below the symbol (figure 18.11). You can find the number of neutrons by subtracting the atomic number from the mass number. How many neutrons does the carbon atom in figure 18.11 have?

What are isotopes?

Many elements have atoms with different numbers of neutrons. These different forms of the same element are called isotopes. Isotopes are atoms of the same element that have different numbers of neutrons. Because of this, the notation shown in figure 18.11 is called *isotope notation*.

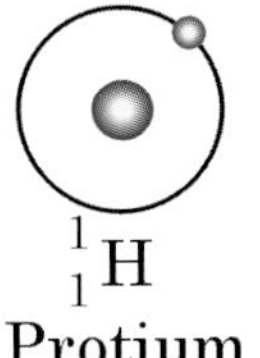

$^{1}_{1}$H
Protium

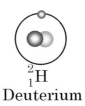

$^{2}_{1}$H
Deuterium

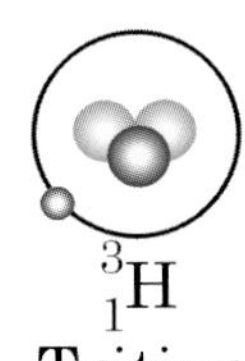

$^{3}_{1}$H
Tritium

The three isotopes of hydrogen are shown here.

Figure 18.10: *The difference between the atomic number and atomic mass is due to the number of neutrons.*

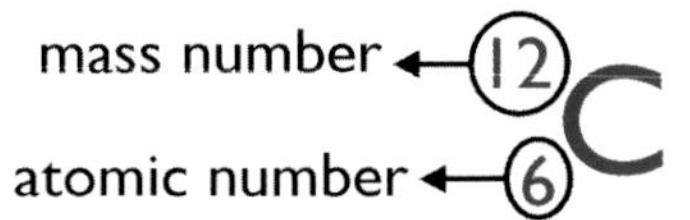

Figure 18.11: *The isotope notation for carbon-12.*

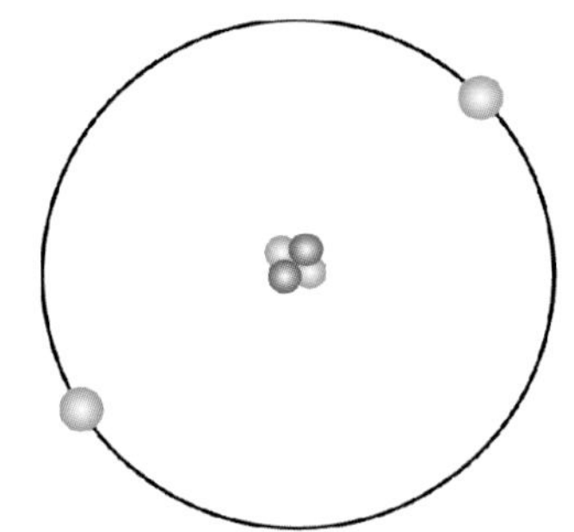

Figure 18.12: *This atom has 2 protons and 2 neutrons. What is the element? What is its mass number?*

Example: finding the number of neutrons

Example: How many neutrons are present in an atom of carbon that has a mass number of 14?

Solution: The mass number is the number of protons plus the number of neutrons.

(1) You are asked for the number of neutrons.

(2) You are given that it is carbon-14. Carbon has 6 protons.

(3) The relationship is $n + p =$ mass number

(4) Solve for n

$n =$ mass number $- p$

(5) Plug in numbers and get answer

$n = 14 - 6 = 8$

There are 8 neutrons in a carbon-14 nucleus.

How many different elements are possible?

Why aren't there infinite numbers of elements?

Why aren't there infinite numbers of elements, each with an atomic number greater than the one before it? The answer may lie in the forces that keep a nucleus together. Remember that positive charges repel each other. In the nucleus, however, positive protons and neutral neutrons sit side by side. Because the protons are repelling each other, they (and the nucleus) should fly apart!

What holds the nucleus of an atom together?

The nucleus stays together because there is another force acting that is stronger than the repulsion of the protons for each other. Because it is stronger than the electromagnetic force, scientists call it the **strong nuclear force**. Unlike gravity, which can reach millions of miles, the strong force only acts on very short distances. The effective distance for the strong force is so short, we do not feel it outside the nucleus of an atom.

What holds the nucleus together?

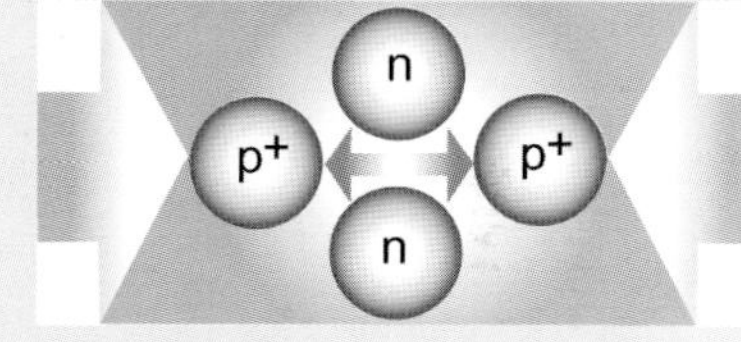

Protons in the nucleus both repel and attract each other. The repulsions are due to electromagnetic force and the attractions are due to the strong nuclear force. The strong nuclear force only acts over very short distances, about the size of an atomic nucleus. Neutrons and protons also attract each other because of the strong nuclear force.

How are electrons arranged in atoms?

Neutral atoms have the same number of electrons as protons

Atoms are electrically neutral. An atom of helium has an atomic number of 2 and two protons in its nucleus. A neutral atom of helium would therefore have two electrons, which stay close to the nucleus because the positive protons and the negative electrons attract each other. An atom of silver has an atomic number of 47 and 47 protons in its nucleus. A neutral atom of silver would therefore have 47 electrons. Are these electrons randomly placed or are they organized in some way?

Electrons are found in the electron cloud

Electrons are never all in one place at the same time. Instead, they literally buzz around the nucleus at a very fast rate, or frequency. Because of this behavior, we can refer to the entire space that electrons occupy as the *electron cloud* (figure 18.13).

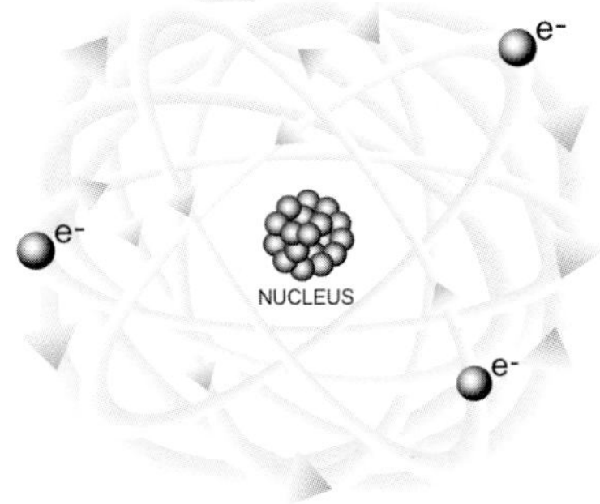

Figure 18.13: *Electrons buzz around the nucleus at a very fast rate.*

The electron cloud is divided into energy levels

The current model of the atom describes the area of the electron cloud that each electron occupies as an *energy state*. The farther away from the nucleus the electron is found, the higher its energy state. Therefore, the electron cloud is divided into *energy levels*. The first energy level is closest to the nucleus and has the lowest energy. Electrons that occupy this level are at a lower energy state than electrons that occupy the second energy level, which is farther from the nucleus. Each energy level can hold up to a specific number of electrons (figure 18.14). Sometimes, when energy is added to an atom, electrons can absorb enough energy to "jump" to a higher energy level. When they fall back to their normal energy level, they release light in a characteristic frequency.

Like the layers of an onion, as the energy levels extend farther from the nucleus, they get larger in diameter and can hold more electrons. The maximum number each level can hold is shown in figure 18.14.

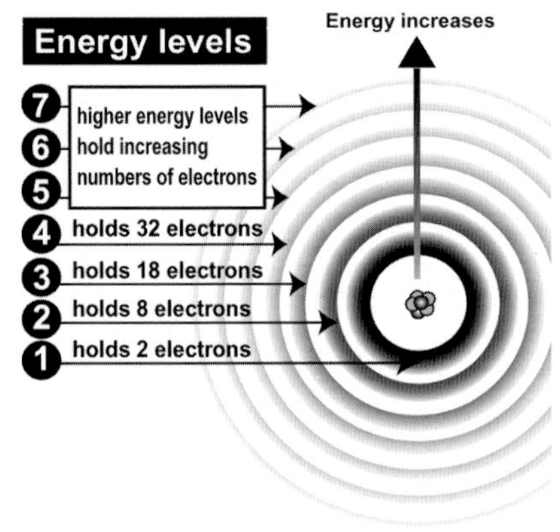

Figure 18.14: *Electrons occupy energy levels around the nucleus. The farther away an electron is, the higher the energy it possesses.*

Energy levels can overlap

It is important to note that some energy levels can overlap. In fact, each energy level is subdivided into smaller regions called *orbitals*. Some orbitals in the third energy level may have higher energy than some in the fourth and so on. Scientists have found out exactly which orbitals are occupied, and by how many electrons, in all 111 elements. You will explore this concept in greater detail in future chemistry courses.

Fireworks and electron energy levels

Almost everyone enjoys the bright colors, noise, and drama of fireworks. The loud noises are caused by a black powder that explodes when burned. What causes the colors? The answer to this question is directly related to energy levels and the strict rules that govern how electrons act around a nucleus.

Electrons will fill up the lowest energy level first, because they are attracted to the nucleus. But just as we can lift a marble to the top of a hill, energy can be used to move an electron farther away from the nucleus. When fireworks burn at a high heat, the energy provided by the heat moves electrons into higher energy levels farther from the nucleus. This process is called *electron excitation.*

When an electron falls back down to its original position, the energy it gained from the heat is released in the form of electromagnetic radiation. The release of electromagnetic energy that occurs when the electrons fall down into a lower-energy position is called *emission.*

Because electromagnetic radiation is a wave, it comes in different frequencies. Some frequencies we can see with our eyes and we call those frequencies light. As you remember from the last unit, light of different frequencies we see as different colors.

Because of the arrangement of the energy levels surrounding an atom, excited electrons can release electromagnetic radiation in a range of frequencies. The trick in building fireworks is to find materials that release radiation at the right frequency for us to see. These materials are metal salts, which are combinations of metal ions with other ions. With energy input, these metal ions release electromagnetic radiation at wavelengths that we see as colors. The colors we see from different elements are listed in figure 18.16.

The fact that different elements, when heated, can release different colors of light tells us that electrons have specific amounts of energy. For example, the wavelengths for different colors are approximately: 610 nanometers for red; 579 for yellow; 546 for green; 436 for blue; and 405 for purple.

The discovery around 1900 that electrons exist at set energy levels changed the way people looked at the physical world. Before then, people believed that objects could have any amount of energy.

The idea that electrons exist at set energy levels has redefined the field of physics and led us to a much deeper understanding of the way the physical universe works. This idea is known as *quantum theory.*

Figure 18.15: *What causes all the different colors in fireworks? Electrons!*

Metal	Color
copper	green
barium	yellow-green
sodium	yellow
calcium	red-orange
strontium	bright red

Figure 18.16: *Metals used in fireworks.*

18.3 The Periodic Table of Elements

Before people understood the internal structure of the atom, they were able to identify elements by how they acted chemically. In this section, you learn how chemists summarize the properties of elements in the *periodic table of elements*, and how an element's chemistry and atomic structure are related.

Elements and compounds In 1808, John Dalton published his theory that all materials were made up of atoms, and that atoms can bond together in different combinations. He supported his theory with experimental results. This work provoked two important questions. Which substances were *elements*, made up of only one kind of atom? Which substances were *compounds*, made up of combinations of atoms?

How many elements are there? In the 18th through 20th centuries, new theories, technologies, and scientific discoveries motivated chemists to find and catalog all the elements that make up our universe. To do so, they had to carefully observe substances in order to identify them, and then try to break them apart by any possible means. If a substance could be broken apart, then they had even more work to do: They observed and tried to break apart each of those materials. If a substance could not be further broken apart, then it most probably was an element.

We now know of 111 different kinds of elements, and the search for new ones continues. Scientist try to build superheavy elements to determine the limits of the internal structure of the atom.

Groups of elements

Elements that are part of the same group act alike As chemists worked on determining which substances were elements, they noticed that some elements acted very much like other elements. For example, one atom of some metals always reacts with two atoms of oxygen. Chemists called these similar elements a group of elements.

By keeping track of how each element reacted with other elements, chemists soon identified a number of groups. At the same time, they also began figuring out ways to determine the relative masses of different elements. Soon chemists were organizing this information into tables. The modern *periodic table of elements* is descended from the work of these early chemists.

Elements & alchemy

On a quest to make gold, the alchemist Hennig Brand (1630-1692) boiled urine and collected the vapor. The cooled vapor condensed and became a white waxy substance that glowed in the dark. Brand had isolated the element phosphorus, the first element discovered in modern times. Scientists know now that phosphorus, while poisonous in its elemental form, is an essential element in DNA, the molecule that carries our genetic makeup.

The periodic table of elements

If you read across the rows of the table, the elements are listed in order of increasing atomic number and weight. Each row indicates how many electrons are in each region of the electron cloud. As you remember, the electrons of an atom are found in an electron cloud around the nucleus. The electron cloud is divided into energy levels. By looking at the row number, you can figure out how many energy levels are filled and how many electrons are partially filling each region of the energy levels. For example, carbon, in row 2, has a filled energy level 1 and four electrons in energy level 2. You know that carbon has four electrons in energy level 2 because it is the fourth element in row 2. Recall that higher energy levels overlap, so this system becomes more complex the higher you go up on the periodic table. The outermost region of the electron cloud contains the valence electrons and is called the *valence shell*.

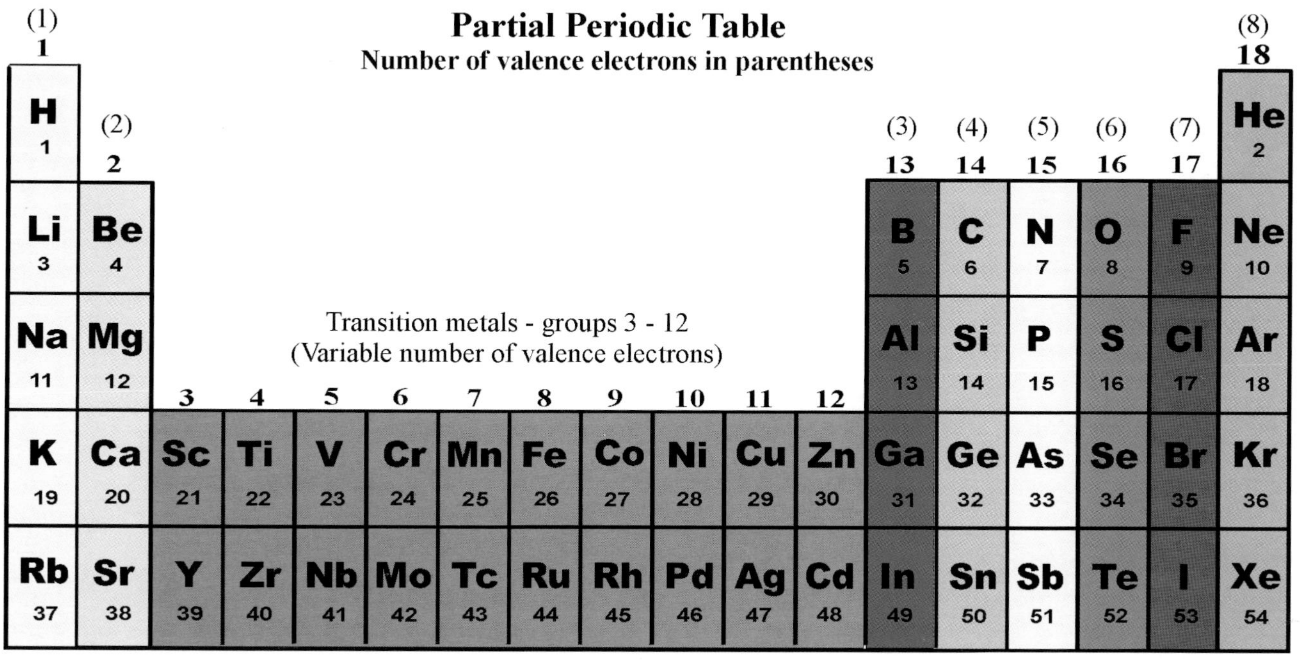

Because the most stable forms of atoms have either full or empty valence shells, the groups of elements relate to the way the valence shells of each element are filled. For example, the last column contains the group known as the noble gases. They don't react easily with any other elements, because this group has atoms with completely filled valence shells. We will study valence electrons in the next chapter.

The periodic table

In 1871, the Russian chemist Dimitri Mendeleev (1834-1907) organized information about all the known elements in a table that visually organized the similarities between them. It became known as the periodic table of elements.

Mendeleev placed each element on the table in a certain row and column based on its properties. Each column represents a group of elements with similar chemical behavior. For example, copper, silver, and gold are in the same column. How are these elements similar?

Reading the periodic table

As you just learned, the arrangement of each element in the periodic table conveys a lot of information about it. The individual listing can tell us even more about the element. A periodic table may show some, or, as in figure 18.17, all of the information for each element.

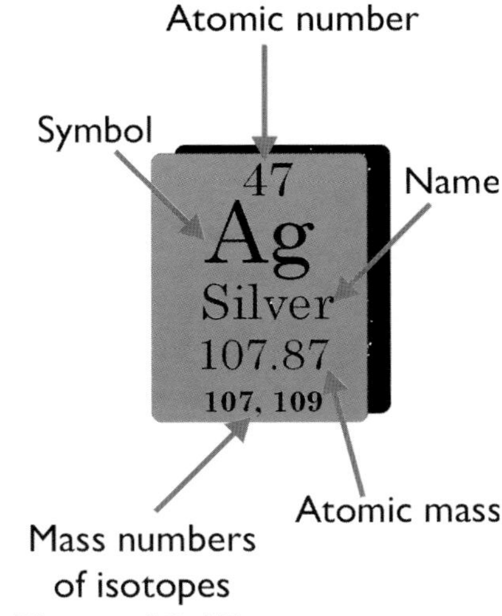

Figure 18.17: *The breadth of information the periodic table can provide.*

Chemical symbol — The chemical symbol is an abbreviation of the element's name. Unlike the abbreviations for a U.S. state, these symbol-abbreviations are not always obvious. Many are derived from the element's name in a language such as Latin or German.

In figure 18.17, Ag is the chemical symbol for the element silver. Its symbol comes from the Latin word for silver, *argentum*. Note that the first letter in the symbol is upper case and the second is lower case. Writing symbols this way allows us to represent all of the elements without getting confused. There is a big difference between the element cobalt, with its symbol Co, and the compound carbon monoxide, written as CO. What is the difference between Si and SI?

Atomic number — As you learned in the last section, the atomic number is the number of protons all atoms of that element have in their nuclei. If the atom is neutral, it will have the same number of electrons as well.

Mass numbers — The mass number of an element is the total number of protons and neutrons in the nucleus. In figure 18.17, you see that silver has two mass numbers, 107 and 109. This means that there are two types of silver atoms, one that has 47 protons and 60 neutrons, and one that has 47 protons and 62 neutrons. Forms of the same element with different mass numbers are called isotopes.

Atomic mass — Although the mass number of an isotope and the atomic number of an element are always whole numbers because they simply count numbers of particles, the atomic mass of an element is not. The atomic mass is the average mass of all the known isotopes of the element. It takes into consideration the relative abundance of the various isotopes. The atomic mass of an element is expressed in atomic mass units, or amu. *Each atomic mass unit is defined as the mass of 1/12 the mass of a carbon-12 atom* (6 protons and 6 neutrons in the nucleus, plus 6 electrons outside the nucleus). Since carbon consists of a mixture of naturally occurring isotopes, the atomic mass of carbon is not exactly 12 amu. You will learn more about how atomic mass is determined in the next chapter.

element	symbol	origin
copper	Cu	*cuprium*
gold	Au	*aurum*
iron	Fe	*ferrum*
lead	Pb	*plumbum*
potassium	K	*kalium*
silver	Ag	*argentum*
sodium	Na	*natrium*
tin	Sn	*stannum*

Figure 18.18: *The symbols for some elements don't always obviously match their names.*

Chapter 18 Review

Vocabulary review

Match the following terms with the correct definition. There is one extra definition in the list that will not match any of the terms.

Set One

1. proton	a. Particle with no charge that exists in nucleus of most atoms
2. neutron	b. Negatively charged particle that exists in nucleus of atom
3. electron	c. Center of atom, contains most of atom's mass
4. subatomic particles	d. Negatively charged particle that exists in space surrounding an atom's nucleus
5. nucleus	e. Positively charged particle that exists in nucleus of atom
	f. Tiny bits of matter that are the building blocks of an atom

Set Two

1. atomic number	a. An atom that has lost some of its electrons; an atom with more protons than electrons
2. strong nuclear force	b. A way to refer to an element; describes the number of protons in the nucleus
3. energy levels	c. The reason that an atom's protons don't break its nucleus apart
4. negative ion	d. The process that moves electrons away from the nucleus
5. positive ion	e. How electrons are arranged around an atom
	f. An atom that has gained extra electrons; an atom with more electrons than protons

Set Three

1. group of elements	a. Atoms of the same element which have different numbers of neutrons in the nucleus
2. periodic table	b. A unit equal to one-twelfth of the mass of carbon-12
3. chemical symbol	c. Elements with similar properties, listed in a single column on the periodic table
4. mass number	d. The total number of protons and neutrons in the nucleus of an atom
5. isotope	e. A chart of the elements, arranged to provide information about each element's behavior
	f. The abbreviation for the name of an element

Concept review

1. Draw a pictorial model of an atom that has 5 protons, 5 neutrons, and 5 electrons. Label the charge of each subatomic particle. What element is this?
2. Two atoms are placed next to each other. Atom A has 6 protons, 6 neutrons, and 5 electrons. Atom B has 6 protons, 7 neutrons, and 6 electrons. Are atoms A and B different elements? How do you know?
3. Why don't the protons in a nucleus repel each other and break the atom apart?
4. Do scientists suspect that there is an infinite number of elements, just waiting to be discovered? What evidence might they give to support such a hypothesis?

Problems

1. How many electron shells would be completely filled by a neutral atom of calcium? How many electrons would be left over?
2. How many electron shells would be completely filled by a neutral xenon atom? How many electrons would be left over?
3. Which element is more likely to combine with other elements, calcium or xenon? How do you know?
4. Use the periodic table on the inside cover of your textbook to answer the following questions:
   a. A magnesium atom will react with two chlorine atoms to form magnesium chloride, $MgCl_2$. Name two other elements that are likely to react with chlorine in a similar manner.
   b. How many completely full electron shells do the elements in the third row contain? Are there any exceptions?
5. For each of the nuclei shown below, do the following:
   a. Name the element.
   b. Give the mass number.
   c. Show the isotope notation.

Atom A

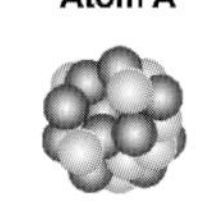

17 Protons
18 Neutrons

Atom B

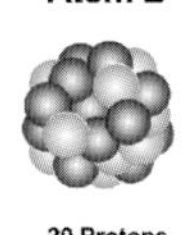

20 Protons
20 Neutrons

Atom C

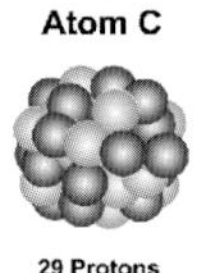

29 Protons
34 Neutrons

Atom D

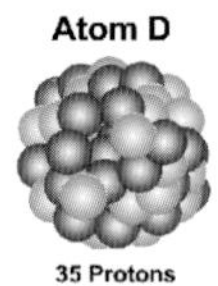

35 Protons
45 Neutrons

Applying your knowledge

1. Make a poster illustrating models of the atom scientists have proposed since the 1800s. Explain how each model reflects the new knowledge that scientists gained through their experiments. When possible, comment on what they learned about charge, mass, and location of subatomic particles.
2. Choose an atom and make a three-dimensional model of its structure, using the Bohr model. Choose different materials to represent protons, neutrons, and electrons. Attach a key to your model to explain what each material represents.

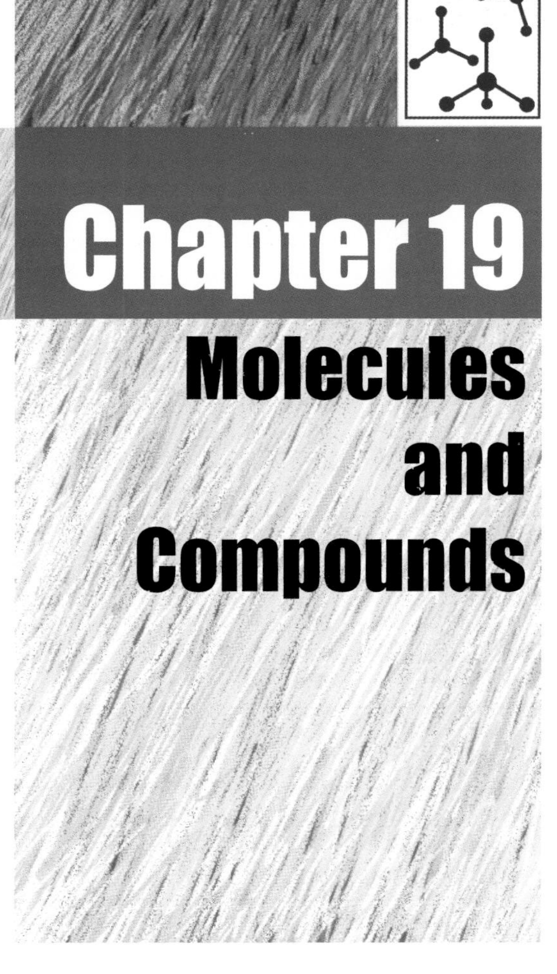

Introduction to Chapter 19

Pure elements are made up of one type of atom. Compounds are made up of molecules which consist of more than one type of atom. Why is it that most of the substances found on earth are compounds? Why do atoms usually associate with other atoms instead of existing alone? In this chapter, you will explore why atoms form chemical bonds to make molecules and compounds.

Investigations for Chapter 19

19.1	**Bonding and Molecules**	*Why do atoms form chemical bonds?*

In this Investigation, you will build models of atoms and discover one of the fundamental ideas in chemistry: How electrons are involved in the formation of chemical bonds.

19.2	**Chemical Formulas**	*Why do atoms combine in certain ratios?*

In this Investigation, you will discover how the arrangement of electrons in atoms is related to groups on the periodic table. You will also learn why atoms form chemical bonds with other atoms in certain ratios.

19.3	**Comparing Molecules**	*How can you determine the chemical formula of a compound?*

Atoms combine in whole number ratios to form chemical compounds. In fact, the same two elements may form several different compounds by combining in different ratios. Chemical formulas show the ratios in which elements combine to form a compound. In this Investigation, you will use nuts and bolts to illustrate the meaning of chemical formulas.

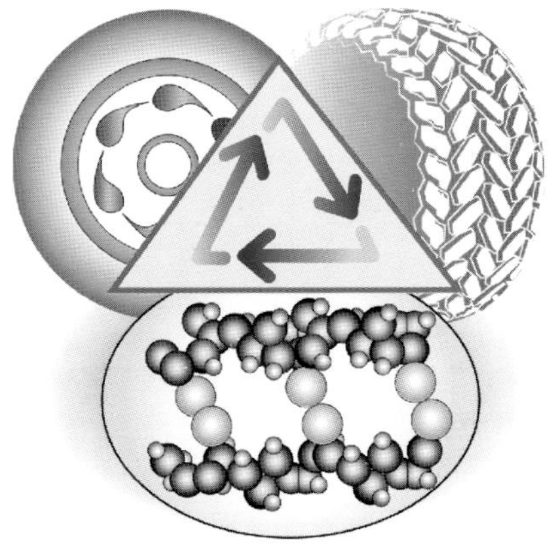

Learning Goals

In this chapter, you will:

- ✔ Relate the chemical behavior of an element, including bonding, to its placement on the periodic table.
- ✔ Identify how elements form chemical bonds and the role of electrons in bonding.
- ✔ Predict the chemical formulas of compounds made up of two different elements.
- ✔ Write chemical formulas for compounds made up of many different types of elements.
- ✔ Calculate the formula mass of a compound and compare different compounds based on their formula masses.
- ✔ Identify the environmental and economic impact of recycling plastics.

Vocabulary

Avogadro number	diatomic molecule	ion	polymer
chemical bond	energy level	monoatomic ion	react
chemical formula	formula mass	octet	subscript
covalent bond	ionic bond	polyatomic ion	valence electron

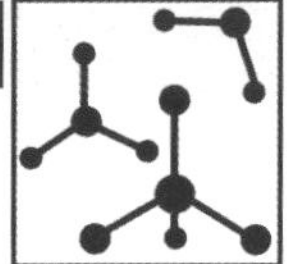

19.1 Bonding and Molecules

Most of the matter around you and inside of you is in the form of compounds. For example, your body is about 80 percent water. You learned in the last unit that water, H_2O, is made up of hydrogen and oxygen atoms combined in a 2:1 ratio. If a substance is made of a pure element, like an iron nail, chances are (with the exception of the noble gases) it will eventually react with another element or compound to become something else. Why does iron rust? Why is the Statue of Liberty green, even though it is made of copper? The answer is fairly simple: Most atoms are unstable unless they are combined with other atoms. In this section, you will learn how, and *why*, atoms combine with other atoms to form molecules. Molecules are made up of more than one atom. When atoms combine to make molecules, they form chemical bonds.

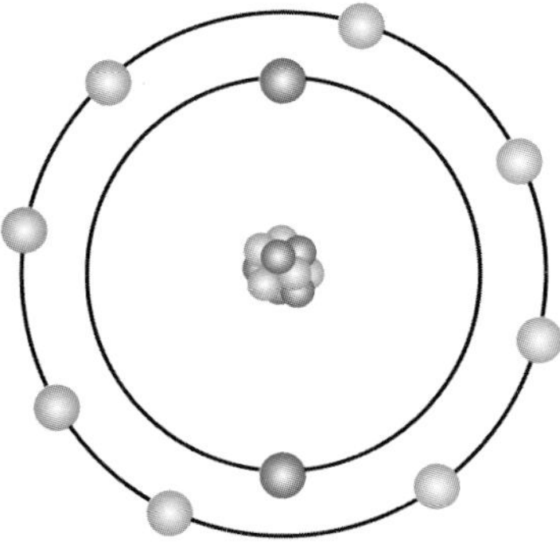

Figure 19.1: *A neon atom is chemically stable because it has a complete octet, or eight valence electrons.*

Why do atoms form chemical bonds?

The outer electrons are involved in bonding

Electrons in atoms are found in energy levels surrounding the nucleus in the form of an electron cloud. The higher the energy level, the more energy is required in order for an electron to occupy that part of the electron cloud. The outermost region of the electron cloud contains the valence electrons and is called the *valence shell*. The maximum number of valence electrons that an atom can have is *eight*. The exception to this rule is the first energy level, which only holds *two* electrons. Valence electrons are the ones involved in forming chemical bonds.

Stable atoms have eight valence electrons

Stable atoms have eight valence electrons. When an atom has eight valence electrons, it is said to have an octet of electrons. Figure 19.1 shows neon with a complete octet. In order to achieve this octet, atoms will lose, gain, or share electrons. An atom with a complete octet is chemically *stable*. An atom with an incomplete octet, like sodium (figure 19.2), is chemically *unstable*. Atoms form bonds with other atoms by either sharing them, or transferring them in order to complete their octet and become stable. This is known as the octet rule.

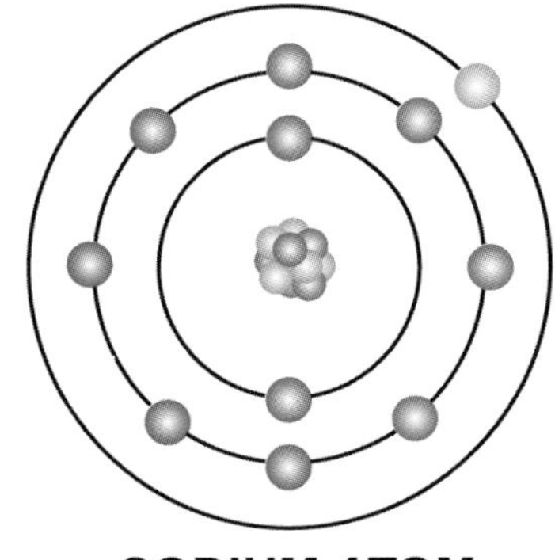

Figure 19.2: *A sodium atom is chemically unstable because it has only one valence electron.*

Exceptions to the octet rule

Look at a periodic table on page 329. Which atoms do you think are an exception to the octet rule? Remember, the first energy level only needs two electrons, not eight. Hydrogen, with only one electron, needs only one more to fill its valence shell. Helium, with two electrons, has a full valence shell (figure 19.3). This means that helium is chemically stable and does not bond with other atoms.

Stable atoms have full valence shells

What about lithium? It has three electrons. This means that its first shell is full but there is one extra electron in the second shell. Would it be easier for lithium (figure 19.4) to gain seven electrons to fill the second shell—or to lose one electron? You probably would guess that it is easier to lose one electron that gain seven. You would be correct in your guess, for lithium loses one electron when it bonds with other atoms. Table 19.1 shows the number of valence electrons and the number needed to complete the octet for the first 18 elements.

Table 19.1: ***Elements, number of valence electrons, and number needed to complete the octet***

element	valence electrons	number needed	element	valence electrons	number needed
H	1	1	Ne	8	0
He	2	0	Na	1	7
Li	1	7	Mg	2	6
Be	2	6	Al	3	5
B	3	5	Si	4	4
C	4	4	P	5	3
N	5	3	S	6	2
O	6	2	Cl	7	1
F	7	1	Ar	8	0

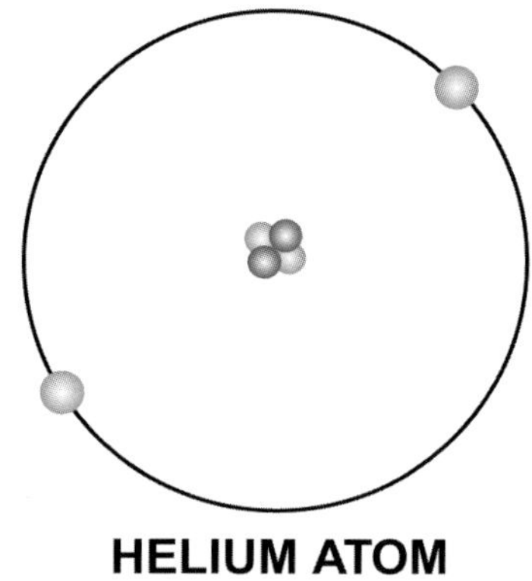

Figure 19.3: *Helium atoms have only two electrons, both of which are in the outermost level. Helium is an exception to the octet rule.*

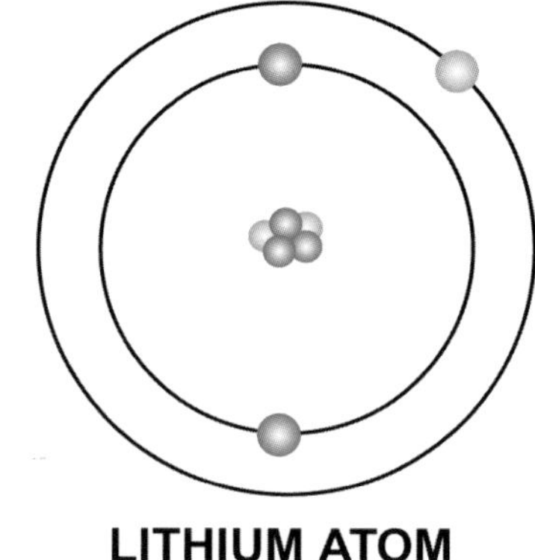

Figure 19.4: *Lithium atoms have three electrons. Since the first energy level only holds two electrons, lithium has one valence electron. If lithium loses that electron, it will have a full valence shell with two electrons.*

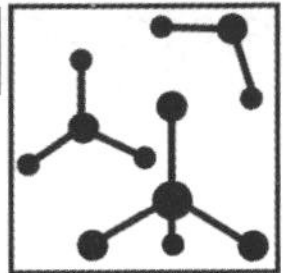

Using the periodic table to determine valence electrons

Do you remember how the periodic table is organized? With the exception of the transition metals, the *column* of the table tells you how many valence electrons each element has. For example, the atoms of the elements in column 1 have only *one* valence electron. Elements in column 2 have *two* valence electrons. Next, we skip to column 13 headed by boron. Atoms in this column have three valence electrons. Columns 14 through 18 have *four*, *five*, *six*, *seven*, and *eight* valence electrons, respectively.

Partial Periodic Table

Number of valence electrons in parentheses

(1) 1	(2) 2	3	4	5	6	7	8	9	10	11	12	(3) 13	(4) 14	(5) 15	(6) 16	(7) 17	(8) 18
H 1																	He 2
Li 3	Be 4											B 5	C 6	N 7	O 8	F 9	Ne 10
Na 11	Mg 12											Al 13	Si 14	P 15	S 16	Cl 17	Ar 18
K 19	Ca 20	Sc 21	Ti 22	V 23	Cr 24	Mn 25	Fe 26	Co 27	Ni 28	Cu 29	Zn 30	Ga 31	Ge 32	As 33	Se 34	Br 35	Kr 36
Rb 37	Sr 38	Y 39	Zr 40	Nb 41	Mo 42	Tc 43	Ru 44	Rh 45	Pd 46	Ag 47	Cd 48	In 49	Sn 50	Sb 51	Te 52	I 53	Xe 54

Transition metals - groups 3 - 12
(Variable number of valence electrons)

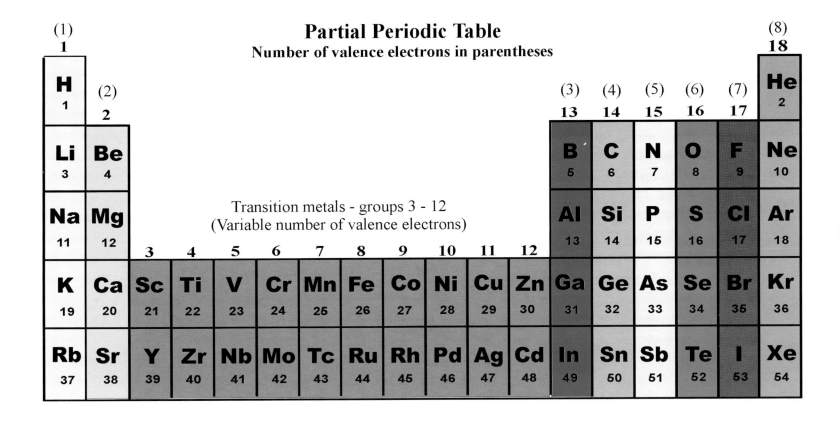

How do you show valence electrons in a diagram?

Valence electrons are often represented using *dot diagrams*. This system was developed in 1916 by G.N. Lewis, an American chemist. The symbol of the element in the diagram represents the nucleus of an atom and all of its electrons except for the valence electrons. The number of dots placed around the symbol of the element is equal to the number of valence electrons. The arrangement of the dots has no special significance and does not show the actual location of the electrons around the nucleus of the atom. Dots are shown in pairs around the four sides of the symbol as a reminder that electrons occur in pairs in the valence shell. Electrons begin to pair up only when no more single spaces are left. This is why the first four electrons are shown as single dots around the symbol, as in the diagram for carbon in figure 19.5.

H· Mg:

·C· :O:

:F: :Ar:

Figure 19.5: *Dot diagrams show the numbers of valence electrons.*

Types of chemical bonds

Chemical bonds result in molecules with different properties

Sodium is a soft, silvery metal so reactive that it must be stored so it does not come into contact with the air. Chlorine exists as a yellow-green gas that is very poisonous. When atoms of these two elements chemically bond, they become the white crystals that you use to make your food taste better: sodium chloride, also known as table salt. When chemical bonds form between atoms, the molecules formed are very different from the original elements they are made out of. What is the "glue" that helps hold atoms together to form so many different compounds? To answer this question, we must study the *types* of chemical bonds.

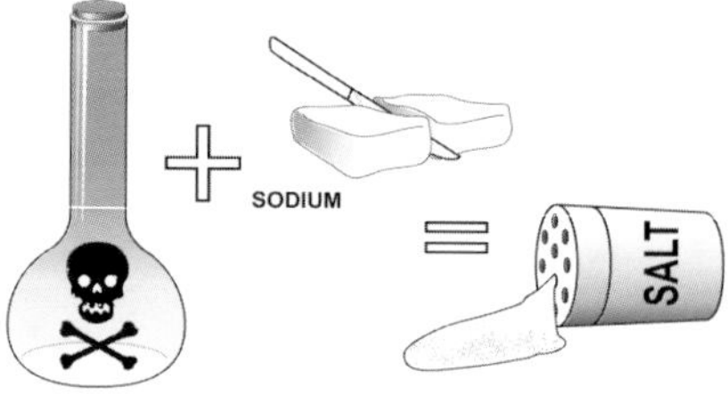

Ionic bonds

Recall that atoms will gain, lose, or share electrons in order to gain eight valence electrons in their outermost shell, that being the most stable configuration. **Ionic bonds** are formed when atoms gain or lose electrons. Sodium has one valence electron in its third energy level. If sodium loses that electron, its second energy level becomes full and stable with eight electrons. Chlorine has seven valence electrons. If chlorine gains only one electron, its valence shell will be full and stable. Do you think these two atoms are likely to bond?

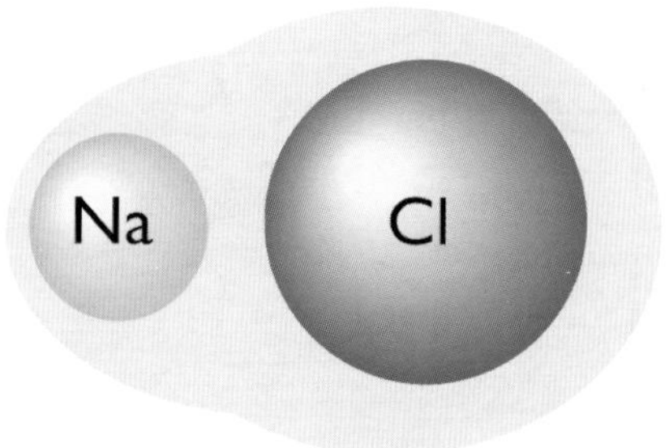

Figure 19.6: *Sodium and chlorine form an ionic bond to make sodium chloride (table salt).*

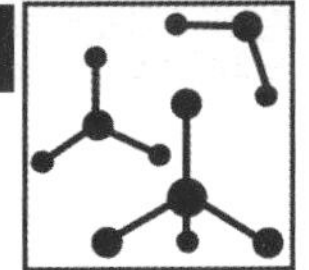

Ionization

In the last unit, you learned that all atoms are electrically neutral because they have the same number of protons and electrons. When atoms gain or lose electrons, they become ions, or atoms that have an electrical charge.

A neutral sodium atom has 11 positively charged protons and 11 negatively charged electrons. When sodium loses one electron to become more stable, it has 11 protons (+) and 10 electrons (-) and becomes an ion with a charge of +1. This is because it now has one more positive charge than negative charges (figure 19.7).

$Na\cdot - \cdot \longrightarrow Na^{+}$

Figure 19.7: *When sodium loses an electron, it becomes an ion with a +1 charge.*

A neutral chlorine atom has 17 protons and 17 neutrons. When chlorine gains one electron to complete its stable octet, it has 17 protons (+) and 18 electrons (-) and becomes an ion with a charge of -1. This is because it has gained one negative charge (figure 19.8).

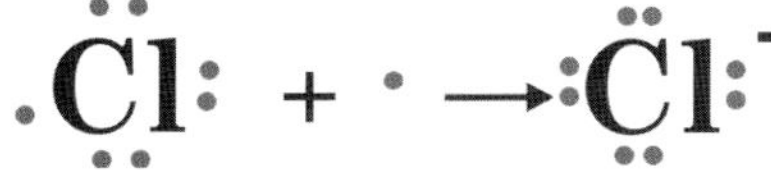

Figure 19.8: *When chlorine gains an electron, it becomes an ion with a -1 charge.*

Opposites attract

Because the sodium ion has a positive charge and the chlorine ion has a negative charge, the two atoms become attracted to each other and form an ionic bond. Recall that opposite charges attract. When sodium, with its +1 charge, comes into contact with chlorine, with its -1 charge, they become electrically neutral as long as they are together. This is because +1 and -1 cancel each other out. This also explains why sodium and chlorine combine in a 1:1 ratio to make sodium chloride (figure 19.9).

Figure 19.9: *Sodium and chlorine form an ionic bond. The compound sodium chloride is electrically neutral as long as the two ions stay together.*

Covalent bonds

Most atoms *share* electrons to in order to gain a stable octet. When electrons are shared between two atoms, a covalent bond is formed. Covalent bonds can form between two different types of atoms, or between two or more atoms of the same type. For example, chlorine, with seven valence electrons, sometimes shares an electron with another chlorine atom (figure 19.10). With this configuration, both atoms can share an electron through a covalent bond to become more stable. Many elemental gases in our atmosphere exist in pairs of covalently bonded atoms. The gases nitrogen (N_2), oxygen (O_2) and hydrogen (H_2) are a few examples. We call these covalently bonded atoms of the same type diatomic molecules (see Table 20.1, "Elements that exist as diatomic molecules," on page 358).

Figure 19.10: *Two chlorine atoms share the pair of electrons between them to form a covalent bond.*

How can you tell whether a bond is ionic or covalent?

Ionic bonds are formed by the attraction of two oppositely charged particles, while covalent bonds are formed when atoms share electrons. Which pairs of atoms are more likely to form ionic bonds? Which are more likely to form covalent bonds? Elements can be classified as *metals, metalloids,* and *nonmetals*. The periodic table inside the cover of this book shows these classifications. Generally, bonds between a metal and a nonmetal tend to be ionic in character while bonds between two nonmetals can be classified as covalent. However, electron pairs are sometimes shared *unequally* in covalent bonds. The attraction an atom has for the shared pair of electrons in a covalent bond is called an atom's **electronegativity**.

○ Empty space
● Valence electron

H Cl
Hydrogen Chlorine

Chemical bond
H Cl

Atoms in column 17 have high electronegativity

For example, in a bond between hydrogen and chlorine, that electron pair is pulled toward the chlorine nucleus. This is because chlorine has very high electronegativity. Atoms in column 17 of the periodic table tend to have very high electronegativity. *Based on what you have learned about valence electrons and stability of atoms, why do you think this is true?* If you suppose that it is because these atoms only need one more electron to complete their octet, you are correct! Atoms with high electronegativity tend to want to *gain* electrons to complete their octet.

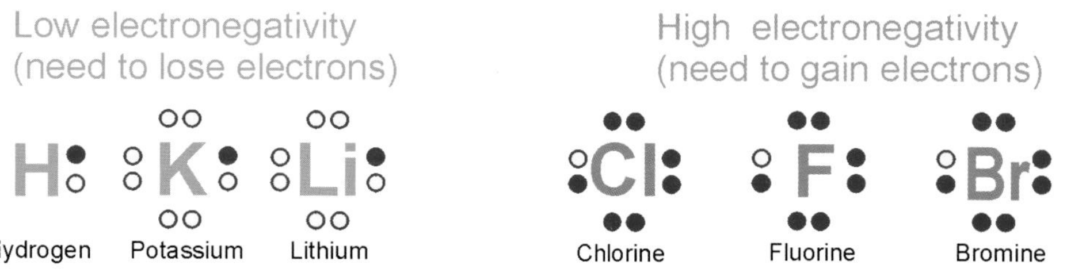

Atoms in columns 1 and 2 have low electronegativity

Conversely, atoms in the first two columns of the periodic table tend to have the lowest electronegativity. This is because they want to *get rid* of the electrons in their highest level so that their next level has a full octet. Bonds between atoms with opposite electronegativities tend to be *ionic*.

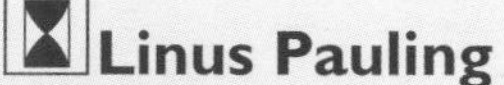

Linus Pauling

Linus Pauling developed a system for assigning electronegativity values for each element. This is just one of his many accomplishments. He is the only person to have won two unshared Nobel prizes, for chemistry in 1954, and for peace in 1962. His passion was to warn the public about the dangers of nuclear weapons, but he was equally dedicated to chemistry as it helps humanity.

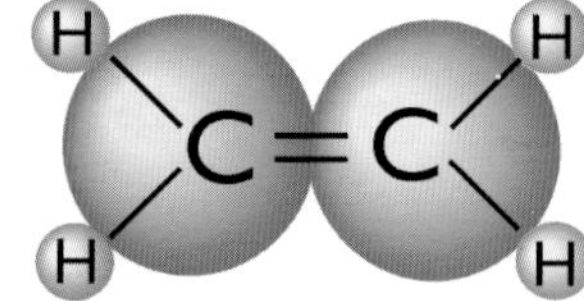

Figure 19.11: *The ethylene molecule is the building block, or subunit, of synthetic plastics. That is why plastics are often referred to as "polyethylenes."*

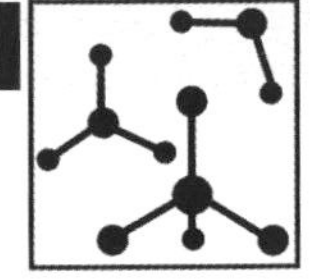

Environmental Issue: Paper or Plastic?

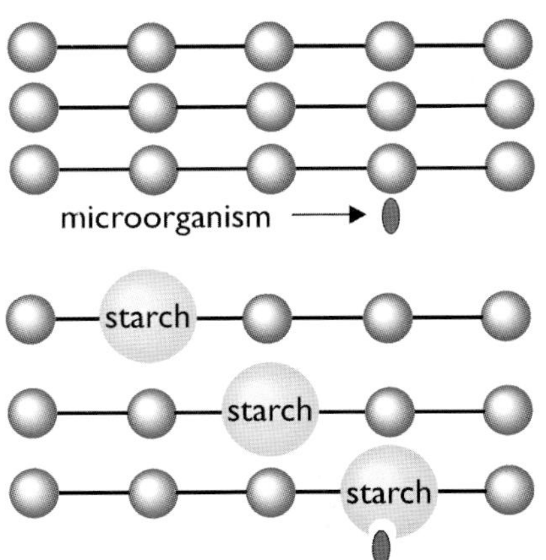

Figure 19.12: *Inserting starch molecules into the polyethylene chain provides a place for microorganisms to begin breaking it down.*

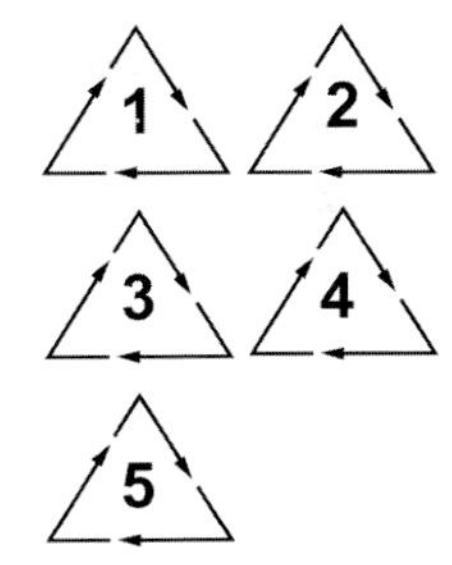

Figure 19.13: *Recycling symbols found on plastic products tell you the type of plastic and are used in sorting the plastics for recycling. Can you find these symbols on products you use every day?*

What is plastic?

Plastics are polymers. You may already know that the prefix *poly-* means "many" and the suffix *-mer* means "unit." A polymer is a large molecule that is composed of repeating smaller molecules. The building block or subunit of synthetic plastics is a molecule called ethylene (figure 19.11). Paper is made out of a natural polymer called cellulose. Cellulose, the most abundant polymer on Earth, is made out of many subunits of glucose molecules. The difference between a natural polymer like cellulose, and the man-made polymer that is used to make a bag or a soda bottle is that cellulose is easily digested by microorganisms. In contrast, synthetic plastics are not easily broken down. For this reason, when you throw a plastic cup away, there isn't much chance it will decompose quickly or at all.

Why can't microorganisms digest plastic?

In order for microorganisms to be able to break down a plastic molecule, they must have access to an exposed end or side branch of the molecule. Because synthetic plastics are such long chains of carbon surrounded by hydrogens, there are no places for microorganisms to begin "biting" on the molecule. Since most plastics we use are man-made, microorganisms are not able to consume them.

Biodegradable plastics

One way to approach the plastics problem is to make them *biodegradable*. This means that microbes such as bacteria and fungi can "eat" the plastic. Making biodegradable plastics involves creating exposed ends on the molecules so microbes can get a start. This is done by inserting a food item that microbes readily eat into into a plastic. For instance, starch can be inserted in the polyethylene molecule. Once microbes have eaten the starch, two ends of polyethylene are exposed. Many plastic grocery bags contain starch.

Recycling plastics

You may be familiar with the recycling symbols on the bottoms of plastic bottles. Those symbols allow you to sort the different plastics that make up each kind of plastic. Choosing the kind of plastic that is used for a certain product is a careful decision. Think about the wide variety of plastic containers (and don't forget their lids) that are used for certain products. In order to recycle plastic, you need to melt it so that it can be remolded into new containers or extruded into a kind of fabric that is used for sweatshirts.

19.2 Chemical Formulas

In the previous section, you learned how and why atoms form chemical bonds with one another. You also know that atoms combine in certain ratios with other atoms. These ratios determine the chemical formula for a compound. In this section, you will learn how to write the chemical formulas for compounds. You will also learn how to name compounds based on their chemical formulas.

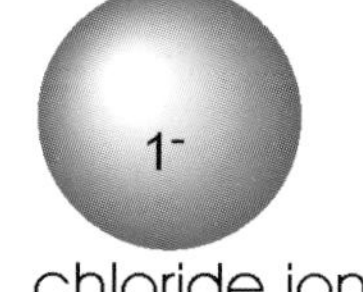

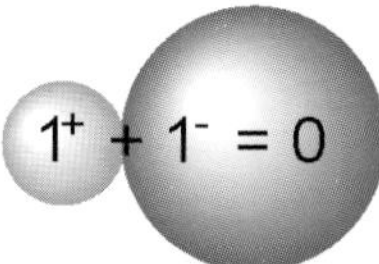

Figure 19.14: *Molecules of all compounds have an electrical charge of zero.*

Chemical formulas and oxidation numbers

What is the chemical formula for sodium chloride?

A sodium atom will form an *ionic bond* with a chlorine atom to make a molecule of sodium chloride. Because sodium chloride is a compound made out of ions, it is called an ionic compound. The chemical formula for sodium chloride is NaCl. This formula indicates that every molecule of sodium chloride contains one atom of sodium and one atom of chlorine, a 1:1 ratio.

Why do sodium and chlorine combine in a 1:1 ratio? When sodium loses one electron, it becomes an ion with a charge of +1. When chlorine gains an electron, it becomes an ion with a charge of -1. When these two ions combine to form an ionic bond, the net electrical charge is zero. This is because (+1) + (-1) = 0.

All compounds have an electrical charge of zero; that is, they are neutral.

Oxidation numbers

A sodium atom always ionizes to become Na+ (a charge of +1) when it combines with other atoms to make a compound. Therefore, we say that *sodium has an oxidation number of 1+*. An oxidation number indicates how many electrons are lost, gained, or shared when bonding occurs. Notice that the convention for writing oxidation numbers is the opposite of the convention for writing the charge. When writing the oxidation number, the positive (or negative) symbol is written *after* the number, not *before* it.

What is chlorine's oxidation number? If you think it is 1-, you are right. This is because chlorine gains one electron, one negative charge, when it bonds with other atoms. Figure 19.15 shows the oxidation numbers for some of the elements.

atom	electrons gained or lost	oxidation number
K	loses 1	1+
Mg	loses 2	2+
Al	loses 3	3+
P	gains 3	3-
Se	gains 2	2-
Br	gains 1	1-
Ar	loses 0	0

Figure 19.15: *Oxidation numbers of some common elements.*

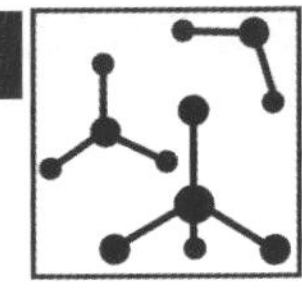

Predicting oxidation numbers from the periodic table

In the last section, you learned that you can tell how many valence electrons an element has by its placement on the periodic table. If you can determine how many valence electrons an element has, you can predict its oxidation number. For example, locate beryllium (Be) on the periodic table below. It is in the second column, or Group 2, which means beryllium has two valence electrons. Will beryllium get rid of two electrons, or gain six in order to obtain a stable octet? Of course, it is easier to lose two electrons. When these two electrons are lost, beryllium becomes an ion with a charge of +2. Therefore, the most common oxidation number for beryllium is 2+. In fact, the most common oxidation number for all elements in Group 2 is 2+.

The periodic table below shows the most common oxidation numbers of most of the elements. The elements known as transition metals (in the middle of the table) have variable oxidation numbers.

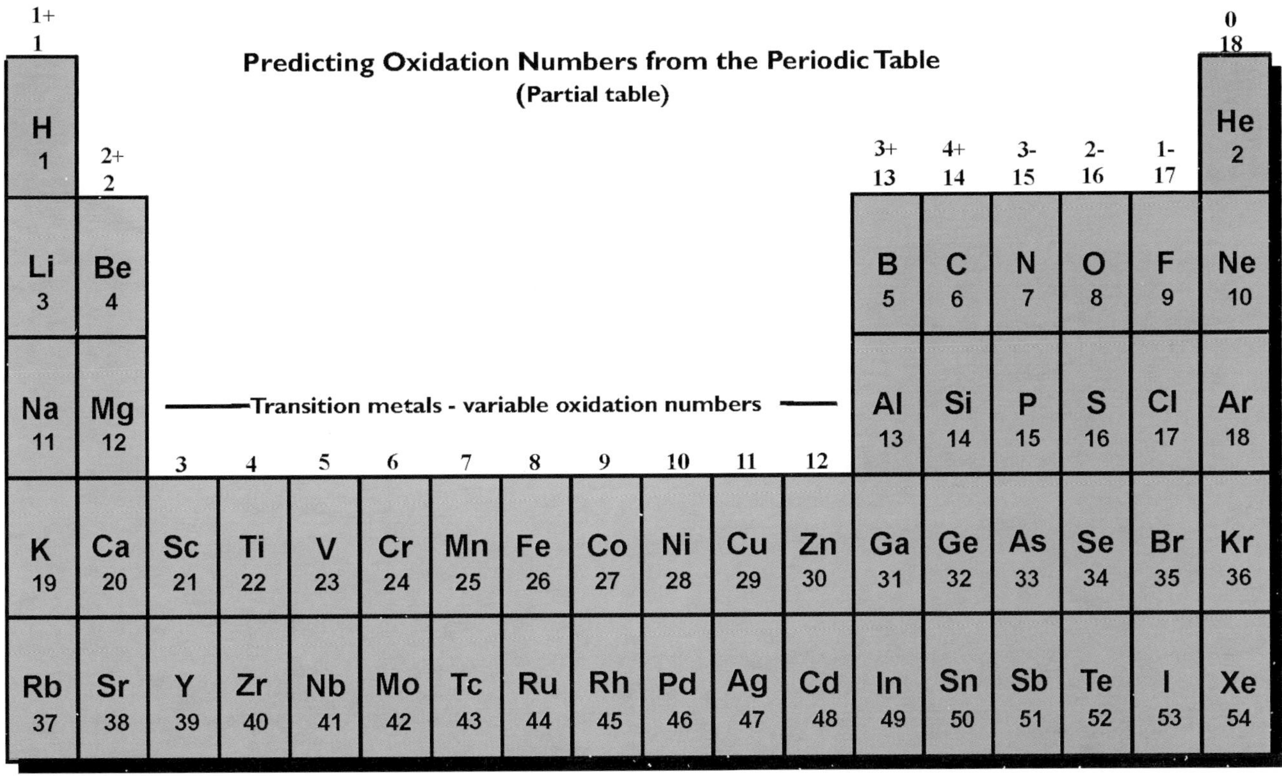

Oxidation number of 1+
(need to lose electrons)

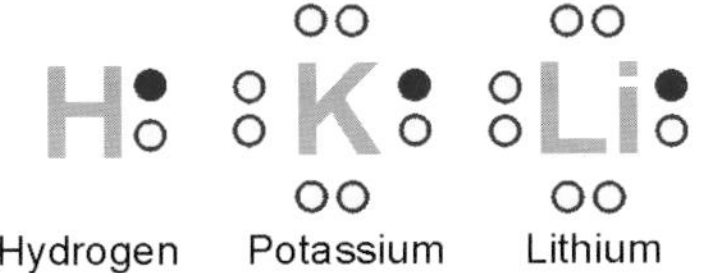

Oxidation number of 2+
(need to lose 2 electrons)

Oxidation number of 2-
(need to gain 2 electrons)

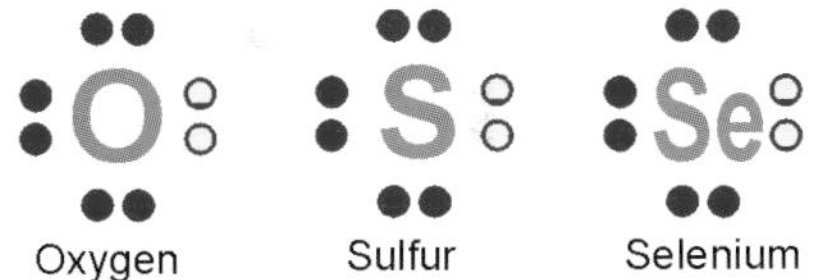

Oxidation number of 1-
(need to gain 1 electron)

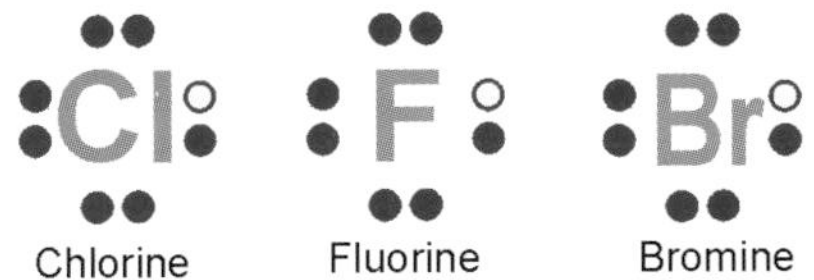

Figure 19.16: *Oxidation number corresponds to the need to gain or lose electrons.*

Writing the chemical formulas of ionic compounds.

Monoatomic ions

Both sodium and chlorine ions are monoatomic ions, that is, ions that consist of a single atom. It's easy to write the chemical formula for compounds made of monatomic ions, if you follow these rules:

1	Write the symbol for the monatomic ion that has a ***positive*** charge first.
2	Write the symbol for the monatomic ion that has a ***negative*** charge second.
3	Add subscripts so that the sum of the positive and negative oxidation numbers is equal to zero—a neutral compound, remember? Note that the subscript tells you how many atoms of that element is in the compound.

Some elements have more than one oxidation number. In this case, roman numerals are used to distinguish the oxidation number. Figure 19.17 shows a few of these elements.

element	oxidation number
copper (I)	Cu^{+}
copper (II)	Cu^{2+}
iron (II)	Fe^{2+}
iron (III)	Fe^{3+}
chromium (II)	Cr^{2+}
chromium (III)	Cr^{3+}
lead (II)	Pb^{2+}
lead (IV)	Pb^{4+}

Figure 19.17: *Elements with variable oxidation numbers.*

Example: Writing a chemical formula

Write the formula for a compound that is made of iron (III) and oxygen.

1. Find the oxidation numbers of each element in the compound.

Iron (III) is a transition metal. The roman numbers indicate that it has an oxidation number of 3+. Its formula is Fe^{3+}.

Oxygen is in group 18 of the periodic table and has an oxidation number of 2-. Its formula is O^{2-}.

2. Determine the ratios of each element and write the chemical formula.

If one iron (III) ion bonds with one oxygen ion, will the compound be neutral? No, since 3+ added to 2- equals 1+. If you have two iron (III) ions for every three oxygen ions, what happens? 2(3+) added to 3(2-) is equal to 0. This means that three iron (III) ions bond with two oxygen ions to get a neutral compound.

The formula for a compound of iron (III) and oxygen is Fe_2O_3.

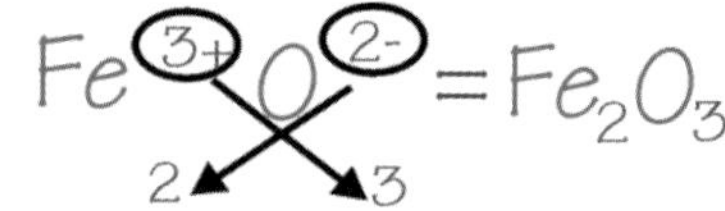

Figure 19.18: *The criss-cross method is a simple way to determine the chemical formula of a compound.*

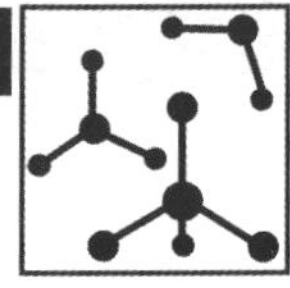

Ionic compounds made of more than two types of atoms

Not all compounds are made of only two types of atoms

Have you ever taken an antacid for an upset stomach? Many antacids contain calcium carbonate, or $CaCO_3$. How many types of atoms does this compound contain? You are right if you said three: calcium, carbon, and oxygen. Some ionic compounds contain polyatomic ions. Polyatomic ions contain more than one type of atom. The prefix *poly* means "many." Table 19.2 lists some common polyatomic ions.

Table 19.2: *Polyatomic ions*

oxidation no.	name	formula
1+	ammonium	NH_4^+
1-	acetate	$C_2H_3O_2^-$
2-	carbonate	CO_3^{2-}
2-	chromate	CrO_4^{2-}
1-	hydrogen carbonate	HCO_3^-
1+	hydronium	H_3O^+
1-	hydroxide	OH^-
1-	nitrate	NO_3^-
2-	peroxide	O_2^{2-}
3-	phosphate	PO_4^{3-}
2-	sulfate	SO_4^{2-}
2-	sulfite	SO_3^{2-}

The positive ion is Ca^{2+}

This is a *monoatomic* ion.

You can determine its oxidation number by looking at the periodic table.

The negative ion is CO_3^{2-}

This is a *polyatomic* ion.

You can determine its oxidation number by looking at the ion chart (Table 19.2).

Figure 19.19: *Which ions does $CaCO_3$ contain?*

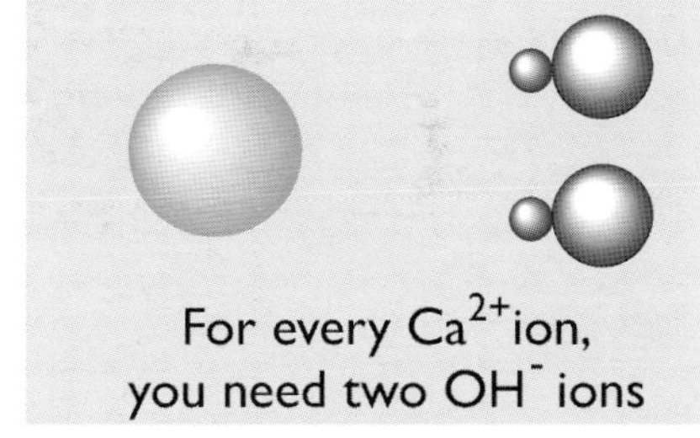
For every Ca^{2+} ion,
you need two OH^- ions

to make a neutral molecule
$Ca(OH)_2$

Figure 19.20: *How to write the chemical formula for calcium hydroxide.*

Rules for writing chemical formulas of ionic compounds that contain polyatomic ions

1 Write the chemical formula and oxidation number of the positive ion. If the positive ion is monoatomic, you can find its oxidation number from the periodic table. If the positive ion is polyatomic, use table 19.2 to find the oxidation number of the polyatomic ion.

2 Write the chemical formula and oxidation number for the negative ion. Again, use the periodic table if the negative ion is monoatomic, or table 19.2 if the negative ion is polyatomic.

3 Add the oxidation numbers of the positive and negative ions. Do they add up to zero? If yes, write the formula for the positive ion first and the negative ion second. Do not include the oxidation numbers in the chemical formula. Be sure to write the subscripts!

4 If the oxidation numbers do not add up to zero, figure out how many of each ion you will need so that the oxidation numbers add up to zero. (**Hint:** *Find the least common multiple between the two oxidation numbers. The number that you have to multiply each oxidation number by to equal the least common multiple tells you how many of each ion you need).*

Example: Writing the chemical formula for *aluminum sulfate*

1. Find the formula and charge of the positive ion.

The positive ion is always the first ion in the name. Where can you find the chemical formula for the aluminum ion? Aluminum is monoatomic and its formula is Al. You can find its oxidation number from the periodic table. Al is in group 13 and contains three valence electrons. When it loses those, its charge becomes +3. Therefore, the oxidation number for Al is 3+.

Chemical formula and oxidation number = Al^{3+}

2. Find the formula and charge of the negative ion.

Sulfate is the negative ion. Where can you find the chemical formula and oxidation number for the sulfate ion? Since sulfate is a polyatomic ion, you must consult an ion chart, unless you can remember the formulas and oxidation numbers for all ions!

Chemical formula and oxidation number = SO_4^{2-}

Writing the chemical formula for aluminum sulfate:

(3+) + (2-) = (1+)
charges do not add up to zero

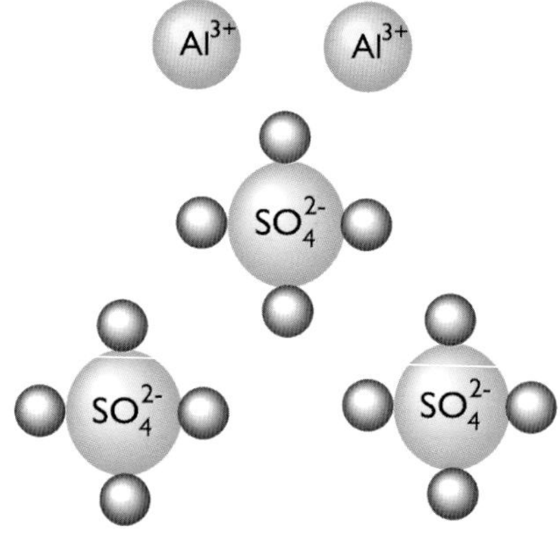

(3+) + (3+) + (2-) + (2-) + (2-) = 0
The combined charges add up to zero

$Al_2(SO_4)_3$

Figure 19.21: *This diagram shows how to determine the chemical formula for aluminum sulfate. How many of each ion does the formula indicate? How many atoms of each element are in one molecule of aluminum sulfate?*

Example, continued

3. Determine how many of each ion are needed so the charges are equal to zero.

The oxidation numbers of (3+) and (2-) add up to (1+), not zero. (3+) + (2-) = (1-)
You need 2 aluminum ions and 3 sulfate ions to make the charges add up to zero.
$(Al^{3+}) \times (2) = (6+)$ $(SO_4^{2-}) \times (3) = (6-)$

4. Write the chemical formula for the compound.

Write the formula, enclosing sulfate in parentheses. Do not change subscripts in the ion.
$Al_2(SO_4)_3$

Example: Name BaF_2

1 The first element is barium.
2 The second element is fluorine.
3 The compound's name is barium fluoride.

Figure 19.22: *Example: Naming a binary compound.*

How do you name ionic compounds?

Compounds with only monoatomic ions

Naming compounds with only monoatomic ions is very simple if you follow these rules:

1	Write the name of the first element in the compound.
2	Write the root name of the second element. For example, ***chlor-*** is the root name of ***chlorine***. Simply subtract the *-**ine*** ending.
3	Add the ending -***ide*** to the root name. ***Chlor***- becomes ***chloride***.

Compounds that contain polyatomic ions

To name a compound that contains polyatomic ions, follow these steps.

1	Write the name of the positive ion first. Use the periodic table or an ion chart to find its name.
2	Write the name of the negative ion second. Use the periodic table or an ion chart to find its name.

1	The positive ion, Mg^{2+}, is **magnesium**.
2	The negative ion, CO_3^{2-}, is **carbonate**.
3	The name of the compound is **magnesium carbonate**.

Figure 19.23: *How to name a compound with the chemical formula $MgCO_3$.*

Covalent compounds

Compounds that are formed through covalent bonds (shared electrons) are called covalent compounds. Covalent compounds are sometimes referred to as *molecular compounds* because they are sometimes made of many smaller molecules, chemically bonded.

Naming covalent compounds

Covalent compounds that are made of more than two types of elements have their own special naming system that you will learn about in more advanced chemistry courses. Naming covalent compounds that consist of only two elements, often called binary compounds, is fairly straightforward. This naming is very similar to the methods used in naming ionic compounds that contain only two elements described on page 336. However, in this case, the *number* of each type of atom is specified in the name of the compound. Figure 19.24 shows how to name a binary covalent compound.

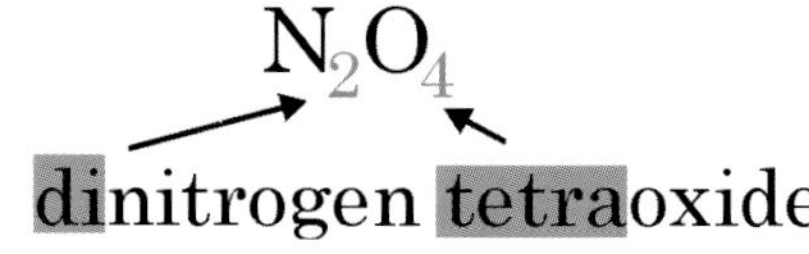

Figure 19.24: *To name a binary covalent compound, specify the number of each type of atom using a Greek prefix. The ending of the name of the second element in the compound is modified by adding the suffix -ide.*

The Greek prefixes in figure 19.24 are used in naming binary covalent compounds. If the molecule contains only one atom of the first element, the prefix *mono-* is not used. It is used in the name of the second element in the compound as in the example below:

CO
carbon monoxide

CO_2
carbon dioxide

prefix	meaning
mono-	1
di-	2
tri-	3
tetra-	4
penta-	5
hexa-	6
hepta-	7
octa-	8
nona-	9

Figure 19.25: *Greek prefixes used in naming binary covalent compounds.*

Empirical and molecular formulas

There are two ways to write chemical formulas

The simplest whole-number ratios by which elements combine are written in a form called the empirical formula. The actual number of atoms of each element in the compound is written in a form called the molecular formula. For some compounds, the empirical and molecular formula is the same as is the case with water, H_2O. A molecule of the sugar glucose has a molecular formula of $C_6H_{12}O_6$. To find the empirical formula of glucose, calculate the simplest whole number ratio of the atoms. The empirical formula for glucose is CH_2O.

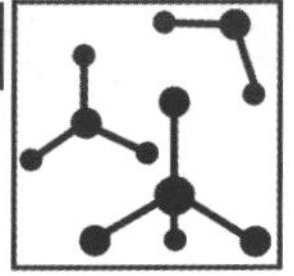

19.3 Comparing Molecules

If you have ever bought paper, you know that it is sometimes sold in a package of 500 sheets called a *ream*. Do you think someone in a factory counts individual sheets of paper and packages them for sale? Instead of counting individual sheets, the paper is packaged according to *mass*. Knowing the mass of 500 sheets of paper allows the paper to be packaged quickly and efficiently by machines. If the machines that make the paper suddenly started making sheets that were twice as heavy, what would happen to the number of sheets in a package? "Counting" by mass is a useful way to deal with large numbers of objects that are uniform in size—like atoms in an element or molecules in a compound. In this section, you will learn how to quantify atoms and molecules using mass.

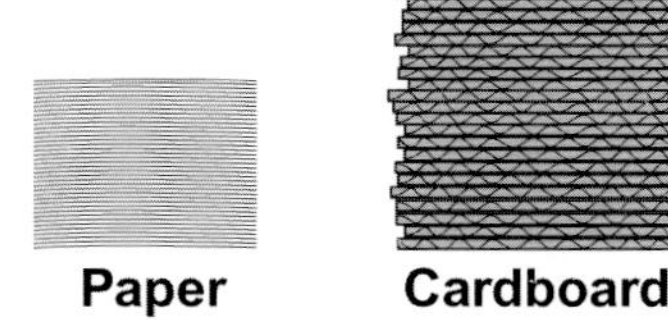

Figure 19.26: *Do 500 sheets of paper have the same mass as 500 sheets of cardboard?*

How do the masses of different molecules compare?

Comparing two different molecules Does a molecule of *water* (H_2O) have the same mass as a molecule of *calcium carbonate* ($CaCO_3$)? Figure 19.27 shows the molecules' comparative sizes. This question seems difficult to answer at first because molecules are so small that you cannot see them. However, you *can* use what you have learned so far to answer the question. You know that atoms of different elements have different *atomic masses*. You also know that molecules are made of different numbers and types of atoms. Based on this knowledge, you can logically conclude that a molecule of water would have a *different* mass than a molecule of calcium carbonate. You can also conclude that 10 grams of water would have a different *number* of molecules from 10 grams of calcium carbonate.

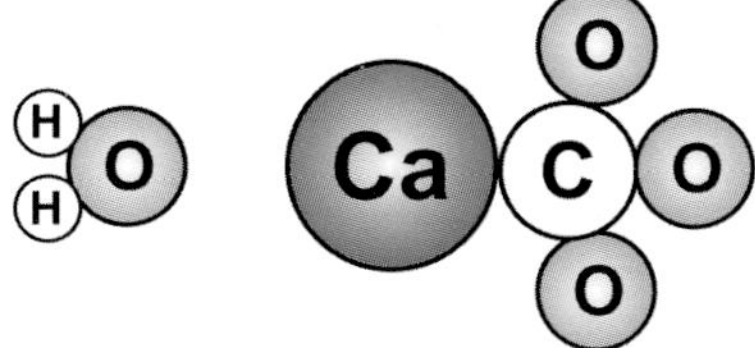

Figure 19.27: *Do you think that a molecule of water has the same mass as a molecule of calcium carbonate?*

Atomic mass units All atoms are assigned a unit of relative mass known as the *atomic mass unit,* or amu. Atomic mass units allow us to compare quantities of matter even though we can't see the molecules and atoms that we want to count or measure.

How is atomic mass determined? Carbon atoms are used as a standard for determining the atomic mass units for the other elements on the periodic table. One carbon atom is equivalent to 12.01 atomic mass units. Because one hydrogen atom is about 1/12 the mass of one carbon atom (figure 19.28), it is represented as having 1.01 atomic mass units. The actual mass of one atomic mass unit is 1.6606×10^{-24} grams—a very small amount!

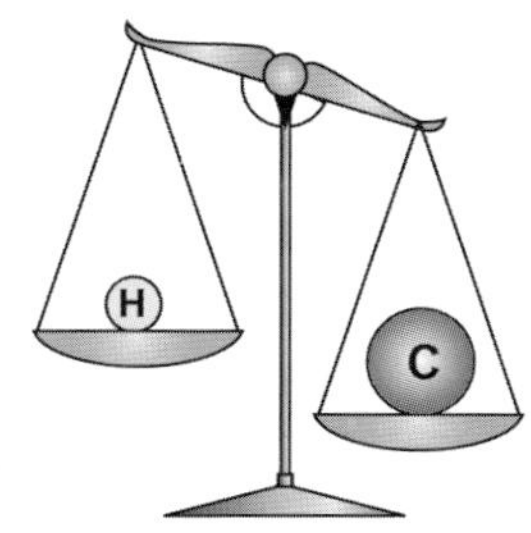

Figure 19.28: *One hydrogen atom is 1/12th the mass of one carbon atom.*

Different objects can be compared by using relative mass

We can use an analogy to explain how the concept of relative mass can be used. Let's say that we have the same number of gumdrops and jawbreakers, and that we will use the variable "x" to represent this number. The sample of x gumdrops has a mass of 100 grams, and the sample of x jawbreakers has a mass of 400 grams. This means that an individual gumdrop has a mass that is 1/4, or 25 percent of, the mass of a jawbreaker. Twenty-five percent can be represented by the number 0.25. This number represents the relative mass of a gumdrop compared with a jawbreaker. Let's call the jawbreaker unit of mass a jmu, for "jawbreaker mass unit." Now, if a single jawbreaker has a mass of 1.0 jmu, then a gumdrop would have a mass of 0.25 jmu. How many jawbreaker mass units would x number of candy bars be if they weighed 800 grams? They would have a mass of 2 jmu.

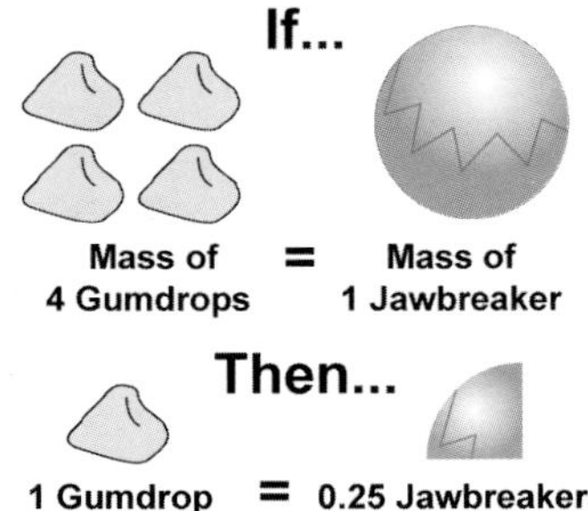

Figure 19.29: *If a single jawbreaker has a mass of 1 jmu (jawbreaker mass unit), what would the mass of 1 gumbdrop be in jmu?*

What does a chemical formula tell you?

Chemical formulas

A chemical formula for a compound gives you three useful pieces of information. First, it tells you which types of atoms and how many of each are present in a compound. Second, it lets you know if polyatomic ions are present. Remember that polyatomic ions are distinct groups of atoms with a collective oxidation number. For example, NO_3 is a polyatomic ion called nitrate with an oxidation number of 1-. As you practice writing chemical formulas, you will start to recognize these ions.

What is formula mass?

Third, a chemical formula allows you to calculate the mass of one molecule of the compound *relative* to the mass of other compounds. Formula mass, like atomic mass, is a way to compare the masses of molecules of different compounds. The formula mass of a compound is determined by adding up the atomic mass units of all of the atoms in the compound as shown in figure 19.30.

Figuring formula mass

The formula for water is H_2O. This means that there are two hydrogen atoms for every one of oxygen in a molecule of water. Using the periodic table, you can see that the atomic mass of hydrogen is 1.007 amu. For our purposes, we will round all atomic masses to the hundredths place. Using 1.01 amu for hydrogen, we can multiply this number by the number of atoms present to determine atomic mass of hydrogen in a water molecule. The atomic mass of oxygen, rounded off, is 16.00. Using this information, the formula mass for water is calculated.

$LiNO_3$

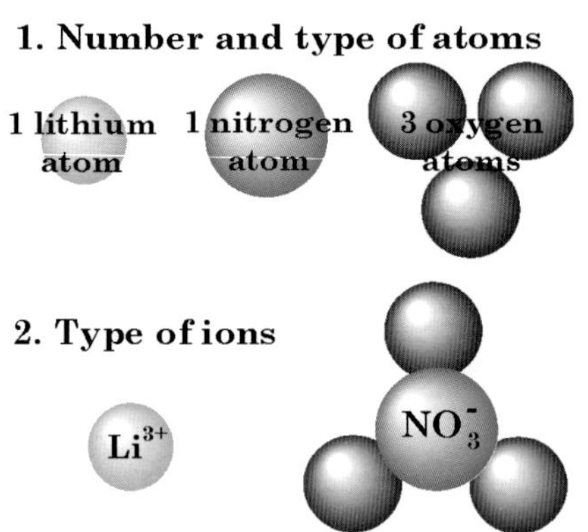

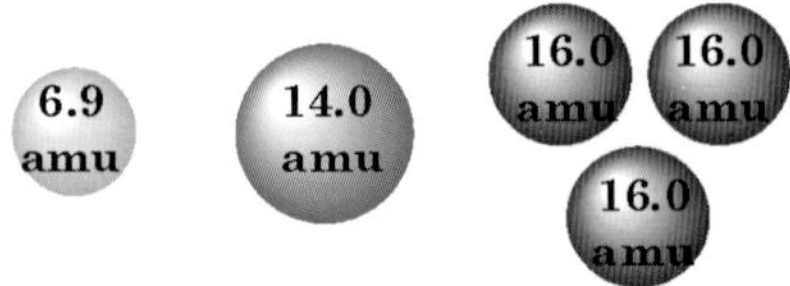

(6.9) + (14.0) + (3 x 16.0) = 68.9 amu

Figure 19.30: *What does a chemical formula tell you?*

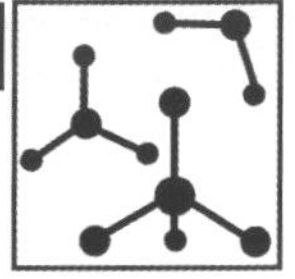

How do we make atomic mass units useful to work with?

The formula mass of H_2O is 18.02 amu

18.02 amu = 1 molecule of H_2O

18.02 grams = 6.02 x 10^{23} molecules of H_2O

Figure 19.31: *The relationship between formula mass, atomic mass units, and grams.*

Atomic mass units and grams

Working with atomic mass units would be very difficult because each atomic mass unit has a mass of 1/12th the mass of a carbon atom. In order to make atomic mass units useful for conducting, using, and evaluating chemical reactions, it would be convenient to set the value of one amu to equal one gram. One gram is, after all, an amount of matter that we can see! For example, one paper clip has a mass of about 2.5 grams.

How do you relate molecules, atomic mass units, and grams?

If we say one water molecule is equal to 18.02 amu, does it make sense to say that one water molecule is equal to 18.02 grams? No, of course not! For this to make sense, we need to come up with a *number* of molecules or atoms that is easy to work with. From here forward, we will say that 18.02 grams of water contains Avogadro's number of molecules. This number is 6.02 x 10^{23}—a very, very large number of molecules! Look at the relationships in figure 19.31 to help you understand the Avogadro number.

Avogadro's number

The Avogadro number is the number of atoms in the atomic mass of an element or the number of molecules in the formula mass of a compound when these masses are expressed in grams. One set of 6.02 x 10^{23} atoms or molecules is also referred to as a mole of that substance. The term mole is used to talk about a number of atoms or molecules just like the term *dozen* is used to talk about quantities of eggs, doughnuts, or cans of soda.

The number, 6.02 x 10^{23}, was named in honor of Count Amedeo Avogadro (1776 - 1856), an Italian chemist and physicist who first thought of the concept of the molecule. A German physicist actually discovered the Avogadro number nine years after Avogadro's death.

Comparing different compounds

If 6.02 x 10^{23} water molecules has a mass of 18.02 grams, how much does the same number of molecules of calcium carbonate weigh in grams? If we calculate the mass of the same number of molecules of each substance, we can compare the relative mass of each molecule. An example of how to calculate the formula mass of a compound is provided on the next page.

Science Facts: How large is Avogadro's number?

Imagine that every person on Earth was involved in counting the Avogadro number of atoms. How long do you think it would take? If all 6 billion people counted 3 atoms per second, it would take 1 million years to count 6.02 x 10^{23} atoms!

Example: Calculating the formula mass of a compound

What is the formula mass of calcium carbonate to the nearest hundredth?

1. Write the chemical formula for the compound.

calcium: Ca^{2+} carbonate: CO_3^{2-}

chemical formula: $CaCO_3$

2. List the atoms, number of each atom, and atomic mass of each atom.

atom	number	atomic mass	total mass (number x atomic mass)
Ca	1	40.08	40.08
C	1	12.01	12.01
O	3	16.00	48.00

3. Add up the values for each type of atom to calculate the formula mass.

40.08 + 12.01 + 48.00 = 100.09 amu

The formula mass of calcium carbonate is 100.09 amu.

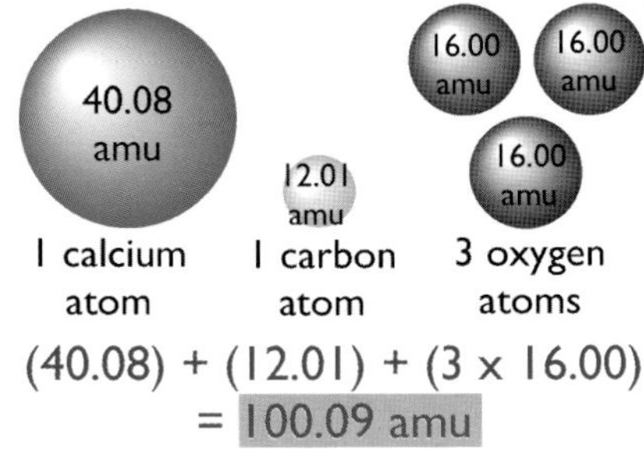

Figure 19.32: *Calculating the formula mass of calcium carbonate.*

How do you compare samples of substances?

The Avogadro number of calcium carbonate molecules would have a mass of 100.09 grams. In other words, if you used a balance to weigh 100.09 grams of calcium carbonate, there would be 6.02 x 10^{23} molecules of calcium carbonate in the sample. Likewise, if you used a balance to weigh 18.02 grams of water, there would be 6.02 x 10^{23} molecules of water in the weighed sample.

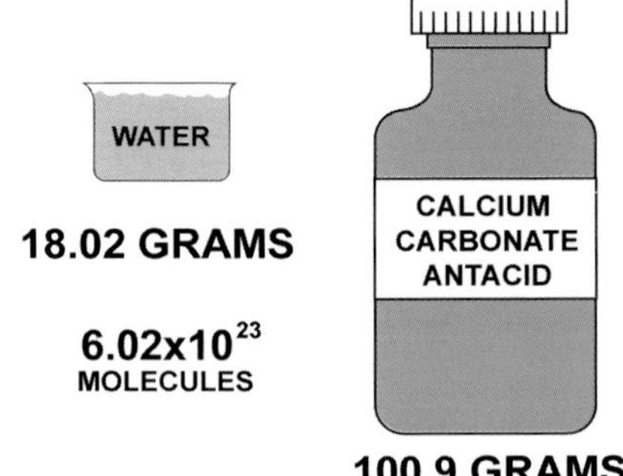

Figure 19.33: *100.09 g of $CaCO_3$ contains the same number of molecules as 18.02 g of H_2O.*

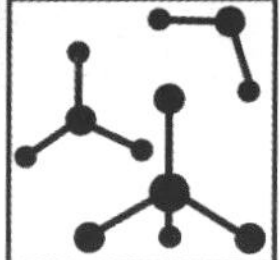

Consumer Chemistry: Hydrates and the Chemical Formulas

Hydrates are ionic compounds that contain precise numbers of water molecules

Have you ever bought a product that contained in the packaging a packet that was labeled: "Silica gel — do not eat"? These packets are often found inside boxes containing electronics equipment—like a DVD player or a stereo receiver. They are found inside shoeboxes, too. What is the purpose of these packets?

The presence of moisture in the packaging of certain products can be a problem. Manufacturers added packets of silica gel to absorb any such water. Ionic compounds like silicon oxide have the ability to incorporate water molecules as part of their structure. Water molecules become chemically bonded to their ions. A hydrate is a compound that has water molecules chemically bonded to its ions. Different compounds can absorb different numbers of molecules, as table 19.3 shows.

Table 19.3: ***Common hydrates***

Name	Formula
Silicon oxide monohydrate	$SiO_2 \cdot H_2O$
Barium chloride dihydrate	$BaCl_2 \cdot 2H_2O$
Calcium nitrate tetrahydrate	$Ca(NO_3)_2 \cdot 4H_2O$
Cobalt chloride hexahydrate	$CoCl_2 \cdot 6H_2O$
Magnesium sulfate heptahydrate	$MgSO_4 \cdot 7H_2O$
Iron (III) nitrate nonahydrate	$Fe(NO_3)_3 \cdot 9H_2O$

prefix	meaning
mono-	1
di-	2
tri-	3
tetra-	4
penta-	5
hexa-	6
hepta-	7
octa-	8
nona-	9

Figure 19.34: *Greek prefixes.*

Note that the chemical formula of a hydrate shows the ionic compound times a certain number of water molecules. This denotes a ratio of the number of molecules of water absorbed for each molecule of the compound. Note also that the name for each compound is followed by a Greek prefix indicating the number of water molecules and the word "hydrate." Figure 19.34 lists some Greek prefixes and their meanings.

Getting rid of the water molecules

You can remove the water molecules from a hydrate by heating it. When all the water leaves the hydrate through evaporation, it is anhydrous, a term that means "without water." Now that you know why packets of silica gel are included with some products, how could you *reuse* a packet of silica gel? How would you know when the packet of silica gel was anhydrous?

How do you calculate the formula mass of a hydrate?

It's easy to calculate the formula mass of a hydrate. First, calculate the formula mass of the ionic compound, then add the formula mass of water times as many molecules of water as are present. The example below shows you how to do this step by step.

Example: Calculating the formula mass of a hydrate

What is the formula mass of $BaCl_2 \times 2H_2O$?

1. Calculate the formula mass of the ionic compound

The ionic compound is $BaCl_2$. To calculate its formula mass:

1 Ba atom × 137.30 amu = 137.30 amu

2 Cl atoms × 35.45 amu = 70.90 amu

137.30 amu + 70.90 amu = 208.20 amu

2. Calculate formula mass of the water molecules

The formula mass for water is:

2 H atoms × 1.01 = 2.02 amu

1 O atom × 16.00 = 16.00 amu

2.02 + 16.00 = 18.02 amu

There are 2 molecules of water in the hydrate. The total formula mass is:

2 molecules H_2O × 18.02 = 36.04 amu

3. Calculate the formula mass of the hydrate

$BaCl_2 \times 2H_2O$ = 208.20+ 36.04 = 244.24 amu

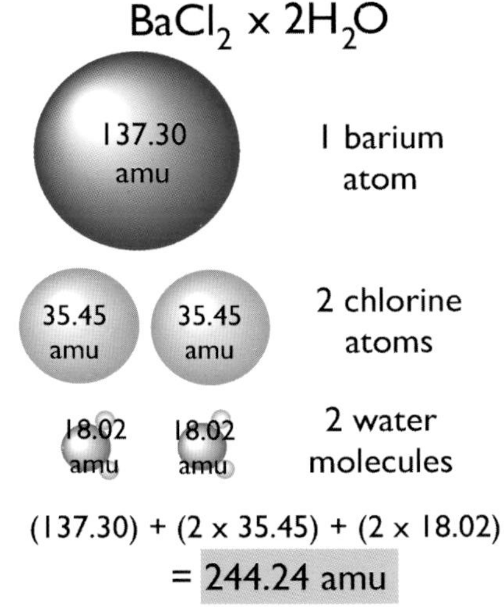

Figure 19.35: *Calculating the formula mass of a hydrate.*

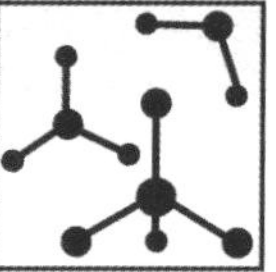

Chapter 19 Review

Vocabulary review

Match the following terms with the correct definition. There is one definition extra in the list that will not match any term.

Set One

1. covalent bond
2. ionic bond
3. octet rule
4. valence electrons

a. The electrons involved in chemical bonding
b. Most atoms need eight valence electrons to be stable
c. A bond between atoms in which electrons are lost or gained
d. A number that represents the number of electrons that are lost or gained in bonding
e. A bond between atoms in which electrons are shared

Set Two

1. Binary compound
2. Monoatomic ion
3. Oxidation number
4. Polyatomic ion

a. An ion like Na+, K+, or Cl-
b. Electrons that are involved in bonding
c. An ion like CO_3^{2-} or OH^-
d. A number that indicates how many electrons will be gained or lost during bonding
e. A molecule composed of two monatomic ions

Concept review

1. Why do atoms tend to combine with other atoms instead of existing as single atoms?
2. Why are atoms in Group 18 considered to be chemically stable?
3. How can you determine the number of valence electrons by looking at the periodic table?
4. What conditions are met when an atom is chemically stable?
5. What is the major difference between ionic and covalent bonds?
6. Provide one general rule for predicting whether or not a bond will be ionic. (Hint: use the periodic table in your rule.)
7. What are polymers? Give an example of a natural polymer and a synthetic polymer.
8. What is an oxidation number? How can you determine an element's oxidation number by looking at the periodic table?
9. In a chemical formula, what do subscripts tell you?
10. What is the relationship between the formula mass of a compound, the Avogadro number of molecules of that compound, and the mass in grams of the compound?

Problems

1. Fill in the table below.

Element	Atomic number	Valence electrons	Lewis dot diagram
Fluorine			
Oxygen			
Phosphorus			
Carbon			
Beryllium			
Nitrogen			
Sulfur			
Neon			
Silicon			

2. Identify which of the following bonds are ionic or covalent and justify your reasoning.
   a. C-C
   b. Na-Br
   c. C-N
   d. C-O
   e. Ca-Cl

3. Fill in the table below.

Element	Number of valence electrons	Electrons gained or lost during ionization	Oxidation number
Potassium			
Aluminum			
Phosphorus			
Krypton			

4. Which group number on the periodic table is represented by each description?
   a. These atoms form compounds with ions that have an oxidation number of 1^-.
   b. The oxidation state of the atoms in this group is 3^-.
   c. Atoms in this group have four valence electrons in the outermost energy level. The atoms in this group form compounds with ions like H^+, Na^+ and Li^+.
   d. If these ions combined with Al^{3+}, you would need three of them and two aluminum ions in the formula.
   e. Atoms in this group lose two electrons during ionization.

5. Which of the following would be a correct chemical formula for a molecule of N^{3-} and H^+?
   a. HNO_3
   b. H_3N_6
   c. NH_3
   d. NH

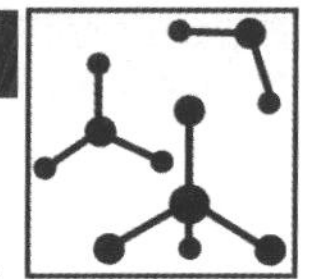

6. What is the simplest ratio of carbon to hydrogen to oxygen in a molecule of glucose ($C_6H_{12}O_6$)?
   a. 1:2:1
   b. 6:12:6
   c. 2:4:2
   d. 6:2:6

7. What is the correct name for the compound $NaHCO_3$?
   a. sodium carbonide
   b. sodium hydrogen carbonate
   c. sodium hydrogen carboxide
   d. bicarbonate

8. Which of the following ion pairs would combine in a 1:2 ratio?
   a. NH^{4+} and F^-
   b. Be^{2+} and Cl^-
   c. sodium and hydroxide
   d. hydrogen and phosphate

9. For each of the compounds below, (1)state whether it is an empirical or molecular formula; and (2)if it is a molecular formula, write the empirical formula.
   a. CH_2O
   b. $(CH_2)_2(OH)_2$
   c. $C_7H_5NO_3S$
   d. $C_{10}H_8O_4$

10. Name each of the following binary covalent compounds.
    a. N_4O_6
    b. SiO_2
    c. S_2F_{10}
    d. $SbCl_5$

11. Write the chemical formula for the following compounds. Consult Table 19.2, "Polyatomic ions," on page 337 when needed.
    a. Sodium acetate
    b. Aluminum hydroxide
    c. Magnesium sulfate
    d. Ammonium nitrate
    e. Calcium fluoride

12. Calculate the formula mass for the following household compounds. Use the periodic table on the inside back cover.
    a. Lye drain cleaner, NaOH
    b. Epsom salts, $MgSO_4$
    c. Aspirin, $C_9H_8O_4$
    d. Plant fertilizer, $Ca(H_2PO_4)_2$
    e. Dampness absorber, $CaCl_2 \cdot 6H_2O$

13. Give the scientific name of compounds (a), (b), and (e) in question 10. Consult Table 19.2 on page 337.

Applying your knowledge

1. Many of the atoms on the periodic table have more than one oxidation number. You can figure out the oxidation number for these elements if you know at least one of the oxidation numbers in the compound. You only need to figure out what the oxidation number would be to make the molecule neutrally charged. Fill in the oxidation numbers for each of the following molecules.

Chemical formula of compound	Oxidation number for positive ion	Oxidation number for negative ion
SiO_2		2-
PBr_3		1-
$FeCl_3$		1-
CuF_2		1-
N_2O_3		2^-
P_2O_5		2^-

2. Suppose you are working in the lab with the following compounds: NaCl and Al_2O_3.
   a. Would the same number of molecules of each compound have the same mass? Explain your reasoning.
   b. Explain how you would measure out Avogadro's number of molecules (6.02×10^{23}) of each compound.
   c. Why is there a difference in the mass of the exact same number of molecules of each compound?

3. Find out about recycling plastics in your community. Prepare a pamphlet or bulletin board for your school that provides information on how to recycle plastics. The pamphlet or bulletin board should include practical information about recycling plastics including: how to get involved in community organizations, and what types of plastics are recycled. If your school does not recycle plastics, see if you can form a committee to develop and implement a plan.

4. Examine the household chemicals that are used in your own home. Make a list of the products your family uses, the names of the chemicals in each product and the hazards associated with each chemical. Research environmentally friendly alternatives to some of the products your family uses and prepare a brief presentation for your class.

UNIT 7

Changes in Matter

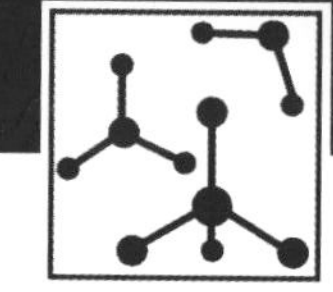

Chapter 20

Chemical Reactions

Introduction to Chapter 20

When you drive a car, the engine is using oxygen and gasoline to produce carbon dioxide and water vapor. This is a chemical reaction that you depend upon to go places. In this chapter, you will learn how to determine what happens during a chemical reaction.

Investigations for Chapter 20

20.1	**Chemical Changes**	*What is the evidence that a chemical change has occurred?*

You will make a list of the evidence for chemical change by carefully observing a series of chemical reactions.

20.2	**Chemical Equations**	*How do you balance chemical equations?*

You will use the Periodic Table Tiles to learn how to balance chemical equations so that the number and type of atoms that react balance with the number and type of atoms that are produced in a reaction.

20.3	**Conservation of Mass**	*How can you prove that mass is conserved in a chemical reaction?*

You will design your own experiment to prove that what you put into a reaction can be accounted for in the products that are produced.

20.4	**Using Equations as Recipes**	*How can you predict the amount of product in a reaction?*

You will discover an important mathematical relationship that will allow you to predict the amount of product based on the amount of one of the reactants.

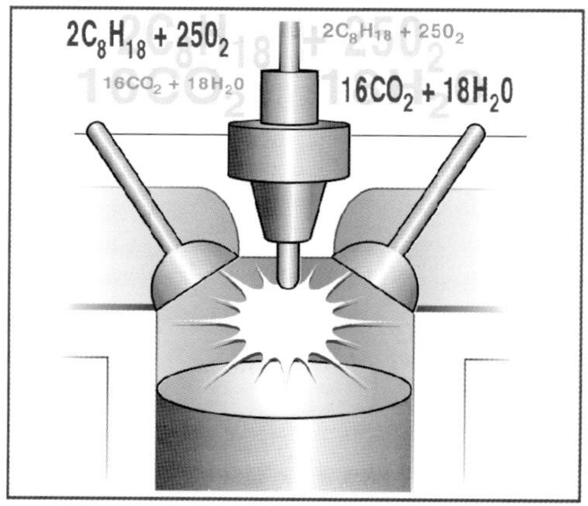

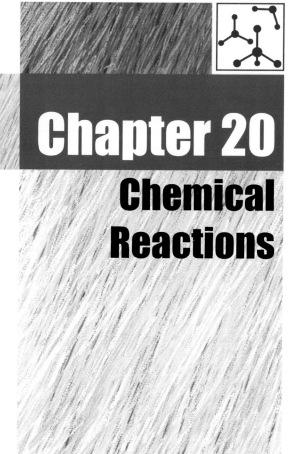

Learning Goals

In this chapter, you will:

- ✔ Distinguish between physical and chemical changes in matter using examples from everyday life.
- ✔ Write and balance chemical equations.
- ✔ Investigate and identify the law of conservation of mass.
- ✔ Use chemical equations to predict the amount of product that will be produced in a reaction.
- ✔ Design an experiment to prove conservation of mass.
- ✔ Identify the mathematical relationship between the mass in grams of reactants and products, the coefficients in a balanced equation, and the formula masses of the reactants and products.
- ✔ Identify economic and environmental reasons for recycling tires.

Vocabulary

balance	coefficient	limiting reactant	reactant
chemical change	conservation of atom	percent yield	
chemical equation	excess reactant	physical change	
chemical reaction	hydrochloric acid	product	

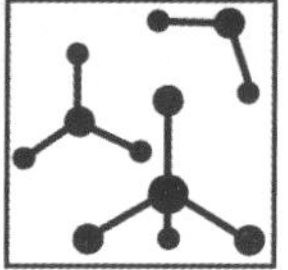

20.1 Chemical Changes

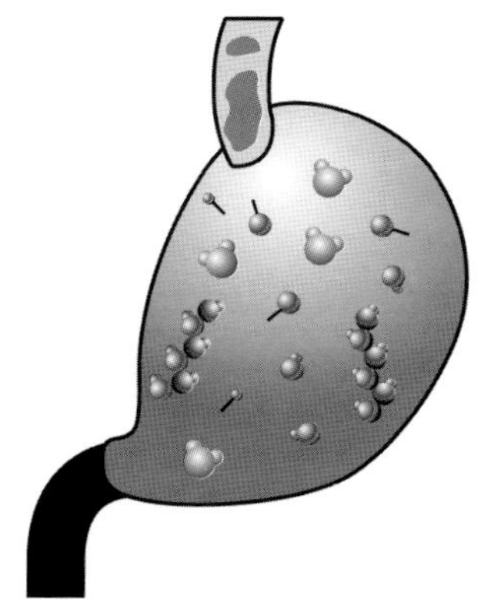

Figure 20.1: *The process of digestion involves both physical and chemical changes to the food. In the stomach, acids are produced which cause chemical changes in the foods you eat.*

Have you ever tried to watch rust forming on a car? You have probably noticed a patch of rust getting larger as weeks or months pass, but chances are, you did not actually *see* the rust form. Can you watch an ice cube melt? Yes, but this process happens much faster than a car rusts. Changes in matter are occurring all around you, all of the time. There are different types of changes in matter that happen. The rusting of a car is much different from the melting of ice. We can classify changes in matter as either chemical changes or physical changes.

Chemical vs. Physical Change

You are what you eat

"You are what you eat." You have heard this many times, but have you ever thought about what it means? How does the food you eat become part of your body? How does the food you eat give you energy? The answer, of course, is that the food you eat goes through many *changes*—from the minute you put it in your mouth, until you eliminate waste. The process of breaking food down so that your body can use it is called *digestion*. It involves many different changes to the food, both physical changes and chemical changes.

Physical changes

If you take a bite out of an apple, have you changed the chemical composition of the apple? Of course not. You have only removed a small piece of the apple. Once the piece of apple is in your mouth, you begin to chew it. Chewing does not alter the chemical composition of the apple either. It only breaks the apple into smaller pieces so that you can swallow it easily. Chewing causes a physical change in the apple. A *physical change* is a change that affects only the physical properties of a substance. Those properties include size, shape, and state. For example, you can change the physical properties of ice by crushing it or by simply letting it melt. The only difference between solid water (ice) and liquid water is the amount of energy involved in each state. Water vapor is the most energetic form of water. Ice, liquid water, and water vapor all have the exact same chemical composition.

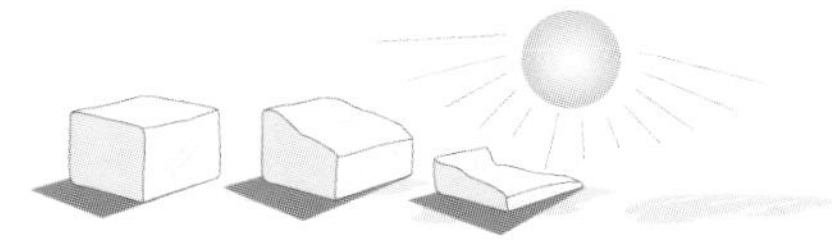

Figure 20.2: *Physical changes affect only the physical properties of a substance.*

Chemical changes

Is the function of chewing only to make the pieces of apple smaller so that you can swallow them? In fact, another function of chewing is to create lots of available surface area for special chemicals called *enzymes* to cause chemical changes in the apple. When you begin chewing, glands in your mouth produce *saliva*. An enzyme in your saliva called *amylase* immediately gets to work to break down complex carbohydrate molecules into simpler carbohydrate molecules by breaking bonds. This causes a chemical change in the apple, altering its chemical composition. Your body actually begins the process of digestion in your mouth. After you swallow the bite of apple, it travels to the next digestion site, the stomach. There, more enzymes and acid further break down the food you have swallowed. The whole process of digestion is very dependent upon chemical changes. Although physical changes are necessary to break any food into bits, chemical changes help release important energy and nutrients from the food you consume. Chemical changes are the result of **chemical reactions**, that is, the breaking of bonds in one or more substances, and the reforming of new bonds to create new substances.

Try this...
Place a saltine cracker in your mouth. Hold it there for about 10 minutes. Then, how does it taste? Is this evidence of a chemical or physical change?

How do you know when a chemical change has occurred?

You know a chemical change has occurred when one or more starting substances are mixed and you get products that appear to be different from those starting substances. Atoms are rearranged when chemical changes occur. Additionally, when you see any evidence that energy has been released or absorbed, a chemical change has probably occurred. You can use your powers of observation to determine that a chemical change has taken place. However, sometimes you need to make sure that the chemical properties of the new substances are different from the ones you started with. If you had never seen ice or water before, would you know that they were the same thing?

Figure 20.3: *When your body "burns" food for energy, carbon dioxide and water are released. This process is called respiration. You need oxygen for this process to occur. Where do the carbon dioxide and water come from?*

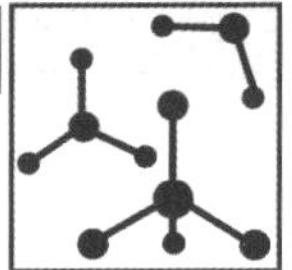

Environmental Issue: Recycling tires

How many tires are thrown away each year?

The next time you travel in a car, think about the tires you are riding on. Did you know that more than 275 million discarded tires are dumped annually into landfills in the United States? Around the world, over 5 million tires are thrown away each day! As the number of cars on the road increases each year, so do the number of tires discarded. For many years, the only alternatives were to throw used tires into landfills, or burn them, which caused air pollution. Today, scientists and engineers are coming up with ways to put a new spin on the discarding of tires. Reusing and recycling scrap tires requires the use of both physical and chemical changes.

What are tires made of?

A typical automobile tire is about 65 percent rubber, 25 percent steel, and 10 percent fiber (plastic). The rubber found in tires is *vulcanized*, or chemically treated to increase the number of sulfur bonds. While this process produces a rigid, strong, and puncture-resistant substance, it also makes it harder to *chemically* break the rubber down into useful substances. Because of this combination of materials, some specialists say that reclaiming the original components from discarded tires is like trying to recycle a cake back to its original ingredients.

How are tires recycled?

Tires can be recycled in two ways: (1) processing them, and (2) using them whole. Whole tire recycling involves using the old tire as is for other purposes, such as landscape borders, playground structures, bumpers, and highway crash barriers. Processing tires for recycling involves chopping them up into pieces, and then separating the rubber and fiber from the steel. While this initial processing is only a *physical change* to the materials found in a tire, it is very challenging because of the way tire manufacturers put the materials together.

An expensive, but very effective way to separate the rubber, fiber, and steel involves cooling the small pieces of tire with liquid nitrogen. This releases the steel, rubber, and fiber pieces from sticking to each other. Next, magnets are used to take out the steel. The pieces of rubber can then be separated from the fiber using density techniques.

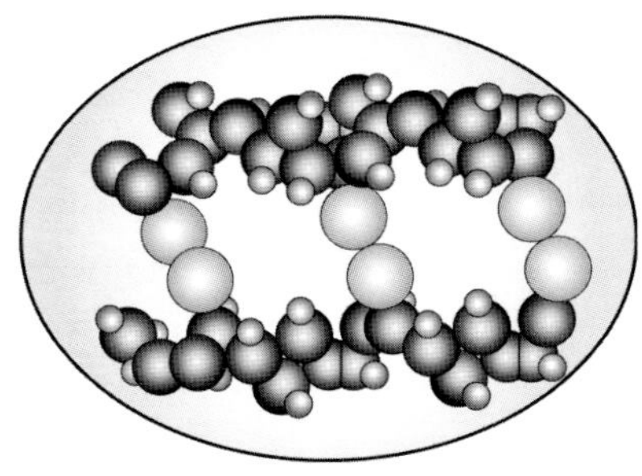

Figure 20.4: *Vulcanized rubber is chemically treated to increase the number of sulfur bonds. This makes the tire harder and more puncture-resistant.*

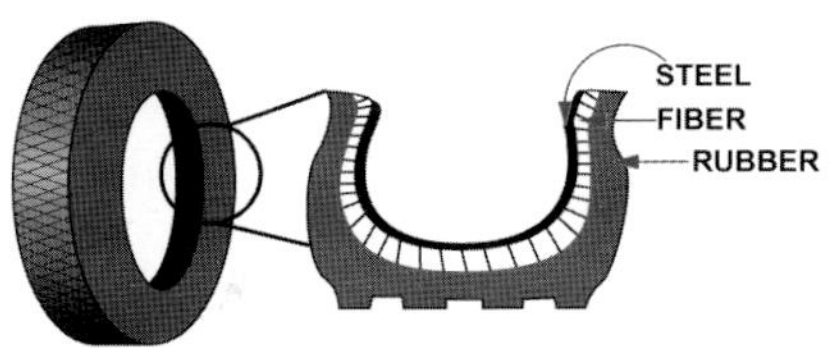

Figure 20.5: *The components of a typical radial tire.*

Use your head...

Based on what you learned in the last unit, can you explain how to separate rubber and fiber using the physical property of density?

Uses for scrap rubber and steel

The small particles of rubber can be used immediately as a substitute for new rubber in products such as footwear, carpet underlay, and waterproofing compounds. It can be mixed with asphalt to make safe and durable road surfaces. In fact, it has been found that adding scrap rubber to the asphalt used to pave roads can significantly decrease braking distances! Asphalt-scrap rubber mixtures are also considered the superior choice for track and field grounds, equestrian tracks, and paved playgrounds.

The steel that is recovered from tires is used to make new steel. In fact, almost everything we make out of steel contains some percentage that is recycled. For nearly as long as steel has been made, recycling has been part of the process.

Recycling 1 ton of steel conserves...
2,500 lbs of iron ore
1,400 lb. of coal
120 lbs of limestone
11 million Btu's of energy

Figure 20.6: *Recycling steel*

Chemically changing rubber

Like plastic, rubber is a polymer. *Polymers* are molecules that consist of long chains of repeating combinations of atoms. Rubber is a polymer that is very difficult to break down—especially vulcanized rubber. Recent advances in technology have created an environmentally friendly process for breaking the carbon-carbon, carbon-sulfur, and sulfur-sulfur bonds in order to produce smaller molecules. These smaller molecules can be used to make liquid and gaseous fuels, ingredients for other polymers, lubricating oils, and a charcoal that can be used to decontaminate water or soil.

A shortage of discarded tires?

Currently, there are so many uses for discarded tires that a better question seems to be, why not recycle *all* of our discarded tires? Perhaps in the near future, instead of an overabundance of discarded tires, there will be a shortage!

For discussion

1 What are the advantages and disadvantages to whole-tire recycling?

2 Describe the physical changes that are used in processing tires for recycling.

3 What are the advantages and disadvantages to chemically changing scrap rubber?

4 How do you think technological advances in tires could present additional challenges to the recycling process?

Exploring further...

- Interview someone from a company that makes asphalt about using scrap rubber from tires.
- Research further about using recycled tires as a fuel source.
- Find out what happens to discarded tires in your community.

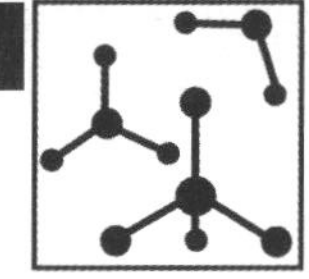

20.2 Chemical Equations

All of the chemical changes you observed in the last Investigation were the result of chemical reactions. A chemical reaction involves a rearrangement of atoms in one or more reactants to form one or more products. All chemical reactions involve the rearrangement of atoms and either use or produce energy. In this section, you will learn how to write "recipes" for such reactions, called chemical equations.

What happens during a chemical reaction?

Did a chemical change take place? In the last Investigation, you observed several chemical reactions. For example, in one of the reactions, you mixed vinegar with baking soda. When you mixed these two substances, you observed a fairly violent bubbling as the baking soda appeared to dissolve into the vinegar. You may have noticed a drop in temperature as the reaction proceeded. These observations provide *evidence* that a chemical change has occurred (figure 20.7).

Proving chemical change In order to prove that a chemical change has occurred, you need to be able to confirm that the chemical and physical properties of one or more of the products are different from those of the reactants. For example, when methane (natural gas) is burned, it reacts with oxygen to form carbon dioxide and water. This is a common reaction used to heat homes, cook food—or heat up chemistry experiments! Upon careful examination, you would conclude that carbon dioxide has different chemical and physical properties from methane.

Methane + Oxygen ⟶ Carbon Dioxide + Water

Reactants	Products
substances that change	substances that are formed

Where does the new substance come from? In ordinary chemical reactions, atoms are rearranged through the breaking and reforming of chemical bonds. In the methane reaction, the bonds between carbon and hydrogen in methane are broken. Carbon reforms a bond with the oxygen to form carbon dioxide, one of the reactants. Hydrogen also forms a bond with additional oxygen atoms to produce water. In addition, heat and light are produced.

Bubbling

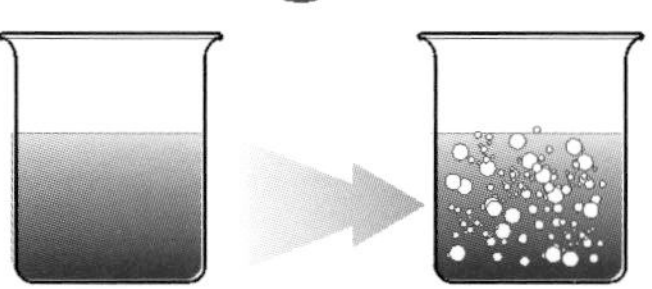

A new gas is forming?

Turns cloudy

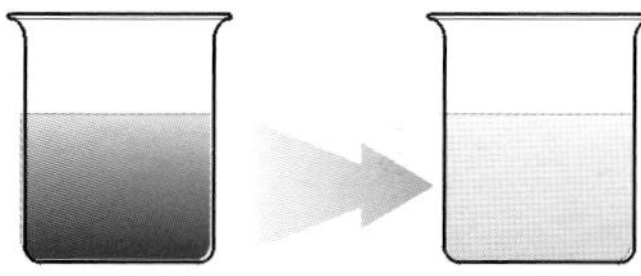

A new solid is forming?

Temperature change

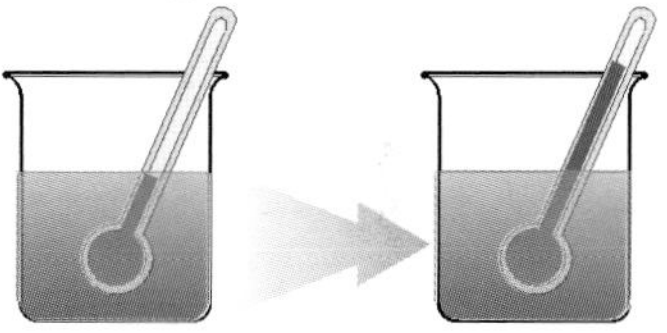

Chemical bonds are changing?

Color change

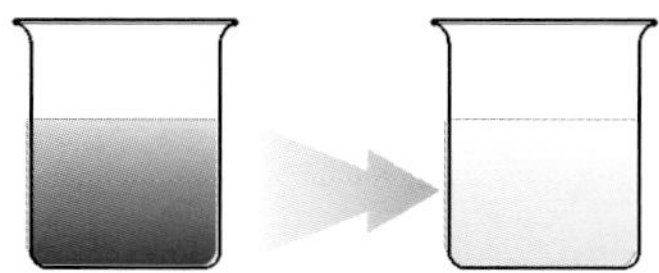

A new substance is forming?

Figure 20.7: *Different kinds of evidence that chemical reactions are occuring.*

How are chemical reactions written?

Chemical reactions as sentences

We could simply write chemical reactions as sentences. For example, we could write the reaction of methane and oxygen as follows:

Methane gas reacts with oxygen gas to produce carbon dioxide and water.

Chemical formulas are more convenient

It is more convenient to use chemical formulas that correspond to the elements and compounds in the reaction. When we use chemical formulas and symbols to represent a reaction instead of using words, it is called a chemical equation.

Remember diatomic molecules?

Do you remember why oxygen is O_2 instead of just O? Recall from the last unit that in nature, most elemental gases do not exist as single atoms (with the exception of the noble gases). Oxygen is called a diatomic molecule, meaning there are two atoms in the molecule. Table 20.1 on page 358 shows some of the elements that exist as diatomic molecules.

Using formulas and symbols, the chemical equation for the reaction of methane with oxygen can be written as:

$$CH_4 + O_2 \longrightarrow CO_2 + H_2O$$

Table 20.1: *Elements that exist as diatomic molecules*

Hydrogen, H_2	Nitrogen, N_2	Oxygen, O_2
Fluorine, F_2	Chlorine, Cl_2	Bromine, Br_2

Chemical equations should show that atoms are conserved in a reaction

The chemical equation above is not completely correct. It does not agree with an important principle in chemistry called conservation of atoms. This principle says that the number of each type of atom on the reactants side of a chemical equation must be equal to the number of each type of atom on the products side of the equation. In other words, you get out of a reaction what you put into it, nothing more, nothing less. If you count the number and type of each atom in the chemical equation above, do they add up on both sides of the equation equally? If you count them carefully, you'll find that the answer is no.

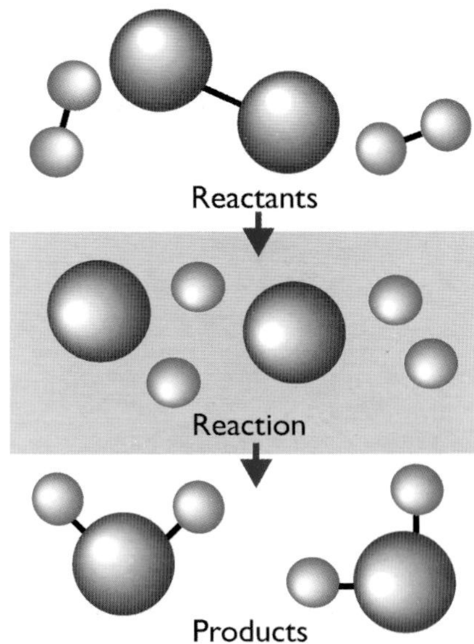

Figure 20.8: *In a chemical reaction, chemical bonds are broken and reformed to make new products.*

:

substance	chemical formula
methane	CH_4
oxygen	O_2
carbon dioxide	CO_2
water	H_2O

Figure 20.9: *Chemical formulas for substances in the methane reaction.*

How do you write a chemical equation that shows conservation of atoms?

Numbers and types of atoms must balance

Since only whole atoms can react—not fractions of an atom—it is necessary to **balance** the number and type of atoms on the reactants and products sides of the equation. Furthermore, by balancing the numbers and types of atoms, you are not allowed to change the chemical composition of any of the substances on the reactants or products sides. To learn about how to balance chemical equations, let's take another look at that methane reaction.

$$CH_4 + O_2 \longrightarrow CO_2 + H_2O$$

The arrow in the chemical equation is read as:

- "to produce" or
- "to yield"

Subscripts below the symbols for elements tell you how many of each type of atom there are in a molecule.

Figure 20.10: *Helpful hints for reading chemical equations.*

Count the number and type of each atom on both sides of the chemical equation

Once again, count the number of each type of atom on both sides of the reaction. The table below summarizes the numbers:

type of atom	total on reactants side	total on products side	balanced?
C	1	1	yes
H	4	2	no
O	2	3	no

When an equation is unbalanced

The chemical equation is not balanced because the number of hydrogen atoms and oxygen atoms are different on both sides of the equation. To make them equal and balance the equation, you must figure out what number to multiply each compound by in order to make the numbers add up. Remember: You cannot change the number of individual atoms in a compound. That would change its chemical formula and you would have a different compound. You can only change the number of molecules of that compound.

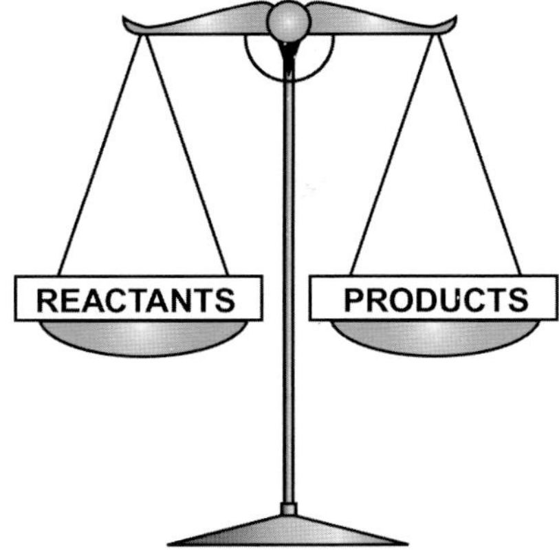

Figure 20.11: *In a chemical equation, the number and type of atoms on both sides of the equation must be equal.*

Balancing equations involves adding coefficients

To change the number of molecules of a compound, you can write a whole number coefficient in front of the chemical formula. When you do this, all of the types of atoms in that formula are multiplied by that number. For example:

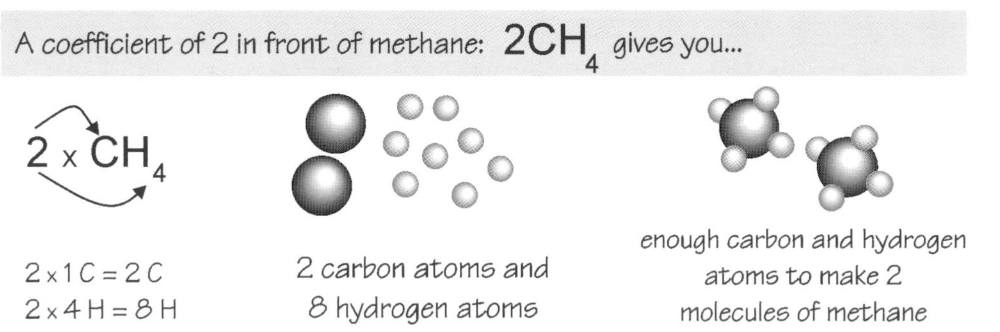

A coefficient of 2 in front of methane: 2CH4 gives you...
2 x CH4
2 x 1 C = 2 C
2 x 4 H = 8 H
2 carbon atoms and
8 hydrogen atoms
enough carbon and hydrogen
atoms to make 2
molecules of methane

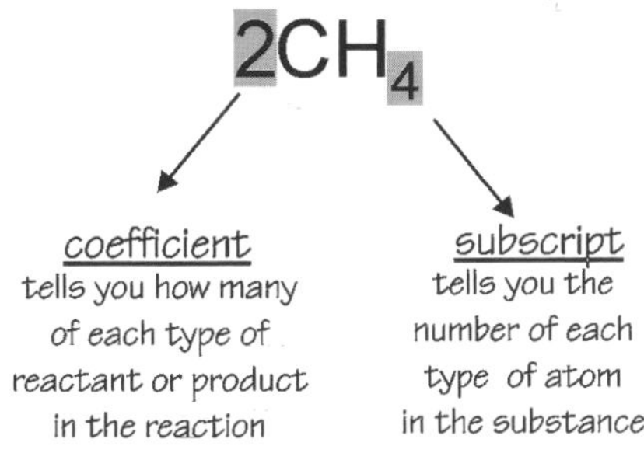

Figure 20.12: *What do coefficients and subscripts mean?*

Multiplying molecules with coefficients

Figuring out where to place coefficients to multiply the numbers of atoms in a chemical formula is largely a process of trial and error. Let's look at the methane reaction after the correct coefficients have been added:

$$CH_4 + 2O_2 \longrightarrow CO_2 + 2H_2O$$

Counting the atoms on both sides again, we see that the equation is balanced.

atom	total on reactants side	total on products side
C	1	1
H	4	2 X 2 = **4**
O	2 X 2 = **4**	2 + (2 X 1) = **4**

How do you read a balanced equation?

The balanced equation above can be read as follows:

One molecule of methane reacts with two molecules of oxygen

to produce

one molecule of carbon dioxide and two molecules of water.

1 Make sure you have written the correct chemical formula for each reactant and product.
2 The subscripts in the chemical formulas of the reactants and products cannot be changed during the process of balancing the equation. Changing the subscripts will change the chemical makeup of the compounds.
3 Numbers called coefficients are placed in front of the formulas to make the number of atoms on each side of the equation equal.

Figure 20.13: *Things to remember when balancing chemical equations.*

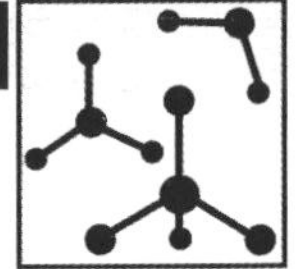

Example: Balancing a common reaction

What happens when you take an antacid?

Hydrochloric acid is a substance your stomach normally produces to help you break down food. Sometimes, if you eat spicy foods or worry excessively about studying chemistry, your stomach produces too much hydrochloric acid and you get acid indigestion. Most people take antacids to relieve this painful condition. Many antacids contain calcium carbonate which neutralizes the hydrochloric acid. The products formed are calcium chloride, carbon dioxide, and water. How do you write and balance the chemical equation for this reaction? The following steps outline this process for you:

1. Write the word form of the equation.

Hydrochloric acid reacts with calcium carbonate to produce calcium chloride, carbon dioxide, and water.

2. Write the chemical equation

Consult an ion chart for some of the chemical formulas. The ion chart on page 337 is useful for solving problems of this type. You need to get the chemical formula for each chemical that appears. The chemical equation for this reaction is:

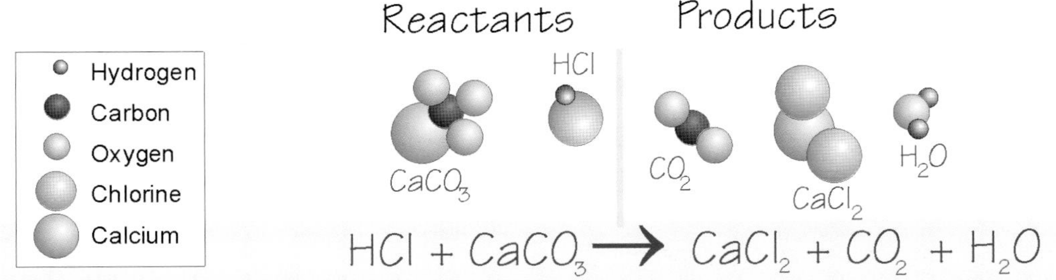

3. Count the number of each type of atom on both sides

What coefficients mean

- A coefficient placed in front of O_2 means that the reaction will require two oxygen molecules for every methane molecule.
- A coefficient placed in front of H_2O means that two molecules of water will be produced for every one molecule of carbon dioxide.
- No coefficient in front of a chemical formula indicates one molecule.

Figure 20.14: *What is a coefficient?*

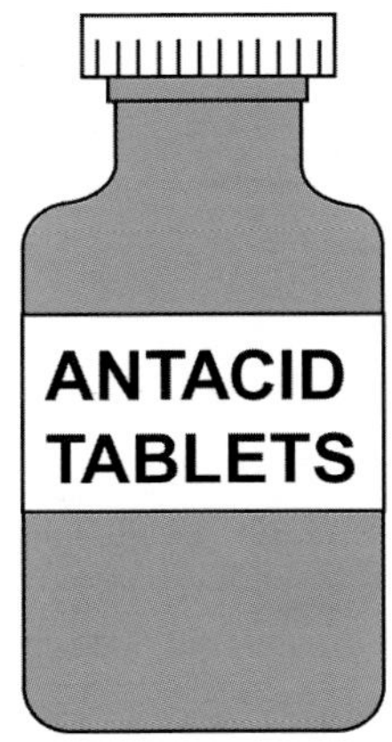

The table below summarizes how many atoms of each type are on the reactants' and products' sides of the chemical equation. Notice that there is an extra hydrogen and an extra chlorine on the products' side. These two extra atoms have to come from somewhere. We need to add something to the reactants that will give us an extra chlorine and hydrogen.

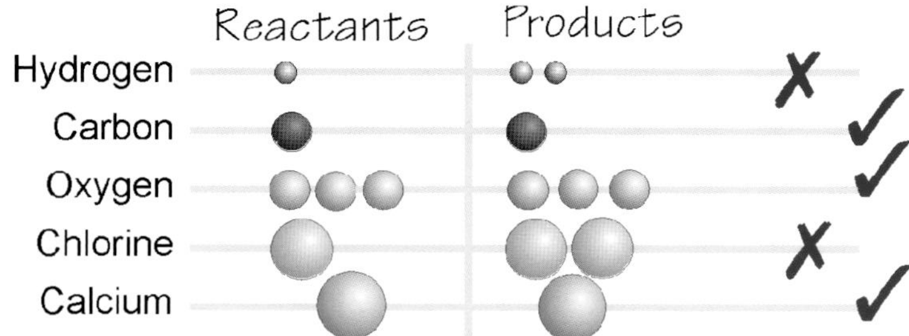

hydrochloric acid	HCl
calcium carbonate	$CaCO_3$
calcium chloride	$CaCl_2$
carbon dioxide	CO_2
water	H_2O

Figure 20.15: *Chemical formulas for each compound in the reaction.*

4. Add coefficients to balance the equation

Fortunately, one of the reactants is HCl so we can add one more molecule of HCl to the reactants side. In the equation we put a '2' in front of the HCl to indicate that we need 2 molecules. You cannot change the subscripts. In this case, you just need to put a coefficient of 2 in front of HCl to balance the equation.

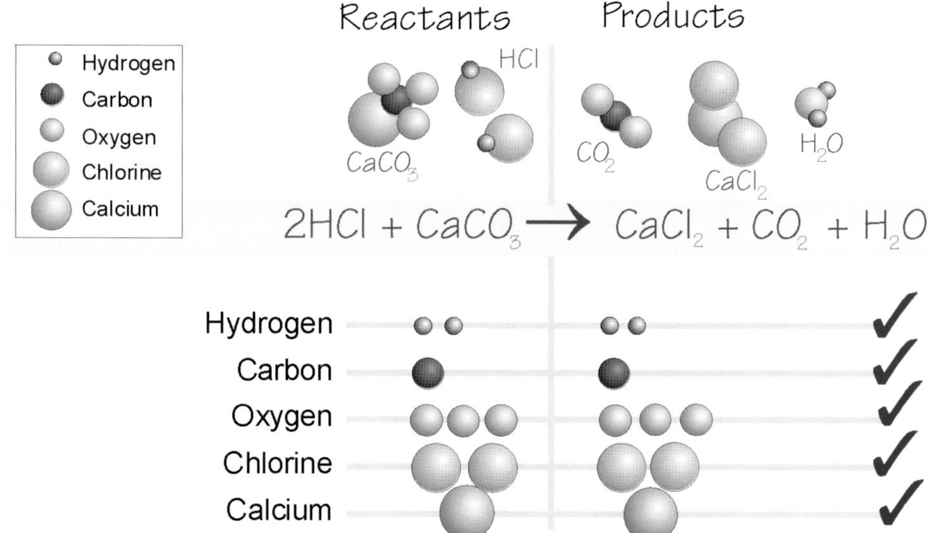

atom	reactants	products
H	1 X 2 = **2**	2
Cl	1 X 2 = **2**	2
Ca	1	1
C	1	1
O	3	3

Figure 20.16: *Is the equation balanced after adding a coefficient of 2 in front of HCl?*

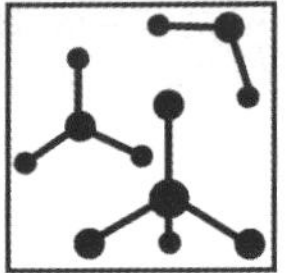

20.3 Conservation of Mass

Have you ever been to a campfire? What happens to the pile of wood after it is finished burning? Of course, it is reduced to a pile of ashes. What happened to the wood? Did it just disappear into the atmosphere? The burning of wood is a chemical reaction. So far, you have learned that every atom in a chemical reaction is accounted for. If this is so, what happened to the mass of the wood in that pile? In this section, you will learn why the mass of the reactants is equal to the mass of the products in any chemical reaction.

Conservation of Mass

What is the law of conservation of mass?

In the eighteenth century, chemical reactions were still a bit of a mystery. A French scientist, Antoine Laurent Lavoisier (1743-94), established an important principal based on his experiments with chemical reactions. He stated that the total mass of the products of a reaction is equal to the total mass of the reactants. This statement is known as the law of conservation of mass. Lavoisier's law of conservation was not obvious to many other scientists of the time.

How can you prove the law of conservation of mass?

You already know that when wood is burned, a chemical reaction is taking place, but do you know what happens to the mass of the wood after it has burned? By now, you also know that much of the mass of the burning wood is converted into a gas such as carbon dioxide. This gas then escapes into the atmosphere. How can you prove that the mass of the reactants is equal to the mass of the products in the reaction of burning wood? Lavoisier showed that a *closed system* must be used when studying chemical reactions. When chemicals are reacted in a closed container, you can show that the mass before and after the reaction is the same.

An example of how mass is conserved in a reaction

In one of his experiments, Lavoisier placed 10.0 grams of mercury (II) oxide into a sealed container. He heated the container so that the mercury (II) oxide reacted to produce oxygen and mercury. As he observed the reaction, the white, powdery mercury (II) oxide bubbled, and turned into a smaller amount of a silvery liquid. In the reaction, 10.0 grams of mercury (II) oxide reacted in the presence of heat to produce 0.7 grams of oxygen gas and 9.3 grams of mercury. How does this data prove the law of conservation of mass?

Antoine Lavoisier

Born in 1743, Antoine Lavoisier was one of the best known French scientists of his time, and an important government official. As a student he stated "I am young and avid for glory." He demonstrated with careful measurements that it was not possible to change water into soil, but that the sediment observed from boiling water came from the container. He also burned sulfur in air and proved that the products of the reaction weighed more than the reactants and that the weight gained came from the air. Despite his contributions to chemistry, he believed that the existence of atoms was philosophically impossible. He became suspicious to leaders of the French Revolution and was beheaded in 1794.

Conservation and petroleum

Why are we in danger of running out of natural resources like petroleum?

In a chemical reaction, *atoms* are conserved, not necessarily molecules. Petroleum is a mixture of many different molecules. Furthermore, the rate of production of these molecules in nature is very small compared to the rate at which we use them. The United States uses many millions of barrels of petroleum each day in a variety of different chemical reactions. Since the mass of petroleum on earth is limited, how long do you think it will take before we run out?

What is petroleum?

Petroleum is our most important *nonrenewable* resource. From it we obtain fuels to burn in our cars, homes and power plants. It also provides us with the chemicals used to manufacture many different products we use every day. Petroleum is a mixture containing hundreds of different compounds, called *hydrocarbons*, that have two important chemical properties. First, when these compounds burn in oxygen, they release large amounts of energy. Second, molecules of these compounds can be modified in a variety of ways to produce useful materials such as plastics, drugs, explosives and even perfumes! It is no wonder that petroleum is often called "black gold."

What are hydrocarbons?

Hydrocarbons are compounds that consist of many carbon atoms bonded together to form a backbone know as a *carbon chain*. Hydrogen atoms are attached to this chain (figure 20.17). Do you see where the name "hydrocarbon" comes from? The chemical formulas for some of the hydrocarbons found in petroleum are given in figure 20.18.

How was petroleum formed?

The formation of petroleum is a chemical reaction that takes millions of years to complete. Many scientists believe that the petroleum we use today originated from animals and plants that lived in the ocean millions of years ago. As these organisms died, they settled to the bottom and were covered with sediments. The plant and animal material was digested by micrscopic organisms and, as more sediments piled up on top of them, pressure and heat converted the organic material into petroleum that is now trapped in porous rocks, deep under the earth. While it is likely that petroleum is continuously being formed, its rate of formation is too slow for it to be considered a *renewable* resource.

A short list of petroleum products...

- Aspirin
- Make-up
- Synthetic rubber
- Chewing gum
- Saccharin
- Fibers for clothing
- Artificial flavors
- Fertilizers
- Plastics

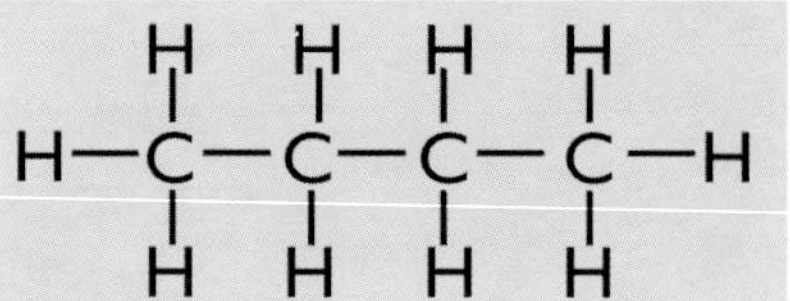

Figure 20.17: *A hydrocarbon*

name	formula
methane	CH_4
ethane	C_2H_6
propane	C_3H_8
butane	C_4H_{10}
pentane	C_5H_{12}
hexane	C_6H_{14}
heptane	C_7H_{16}
octane	C_8H_{18}

Figure 20.18: *Some of the hydrocarbons found in petroleum.*

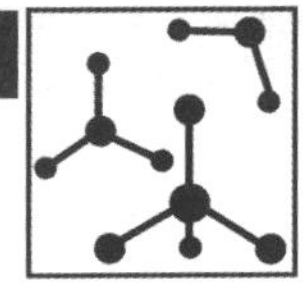

20.4 Using Equations as Recipes

Have you ever tried to make something from a recipe—say, a chocolate cake—and it didn't turn out quite the way you hoped? Some recipes require you to follow directions and add the correct amounts and types of ingredients. If you left out the eggs, for example, your cake wouldn't turn out at all. A balanced chemical equation is just like a recipe. It tells you the ingredients needed and the amount of each. It also tells you how much of each product will result if the precise amount of reactants are added. In this section, you will learn what chemical equations tell you and how to use them much like you would a recipe for a chocolate cake, although your products won't be as tasty!

Figure 20.19: *What happens when you leave out an ingredient in a recipe?*

What can a chemical equation tell you?

Recipe #1: Chocolate Cake	Recipe #2: Water
1 cup flour 1/2 cup cocoa powder 1/2 cup butter 1 tsp vanilla 1 cup sugar 1 teaspoon baking powder 1/2 cup milk 1 egg	2 molecules of hydrogen gas 1 molecule of oxygen gas $2H_2 + O_2 \longrightarrow 2H_2O$
In a bowl, combine flour, sugar, cocoa powder, and baking power. Add butter, milk, vanilla, and egg. Mix until smooth. Bake in a 350°F oven for 35 minutes. *Makes 8 servings*	Combine the molecules in a closed container. Add a spark of electricity. *Makes two molecules of water.*

Chemical equations are like recipes

How are the two recipes above alike? How are they different? Both recipes give you the ingredients needed, the instructions, and the product that will be produced. Both recipes also give you the *quantities* of ingredients needed and the *quantities* of products that are produced.

Recipes tell you the ratios of ingredients

The recipe for chocolate cake shows the *ratios* among the various ingredients needed to make eight servings. If you double the ingredients, you will make twice as many servings. Suppose you only had half a cup of flour. Could you still make eight servings? If you tried it, the cake would probably not turn out like the recipe intended. What would you need to do to make the same final product? Of course, you would use half as much of the rest of the ingredients since you only have half as much flour.

Figure 20.20: *If you had half as much flour, you could only make half the amount of cake.*

Proportional relationships in balanced equations

Just like recipes which show the ratios of the amounts of each ingredient, balanced equations show the ratios of the number of molecules of reactants needed to make a certain number of molecules of products. *The ratios are determined by the coefficients of the balanced equation.* In the formation of water, two molecules of H_2 react with one molecule of O_2 to produce two molecules of H_2O. If you reacted four molecules of H_2 with two molecules of O_2, you would produce four molecules of H_2O instead of two. Doubling the number of each reactant doubles the amount of product formed. What happens if you only double the number of H_2 molecules and not the number of O_2 molecules? How many H_2O molecules could you make? Would you have anything left over? (figure 20.21)

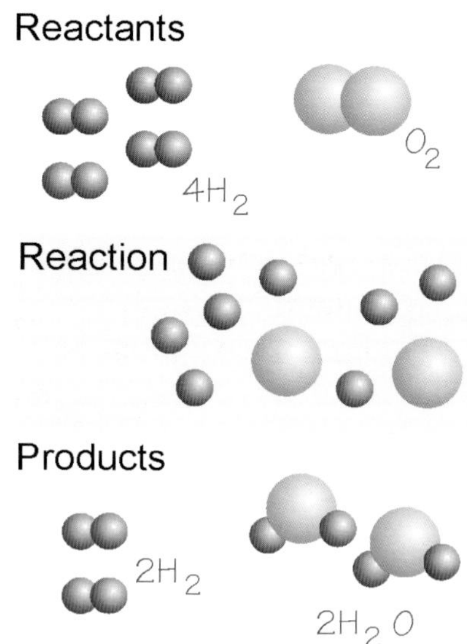

Figure 20.21: *What happens if you double the number of hydrogen molecules in the reaction for the formation of water?*

Balanced equations also show the ratio of relative masses

You have learned that the formula mass of a substance is *relative* to the formula mass of another substance. This is because individual atoms of different elements have an atomic mass relative to the size of their nuclei. Both atomic and formula mass are measured in atomic mass units, or amu. You should also remember that the avogadro number (6.02×10^{23}) of atoms or molecules is equal to the mass of the substance, in grams. For example, the formula mass of water is 18.02 amu. If you had a beaker with 6.02×10^{23} molecules of water, the water would have a mass of 18.02 grams. You have also learned that the coefficients in a balanced equation tell you the ratio of each substance in the equation. If you have a coefficient of 2 in front water in an equation, this means that you have two times the amount of water molecules. Therefore, the molecular mass of water would be 36.04 amu's and 2 x (6.02×10^{23}) molecules would have an actual mass of 36.04 grams.

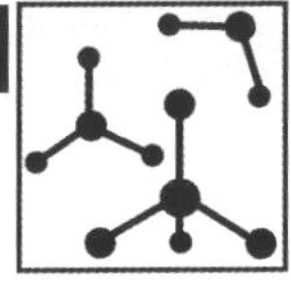

Let's take a closer look at the formation of water using this logic:

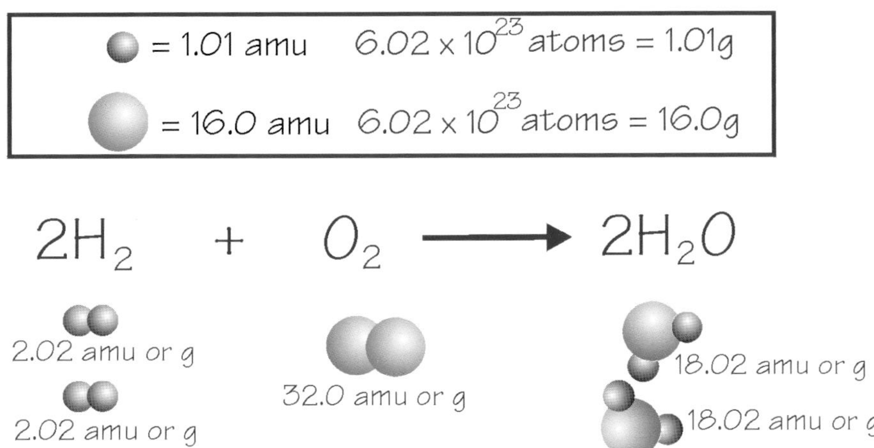

total reactants: 36.04 amu or g = total products: 36.04 amu or g

Balanced equations show how mass and atoms are conserved

As you can see from the balanced equation of the formation of water, there are an equal number of hydrogen and oxygen atoms in the reactants and products. By adding up the atomic masses, you can determine the formula mass in atomic mass units. You can also see that the masses in atomic mass units are equal on both sides of the equation. Therefore, if you have 6.02×10^{23} of each molecule represented in the diagram, a total of 36.04 grams of reactants, will produce 36.04 grams of water—providing all goes as planned. Can you see how a balanced equation can be used like a recipe?

What doesn't a balanced equation tell you?

It is important to note that a balanced equation does not describe the exact conditions under which a reaction will occur. For example, simply putting hydrogen and oxygen molecules together does not always produce water. A jolt of energy will usually result in the formation of water. Many reactions require specific conditions to occur and these are not shown in the balanced equation. Some reactions may not occur at all, even though you can write a balanced equation for them. If this were the case, we could make just about anything we need! Most of the reactions that are used in science and industry are the result of research and experimentation.

What happens if one reactant is used up before another?

If a cookie recipe calls for two eggs and you only have one, can you make a whole batch of cookies? Of course you could only make half as many. The fact that you only have one egg *limits* the amount of cookies you can make. The same is true of chemical reactions. When a chemical reaction occurs, the reactants are not always present in the exact ratio indicated by the balanced equation. In fact, this is rarely the case unless the reaction is performed in a lab with specific amounts of reactants measured. The reaction will run until the reactant that is in short supply is used up.

The reactant that is in short supply is called the limiting reactant

The reactant that is used up first is called the limiting reactant because it is used up first and thus, limits the amount of product that can be formed. A reactant that is not completely used up is called an excess reactant because some of it will be left over when the reaction is complete.

Because it is used up first, the limiting reactant determines the amount of product formed.

Do reactions always turn out as expected?

Not all reactions turn out exactly as planned. In other words, if you use a specific amount of a limiting reactant and expect the exact amount of product to be formed, you will usually be disappointed. There are many factors involved in the occurrence of reactions that affect the amount of product formed. Usually the amount of product that is formed is less than the amount you would expect. If you can measure the amount of product produced in a reaction, you can determine the percent yield. The percent yield is defined as the actual yield divided by the predicted yield and then divided by one hundred as in the equation below:

$$\text{percent yield} = \left(\frac{\text{actual yield}}{\text{predicted yield}}\right) \times 100$$

The predicted yield can be determined from the balanced equation for the reaction. The actual yield is determined by simply measuring the mass, in grams, of the product produced in the actual reaction.

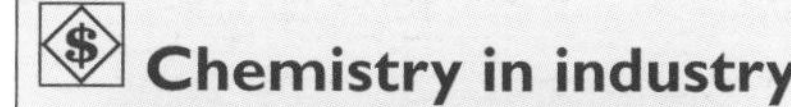

Chemistry in industry

When a chemical reaction is carried out by an industry, the more expensive reactant is usually the limiting reactant and the cheaper one is the excess reactant. For example, in the manufacture of artificial flavorings such as vanillin (artificial vanilla) or artificial almond flavoring, acetic acid is reacted with a chemical called an ester to produce the desired flavor. There are many different types of esters that are used, but all of them are more expensive than acetic acid (found in vinegar). Which chemical do you think is used for the limiting reactant?

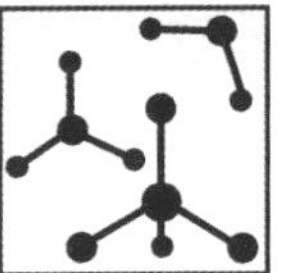

Chapter 20 Review

Vocabulary review

Match the following terms with the correct definition. There is one extra definition that will not match any of the terms.

Set One

1. chemical change
2. enzyme
3. physical change
4. physical property

a. The type of bonding that an element typically undergoes is an example of this kind of property
b. The state, size, or shape of a substance
c. What happens when two substances react to produce entirely different substances
d. Ice melting is an example of this kind of change
e. A special molecule that can speed up chemical reactions

Set Two

1. balanced equation
2. coefficient
3. subscript
4. Law of conservation of mass

a. The "3" in $CaCO_3$
b. The "6" in $6H_2O$
c. An equation with an equal number of atoms in the reactants and products
d. The number that represents the number of electrons the atom will lose or gain
e. You cannot create or lose mass in a reaction

Set Three

1. actual yield
2. limiting reactant
3. percent yield
4. predicted yield
5. ratio

a. The reaction that uses carbon dioxide and water to make sugar
b. The amount of product that should be produced in a chemical reaction
c. The reactant that is in short supply for a chemical reaction
d. The numerical relationship between two objects or substances
e. The ratio of actual yield to predicted yield times 100
f. The amount of product that you can measure after a chemical reaction

Concept review

1. How can you tell the difference between a physical change and a chemical change?
2. List three examples of a physical change.
3. List three examples of a chemical change.
4. List two differences and two similarities between a recipe for a food item and a chemical reaction.
5. What happens to chemical bonds during a chemical reaction?
6. What is meant by the phrase, "atoms are conserved in chemical reactions"?
7. Describe the contributions of Antoine Laurent Lavoisier to our current knowledge of chemical reactions.
8. Describe three things you can tell from a chemical equation.
9. What is the difference between a limiting reactant and an excess reactant?
10. Give three reasons the actual yield for a product in a reaction is usually lower than the predicted yield.

Problems

1. The process of digestion involves:
   a. Only chemical changes.
   b. Only physical changes.
   c. Both physical and chemical changes.
2. How are ice, liquid water, and water vapor *different* from each other?
   a. Each is a physical state of water.
   b. A chemical change has to occur for ice to become liquid and then for liquid water to become water vapor.
   c. Each of these states of water has a different amount of energy.
3. Which of the following events is *not* evidence that a chemical change has occurred?
   a. When you eat and breathe in oxygen, you have energy and breathe out carbon dioxide.
   b. You mix two solutions and a bright yellow precipitate appears.
   c. You notice that your grandmother's silver is very dark in places and needs polishing.
   d. Your cup of hot chocolate gives off steam.
4. Which of the following events is *not* evidence that a physical change has occurred?
   a. When you accidentally leave a soft contact lens on the bathroom sink overnight, it becomes dry and brittle.
   b. When you mix baking soda and vinegar, the two substances fizz and produce bubbles.
   c. When you take take the cap off a soda bottle for the first time, bubbles suddenly appear and rush to the surface of the soda.
   d. Baby food carrots no longer look like carrots because the carrots have been nearly liquefied.

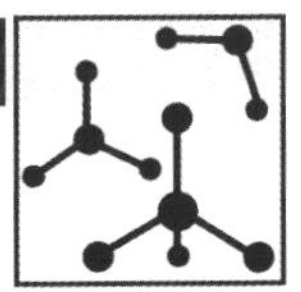

5. Fill out the table for this reaction: $Al + Br_2 \longrightarrow AlBr_3$

type of atom	total on reactants side	total on products side	balanced? (yes or no)
Al			
Br			

6. Which of the following equations is balanced?
   a. $Al + Br_2 \longrightarrow 2AlBr_3$
   b. $2Al + 2Br_2 \longrightarrow 3AlBr_3$
   c. $2Al + 3Br_2 \longrightarrow 2AlBr_3$
   d. $Al + Br_2 \longrightarrow AlBr_3$

7. How would you express the following combustion of ethane, C_2H_6, as a sentence: $2C_2H_6 + 7O_2 \longrightarrow 4CO_2 + 6H_2O$?
   a. Two ethane molecules combine with oxygen to produce carbon dioxide molecules and six water.
   b. Two ethane molecules combine with seven oxygen molecules to produce four carbon dioxide molecules and six water molecules.
   c. Ethane combusts to produce carbon and water.
   d. Four carbon dioxide molecules and six water molecules can be mixed to make oxygen and ethane.

8. Which of the following reactions is balanced?
   a. $CS_2 + 3O_2 \longrightarrow CO_2 + SO_2$
   b. $2N_2O_5 + NO \longrightarrow 4NO_2$
   c. $P_4 + 5O_2 \longrightarrow P_2O_5$
   d. $4Fe + 3O_2 \longrightarrow 2Fe_2O_3$

9. What coefficient for oxygen would balance the equation below?

   $4Fe +$ ____ $O_2 + 6H_2O \longrightarrow 2(Fe_2O_3 \cdot 3H_2O)$

10. Balance the following equations. If an equation is already balanced, say so in your answer.
    a. $Cl_2 + Br \longrightarrow Cl + Br_2$
    b. $CaO + H_2O \longrightarrow Ca(OH)_2$
    c. $Na_2SO_4 + BaCl_2 \longrightarrow BaSO_4 + NaCl$
    d. $ZnS + O_2 \longrightarrow ZnO + SO_2$

11. Balance these chemical equations:
    a. $Cl_2\,(g) + KBr\,(aq) \longrightarrow KCl(aq) + Br_2(l)$
    b. $NH_3\,(g) + O_2\,(g) \longrightarrow NO\,(g) + H_2O\,(g)$

12. Calculate the formula mass for each of the molecules listed in the *balanced* equation for 11b (above). Hint: Multiply the coefficient for each molecule times the formula mass for the molecule.

    a. NH_3 __________ amu   c. NO __________ amu
    b. O_2 __________ amu   d. H_2O __________ amu

13. If you had Avogadro's number of each molecule in question 12, what would the masses of these molecules be? Include the coefficient from question 11b in your calculation. Hint: You don't need a calculator for this question!

    a. NH_3 __________ g   c. NO __________ g
    b. O_2 __________ g   d. H_2O __________ g

14. If oxygen was the limiting reagent in equation 11b and you had only 20 grams of oxygen, what would be the predicted yield of water in this reaction? Be sure to show your work.

15. In the equation to the right, the actual yield of bromide (Br_2) was 19.8 grams when the reaction was performed with 10 grams of chlorine (Cl_2). Calculate the predicted yield for the reaction and then calculate the percent yield.

$$Cl_2\,(g) + KBr\,(aq) \longrightarrow KCl(aq) + Br_2(l)$$

Applying your knowledge

1. List the steps for preparing and eating a salad. Identify which steps have chemical changes and which have physical changes.
2. Identify whether or not a chemical reaction has occurred or will occur in the following situations.
   a. By activating a heat pack, you generate heat to warm your hands.
   b. An orange precipitate forms when two solutions are mixed.
   c. A glass of water turns red when you add dye to it.
   d. The recipe calls for adding sugar and butter to flour.
   e. When you add an effervescent tablet to water, it immediately starts to fizz.
3. Aspirin can be made in the laboratory through a series of reactions. If the actual yield for aspirin was 461.5 grams when the reactions were performed, and the predicted yield was 500 grams, what was the percent yield?
4. The source of fuel in a science lab is methane gas, CH_4, which burns in oxygen gas, O_2, to produce carbon dioxide, CO_2, and water, H_2O. The equation for this reaction is:

   $$CH_4\,(g) + 2O_2\,(g) \longrightarrow CO_2\,(g) + 2H_2O\,(g)$$

   If you have ever heated glassware in the lab, you may have noticed a black soot forming on the surface of the glass. This happens when there is insufficient oxygen and not all of the carbon combines with oxygen to form carbon dioxide.
   a. Which element do you think makes up the soot?
   b. Which substance is the limiting reactant in this reaction?
   c. Which substance is the excess reactant?
5. A chocolate sundae is prepared by combining 1/2 cup of ice cream, 2 ounces of chocolate sauce and 1 cherry. Assume you have 10 cups of ice cream, 25 ounces of chocolate sauce and 10 cherries.
   a. What is the maximum number of sundaes you can make?
   b. Which ingredient is the limiting component of the system?
   c. What quantities of the other two "reactants" will be left over when you are finished?
6. Look for situations that demonstrate chemical change. List each situation and describe the evidence of chemical change that you observe. Try to identify the reactants and products.
7. Identify an industry in your community that uses chemical reactions (Actually, it would be more difficult to find one that does not use them!) Examples include: hospitals, sewage or water treatment plants, dry cleaners, photo developers and manufacturers of any product. Research the chemical reactions the facility uses. Write balanced equations for each reaction you identify.

Types of Reactions

Introduction to Chapter 21

There are many different types of reactions that occur around you all of the time. For example, when you breathe you take in oxygen, which reacts with the sugar in your cells. This produces carbon dioxide and water. It also releases energy for your cells to use or store. This type of reaction is called a combustion reaction. In this chapter you will learn how to classify reactions based on the reactants and products, and whether or not they produce or use energy.

Investigations for Chapter 21

21.1	**Classifying Reactions**	*How can you predict the products in a reaction?*

A double-displacement reaction is a chemical reaction in which the ions from the two reactants change places. One of the new compounds formed is sometimes insoluble and forms a cloudy precipitate. In this Investigation, you will develop a set of rules for precipitate formation that will allow you to make predictions about the types of products in double-displacement reactions.

21.2	**Energy in Reactions**	*How can you classify reactions based on energy?*

You will measure the energy changes in reactions and classify reactions according to how they use or produce energy.

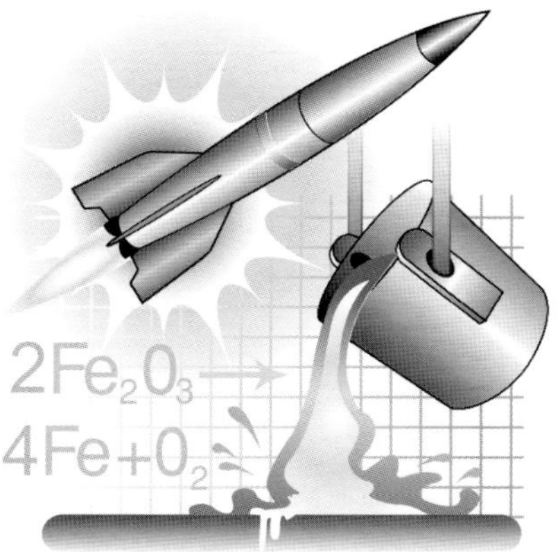

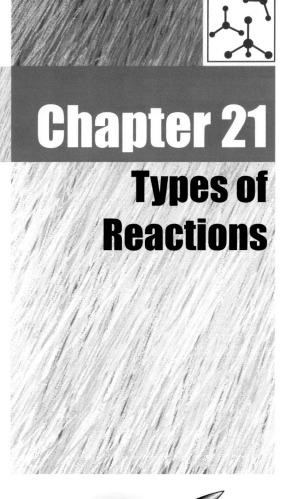

Learning Goals

In this chapter, you will:

- ✔ Distinguish between different types of reactions.
- ✔ Given the reactants, identify the type of reaction that will occur and predict the products that will be produced.
- ✔ Analyze energy changes that accompany chemical reactions and classify them as exothermic or endothermic.
- ✔ Observe reactions of household chemicals to develop a set of rules for precipitate formation. Use these rules to make predictions.
- ✔ Demonstrate safe practices during laboratory investigations.

Vocabulary

addition reaction	dissolution reaction	exothermic reaction	precipitate
combustion reaction	double-displacement reaction	insoluble	single-displacement reaction
decomposition reaction	endothermic reaction	polymerization	

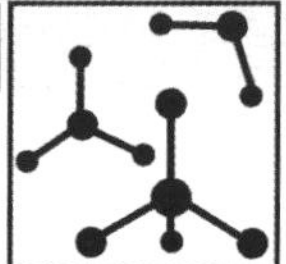

21.1 Classifying Reactions

Most of the products you use every day are the result of chemical reactions. How do manufacturers know which chemical reactions to use when they make their products? In this section, you will learn how to classify reactions. Being able to recognize the types of reactions will help you predict what types of substances will be produced.

Addition reactions

Compounds are made in addition reactions

In an addition reaction, two or more substances combine to form a new compound. A good example of an addition reaction is the formation of rust:

$$Fe_{(s)} + O_{2(g)} \longrightarrow Fe_2O_{3(s)}$$

A general equation for addition reactions is:

$$A + B \longrightarrow AB$$

A and B are elements or compounds, and AB is a compound

Acid rain

Some fossil fuels, like coal, contain sulfur. When these fuels are burned, the sulfur reacts with oxygen in the air to form the compound sulfur dioxide in the following addition reaction:

$$S_{(s)} + O_{2\,(g)} \longrightarrow SO_{x\,(g)}$$

In air polluted with sulfur dioxide, acid rain is produced in the reaction below:

$$SO_{x(g)} + H_2O_{(l)} \longrightarrow H_2SO_{x\,(aq)}$$

The “x” indicates that the subscript for oxygen varies.

(s)

(l)

(g)

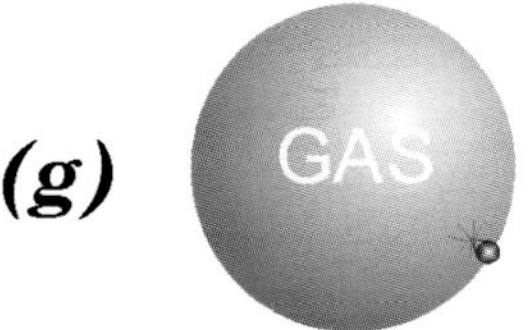

(aq)

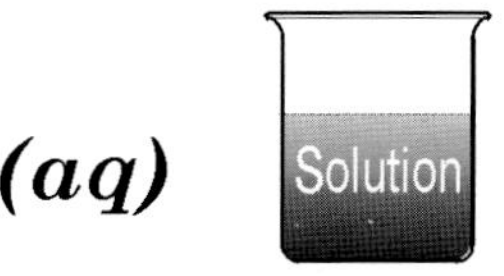

symbol	meaning
(s)	substance is a solid
(l)	substance is a liquid
(g)	substance is a gas
(aq)	substance is dissolved in solution (aqueous)

Figure 21.1: *What do the symbols shown in parenthesis in equations mean?*

Polymerization is an addition reaction

In the last chapter, you learned that polymers are large molecules made up of repeating segments. Polymerization, or the formation of polymers, is a series of addition reactions taking place to produce a very large molecule. Polymers are made by joining smaller molecules called monomers.

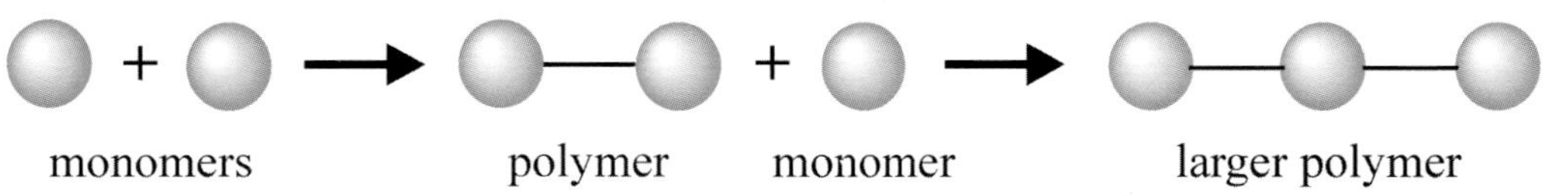

polymer	products
polystyrene	foam containers
polyethylene	food packaging
polyester	clothing
polyvinyl chloride	plumbing (PVC pipes)
polyvinyl acetate	chewing gum

Figure 21.2: *Polymers you'll find around your house.*

Decomposition reactions

Compounds are broken down in decomposition reactions

A chemical reaction in which a single compound is broken down to produce two or more smaller compounds is called a decomposition reaction. The simplest kind of decomposition is the breakdown of a binary compound into its elements, as in the decomposition of water with electricity into hydrogen and oxygen:

$$2H_2O_{(l)} \longrightarrow 2H_{2(g)} + O_{2(g)}$$

Larger compounds can also decompose to produce other compounds, as in the decomposition of baking soda with heat:

$$NaHCO_{3(s)} \xrightarrow{heat} 2H_{2(g)} + NaCO_3$$

The general equation for decomposition is:

$$AB \longrightarrow A + B$$

AB is a compound, and A and B are elements or compounds.

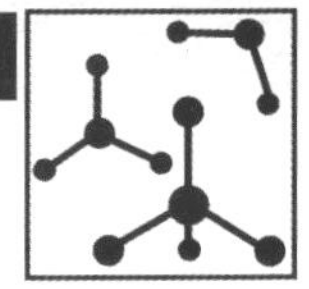

Single-displacement reactions

In single displacement reactions, one element replaces another in a compound

In **single-displacement reactions**, one element replaces a similar element in a compound. For example, if you place an iron nail into a beaker of copper (II) chloride, you will begin to see reddish copper forming on the iron nail. In this reaction, iron *replaces* copper in the solution and the copper *falls out* of the solution as a metal:

$$Fe_{(s)} + CuCl_{2\,(aq)} \longrightarrow FeCl_{2(aq)} + Cu_{(s)}$$

Single-displacement reactions can be represented with the general equation:

$$AX + B \longrightarrow BX + A$$

Where AX is a compound, B is an element, BX is a compound, and A is an element.

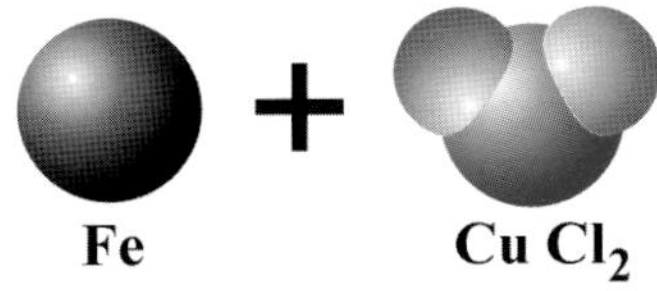

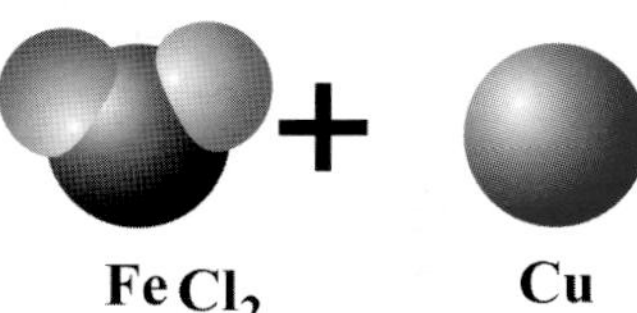

Figure 21.3: *The reaction between iron and copper chloride is a single-displacement reaction.*

Double-displacement reactions

In double-displacement reactions, ions switch places

In **double-displacement reactions**, ions from two compounds in solution exchange places to produce two new compounds. One of the compounds formed is usually a precipitate that settles out of the solution, a gas that bubbles out of the solution, or a molecular compound such as water. The other compound formed often remains dissolved in the solution.

The general formula for a double-displacement reaction is:

$$AB + CD \longrightarrow AD + CB$$

Where AB and CD are ionic compounds in a solution, and AD and CB are ionic compounds in a solution as well.

What is a precipitate?

The formation of a **precipitate** occurs when one of the compounds formed in a double-displacement reaction is **insoluble**, or does not dissolve in water. Precipitates are first recognizable by the cloudy appearance they give to a solution.

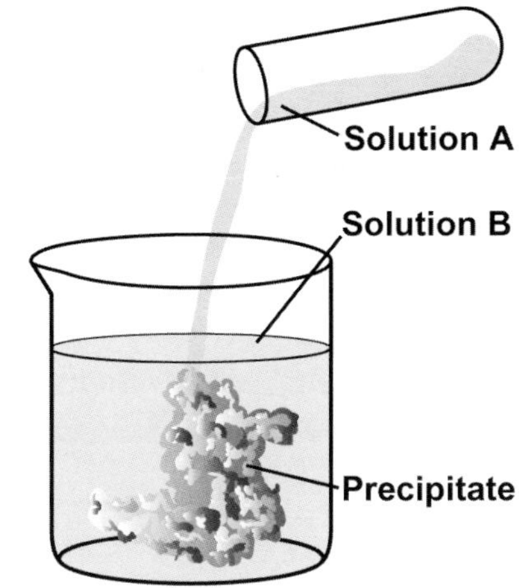

Figure 21.4: *The formation of a cloudy precipitate is evidence that a double-displacement reaction has occurred.*

If undisturbed in a beaker, a precipitate will settle to the bottom. Depending on the compound formed, the precipitate can be many different colors from white to fluorescent yellow, as in the reaction between lead (II) nitrate and potassium iodide:

$$Pb(NO\ )_{3(aq)} + 2KI_{(aq)} \longrightarrow PbI_{2(s)} + 2KNO_{3(aq)}$$

Use your head...

Which product is the "precipitate" in the dried fruit reaction to the left?

Consumer chemistry: Preserving dried fruit

Have you ever opened up a box of dried fruit such as golden raisins or apricots and smelled a slight "sulfur" odor, like a lit match? The odor is caused by *sulfur dioxide*, a gas that is used to preserve the color of dried fruits. This gas is produced in a double-displacement reaction between sodium sulfite and hydrochloric acid:

$$Na_2SO_{3(aq)} + 2HCl_{(aq)} \longrightarrow 2NaCl_{(aq)} + H_2O_{(l)} + SO_{2(g)}$$

The fruit is exposed to the gas, which is absorbed into the skin of the fruit. When you open the box for the first time, some of the gas that has escaped the fruit may not escape your nose!

Combustion reactions

In a combustion reaction, a substance combines with oxygen to release energy

It's hard to imagine where our society would be without combustion reactions. A substance such as wood, natural gas, or propane combines with oxygen, releasing a large amount of energy in the form of light and heat, thus completing a combustion reaction. For example, in the combustion of natural gas to heat a house, methane (natural gas) combines with oxygen to produce carbon dioxide and water:

$$CH_4 + 2O_2 \longrightarrow CO_2 + 2H_2O$$

The general formula for a combustion reaction is:

$$\text{Carbon Compound} + O_{2(g)} \longrightarrow CO_{2(g)} + H_2O_{(g)}$$

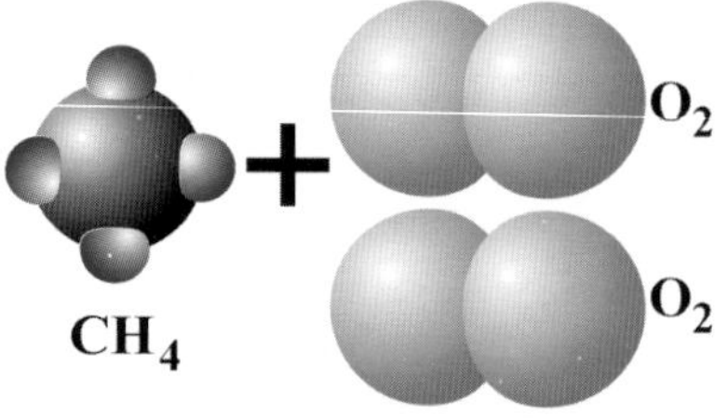

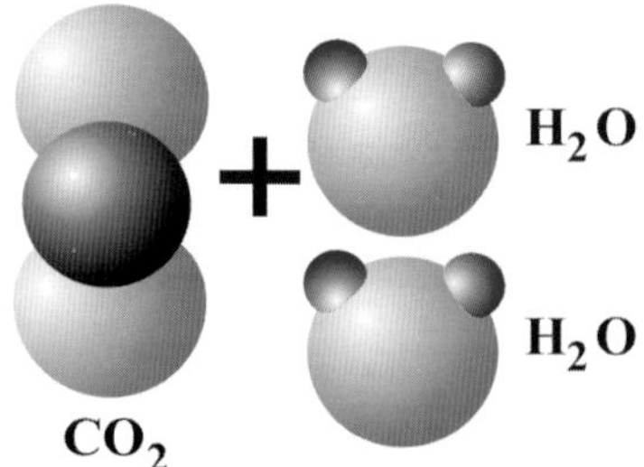

Figure 21.5: *The combustion of meathane gas, in oxygen, produces carbon dioxide and water.*

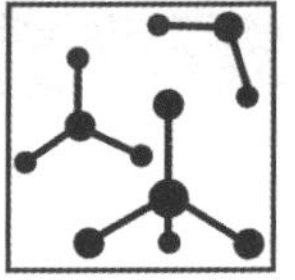

Energy and the environment: Hydrogen-powered cars

Not all combustion reactions produce carbon dioxide. For example, when hydrogen gas is burned in oxygen, water is the only product:

$$2H_{2(g)} + O_{2(g)} \longrightarrow 2H_2O_{(l)}$$

Perhaps in the future, some of our cars will run by this reaction. In fact, automobile manufacturers are developing hydrogen-powered cars right now using a technology called "fuel cells."

- How would hydrogen-powered cars impact global warming?
- Do some Internet research to find out about fuel cells and hydrogen-powered cars.

Try this...

You get energy from a combustion reaction known as respiration. In this reaction, you "burn" glucose ($C_6H_{12}O_6$) in oxygen to produce carbon dioxide and water. Can you write the balanced equation for this reaction?

Summary of the types of reactions

Use your head...

Have you ever noticed water dripping from the tailpipe of a car? Could combustion be responsible for some of that water?

Table 21.1: ***Summary of the types of reactions***

Type	General equation	Example
addition	$A + B \rightarrow AB$	$2H_2 + O_2 \rightarrow 2H_2O$
decomposition	$AB \rightarrow A + B$	$2NaHCO_3 \rightarrow H_2 + 2NaCO_3$
single-displacement	$AX + B \rightarrow BX + A$	$Fe + CuCl_2 \rightarrow FeCl_2 + Cu$
double-displacement	$AB + CD \rightarrow AD + CB$	$Pb(NO_3) + 2KI \rightarrow PbI_2 + 2KNO_3$
combustion	carbon cpd $+ O_2 \rightarrow CO_2 + H_2O$	$C_6H_{12}O_6 + 6O_2 \rightarrow 6CO_2 + 6H_2O$

Example: predicting the products of a reaction

Can you predict the products of this reaction?

Silver becomes tarnished as time passes. Have you ever eaten something with a tarnished fork or spoon? The black tarnish is silver sulfide, the result of a reaction between the silver metal and sulfur in foods. Some products claim to be able to remove the tarnish without destroying the silver. One product contains aluminum metal in a solution. Write the complete reaction for removing tarnish with this product.

1. Write the chemical formulas for the reactants

Silver sulfide reacts with the aluminum metal in the product.

Silver = Ag^{+} ion; sulfide = S^{2-} ion

The chemical formula for silver sulfide is Ag_2S

Aluminum is an element so its formula is Al

Chemical formulas for reactants: $Ag_2S + Al$

2. Identify the type of reaction

This is a *single replacement* reaction because of the general formula:

$$AX + B \longrightarrow BX + A$$

3. Predict the products and write their chemical formulas

Ag_2S is a compound and Al is an element so Al will replace Ag.

The products formed will be aluminum sulfide and silver metal.

Aluminum ion = Al^{3+}; sulfide ion = S^{2-}

Chemical formulas for products: $Al_2S_3 + Ag$

4. Write and balance the complete equation

Unbalanced equation:

$Ag_2S + Al \rightarrow Al_2S_3 + Ag$

Balanced equation:

$3Ag_2S + 2Al \rightarrow Al_2S_3 + 6Ag$

Reactants

+

$CuCl_2(aq)$ Zn(s)

Ions

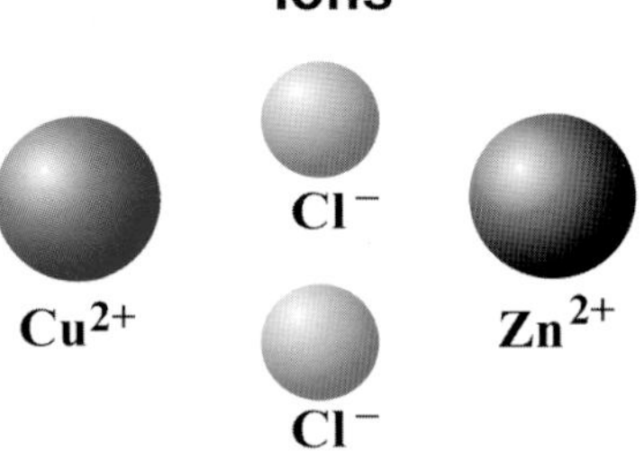

Products

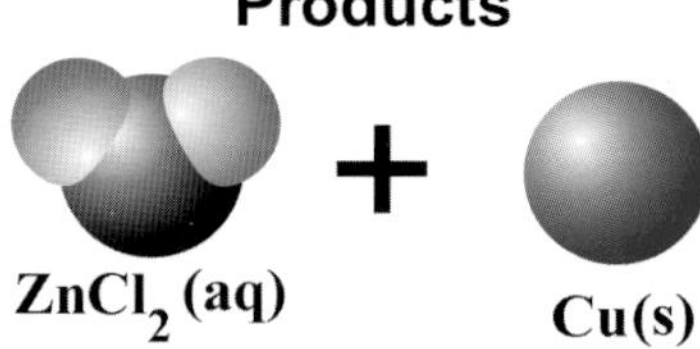

Figure 21.6: *The reaction of copper chloride (in solution) with zinc metal is another example of a single-displacement reaction.*

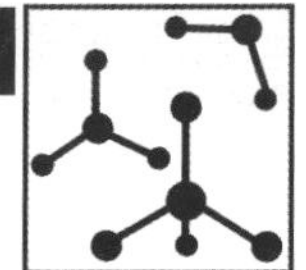

21.2 Energy in Reactions

You have learned that when most reactions take place, chemical bonds must be broken and new chemical bonds must be formed. Breaking chemical bonds requires energy. When new bonds are formed, energy is released. Why do some reactions *produce* more energy than others? Why do some reactions *use* more energy than they produce? In this section, you will learn about both these types of reactions and some ways we use them in household products.

Exothermic reactions

Exothermic reactions produce energy

In many reactions, less energy is required to break the bonds in the reactants than is released when bonds are formed to make new products. In these types of reactions, called exothermic reactions, some type of energy is released. The combustion of gasoline to run automobiles is an exothermic reaction. Some other exothermic reactions happen so slowly that you cannot feel the heat, like the formation of rust. Exothermic reactions can be detected by measuring a rise in temperature.

What are some useful exothermic reactions?

It is fairly obvious that we use exothermic reactions every day to heat our homes, drive our cars, and cook our food. These reactions are all combustion reactions that produce tremendous amounts of heat and light. Some other exothermic reactions may not be so obvious.

Meals ready to eat

The US Army developed a Meal, Ready to Eat (or MRE) for the 1991 Gulf War. These meals have a special sleeve placed around the food, which is wrapped in aluminum foil. When water is added to the sleeve, the resulting chemical reaction produces enough heat to cook the food inside the foil. What's in that sleeve? It is a pad that contains suspended particles of magnesium metal. When the magnesium reacts with the water to produce magnesium hydroxide, heat is released. The heat is conducted through the aluminum to heat the food. The result is a piping hot meal, ready to eat!

Clogged drain?

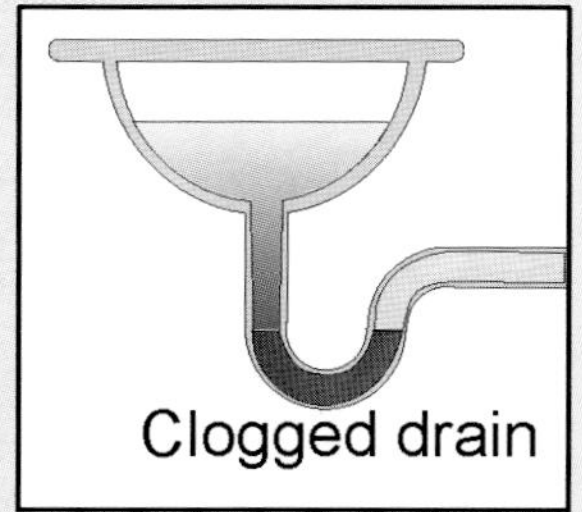

Many drain cleaners are a mixture of sodium hydroxide and aluminum filings. When these two substances mix in water, they react to produce enough heat to melt the fat in your clogged drain. The bubbles produced are hydrogen gas.

Can you write the balanced equation for this reaction?

$$Mg_{(s)} + 2H_2O_{(l)} \longrightarrow Mg(OH)_{2(aq)} + H_{2(g)}$$

Figure 21.7: *The MRE reaction.*

Endothermic reactions

How does a cold pack work?

Have you ever used an "instant cold pack" as a treatment for aching muscles? These products, found in your local drugstore, uses a special chemical reaction that has to do with energy. The product usually comes in a plastic bag. Inside of the bag is a packet of water surrounded by crystals of ammonium nitrate. To activate the cold pack, you squeeze the plastic bag to release the water. When the water contacts the ammonium nitrate crystals, a reaction occurs and the pack becomes icy cold. Why does this reaction get so cold?

$$NH_4NO_{3(s)} + H_2O_{(l)} + \text{Energy} \longrightarrow NH_{4(aq)}^{+} + NO_{3(aq)}^{-}$$

Figure 21.8: *The "cold pack" reaction.*

Endothermic reactions require more energy than they produce

Sometimes more energy is required to break the bonds in the reactants than is released from the formation of new bonds in the products. In these reactions, called endothermic reactions, more energy must be provided for the reaction to take place than is released. You can detect an endothermic reaction by measuring a decrease in the temperature. The cold pack reaction can be classified as an endothermic reaction.

Look at the cold pack reaction in figure 21.8. Besides being endothermic, this reaction is also called a dissolution reaction. Dissolution reactions occur when an ionic compound dissolves in water to make an ionic solution.

NaCl

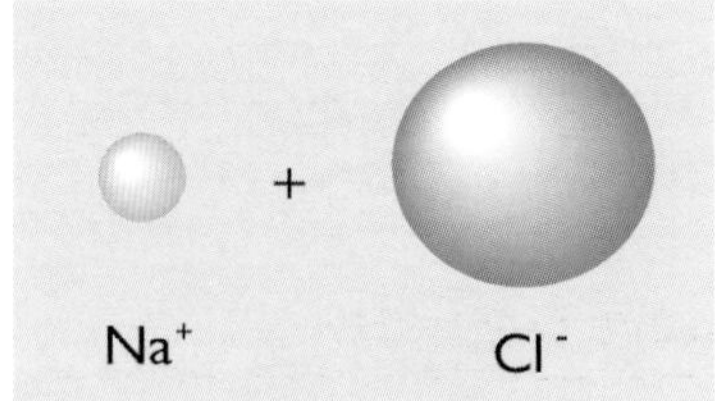

NaCl in water

Figure 21.9: *When NaCl is in water, it dissolves into positive and negative ions. This is an example of a dissolution reaction.*

What are some useful endothermic reactions?

Most of the reactions used in industry to produce useful materials and products require more energy than they produce. This is one of the reasons sources of energy are so important to industry. For example, the refining of ores to produce useful metals frequently uses an endothermic reaction, as in the refinement of aluminum ore:

$$2Al_2O_{3(s)} + \text{Energy} \longrightarrow 4Al_{(s)} + 3O_{2(g)}$$

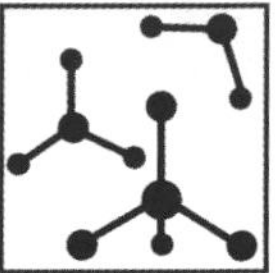

Chapter 21 Review

Vocabulary review

Match the following terms with the correct definition. There is an extra definition that will not match any term

Set One	
1. combustion reaction	a. A large molecule with repeating units of smaller molecules
2. decomposition reaction	b. A molecule that is used to speed up reactions
3. double-displacement reaction	c. The process of attaching small molecule units together to make a large molecule
4. polymer	d. $AB \longrightarrow A + B$
5. polymerization	e. $AB + CD \longrightarrow AD + CB$
	f. A reaction that is used to obtain energy from fuel

Set Two	
1. precipitate	a. A reaction that uses more energy than it produces
2. single-displacement reaction	b. $AB + CD \longrightarrow AD + CB$
3. endothermic reaction	c. $A + B \longrightarrow AB$
4. addition reaction	d. $AX + B \longrightarrow BX + A$
5. exothermic reaction	e. The insoluble product of a double-displacement reaction
	f. A reaction that produces more energy than it uses

Concept review

1. Are combustion reactions usually exothermic or endothermic?
2. The formation of rust is represented by the following reaction:
   $4Fe(s) + 3O_2(g) \longrightarrow 2Fe_2O_3(s) + \text{energy}$
   a. Classify this reaction as either: single-displacement, decomposition, addition, combustion or double-displacement.
   b. Is this reaction exothermic or endothermic?
3. What conditions must be met in order for a reaction to be considered exothermic?
4. A reaction that requires more energy to break the bonds in the reactants than is released when new bonds are formed in the products is a(n):
   a. MRE reaction.
   b. endothermic reaction.
   c. silver reaction.
   d. exothermic reaction.

Problems

1. Identify the following reactions as: addition, decomposition, single-displacement, double-displacement, or combustion reactions.
   a. $NaS (aq) + ZnNO_3(aq) \longrightarrow NaNO_3(aq) + ZnS (s)$
   b. $6Li(s) + N_2 \longrightarrow 2Li_3N$
   c. $2KClO_3 \longrightarrow 2KCl + 3O_2$
   d. $2C_3H_7OH + 9O_2 \longrightarrow 6CO_2 + 8H_2O$
   e. $Mg + 2AgNO_3 \longrightarrow Mg(NO_3)_2 + 2Ag$
2. Complete the reactions below. You are not required to balance this set.
   a. $H_2SO_4(aq) + BaCl(aq) \longrightarrow$
   b. $ZnSO_4(aq) + Na_3PO_4(aq) \longrightarrow$
   c. $HCl (aq) + K_2SO_3 \longrightarrow$
   d. $SnCl_2 + Fe_2(SO_4)_3 \longrightarrow$
3. Use the solubility rules to identify the precipitate, if any, for each reaction in question 2.
4. Complete and balance the following reactions:
   a. $Fe(s) + CuCl_2(aq) \longrightarrow$
   b. $C_2H_6(g) + O_2(g) \longrightarrow$
   c. $NaCl(aq) + NH_4OH(aq) \longrightarrow$
   d. $H_2O \longrightarrow$
   e. $Cu(s) + O_2(g) \longrightarrow$
   f. $Al_2O_3 \longrightarrow$
   g. $Mg(s) + HCl(aq) \longrightarrow$
   h. $LiNO_3(aq) + MgCl_2(aq) \longrightarrow$

Applying your knowledge

1. Many drain cleaners are a mixture of sodium hydroxide and aluminum filings. When these two substances mix in water, they react to produce enough heat to melt the fat in a clogged drain. The bubbles produced are hydrogen gas. The complete reaction occurs in two steps:

   step 1: $Al(s) + NaOH(aq) \rightarrow Al(OH)_3(s) + Na^+ (aq)$

   step 2: $Na^+(aq) + H_2O \rightarrow Na_2O(s) + H_2(g)$

   a. Classify step 1 of the reaction as: addition, single-displacement, double-displacement or decomposition.
   b. Is this an endothermic or an exothermic reaction?
   c. Balance each equation for each step of the reaction.
2. Propane, C_3H_8, is a gas that is used by cooks and campers every day. It is burned in oxygen in order to cook food, provide heat and light, and even to run refrigerators in areas that do not have electricity. Write the complete, balanced equation for the combustion of propane.
3. Light bulb filaments are made of the element tungsten. When this metal is heated, it usually forms an oxide with the oxygen in the air. This causes the metal to become brittle and fall apart. Can you explain why the filament of tungsten inside of a light bulb does not form an oxide? (Hint: think about the structure of a light bulb.)

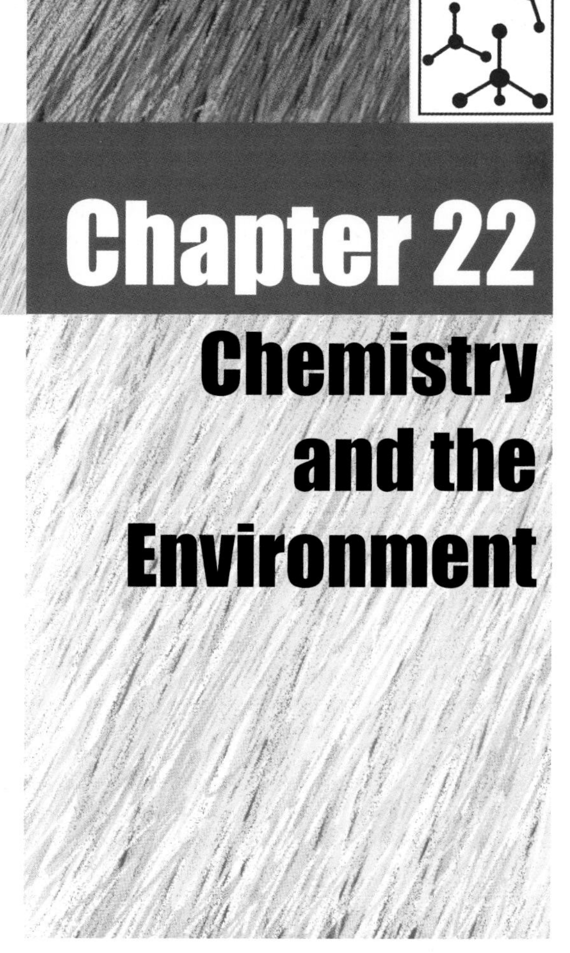

Introduction to Chapter 22

The reactions of elements and compounds are everywhere in the environment. In fact, the Earth's environment as we know it is the result of the reactions of organisms. Plants, for example, produce the atmospheric oxygen that we depend on. In this chapter you will learn that nuclear reactions in the sun produce the energy that eventually leads to this oxygen production. As you learn more about nuclear and carbon reactions, you will see the role they play in improving and affecting our environment and lifestyles.

Investigations for Chapter 22

22.1	**Nuclear Reactions**	*How do you simulate nuclear decay?*

With 92 protons and 146 neutrons, the nucleus of uranium-238 has a tendency to fall apart or "decay." It emits radiation in the forms of particles and energy until it becomes an atom with a more stable nucleus. The entire radioactive decay process for uranium-238 takes about 5 billion years! In this Investigation, you will simulate the radioactive decay of an element.

22.2	**Carbon Reactions**	*How do your choices impact the environment?*

If you needed to buy a car to drive to school or work, what would you buy? How would you make your decision? In this Investigation, you will use consumer information to evaluate how your decision affects the environment and your personal finances. You will calculate how much carbon dioxide your car or truck would produce. In the last part of the Investigation, you will see how the sun's energy may be used to reduce carbon dioxide in the atmosphere.

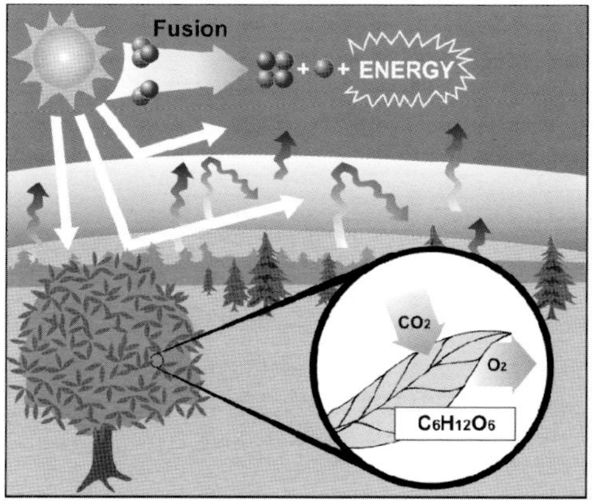

Learning Goals

In this chapter, you will:

- ✔ Compare and contrast nuclear reactions with chemical reactions.
- ✔ Describe the environmental impact of nuclear reactions.
- ✔ Research and describe the environmental and economic impact of the end-products of chemical reactions.
- ✔ Identify how personal choices about products can have an impact on the environment.
- ✔ Evaluate the impact of scientific research on society and the environment.
- ✔ Organize data and use it to predict trends.

Vocabulary

alpha decay	emissions	half-life	radioactive
alpha particles	fission	neutral	radioactive isotope
beta decay	fossil fuels	nuclear reactions	radiation
beta particles	fusion	nucleons	stable
carbon dating	global warming	photosynthesis	unstable

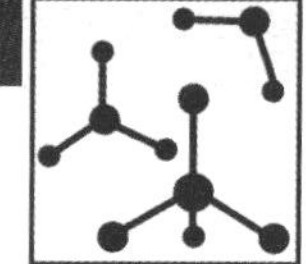

22.1 Nuclear Reactions

In the Middle Ages, individuals called alchemists spent a lot of time trying to make gold. Often, they fooled people into believing that they had made gold. Although alchemists never succeeded in making gold, their experimental techniques laid the foundation for the field of chemistry.

Gold is an element. Is it possible to make an element? What do you think?

Making an element is possible only if you can achieve a nuclear reaction, something the alchemists could not do. Nuclear reactions involve either combining or splitting the nuclei of atoms. In this section, you will learn about nuclear reactions as well as nuclear energy and radioactivity.

Figure 22.1: *Gold is a precious metal. In the Middle Ages "alchemists" tried to turn ordinary substances into gold. Using the means they had at the time, alchemists never succeeded in making gold. Today it is possible, but not economically reasonable to make gold!*

Making gold is not a simple task

Gold on the periodic table Do you know where to find gold on the periodic table? Unlike what you might expect, its symbol is not Ga, nor Ge, or Gd. The symbol comes from the Latin word ***aurum***. The Romans used this word to refer to gold, but it also meant "shining dawn."

Atoms are distinguished by number of protons Although gold's ancient name is descriptive, an atom of gold is defined by its atomic number, 79. This number identifies how many protons an atom has in its nucleus. All atoms that have 79 protons are gold atoms. Atoms with one more proton are mercury (Hg) atoms, and atoms with one fewer proton are platinum (Pt) atoms. In these terms, it seems that it would be easy to make gold. You could simply combine nuclei (the plural form of nucleus) of different atoms until you made an atom with 79 protons. Which atoms do you think could be combined to make gold?

Fusion and fission reactions provide a way to make gold To make gold, you would need to perform a nuclear reaction. There are two kinds of nuclear reaction: fusion and fission. The process of combining the nuclei of atoms to make different atoms is called *fusion*. To make gold, you could also split the nucleus of an atom that has more protons and neutrons than gold. Breaking up the nucleus of an atom is called *fission*. Scientists can use a special machine called a particle accelerator to bombard particles and atoms in order to achieve fusion and fission reactions. However, only a very small number of atoms can be made in this way at one time.

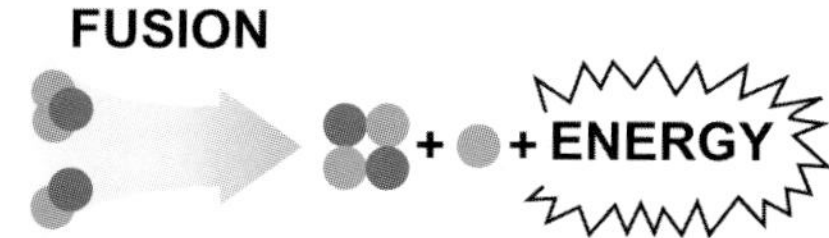

Figure 22.2: *In fusion, nuclei are "fused," a particle is emitted, and a lot of energy is released. The reaction shown above shows the fusion of hydrogen-3 (1 proton + 2 neutrons) with hydrogen-2 (1 proton + 1 neutron) to make a helium nucleus, a neutron and energy. In the graphic, the dark blue dots are protons; the lighter blue dots are neutrons.*

What is a nuclear reaction?

Nuclear vs. chemical reactions

Fission and fusion are nuclear reactions. Protons and neutrons—the two most important subatomic particles in the nucleus—participate in these reactions. Collectively, the protons and neutrons in the nucleus are called nucleons. Chemical reactions involve only the outermost electrons of atoms. A summary of the differences between chemical and nuclear reactions is listed in the table below.

	chemical reactions	nuclear reactions
What part of the atom is involved?	Outermost electrons	Protons and neutrons in the nucleus
How is the reaction started?	Atoms are brought close together with high temperature or pressure, or catalysts, or by increasing concentrations of reactants	High temperature is required or atoms are bombarded with high-speed particles
What is the outcome of the reaction?	Atoms form ionic or covalent bonds	The number of protons and neutrons in an atom usually changes
How much energy is absorbed or released?	A small amount	A huge amount
What are some examples?	Burning fossil fuels, digesting food, housecleaning, making medicines and commercial products	Nuclear energy, taking x-rays, treating cancer, irradiating food to sterilize it, the sun generating heat and light

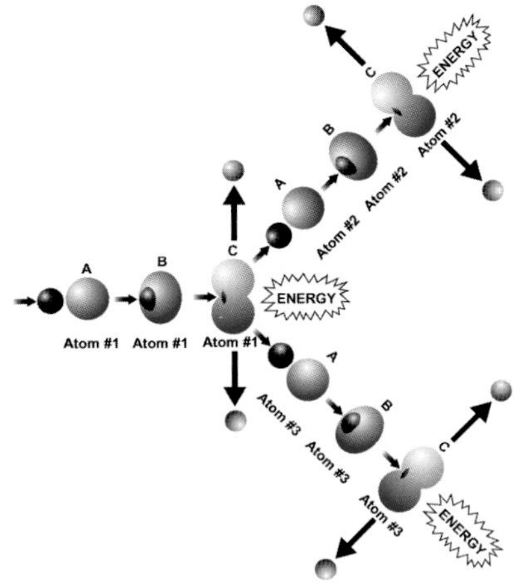

Figure 22.3: *Nuclear fission can be started when a neutron (dark ball) bombards a nucleus (blue ball). A chain reaction results. A free neutron (step A) bombards a nucleus (step B) and the nucleus splits releasing more neutrons (step C). These neutrons then bombard other nuclei. Fission and (energy production) in nuclear reactors is controlled by releasing neutrons to start a chain reaction or by capturing neutrons to slow or stop a chain reaction.*

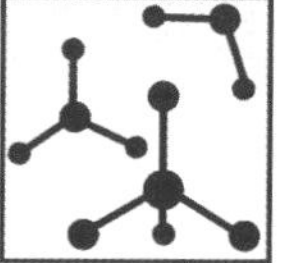

Forces in the nucleus

Opposites attract to form neutral atoms

Protons are positively charged particles. Consider an atom like boron with an atomic number of 5. The nucleus of a boron atom has five positively charged protons. What keeps these positive particles packed together? If "likes repel," shouldn't the protons fly apart from each other?

Strong nuclear force is the key

The nucleus stays together because of the *strong nuclear force*. The strong nuclear force attracts every proton and neutron to every other proton and neutron. The attractive forces from the neutrons and protons together are stronger than the electromagnetic force that cause the protons to repel each other.

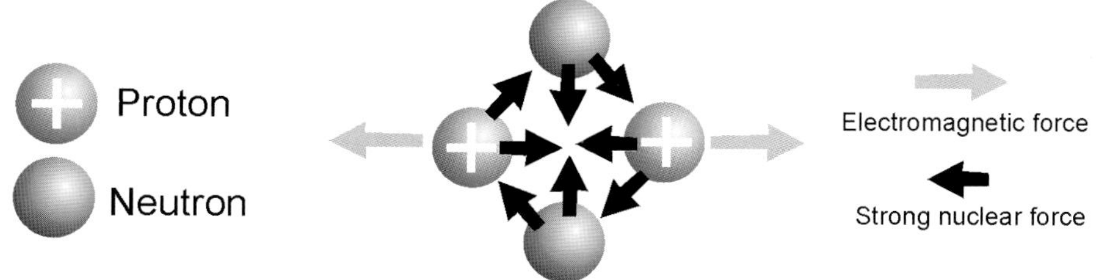

Figure 22.4: *The theoretical physicist, Hideki Yukawa (1907-1981) was the first Japanese to receive a Nobel Prize. He won the award in 1949 for his theory of strong nuclear force. This theory predicted the meson, a elementary particle that was later discovered.*

The importance of neutrons

For every atom heavier than helium there needs to be at least as many neutrons as protons to hold the nucleus together. For example, calcium-40 has 20 protons and 20 neutrons. For heavier atoms, more neutrons are needed than protons. This is because neutrons add attractive force without electromagnetic repulsion. For atoms with more than 83 protons, even the added strong nuclear force from neutrons is not enough to hold the nucleus together. Every nucleus with more than 83 protons is unstable.

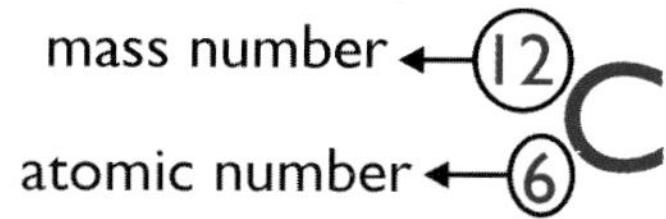

Figure 22.5: *The isotopes of carbon can written with the mass number above the atomic number. Here, we will call this format the "isotope notation." The diagram above is for carbon-12, one of the common and stable isotopes of carbon.*

Different atoms of an element can have different numbers of neutrons

You may already know that the atoms in an element can have different numbers of neutrons. For example, all carbon atoms have six protons, but some have six neutrons and some have seven neutrons. Atoms of the same element that differ in their number of neutrons are called **isotopes**. The best way to identify isotopes is by their atomic mass number. A carbon atom with six neutrons is referred to as carbon-12 and one with seven neutrons is carbon-13. The *atomic mass number* of an isotope is the number of protons plus the number of neutrons in an atom.

What is radioactivity?

An unstable nucleus is radioactive

Radioactivity is how we describe any process where the nucleus emits particles or energy. The nucleus of a uranium-238 atom is radioactive. It emits radiation in the forms of particles and energy as it transforms itself into an atom with a more stable nucleus. In figure 22.6, uranium-238 emits two protons and two neutrons to become a thorium-234 atom. Eventually, uranium-238 decays naturally to lead-206, which is not radioactive. The entire decay process takes about 5 billion years!

The three kinds of nuclear decay

Unstable isotopes emit three kinds of radioactive decay. These include alpha particles, beta particles, and gamma rays.

Alpha decay

In alpha decay, a particle that has two protons and two neutrons is released from an unstable nucleus. This particle is called an *alpha particle*. When a radioactive isotope undergoes alpha decay, it ejects an alpha particle. Uranium-238 undergoes alpha decay to become thorium-234 (figure 22.6).

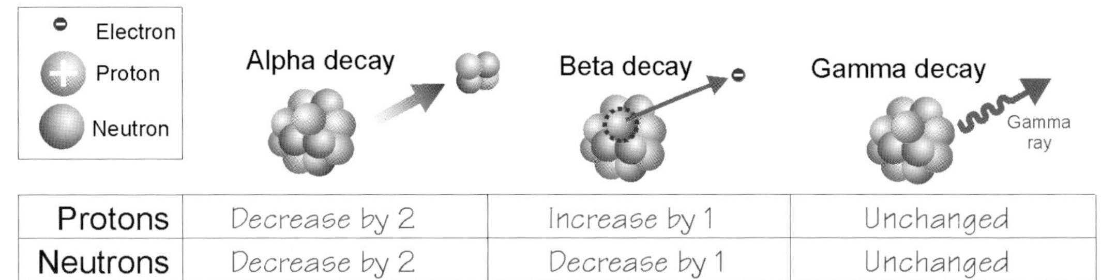

	Alpha decay	Beta decay	Gamma decay
Protons	Decrease by 2	Increase by 1	Unchanged
Neutrons	Decrease by 2	Decrease by 1	Unchanged

Beta decay

Beta decay occurs when a neutron in the nucleus of a radioactive isotope splits into a proton and an electron. The proton stays behind in the nucleus, but the electron is emitted. The electron is called a *beta particle*. Carbon-14 (a radioactive form of carbon) undergoes beta decay to become nitrogen-14. Why are the atomic masses of the carbon and nitrogen atoms both 14?

Gamma decay

Gamma decay involves the release of high-energy, electromagnetic radiation from the nucleus of an atom. Gamma rays have shorter wavelength than X rays and have much more energy.

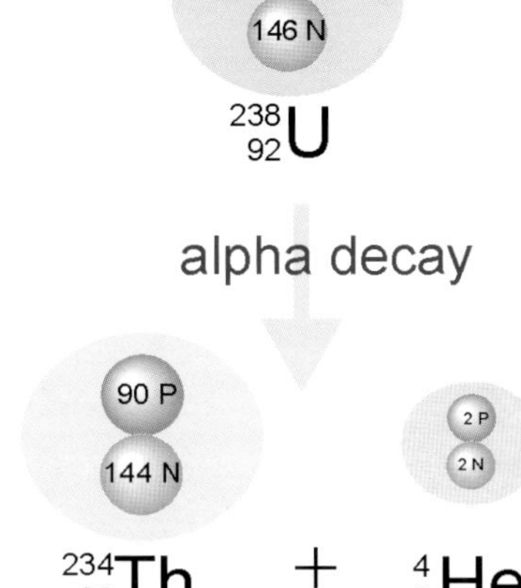

Figure 22.6: *When uranium-238 undergoes alpha decay, it becomes thorium-234 and releases a helium nucleus. Additionally, a lot of energy is released. The helium nucleus is called an alpha particle. The mass number for the elements on one side of the equation above equal the mass numbers on the other side. Nuclear reactions follow the law of conservation of mass.*

Use your head...

Gold-185 decays to iridium-181. Is this an example of alpha or beta decay?

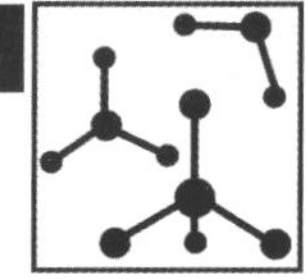

Using nuclear reactions for our energy needs

Sun power is nuclear power Nuclear reactions are more common in everyday life than you might think. For example, consider that we all depend on the energy from the sun. We need the sun to warm us. What we and other animals eat depends on plants and algae converting energy from the sun into food. Even the fuel we use in our cars, derived from the fossil remains of plants and animals, can be attributed to the sun's energy. The huge amount of energy produced in the sun is the result of a multi-step fusion reaction in which hydrogen isotopes are forced together in the extremely hot interior of the sun to make helium.

Nuclear reactors Some of our energy production on Earth involves nuclear reactors that use fission to produce heat. This heat is then used to generate steam for running turbines. In turn, the turbines generate electricity for homes and businesses.

Nuclear reactors produce hazardous nuclear waste Almost all of our energy technologies also produce some harmful waste products. Burning coal and oil creates waste gasses that contribute to global warming and acid rain. Although nuclear reactors do not normally produce harmful emissions, they do produce nuclear waste. What is nuclear waste and why is it a problem?

Half-life To understand nuclear waste, you have to understand the term half-life. All radioactive elements have a half-life. This means that there is a certain length of time after which *half* of the radioactive element has decayed. For example, the half-life of carbon-14 (one of the radioactive isotopes of carbon) is 5,730 years. This means that if you start out with 100 atoms of carbon-14, 5,730 years from now only 50 atoms will still be carbon-14. The rest of the carbon will have decayed to nitrogen-14 (a stable isotope). As a radioactive element decays, it emits harmful radiation (alpha and beta particles, and gamma rays). By breaking chemical bonds, radiation can damage cells and DNA. Exposure to radiation is particularly harmful if it is too intense or for too long a period of time.

The half-life of uranium The radioactive element in nuclear reactor fuel is uranium. When a uranium atom breaks up (fission), giving off energy, the resulting smaller atoms are also radioactive. Many of the atoms which are decay products of uranium fission have long half-lives. That means spent fuel from a reactor stays radioactive for a long time, which is why it is dangerous .

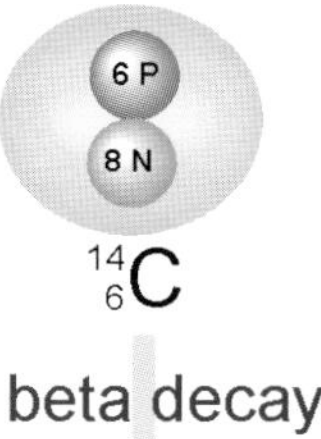

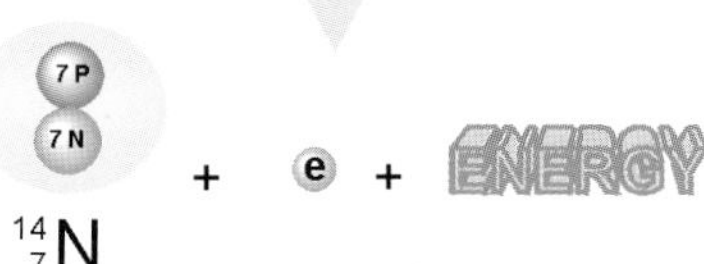

Figure 22.7: *When carbon-14 undergoes beta decay, it becomes nitrogen-14. This is because one of the neutrons in the carbon nucleus becomes a proton and an electron. The proton stays in the nucleus and an electron and energy are emitted.*

Radiation all around

Because you can not see or feel radiation, you may not be aware that it is all around you. Many common objects contain radioactive isotopes. Exposure to radiation can come from space (radiation entering the Earth's atmosphere), having an x ray, brick or stone buildings, or brazil nuts! Fortunately, exposure to radiation from these sources is very low.

A plan for storing nuclear waste

In 1974, the U.S. Congress established the Nuclear Regulatory Commission (NRC) as a monitoring organization for nuclear fuel use and the storage of nuclear waste. There is a proposed permanent storage facility for highly radioactive nuclear waste that may be built by 2007 in Yucca Mountain, Nevada. Presently, nuclear waste is stored in special facilities around the country in containers meant to last 100 years. Storing nuclear waste is a very controversial issue. What do you think should be done about storing it?

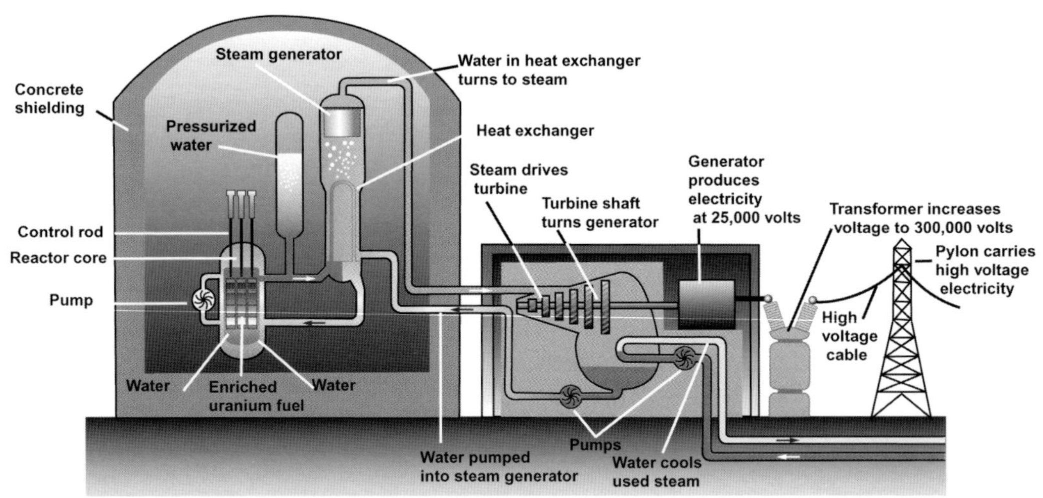

How much energy comes from nuclear reactors?

The US gets about 1/5 (20%) of its energy from nuclear fission reactors. The remaining energy comes from coal, natural gas, oil, and hydroelectric dams. Many foreign countries get more of their electricity from nuclear fission reactors. France is the most dependent on nuclear power. About 75% of electricity generated in France comes from nuclear fission. Sweden and Belgium also get more than 50% of their energy from nuclear fission.

What is nuclear fusion?

Nuclear fission is one of two ways to get energy from the atomic nucleus. The other process is called nuclear fusion. In nuclear fusion, light atoms are heated up to extremely high temperatures so their nuclei can fuse together to create heavier atoms. The process gives off tremendous amounts of energy, and is what powers the Sun and the stars.

Science Fact

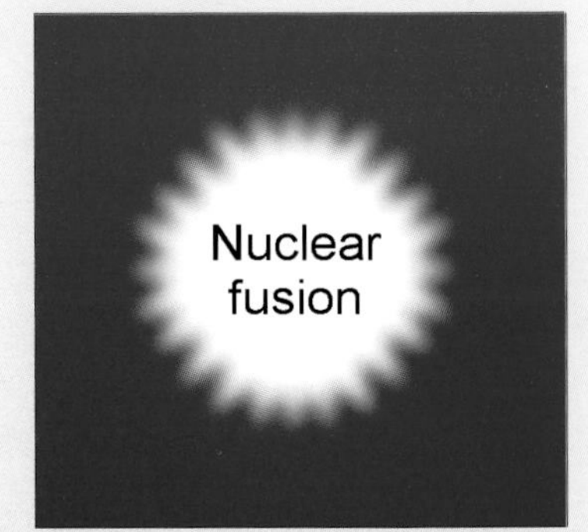

Fusion is a nuclear reaction that does not produce nuclear waste. However, causing a fusion reaction is very difficult. The interior of the sun where fusion takes place is about 15 million degrees Celsius. On Earth, we would need to generate about 100 million degrees Celsius to create fusion of hydrogen for producing energy. This high temperature is necessary to overcome the difficulty of forcing positively charged protons together! Many countries are working together in fusion research Someday we may get our energy from clean power plants using nuclear fusion. .

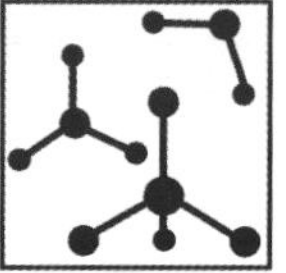

Using nuclear reactions in medicine and science

Radioactive isotopes can be used to detect problems in systems

Radioactive isotopes (also called *radioisotopes*) are commonly used as tracers in medicine and science. By adding a radioactive isotope into a system (such as the human body or an underground water supply), problems can be detected. The tracer's radiation allows it to be detected using a Geiger counter or other machine and followed as it travels through the system. In the food industry, nuclear reactions are used to sterilize packaged foods.

The age of some fossils can be determined by measuring carbon-14

It is possible to figure out the age of objects made from plants or animals that are between 50,000 and a few thousand years old using carbon dating. Plants and animals absorb carbon into their tissues. Much of the carbon they absorb is carbon-12 and carbon-13 because these are the most abundant carbon isotopes. However, some carbon-14 is also absorbed. Carbon-14 undergoes radioactive decay and has a half-life of 5,730 years. By measuring the amount of carbon-14 remaining in a plant or animal fossil, the age of the fossil can be estimated if it isn't too old. Why do you think very old fossils cannot be dated using carbon dating?

Did you know?

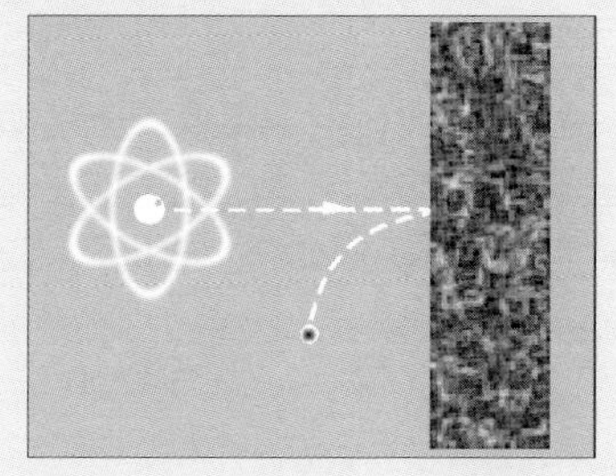

You don't always need thick walls of lead or concrete to block radiation. It depends on what kind of radiation you are trying to stop. A simple sheet of paper or your skin can block alpha particles. Your clothing or wood can block beta particles. However, gamma rays and high-speed neutrons will pass right through you, potentially causing damage along the way. Nuclear reactors use thick walls of concrete to block neutrons and gamma rays.

Historical Perspective: Marie Curie

The field of nuclear chemistry began when Marie Curie (1867-1934) and her husband, Pierre Curie (1859-1906), discovered radioactivity. In 1898, Marie Curie, a Polish-born chemist, coined the word "radioactivity" to describe peculiar behavior of elements she and her husband had discovered. They shared a Nobel Prize in 1903 for their discovery of radioactivity. Marie Curie was awarded a second Nobel in 1911 for her discovery of the elements radium and polonium.

Marie Curie began her career as a scientist at the University of Sorbonne in Paris. There, she was the first woman to graduate with a degree in physics (1893). Later in 1894, she received a degree in mathematics. For her work on radioactivity, she was the first woman to receive a Nobel Prize and the first person to receive two Nobel prizes. She was also the first woman professor at the University of Sorbonne. During World War I, she used her knowledge of radioactivity and her passion for applying this technology to medicine to organize mobile X-ray machines that could go from hospital to hospital. She championed radiation therapy as a treatment for cancer.

22.2 Carbon Reactions

What would the world be like without the sun? The world relies on the sun's energy more than you may realize. In fact, 99 percent of our energy needs are met by the sun. We get the rest of our energy namely by using fossil fuels—which were derived from the sun's energy millions of years ago. In this section you will learn about carbon reactions, such as the combustion of fossil fuels. Your body also happens to use a combustion reaction to get energy from the food you eat. By the end of the section, you will better understand the role of carbon reactions in food production, air pollution, and global warming.

Figure 22.8: *Whether you walk or ride in a car, you are using carbon reactions to travel from place to place.*

We all depend on the carbon reactions performed by plants

Plants convert the sun's energy into products we use

You may be familiar with a nuclear reaction called fusion. In this reaction hydrogen atoms "fuse" to produce helium and a lot of energy. The fusion reactions in the sun produce enough energy to illuminate and warm our planet Earth. This energy reaches the planet as visible and ultraviolet light, and infrared radiation (heat). It is easy to take all this energy for granted because is it free and clean. Most importantly, plants, using the process of photosynthesis, can convert this abundant energy source into things we like to eat, wear, and use. Fruits, vegetables, cotton, and wood are just some of the many plant products you may consume or make use of during a single day.

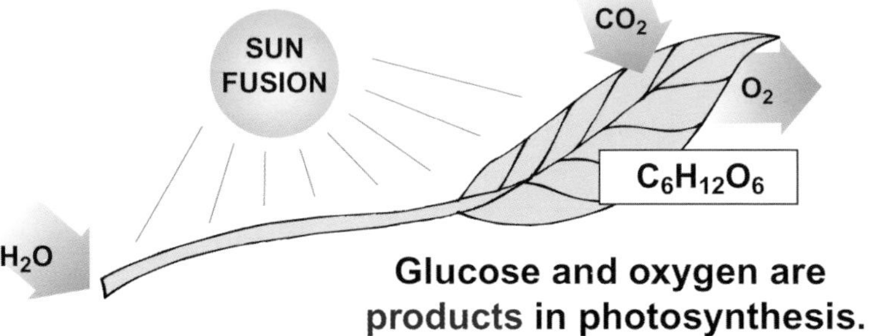
Water and carbon dioxide are reactants in photosynthesis.
SUN FUSION
CO_2
O_2
$C_6H_{12}O_6$
H_2O
Glucose and oxygen are products in photosynthesis.

Photosynthesis

Photosynthesis is a process that is performed by plants, fresh water algae, saltwater algae, and some bacteria. In this process, special pigments absorb energy from the sun. This energy is used to convert water and carbon dioxide (CO_2) to glucose ($C_6H_{12}O_6$) and oxygen (O_2). Photosynthetic organisms (those that perform photosynthesis) produce glucose for their own energy and structural needs. Humans then use what plants produce for food, building materials, writing materials, clothing, and even medicines.

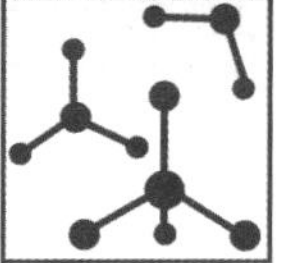

We depend on carbon reactions for transportation

Cars burn fossil fuels for energy

The sun helps make Earth very livable. More and more, however, we are requiring additional energy in the form of fossil fuels. The world's reliance on fossil fuels has increased steadily since the beginning of the Industrial Revolution in the mid-eighteenth century. Today, we use fossil fuels (like natural gas, kerosene, and coal) for home heating, for the production of electricity, and to run our machines. The machine we depend on most—the automobile—allows us to ride instead of walk to the places we want to go. A car converts the energy stored in fossil fuel (gasoline) into motion through a common chemical reaction called *combustion*.

Use of fossil fuels affects the environment

Unfortunately, our dependence on fossil fuels comes at a cost. When you put gasoline into a car, you are providing one of the reactants for a combustion reaction. Gasoline and oxygen react to produce carbon dioxide and water. Because combustion occurs in the engine at a high temperature and pressure, other products are produced as well. Because we can't see some of these products, it is easy to forget they are there.

Global warming

Natural sources release about 150 billion tons of carbon dioxide each year. Much of this carbon dioxide is absorbed by natural processes, such as photosynthesis. By burning fossil fuels and clearing land for development, we put a strain on Earth's ability to manage CO_2 levels. For example, the amount of CO_2 in the atmosphere has increased by 30 percent since the beginning of the Industrial Revolution. Additionally, the average surface temperature of the planet has increased 0.6 to 1.2°F since the mid-1800s. These increases are not huge, but they are enough to have warmed the north pole and caused the sea level to rise 4 to 10 inches. What other consequences of global warming have you heard about?

The chemistry of the atmosphere

Earth's atmosphere is a mixture of gases. The composition of the air is 78 percent nitrogen gas (N_2), 21 percent oxygen (O_2), 0.036 percent carbon dioxide (CO_2), 1 percent argon (an unreactive gas), traces of other gases, and some water vapor.

The atmosphere is mostly nitrogen gas

Nitrogen gas (N_2) is particularly abundant in the atmosphere because it isn't very reactive. However, nitrogen is essential for making molecules called proteins. Plants called legumes (like beans and peas) incorporate airborne nitrogen into protein for their own use. Other plants obtain nitrogen from fertilized soil. Your body obtains nitrogen for making proteins when you eat foods (vegetables and meat) that are high in protein.

O_2 comes from photosynthesis

Unlike nitrogen, oxygen (O_2) is a reactive, flammable gas. The great abundance of nitrogen (N_2) in the atmosphere effectively dilutes the O_2 so that things don't burn out of control every time a fire is started! Living plants and organisms are responsible for keeping enough oxygen in the atmosphere.

Carbon dioxide

Too much CO_2 in the atmosphere causes global warming

Compared to N_2 and O_2, there is very little carbon dioxide (CO_2) in the atmosphere. This may be surprising to you because you have heard that increases in CO_2 in the atmosphere cause global warming. The amount of CO_2 that we have in our atmosphere is just enough to trap heat from the sun to make Earth warm and comfortable. The planet would be too warm with more CO_2 and too cold with less CO_2. When we use fossil fuels, we add more CO_2 to the atmosphere. The phrase **global warming** refers to our ability to increase the temperature of the planet's climate by increasing the amount of CO_2 in our atmosphere. In the United States, each person contributes about 6.6 tons of CO_2 every year! The world produces about 7 billion tons per year.

Car emissions are pollutants

The amount of CO_2 produced by a single car is less than that produced by a large factory or power plant. However, many of us use cars every day and carbon dioxide emissions add up. The word **emissions** refers to the airborne gases and particles that come out of the car's tailpipe when it runs. The combined CO_2 emissions and other pollution from cars on a day-to-day basis have caused many of our large cities to be noticeably hazy and smoggy.

Auto emissions	harm
carbon dioxide	major contributor to global warming
carbon monoxide	deadly gas
nitrous oxides	contribute to acid rain
ozone	irritation to eyes and lungs
hydro-carbons	cancer causing

Figure 22.9: *Ways in which automobile emissions affect air quality.*

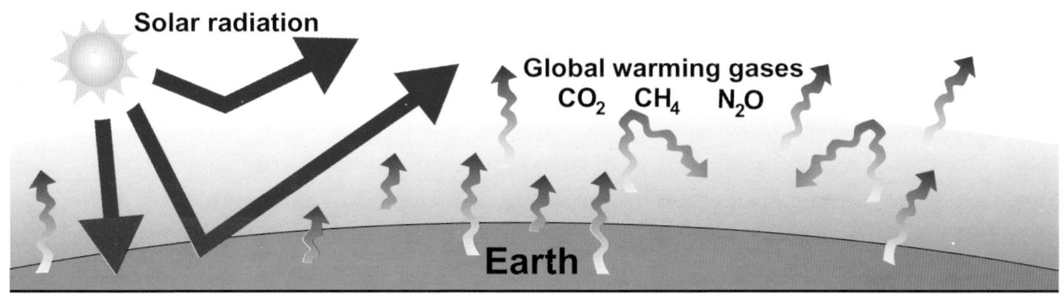

Global warming

Some of the solar radiation that reaches Earth is absorbed by its surface, and some is reflected and exits the atmosphere. However, heat that builds up within the Earth's atmospheres is trapped by global warming gases. The main global warming gases are carbon dioxide (CO_2), methane, (CH_4), and nitrous oxide (N_2O).

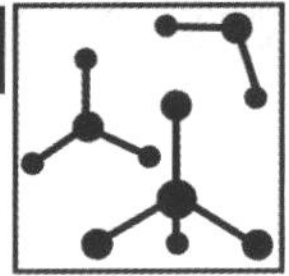

The combustion reaction in cars

Incomplete combustion means more air pollution

Fuel is a mixture of molecules called hydrocarbons. As the name suggests, these molecules only contain hydrogen and carbon. The energy of these valuable molecules is stored in the carbon-carbon and carbon-hydrogen bonds. Hydrocarbons become pollutants when they are incompletely burned during combustion or when they evaporate during refueling or from the engine while it cools. Hydrocarbons can react with nitrogen oxides and sunlight to make ozone. Both ozone and hydrocarbons are toxic pollutants.

The problems with nitrogen oxides

During combustion of fuel in a car, the high temperature and high pressure in the engine causes nitrogen in the air (which is typically unreactive) to convert to nitrogen oxides. Nitrogen oxides are reactants in the formation of ozone, a irritant to eyes and lungs. Nitrogen oxides also mix with water in the atmosphere, forming nitric acid, a component of acid rain.

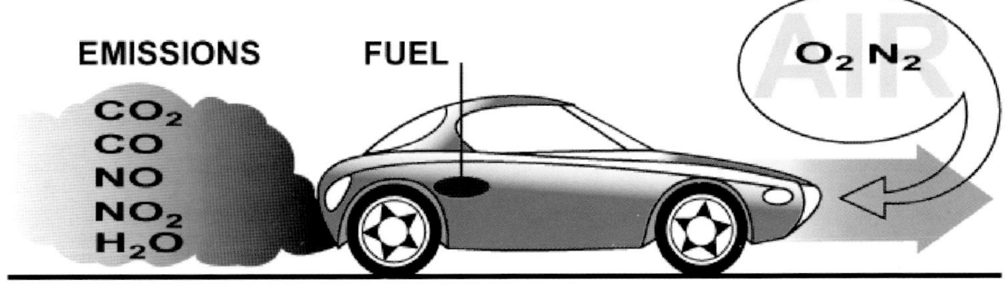

Carbon monoxide is a toxic gas

Complete combustion reactions produce only carbon dioxide. Incomplete combustion reactions also produce carbon monoxide (CO). This small molecule "looks" like oxygen to your body so your body uses CO instead of oxygen. For this reason, high concentrations of CO can be deadly. Lower concentrations found in areas with heavy traffic can be harmful to people with heart or lung disease.

The catalytic converter

The catalytic converter, introduced in the 1970s, reduces hydrocarbon and carbon monoxide emissions by converting these molecules to carbon dioxide and water. Improvements to the catalytic converter over the years have greatly reduced these emissions.

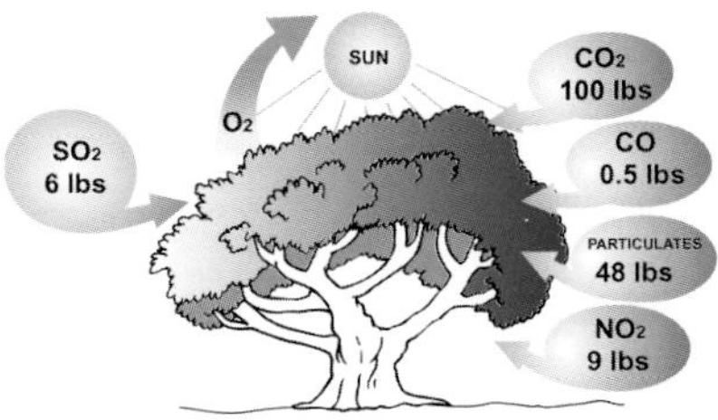

Figure 22.10: *Trees help consume carbon dioxide and other pollutants.*

What can we do to reduce CO_2?

One acre of trees provides oxygen for about 20 people each day. This same acre can absorb emissions, including CO_2 (see figure 22.10).

Questions to discuss with your friends:

- Trees greatly benefit our air quality, but can they solve global warming?
- Why might trees not be a good enough solution to global warming?
- What can you do to reduce how much CO_2 you produce?

Chapter 22 Review

Vocabulary review

Match the following terms with the correct definition. There is one extra definition in the list that will not match any of the terms.

Set One	
1. alpha particle	a. A word to describe isotopes that undergo fission
2. radioactive	b. The part of an atom that contains protons and neutrons
3. beta particle	c. Two neutrons and two protons released from the nucleus of an atom
4. radioactive decay	d. An electron that splits off of a neutron and is released from the nucleus of an atom
5. fission	e. A nuclear reaction that involves the splitting of a heavy nucleus into a lighter nucleus
	f. Radioactive isotopes experience this when they undergo fission

Set Two	
1. fusion	a. This type of nuclear reaction occurs in the sun
2. gamma rays	b. The average time for half the amount of a radioactive element to decay
3. half-life	c. An atom that is distinguished by the number of neutrons in its nucleus
4. isotope	d. A form of electromagnetic radiation released during radioactive decay
5. nuclear reaction	e. The mixing of baking soda and vinegar causes this kind of reaction
	f. Fission and fusion are examples of this kind of reaction

Concept review

1. In your own words, describe the difference between fusion and fission. Why do elements undergo fusion or fission spontaneously?
2. In a short paragraph, contrast nuclear reactions with chemical reactions.
3. Write the isotope notation for hydrogen-3, hydrogen-2 and hydrogen-1. List the number of neutrons, protons and electrons in each of these isotopes.
4. What are the differences between alpha decay and beta decay? Draw a labeled diagram showing each of these particles.
5. Explain how photosynthesis and respiration are related carbon reactions. Write out these reactions in your response.
6. Describe the chemical composition of the Earth's atmosphere.
7. Explain why our use of cars can be cited as one cause of global warming.
8. List 10 products that you use or consume that are made from plants.

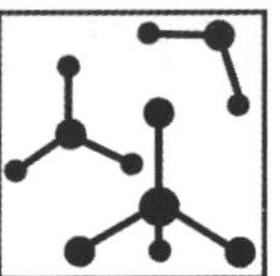

Problems

1. At the beginning of the student reading you were asked, "Which atoms could you combine to make gold?" Use a periodic table with the mass numbers of stable isotopes to write out a fusion reaction and fission reaction for gold. Use the isotope notation for referring to each isotope in the reaction (i.e., the notion for hydrogen-2 would be ${}^{2}_{1}\text{H}$). Additionally, if your reactions involve alpha or beta decay, or the gain or loss of a neutron, be sure to indicate these aspects in your written reaction.
   a. Fusion:
   b. Fission:

2. An isotope decreased to one-fourth its original amount in 18 months. What is the half-life of this radioactive isotope?

3. The decay series for uranium-238 and plutonium-240 are listed below. Above each arrow, write "a" for alpha decay or "b" for beta decay to indicate which type of decay took place at each step.

   a. ${}^{238}_{92}\text{U} \rightarrow {}^{234}_{90}\text{Th} \rightarrow {}^{234}_{91}\text{Pa} \rightarrow {}^{234}_{92}\text{U} \rightarrow {}^{230}_{90}\text{Th} \rightarrow$

   ${}^{226}_{88}\text{Ra} \rightarrow {}^{222}_{86}\text{Rn} \rightarrow {}^{218}_{84}\text{Po} \rightarrow {}^{214}_{82}\text{Pb} \rightarrow {}^{214}_{83}\text{Bi} \rightarrow$

   ${}^{214}_{84}\text{Po} \rightarrow {}^{210}_{82}\text{Pb} \rightarrow {}^{210}_{83}\text{Bi} \rightarrow {}^{210}_{84}\text{Po} \rightarrow {}^{206}_{82}\text{Pb}$

   b. ${}^{240}_{94}\text{Pu} \rightarrow {}^{240}_{95}\text{Am} \rightarrow {}^{236}_{93}\text{Np} \rightarrow {}^{232}_{91}\text{Pa} \rightarrow {}^{232}_{92}\text{U} \rightarrow$

   ${}^{228}_{90}\text{Bi} \rightarrow {}^{224}_{88}\text{Ra} \rightarrow {}^{224}_{89}\text{Ac} \rightarrow {}^{220}_{87}\text{Fr} \rightarrow {}^{216}_{85}\text{At} \rightarrow$

   ${}^{212}_{83}\text{Bi} \rightarrow {}^{212}_{84}\text{Po} \rightarrow {}^{208}_{82}\text{Pb} \rightarrow {}^{208}_{83}\text{Bi}$

4. All plants use the process of photosynthesis. However, this process wasn't always understood. In one classic experiment, a small plant and its soil were weighed. The plant was only given water for a solid year. At the end of the year, the plant weighed much more than it did at the first of the year. The soil weighed the same amount. Where did the extra weight of the plant come from?

5. Could you get rich making gold from fission and fusion reactions? Why or why not?

6. Due to radioactive decay, a sample of an isotope decreased to one-half its original amount in 6 days. What is the half-life of this radioactive isotope?

7. Answer the following:
   a. Cesium-137 is used to investigate soil erosion. This radioactive isotope naturally undergoes beta decay to become a different element. How many neutrons and protons will the different element have? What is this element?
   b. The half-life of cesium-137 is 30 years. Make a graph that shows the radioactive decay of cesium-137 over a period of 300 years. Place time on the x-axis of the graph, and amount of cesium-137 on the y-axis. The starting amount of cesium-137 is 100 atoms. Be sure to title the graph and label the axes.

Applying your knowledge

1. Mining for gold is an active industry. In order for mining companies to grow as businesses, they need to discover new sites that are rich in gold or other valuable minerals and element. Research in your library or on the Internet to find out about mining for gold. What do experts say about how much gold remains to be discovered?

2. Organize a debate in your class on the topic of nuclear energy and technology. What are the pros of using nuclear energy and technology? What are the cons? Prior to the debate, assign teams to the pro or con side and figure out with the class how the debate will be scored.

3. What is the difference between strong nuclear force and gravity? Are there other forces in the universe besides strong nuclear force and gravity? If so, what are these forces and how are they different from gravity and strong nuclear force?

4. The Earth's atmosphere differs from the atmospheres of Mars and Venus. Find out the chemical composition of the atmospheres on these planets. Explain why Earth's atmosphere is suitable for life, but the atmospheres of Mars and Venus are not.

5. Read a recent article about global warming. Write a short summary about the article and a brief paragraph explaining your opinions about the article and global warming.

6. Make a brochure that describes the causes of, the consequences, and the solutions to global warming. Include the economic impact of global warming in your brochure. Do careful research in your library and on the Internet to make this brochure. Include quotations from individuals who are experts on this subject. Experts might be individuals who study global warming at a local college or university. Add your own color graphics to your brochure.

7. The Clean Air Act is an important piece of environmental law. The act was passed in 1970 and then amended in 1990. The purpose of this act is to reduce the number of airborne pollutants in our atmosphere. Most of these pollutants are end-products of chemical reactions that result from industrial processes and our use of gasoline-powered cars.

   Identify three chemical reactions that are used in industry that result in airborne pollutants. Find out how the Clean Air Act has regulated the industries that produce these pollutants
   .

   Obeying the Clean Air Act means that a polluting company, consumers (you), and/or tax-payers have to pay for fixing the causes of the pollutants. This could mean cleaning facilities or changing to newer, non-polluting technologies.

   List five things companies could do to reduce pollution. These costs are usually passed on to consumers through higher prices.

   List five additional problems caused by airborne pollutants that society must pay for. Is the cost of each problem paid by taxes or by the individuals affected by the pollution?

UNIT 8

Water and Solutions

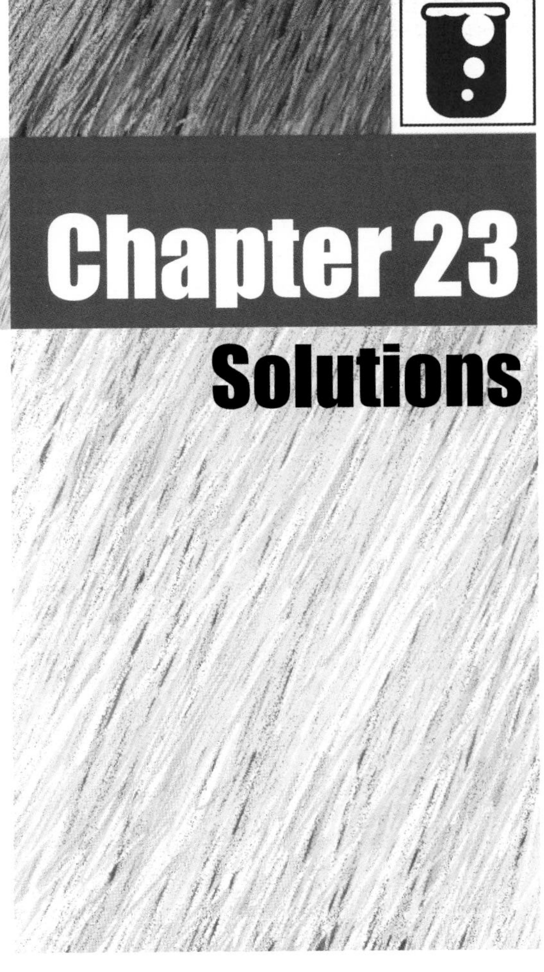

Chapter 23

Solutions

Introduction to Chapter 23

Many of the foods you eat and the products you use (like shampoo) are solutions or other types of mixtures. In this chapter you will learn about solutions and solubility. Since many solutions are critical to the human body, you will also learn how solutions affect health and athletic performance.

Investigations for Chapter 23

23.1	**What is a Solution?**	*Can you identify mixtures as solutions, suspensions, or colloids?*

In this Investigation you will construct an apparatus to view the Tyndall effect. The Tyndall effect is a test for determining the characteristics of a mixture. Your tests will tell you whether the mixture is a solution, colloid, or suspension.

23.2	**Dissolving Rate**	*How can you influence dissolving rates?*

In this Investigation you will design three methods for dissolving rock salt in water and calculate the dissolving rates for each method. Your tests will determine the effect of changing conditions on solubility, such as heat and stirring.

23.3	**Solubility**	*What factors affect solubility?*

When you want to dissolve sugar in water, it helps to heat things up. In this Investigation, you will observe how temperature influences how fast a substance dissolves. Using your observations, you will develop an explanation for how temperature affects solubility. In addition, using carbonated water and a balloon, you will have the opportunity to explore how pressure affects the solubility of a gas in a liquid.

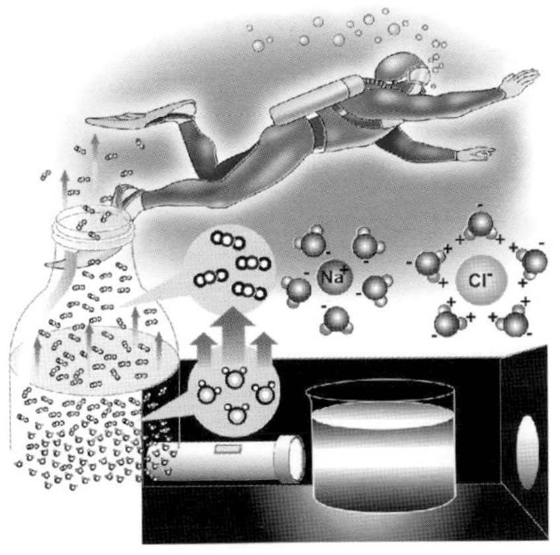

Learning Goals

In this chapter, you will:

- ✔ Categorize mixtures as solutions, suspensions, or colloids.
- ✔ Define solubility.
- ✔ Describe saturated, unsaturated, and supersaturated solutions.
- ✔ Define and calculate dissolving rate.
- ✔ List factors which influence dissolving rate.
- ✔ Evaluate the effectiveness of different methods of influencing dissolving rates.
- ✔ Explain how temperature and pressure influence solubility.
- ✔ Understand solubility values.
- ✔ Interpret temperature-solubility graphs.

Vocabulary

alloys
atmospheres
colloid
dissolved
dissolving rate
equilibrium
hydrated
saturated
solubility
solubility value
solutes
solution
solvent
supersaturated
system
Tyndall effect
unsaturated

23.1 What is a Solution?

If you walk down the beverage aisle of your local grocery store, you might be surprised by the many different ways water is bottled for sale. You might see mineral water, spring water, potable water, distilled water, and carbonated (or seltzer) water. To complicate matters more, there may be several brands of each kind of water to choose from! Is there truly any difference between them?

Figure 23.1: *The variety of containers for bottled water. Spring water and seltzer are often purchased for drinking. Distilled water is used in steam irons and for performing experiments in the laboratory. Why would distilled water be a good choice for these uses?*

What is in bottled water?

Bottled water contains more than pure H_20

The types of bottled water mentioned above have unique characteristics. Mineral water, potable water (that is, water suitable for drinking), and carbonated water contain elements other than pure H_20.

Mineral water contains naturally present minerals

Mineral water, according to government regulations, must contain at least 250 milligrams per liter of dissolved minerals such as calcium, potassium, and magnesium. The minerals must be present naturally and cannot be added at the bottling plant to make mineral water. Also, the water must be collected from an underground source.

Potable water contains additives

Potable water is bottled from a city or town water source. In addition to minerals, potable water may contain sodium fluoride, chlorine, or other additives. Consumers sometimes purchase this water if they know their home plumbing contains lead pipes or lead solder and they want to avoid ingesting any traces of lead that might be present in their tap water.

Distilled water is nearly mineral-free

Distilled water has had most of the minerals removed. First, the water is boiled. The minerals are left behind when the water molecules enter the gas phase. The water vapor is then collected and cooled to room temperature so that it exists once again as a liquid. Sometimes the water is further purified by processes called *deionization* and *reverse osmosis*. Salt water is converted to fresh water using these processes. However, even treated water contains traces of other elements.

Carbonated water

Carbonated water contains carbon dioxide gas evenly distributed throughout the liquid to make it bubbly.

Types of bottled water are examples of solutions

A solution is homogeneous at the molecular level

In chemistry terms, we call mineral water, potable water, tap water, carbonated water, and even distilled water *solutions*. A solution is a mixture of two or more substances that is homogeneous at the molecular level. The word *homogeneous* means the particles in the water are evenly distributed. For example, in mineral water, there are no clumps of hundreds of mineral ions. The particles in a solution exist as individual atoms, ions, or molecules. Each has a diameter between 0.01 and 1.0 nanometer.

An alloy is a solution of two or more metals

Although we often think of solutions as mixtures of solids in liquids, solutions exist in every phase, be it solid, liquid, or gas. Carbonated water is a solution of a gas in a liquid. Fourteen-karat gold is a solution of two solids, silver and gold. "Fourteen-karat" means that 14 out of every 24 atoms in the solution are gold atoms. Likewise, ten-karat means that 10 out of every 24 atoms in the solution are gold. Solutions of two or more metals are called alloys.

A solution is a mixture of solute dissolved in a solvent

Scientists generally refer to the component of the mixture that is present in the greatest amount as the solvent. The remaining components are called the solutes. When the solute particles are evenly distributed throughout the solvent, we say that the solute has dissolved.

Table 23.1: *Different solutions*

Solution	Solvent	Solute(s)	State of solution
air	nitrogen (gas)	O_2, CO_2, He, H_2, H_20, etc. (gases)	gas
carbonated water	water (liquid)	CO_2 (gas)	liquid
saline solution	water (liquid)	salt (solid)	liquid
rubbing alcohol	alcohol (liquid)	water (liquid)	liquid
sterling silver	silver (solid)	copper (solid)	solid

What is a nanometer?

A nanometer is one-billionth of a meter. It is represented by writing "nm." In addition to particles, wavelengths of light are measured in nanometers. For example, the range of wavelengths of visible light is 400 to 700 nm.

Figure 23.2: *Solutions are made when solutes dissolve in solvents. Here, salt is the solute, and water is the solvent.*

Colloids and suspensions

Colloid particles are larger than those in true solutions, but smaller than those in suspensions

Mixtures such as mayonnaise, egg whites, and gelatin are colloids. They look like solutions, but the particles in these mixtures, at one to 1,000 nanometers, are larger than those found in solutions. True solutions contain single atoms and molecules (less than 1 nanometer in size). By comparison, colloid particles are formed of *clusters* of atoms or molecules. Nevertheless, colloid particles are too small (1-1,000 nanometers) to settle to the bottom of their container. Instead, they stay evenly distributed throughout the mixture because they are constantly tossed about by the movement of the liquid particles.

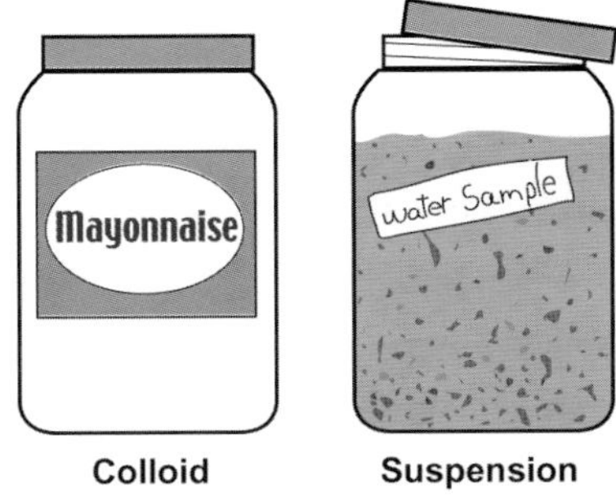

Figure 23.3: *Mayonnaise is a colloid. Water and silt make a suspension.*

Suspensions settle upon standing

You may have noticed that when you step into a pond or lake to go swimming, you suddenly make the water cloudy. Your feet cause the mud on the bottom of the pond or lake to mix with the water. However, if you stand very still, eventually the water becomes clear again. This is because the individual mud particles sink. In suspensions like muddy water, the particles are greater than 1,000 nanometers in diameter. Atoms and molecules are much smaller than 100 nanometers. Suspensions are mixtures that settle upon standing (figure 23.3). Suspensions can be separated by filtering.

Figure 23.4: *The Tyndall effect helps you tell the difference between colloids and solutions. Here, the beam of the flashlight is visible as it shines through the colloid in the beaker. The beam would not be visible if the beaker contained a solution.*

The Tyndall effect

It isn't possible to separate colloids by filtering. However, there is a way to visually distinguish colloids from true solutions. It is called the Tyndall effect. If you shine a flashlight through a jar of a translucent colloid, the particles scatter the light, making the beam visible. Fog is an example of a colloid. This is why an automobile's headlight beams can be seen on a foggy evening.

Table 23.2: *Properties of solutions, suspensions, and colloids*

	Approximate size of solute particles	Solute particles settle	Can be separated by filtering	Particles scatter light
solutions	0.01 - 1.0 nm	no	no	no
colloids	1.0 - 1,000 nm	no	only with special equipment	yes, if transparent
suspensions	>1000 nm	with time	yes	yes, if transparent

23.2 Dissolving Rate

On long backpacking trips, hikers must make sure that they have a safe, reliable source of drinking water. Drinking from an icy cold mountain stream may seem appealing to a hot, tired backpacker, but it could bring the trip to an unpleasant end. Most streams, rivers, and lakes in the United States contain Giardia and other microorganisms that can cause serious intestinal disturbances.

Consequently, wise backpackers always carry water-treatment supplies. One of the safest and least expensive ways to purify the water is to add an iodine tablet. Iodine tablets are effective against many microorganisms, bacteria, and viruses. These tablets are especially useful because they add so little weight to the pack and can be used with refreshingly cold water.

What could a thirsty backpacker do to get an iodine tablet to dissolve faster? In this section, you will learn about factors that affect the dissolving rate of various substances.

Figure 23.5: *Water from lakes, rivers, and streams must be treated to make it safe to drink. A microscopic view of two Giardia in water is shown in the upper left corner of the figure. Giardia is a parasite that lives in the small intestine of wild animals. You can become infected with Giardia if you drink untreated water that contains infective cysts, a life stage of Giardia that permits this parasite to spread from animal to animal or from animals to humans.*

Molecular motion and dissolving rate

Stirring a mixture speeds dissolving

One of the simplest ways to increase the dissolving rate of the iodine tablet is to stir the water or shake the water bottle. To understand why this method works, we need to take a look at what is happening on a molecular level.

A solute such as iodine can dissolve when solvent molecules collide with clumps of solute particles. In this case, water molecules collide with iodine ions in the tablet. Stirring helps this process by increasing the rate of the collisions. The result of collisions between molecules is that solute particles are "pulled" into solution and surrounded by solvent molecules.

Stirring exposes fresh solvent to newly exposed solute

Stirring a solution does more that just increase collisions between solute and solvent molecules. Stirring moves the molecules around. Solvent molecules that have collided with the solute have to get out of the way so that new ones can collide with the exposed surface of the solute.

Surface area and dissolving rate

Crushing a solute tablet increases the surface area exposed to the solvent

If the hiker were to crush the iodine tablet, the dissolving rate would increase dramatically. When the tablet is whole, many billions of iodine atoms remain completely surrounded by other iodine atoms, but the atoms inside the tablet are protected from the water molecules. Crushing the tablet increases the surface area that is available for solvent molecules to interact with solute molecules.

Here is a 1-centimeter cube. This means that each edge of the cube is 1 centimeter wide. The area of each face of the cube is 1 cm by 1 cm or 1 cm^2. Cubes have six faces. Therefore, the total surface area of the cube is: $6 \times 1\ cm^2 = 6\ cm^2$.

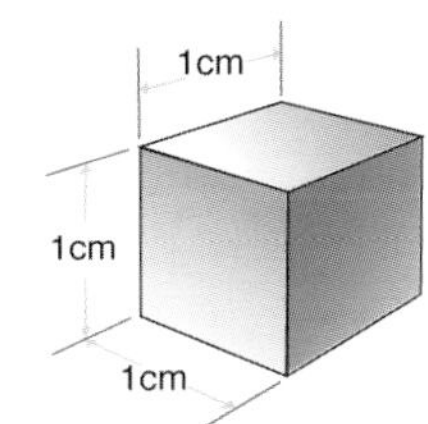

Every time the piece is divided the surface area increases

What do you think happens to surface area if we cut the cube in half? Now, in addition to the original 6 cm^2, you have added two additional faces of 1 cm^2 each, for a total surface area of 8cm^2.

Cut the halves of the cube in half, and you have four new faces for a total surface area of 12 cm^2.

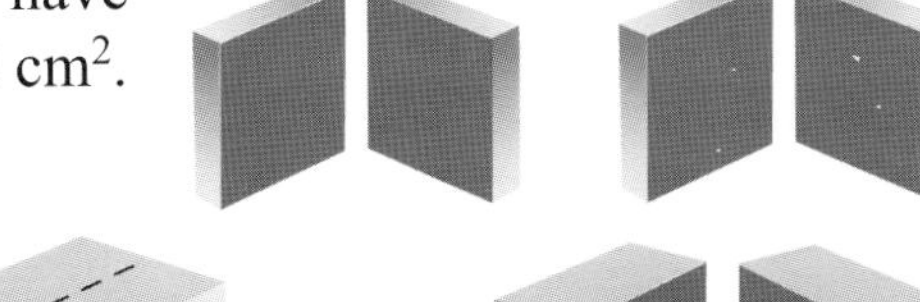

Stack up the four pieces and make a vertical cut down the center. You have added two new faces, for a total surface area of 14 cm^2.

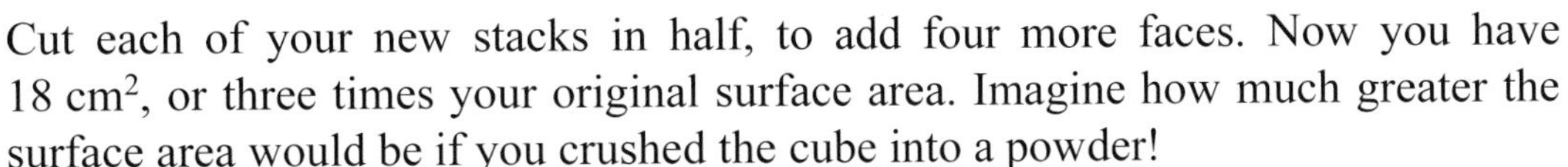

Cut each of your new stacks in half, to add four more faces. Now you have 18 cm^2, or three times your original surface area. Imagine how much greater the surface area would be if you crushed the cube into a powder!

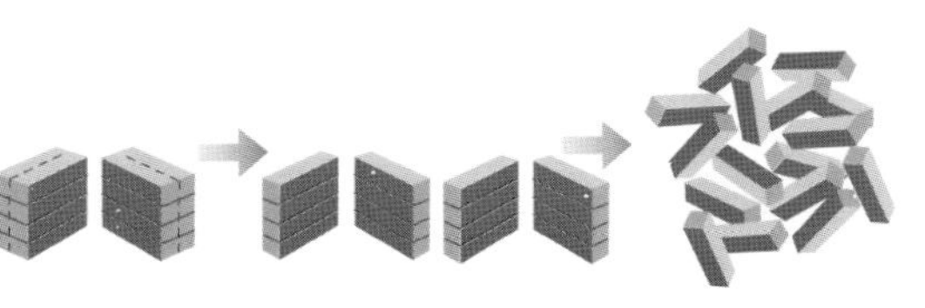

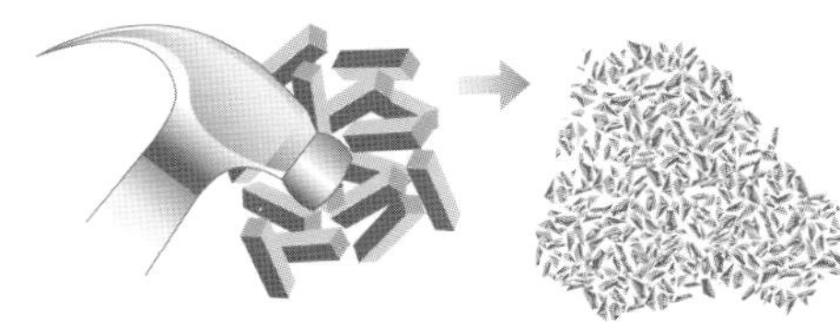

Disinfecting with iodine

Iodine, like all halogens (fluorine, chlorine, and bromine), has seven valence electrons. It reacts with substances to gain an electron and satisfy the "octet rule"—the need for eight electrons in the outermost energy level of an atom.

Halogens are so reactive that they can be used as disinfectants. However, of the halogens, iodine (the only one existing as a solid at room temperature) and chlorine (in combination with other elements) are the most easily used in this way. In the proper concentrations, chlorine and iodine tablets dissolved in water can kill microorganisms like Giardia without being toxic to the person drinking the water.

Fluorine and bromine are not useful for sterilizing water. Fluorine is a highly reactive gas, and bromine is a liquid that is very damaging to skin.

Timed-release capsules: making less medicine more effective

Timed-release medicine

Have you ever taken cold or allergy medicine in the form of a clear capsule with multi-colored round beads inside? If so, you are familiar with timed-release medicine. Understanding dissolving rates made the invention of this type of medicine possible.

What is micro-encapsulation?

There are several ways to manufacture timed-release medication. One of the most common is called *microencapsulation*. Using this method, pharmaceutical manufacturers divide a dose of medicine into tiny particles. Some of these particles are placed into the capsule unchanged. These particles of medicine become active in the patient's body soon after the capsule is swallowed. The remaining particles are coated with a *polymer* usually derived from gelatin, cellulose, or silicone. The coating dissolves slowly in the stomach, releasing the medicine inside over a period of time. By changing the thickness or varying the coating material, manufacturers alter the dissolving rate of the coating. This allows them to control the amount of time it takes for the medicine to be released in the body. The different colored beads inside the capsule show the different coatings used to encapsulate the medicine particles.

Timed-release capsules mean that you can take less medicine to feel better

Timed-release capsules have several advantages. First, they make smaller doses of medicine more effective. Previously, when a patient swallowed a dose of medicine, there would be a peak level in the body followed by a steady decline until the next pill was swallowed. To maintain the minimum effective amount of the medicine in the body at all times, the peak level had to be significantly higher than the ideal dose. This meant the patient had to consume larger quantities of the medicine, thereby increasing the risk of side effects. Timed-release capsules help to ensure a steady supply of the minimum effective dose.

Timed-release capsules are safer and more cost-effective

Timed-release capsules are safer and more convenient for the patient. For example, a patient who previously had to take a pill four times a day might switch to a once-a-day, timed-release capsule. Taking only one capsule reduces the chances of forgetting how much medicine you have taken.

Figure 23.6: *Grinding substances to make medicines is an ancient practice that is still used today. Powdered substances dissolve quickly.*

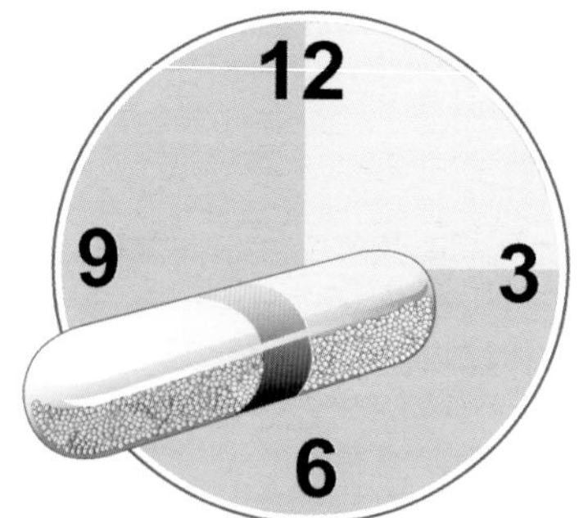

TIMED- RELEASE CAPSULE

Figure 23.7: *Timed-release capsules contain microencapsulated medicine that appear as tiny beads within the capsule. The different dissolving rates of the beads allow you to take less medicine to feel better.*

23.3 Solubility

The human body is mostly water. For every hour of vigorous exercise, you may lose as much as a half-gallon of your body's water supply through sweating and exhaling! You also lose small amounts of salts, lactic acid, and urea when you sweat. Lactic acid and urea are the breakdown products of sugar and proteins, respectively. The more you exercise, the more water and salts you lose, and the more you break down sugar and protein. You can replenish lost fluid by drinking water. To quickly replace salts and sugar as well, many athletes consume sports drinks. Sweat and sports drinks are both examples of solutions—both are mostly water with dissolved substances. In this section, you will learn about the factors that affect how solutes dissolve in solutions.

1/2 GALLON OF WATER PER HOUR

Figure 23.8: *With vigorous exercise, you can lose up to a half-gallon of water per hour by sweating and exhaling.*

Using systems to talk about solutions

Systems are collections of matter and processes that can be studied

Your body is a system. A system is a collection of matter and processes that take place in a certain space and can be observed and studied. Your body with its numerous metabolic activities is an excellent example of a system that is "open." This means that your body constantly interacts with its environment by taking in and releasing substances. For example, you eat food, exhale carbon dioxide, and give off heat.

Systems can be open or closed

Scientists often find open systems difficult to work with because it is hard to control the variables in open systems. Scientists have an easier time studying closed or nearly closed systems. A reaction that takes place in a stoppered test tube is a good example of a closed system.

A solute and a solvent make up a system

The system of a solution includes the solute and the solvent. The kind of container that holds the solute and solvent is not important. For the rest of this section, the factors that affect the system of a solute and a solvent will be discussed.

What happens when a solute dissolves in a solvent?

NaCl is an example of a solute

Let's use sodium chloride (NaCl) as an example of a solute being dissolved in the solvent, water. If you look closely at a single crystal of NaCl, you will notice that it is a cube. Millions of sodium (Na) and chlorine (Cl) atoms, each too small to see with your naked eye, are a part of a single crystal of NaCl.

The bond between Na and Cl is ionic

Within a crystal of NaCl, ionic bonds are formed between Na and Cl. The oxidation state of Na is (1^+), and the oxidation state of Cl is (1^-). Na and Cl are a good match because their oxidation states add up to zero: (1^+) + (1^-) = 0. This means that a single NaCl molecule is neutral and stable. However, the Cl end of the molecule is more negatively charged than the Na end because the Cl has attracts an electron away from Na to form the ionic bond.

Water molecules bond with each other

Although a water molecule does not have ionic bonds, the molecule does have a partially charged positive end and a partially charged negative end. Water molecules weakly connect to each other by matching their partial positive end to the partial negative end of a neighboring molecule. These links between water molecules are called *hydrogen bonds*.

Water molecules hydrate Na and Cl

When a NaCl crystal is mixed with water, a reaction occurs. The partially charged ends of the water molecules are attracted to Na and Cl in the crystal. The process results in the formation of Na^+ and Cl^- ions that are completely surrounded by water molecules. When this happens, we say the ions are hydrated and write "aq" next to the ions. "Aq" stands for aqueous which refers to a water solution. Hydrated $Na_{(aq)}^+$ and $Cl_{(aq)}^-$ ions are able to freely move in a solution.

Hydration continues until the solution is saturated

As one layer of molecules on a NaCl crystal is brought into solution by water molecules, another layer is exposed. If the conditions are right, this process continues until the entire crystal is dissolved. It seems, in fact, to have disappeared! All that has happened, however, is that Na^+ and Cl^- ions from NaCl have been separated and completely surrounded by water molecules.

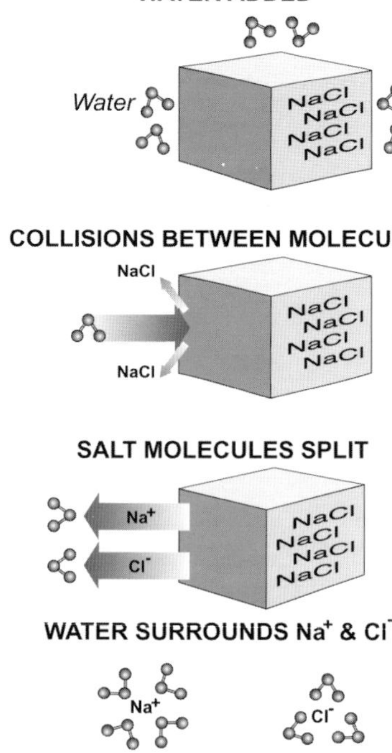

Figure 23.9: *When a crystal of NaCl molecules is mixed with water, hydrated Na+ and Cl- ions are formed.*

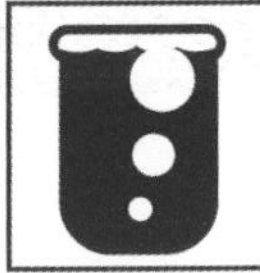

Solubility

What is solubility? The term solubility means the amount of solute that can be dissolved in a specific volume of solvent under certain conditions. A solute's solubility depends on the chemical nature of the solvent. Another important factor that influences solubility is the temperature of the system (the solute and solvent).

Volume affects solubility For a solute to dissolve completely, you need a certain volume of solvent. The volume of solvent provides enough solvent molecules to surround all the solute molecules. For example, to dissolve an amount of sodium chloride (NaCl), you need enough water molecules to pull apart and surround all the Na^+ and Cl^- ions.

The solubility of a solid usually increases with temperature The solubility of a solid substance usually increases as temperature increases. The effect of temperature on solubility has to do with molecular motion and the energy of the solute-solvent system. At higher temperatures, molecules move faster so that there are more molecular collisions between solute and solvent molecules. The rate of collisions between these molecules is usually directly related to the rate at which the solute dissolves.

Solubility values The solubility value for table salt (NaCl) is 1 gram per 2.8 milliliters of water at 25°C. The solubility value for NaCl tells you how much can dissolve in a certain volume (or, sometimes, mass) of water as long as the water is at 25°C. Using this information, how much salt would dissolve in 280 milliliters of water at that temperature? If you said 100 grams, you are correct!

Some substances do not dissolve in water The table in figure 23.10 shows the solubility values for common substances. Notice that chalk and talc do not have solubility values. Because these substances do not dissolve in water, they are said to be *insoluble*.

Common name	Solubility at 25 °C (grams per 100 mL H_2O)
table salt (NaCl)	37.7
sugar ($C_{12}H_{22}O_{11}$)	200
baking soda ($NaHCO_3$)	approx. 10
chalk ($CaCO_3$)	insoluble
talc (Mg silicates)	insoluble

Figure 23.10: *Solubility values for common substances.*

Temperature-solubility graphs

Temperature-solubility graphs show how much substance dissolves at a given temperature

The solubility values for solutes are easily determined if you have a temperature-solubility graph. The *y*-axis on these graphs represents how many grams of solute (in this case, salts) will dissolve in 100 milliliters of water. The *x*-axis represents temperature in degrees Celsius.

You will notice in the graph that the salts (NaCl, KNO_3, $NaNO_3$) dissolve differently as temperature increases. For something to dissolve in water, the water molecules need to break the bonds between the solute molecules. Water dissolves substances differently because the chemical bonds between atoms are not all the same.

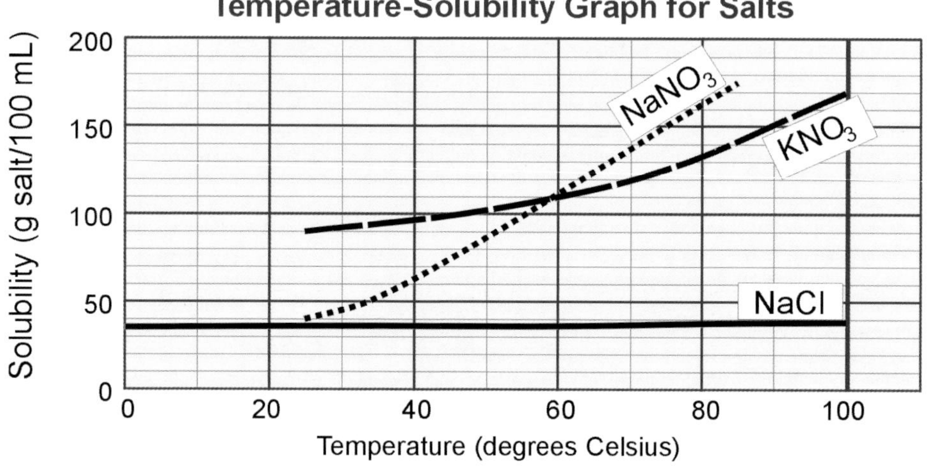

Interpreting the graph

The graph above is a temperature-solubility graph for sodium chloride (NaCl), potassium nitrate (KNO_3), and sodium nitrate ($NaNO_3$). The solubility of NaCl does not change much as temperature increases. The effect of temperature on the solubility of KNO_3 and $NaNO_3$ is more noticeable. More KNO_3 and $NaNO_3$ will dissolve in 100 milliliters of water at higher temperatures than NaCl.

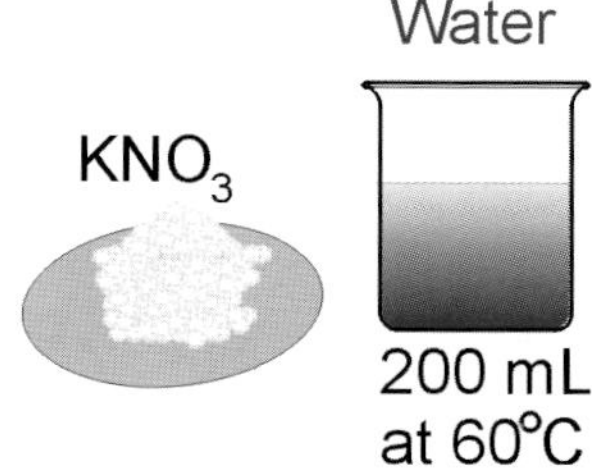

Example

How many grams of potassium nitrate (KNO_3) will dissolve in 200 mL of water at 60°C?

Solution:

(1) You are asked for the mass in grams of solute.

(2) You are given temperature and volume.

(3) The relationship between solubility and temperature for KNO_3 can be seen on a graph to the left.

(4) From the graph, you see that 110 grams of KNO_3 dissolve in 100 mL of water at 60°C.

(5) Plug in numbers.

200 mL / 100 mL = 2

2 x 110 g = 220 g

(6) Answer:

220 grams of KNO_3 will dissolve in 200 mL of water at 60°C.

The solubility of gases

For the same reasons that temperature tends to increase the solubility of solids in liquids, temperature tends to decrease the solubility of gases in liquids. You may have noticed that a can of soda at room temperature is more likely to fizz and spill over when opened than a cold can of soda. As temperature increases, the gas molecules and water molecules begin to move around more. The increased motion means that more dissolved gas molecules encounter the surface of the soda and escape.

Figure 23.11: *The CO_2 in a can of soda like ginger ale has been dissolved in water with the use of pressure.*

Pressure influences the solubility of gases

The solubility of gas depends on temperature and pressure

The solubility of gases depends on temperature and pressure. When you drink fizzy, carbonated beverages, you are consuming carbon dioxide (CO_2) that has been dissolved in water with the use of pressure (figure 23.11). Soda is fizzy because carbon dioxide has been dissolved in the liquid by using pressure. When you pop the tab on a can of soda, you release pressure. You can hear carbon dioxide rapidly escaping. Shaking a can of soda before opening it also forces some carbon dioxide to come out of solution by getting more carbon dioxide molecules to the surface of the liquid.

★ Fish and other aquatic organisms in lakes, rivers, and oceans need dissolved oxygen to live

Dissolved oxygen is an important component of lake, river, and ocean water. Oxygen is mixed into the water through wave action and produced by underwater plants as a by-product of photosynthesis. When the water temperature rises, the amount of dissolved oxygen decreases. Less dissolved oxygen means less oxygen for fish, and they depend on this dissolved oxygen for respiration. When the weather is very warm, fish stay near the bottom of ponds and rivers where there is cooler, more oxygenated water.

How temperature affects the amount of dissolved oxygen in water

Electrical generating facilities are often built near bodies of water so that they have an inexpensive source of water for their cooling system. However, when this water is discharged back into the river or bay while it is still warm, it can significantly reduce the amount of dissolved oxygen available in the waterway. At the same time, the warming of the water increases the metabolic rate of the fish so that their need for dissolved oxygen increases. The combination of these two factors can spell trouble for the fish and cause large disturbances to the local ecosystem.

How did soda get its name?

In 1767, Joseph Priestly, an English chemist best known for discovering oxygen, figured out how to artificially carbonate beverages. Initially, carbon dioxide was obtained by acidifying baking soda (sodium bicarbonate). This is why we often use the name "soda" for carbonated beverages.

How much will dissolve?

The solubility of a substance stops at equilibrium

When talking about solubility, equilibrium is the balance of solute molecules coming and going from a solution for a given set of conditions. In other words, the process of dissolving a solute is a "two-way street." For every set of conditions, a solute will dissolve in and come out of solution at a certain rate. When the rate of dissolving equals the rate of coming out of solution, we say equilibrium has been reached (figure 23.12).

Saturated means the maximum amount has dissolved

One way to describe a solution that contains 100 grams of NaCl in 280 milliliters of water at 25°C is to say that it is saturated, meaning no more salt will dissolve under these conditions. If you raise the temperature of this system, however, you will be able to dissolve a little more salt. What happens when the solution cools back down again? Some of the dissolved salt will recrystallize (figure 23.12).

Unsaturated means more solute can be dissolved

This sequence of processes also describes how rock candy is made. Rock candy consists of large sugar crystals usually attached to a rough surface such as a piece of cotton string. The candy is made by heating water to boiling and then stirring in granulated sugar. As long as the sugar dissolves, the solution is said to be unsaturated. When no more sugar will dissolve, the solution is said to be saturated. Next, the saturated, sugar-water solution is poured into a jar with a suspended cotton string. As the solution cools, it becomes supersaturated.

Supersaturated means more is dissolved than normally possible

Supersaturated solutions are unstable. In this case, if the jar of supersaturated sugar-water is jiggled, the suspended string moves even slightly, or another granule of sugar is dropped in, crystals of solute begin to form. The crystals stick to the rough surface of the string. After five to seven days, all the excess sugar returns to its solid form, and the string is covered with large crystals. The solution left behind now contains only the amount of sugar that can remain dissolved at room temperature. It is once again a *saturated* solution.

Figure 23.12: *A solute dissolves until equilibrium is reached. This diagram shows gas molecules (the open circles) dissolving and coming out of solution at the surface of the solution. At the bottom of the glass, molecules of a solid (the closed circles) are dissolving and recrystallizing.*

Science in the Real World: Scuba diving

You now know that gases dissolve in liquids and that pressure is an important factor in determining how much gas will dissolve in a liquid. In scuba diving, a deep descent underwater poses some problems that have to do with the solubility of gases in blood.

Atmospheric pressure is measured in units called **atmospheres**. The abbreviation of this unit is "atm." At the Earth's surface, atmospheric pressure is 1 atm. The pressure increases by 1 every 10 meters (about 33 feet) as a diver descends through sea water. In other words, at a depth of 10 meters, the pressure acting on the diver has doubled to 2 atmospheres, or twice what we are used to on the Earth's surface. At 30 meters (99 feet), the pressure has quadrupled to 4 atm. Because one atm is equal to 14.5 pounds per square inch (psi), at 40 meters, you would be under 72.5 psi. That's equal to about twice as much air pressure as a car tire!

Depth (meters)	Pressure (atm)
0	1
10	2
20	3
30	4
40	5

Figure 23.13: *How pressure changes with water depth.*

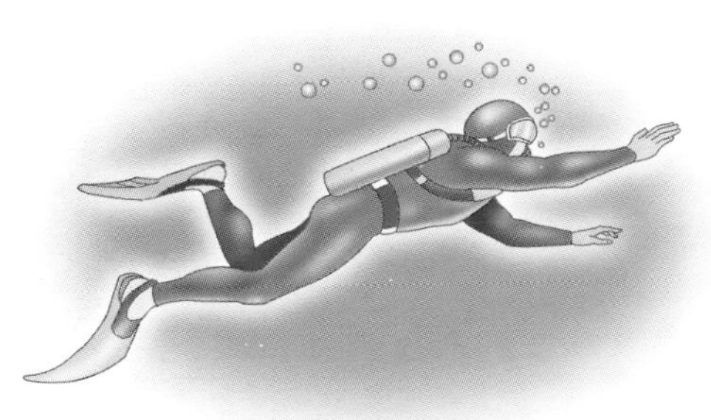

Because a diver is under increased pressure during a dive, the concentrations of gases in the blood and tissues of the diver are higher. The diver can easily process oxygen and carbon dioxide. However, nitrogen is an unreactive gas. It stays in the tissues when a diver is in deep water. High concentrations of nitrogen in the body cause a condition called *nitrogen narcosis*. This causes divers to be either extremely carefree, extremely suspicious, or fearful. In either case, the diver loses his or her ability to function safely underwater. Diving partners (called "dive buddies") keep up constant communication to check that they are not confused because of nitrogen narcosis. The best way to treat nitrogen narcosis is to slowly rise to the water surface with a partner or dive buddy. A slow ascent with normal breathing allows gases to come back out of the blood and tissues easily. Scuba divers should never hold their breath underwater. Expanding gases as a diver rises to the surface can rupture lung tissue!

Decompression sickness occurs when body tissues get supersaturated with nitrogen. Bubbles of nitrogen form in the bloodstream and tissues. These bubbles can block important arteries and cause a stroke or heart attack. When they are trapped in one's joints or back or abdomen, the bubbles are painful. To release pressure in the back or stomach due to bubble formation, individuals with decompression sickness bend over, which is why decompression sickness is often called "the bends."

How did scuba get started?

SCUBA stands for self-contained underwater breathing apparatus. A number of inventors have contributed to developing the technology for scuba diving. The invention of the aqualung by Jaques-Yves Cousteau and Emile Gagnan in 1943 made scuba diving available to anyone who wanted to do underwater exploring. This device made breathing air underwater easy, safe and reliable.

Chapter 23 Review

Vocabulary review

Match the following terms with the correct definition. There is one extra definition in the list that will not match any of the terms.

Set One

1. solution
2. solvent
3. solute
4. suspension
5. colloid

a. A substance particles that dissolves in a solvent
b. A solution of two or more metals
c. A mixture of two or more substances that is homogeneous at the molecular level
d. A mixture that cannot be separated by filtering but does scatter light rays
e. The component of a solution that is present in the greatest amount
f. A mixture that will separate if left to stand for a period of time

Set Two

1. dissolve
2. solubility
3. unsaturated
4. saturated
5. supersaturated

a. Contains less than the maximum amount of solute that can dissolve for a given set of conditions
b. To spread a solute evenly throughout a solvent
c. Unstable solution containing more solute than will usually dissolve for a given set of conditions
d. To undergo a phase change
e. Contains the maximum amount of solute that will dissolve for a given set of conditions
f. The amount of solute that will dissolve in a given amount of solvent for a given set of conditions

Set Three

1. soluble
2. solubility value
3. equilibrium

a. A substance in a solution that is in the smallest amount
b. The ability of a substance to be dissolved by a solvent
c. The state of the formation of a solution in which as many solute molecules are dissolving as are coming back out of the solution
d. A number indicating the mass of solute that can dissolve in a mass or volume of solvent at a certain temperature

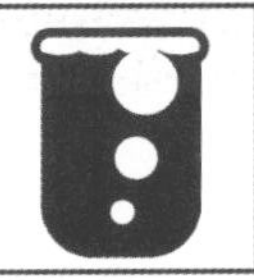

Concept review

1. Give an example of a solution in which the solute is not a solid and the solvent is not a liquid.
2. Name two ways to distinguish between suspensions and colloids.
3. What would happen to the solubility of potassium chloride in water as the water temperature increased from 25°C to 100 °C?
4. What happens to the solubility of oxygen in a pond as the pond temperature decreases from 25°C to 10°C?
5. When you open a can of orange soda at room temperature, why is it more likely to fizz and spill over than a can that has been refrigerated?
6. What happens to a supersaturated solution when more solute is added?
7. Name three ways to increase the dissolving rate of sugar in water.
8. What information goes on the x-axis and on the y-axis of a temperature-solubility graph?
9. A piece of rock candy in a sugar solution is at equilibrium with the solution. What does this mean on a molecular level? In other words, what are the rock candy molecules doing, and what are the sugar molecules in solution doing? You may want to draw a picture to help answer this question.

Problems

1. If you had a cube measuring 10 centimeter per side, what is its total surface area?
2. If you cut the cube into eight identical small cubes, what is its total surface area?
3. One solubility value of NaCl is 1 gram/2.8 milliliters of water at 25°C. Use this value to figure out the following: (a) The volume of water needed to dissolve 100 grams of NaCl, (b) The mass of NaCl that would dissolve in 100 ml of water.
4. Use the temperature-solubility graph on page 412 to answer the following questions:
   a. What is the solubility value of $NaNO_3$ at 25°C?
   b. Which salt has the highest solubility value at 75°C?
   c. Temperature affects the solubility of which salt the least?
   d. Temperature affects the solubility of which salt the most?

Applying your knowledge

1. Create an interesting handout for fourth graders that explains how to make rock candy. The handout should include safety instructions, including supervision, and definitions of these words: *dissolve*, *unsaturated*, *saturated*, and *supersaturated*.
2. Part of a drug manufacturer's job is designing medicines that are easy to take and work effectively.
   a. Design a medicine that dissolves quickly in water. What features allow it to dissolve quickly?
   b. Design a timed-release medicine. What features allow the medicine to be released in small doses once it is taken?
3. In scuba diving, a counting test is performed by dive buddies to check to see if both buddies are thinking clearly. The test is performed correctly when the buddies are able to count together with their fingers because in scuba diving, it is easier to communicate with hands than with voices. For example, if one buddy holds up two fingers, the other buddy should hold up three fingers. If one buddy holds up four fingers, the other buddy should hold up five fingers, and so on. Use this information to answer this question:
   You are scuba diving with a buddy in deep water and decide to check if she is all right by doing the counting test with her. You hold up two fingers. She should hold up three fingers, but she holds up five fingers! You suspect your buddy has nitrogen narcosis. You decide to take your buddy slowly to the surface. At the surface, you check again to see if she is all right. You hold up two fingers, and she holds up three fingers. You are relieved she is thinking clearly! When someone asks what happened, you tell the story in detail. Explain what you think happened to your friend and why. Also, explain why you brought her to the surface slowly instead of quickly.
4. Why should scuba divers never hold their breath when underwater?

Rock Candy Recipe

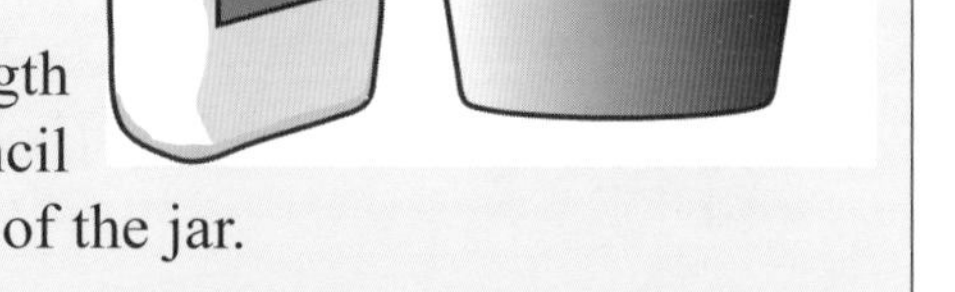

You will need: *1 kg sugar, 450 mL water, saucepan, 2 liter glass jar, candy thermometer, cotton string, plastic wrap, pencil*

Prepare the jar: Tie one end of the clean cotton string to the middle of the pencil. Cut the string to a length equal to the height of the jar. Tie a knot in the end of the string to serve as a small weight. Place the pencil on top of the jar so that the string is suspended inside. The string should not touch the sides or bottom of the jar.

Heat the water to boiling. Slowly stir in the sugar until the solution is saturated. When no additional sugar will dissolve, pour the solution into the jar. Make sure the string does not stick to the side of the jar. Cover with plastic wrap.

Set the jar aside where it can rest undisturbed for 5 to 7 days. At the end of this time, remove the string from the solution. Examine the large crystals with a magnifying glass.

UNIT 8

Water and Solutions

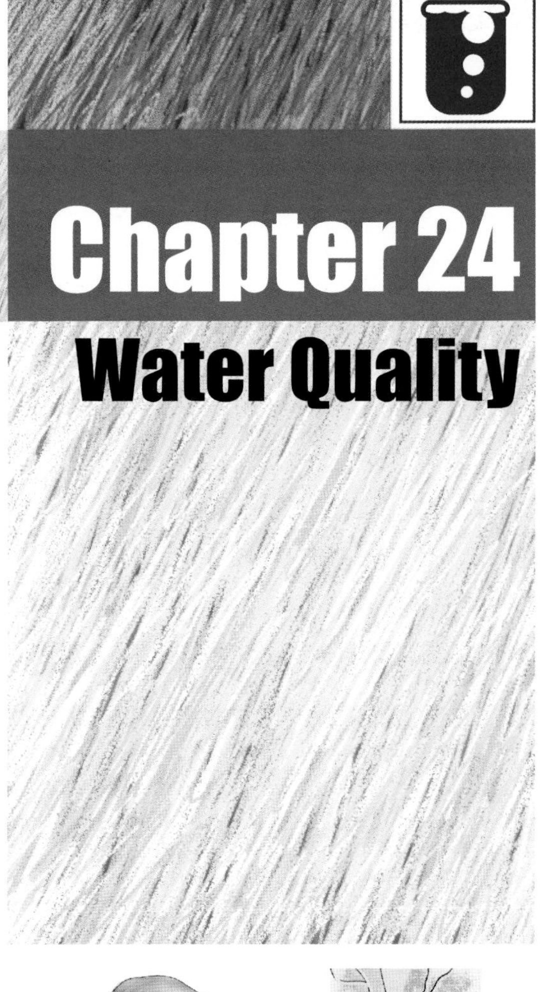

Chapter 24

Water Quality

Introduction to Chapter 24

This chapter is about water and how the quality of water is measured. You will first learn about water on a molecular level. In the second section, the focus becomes the water cycle and how water is distributed. You will learn to recognize and use standard water quality tests in both Investigations to assess the quality of water you use at home and water that exists naturally in your community.

Investigations to Chapter 24

24.1	Water	*What is the quality of your tap water?*

How pure is the water you drink? In this Investigation, you will collect hot and cold water samples at home. You will then test the pH, hardness, and levels of chlorine, copper, and iron in your water samples.

24.2	The Water Cycle	*What is the quality of your local surface water?*

In this Investigation, you will do research and field work. Your task is to meet with a local water quality official and learn how water is tested. You will monitor data for levels of coliform bacteria, pH, dissolved oxygen, biological oxygen demand, nitrate, phosphate, and turbidity. Since this data is extremely important to public health, you will summarize your findings in a report.

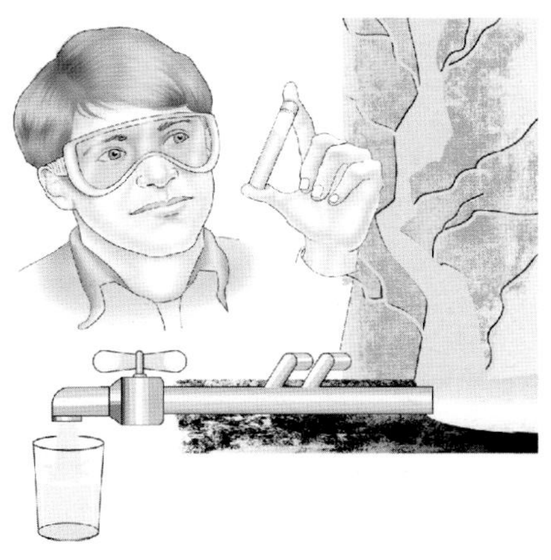

Learning Goals

In this chapter, you will:

- ✔ Describe the properties of water including its function as a nearly universal solvent.
- ✔ Understand what factors are important to water quality.
- ✔ Use and interpret basic water quality tests.
- ✔ Describe how water moves through the water cycle.
- ✔ Explain why maintaining our water quality is important.

Vocabulary

aquifer	groundwater	nonpolar	surface runoff
condensation	hydrogen bond	polar	surface water
evaporation	hydrologic cycle	precipitation	transpiration

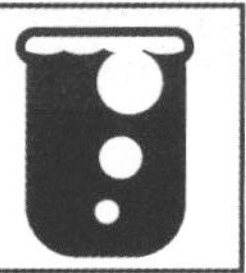

24.1 Water

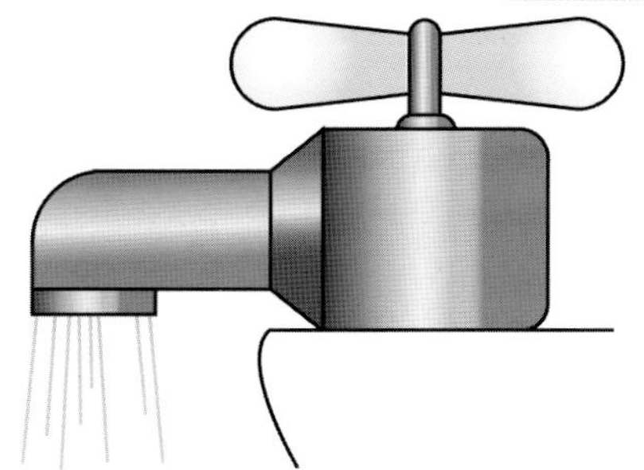

Water is one substance that makes our planet unique. All life on Earth depends on this useful combination of hydrogen and oxygen atoms. In our solar system, only Earth has water in such great abundance. Because we seem to have so much water, it is easy to take it for granted. Think about what you did yesterday. How often did you use water and how much? Now think about how yesterday would have been different if you had had no access to water!

Water is a nearly universal solvent

Water dissolves most solutes We rely on water to clean fruits and vegetables, clothes, cars, and dogs, and ourselves. Also, if you like to cook, you know that certain substances like salt and sugar dissolve easily in water. This is why water is so useful for cooking. We get most of our nutrients dissolved in water. Water is useful because it dissolves many things. In other words, *water is an excellent solvent of many solutes.* This is what is meant when water is described as a nearly universal solvent.

A water molecule is V-shaped A water molecule forms a "V." An oxygen atom forms the point of the "V," and the bonds with the two hydrogen atoms are the two legs. Oxygen atoms have an oxidation state of 2^- and hydrogen atoms have an oxidation state of 1^+. The combination of two hydrogen atoms and one oxygen atom makes a water molecule that is neutral. However, because of different electronegativity values for oxygen and hydrogen atoms and the V-shape, a water molecule is slightly positive on one end and slightly negative on the other.

A water molecule is polar Because one end of a water molecule is partly positive and one is negative, we say water is a polar molecule because it has a two poles, each with a different partial charge (see Figure 24.1). The polar characteristic of a water molecule helps explain why water dissolves so many things.

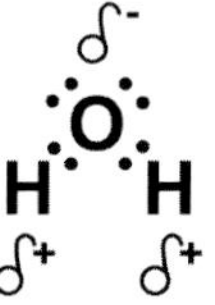

A bond between O and H is polar covalent.

H
H :C: H
H

A bond between C and H is nonpolar covalent.

Figure 24.1: *The bond between oxygen and hydrogen in a water molecule (H_2O) is polar covalent. The oxygen end of the O-H bond has a partial negative charge (represented as δ^-), while the hydrogen end has a partial positive charge (represented as δ^+). Water has two polar covalent bonds. The bond between carbon and hydrogen in a methane molecule (CH_4) is nonpolar covalent. This kind of bond does not have partial charges. Methane has four nonpolar covalent bonds.*

The nature of water and hydrogen bonding

Hydrogen bonds

A water molecule is like a battery with a negative and a positive terminal. Water molecules connect the way you put batteries end to end in a battery-powered device. The partial positive end of one water molecule is attracted to the partially negative end of another water molecule. This connection between water molecules is called a hydrogen bond. Hydrogen bonds are relatively weak. They are broken and constantly re-form as water molecules collide.

Nonpolar molecules do not dissolve in water

Think about what a water droplet looks like on a waxy surface. The water forms nearly round beads that easily roll off the surface. The beads form because the water molecules bind to each other more tightly than to the waxy surface. Because wax is a nonpolar substance, its molecules do not have positive and negative ends that can be attracted to the partially charged poles of a water molecule.

Hydrogen bonding is important to plants

Hydrogen bonding between water molecules is important to the function of plants. Plants obtain water from their roots. How then does a plant get water to its leaves? Plants have cells in their stems that are like soda straws. These sets of cells are microscopically thin. If a plant stem was transparent, you would see streams of water going from the roots to the leaves. As water molecules evaporate from the leaves, more water molecules are pulled into place. It is as if water molecules hold hands. If one molecule moves, the ones behind follow because they are connected by hydrogen bonds!

Water is a network of hydrogen-bonded molecules

In Figure 24.2, you can see that the oxygen atom in a water molecule has two pairs of electrons on one side. Each pair of electrons is available to form a hydrogen bond with the partially positive hydrogen atom of a neighboring water molecule. Many neighboring water molecules connected by hydrogen bonds form a lattice of water molecules. In fact, ice is often described as having a honeycomb structure.

Ice is less dense than water

There is more space between molecules in ice than in water. This explains why water expands when it is frozen and why ice floats on water! The density of ice is about 0.9 g/cm^3 whereas the density of water is about 1 g/cm^3. What would the world be like if ice were denser than water?

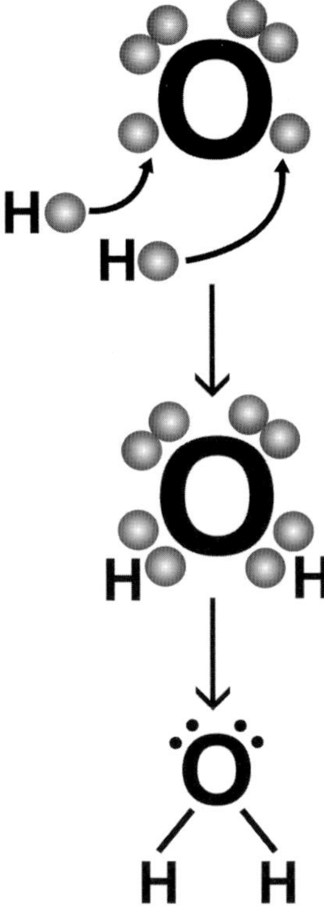

Figure 24.2: *In the formation of water, hydrogen atoms contribute two electrons to the molecule. Oxygen has six valence electrons. Hydrogen needs two valence electrons to be stable, but oxygen needs eight. By forming water, all three atoms (one oxygen and two hydrogens) become stable. Two electrons form a bond between two atoms. Bonds between atoms are represented by a line. The oxygen end of the molecule is partially negative. The hydrogen end of the molecule is partially positive.*

What dissolves in water?

Water dissolves polar substances

The fact that water molecules have partially positive and negative ends allows them to dissolve molecules and ions that have positive or negative charges. In other words, polar molecules like water dissolve other polar molecules.

A salt is a molecule formed by combining a positive ion with a negative ion. For this reason, many salts dissolve easily in water. The diagram below is an illustration of a sodium chloride (NaCl) crystal dissolving in water. The partial charges on the water molecule are shown. The orientation of water molecules as they surround the Na^+ and Cl^- ions is related to these partial charges.

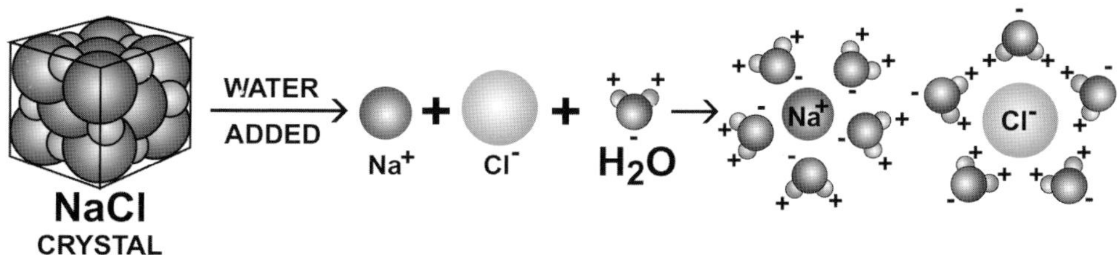

Common beverages	What's dissolved?
soda	carbon dioxide, sugar, dyes
water	minerals, fluorine
orange juice	Vitamin C, sugars
milkshake	milk protein, sugar, calcium

Figure 24.3: *Some substances that are dissolved in common beverages*

Oil and water do not mix

Fat and oil molecules do not dissolve in water. These substances are nonpolar. Have you ever tried to wash butter off of a knife with only water? It is hard to do! Soap is always necessary when washing away fats and oils. Soap molecules have a polar end and a nonpolar end. The polar end of the soap molecule is available for combining with polar molecules like sugars, salts, and proteins. The nonpolar end is available for combining with nonpolar molecules like oils and fats. For this reason, soap can clean most molecules off your hands, dishes, and clothes.

Solubility rules and ionic compounds

In addition to nonpolar molecules like fat and oil, some ionic compounds do not dissolve in water. A set of solubility rules determines which combinations of ions form soluble or insoluble ionic compounds. Figure 24.4 lists some of the solubility rules. Additional soluble compounds include these ions: acetate, chlorate, and sulfate (unless the sulfate is paired with barium, strontium, calcium, lead, or mercury). Carbonate, hydroxide, oxide, silicate, and phosphate compounds are insoluble with the exception of those that follow rule one listed in figure 24.4. Sulfide compounds are soluble only if they contain calcium, barium, strontium, magnesium, sodium, potassium, or ammonium.

What is soluble?

1. Common compounds formed with Group 1 elements and ammonium ions (NH^{4+}).
2. Compounds formed between Group 7 elements (except fluorine) and most metals.
3. All nitrates (compounds with NO_3^-).

Figure 24.4: *Some solubility rules.*

Water at home

What gives tap water its taste? Your tap water has certain dissolved ions such as calcium, iron, zinc, copper, and sodium depending on where you live. Additionally, tap water is treated with sodium fluoride to prevent tooth decay and with chlorine to kill bacteria. These ingredients in water give it a certain taste.

Why do some people filter their tap water? The water that comes to your house from your town or city is treated so that it is safe to drink. However, the plumbing of a house often introduces substances like iron, lead, and copper that you may not want to drink. If you get your water from a well, you may not be sure about its quality. Below is a table of the types of things that may be in your tap water.

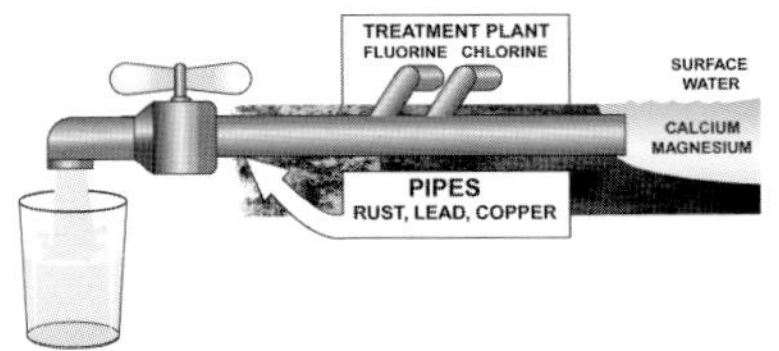

Figure 24.5: *Water treatment plants add sodium fluoride and chlorine. Iron (rust), lead and copper can dissolve into your water supply from your pipes.*

Table 24.1: ***What is in your water?***

Possible component of tap water	Source	Description
acid (high H+)	dissolved carbon dioxide from soils	corrodes pipes; leaches lead and copper into water supply; causes deposits in pipes
base (high OH-)	calcium and magnesium occurring naturally in the water supply	components of hard water; essential minerals for human health
chlorine (Cl-)	an additive in water treatment	changes taste; smells; kills bacteria
fluorine (F-)	added as sodium fluoride in water treatment	prevents tooth decay by making teeth stronger
iron (Fe^{2+} and Fe^{3+})	from pipes	causes orange stains
copper (Cu^{+} and Cu^{2+})	from copper pipes	changes taste in high concentrations; causes blue stains; an essential element for human health
lead (Pb^{4+})	from pipes or the solder for pipes	toxic even in very low concentrations

24.2 The Water Cycle

In the summer of 2000, the state of Texas endured a severe, record-setting drought and many hot days with the temperature of 100°F. Relief came in November—and it was overwhelming. In the first eight days of the month, the Texas offices of the National Weather Service issued hundreds of weather statements and advisories and a total of 324 warnings: 25 tornado, 76 severe thunderstorm, and 223 flash flood warnings (http://www.noaanews.noaa.gov/stories/s525.htm).

The abundance or shortage of rain in Texas or anywhere else in the world is unpredictable. However, research has shown that it is possible to influence weather patterns. Rain can be coaxed out of a cloud by introducing silver iodide crystals from an airplane. This is called cloud seeding. In one 29-year cloud seeding program in Texas, rain increased by 20 to 30 percent. The transformation of water vapor in clouds to rain is just one important part of the water cycle.

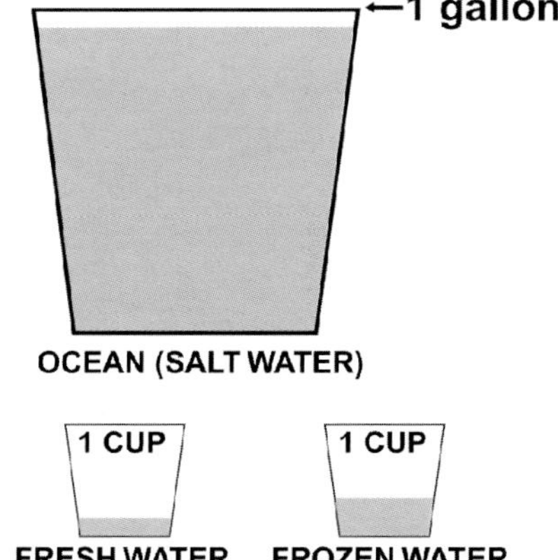

Figure 24.6: *If all the water on the Earth could fit into a one-gallon container, the amount of fresh water available for human consumption would be equal to about one-sixth of a cup! The amount of water frozen at Earth's poles would equal about one-third of a cup.*

Earth is a water planet

About 1% of the planet's water supply can be used for human consumption

The amount of water on Earth is about the same as during the age of the dinosaurs, 65 to 220 million years ago. With about 80 percent of its land submerged, Earth is truly a water planet. However, the amount of water available for human use is small. Of the total amount of water on the planet, less than 1 percent is available for our consumption because all the rest is either in the oceans, which are very salty, (97 percent) or frozen at the planet's two poles (about 2 percent). Imagine that a one-gallon jug of water represents Earth's entire water supply. How much of this gallon would be available to drink? There are 128 ounces of water in a gallon. One percent is 1.28 ounces, or one-sixth of a cup.

Water supplies vary with seasons and geography

Most of us are used to having water on demand from our faucets at home. However, in hot, dry climates or on islands, water use is restricted. Local governments sometimes have to limit the use of water for watering lawns, washing cars, and even for use in the home. These water restrictions are related to the availability of water at a given time in the year. For example, water is usually in short supply during the summer when higher temperatures cause more water to evaporate, making it less available for consumption. At cooler air temperatures, chances are greater that water will be available for human use.

What is the water cycle?

When you turn on a faucet, you usually expect to get fresh water. But is this water really all that fresh? Remember that our water supply today is the same as when the dinosaurs were around. Because of the water cycle, also known as the **hydrologic cycle**, the water you drink today was used millions of years ago!

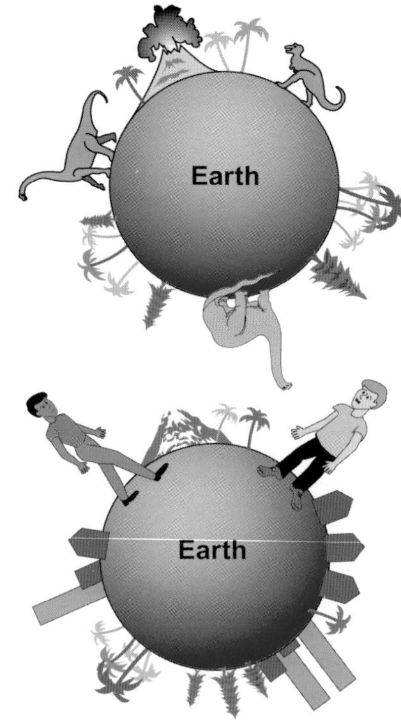

Figure 24.7: *The amount of water on Earth is about the same as it was when dinosaurs lived on Earth 65-220 million years ago.*

Aquifers contain groundwater

To better understand the water cycle, let's begin with **groundwater**. As water seeps through soils and rocks, disease-causing microorganisms are filtered out. At the same time, this water picks up some carbon dioxide from the soils and becomes slightly acidic. Acidic water is capable of dissolving minerals. The destination of this water is an underground area of sediment and rocks called an **aquifer**. It takes about 300 years to replenish the groundwater supply in an aquifer. Now you know how the water gets into the aquifer, but how does it leave?

Water vapor in the atmosphere comes from surface water and transpiration

Some groundwater is collected for human consumption. The rest of it continues to flow through sediments and eventually enters the ocean. The cycle continues when water is evaporated from the ocean. Other sources of water vapor in the atmosphere include evaporation from **surface water** such as lakes, ponds, rivers, streams, and reservoirs. Plants also contribute water to the atmosphere. You may recall that plants need carbon dioxide (CO_2) to make sugar. Whenever plants open tiny pores on their leaves to get CO_2, they also lose some water through a process called **transpiration**. The water vapor in the atmosphere eventually falls back to Earth's surface as **precipitation** in the form of rain, hail, sleet, or snow.

Water vapor leaves the atmosphere as precipitation

Surface water areas are replenished when precipitation reaches Earth's surface. Water, as you might expect, flows over land until it flows into lakes and rivers. The water that reaches surface water areas this way is called **surface runoff**. As this water flows over the ground, it picks up minerals and nutrient-rich soil (thereby causing some soil erosion). Many of the nutrients in freshwater and saltwater come from surface runoff. At low air temperatures, water from precipitation does not evaporate quickly but is also available to percolate back down through the Earth to once again become groundwater.

What drives the water cycle?

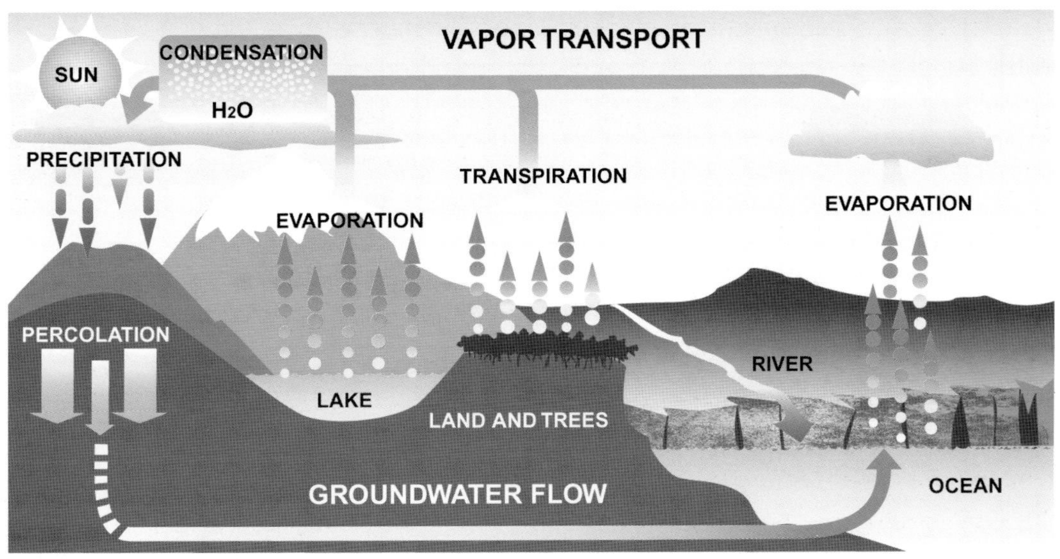

Figure 24.8: *If you have ever watched a puddle of water dry in the sun, you have witnessed the hydrologic or water cycle. Through the processes of precipitation, evaporation, transpiration, and condensation, water moves around the Earth.*

The sun is the source of energy for the water cycle

The sun is the source of energy that keeps water moving through different phases and different places. The four main processes of the water cycle are *evaporation*, *transpiration*, *condensation*, and *precipitation*. Evaporation and transpiration (defined on the preceding page) occur when the water molecules have enough kinetic energy to leave the liquid phase and become a gas. The sun provides the kinetic energy as heat. The condensation of water occurs when water in its gaseous state loses energy. Water vapor molecules slow down so much that they group and form droplets of liquid. When these droplets are heavy enough, they fall to Earth as precipitation.

Cloud seeding—a way to modify the weather

Many variables control weather

On average, water vapor is replenished in the atmosphere every 8.9 days. If we could depend on water vapor becoming rain every 8.9 days, we wouldn't need weather forecasters. Because there are so many variables associated with weather patterns, meteorologists depend on computers to make their predictions.

Weather can be predicted but not controlled

Technology and other scientific breakthroughs make weather prediction easier. For instance, satellite images allow meteorologists to forecast hurricanes. In the past, hurricanes often came without warning. Rain is a milder form of weather that can often be predicted. Whether or not it will rain is very important information. Vacationers usually hope it does not rain. However, if you are a farmer, frequent rain means enough water for a good harvest and a steady income.

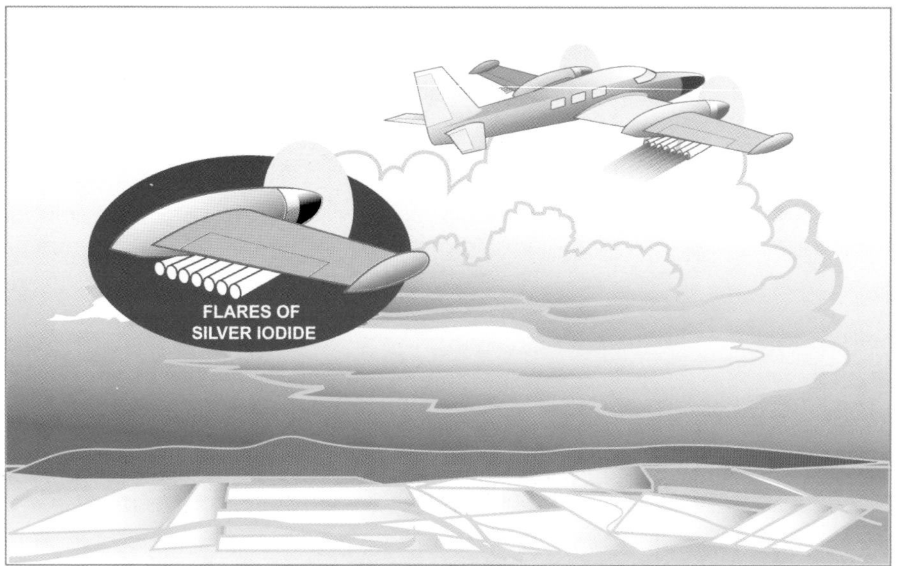

Figure 24.9: *Often planes are used for cloud seeding. Flares of silver iodide can be attached to the wing of the plane and dropped once the plane is above a cumulus (or convective) cloud. These kinds of clouds signal rain. The presence of silver iodide crystals in the clouds encourages the condensation of more water droplets and increases the chance that rain will fall.*

Cloud seeding increases the chance of rain

Rain is very important weather in the agricultural areas of the United States. To encourage rain to fall, meteorologists and airplane pilots work together. Cloud seeding is a way to produce more raindrops in cumulus clouds (also called convective clouds). Using this process increases the chances that rain will fall by 5-20 percent in continental areas and 5-30 percent in coastal areas.

Silver iodide is used to seed clouds

Flares of silver iodide (AgI) are either dropped from an airplane at the top of a cloud or shot from the plane's wing into the base of the cloud. Silver iodide forms crystals that are very similar in shape to ice crystals. Very cold water droplets in the cloud (particularly at the top of the cloud) are attracted to the crystals. When enough water droplets gather around a crystal, raindrops form and fall.

Cloud seeding provides crystals for large water droplets to form

You may be wondering why silver iodide is used. Seeding clouds provides more crystals around which large, heavy water droplets can form. Sometimes cumulus clouds do not release their water vapor as rain because there are not enough water crystals for "seeding" water droplets into big raindrops.

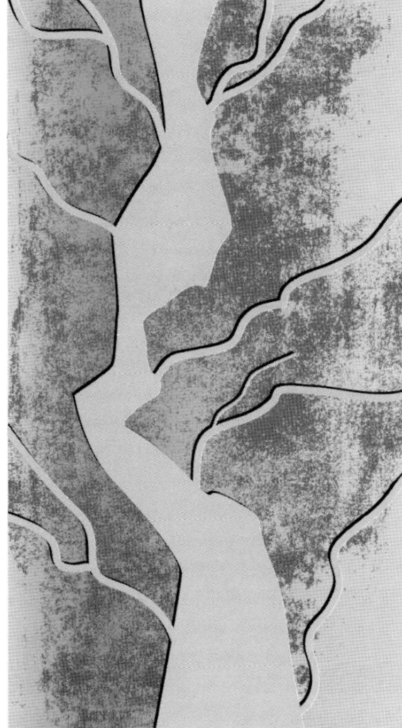

RIVERS AND TRIBUTARIES

Figure 24.10: *What is the value of rivers? Rivers are good routes for travel and moving products from one place to another. As a source of power, rivers can be dammed to provide water energy to run turbines for generating electricity. A river also can be mined for resources like gold and quartz. Regarding the environment, rivers are important in that they provide a habitat for fish, birds, and other wildlife. What other uses for rivers do you know about?*

The distribution of water on Earth

What is the water like where you live?

How you use and appreciate water often depends on where you live. If you grow up in the Midwest of the United States, you may be more familiar with rivers or lakes than with the ocean. Ocean experiences are more common for people who live on one of the coasts of the United States.

Table 24.2 lists how water is distributed on Earth. Do these distribution percentages surprise you? Why or why not?

Table 24.2: ***The distribution of water on Earth***

Body of water	Description
ocean	97.1%
polar ice	2.24%
groundwater	0.61%
lakes	0.016%
moisture in the atmosphere	0.001%
rivers	0.0001%

The importance of water quality

Special standards are used to judge water quality

Because water is so important to our health and way of living, state and federal governments have set strict standards for water quality. Water that meets these standards is safe for drinking, cooking, and other household activities. Like water quality tests for tap water, other tests determine the quality of natural bodies of water like rivers, streams, lakes, and ponds.

Analyzing water quality: Using a pond as an example

Make observations and ask a question

One of the most important things you can do when you assess a situation is to make careful observations. You can guide your observations by asking simple questions. In this case, you could ask, "What does the pond water look like? What animals and plants are living in the pond? Where is the pond located? Are there houses or farms nearby? Is the pond near any industry?"

The time of year that the pond is analyzed is also important. Be sure that you record the date and time that you perform your tests. It is also important to document the weather for that day and for previous days. Sometimes, a storm that has occurred a few days before can cause significant changes in a body of water.

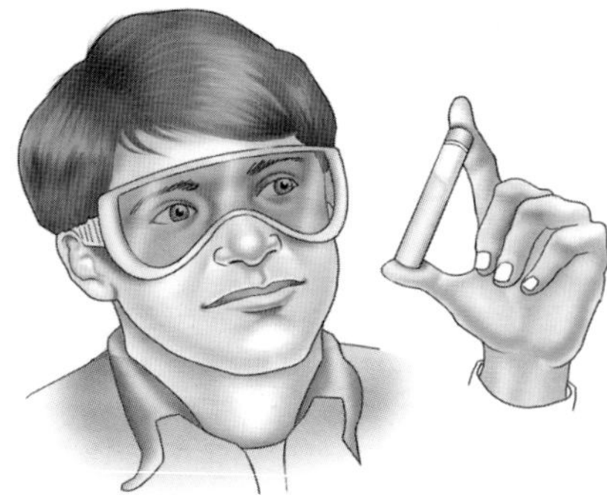

Figure 24.11: *Many tests for water quality are performed by adding an indicator to a water sample. The color change that results is related to how much of a substance is in the water. Indicators can be harmful if they get in your eyes. Always wear goggles when working with these chemicals.*

Water temperature

Water temperature should be measured three or more inches below the surface of the water. The higher the water temperature, the less dissolved oxygen there may be in the water. Dissolved oxygen is required by all organisms living in the pond.

Dissolved oxygen test

Oxygen enters surface water mainly from the air. The solubility of oxygen in water is higher at cooler temperatures. As you might expect, the quality of water in a pond is higher when levels of dissolved oxygen are high. Water samples for dissolved oxygen should be taken away from the edge of the pond and three or more inches below the surface of the water. Dissolved oxygen is measured in parts per million (or ppm). A good level of oxygen is 9 ppm, meaning there are 9 milligrams of oxygen for every one liter of water.

Biological oxygen demand test The biological oxygen demand (BOD) test measures dissolved oxygen in two water samples taken at the same time. Oxygen is measured in the first sample when it is collected. The second sample is protected from light (to prevent photosynthetic organisms from producing oxygen) and measured at a later time. The amount of oxygen in the first and second samples is compared to find out how much oxygen is being used by bacteria as they decompose organic material. When a pond or lake contains a lot of organic material, the bacteria consume too much oxygen and endanger other organisms, like fish, that also need oxygen.

Turbidity test The turbidity test measures the cloudiness of water. The easiest way to measure turbidity is with a Secchi disk. The disk is lowered into the water until the black and white panels on the disk are no longer visible by a person looking into the water from above the water's surface. The rope holding the disk is marked at meter or half-meter intervals to measure the depth of the Secchi disk when it disappears from view underwater.

Nitrate test Nitrogen is used by all organisms to make protein. Nitrogen is most available to organisms when it is combined with oxygen-forming nitrate (NO_3^-). Fertilizers are high in nitrates. If a pond is near a lawn or farm, the pond may have too much nitrate. Excess nitrate can cause *algal blooms*, large growths of algae in a body of water. Because the algae use oxygen, the algal bloom endangers fish and other organisms in the pond.

Phosphate test Phosphate (PO_4^{3-}) is the form in which organisms get phosphorus. Phosphorus is an essential element in DNA. Although all organisms use phosphorus, this element tends to enhance the growth of algae in particular. As with excess nitrogen, excess phosphorus in a body of water can cause algal blooms.

pH test The pH scale ranges from 0 to 14. The pH of pure water is 7 (a neutral pH value). The pH values of acids are below 7 and the values for bases are above 7. Surface water ranges from 6.5 to 8.5. If water is too acidic or basic, organisms are not able to survive. Acidic rain (called "acid rain") is a serious threat to the health of ponds and lakes that sustain wildlife. Acid rain is caused by car and industry emissions such as nitrogen and sulfur oxides. These pollutants mix with water in the atmosphere to produce strong acids like nitric and sulfuric acid.

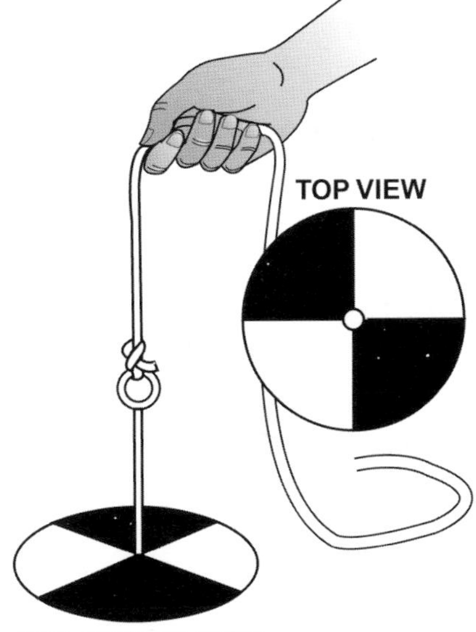

Figure 24.12: *A Secchi disk can be used to measure the turbidity of water. If water is too cloudy, sunlight is blocked. Photosynthetic organisms use sunlight to grow. These organisms are food for larger animals in the pond or lake.*
How to use a Secchi disk: The disk is lowered into the water until it is no longer visible. Then, it is pulled up slightly until it is seen again. The length of the rope between the disk and the surface of the water is related to the clarity of the water. Secchi disks usually have an alternating black and white pattern. Why is it important that a portion of the disk is white?

Chapter 24 Review

Vocabulary review

Match the following terms with the correct definition. There is one extra definition in the list that will not match any of the terms.

Set One

1. polar
2. nonpolar
3. hydrogen bond
4. aquifer
5. groundwater

a. A molecule that has partial charges
b. Water that filters through soil and rock and eventually enters an aquifer
c. The measure of the clearness of water
d. A bond between the partial positive end of one H_2O molecule and the partial negative end of another H_2O molecule
e. An underground area of rock and sediment where groundwater concentrates
f. A molecule that has no partial charges

Set Two

1. hydrologic cycle
2. precipitation
3. transpiration
4. condensation
5. surface runoff

a. The process by which water vapor transforms to liquid water
b. The sun-driven process by which water is moved from place to place on Earth
c. The process by which water vapor enters the atmosphere from plants
d. A general term for water (frozen or in liquid form) released from clouds
e. Natural formations of water including streams, rivers, ponds, and lakes
f. Water, usually resulting from precipitation, that flows from land to surface water

Set Three

1. surface water
2. evaporation
3. biological oxygen demand
4. dissolved oxygen
5. turbidity

a. The concentration of oxygen in a body of water
b. The measure of the clearness of water
c. The amount of oxygen consumed by bacteria in a body of water over a certain time period
d. Natural formations of water including streams, rivers, ponds, and lakes
e. The process by which a liquid becomes a gas
f. The process by which water molecules transform from liquid to ice

Concept review

1. Draw a Lewis dot diagram of a water molecule and indicate the location of the partially positive charges and the partially negative charges.
2. Make a diagram that shows two water molecules joined by a hydrogen bond. Represent this bond with a dotted line. Be sure to include the locations of the partially positive and negative charges.
3. Explain the phrase *oil and water don't mix* using the terms *nonpolar*, *polar*, and *partial charge*.
4. List two reasons to support and two reasons to refute the statement: *Water is a nearly universal solvent.* Hint: Brainstorm by writing down how you have used and consumed water today.
5. How important is the water cycle? Give three reasons to support your answer. Be sure to explain your reasons clearly.

Problems

1. Water is the product of hydrogen gas combining with oxygen gas.
   a. Balance the equation for this reaction.
      ________ H_2 (g) + ________ O_2(g) → ________ H_2O
   b. To make a water molecule, what bonds need to be broken and reformed in this reaction?
2. Identify the following substances as containing polar or nonpolar molecules. Use a *P* for polar and an *N* for nonpolar.
   a. water
   b. vegetable oil
   c. butter
   d. maple syrup
   e. turpentine
   f. vinegar
3. Design an original diagram to illustrate how water is distributed on Earth. Use the percentages provided in table 24.2 to make your diagram.

Applying your knowledge

1. After writing a short note with a ballpoint pen, you accidentally spill some water on the paper. You are happy to see that the ink doesn't run! Come up with a hypothesis to explain why the ink did not run.
2. A common stain removal tip is to use hair spray or rubbing alcohol to remove ink stains from clothing. Why do you think this method works?

3. Imagine you are a droplet of water in a puddle. Trace your path through the water cycle. Be sure to include the terms *evaporation*, *transpiration*, *condensation*, and *precipitation* in your answer.
4. Some areas in the United States do not get enough rain. For this reason, these areas may have cloud seeding programs or water-use restrictions. Does a water shortage in an area mean that the Earth is running out of water? Justify your answer.
5. What is the history of your community's water supply or water treatment? Go to the library to read your local newspapers or magazines from the past and present. Look for stories about the water supply or water treatment. Write a one or two page report about your findings.
6. Zoos often use large aquaria, man-made ponds, or other water areas for the animals they keep. To help keep the animals healthy, it is very important that the water quality be high. Research how your local zoo maintains water quality in one of its exhibits. Choose one animal and its habitat to research. Ways to find information include talking to a zookeeper, visiting the zoo, searching the Internet, and checking your local library for information about how zoos maintain water quality in their exhibits. When you have finished your research, organize it into a two to three-page report.
7. JAN FEB MAR Many businesses, schools, and homes use the services of bottled water companies. These companies provide drinking water dispensers and the water for monthly fees. Bottled water services cost much more than tap water. Why do people pay for a bottled water service? In answering this question, you will make *inferences* based on information that you collect. An inference is a statement that can be made based on observations and known facts. Inferences can be used to make a hypothesis that can be tested in an experiment.

Collecting your data:

a. Interview three people who use the services of a bottled water company. Ask them why they use the service.
b. Look in your local phone book to find advertisements for three bottled water services. Call each company and ask them why they recommend using bottled water in your area.
c. Perform an Internet search for information about bottled water and tap water. For example, search according to the phrase "bottled water versus tap water." Make a table that lists three reasons why you *would* use a water service (pros) and three reason why you *would not* use a bottled water service (cons).
d. Examine the data from parts 7(a) - (c). Based on your data, make three inferences as to why people might purchase bottled water services.
e. Based on your data, make at least one inference as to why someone might *not* choose to use a bottled water service.

UNIT 8 Water and Solutions

Chapter 25 Acids and Bases

Introduction to Chapter 25

This chapter explores the chemistry of acids and bases and explains the pH scale. In the first Investigation, you will create a pH scale using a natural indicator solution. You will learn about the applications of acid-base chemistry in household products, medicine and the environment. In the second section and Investigation, you will learn about and simulate the effects of acid rain.

Investigations to Chapter 25

25.1	**Acids, Bases, and pH**	*What is pH?*

In this Investigation, a natural indicator and household chemicals are used to create a color-based pH scale. You will use your pH scale to figure out the pH of additional household chemicals and two mystery solutions.

25.2	**Acid Rain**	*What is acid rain?*

In this Investigation, you will model the effects of acid rain on a natural ecosystem. You will observe the effect of different dilutions of an acid on the activity of water fleas (*Daphnia magna*). Water fleas are an important source of food for fish and other organisms in fresh water environments. In this Investigation, you will also have the opportunity to research topics related to acid rain on the Internet.

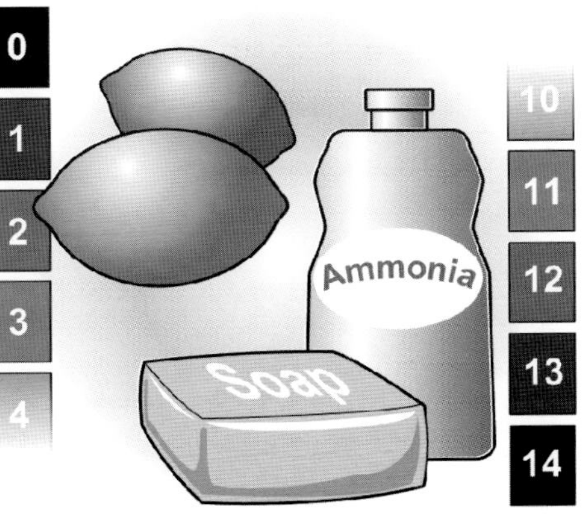

Learning Goals

In this chapter, you will:

- ✔ Describe pH as a way to measure the strength of acids and bases.
- ✔ Understand the definitions of an acid and a base.
- ✔ Identify pH of common household chemicals.
- ✔ Understand the cause of acid rain.
- ✔ Understand the environmental effects of acid rain.
- ✔ Demonstrate the effect of acid on a natural ecosystem.

Vocabulary

acid	base	pH	smog
acid precipitation	electrolytes	pH indicator	
acid rain	neutral	pH scale	

25.1 Acids, Bases, and pH

In the Investigations, you measured several indicators of water quality, including the pH. You may remember that pH values range from 0 to 14. Low values (0 to 6) indicate that a solution is acidic whereas high values (8 to 14) indicate that a solution is basic. Your stomach secretes one of the stronger acids, hydrochloric acid (HCl). As acidic solutions of digested food leave your stomach, other organs in your digestive system secrete bicarbonate, a base. The added base neutralizes the strong, corrosive acid.

As you can see, acids and bases play a significant role in how your body works. What exactly are acids and bases? What does pH mean?

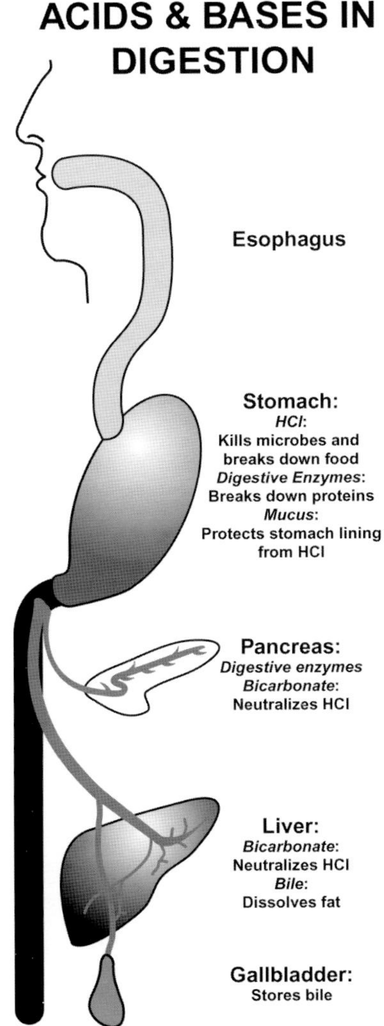

Figure 25.1: *Acids and bases play important roles in digestion.*

Why is pH important?

The pH of water indicates its quality

Water quality is evaluated using pH values for many reasons. For example, if the pH of your tap water is too high, it might indicate that calcium or magnesium deposits are forming in and may clog your water pipes. On the other hand, if the pH is too low, the water may be corroding your pipes.

The pH of water is important to life. The pH of natural bodies of water also has to be just right—neither too high nor too low. For example, at a pH of 4 or 5, fish have trouble reproducing. At even lower pH values, they die.

Acids and bases are defined by pH values

The pH of water is related to the action of a class of chemicals called *acids* and *bases*. A solution with a pH value that is less than 7 contains an acid, and a solution with pH values greater than 7 contains a base. You will learn how pH is determined later on in this section.

What are acids and bases?

Acidic solutions have more H+ ions, and basic solutions have more OH- ions

An acid is a chemical that contributes hydrogen ions, H+, to a solution. A base is a chemical that contributes hydroxyl ions, OH-, to a solution. Therefore, solutions can be described as "acidic" or "basic" according to the concentrations of H+ and OH- ions in the solution. A solution with a high concentration of H+ ions and few OH- ions is strongly acidic. A strongly basic (or alkaline) solution has a high concentration of OH- ions and few H+ ions.

HCl is an acid

Hydrochloric acid (HCl) is a very strong acid which can seriously irritate your nose if you smell it and your skin if it spills on you! When HCl dissolves in water (as indicated by the symbol "aq"), it ionizes to become H+ ions and Cl- ions:

$$HCl \longrightarrow H^{+}_{(aq)} + Cl^{-}_{(aq)}$$

An acid such as HCl ionizes almost completely when dissolved in water and therefore contributes many H+ ions to a solution. Because of this, HCl is a known as a *strong acid.*

NaOH is a base

Sodium hydroxide (NaOH) is a base commonly used for rigorous housecleaning and for unclogging drains. As you can see from the chemical formula, NaOH will release OH- ions when it dissolves in water:

$$NaOH \longrightarrow Na^{+}_{(aq)} + OH^{-}_{(aq)}$$

Since NaOH ionizes almost completely when dissolved in water and contributes many OH- ions to a solution, it is known as a *strong base*.

Weak acids and bases

Many acids and bases do not ionize completely in water and are known as weak acids and bases.

Vinegar, also known as *acetic acid,* is a weak acid because it contributes a few H+ ions to solution. Vinegar is sometimes used for cleaning but is not very irritating to the skin. Your nose may not like it, however!

$$HC_2H_3O_{2(aq)} \rightleftharpoons H^{+}_{(aq)} + C_2H_3O_2^{-}{}_{(aq)}$$

A weak acid or base ionizes *incompletely* when dissolved in water as shown by the double arrows in the chemical equation above.

Household ammonia is an example of a *weak base* because it does not completely ionize in water.

Hydronium Ions

In an acid solution, separate hydrogen ions (H+) do not exist by themselves for very long. Each hydrogen ion is attracted to the oxygen end of a water molecule. The two combine to form a hydronium ion. In chemistry, it is common to refer to H_3O+ ions as H+ ions.

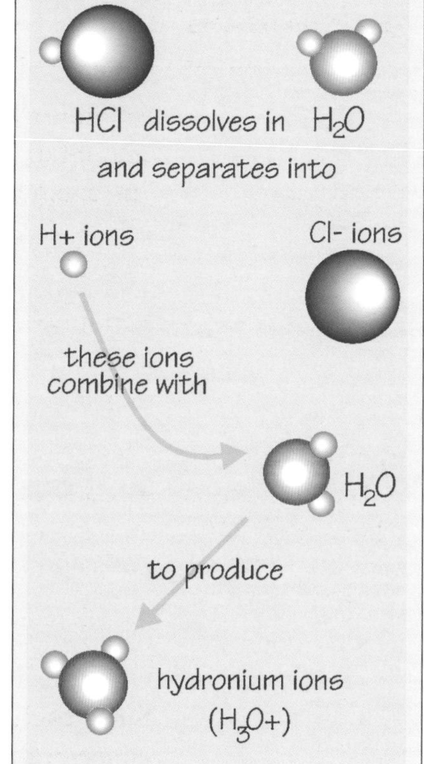
HCl dissolves in H2O
and separates into
H+ ions
Cl- ions
these ions combine with
H2O
to produce
hydronium ions (H3O+)

pH and the pH scale

pH is based on the concentration of H+ ions in solution

Just as centimeters describe length, pH describes the exact concentrations of H+ ions in a solution. Most instruments that measure pH use a pH scale that runs from 0 to 14. At pH 1, a solution is strongly acidic. At pH 14, a solution is strongly basic, or alkaline.

pH 7 means equal H+ and OH- ions

A solution that has a pH of 7 has equal numbers of H+ and OH- ions and is called a neutral solution.

Low pH means high H+ concentration

Everyone is familiar with using a ruler to measure things. However, a pH scale is different from a ruler in that the *more* H+ ions there are in a solution, the *lower* the pH value. Conversely, *fewer* H+ ions in a solution means a *higher* pH value.

The pH scale is based on powers of 10

A pH scale is based on powers of ten. A solution that is pH 1 has *10 times* more hydrogen ions than a solution of pH 2. In turn, the pH 2 solution has *10 times* more hydrogen ions than a solution of pH 3.

Another way of looking at the scale is to see that as the pH numbers *increase*, the amount of H+ ions *decreases* by powers of 10. Figure 25.2 illustrates the pH scale. For example, a solution at pH 1 has 10 million times more hydrogen ions than a solution at pH 7, and a solution at pH 7 has 10 million times more hydrogen ions than a solution at pH 14!

You now know that the amount of H+ in a solution at pH 6 is 10 times the amount in a solution at pH 7. But a solution at pH 7 is neutral. What is the amount of OH- ions in a neutral solution? What is the amount of OH- ions in a solution at pH 6?

Acids have more H+ ions, bases have more OH- ions

The answers to these questions are that the amount of OH- ions in a neutral solution is equal to the amount of H+ ions. If you go down the pH scale to 6, the amount of OH- ions decreases by a power of 10 whereas the amount of H+ increases by a power of 10. Remember:

- pH values *below* 7 means H+ ions outnumber OH- ions, and
- pH values *higher* than 7 means OH- ions outnumber H+ ions.

Since each pH is an increase or decrease by tenfold, there is a big difference in ion concentration between each pH value.

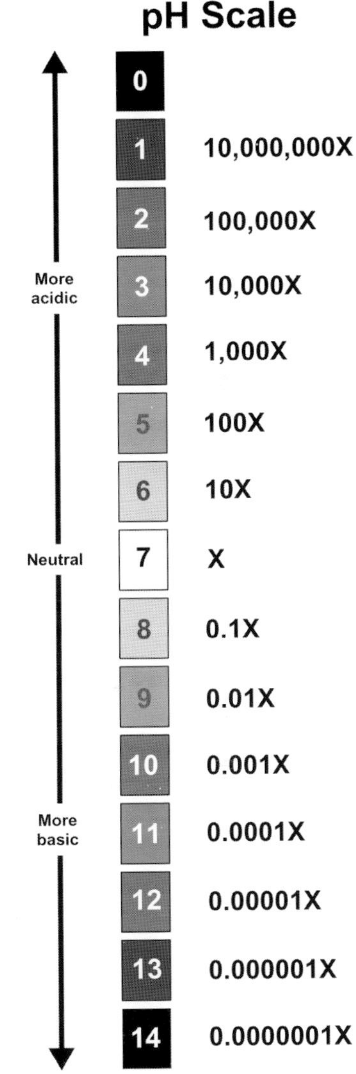

Figure 25.2: *The pH scale is based on the concentration of hydrogen ions in solution.*

The ionization of water

Water is both a weak acid and a weak base

Water plays an important role in acid and base chemistry. Water itself is both a weak acid and a weak base. A water molecule can split or ionize into H+ and OH- ions. Because the H+ ions immediately attach themselves to water molecules, the equation for the ionization of water is written as:

$$2H_2O \leftrightarrow H_3O^+ + OH^-$$

What does the double-headed arrow mean?

The double-headed arrow in the equation means that water, if left alone, is always in *equilibrium* with its ions. The rate at which water breaks down into ions is the same as the rate at which the ions re-form into water. However, water ionizes so slowly that most water molecules exist whole, not as ions.

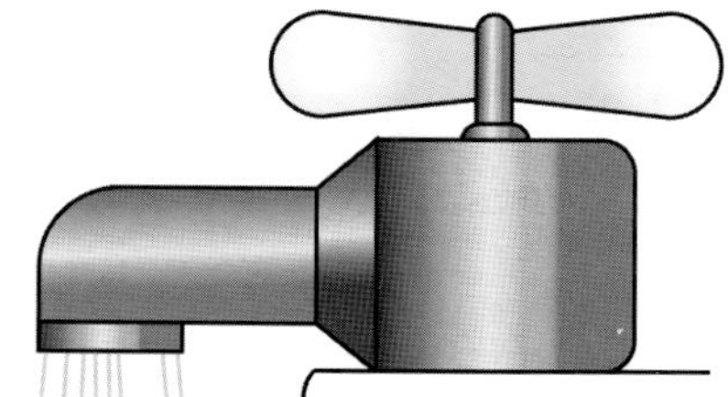

Figure 25.3: *.Water ionizes into H+ and OH- ions. Therefore, it acts like both a weak acid and a weak base. Pure water has a neutral pH (pH 7) because the concentrations of H+ and OH- ions are equal.*

Examples of acid and base chemistry

Acids and bases play a role in digestion

Many reactions, such as the ones that occur in your body, work best at specific pH values. For example, acids and bases are very important in the reactions involved in digesting food (see figure 25.1). As you may know, the stomach secretes hydrochloric acid (HCl), a strong acid (pH 1.4). The acidity of our stomachs is necessary to break down the protein molecules in our food so that they can be absorbed. A mucus lining in the stomach protects it from the acid produced. As food and digestive fluids leave the stomach, however, other organs in the digestive system also need to be protected from the acid. This is accomplished by two parts of the system—the pancreas and liver. These two organs secrete bicarbonate to neutralize the stomach acid before it reaches other organs.

Acids and bases have many uses

The reactivity of acids and bases means that these chemicals have many uses. They react with each other and other chemicals. Metals and glass can be etched with corrosive acids. Lye (pH 13) is used to unclog drains, and sulfuric acid (pH 1) is used throughout industry. Millions of tons of sulfuric acid are produced each year (40 million tons in 1990). Its uses range from making rayon to cleaning impurities from gasoline.

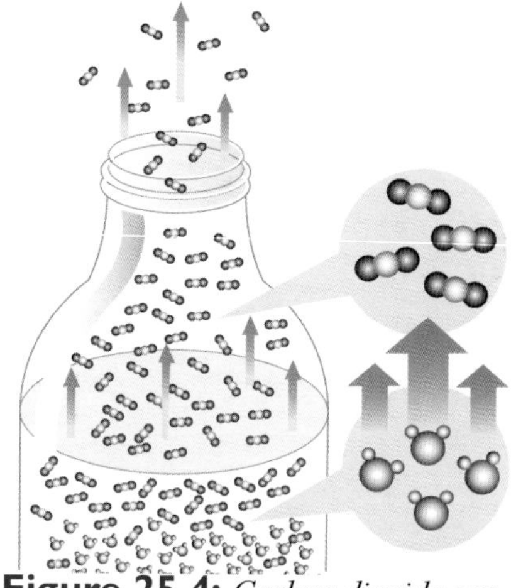

Figure 25.4: *Carbon dioxide gas (CO_2) escaping from carbonated water. The CO_2 molecules are chains of three atoms, and the water molecules have a triangular shape. CO_2 makes soda fizzy and reacts with water to form carbonic acid, which gives the soda a sharp, or acidic, taste. This and other acids in soda, like phosphoric acid, can dissolve tooth enamel. Be sure to brush your teeth after drinking soda!*

Electrolytes and nonelectrolytes

Electrolytes conduct current

Current is the flow of charge. When a solution contains dissolved ions (charged particles), it can conduct current. Chemicals that conduct current when dissolved in water are called electrolytes. These chemicals form ions when dissolved.

Salt dissociates in water

Ionic compounds, molecular compounds, and even atoms can contribute ions to a solution. When an ionic compound is dissolved in water, the polar ends of the water molecule attract the positive and negative ions in the solution. In previous sections, you learned how water dissolves table salt (NaCl). Recall that the attraction of the polar ends of the water molecule is strong enough to break the weak ionic bonds of NaCl. When an ionic compound is brought into solution by water it is said to *dissociate*. The term *ionization* is used if a molecular compound or atom forms an ion.

For example, when NaCl dissolves in water we say it *dissociates*. When the element Na loses an electron, it *ionizes* to Na+.

Acids and bases are electrolytes

All acids and bases are electrolytes because they contribute ions to a solution. Some chemicals, like salt (NaCl), dissociate to form ions in solution but are not acidic or basic. Acids, bases, and salt water are examples of electrolytes.

Non-electrolytes do not have ions and are not acidic or basic

Other chemicals do not form ions when they are dissolved in solution. They are called *non-electrolytes*. Non-electrolytes are not acidic or basic. Sugar dissolved in water is an example of a non-electrolyte.

Electrical appliances and water

Because tap water contains small amounts of dissolved ions, it is an electrolyte. Remember that even a small amount of current is dangerous if it enters your body directly? Water provides a way for electric current to enter your body, so always take care when using electrical appliances near water!

Electrolytes and your body

When you perform a strenuous activity, your body cools itself by sweating. Sweat contains water and dissolved salts (or electrolytes) like sodium and potassium. Before, during, and after exercising, you can replenish fluids and your body's electrolytes by drinking diluted fruit juice, slightly salty water, or by consuming a sports drinks. The water in these fluids helps your body continue to cool itself so that you don't get overheated. By replacing electrolytes, you may be helping your body speed up resorption of fluids. Diluted fruit juice or a sports drink contains small amounts of carbohydrates to give your body the energy boost it may need during strenuous exercise.

The pH of substances you use or consume

Many foods are acidic and many cleaning products are basic

Table 25.1 contains a list of some common chemicals and their pH values. What do you notice about this list of substances? Where would you find acids in your kitchen? Where would you find bases?

Table 25.1: ***The pH of some common chemicals.***

Household chemical	Acid or base	pH
lemon juice	acid	2
vinegar	acid	3
soda water	acid	4
baking soda	base	8.5
bar soap	base	10
ammonia	base	11

It turns out that many of the foods we consume or use for cooking are acidic. On the other hand, many of our household cleaning products are basic.

A pH indicator

In the Investigation, you will be testing the pH of common chemicals using another item that you may find in your kitchen. You will measure pH using a pH indicator—a chemical that changes color at different pH values.

Common foods can also be used as pH indicators. In the Investigation, the indicator you will use is made from the juice of a red cabbage.

Acids, bases, and taste

Our taste buds are sensitive to acids and bases. We taste acids as sour and bases as bitter. Lemon juice is strongly acidic, and soap is strongly basic. Acids that are stronger than lemon juice and bases that are stronger than ammonia are so reactive that they can harm your skin and damage clothing.

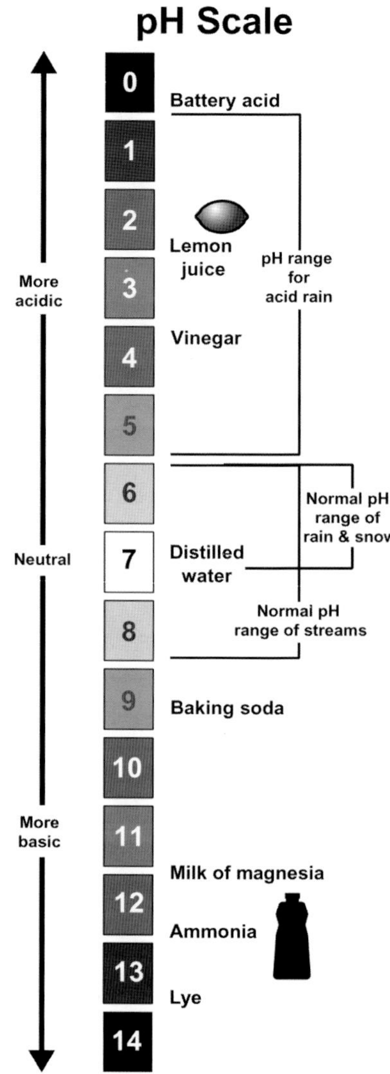

Figure 25.5: *The pH scale showing common substances.*

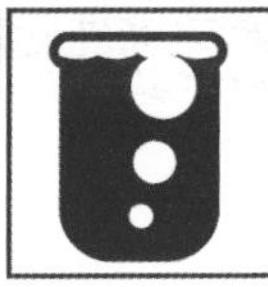

Health Perspective: pH and your blood

It is very important for your blood pH to stay within the normal range. At higher or lower pH values, your body does not function properly. Fortunately, you can regulate the pH of your blood simply by breathing!

Blood is a watery solution that contains many solutes including the dissolved gases carbon dioxide and oxygen. Carbon dioxide appears in your blood because it is produced by respiration. Recall that respiration is the combustion of sugar by your body. You breathe in oxygen to get this process going. The end products of this reaction are energy, water, and carbon dioxide.

$C_6H_{12}O_6 + 6O_2 \rightarrow 6CO_2 + 6H_2O + \text{energy}$

The rate at which you breathe controls the concentration of carbon dioxide in your blood. For example, if you hold your breath, more carbon dioxide enters your blood. If you hyperventilate, you blow off carbon dioxide, so that significantly less is in your blood. These two processes influence blood pH. The equation below illustrates how carbon dioxide dissolves in an aqueous (watery) solution like blood:

CO_2	+	H_2O	$\leftrightarrow$	H_2CO_3	$\leftrightarrow$	H^+	+	HCO_3^-
carbon dioxide	+	water	$\leftrightarrow$	carbonic acid	$\leftrightarrow$	hydrogen ion	+	bicarbonate ion

When CO_2 dissolves, H+ ions are produced in solution. Therefore, the more CO_2 in your blood, the more acidic your blood will become. If you breathe slowly, the added CO_2 makes your blood more acidic. However, if you breathe too often and too quickly (hyperventilating), the loss of CO_2 makes your blood more basic. You can offset this effect by breathing into a paper bag. This forces you to re-breathe carbon dioxide.

When you breathe normally, your blood pH ranges between 7.35 and 7.45.

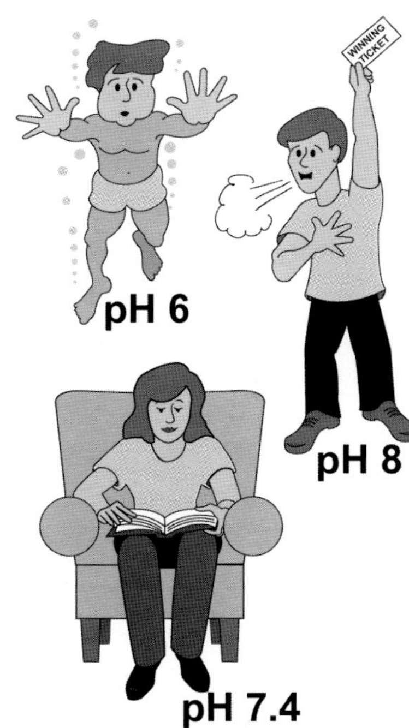

Figure 25.6: *Some causes of low blood pH (acidosis) include holding your breath, excessive lactic acid produced during heavy exercise, and production of ketone acids because of fasting or having low levels of insulin (diabetes). High blood pH (alkalosis) can be caused by hyperventilating. Under normal conditions, your blood pH ranges between 7.35 and 7.45.*

25.2 Acid Rain

You have probably heard about acid rain. You might know that acid rain harms the environment. But what is acid rain?

Life occurs within certain ranges of pH. Most plants and animals function best when pH is nearly neutral. At the extreme ends of the pH scale, where you find strong acids and strong bases, many life processes will not occur. For example, fish have trouble reproducing when the pH of their watery environment is too acidic.

Also, plants have trouble growing if soil is acidified below 5.1, and aquatic animals have difficulty surviving in water below pH 5.5. It was recently discovered that lakes and forests in certain parts of the world were not as healthy as they once had been. The cause was higher acidity in the lakes, resulting from rainfall, snowfall, or fog that was highly acidic. How can rain or snow be harmful to the environment?

Figure 25.7: *If a body of water has a pH of 4.5 or lower, almost nothing can grow in it. Other animals that live near the water, such as frogs and insects, often die as well.*

The definition of acid rain

Rain and snow are naturally acidic

Rainfall, snowfall, or any precipitation happens to be naturally acidic. This is because the rain, snow, or fog mixes with carbon dioxide, a gas present in air, and forms small amounts of carbonic acid. The pH of precipitation before the Industrial Revolution (which started in the mid-1700's) was probably around 5.6. Therefore, the normal pH of rain and other forms of precipitation is considered to be 5.6. Any rain, snow, or fog that has a pH *lower* than 5.6 is called acid rain or acid precipitation.

Acid rain results from gases produced during combustion reactions

The chief indicators of acid rain in the atmosphere are the gases sulfur dioxide (SO_2), sulfur trioxide (SO_3), nitrogen oxide (NO), and nitrogen dioxide (NO_2). A large part of SO_2 in the atmosphere is created by the burning of coal and oil that contain sulfur, and by industrial processes such as metal purification. Nitrogen oxide is a leading by-product of fuel combustion from traffic and power plants.

Sulfur trioxide and nitrogen dioxide are created from the reactions of sulfur dioxide and nitrogen oxide, respectively, with oxygen-containing compounds in the atmosphere. Both of these reactions speed up due to chemicals present in particulate matter, a common pollutant released by traffic and industrial processes.

Figure 25.8: *Ideally, fish require water within the 6 - 8 pH range.*

Sulfur and nitrogen gases mix with water to form sulfuric and nitric acids

Sulfur oxides in the air mix with water, ozone, or hydrogen peroxide to form sulfuric acid (H_2SO_4). This strong acid is the number one cause of acid rain. Even before acid rain is formed, the four gases that cause acid rain (SO_2, SO_3, NO, and NO_2) create health problems in cities. They are irritants to the respiratory system and may increase the incidence of asthma and other respiratory ailments.

$$SO_3 \text{ (air pollutant)} + H_2O \text{ (rain)} \longrightarrow H_2SO_4 \text{(acid rain)}$$

Nitrogen oxides react with components in the atmosphere to form nitric acid (HNO_3), the second greatest cause of acid rain.

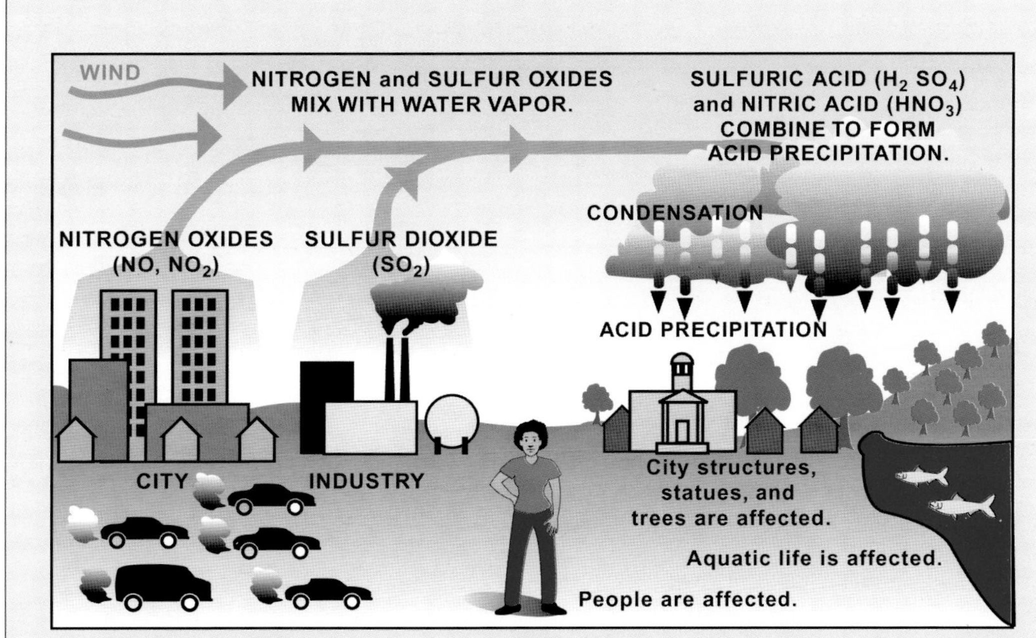

Nitric and sulfuric oxides are produced by cars and industry. These airborne chemical react with water to form nitric and sulfuric acids. Weather patterns (i.e., wind) can transport these acids to other areas where they will fall as precipitation. Acid precipitation can affect the health of people, trees, and aquatic life and erodes buildings and statues.

Figure 25.9: *You can help reduce the emission of acid rain gases by using these alternative means of transportation.*

Chapter 25 Review

Vocabulary review

Match the following terms with the correct definition. There is one extra definition in the list that will not match any of the terms.

Set One

1. acid	a. A chemical that contributes H+ ions to a solution
2. base	b. A solution that has no H+ or OH- ions
3. pH	c. A solution that has equal numbers of H+ and OH- ions
4. neutral	d. A chemical that conducts current when dissolved in a solution
5. electrolyte	e. The measurement of the amount of H+ and OH- ions in a solution
	f. A chemical that contributes OH- ions to a solution

Set Two

1. acid rain	a. The naturally occurring rock that protects some areas of the country from acid rain
2. acid precipitation	b. Rain with a pH lower than 5.6
3. smog	c. The process of turning an acidic or basic solution into a neutral (pH 7) solution
4. acid shock	d. A sudden increase of acid precipitation into a lake or other ecosystem
5. neutralization	e. A combination of gases produced by industry and automobiles; a combination of smoke and fog
	f. Rain, snow, or fog with a pH lower than 5.6

Concept review

1. Many foods are acidic. List four examples.
2. Explain the meanings of a strong acid and a weak acid. Give examples of each.
3. Explain the meanings of a strong base and a weak base. Give examples of each.
4. Is water an acid, a base, neither, or both? What is the pH of water?
5. Explain why a single number on the pH scale can describe both the concentration of H+ ions and OH- ions.
6. What is the difference between an electrolyte and a nonelectrolyte? Give an example of each.
7. Describe in your own words how the amount of CO_2 dissolved in your blood affects your blood pH. Consider what happens if a person breathes very slowly and when a person breathes very quickly (hyperventilating).
8. Explain why acid rain is defined as rain with a pH less than 5.6.
9. List the four gases formed from human processes that result in acid precipitation.
10. List the two most common acids found in acid rain.
11. Describe four examples of the harmful effects of acid precipitation.

Problems

1. You have solution A, pH 3, and solution B, pH 4. Which solution has more H+ ions? How many more H+ ions does one solution have than the other?
2. Of the solutions in question 1, which solution (A or B) has more OH- ions? How many more OH- ions does one solution have than the other?
3. You have solution C, pH 2, and solution D, pH 5. Which solution has more H+ ions? How many more H+ ions does one solution have than the other?
4. You have 10 milliliters of an acidic solution E and a large beaker full of a basic solution F. Solution E has twice as many H+ ions as solution F has OH- ions. How many milliliters of solution F would you add to solution E to make a solution with a neutral pH? Hint: You need to have an equal amount of H+ ions and OH- ions for the solution to have a neutral pH.
5. If you add an acidic solution to a basic solution, you have a solution with high levels of both H+ and OH- ions. These ions react to form a common compound. Write down the equation that occurs.

Applying your knowledge

1. One remedy for a stomachache is to take an antacid. Find out the definition of this word. Explain why an antacid might make someone's stomach feel better.

2. Blood pH values that are too high or too low indicate a health problem. Acidosis occurs when your blood pH is less than 7.4. Alkalosis occurs when your blood pH is more than 7.4. Sometimes the way your body works affects your blood pH. For instance, individuals with diabetes mellitus do not produce enough insulin to help them metabolize nutrients. This is why diabetics need to administer insulin to themselves on a regular basis. They can gauge whether they have enough insulin by testing their blood pH. If their blood is too acidic, they are producing ketone acids—a condition that occurs when their blood doesn't have enough insulin. Use the Internet or your local library to research body metabolism and ketone production as it relates to diabetes and blood pH.

3. Two years ago, you joined a project to study the water quality of a local pond. During the second spring, you notice that there are not as many tadpoles as there were last year. You want to know if the number of tadpoles in the pond is related to the pH of the pond. The records that document the water quality and wildlife started ten years ago. Describe the steps you would take to determine whether a change in pH of the pond water is affecting the population of frogs and their ability to reproduce.

4. Research the issue of acid rain and prepare a short report or presentation on the topic. Use one or more of the questions below to focus your research:

   - Is acid rain a problem in your community? (Parts of the United States that have fewer problems with acid rain are protected by the limestone (a base) that exists naturally in the soil.)
   - Gases that cause acid rain are all end-products of chemical reactions. These reactions are useful for our economy in that they are involved in keeping cars and industry going. However, what is the economic cost of producing these gases? Do the benefits of keeping cars and industry going outweigh the economic impact of acid rain?
   - What can you or your class do to raise awareness about acid rain and its effects on human health and the environment?
   - What can you do to help reduce the problem of acid rain?
   - Search the Internet to find the answer to the questions listed above and to find out how the United States and other countries are addressing the problem of acid rain.

     Two Internet sites that address acid rain are *http://www.epa.gov/airmarkets* (for the United States) and *http://www.brixworth.demon.co.uk/acidrain2000* (in Europe). The second site is maintained by students who are studying acid rain in Europe.

UNIT 9

Heating and Cooling

Chapter 26

Measuring Heat

Introduction to Chapter 26

In this chapter, you will learn how heat and temperature are measured. Many people believe that heat and temperature are the same thing, but these two properties are different. Temperature measures the average kinetic energy of a substance, whereas heat describes the flow of thermal energy from one substance to another.

Investigations for Chapter 26

26.1	Temperature Scales	*How is temperature measured?*

In this Investigation you will graph the Celsius temperature scale as a function of the Fahrenheit temperature scale. From this graph you will develop a mathematical relationship between the Fahrenheit and Celsius temperature scales.

26.2	Measuring Changes in Heat	*How efficient is an immersion heater?*

In this Investigation you will explore how much thermal energy is supplied to water by an immersion heater. You will also make some predictions on the change in temperature if the amount of water is changed. In addition, you will revisit the concept of efficiency to calculate the efficiency of the system.

26.3	Specific Heat	*How much heat flows between liquids at different temperatures?*

In this Investigation you will observe what happens to the final temperature when you mix hot and cold liquids. Next you will analyze how much heat flows from the hot liquid to the cold liquid. You will also determine the specific heat of alcohol.

Learning Goals

In this chapter, you will:

- ✔ Measure temperature.
- ✔ Convert between the Celsius and Fahrenheit temperature scales.
- ✔ Understand and demonstrate physical changes due to temperature.
- ✔ Develop a mathematical relationship that describes how much the temperature of water increases when heat is added to the water.
- ✔ Discuss the relationship of heat and energy.
- ✔ Calculate the efficiency in a heating system.
- ✔ Predict the final temperature when two containers of water of different temperatures are mixed.
- ✔ Quantify the flow of heat from one container of water to another where there is an initial temperature difference between the two containers.
- ✔ Analyze temperature changes in terms of the flow of heat.
- ✔ Calculate the specific heat of a substance if a known quantity of that substance is mixed with water.
- ✔ Predict the equilibrium temperature of a mixture of water and another substance.

Vocabulary

British thermal unit (Btu)	first law of thermodynamics	latent heat	thermal equilibrium
calorie	heat	temperature	thermometer
Celsius scale	heat-temperature rule	thermal energy	thermostat
Fahrenheit scale			

26.1 Temperature Scales

You have probably used a thermometer. However, did you ever stop to think about how it works? In this section, you will learn how temperature is measured and how the devices we use to measure temperature work.

Temperature

What is temperature?

Many people use a thermometer to find the temperature outside. Temperature is the measurement we use to quantify the sensations of hot and cold. A hot cup of coffee has a higher temperature than a cold glass of iced tea. But what does temperature actually measure?

What does temperature measure?

If we were to blow up a balloon we would fill it with billions upon billions of molecules of air. All of these molecules are constantly moving. If they are moving, they have kinetic energy. Some of the molecules are moving fast, some are moving slowly. They can move up, down, and sideways. Fast particles have more kinetic energy than slow particles. If we were to take the kinetic energy of every single molecule in a balloon, and divide it by the total number of molecules, we would have an average of the kinetic energy for molecules in the balloon. This average is what temperature measures.

If average kinetic energy increases, so does temperature

If we were to heat up a balloon, all of the molecules inside of it would start to move faster and faster. What does this tell you about the relationship between average kinetic energy and temperature? It tells you that increasing the temperature increases the random motion of the molecules, and so increases the average kinetic energy of the molecules.

The temperature of an object measures the average kinetic energy of its molecules.

Celsius scale

The Celsius scale is also called the centigrade scale because the difference in temperature between the freezing and boiling points of water is divided into 100 degrees.

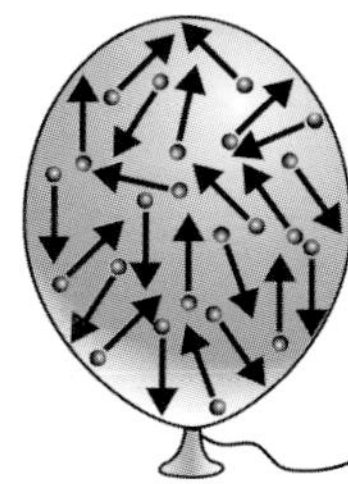

Figure 26.1: *As temperature increases, so does the average kinetic energy of the molecules.The sizes of the arrows in the balloons represent the amount of kinetic energy of the molecules they contain.*

Temperature scales

The Fahrenheit scale You are probably most familiar with the English system of measuring temperature, known as the Fahrenheit scale. In the Fahrenheit scale, water freezes at 32 degrees (or 32°F) and water boils at 212°F. You have probably also taken your own body temperature, which is normally about 98.6°F. Room temperature is about 68°F.

The Celsius scale The SI, or metric, unit used to measure temperature is the degree centigrade, also known as the degree Celsius. In the Celsius scale, water freezes at zero degrees Celsius (or 0°C) and water boils at 100°C. Room temperature is about 25°C.

The history of temperature scales Ole Roemer created the first commonly used temperature scale (the Roemer scale) in 1702 in Denmark. Roemer used a thermometer containing alcohol with a red dye. He created his scale by dividing the temperature between the freezing and boiling points of water into 80 degrees.

Gabriel Fahrenheit, a German physicist, was the first person to use a mercury thermometer. In 1714, in Holland, he developed the Fahrenheit scale. However, he did not base his scale on the freezing and boiling points of water. Instead, for his zero point he used the lowest temperature he could create in the laboratory from a mixture of water, salt, and ice. For the other end of his scale he used the temperature of the human body for 100 degrees.

Eventually the Fahrenheit scale was redesigned so that water freezes at 32 degrees, water boils at 212 degrees, and the scale between freezing and boiling is divided into 180 degrees. In 1742, Anders Celsius, a Swedish astronomer, invented a scale in which there were 100 degrees between freezing and boiling. This scale was called the centigrade scale. In 1948 this official scale of the metric system was named the Celsius scale in honor of Anders Celsius. Most countries in the world use the Celsius scale.

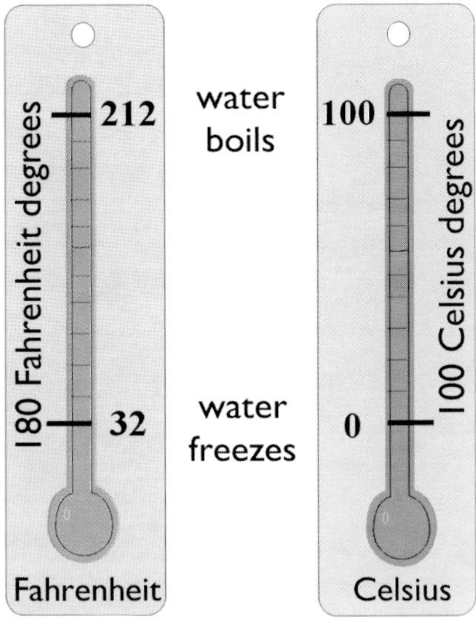

Figure 26.2: *A comparison of the Fahrenheit and Celsius temperature scales.*

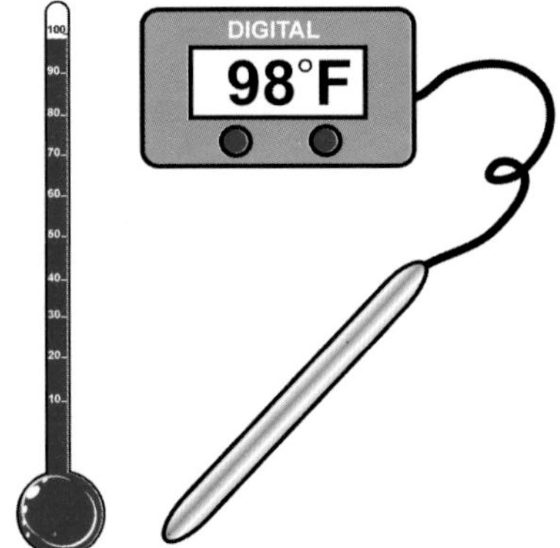

Figure 26.3: *Different types of thermometers measure different physical changes in substances.*

Thermometers

Thermometers You have used a thermometer all your life but might not know how it works. The most common thermometers contain either a red fluid, which is alcohol containing a small amount of red dye, or a silvery fluid, which is mercury. You may have also used a thermometer with a digital electronic readout. Thermometers can detect the physical changes in materials due to change in temperature. Different types of thermometers measure different physical changes.

Most materials expand with temperature Most materials expand when you raise the temperature. The expansion comes from the increase in molecular motion that goes with the rise in temperature. If atoms are moving around more, they tend to bump each other apart and take up more space. The most obvious example is that gas expands when it heats up. You can see this if you heat or cool a balloon. The expansion of a liquid is not as great, but we can easily observe it.

How does a common thermometer work? Thermal expansion is the basic principle of a thermometer. The expansion of the liquid is directly proportional to the change in temperature. For example, for every degree the thermometer heats up, the fluid inside might expand so that it takes up one more millimeter of space in the tube.

Temperature changes and bridges

Most solids also expand due to an increase in temperature, but the increase is very small. For solid steel the thermal expansion in on the order of one ten-thousandth. This means that a 1-meter steel rod will expand 0.01 millimeters for every degree Celsius of temperature increase. Although this may be difficult to detect, temperature changes can have dramatic effects on larger structures such as buildings and bridges. For instance, a 100-meter-long bridge could be up to 10 centimeters longer on a hot summer day than on a cold winter day. In order to prevent damage to the bridge, civil engineers use expansion joints in bridges as shown in figure 26.5.

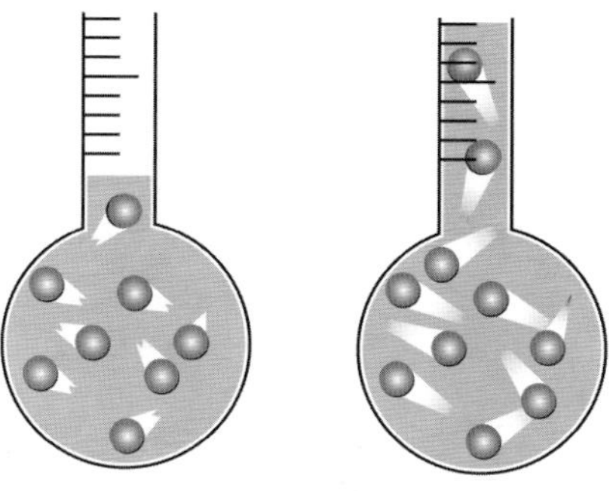

Figure 26.4: *The expansion of the liquid in a thermometer is directly proportional to increase in temperature.*

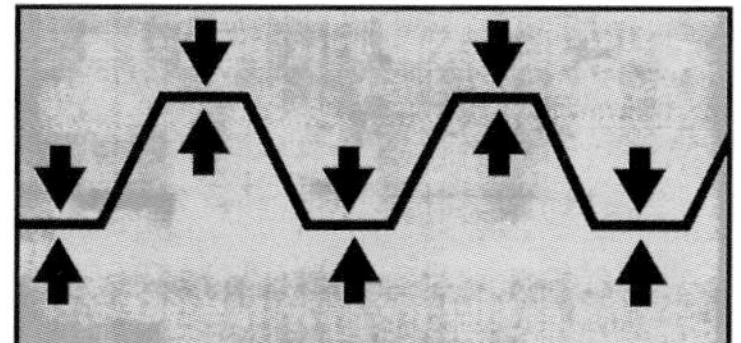

Figure 26.5: *In order to prevent damage due to temperature changes, civil engineers use expansion joints in bridges.*

Digital thermometers

Another physical property that changes with temperature is electrical resistance. The resistance of a metal wire will increase with temperature. Since the metal is hotter, and the metal atoms are shaking more, there is more resistance to electrons passing through the wire. Digital thermometers measure this change in resistance. Most commonly, platinum metal is used in digital thermometers.

How does a thermostat work?

You probably have a thermostat in your home. A thermostat turns on a heater (or air conditioner) based on the temperature. If the temperature in the room is too hot, the thermostat sends an electrical signal to your furnace to shut it off.

Simple thermostats use a bi-metallic strip to make a switch. We mentioned earlier that metals expand with an increase in temperature. Different metals expand at different rates. If you take two different metals and fix them together in a strip, the strip will bend when heated. The metal on the bottom (dark) expands more than the metal on the top (blue) and the difference is what causes the bending. In a thermostat, this bending moves a switch.

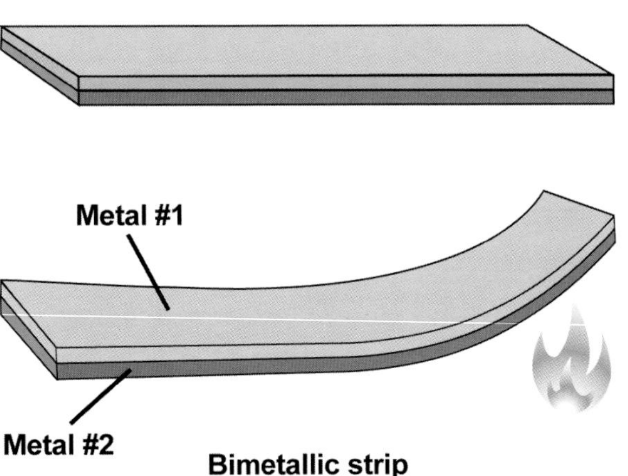

Bimetallic strip

Science in your home

Have you ever had trouble opening a jar of salsa or mayonnaise because the lid was put on too tight? One method of opening the jar is to run the it under warm water. As the glass jar and the metal lid heat up, they will both expand. However, the rate of expansion of metal is over twice the rate of expansion of glass. Thus the lid will loosen as you heat up the jar!

Liquid-crystal thermometers

Some thermometers, often used on the outside of aquariums, contain liquid crystals that change color based on temperature. These liquid crystals are derived from cholesterol and were discovered in 1838 by Austrian botanist Freidrich Reinitfer. We now use these crystals by trapping them between two thin sheets of plastic, in a layer one-tenth of a millimeter thick. These are the same crystals that can be found in a "mood ring." If you place a liquid crystal thermometer on your skin you will see it change color. As temperature increases, the molecules of the liquid crystal bump into each other more and more. This causes a change in the structure of the crystals, which in turn affects their color. These thermometers are able to accurately determine the temperature between 65°F and 85°F.

26.2 Measuring Changes in Heat

You know that energy can take many forms such as kinetic energy, gravitational potential energy, electrical potential energy, and chemical potential energy. In this section, we explore thermal energy and how electrical energy becomes thermal energy. You will see how thermal energy increases the temperature of an object. You will also develop a relationship between the rate of increase in temperature of water and the increase in thermal energy of water.

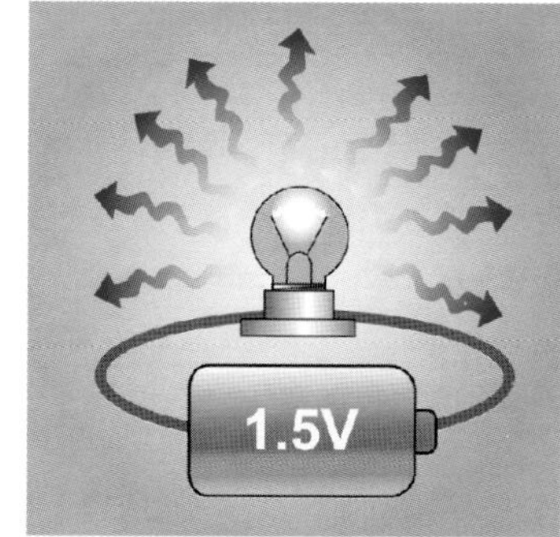

Figure 26.6: *What energy changes are involved in this scenario?*

Figure 26.7: *Where does the energy come from? Where does it go?*

Figure 26.8: *On a hot day, the flow of thermal energy can turn your ice cream cone into a puddle if you don't eat it fast!*

Temperature, thermal energy, and heat

Changing temperature changes energy

Nature never creates or destroys energy; energy only gets converted from one form to another. Changes in temperature involve changes in energy. When you heat a pot of soup with an electric hot plate, *electrical energy* is converted into *thermal energy*. What, exactly, is thermal energy?

What is thermal energy?

Thermal energy and temperature are not the same. Temperature, as you have learned, measures the *average* kinetic energy of the molecules inside an object. Thermal energy is the *sum* of all the kinetic and potential energies of the molecules of a substance. The amount of thermal energy stored in an object depends on three things: the mass, the temperature, and the amount of energy that a particular material stores per degree.

Suppose you are asked to heat up a single cup of soup or a huge pot of soup. Both have to get to the same temperature. Which takes more energy? Heating up the huge pot takes more energy because it is like heating up 100 individual cups! Because it took more energy to heat the pot of soup, it now contains more thermal energy than the cup of soup, even though they are at the same temperature.

Heat and thermal energy

What happens when you hold an ice cream cone on a hot day? Thermal energy flows from your hand and the surrounding air to melt the ice cream. We call this flow of thermal energy heat. In the scientific sense, heat occurs only when there is a difference in temperature. Heat always flows from the warmer object to the cooler one.

Measuring heat

Understanding heat is important

The flow of thermal energy (which we call heat) is happening around us all the time. When you cook a pot of soup, thermal energy flows from the burner to the soup and to the surrounding air. You might have a fan above the stove to remove the hot air from the kitchen. A lot of the energy we consume goes toward heating or cooling our homes, businesses, and schools.

The calorie

Because heat is such an important concept in our lives there are three units of energy that relate directly to heat. The metric unit used to measure heat or energy is the calorie. The **calorie** is defined as the quantity of heat needed to increase the temperature of 1 gram of water by 1 degree Celsius. Both calories and joules are units of energy: 1 calorie = 4.184 joules.

The British thermal unit

Still another unit of heat you may have heard of is the **British thermal unit**, or Btu. The Btu is often used to describe heat produced by heating systems or heat removed by air-conditioning systems. A Btu is the quantity of heat it takes to increase the temperature of 1 pound of water by 1 degree Fahrenheit.

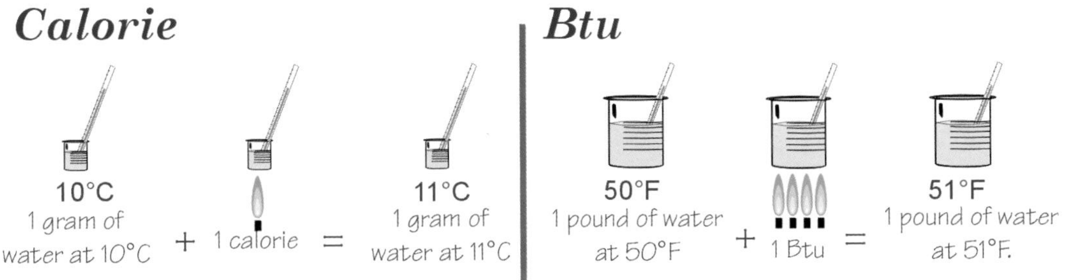

How do you quantify amounts of heat?

If you add heat to an object, how much will its temperature increase? Based on our definition of the calorie we can say that the amount of heat that flows into an object is proportional to the *mass of the object times the change in temperature.* This statement is known as the **heat-temperature rule**. Simply stated, the more heat you add to an object, the greater the increase in temperature. If you have twice as much mass of object to heat, you need twice as much energy to increase the temperature by the same amount.

James Prescott Joule

In the 1840s, James Prescott Joule proved that the law of conservation of energy also applied to heat. Until that time, physicists only considered the law of conservation of mechanical energy, which did not include heat. Joule showed that when he converted electrical energy and kinetic energy into thermal energy, energy was still conserved. The unit for heat and energy is named in his honor.

Unit	Equals
1 calorie	4.186 joules
1 Calorie	1000 calories
1 Btu	1055 joules
1 Btu	252 calories

Figure 26.9: *Conversion table for units of heat*

Differences in materials The amount of temperature increase also depends on what you are heating. It takes more energy to raise the temperature of some materials than others. For example, suppose you put 100 calories of heat into a beaker with 100 grams of water. The temperature goes up one degree. If you apply the same amount of heat to 100 grams of iron, the temperature goes up 20 degrees!

What is specific heat? As water and iron illustrate, substances vary greatly in their ability to store thermal energy. The **specific heat** is a property of a substance that tells us how much the temperature goes up when a given amount of heat is added. A large specific heat means you have to put in a lot of energy for each degree increase in temperature.

The heat equation The whole story is told by the heat equation below. The equation tells you how much heat (Q) it takes to change the temperature (Δ T) of a mass (m) of a substance with specific heat (c).

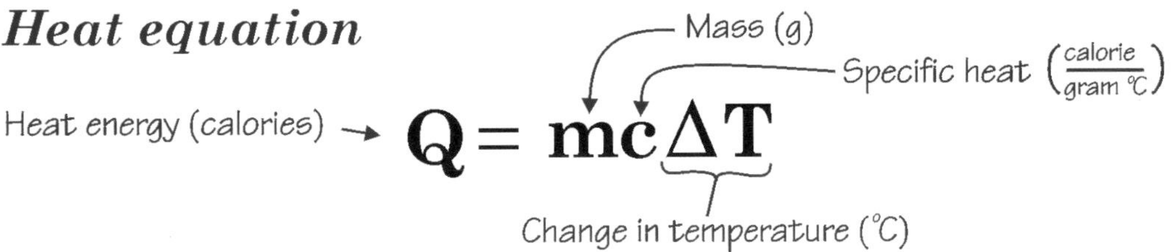

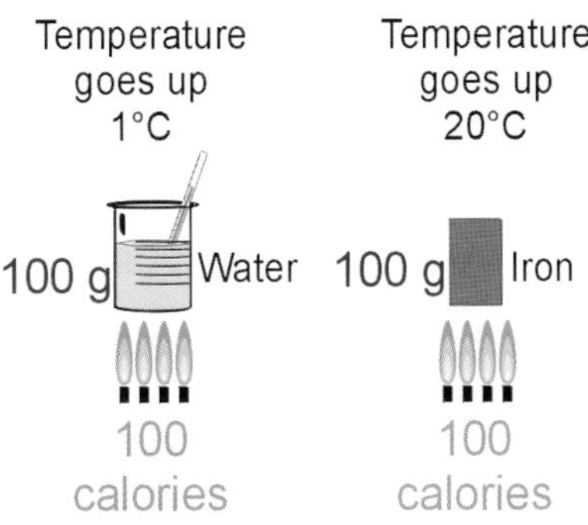

Figure 26.10: *The temperature gains in iron and water for equal amounts of heat.*

Example:

How much heat is needed to raise the temperature of 250 grams of water from 20 °C to 40 °C?

1. Identify the variables in the equation.

   Heat equation: $Q = mc\Delta T$

   Q = trying to determine

   m = mass of water = 250 grams

   c = specific heat of water = 1 calorie/g °C

   $\Delta T = 40\ °C - 20\ °C = 20\ °C$

2. Plug the variables into the equation and solve.

   $Q = (250\ g) \times (1\ \text{calorie/g °C}) \times (20\ °C)$

   Q = 5000 calories

Specific heats of materials

substance	specific heat $\frac{\text{calorie}}{\text{gram°C}}$
water	1.00
ice	0.493
benzene	0.416
methanol	0.586
ethanol	0.584
aluminum	0.215
carbon	0.170
silver	0.052
gold	0.031

26.3 Specific Heat

Energy is always conserved and can take many forms. Energy can be converted from kinetic energy into potential energy. Electrical energy can be converted into thermal energy. In this section, you will learn about the transfer of thermal energy from one body to another body.

Flow of heat and equilibrium

Energy can change from one object to another

When heat flows from a warm mug of hot chocolate to your hand, there is an exchange of energy for both objects. The warm mug loses energy and cools down. Your hand gains energy and warms up. When you touch the mug, your hand is in *thermal contact* with it.

Energy loss is equal to energy gain

Suppose you were able to take some objects or substances in thermal contact with each other and place them in a container that would not allow any energy to leave the system. For example, you place a cup of hot coffee mixed with a cup of ice into your container. Because the mixed drink is isolated from the outside, the energy that the hot coffee loses must equal the energy that the ice gains. This is an example of the law of conservation of energy. When we are talking about heat, this law is also known as the **first law of thermodynamics**. Both laws state that the energy in an isolated system is conserved.

What is thermal equilibrium?

Have you ever filled your kitchen sink with hot water to wash dishes? If the water was too hot, you may have added cold water to cool down the hot water. The temperature of the water in the sink eventually reaches a balance where everything is evenly warm. Whenever you have a hot object or substance in thermal contact with a cold one, heat will flow from the hot object to the cold object until they are at the same temperature, which means they are in **thermal equilibrium**.

When do objects reach thermal equilibrium?

Objects reach thermal equilibrium when they reach the same temperature. When you submerge a thermometer in water to measure its temperature, you need to wait for a few seconds until you see the mercury or alcohol level of the thermometer stops rising. At that point, the thermometer and the water will have reached the same temperature. Both objects transfer energy (heat) until they reach thermal equilibrium. Thus, the reading you get is the thermometer's own temperature.

Heat flow and the origin of the word *calorie*

We now understand that the flow of heat is due to the transfer of energy. However, until the 1840s scientists thought that heat traveled by an invisible fluid called *caloric*, which comes from the Latin word for heat. We still use the word *calorie* even though we no longer believe in a fluid called caloric.

Figure 26.11: *When you hold a mug of hot chocolate, your hand is in thermal contact with the cup.*

Specific heat

What does specific heat mean?

You learned in the last section that when heat flows it raises the temperature of some substances more than others. We refer to this property of a substance as its specific heat. For example, the specific heat for water is equal to $1\frac{\text{calorie}}{\text{gram°C}}$.

Water has a high specific heat

It is important to point out that other substances have very different specific heat values. Water has a very high specific heat, which is why it is used as a coolant. It takes more energy to increase the temperature of water than for other substances in nature.

Metals have low specific heats

Figure 26.12 shows the specific heats for different substances. For example, aluminum has a specific heat $0.215\frac{\text{calorie}}{\text{gram°C}}$. Like most metals, aluminum has a specific heat that is five times smaller than the specific heat of water. If we add 1 calorie of energy to one gram of water, the temperature of the water will increase 1°C. However, if we add 1 calorie of energy to 1 gram of aluminum, the temperature will increase almost 5°C!

Although the temperature of water did not go up by very much, the water still absorbed the heat that flowed into it. Therefore, water at a certain temperature will transfer more heat to a cooler object than most other substances. For example, 10 grams of water at 90°C will raise the temperature of a cup of cold water much higher than would 10 grams of aluminum at 90°C.

substance	specific heat $\frac{\text{calorie}}{\text{gram°C}}$
water	1.00
ice	0.493
benzene	0.416
methanol	0.586
ethanol	0.584
aluminum	0.215
carbon	0.170
silver	0.052
gold	0.031

Figure 26.12: *The specific heats of some common substances.*

Joseph Black

Scottish chemist Joseph Black developed the theory of specific heat in 1760. Black realized the difference between heat that increases the temperature of a substance, and heat that melts or boils a substance. For instance, if we add heat to water, initially the temperature of the water increases. Black called this heat *sensible* heat because it could be sensed with a thermometer. Once the temperature of water reaches 100°C, it boils. Any heat added to boiling water causes water to vaporize, but does not raise the temperature. Black called the heat for melting and boiling latent heat because it could not be sensed with a thermometer. Latent means "hidden."

More about specific heat: the law of Dulong and Petit

The specific heat of an element

Every substance has a different specific heat, but what physical principle gives rise to these differences? The answer was discovered in 1819 by the French physicists Pierre Louis Dulong and Alexis Therese Petit. They showed that the specific heat of an element depends on how many atoms there are per gram. One gram of a heavy element, like silver, will have fewer atoms than 1 gram of aluminum.

How energy is divided

Suppose you add one calorie of heat to two samples (aluminum and silver) of equal mass. The temperature of the silver goes up by 18°C while the aluminum only goes up by 5°C (figure 26.13). The silver sample has fewer atoms than the aluminum sample because silver atoms are heavier. When you add heat, each atom gets an equal share of the energy. If there are more atoms, each atom gets less energy. Because the energy added to the two samples is the same, each silver atom gets more energy that each aluminum atom.

More atoms per gram means higher specific heat

The temperature depends on the amount of energy per atom. If each atom gets more energy, the temperature change will be greater. This explains why the specific heat of aluminum is greater than the specific heat of silver. Aluminum has more atoms per gram, therefore it takes more energy per gram to raise the temperature.

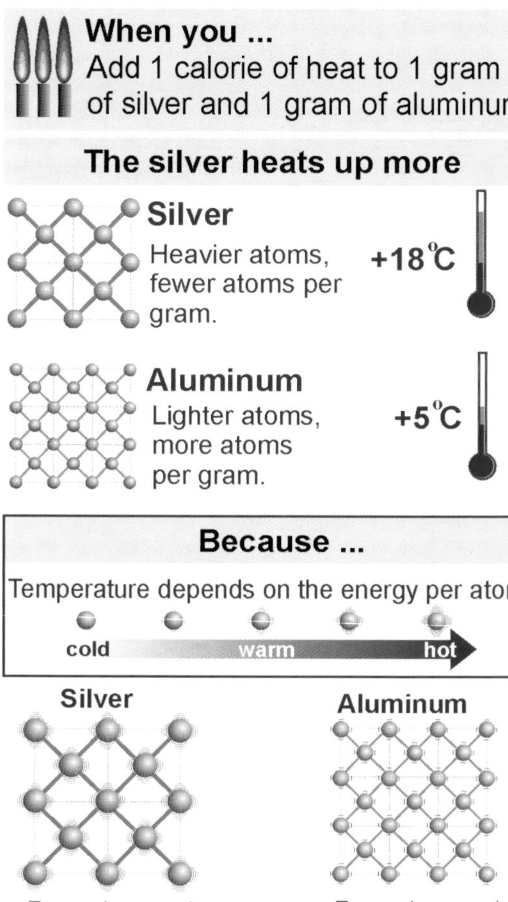

Figure 26.13: *The specific heat of aluminum is greater than that of silver because aluminum has more atoms per gram than silver.*

Chapter 26 Review

Vocabulary review

Match the following terms with the correct definition. There is one extra definition in the list that will not match any of the terms.

Set One

1. Fahrenheit scale	a. Temperature scale where the freezing point of water is 0° and the boiling point is 100°
2. Celsius scale	b. A quantity used to describe the sensations of hot and cold
3. thermometer	c. A device that converts temperature differences into electrical energy for running machines
4. electrical resistance	d. Temperature scale where the freezing point of water is 32° and the boiling point is 212°
5. temperature	e. Instrument that measures temperature changes
	f. A physical property that changes with temperature change

Set Two

1. thermal energy	a. The temperature rises proportionally to the mass and amount of heat added
2. heat	b. The sum of the kinetic and potential energies of the molecules of a substance
3. heat-temperature rule	c. Quantity of heat needed to raise the temperature of 1 gram of water by 1° Celsius
4. joule	d. Energy transferred because of a temperature difference
5. calorie	e. Unit of energy smaller than the calorie
	f. Quantity of heat needed to raise the temperature of 1 pound of water by 1° Fahrenheit

Set Three

1. law of conservation of energy	a. The amount of energy it takes, per unit mass, to raise the temperature of a material one degree
2. thermal equilibrium	b. Energy per unit mass that flows at the melting or boiling points of a substance
3. specific heat	c. Heat flows from a hot object to a cold object until they have the same temperature
4. specific heat of water	d. Energy lost by one part of a system must equal the energy gained by another part of the system
5. latent heat	e. Instrument that measures temperature changes
	f. $1.00 \frac{\text{calorie}}{\text{gram°C}}$

Concept review

1. How would you define temperature?
2. What happens to the volume of the gas in a balloon when it is heated?
3. What happens to the length of a bar of iron when it is heated?
4. How would you define heat?
5. How would you define thermal energy?
6. Why is water used as a coolant?
7. On the Celsius scale, water boils at what temperature?
   a. 0°
   b. 32°
   c. 100°
   d. 212°
8. Normal human body temperature on the Fahrenheit scale is closest to:
   a. 37°F
   b. 68°F
   c. 150°F
   d. 100°F
9. Water at 40°C is mixed with an equal amount of water at 40°F. The final temperature of the mixture:
   a. remains constant at 40°C.
   b. remains constant at 40°F.
   c. gets warmer than 40°C.
   d. gets warmer than 40°F.
10. Describe what happens to the individual molecules in an object when you increase its temperature, and why this causes the object's size to increase.
11. What is thermal equilibrium?
12. What does the law of conservation of energy tell us about heat transfer?
13. How does a thermometer work?
14. One liter of water at 10°C is added to 1 liter of water at 80°C. What is the final temperature of the mixture?
    a. 10°C
    b. 45°C
    c. 5°C
    d. 90°C
15. When you hold a cold can of soda in your hand, thermal energy flows:
    a. from the can of soda to your hand.
    b. from your hand to the can of soda.
    c. in both directions.
    d. There is no flow of thermal energy.
16. Due to its large mass, an iceberg has more thermal energy than a hot cup of coffee. If the cup of coffee is placed in thermal contact with an iceberg, where is energy exchanged?
    a. Thermal energy flows from the iceberg to the cup of coffee.
    b. Thermal energy flows from the cup of coffee to the iceberg.
    c. Thermal energy flows in both directions.
    d. There is no exchange of thermal energy.

Problems

1. Convert the Celsius temperature at which water freezes, 0°C, to degrees Fahrenheit.
2. Convert the Fahrenheit temperature at which paper burns, 451°F, to degrees Celsius.
3. Convert the Celsius temperature of the surface of the sun, which is 5,500°C, to degrees Fahrenheit.
4. Convert today's highest temperature from Fahrenheit to Celsius.
5. A teapot contains 500 milliliters of water. Five thousand calories of heat are added to the teapot. What is the increase in the temperature of the water?
6. How much energy will it take to increase the temperature of 200 milliliters of water by 12°C?
7. The power of a coffee pot is rated at 900 watts. It can heat 1 liter of water in 2 minutes.
   a. How much electrical energy does the coffee pot use in this process?
   b. Assuming the coffee pot has an efficiency of 30 percent, how much of the electrical energy becomes thermal energy in the water?
   c. What is the increase in the temperature of the water?
8. One liter of water at 10°C is added to 4 liters of water at 80°C. What is the equilibrium temperature of the mixture?
9. One liter of water at 20°C is mixed with 3 liters of water at 80°C. What is the equilibrium temperature of the mixture?
10. In the problem above, how many calories of heat are transferred from the hot water to the cold water?
11. Two liters of water at 40°C are added to 2 liters of water at 80°C. The final temperature of the mixture is 60°C. How many calories of heat flow from the hot water to the cold water? (Hint: The mass of 1 liter of water is 1000 grams.)
12. Two beakers each contain 1 kilogram of water at 0°C. One kilogram of gold at 100°C is dropped into one beaker. One kilogram of aluminum at 100°C is dropped into the other beaker.

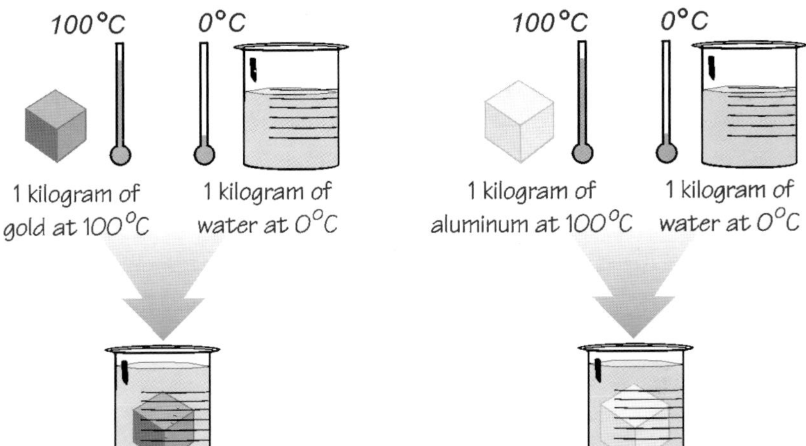

   a. Compare the amount of thermal energy contained in the aluminum and gold.
   b. After each beaker has reached thermal equilibrium, describe whether the temperatures are the same, or different. If they are different, describe which is warmer and which is colder.
   c. Explain why you gave you answer to part (b). Use the concept of specific heat in your explanation.

Applying your knowledge

1. Look at or have someone show you the water level in an automobile radiator. You will notice that the radiator is filled up to the cap with water. Next to the radiator there is an overflow container. As the car runs and the water get very hot, what happens to the water? What have engineers included in the design of an automobile radiator system to return the water from the overflow into the radiator?
2. The first settlers in Colorado were very concerned about fruits and vegetables freezing in their root cellars overnight. They soon realized that if they placed a large tub of water in the cellar, the food would not freeze. Explain why the food would not freeze.
3. If you keep lowering the temperature of a material, the atoms vibrate less and less. If you could eventually reach a low enough temperature, the atoms might not vibrate at all. Is this possible, and what does it mean for the temperature scale? Is it possible to keep lowering the temperature indefinitely?
4. For one or more of the following, write a short paper or give a presentation on your research:
   a. In the 1860s, the English physicist James Clerk Maxwell (1831-1879) and the Austrian physicist Ludwig Boltzmann (1844-1906) first gave a rigorous analysis of temperature in terms of the average kinetic energy of the molecules of a substance. Explore their lives and their contributions to the development of the theory of temperature.
   b. Lord Kelvin (1824-1907), a British physicist, developed the idea of absolute zero, the coldest temperature attainable. The Kelvin temperature scale is named in his honor. Research absolute zero, the Kelvin scale, and the life of Lord Kelvin.
   c. Scottish chemist Joseph Black developed the theories of specific and latent heat. Research his life and how he made these discoveries.

Chapter 27

Heat Transfer

Introduction to Chapter 27

What process does a hot cup of coffee undergo as it cools? How does your bedroom become warm during the winter? How does the cooling system of a car work? Understanding heat transfer will help you answer these questions. This chapter will look into three types of heat transfer: convection, conduction and radiation.

Investigations to Chapter 27

27.1	Conduction	*How well do common materials conduct heat?*

In this Investigation you will compare heat conduction in several materials by using your sense of touch and then rank their thermal conductivity.

27.2	Convection	*How much heat is transferred through convection?*

In this Investigation you will observe both natural convection and forced convection. A flask of hot water with red dye will be placed in a beaker filled with cool water. The hot red water will rise into the cooler water due to natural convection. You are going to observe the process and take temperature data to analyze how much heat is transferred via convection. You will also blow through a straw to force the red dye out of the flask into the larger beaker to explore forced convection.

27.3	Radiation	*Which materials are good absorbers of radiation?*

In this Investigation you will use a 100-watt light bulb as the source of radiation. You will observe and compare the increase in temperature (using a temperature probe) in air, water, sand, and soil.

Learning Goals

In this chapter, you will:

- ✔ Describe how thermal energy is transferred by conduction.
- ✔ List various kinds of materials that are heat conductors or insulators.
- ✔ Explain why thermal and electrical conductivity of a material are related.
- ✔ Analyze how energy can be transferred through convection.
- ✔ Describe the motion of liquid because of temperature differences within the system.
- ✔ Describe applications of convection.
- ✔ Explain what properties make a good absorber of heat.
- ✔ Explain the color-temperature relationship.

Vocabulary

absorbers	forced convection	reflectors	thermal insulators
conduction	heat transfer	sea breeze	ultraviolet light
convection	infrared light	thermal conductivity	
emitters	natural (or buoyant) convection	thermal conductors	

27.1 Conduction

Thermal energy travels as heat from a material at a higher temperature to a material at a lower temperature. This general process is called heat transfer. How is heat transferred from material to material, or from place to place? What materials do we use to keep things warm or cold? It turns out there are three quite distinct mechanisms of heat transfer. In this section, you will learn about conduction, which is the transfer of heat by the direct contact of particles of matter. By comparing the heat conduction of different materials, you can rank their thermal conductivity.

Figure 27.1: *A metal spoon placed in hot water quickly transmits the heat to your hand.*

What is conduction?

What is conduction?

Conduction is the transfer of heat by the direct contact of particles of matter. Conduction occurs between two materials at different temperatures when they are touching each other. Conduction can also occur through one material, if one part of the material is hotter than another part. For example, a metal spoon placed in hot water quickly transmits the heat to your hand.

Conduction is the transfer of heat by the direct contact of particles of matter.

How is thermal energy transferred?

Imagine that you are the size of an atom. Things that used to look unmoving like a table or even air now appear as a sea of atoms and molecules in constant motion. In solids the molecules and atoms vibrate in place, in liquids they move over and around each other, and in gases they shoot around. Collisions are occurring everywhere as atoms and molecules jiggle and zoom.

All these moving atoms and molecules have *kinetic energy*. Now imagine what happens at the atomic level when a warmer material comes in contact with a cooler material. The atoms and molecules of the warmer material are moving around faster than the atoms and molecules of the cooler material. Where the two materials are in contact there are lots of collisions between the atoms and molecules of each.

Figure 27.2: *When a warmer material, like the hot water in this cup, comes in contact with a cooler material, like the spoon, there are lots of collisions between the atoms and molecules of each.*

What happens as these collisions take place?

Imagine the beginning of a giant bumper car rally. Some cars start out fast and others start out slow. Soon they are all hitting each other. When a fast car bounces into a slow car, the fast car slows down a bit and the slow car speeds up a bit. The cars may even change direction as well! As each car changes direction it then hits other cars around it. Pretty soon all the cars in the giant rally are bouncing off each other at about the same average speed. When this happens, they are in equilibrium.

The collisions happen until thermal equilibrium is reached

The same thing happens at the atomic level. As collisions occur, the atoms and molecules of the warmer material slow down, and the atoms and molecules of the cooler material speed up. Some of the kinetic energy of the hotter material is transferred, one collision at a time, to the cooler material. Soon, both materials are at the same temperature (figure 27.3). This is how two materials reach thermal equilibrium by conduction.

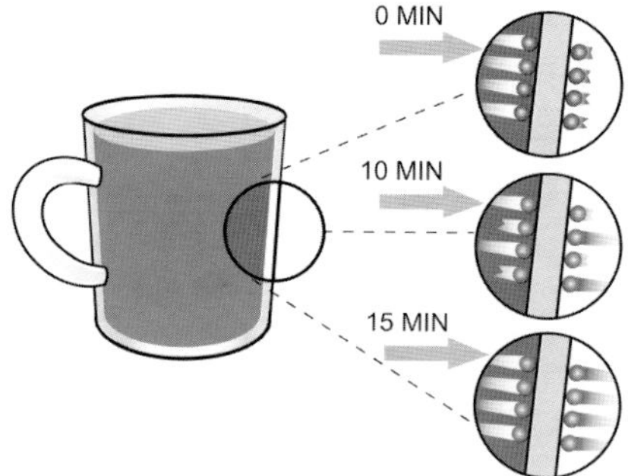

Figure 27.3: *In a hot glass of cocoa, the particles in the liquid and air collide with the particles in the glass. Because kinetic energy is transferred by these collisions, cocoa, glass and air eventually reach the same temperature.*

Conductors and insulators

Which state of matter conducts best?

Conduction can take place in solids, liquids and gases. However, the more densely packed atoms or molecules of a solid can conduct more heat because there are many more collisions taking place. The low density of gases mean that relatively few collisions take place per second and therefore air is a poor conductor of heat. This explains why many things we use to keep things warm or cold, such as foam, fiberglass insulation, and down jackets, contain air pockets that slow down the transfer of heat.

What are thermal insulators and thermal conductors?

In general, materials that conduct heat easily are called **thermal conductors** and those that conduct heat poorly are called **thermal insulators**. For example, metal is a thermal conductor, and foam is a thermal insulator. You may remember that the words *conductor* and *insulator* are also used to describe a material's ability to conduct electrical current. There is a reason for this common usage. In general, good electrical conductors are also good heat conductors. Remember, metals are good conductors of current because the metal atoms have electrons that escape easily from the atom. When a metal conducts heat, these free electrons also transfer kinetic energy easily.

Figure 27.4: *Styrofoam is a better thermal insulator than glass. Therefore, liquid in a foam container will retain heat longer than it would in a glass container.*

Thermal conductivity in the building and manufacturing industries

Different materials conduct thermal energy at different rates

Thermal conductivity is a measure of how well a material conducts heat. Although solids in general are better conductors of heat than liquids or gases, each material conducts heat at a different rate. We can compare thermal conductivities by measuring how fast a certain amount of thermal energy flows through uniformly sized pieces of various materials.

Thermal conductivity in your home

Measuring the thermal conductivity of different materials is important in the building and manufacturing industries. We don't want hot air to leave our home when it's cold outside and we also don't want hot air to enter our home when it's very hot outside. A home built with good insulators lessens heat transfer in both directions.

Windows and energy loss

The thermal conductivity of a single-pane glass window is very high and heat is easily transferred through it. Air leakage also occurs around windows, which results in even more heat transfer. This means that about one-third of home heat in the United Sates is lost through windowpanes and window frames. This energy loss is about equal to all the energy available from the oil flowing through the Alaskan pipeline in an entire year.

Thermal conductivity in the workplace

Sometimes you want to conduct heat away quickly. Did you know that hammering a penny or paper clip makes it hot? Some of the work done on the penny or paperclip is converted to thermal energy. Drilling, hammering, and many other manufacturing processes create unwanted increases in temperature. If the heat has to be transferred away quickly, structures like metal grills and fins are often used. Metal is a good conductor of heat, and grills and fins add surface area to increase cooling by *convection*, another form of heat transfer.

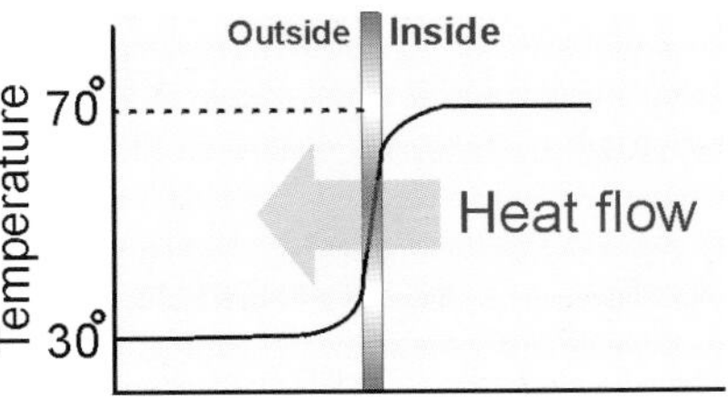

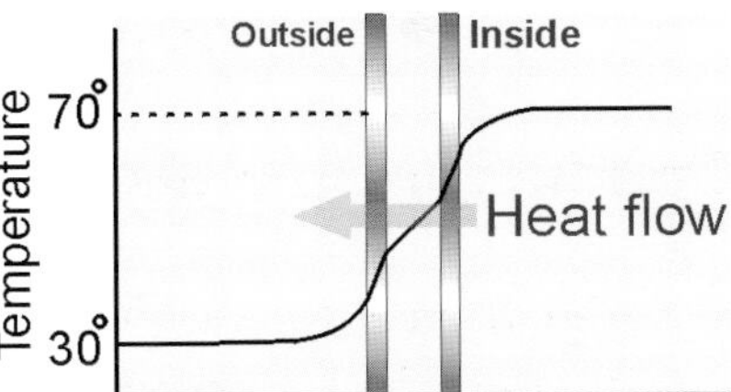

Figure 27.5: *Heat flows from hot to cold. On a cold winter day, heat flows through the window from inside to outside.*

Heat flows quickly if the temperature changes a lot over a short distance. With single pane glass the temperature changes from inside to outside over the thickness of the glass, resulting in a large heat flow.

Double pane glass spreads the temperature change over a much longer distance, and puts a layer of insulating air between the glass panes. As a result, much less heat is lost through the window.

27.2 Convection

Another type of heat transfer that is due to temperature differences is called convection. This type of heat transfer is responsible for global weather patterns, the heating of our homes and the circulation of waters in the oceans.

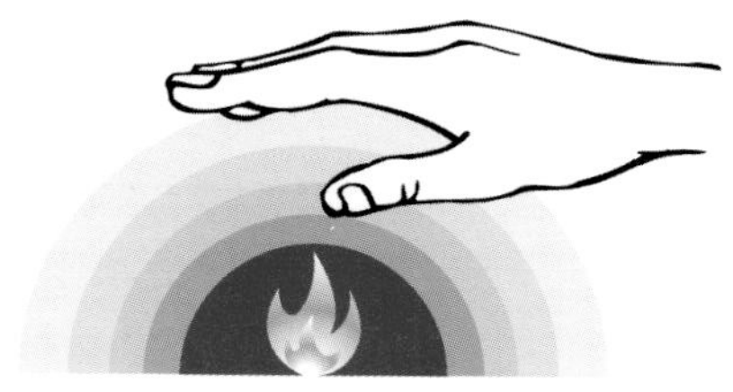

Figure 27.6: *The air right above the flame heats up and expands, transferring heat to your hand.*

What is convection?

What is convection?

Have you ever warmed up your hands by putting them over an open flame? You can do this because the air right above the flame heats up and expands. Because the expanded air is less dense, it rises, bringing the heat to your hand (figure 27.6). This heat transfer process is called convection. Unlike conduction, which occurs mostly in solids, convection occurs only in liquids and gases. Convection comes from a Latin word meaning *to carry together.*

Convection is the transfer of heat by the actual motion of a fluid (liquid or gas) in the form of currents.

Convection can occur in all fluids, whether liquids or gases. Convection occurs because warmer fluids are less dense, and rise. Cooler fluids are more dense, and sink. This motion of fluids causes currents.

Convection causes the weather patterns on Earth

The currents caused by convection occur constantly in our atmosphere and are responsible for much of our weather. On a global scale, hot air near the equator rises and is forced toward the poles as shown in figure 27.7. The sinking air forces cold air at the poles toward the equator. Combined with forces due to the rotation of the Earth, convection and unequal heating are the primary causes of weather.

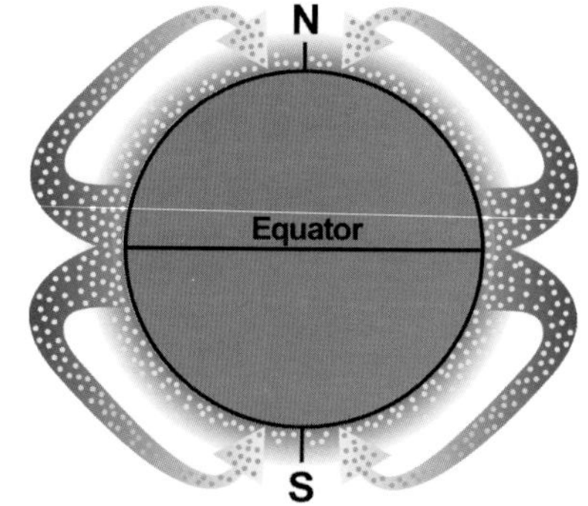

Figure 27.7: *Currents caused by convection are responsible for much of our weather. Warm air rises off the surface of the Earth. As it cools, it sinks back down and replaces warmer air.*

Natural convection

Why does warmer air rise?

There is a natural upward force called buoyancy. This force occurs whenever you have an object submerged in a denser medium. An example is an inflated ball under water. The ball is less dense than the water. There is an upward force equal to the weight of the displaced medium that pushes the ball out of the water. But this force not only applies to solids, it also applies to fluids and gases. As heated air or a fluid rises, there are density differences, which act with gravitational forces to produce **natural or buoyant convection**.

Sea breezes are due to convection

On a smaller scale near coastlines, convection is responsible for sea breezes. During the daytime, land is much hotter than the ocean. A sea breeze is created when hot air over the land rises due to convection and is replaced by cooler air from the ocean. In the evening, the ground cools rapidly but the ocean remains warm, due to water's high specific heat. Warm air rises over the water and is replaced with cooler air from over the land. This is known as the land breeze.

Heating a room

As a clear example of natural convection, we can analyze how a room radiator heats a room during winter (figure 27.8). As the temperature of the air around the radiator is increased by conduction, it becomes less dense than the cold air in the room. This warmer air rises and cooler air from the far side of the room replaces it. This air circulation transfers heat from the radiator to the cooler parts of the room.

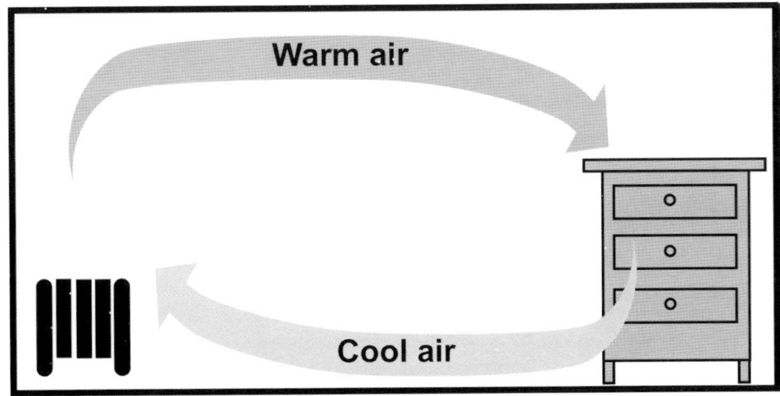

Figure 27.8: *During the day, a sea breeze is created when hot air over the land rises due to convection and is replaced by cooler air from the ocean. At night, temperatures reverse and a land breeze occurs. This happens because the land cools more rapidly than the ocean.*

Convection in the kitchen

Another application of natural convection is cooking on a gas stovetop. As with a candle, the heat from the burning gas rises to boil the water in the pot above it. Even the water in the cooking pot itself experiences convection. The hot water at the bottom of the pot rises to the top of the pot, replaced by the cooler water. Next the cooler water is heated. If this did not happen, we would have to rely on the slower method of conduction to boil a pot of water.

Figure 27.9: *Convection in water. The hot water at the bottom of the pot rises to the top and replaces the cold water.*

Why wearing a sweater keeps you warm

Through the process of convection, air carries heat away from your body. A wool sweater prevents this from happening by trapping air in many small pockets so that it cannot flow and carry the heat away. Similarly, in cold weather birds trap pockets of air by fluffing their feathers.

Wind chill

If you expose bare skin to cold temperatures, natural convection can quickly become dangerous. As the air surrounding your body warms up, it rises and carries heat away. The effect of air carrying heat away is greatly increased on a windy day when a steady stream of air flows. The faster the wind speed, the more effectively heat is carried away. Antarctic explorers created a commonly used method for "measuring" the chilling effects of the wind, called the Wind Chill Equivalent Temperature or wind chill factor. The wind chill factor was originally based on the temperature at which plastic jugs of water placed on top of a high pole would freeze, given a certain wind speed.

Why does smoke rise up the chimney?

Convection causes the smoke from the fire in a fireplace to rise up the chimney instead of entering your home. This is because convection is extremely efficient in focusing the heat in one direction: up! Smoke particles are carried upward by the rising hot air. If you have ever toasted marshmallows on a campfire, you may have noticed that if you hold the marshmallow on the stick right next to the fire, it gets nice and toasty. However, if you hold the marshmallow directly above the fire, it quickly catches fire and burns to a crisp. The air directly above the fire carries much more heat by convection. At the edge of the fire, the heat is mostly carried by a different kind of heat transfer called radiation.

Figure 27.10: *Convection is extremely efficient at focusing heat in one direction: up.*

Forced convection

What is forced convection?

Another type of convection is the one in which a mechanical device is used to *force* the fluid or gas to move, as opposed to the buoyant force. This is called forced convection. Air or liquids can be forced with fans or pumps. Warm fluids can carry heat to cooler regions and cool fluids can take heat away from hot regions.

Applications of forced convection

Most heating systems use a combination of forced and natural convection. Let's return to the example of a radiator for home heating. Water is heated in the basement and pumped into the rooms of the house. The process of pumping the hot water through the house is forced convection. In a room, the hot water releases heat to the air surrounding the radiator through conduction. The heat is then carried away from the radiator by natural convection (figure 27.11).

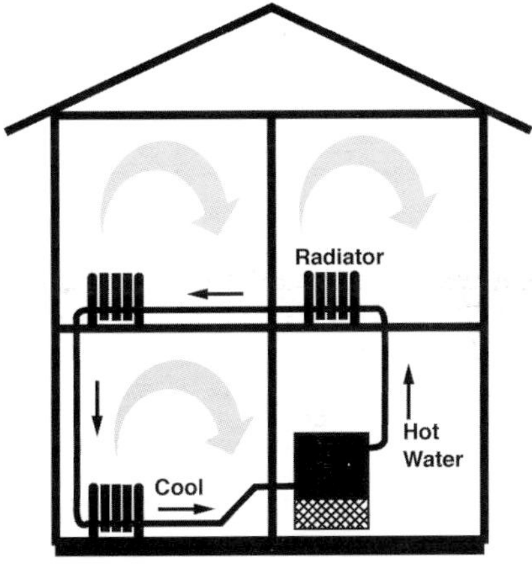

Figure 27.11: *Both natural and forced convection help to heat a house.*

The opposite occurs in an air-conditioning system, where cool air is blown through a room with a fan. This forces the cooler air to replace the warmer air in the room.

Forced convection in a car

In the radiator of a car, there are two examples of forced convection. In the cooling system of a car, heat is transferred from the engine to the water by conduction. Then the heated water is pumped to the radiator by forced convection. After the water is inside the radiator, heat from the water is conducted to the radiator fins. The radiator fins are cooled by air blowing over the radiator.

27.3 Radiation

Have you ever stood in the sun on a cold day? If it is not too windy, you will feel the sun's warmth, no matter how cold it is outside. On a warm day, you will feel even hotter if you stand in the sun. How does the warmth of the sun reach the Earth? In this section, you will learn about another type of heat transfer known as *radiation* that is responsible for the way the sun warms our planet. Radiation is a type of heat transfer that does not require matter to travel through.

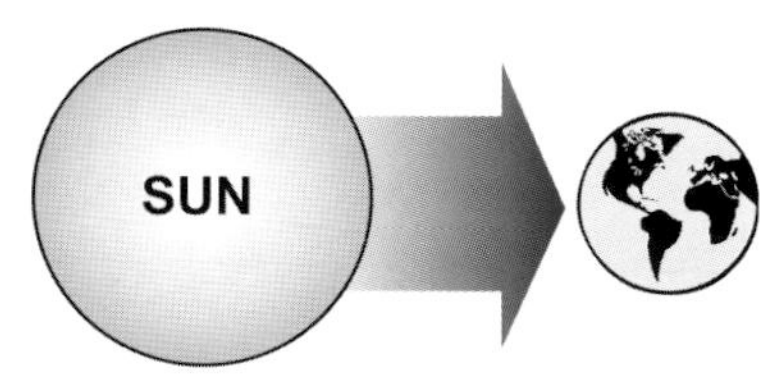

Figure 27.12: *Most of the Earth's heat is electromagnetic radiation that comes from the sun.*

Electromagnetic radiation

Radiation is heat transfer by electromagnetic waves.

What is electromagnetic radiation?

One form of heat transfer due to radiation comes from electromagnetic radiation such as light, ultraviolet rays, X rays, and infrared rays. You know that conduction and convection require matter to transfer heat. However, as you learned previously, electromagnetic waves can travel through a vacuum. This is fortunate because the Earth receives most of its heat in the form of electromagnetic radiation from the sun. Since space is a vacuum, radiation is the primary way we can receive heat from the sun.

Where does solar radiation go?

Of the total incoming solar radiation:

- 30% is returned to outer space.
- 47% is absorbed by the Earth.
- 23% is used to drive the hydrologic cycle.
- 0.2% drives the winds.
- .02% is absorbed by plants to be used in photosynthesis.

Energy-radiation relationships

What types of radiation do objects emit?

All objects emit radiation due to their thermal properties, or because they have some internal thermal energy. Some objects emit mostly visible light, some ultraviolet, and some infrared. The type of radiation an object emits depends on its temperature. Hotter objects have more energy per molecule than cold objects. Thus hot objects emit light with a higher frequency than cold objects. Ultraviolet photons have more energy than visible light. Visible light has more energy than infrared light. You learned previously how the colors of the rainbow, Red, Orange, Yellow, Green, Blue, and Violet (ROYGBV) are related to the energy of the visible light.

What is infrared radiation?

Infrared radiation has lower energy than visible light. While human eyes cannot detect infrared radiation, certain species of snakes can. You may have seen popular spy movies where the hero uses an infrared viewer to see people in the dark. In addition, firefighters use infrared equipment to find people in smoke-filled rooms.

Color-temperature relationships

You may have noticed that when a light bulb on a dimmer is turned on slowly, the bulb will begin to heat up, then glow in the red, then orange, and then yellow areas of the electromagnetic spectrum. This is because different temperatures cause the filament in the light bulb to glow at different colors (figure 27.13).

Why do stars appear in different colors?

Stars also have different colors. The coolest stars are red, such as Antares in the heart of Scorpio the scorpion. The warmest stars are blue. A bright blue star is Betelgeuse, in the knee of Orion the hunter. Astronomers can tell the temperature of a star by looking at its color. But that does not mean the star only emits light at that color. The star emits light in a range of colors; however, the peak color is what we actually detect with our eyes. The light emitted by a star can be represented using a spectral diagram, like the diagram at the right.

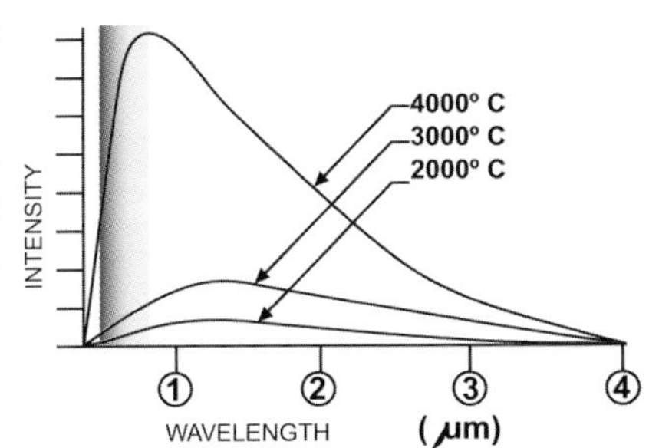

Light bulbs

If objects have to be incredibly hot in order to glow in the visible spectrum, why doesn't the filament in a light bulb burn up? Remember that a fire requires two things, fuel and oxygen. One of Thomas Edison's contributions to engineering was developing the tungsten filament, which could withstand high temperatures. He also had the idea of removing the air from the bulb to prevent the filament from reacting with oxygen too quickly. Edison invented the incandescent light bulb in 1879.

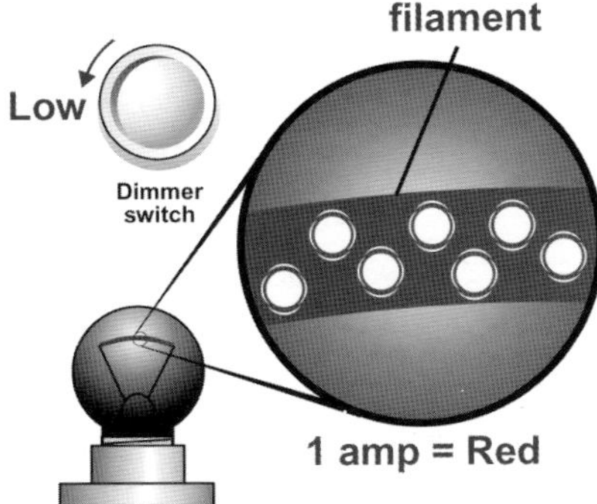

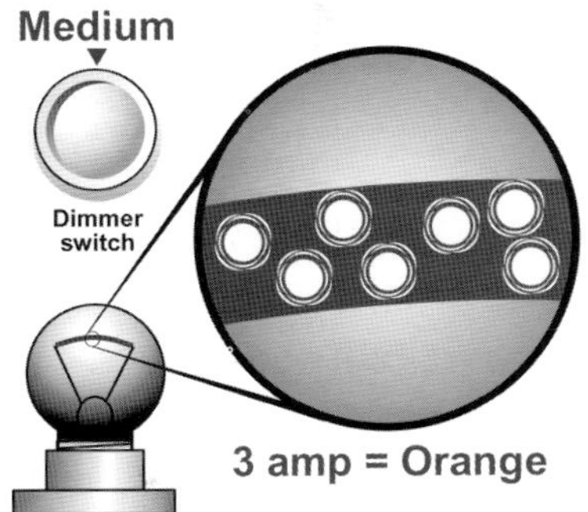

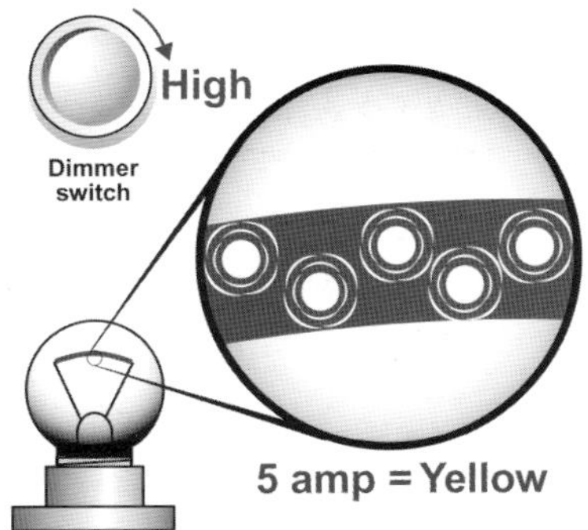

Figure 27.13: *As the temperature of the light bulb increases, the light glows in the red, then orange, then yellow areas of the spectrum.*

Absorption and emission

Absorbers and reflectors

Some objects are good absorbers and some objects are good reflectors. Good reflectors reflect most of the radiation that hits the object. Shiny metallic objects are great reflectors. Generally, materials that are good conductors of electricity and heat are also good reflectors. White and light colored objects also make good reflectors.

Color and absorption

Remember that white objects reflect light of all wavelengths. Black and dark objects tend to absorb all light that falls upon them. They take the radiation and convert it into thermal energy, increasing the temperature of the object. Solar cells, which convert sunlight to electricity, are black so that they will absorb as much light energy as possible.

Emitters of radiation

Objects that are good absorbers of radiation are also good emitters of radiation. Thus, after sunset, a black road surface emits radiation and cools quickly, whereas a white sandy surface of the beach would not emit radiation efficiently and would cool slowly (figure 27.14).

Reflection and planets

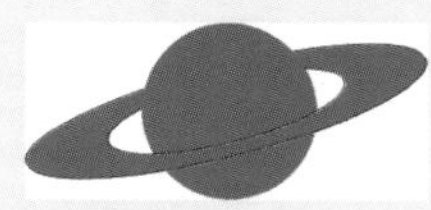

When we look up in the nighttime sky, we can see stars, planets and our moon. The stars generate their own light, just like our sun. The planets and our moon only reflect light that the sun emits. The albedo of a planet is the percentage of the sun's light reflected from its surface. A planet with little or no atmosphere (such as Mercury or our moon) reflects very little light because rocks tend to absorb light. Clouds tend to have a high reflectivity, thus Venus, Jupiter, and Saturn have very high albedos because they have lots of clouds. Ice and snow also have a very high reflectivity. The icy moons of Saturn reflect over 90 percent of the light that hits their surface. The albedo of Earth varies with the constantly changing cloud cover and the amount of snow covering the planet's surface. Given the low albedo of the cloudless moon, why do you think it appears so bright in our nighttime sky?

Figure 27.14: *A black road surface is a good absorber and good emitter of radiation. A white sand beach is a poor absorber and poor emitter of radiation.*

Chapter 27 Review

Vocabulary review

Match the following terms with the correct definition. There is one extra definition in the list that will not match any of the terms.

Set One	
1. heat transfer	a. A method of heat transfer by direct contact of particles of matter
2. thermal conductors	b. When energy in the form of heat travels from a hot object to a cold object
3. conduction	c. Materials that conduct heat poorly
4. thermal insulators	d. Property of a material that describes how well (or poorly) it conducts heat
5. thermal conductivity	e. Heat transfer by the movement of particles
	f. Materials that conduct heat easily

Set Two	
1. convection	a. The transfer of heat by electromagnetic waves
2. forced convection	b. The process by which radiant energy raises the temperature of a material
3. natural convection	c. A process where the buoyancy of warmer air causes a current of air to carry away heat
4. absorption	d. A process where a mechanical device is used to move a fluid or gas to transfer heat
5. radiation	e. Heat transfer caused by the actual movement of matter
	f. Heat transfer due to density differences in solid materials

Concept review

1. What properties make a material a good thermal conductor? Give three examples of good thermal conductors.
2. What properties make a material a good thermal insulator in a solid? Give three examples of solids that are insulators.
3. Why is air a bad conductor of heat? How can air be used as an insulator? Give two examples.
4. Why does hot air rise?
5. Why doesn't convection occur in a solid?
6. What is a sea breeze? When and why does it happen?
7. What is a land breeze? When and why does it happen?
8. What is forced convection?
9. Explain the color-temperature relationship.
10. What properties make a material a good absorber?
11. What properties make a material a good reflector?

Problems

1. You pour some water into a metal cup. After a minute, you notice that the handle of the cup has become hot. Explain, using your knowledge of heat transfer, why the handle of the cup heats up. How would you design the cup so that the handle does not heat up?
2. Explain how both natural and forced convection can help heat your home.
3. You observe three stars in the sky: a red, a yellow, and a blue. Which of the stars is the hottest? Which of the stars is the coolest? Explain your reasoning.
4. A computer CPU chip creates heat because of the electric current it uses. The heat must be carried away, or the chip will melt. To keep the chip cool, a finned heat sink is used to transfer heat from the chip to the air. Which of the materials below would make the BEST heat sink (transfer the most heat)? Which would be the WORST material to use?

Thermal Conductivities of Materials (W/m-C)		
Concrete = 1.2	Aluminum = 240	Asbestos = 0.1
Glass = 0.8	Copper = 400	Gold =310
Wood = 0.1	Rubber = 0.2	Silver = 430

Applying your knowledge

1. In an automobile, water and antifreeze are pumped through the engine block as a coolant. The mixture is pumped back to the radiator where a fan blows air through the radiator. Explain, using conduction, convection, and radiation, how this system works to transfer heat from the engine to the air.
2. In a home aquarium, regulating the temperature of the water is critical for the survival of the fish. To keep a fish tank warm, a heating element with a thermostat is often placed on the bottom of the tank. Why is a heating element placed on the bottom of the tank instead of at the top?
3. A thermostat controls the switch on a furnace or air conditioner by sensing the temperature of the room. Explain, using conduction, convection and radiation, where you would place the thermostat in your science classroom. Consider windows, inside and outside walls, and where the heating and cooling ducts are located. You can also sketch your answer—draw your classroom, showing room features and placement of the thermostat.
4. Building materials such as plywood, insulation, and windows are rated with a number called the "R value." The R value has to do with the thermal conductivity of the material. Higher R values mean lower conductivity and better insulation properties. Design a window with a high R value. Sketch your window, and label its features and the materials it is made from. Explain the reasons for each of your design choices.

Chapter 28

Heating, Cooling, and Systems

Introduction to Chapter 28

What do the weather, your body and a machine have in common? First, they are all systems with different components that work together. Second, they are all affected by heating and cooling. In this chapter you will learn how heating and cooling affect these three types of systems.

Investigations for Chapter 28

28.1	Weather	*How does heating and cooling affect the weather?*

In this Investigation you will need to bring in the weather forecast from a newspaper. In class you will analyze the weather map and the forecast in terms of heating and cooling. You will explore the relationship between fronts, high- and low-pressure air masses, temperature, and storm systems.

28.2	Living Systems	*Which types of food contain the greatest amount of energy?*

In this Investigation you will discover which foods contain more energy. You will derive the relationship between energy generated by burning food items and energy in calories. In addition, you will compare the energy obtained from different foods.

28.3	Mechanical Systems	*How much energy is lost as heat in a mechanical system?*

In this Investigation you will explore energy loss as heat in mechanical systems. You will try to calculate how much heat was generated. Additionally, you will generate heat by shaking sand inside a soda can to observe how mechanical friction creates heat.

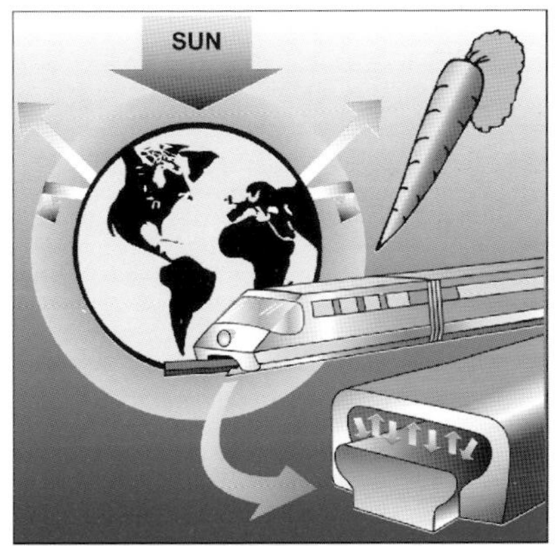

Learning Goals

In this chapter, you will:

- Explain how heating and cooling affect weather on a global scale.
- Explain how heating and cooling affect weather on a local scale.
- Interpret a daily newspaper weather forecast.
- Calculate how many Calories you take in and use on a daily basis.
- Measure by calorimetry how many calories are stored in such food items as a marshmallow, a potato chip, and a cashew nut.
- Analyze and explain the loss of energy in the mechanical systems.
- Explain how a steam engine works.
- Explain how an internal combustion engine works.

Vocabulary

calorie	dew point	kilocalories	metabolic rates
carbohydrates	humidity	latent heat	

28.1 Weather

Why does the Earth remain at a relatively constant temperature? Why does the temperature vary according to latitude? What causes weather? In this section you will learn how the heating and cooling of the Earth and its position in space creates our seasons, climates, and weather. To understand this complex system, you will build on what you know about radiation, convection, and specific heat.

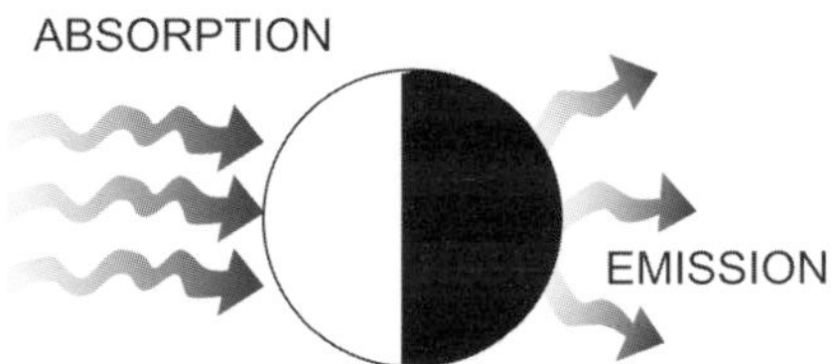

Figure 28.1: *The sun heats up the surface of the Earth during the day. At night, the Earth emits much of the radiation that was absorbed during the day.*

Global heating and cooling

Where does Earth receive its thermal energy? Even though Earth receives only a tiny part of the sun's radiation, the radiation that reaches us provides most of Earth's thermal energy. Slightly less than half (45 percent) of the radiation is actually absorbed by the Earth. Fifty-five percent of the radiation is reflected back into space. If the sun were to disappear, the Earth would gradually cool by radiation emitted into space.

Why is the temperature of Earth relatively constant? Despite all this absorption of energy, the temperature on Earth is relatively constant. For the temperature of any isolated object to remain constant, the rate at which energy is added to the object must be equal to the rate of energy leaving the object. Earth's temperature remains at an average of 27°C because Earth re-emits the heat as infrared radiation. Some of the emitted heat is reabsorbed in our atmosphere and the rest goes into space. If our atmosphere were thicker, less radiation would escape into space, and the average temperature of Earth would be higher.

Global warming Global warming occurs when a thickened atmosphere reabsorbs too much of the radiation. The planet Venus, which has a very thick atmosphere, is a prime example of tremendous global warming. The atmosphere of Venus, which is 90 times denser than that of the Earth, is mostly carbon dioxide with a little nitrogen. This large amount of carbon dioxide prevents radiation from escaping the atmosphere. As a result, the surface temperature of Venus is more than 500°C!

Figure 28.2: *Because our atmosphere is relatively thin, it allows much of the radiation to be reflected or re-emitted back into space.*

Global warming

The composition of the Earth's atmosphere is changing because of the high amounts of carbon dioxide (CO_2) that are released due to the combustion of fossil fuels. Carbon dioxide traps heat that is emitted from the Earth's surface. The CO_2 in our atmosphere has increased 30 percent since the beginning of the Industrial Revolution. As a result, the average surface temperature of Earth has increased between 0.6°C and 1.2°C since the mid-1800s. This increase does not seem huge, but if it continues, it could result in a rise in sea level and changes in the distribution of plants and animals. What possible effects of global warming have you heard about?

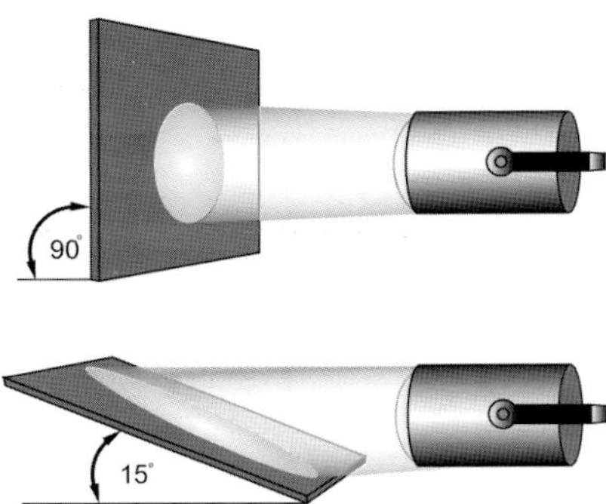

Figure 28.3: *If you hold a piece of paper at a 90° angle to a lamp and then at a 15° angle, where does the light have a larger area? Where is the light the brightest and hottest?*

Variations in the heating and cooling of the Earth

Day heating and night cooling

There are several variations in the heating and cooling of the Earth. The most obvious is that heating occurs during the daytime and cooling occurs in the nighttime. As the Earth rotates, all parts of the planet get heated, but not overheated. The atmosphere and the oceans help to keep the nighttime side of Earth warm. On the other hand, the planet Mercury rotates very slowly, has no oceans, and very little atmosphere. During the daytime, Mercury is over 800°F. Since each day on Mercury is almost 60 Earth-days long, the surface is exposed to the extreme heat of the sun for half that time (almost 30 Earth-days). The nighttime on Mercury is also 30 days long and Mercury has very little atmosphere to retain any heat, and thus cools down to –280°F. We should be thankful that we have an atmosphere, oceans and short 24-hour days!

Why does temperature vary according to latitude?

There are variations in heating due to latitude. The hottest part of the Earth is near the equator, where the sun is closest to directly overhead year round. At the poles, the sun is lower on the horizon. The light from the sun does not hit the poles directly. To understand how this affects the heating of the Earth, imagine shining a flashlight on a sheet of paper as in figure 28.3. It makes a very bright, small spot. However, if the piece of paper were at an angle, the light is spread out over a larger spot and is less intense. The same thing happens to the sun's energy, which reaches the north and south poles at an angle. The sunlight is spread out and thus less intense, while at the equator, the sunlight is direct and more intense (figure 28.4).

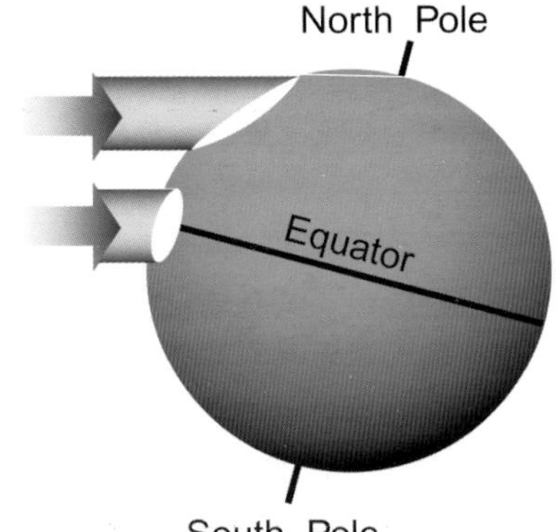

Figure 28.4: *The example in figure 28.3 shows how the sun's radiation reaches the Earth. Sunlight is more intense at the equator. Do you see why?*

The uneven heating of the Earth creates wind patterns

Pressure gradients and wind are consequences of uneven heating of the Earth. The hot air over the equator is less dense. The polar regions are cooler and denser. The difference in density causes movement of air from the poles to the equator. The hot air at the equator also has a tendency to rise due to convection. As a result, colder air tends to flow close to the ground, making wind. Due to the Earth's rotation there are also several other factors affecting the wind, such as friction between the air and the Earth's surface.

How does altitude affect temperature?

Believe it or not, some of the colder spots on Earth are on the equator. For example, in Quito, the capitol of Ecuador, the average temperature is from 3°C to 9°C. Higher up in the Andes Mountains, the temperature ranges from zero to 3°C and there is frequently snow. If you have ever visited the mountains, you have experienced the decrease in temperature with altitude.

Why does the Earth have seasons?

Why is it cold in the winter and hot in the summer? The reason for the seasons is that the Earth spins on its axis at an angle. In January, the northern hemisphere is tilted away from the sun. Each ray of sunlight is spread out over a larger surface so there is less heat per unit area and we have winter. The opposite is true in the southern hemisphere, where it is summer in January. In June, the Earth is on the opposite side of its orbit and the northern hemisphere tilts toward the sun. In the northern hemisphere we see the sun bright and overhead in June, and it is summer.

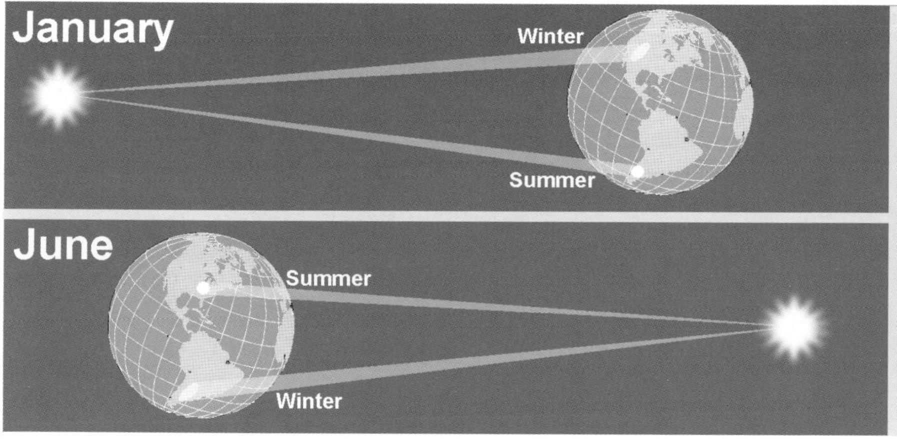

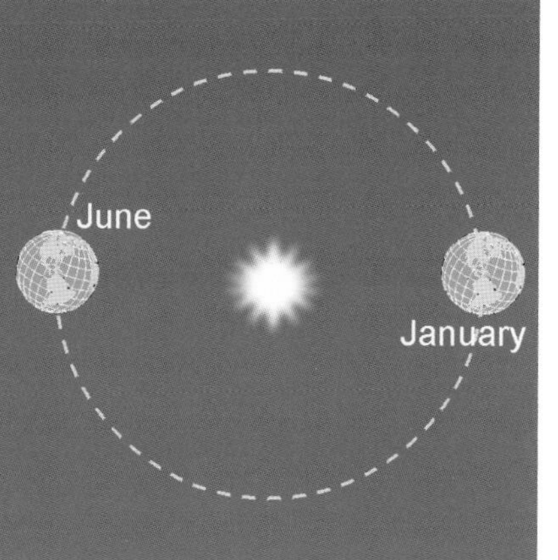

Figure 28.5: *Altitude affects temperature. There is snow on the tops of tall mountains even in warm climates.*

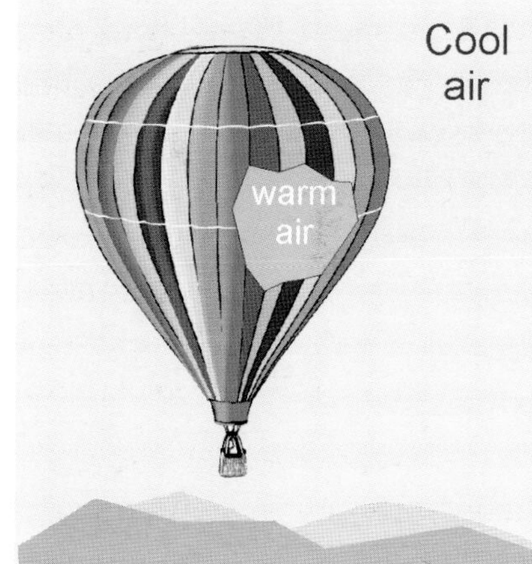

Figure 28.6: *The warmer air inside the balloon is less dense than the cooler air outside it. This is why a balloon with hot air will rise until the density of the air inside the balloon is the same as the density of the air outside it.*

The effects of bodies of water on weather

Water has a large impact on climate

Water has a very high specific heat. This physical property of water has a large impact on the Earth's climate since three-fourths of our planet is covered with water. One of the fundamental reasons our planet is habitable is that the huge amount of water helps regulate the temperature of the Earth.

How does water help regulate temperature?

Land, because it has a low specific heat, experiences large changes in temperature due to absorbing heat from the sun. Water tends to have smaller changes in temperature when it absorbs the same amount of heat. During the daytime, the oceans keep the Earth cool, and at night, they keep it warm so all the heat is not emitted into outer space. The difference in specific heat means the variation in temperature over land is much larger than the variation in temperature over water. Typically, the change in temperature near the water between day and night is only 10°F. This is also why temperatures tend to vary less in coastal areas from season to season compared with inland areas.

The terrain of the land also influences temperature variation

There is a wide variety in the terrain of land on Earth that also influences temperature variations. Wet areas like marshes and swamps do not experience great changes in daily temperature. Forests, with all the trees (which contain water) do not vary as much in daily temperature when compared with dry, sandy desert. In Tucson, Arizona, a desert region, the temperature variation over 24 hours in May averages over 40°F, from 53°F at night to 94°F during the daytime. In Southern California on the coast, the average nighttime temperature is 55°F and the average daytime temperature is about 70°F. The range of temperature variation for Southern California is only 15 degrees. Can you explain the differences in temperature variation between Tucson (desert) and California?

Volcanoes and the Earth's temperature

A small amount of the Earth's energy does not come from the sun but from inside the planet. The core is very hot due to a combination of gravitational pressure and the energy released in radioactive decay. The exact processes for the internal heating of the Earth are not well understood. However, the internal thermal energy is responsible for occasional volcanic activity, which affects the weather. Whenever a volcano erupts, tons of dust are thrown into the air. This dust prevents the sun's radiation from reaching the Earth and actually has a cooling effect.

Weather and humidity

What is humidity? The air in our atmosphere is made from several different substances. The average composition of the atmosphere is 78 percent nitrogen, 21 percent oxygen, 1 percent argon, 0.03 percent carbon dioxide and trace amounts of water vapor, neon, helium, krypton, hydrogen, and ozone. **Humidity** describes how much water vapor is in the air.

How much water vapor can the air hold? The air can hold only a certain amount of water vapor before it becomes *saturated.* When you dissolve sugar in water in a cup, after a certain point the sugar-water solution becomes saturated. At this point, the sugar will no longer dissolve in the water and then collects in the bottom of the cup. When the air becomes saturated with water vapor, the water vapor condenses into a liquid form. On the news, you hear about the **relative humidity** index. If the relative humidity is 51 percent, that means that the amount of water vapor in the air is 51 percent of what the air could possibly hold. When the relative humidity reaches 100 percent, the air is saturated and can hold no more water vapor.

What is the dew point? The amount of water vapor the air can hold depends on the temperature. Warm air can hold more water vapor than cold air. Suppose you have warm air at 100 percent humidity. If the air gets cooler, the amount of water vapor it can hold goes down. That means some of the water vapor must convert back to liquid water. Cooling of saturated air is part of the explanation for both clouds and fog. The temperature at which a given mixture of air and water vapor is 100 percent saturated is called the **dew point**.

How does rain form? If you cool air to a temperature lower than the dew point, some water vapor condenses into liquid. The water often condenses on particles of dust in the atmosphere. Once one water molecule condenses, it creates a site for other molecules to condense too. What started as one water molecule on a speck of dust quickly grows to millions of molecules that form a water droplet with the dust in the center. When the droplet becomes too large, the strength of gravity overcomes wind forces and the droplet falls as a rain drop (figure 28.8).

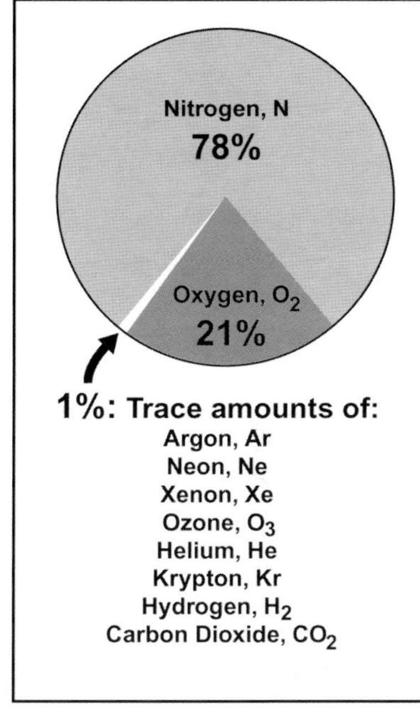

Figure 28.7: *The composition of the Earth's atmosphere.*

Figure 28.8: *Water droplets often condense around dust specks.*

Condensation warms the air Condensation is actually a warming process. When vapor condenses into a liquid, it releases latent heat, warming the air around it. This is why it sometimes warms up a few degrees when any type of precipitation (like rain or snow) is falling.

Why does dew form? Because the ground cools quickly, late at night or early in the morning the temperature of the ground is often below the dew point. Air near the ground gets cooled and some water vapor condenses in the form of *dew* (figure 28.10). If the temperature is low enough, the dew freezes and we get frost.

Where does fog come from? If air within a few hundred meters of the ground is cooled below the dew point, fog will form. Fog can form under several conditions. Warm moist air could move over a cooler surface. The ground below could cool below the dew point at night. Another way for air to cool to the dew point is via convection. As air rises it will cool. So the moist rising air will cool below the dew point, and that is how clouds form. When the particles of condensed water get too big, it rains.

Figure 28.9: *Water usually condenses on particles of dust in the atmosphere to form condensation nuclei. When the droplets are large enough, they fall as rain.*

What is a weather front? Large bodies of air often move across the Earth's surface. When two air masses collide, the result is called a *front.* The front is the boundary between the two moving air masses, which usually have different temperatures, pressures, and humidity. In a warm front, warm air overtakes cold air. The cold air is denser and hugs the ground. In a cold front, a mass of cold air lifts and pushes warm air aside. Because of the different conditions, fronts can produce dramatic weather. Tornadoes and thunderstorms are examples of weather patterns that often result from the collision of two different air masses.

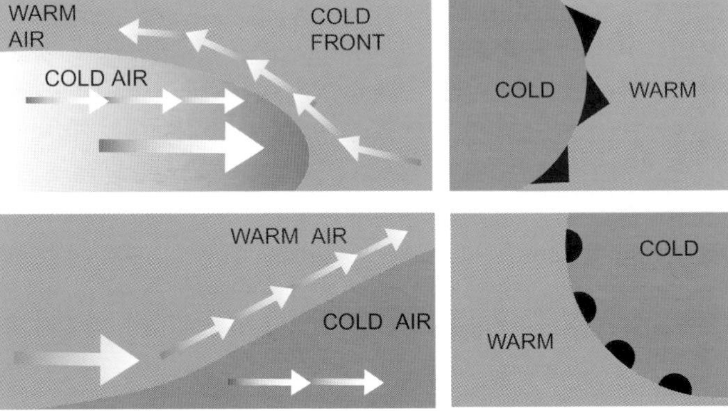

Figure 28.10: *Dew forms because the ground temperature is lower than the dew point.*

28.2 Living Systems

Your everyday activities, such as walking, thinking, and even sleeping, all require energy. The cells within your body harvest the chemical energy stored in food. This energy is then stored by your cells and released as you need it to perform daily functions. We measure the energy stored in foods, and the energy required to perform activities, in a unit called calories.

Food and energy

How is the energy in foods measured?

Humans need the chemical energy stored in food to survive. How many Calories do you consume in your food on a daily basis? You might recall from previous lessons, a calorie is the amount of heat required to raise the temperature of 1 gram of water by 1°C. However, you might have noticed that the caloric values on a food nutrition label are expressed as calories with an uppercase C. These Calories are a thousand times larger than a calorie or, in other words, they are kilocalories. All of the food labels you examine will measure the amount of energy in foods using Calories.

1000 calories (cal) = 1 kilocalorie (kcal) = 1 Calorie (Cal)

How does your body get energy from food?

The chemical compounds in the foods you eat provide you with energy. These compounds react with oxygen in your cells and energy is released by the reactions. Your lungs take oxygen from the air you inhale and deliver it to your cells through the blood stream. Your digestive system breaks down fat, protein, and carbohydrates into simple sugars such as glucose ($C_6H_{12}O_6$), which are then transported to your cells. In your cells, oxygen and glucose are combined in an exothermic reaction. The products of this chemical reaction are water, carbon dioxide, and energy. Here is what the balanced chemical equation looks like:

$$\text{glucose} + \text{oxygen} \longrightarrow \text{carbon dioxide} + \text{water} + \text{energy}$$

$$C_6H_{12}O_6 + 6O_2 \longrightarrow 6CO_2 + 6H_2O + \text{energy}$$

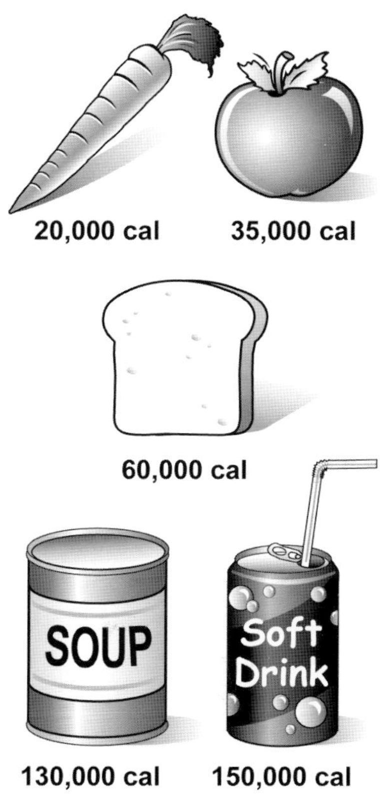

Figure 28.11: *A serving of soup, for example, is 130 Calories or 130,000 calories. Can you see why food manufacturers display energy values in Calories instead of calories?*

How is the Calorie information on food labels gathered?

We can analyze the Calories you consume by measuring how much fat, protein, and carbohydrates (fiber and sugars) are in the food. Fats provide about 9 Calories per gram. On the other hand, 1 g of protein contains about 4 Calories and carbohydrates provide 4 Calories per gram. Table 28.1 lists the Calories you get from certain foods. But how are these values determined? The energy content in food is measured by burning the food in a closed system, and carefully measuring the amount of thermal energy released. This procedure is called *calorimetry*, and the apparatus used in the experiments is called a *calorimeter*. In most calorimeters, the food burned heats up a known mass of water. The temperature increase of the water is measured and the heat released is calculated using the same equation you used earlier to calculate heat gain: $Q = mc\Delta T$

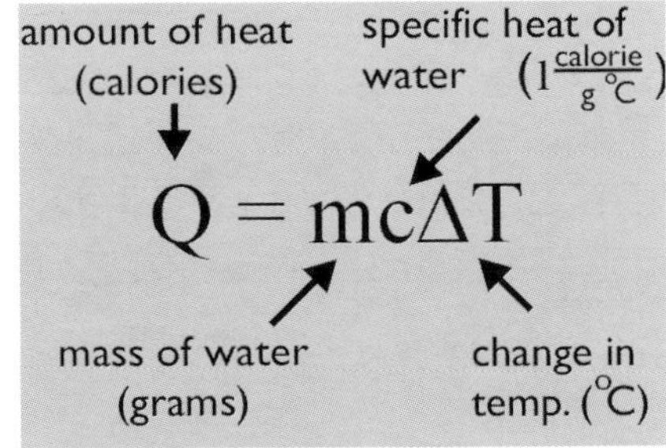

Figure 28.12: *The equation used to determine the amount of energy in food products using calorimetry. What do you need to do to convert the answer to Calories from calories? Answer: Divide by 1000!*

Calories and work

Calories are burned by doing work

So where do all those Calories go? Only 20 to 30 percent of the Calories are used to do work. How much work is needed to carry a heavy box horizontally across a room with no change in height? One standard definition of work is the application of a force over a certain distance. According to this definition, you do work if you push a box across the room or carry it up some stairs, but not if you carry it across a room. However, even though you do no work when you carry something, your muscle fibers do! Therefore the Calories used to do this work go into moving your muscles, not the box.

In addition to doing work, your body gives off heat

But what happens to the other 70 to 80 percent of the Calories? Many are converted into heat. Some of the heat is radiated away or carried away by conduction into the nearby air. When you exercise, your body actually heats up. During such times, your body uses other mechanisms to remove the excess heat, such as perspiration. When your body perspires, the sweat carries heat away from your body. If the sweat evaporates on your skin, there is a tremendous cooling effect. Remember, it takes energy to cause water to evaporate, which is why evaporation is a cooling process. Every liter of evaporated sweat carries away 500 Calories of energy. Drinking lots of fluids when you are exercising replaces lost fluids and helps cool your body down. Figure 28.13 summarizes how your body uses its Calories.

60-70% of Calories are used for life functions such as breathing, pumping blood, and maintaining body temperature.

20-30% of Calories are used for activities like sitting, walking, running, dancing and playing basketball.

5-10% of Calories are used for processing and extracting nutrients and energy from food, and for dealing with environmental factors such as extreme heat and cold.

Figure 28.13: *How does your body use Calories?*

Biology connection: storing energy for later

The complex mechanisms in your body have to balance the Calories you eat and the Calories you use. This is not an easy task! Your daily routine probably consists of many different activities, some of which require many Calories and others which require only a few.

You need different amounts of energy

What happens to you when you run? Your body demands more energy than if you were sitting down. Your body needs some time to deliver glucose to the muscles cells so they can burn it to release energy. But these muscle cells cannot wait too long to obtain the needed glucose.

Your body stores energy in different forms

How do your cells get the glucose they need when their supplies are running low? In this case, the cells obtain energy that has been *stored* for future needs. The human body stores energy in three forms—glycogen, which is used first, fat, which is used second, and protein, which is used last.

Energy storage and transfer in cells

Because there are many reactions relating to energy capture and storage, cells use a small high-energy molecule that can easily hold and transfer energy from one place to another. This molecule is called *adenosine triphosphate* or ATP. Larger quantities of ATP are stored in your muscle cells for short bursts of energy.

When you are fit, your cells are more efficient

During exercise, if oxygen or glucose is in short supply, you will get tired quickly. Usually enough energy is stored for the body to function without enough oxygen for a couple of minutes. When you use energy faster than your body can produce it, your energy reserves (such as ATP) decrease. When you stop exercising, your energy demand and supplies return to normal. When you are physically fit, the efficiency of your body improves and your ability to harness energy from small amounts of sugar and oxygen improves.

Gerty Theresa Cori

Gerty Cori studied how cells in our bodies convert glucose (sugars) to glycogen (a complex sugar based on glucose). If either of these sugars or oxygen is absent, the production of energy in muscles stops. Cori was born in Prague, Czechoslovakia. In 1922, she emigrated to the United States with her husband, Carl. The Coris, both chemists, researched how the chemical reactions of sugars release energy in cells. The Coris won the Nobel Prize in 1947 for their work on these chemical reactions.

Energy use in our bodies

What is a metabolic rate?

Different people have different metabolic rates. This is defined as the rate of energy consumption at all times (resting or awake) within the body. A person's metabolic rate depends upon age and the level of fitness. For example, the average male teenager has a metabolic rate of 2.9×10^{-4} Calories/second-kilogram and the average female teenager has a rate of 2.6×10^{-4} Calories/second-kilogram.

Why do metabolic rates vary from person to person?

One important factor that influences a person's average metabolic rate is the percentage of body fat. This is because every kilogram of muscle uses up over three times as many Calories as every kilogram of fat. This means that the higher the percentage of body fat, the lower your metabolic rate. People with a low percentage of body fat will require more calories every day than a person of the same weight with a higher percentage of body fat.

Table 28.1: *Energy content of some food items*

Food	Quantity	Joules	Calories
soda	12 ounces	502,000	120
tortilla chips	about 15 chips	585,000	140
spaghetti	1/2 cup	836,000	200
peanut butter	1 tablespoon	418,000	100
carrot	1 small	83,000	20
beans	1/2 cup	376,000	90
beef (lean)	3 ounces	711,000	170
chicken	3 ounces	711,000	170
broccoli	1 spear	124,000	30
milk	1 cup	376,000	90
bread	1 slice	251,000	60

Activity	Cal/hr.
running	850
swimming	300
biking	600
walking	210
studying	100
sitting	84
dancing	350
sleeping	56

Figure 28.14: *Calories used per hour for certain activities.*

28.3 Mechanical Systems

Most mechanical systems such as automobiles, simple and complex machines, and power generators contain many moving parts that are in contact with each other. In addition, some of these mechanical systems are designed to perform tasks such as heavy lifting or harsh movements. All of this work is accomplished by the input of energy. In the process of doing work, mechanical systems also generate thermal energy in the form of heat. The heat is wasted energy that dissipates into the atmosphere. Where does this heat come from?

In this section, you will learn about the heat generated in mechanical systems, and some of the technology developed to solve the problems associated with heat loss. You will also learn how heat can be used to generate mechanical work.

Where does the heat in mechanical systems come from?

Most of the heat comes from friction

If you rub your hands together for a minute they will soon feel very warm. This warmth is due to friction. In most mechanical systems, the major loss of energy, in the form of heat, is due to friction. Friction not only occurs with sliding objects but also with rotating objects. When a pulley turns on an axle, the axle rubs against the pulley, generating friction.

The deformation of objects generates heat

Heat can also be generated from the *deformation* of an object. When you drop a basketball, as shown in figure 28.15, it does not return to the same height after a few bounces. Every time the basketball hits the ground, it is compressed. The change in shape of the ball causes friction between the individual molecules in the ball, thus generating heat.

Figure 28.15: *Heat can be generated from the deformation of an object.*

Fluid or air friction is another cause of heat in mechanical systems

Another source of heat can be fluid resistance such as air resistance. When the space shuttle returns from orbit as shown in figure 28.16, it enters the atmosphere at a very high speed. The air molecules are moving so fast over the bottom of the shuttle, that if there were no heat resistant tiles, the space shuttle would burn up. Whenever meteorites enter the atmosphere they burn up. Most meteorites are no larger than a grain of sand, but if you have ever seen one in the sky, they radiate enough heat and light that we can see them from miles away.

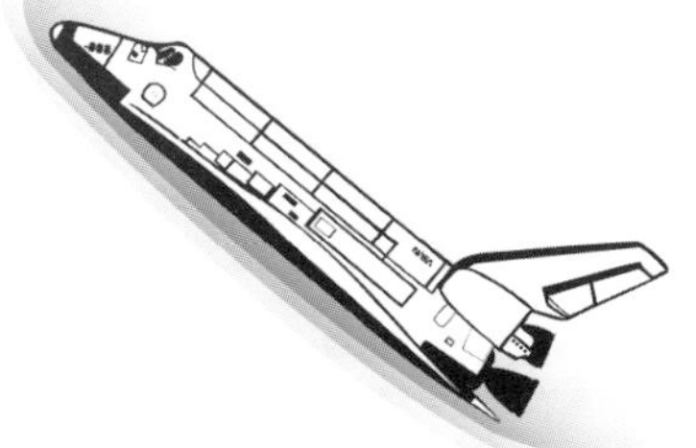

Figure 28.16: *As the space shuttle enters the atmosphere, heat is generated by air resistance.*

Reducing losses due to friction

Why do we lubricate machines?

Two dry surfaces sliding against each other can quickly generate a lot of friction and heat. To reduce friction we use lubricants, like oil. You add oil to a car engine so the pistons can slide back and forth with less friction. Even water can be used as a lubricant under conditions where there is not too much heat. Powdered graphite is another lubricant. A common use of graphite is to spray it into locks so a key will slide better.

Ball bearings are used to reduce friction

In systems where there are axles, pulleys, and rotating objects, ball bearings are used to reduce friction. A rotating shaft in a plain hole would rub and generate a great amount of heat from friction (figure 28.17, top picture). Oil helps, but can leak out the sides of the hole. Ball bearings are small, hard balls of steel that go in between the shaft and the hole it turns in. The shaft rolls on the bearings instead of rubbing against the walls of the hole. The bearings rotate easily and greatly reduce friction in the system (figure 28.18, bottom picture). Some oil (or grease) is still required to keep the bearings rolling smoothly.

Reducing friction by floating on air

Another method of reducing friction is to separate two surfaces with a cushion of air. A hover-craft, floats on a cushion of air created by a large fan. Electromagnetic forces can also be used to separate surfaces. Working prototypes of a magnetically levitated train, or maglev, have been built from several designs. A maglev train floats on a cushion of force created by strong electromagnets (figure 28.19). Once it gets going, the train does not actually touch the rails. Because there is no contact, there is far less friction than in a normal train. The ride is also smoother, allowing much faster speeds.

Is friction always harmful?

Despite efforts to get rid of friction in machines, there are many applications where friction is very useful. In a bicycle, when you apply the brakes, two rubber pads apply pressure to the rim. Friction between the brake pads and the rim slows down the bicycle. The kinetic energy of the bicycle becomes heat in the brake pads. Without friction, the bicycle would not be able to slow down.

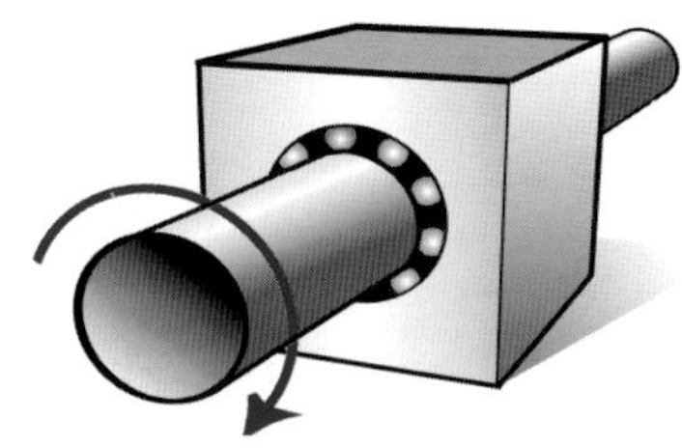

Figure 28.17: *The friction between a shaft (the long pole in the picture) and an outer part of a machine produces a lot of heat. Friction can be reduced by placing ball bearings between the shaft and the outer part.*

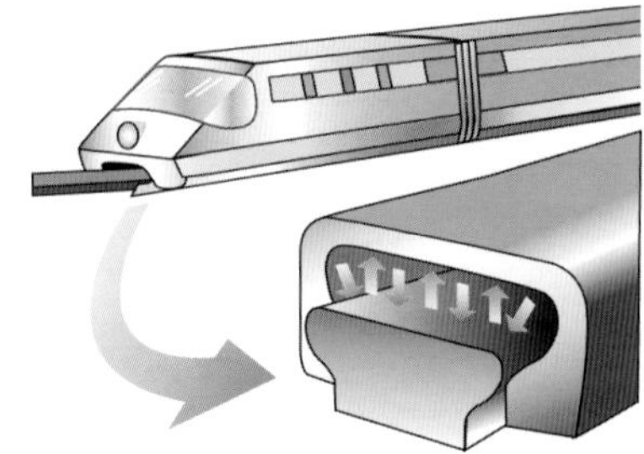

Figure 28.18: *In a maglev train, there is no contact between the moving train and the rail. This means that there is very little friction.*

Using heat to do mechanical work: external combustion engine

Steam engines

One of the most important practical inventions to harness the power of heat was the steam engine. The steam engine is an example of an external combustion engine, because the action of heating takes place outside the engine. Originally, wood and coal were burned to create steam. In modern steam engines, coal is still burned, along with oil and even garbage! In a nuclear power plant, nuclear reactions in uranium generate heat to boil water into steam to turn a turbine and make electricity.

How a steam engine works

In a simple steam engine, heat boils water to create steam. The hot steam is created at high pressure and passes through a valve into the cylinder, pushing back the piston. When the piston reaches the bottom it opens a valve to exhaust the expanded steam. The inertia of the flywheel then carries the piston back up the cylinder. When it gets to the top, the piston opens the intake valve and a fresh charge of hot steam pushes it back down again. The exhausted steam is condensed back to liquid water and pumped back into the boiler to repeat the cycle.

How a steam engine works

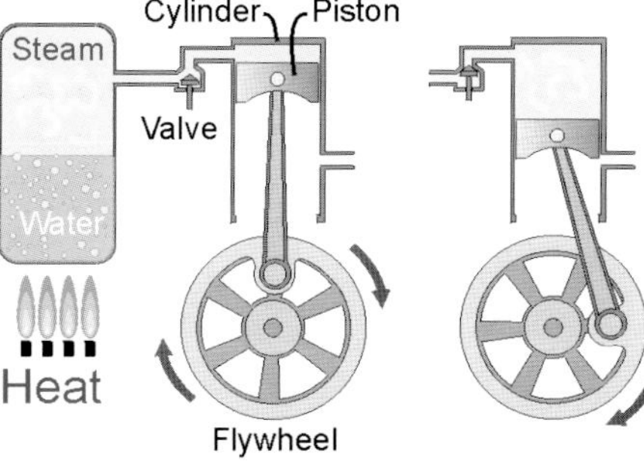

The valve opens and hot steam pushes the piston down

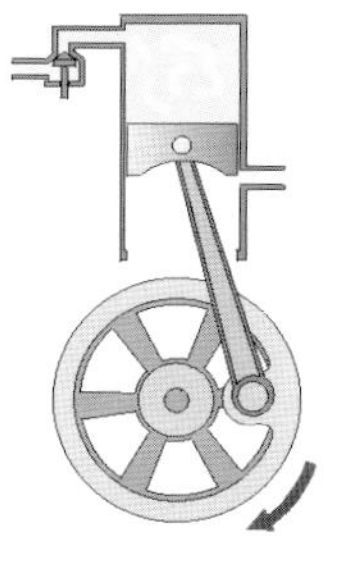

The piston goes down

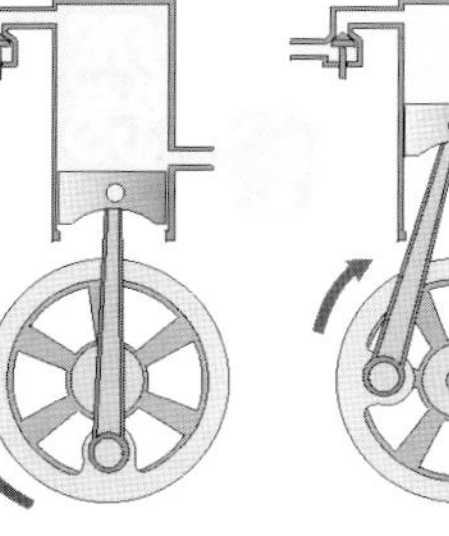

At the bottom, the piston opens a vent to exhaust the steam

The inertia of the flywheel carries the piston back up

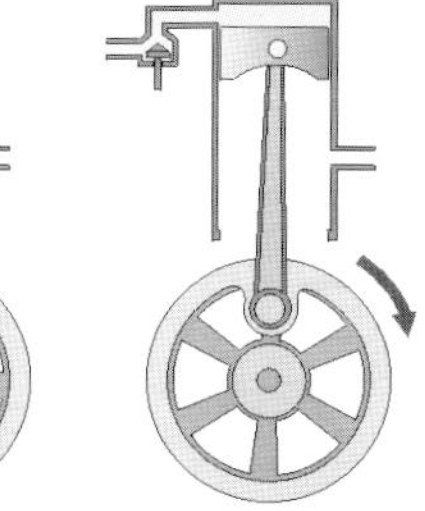

The valve opens, letting in new steam to start the cycle again

James Watt

James Watt was a Scottish engineer who perfected the steam engine. Watt's first contribution to the steam engine, in 1769, involved building separate chambers for the condensing of water. This allowed the cylinder to always remain at the temperature of steam, while the cooling of the steam took place in a separate chamber.

Early steam engines were used in trains and boats. Before the invention of the gasoline-powered internal combustion engine, even early cars used steam engines. In parts of the world, steam locomotives are still used today.

Modern steam engines use a turbine instead of a piston and cylinder

In the modern steam engine, the hot steam passes through fins in a giant turbine. As the steam expands, it turns the turbine. The turbine turns an electric generator which produces electricity. Turbines are much more efficient than pistons. More of the heat of the steam is converted to useful energy.

When the steam leaves the turbine it is still warm and must be cooled to condense back into liquid water. The liquid water can be pumped back into the boiler to be reheated into steam. In some cases water from a flowing river is used to cool and condense the steam. In other cases cooling towers are built where water passes down the inner walls of a giant tube and is cooled by the air as it falls (figure 28.19). Most of the wasted heat goes to the atmosphere or nearby rivers. What are some the environmental consequences to these strategies for releasing wasted heat?

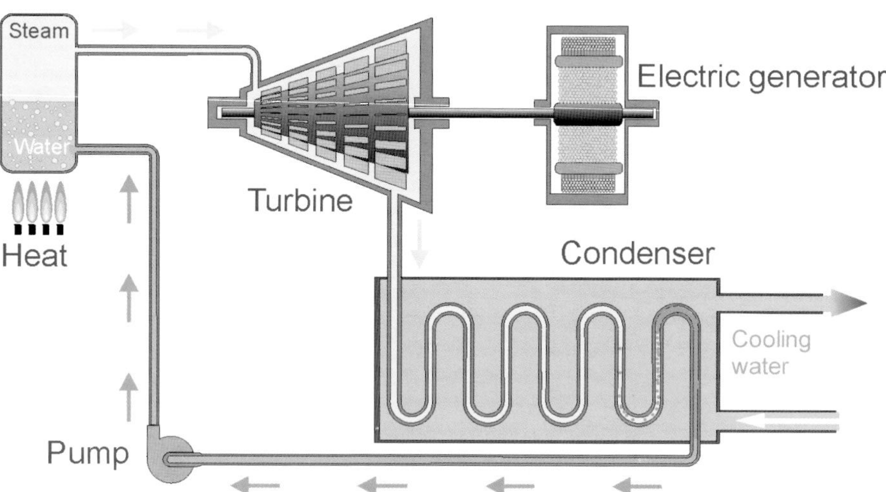

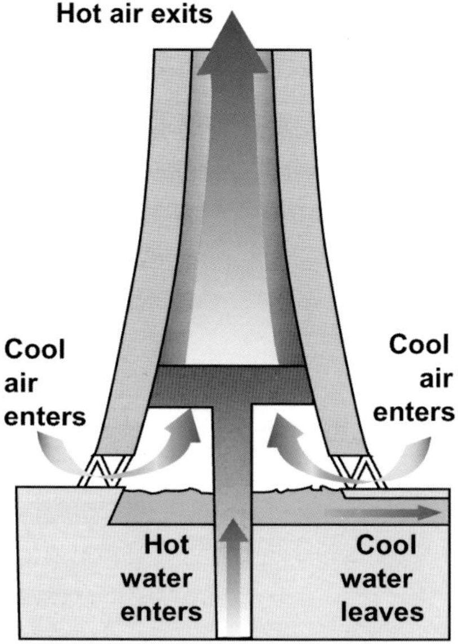

Figure 28.19: *Giant cooling towers are built to cool hot water before it leaves the power plant.*

What do you think?

Other methods of turning the turbine in an electric power plant include using gravitational potential energy (hydroelectric power plants), harnessing the wind (windmills), and splitting uranium atoms (nuclear energy). What are the pros and cons of each of these methods?

The efficiency of a turbine

Because some heat is always rejected at the end of the cycle, not all the original heat energy is converted to mechanical energy by the turbine. The efficiency of the turbine is the ratio of how much useful energy is extracted compared with how much energy is available. Typically, the best turbines are only 40 percent efficient, meaning almost two-thirds of the heat energy from fuels gets wasted.

Using heat to do mechanical work: internal combustion engine

Internal combustion engines

The internal combustion engine was developed in Germany in the late nineteenth century. In an internal combustion engine, the burning process takes place inside the cylinder (see graphic at the bottom of page 493). The most common engine is the four-stroke engine. Almost every car and motorcycle is powered by this kind of engine. Credit for inventing the internal combustion engine is given to Nikolaus Otto, who constructed the first practical engines in 1877.

Intake stroke

First, the vapors from a fuel such as gasoline are mixed with air to create a highly explosive mixture. This mixing is done in a carburetor. In modern automobiles, a precise mixture of fuel and air is injected directly into each cylinder. During the intake stroke, the intake valve opens, allowing fuel and air into the cylinder. As the piston goes down, it draws the fuel and air into the cylinder.

Compression stroke

Once the piston reaches the bottom, the intake valve closes. On the way back up for the compression stroke, the piston compresses the fuel-air mixture. At the top of the stroke, the mixture is compressed almost 10 times and is ready to ignite. A spark plug creates a spark in the mixture, igniting the compressed fuel and air in a small but powerful explosion.

Power stroke

After ignition comes the power stroke and the exploding fuel expands quickly due to the heat released by the chemical reaction of burning. The piston is pushed with great force back down, turning the shaft of the engine and making your car go forward. The bigger the cylinder and piston, the more forceful the explosion stroke and the more powerful the engine.

Exhaust stroke

When the piston gets to the bottom, the fuel is all burned. As it moves up again for the exhaust stroke, a second valve opens, and the piston pushes the burned fuel and air out. The flywheel in the engine keeps the piston moving to begin the cycle again. The intake valve opens and the piston draws fresh fuel and air into the cylinder. Modern car engines routinely turn at speeds of 3,000 revolutions per minute or more. Since the spark plug fires every second revolution, each cylinder in your engine experiences 1,500 explosions every minute you are driving!

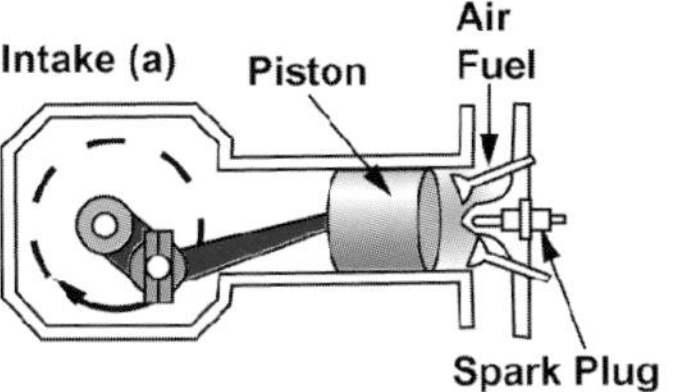

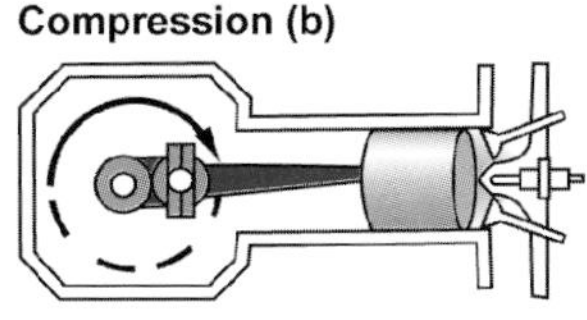

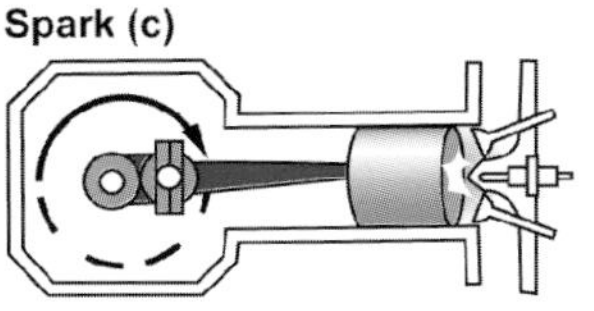

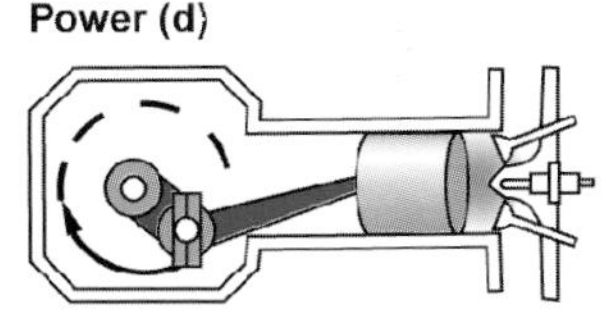

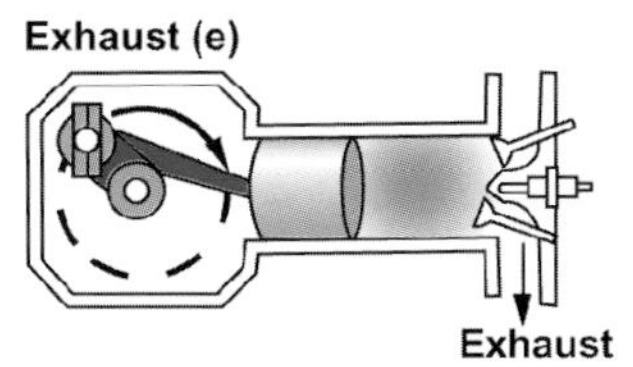

Figure 28.20: *The four strokes of an internal combustion engine.*

Chapter 28 Review

Vocabulary review

Match the following terms with the correct definition. There is one extra definition in the list that will not match any of the terms.

Set One

1. global warming	a. A number that describes how much water vapor is in the air as a percentage of the total water vapor that the air could possibly hold
2. humidity	b. The temperature at which air is saturated with water
3. relative humidity	c. Many water molecules that condense onto one big molecule
4. front	d. Amount of water vapor in the air
5. dew point	e. The edge between two masses of air
	f. Increase in the Earth's average temperature due to increased CO_2 in the atmosphere

Set Two

1. Calorie	a. Apparatus used to get the energy content of food
2. metabolic rate	b. High energy molecules that help in storing and releasing energy
3. Gerty Cori	c. A unit that is 1,000 times larger than a calorie; a kilocalorie
4. adenosine triphosphate	d. The rate of energy consumption at all times within the body
5. calorimetry	e. Scientist who studied how cells take glucose and convert it into energy
	f. Process in which food is burned to obtain the energy content of food

Set Three

1. friction	a. Mechanical device in which steam passes through
2. external combustion engine	b. A machine developed in Germany where burning of fuel takes place inside a cylinder
3. turbine	c. Engineer who perfected the steam engine
4. internal combustion engine	d. The rubbing of one object against another to produce heat
5. James Watt	e. Engine in which heating takes place outside the engine
	f. Stroke in which the piston compresses

Concept review

1. What is topography?
2. What is the dew point?
3. What is relative humidity?
4. If you look at nutritional labels from different foods, you will notice that they list the amount of Calories that food has. How do scientists calculate the amount of Calories in food?
5. Which has the most calories per gram: fats, protein, or carbohydrates?
6. What is the chemical equation that describes how our bodies get energy from food?
7. What are some sources of heat loss in a mechanical system?
8. What are some ways to reduce the loss of energy by heat in a mechanical system?
9. Explain how an internal combustion engine works.
10. Explain how a steam engine works.

Problems

1. Using data from a national weather forecast, give examples of cities that are hotter because of their latitudes.
2. Using data from a national weather forecast, give examples of cities that are cooler because of their proximity to water.
3. Using data from a national weather forecast, give examples of cities that experience big temperature changes. Explain why they have such large changes.
4. Imagine you and 30 classmates are all dancing. Dancing uses 350 Calories per hour.
    a. If there are 3,600 seconds in an hour and 4,187 joules in a Calorie, how many watts of power are produced by your dancing?
    b. If a space heater has a power of 500 watts, you and your friends produce as much heat as how many space heaters?
5. The process of sitting down and doing your homework burns 100 Calories per hour. How many watts of power are you currently producing?
6. You design a mechanical system with several pulleys to move a heavy load. You do 4,000 joules of work to lift the load. In the process, you give the load 1,000 joules of gravitation potential energy. What is the efficiency of your machine?
7. How much energy is lost as heat in your machine?
8. Given how much energy is lost as heat, what could possibly be the advantage of using a machine like this?
9. Which form of generating electricity is the best from an economic standpoint?
10. Which form of generating electricity is the best from an environmental standpoint?

Applying your knowledge

1. The planets below are all in the same solar system and are all the same distance from their sun. The atmospheric composition of each planet is given. Which planet has the warmest surface temperature? Explain your reasoning.

Calorea	Galatia	Hydro
25% nitrogen 70% oxygen 5% carbon dioxide	80% hydrogen 10% carbon dioxide 10% neon	60% carbon dioxide 20% nitrogen 20% krypton

2. JAN FEB MAR Keep track of your daily intake of food (type and amount) for three days. Also keep track of your activities for the same period. Calculate your total Calories taken in for the three-day period and your total Calories used for the three-day period. To find the Calories in the foods you eat, consult the food labels on the packages. The table below shows the number of Calories used for certain activities.

Activity	Cal/hr.	Activity	Cal/hr.
running	850	sitting	84
swimming	300	dancing	350
biking	600	sleeping	56
walking	210	light chores	180
studying	100	standing	140

3. Calculate the number of Calories that your body needs to metabolize from food on a daily basis by following the steps below. This is not an exact calculation as your height, weight, age, sex, health, and fitness level influence your basic metabolic rate (BMR).

1. State your weight in pounds.
2. Multiply your weight in pounds × 0.45 to get your mass in kilograms.
3. Use your mass in kilograms in the following equation:

$$\text{kg} \times \frac{1 \text{ Calorie}}{\text{kg}^2\text{ hr}} \times \frac{24 \text{ hours}}{\text{day}} = \text{BMR in Calories per day}$$

4. Multiply your BMR by your activity level coefficient (see table below) to get the number of Calories spent in physical activity per day.
5. Add your BMR and physical activity Calories. Multiply this total by 0.1 to calculate the number of Calories spent in processing food per day.
6. Add your BMR, physical activity Calories per day, and food processing Calories per day. This sum is the number of total Calories your body needs per day.

The following table gives your activity level coefficient:

Physical Activity	Not active	Moderate	Very active
Activity Level	0.3	0.5	0.7

Reference

Reference

Safety

The Investigations that you will be doing as part of the CPO Integrated Physics and Chemistry curriculum are designed to reduce safety concerns in the laboratory. The physics investigations use stable equipment that is easy to operate. The chemistry investigations use household supplies and chemicals. Although these chemicals might be familiar to you, they still must be used safely!

You will be introduced to safety by completing a skill sheet to help you learn the safety aids and important information in your science laboratory. In addition to this skill sheet, you may be asked to check your understanding and complete a safety contract. Your teacher will decide what is appropriate for your class.

Throughout the Investigation Guide, icons and words and phrases like *caution* and *safety tip* are used to highlight important safety information. Read the description of each icon carefully and look out for them when reading your Student Edition and Investigation Guide.

Safety is a very an important part of doing science. The purpose of learning and discussing safety in the lab is to help you learn how to protect yourself and others at all times.

	Use extreme caution: Follow all instructions carefully to avoid injury to yourself or others.
	Electrical hazard: Follow all instructions carefully while using electrical components to avoid injury to yourself or others.
	Wear safety goggles: Requires you to protect your eyes from injury.
	Wear a lab apron: Requires you to protect your clothing and skin.
	Wear gloves: Requires you to protect your hands from injury from heat or chemicals.
	Cleanup: Includes cleaning and putting away reusable equipment and supplies and disposing of leftover materials.

Safety in the science lab is the responsibility of everyone! Help create a safe environment in your science lab by following the safety guidelines from your teacher and on the safety skill sheet.

CPO Science Safety Quiz

A. Knowing your science lab

1. Draw a diagram of your science lab on a separate piece of paper. Include in your diagram the following items:

Exit/entrance ways	Fire extinguisher(s)	Fire blanket
Eye wash and shower	Location of eye goggles and lab aprons	First aid kit
Location of special safety instructions (example: bulletin board, chalk board, etc.)	Sink	Trash cans

2. Include notes on your diagram that explain how to use these important safety items.

B. Quiz

1. How many fire extinguishers are in your science lab?
2. List the steps that your teacher and your class would take to safely exit the science lab and the building in case of a fire.
3. Before beginning certain Investigations, why should you put on protective goggles and clothing first?
4. Why is teamwork important when you are working in a science lab?
5. Why should you always clean up after every Investigation?
6. List at least three things you should you do if you sense danger or see an emergency in your classroom or lab?
7. Five lab situations are described below. What would you do in each situation? Explain how you would be careful and safe in each situation.

   a. You accidentally knock over a beaker and it breaks on the floor.

   b. You accidentally spill a large amount of water on the floor.

   c. You suddenly you begin to smell a chemical odor that gives you a headache.

   d. You hear the fire alarm sound while you are working in the lab. You are wearing your goggles and lab apron.

   e. While your lab partner had her lab goggles off, she gets some liquid from the experiment in her eye.

   f. A fire starts in the lab.

Reference

Unit Conversions (Dimensional Analysis)

Scientific terminology is like any other language in that there are often many ways to say one thing. For instance, when measuring the width of a window, you can say that it measures 36 inches. You can also say it measures one yard. Of course, we are not saying that the actual length of the window has changed—the only thing that has changed is the unit of measure.

In a typical language—English, for example—we can substitute one word for another, like saying *car* instead of *automobile*. In the language of science, however, there is always a numeric quantity that is associated with the unit of measure. So in describing something in science (an object, action, or phenomena), when we want to change from one unit of measure to another, we need to adjust the quantity as well. For example, when we changed the description of the window's width from inches to yards, we had to change the quantity from 36 to 1. There is a system one can use to make the change. We can call it *dimensional analysis*.

Example: If you need 12 eggs, you can refer to the 12 eggs as one (1) dozen since 12 items equals a dozen. Mathematically, we say 12 eggs = 1 dozen eggs.

What happens if you take the units out of the expression? You will get 12 = 1. If you take away the units, the equation is no longer true. *Units are essential in the language of science.*

In mathematics, we know this to be true: Any quantity (other than zero) divided into itself always results in one (or unity). That is:

$$\frac{4}{4} = 1 \qquad \frac{1{,}760}{1{,}760} = 1$$

You can also write this as:

$$4 \div 4 = \frac{4}{4} = 1$$

Suppose you have two units that are shown to be equal, like:

$$\left(\frac{12 \text{ eggs}}{1 \text{ dozen eggs}}\right) = 1 = \left(\frac{1 \text{ dozen eggs}}{12 \text{ eggs}}\right)$$

When you multiply any quantity by one, the size or degree of that quantity is unchanged.

So you can use the expressions in the parentheses to exchange (or convert) your units. We call these expressions *conversion factors*.

Example: If you are being offered 10 dozen eggs and you want to know how many individual eggs you will receive, you can use dimensional analysis to determine the correct number.

$$10 \text{ \sout{dozen eggs}} \times \left(\frac{12 \text{ eggs}}{1 \text{ \sout{dozen eggs}}}\right) = \frac{10 \times 12 \text{ eggs}}{1} = 120 \text{ eggs}$$

Note that a unit that appears in both the numerator and denominator is *cancelled out*.

Also, when choosing which conversion factor to use, we had two options:

$$\left(\frac{12 \text{ eggs}}{1 \text{ dozen eggs}}\right) \text{ or } \left(\frac{1 \text{ dozen eggs}}{12 \text{ eggs}}\right)$$

We chose the factor with the units (*eggs*) that we wanted in the numerator.

When converting one unit to another, you need to drop the current unit in favor of another. This is done by canceling out units.

In the example above, we cancel the units "dozen eggs," but not the quantity associated with it.

More examples:

1 If you drop an egg 72 inches, how many feet is that?

1 foot = 12 inches, so use one of the following factors to answer in feet:

$$\left(\frac{1\text{ ft}}{12\text{ in.}}\right) = \left(\frac{12\text{ in.}}{1\text{ ft}}\right) = 1$$

$$72\text{ in.} \times \left(\frac{12\text{ in.}}{1\text{ ft}}\right) = \frac{864\text{ in.}^2}{\text{ft}}$$

Incorrect: This has the wrong units.

$$72\,\cancel{\text{in.}} \times \left(\frac{1\text{ ft}}{12\,\cancel{\text{in.}}}\right) = \frac{72 \times 1\text{ ft}}{12} = 6\text{ ft}$$

Correct: This has the right units.

2 How many feet are in 60 miles?

1 mile = 5,280 feet, so use one of the following factors:

$$\left(\frac{1\text{ mile}}{5{,}280\text{ ft}}\right) = \left(\frac{5{,}280\text{ ft}}{1\text{ mile}}\right) = 1$$

$$60\,\cancel{\text{miles}} \times \left(\frac{5{,}280\text{ ft}}{1\,\cancel{\text{mile}}}\right) = \frac{60 \times 5{,}280\text{ ft}}{1} = 316{,}800\text{ ft}$$

3 How many seconds are in an hour?

1 hour = 3,600 seconds, so use one of the following factors:

$$\left(\frac{1\text{ hr}}{3{,}600\text{ sec}}\right) = \left(\frac{3{,}600\text{ sec}}{1\text{ hr}}\right) = 1$$

$$1\,\cancel{\text{hr}} \times \left(\frac{3{,}600\text{ sec}}{1\,\cancel{\text{hr}}}\right) = 3{,}600\text{ sec}$$

4 Suppose you want to exchange one unit of speed for another. You can do it by breaking the problem down into steps.

Say you are in a car traveling 60 miles per hour, and you want to know the distance in feet that you are traveling each second.

We will start by converting your speed from miles-per-hour to feet-per-hour:

$$\frac{60\,\cancel{\text{miles}}}{1\text{ hr}} \times \left(\frac{5{,}280\text{ ft}}{1\,\cancel{\text{mile}}}\right) = \frac{60 \times 5{,}280\text{ ft}}{1 \times 1\text{ hr}} = \frac{316{,}800\text{ ft}}{\text{hr}}$$

Now let's change hours to seconds:

$$\frac{316{,}800\text{ ft}}{\cancel{\text{hr}}} \times \frac{1\,\cancel{\text{hr}}}{3{,}600\text{ sec}} = \frac{88\text{ ft}}{\text{sec}}$$

You could also combine all of your conversion factors in one long expression:

$$\frac{60\,\cancel{\text{miles}}}{1\,\cancel{\text{hr}}} \times \left(\frac{5{,}280\text{ ft}}{1\,\cancel{\text{mile}}}\right) \times \frac{1\,\cancel{\text{hr}}}{3{,}600\text{ sec}} = \frac{60 \times 5{,}280\text{ ft}}{1 \times 1\text{ sec}} = \frac{88\text{ ft}}{\text{sec}}$$

In the example here, we wanted to convert hours to seconds.

So why did we use the conversion factor with seconds in the denominator?

The answer is that we want a result that puts seconds in the denominator position, not the numerator (feet *per* second).

Quantity	Unit 1	Unit 2	Relationship	Conversion Factor 1 Unit 1 / Unit 2	Conversion Factor 2 Unit 2 / Unit 1
length	inch (in)	millimeter (mm)	1 in = 25.4 mm	$\left(\frac{25.4 \text{ mm}}{1 \text{ in}}\right)$	$\left(\frac{0.0394 \text{ in}}{1 \text{ mm}}\right)$
	inch (in)	centimeter (cm)	1 in = 2.54 cm	$\left(\frac{2.54 \text{ cm}}{1 \text{ in}}\right)$	$\left(\frac{0.394 \text{ in}}{1 \text{ cm}}\right)$
	foot (ft)	inch (in)	1 ft = 12 in	$\left(\frac{12 \text{ in}}{1 \text{ ft}}\right)$	$\left(\frac{0.083 \text{ ft}}{1 \text{ in}}\right)$
	meter (m)	centimeter (cm)	1 m = 100 cm	$\left(\frac{100 \text{ cm}}{1 \text{ m}}\right)$	$\left(\frac{0.01 \text{ m}}{1 \text{ cm}}\right)$
	meter (m)	inch (in)	1 m = 39.37 in	$\left(\frac{39.37 \text{ in}}{1 \text{ m}}\right)$	$\left(\frac{0.0254 \text{ m}}{1 \text{ in}}\right)$
	meter (m)	foot (ft)	1 m = 3.281 ft	$\left(\frac{3.281 \text{ ft}}{1 \text{ m}}\right)$	$\left(\frac{0.3048 \text{ m}}{1 \text{ ft}}\right)$
	meter (m)	yard (yd)	1 m = 1.094 yd	$\left(\frac{1.094 \text{ yd}}{1 \text{ m}}\right)$	$\left(\frac{0.9144 \text{ m}}{1 \text{ yd}}\right)$
	mile (mi)	foot (ft)	1 mi = 5,280 ft	$\left(\frac{5{,}280 \text{ ft}}{1 \text{ mi}}\right)$	$\left(\frac{0.0001894 \text{ mi}}{1 \text{ ft}}\right)$
	mile (mi)	meter (m)	1 mi = 1,609 m	$\left(\frac{1{,}609 \text{ m}}{1 \text{ mi}}\right)$	$\left(\frac{0.0006214 \text{ mi}}{1 \text{ m}}\right)$
	mile (mi)	kilometer (km)	1 mi = 1.609 km	$\left(\frac{1.609 \text{ km}}{1 \text{ mi}}\right)$	$\left(\frac{0.6214 \text{ mi}}{1 \text{ km}}\right)$
area	square inch (in^2)	square centimeter (cm^2)	1 in^2 = 6.452 cm^2	$\left(\frac{6.452 \text{ cm}^2}{1 \text{ in}^2}\right)$	$\left(\frac{0.1550 \text{ in}^2}{1 \text{ cm}^2}\right)$
	square foot (ft^2)	square inch (in^2)	1 ft^2 = 144 in^2	$\left(\frac{144 \text{ in}^2}{1 \text{ ft}^2}\right)$	$\left(\frac{0.006944 \text{ ft}^2}{1 \text{ in}^2}\right)$
	square meter (m^2)	square inch (in^2)	1 m^2 = 10.76 in^2	$\left(\frac{1{,}550 \text{ in}^2}{1 \text{ m}^2}\right)$	$\left(\frac{0.0006452 \text{ m}^2}{1 \text{ in}^2}\right)$
	square meter (m^2)	square foot (ft^2)	1 m^2 = 10.76 ft^2	$\left(\frac{10.76 \text{ ft}^2}{1 \text{ m}^2}\right)$	$\left(\frac{0.0929 \text{ m}^2}{1 \text{ ft}^2}\right)$
volume	milliliter (mL)	cubic centimeter (cm^3)	1 mL = 1 cm^3	$\left(\frac{1 \text{ cm}^3}{1 \text{ mL}}\right)$	$\left(\frac{1 \text{ mL}}{1 \text{ cm}^3}\right)$
	cubic inch (in^3)	cubic centimeter (cm^3)	1 in^3 = 16.39 cm^3	$\left(\frac{16.39 \text{ cm}^3}{1 \text{ in}^3}\right)$	$\left(\frac{0.0610 \text{ in}^3}{1 \text{ cm}^3}\right)$
	liter (L)	milliliter (mL)	1 L = 1,000 mL	$\left(\frac{1{,}000 \text{ mL}}{1 \text{ L}}\right)$	$\left(\frac{0.001 \text{ L}}{1 \text{ mL}}\right)$
	liter (L)	quart (qt)	1 L = 1.057 qt	$\left(\frac{1.057 \text{ qt}}{1 \text{ L}}\right)$	$\left(\frac{0.9464 \text{ L}}{1 \text{ qt}}\right)$
	U.S. gallon	quart (qt)	1 gallon = 4 qt	$\left(\frac{4 \text{ qt}}{1 \text{ gallon}}\right)$	$\left(\frac{0.250 \text{ gallon}}{1 \text{ qt}}\right)$
	U.S. gallon	liter (L)	1 gallon = 3.785 L	$\left(\frac{3.785 \text{ L}}{1 \text{ gallon}}\right)$	$\left(\frac{0.2642 \text{ gallon}}{1 \text{ L}}\right)$
time	minute (min)	second (sec) or (s)	1 min = 60 sec	$\left(\frac{60 \text{ sec}}{1 \text{ min}}\right)$	$\left(\frac{0.01667 \text{ min}}{1 \text{ sec}}\right)$
	hour (hr)	min (min)	1 hr = 60 min	$\left(\frac{60 \text{ min}}{1 \text{ hr}}\right)$	$\left(\frac{0.01667 \text{ hr}}{1 \text{ min}}\right)$

Quantity	Unit 1	Unit 2	Relationship	Conversion Factor 1 Unit 1 / Unit 2	Conversion Factor 2 Unit 2 / Unit 1
mass	kilogram (kg)	gram (g)	1 kg = 1,000 g	$\left(\frac{1{,}000\ g}{1\ kg}\right)$	$\left(\frac{0.001\ kg}{1\ g}\right)$
weight & force	**Weight** is actually a unit of force. A mass under the influence of the earth's gravity results in the force we call ***weight.***				
	ounce (oz)	gram (g)	1 oz = 28.35 g	$\left(\frac{28.35\ g}{1\ oz}\right)$	$\left(\frac{0.03527\ oz}{1\ g}\right)$
	pound (lb)	ounce (oz)	1 lb = 16 oz	$\left(\frac{16\ oz}{1\ lb}\right)$	$\left(\frac{0.0625\ lb}{1\ oz}\right)$
	pound (lb)	newton (N)	1 lb = 4.448 N	$\left(\frac{4.448\ N}{1\ lb}\right)$	$\left(\frac{0.2248\ lb}{1\ N}\right)$
	kilogram (kg)	pound (lb)	1 kg = 2.205 lb	$\left(\frac{2.205\ lb}{1\ kg}\right)$	$\left(\frac{0.4535\ kg}{1\ lb}\right)$
pressure	pounds per sq. inch (psi)	pascals (pa) or (N/m^2)	1 psi = 6,895 pa	$\left(\frac{6{,}895\ pa}{1\ psi}\right)$	$\left(\frac{0.0001450\ psi}{1\ pa}\right)$
	pounds per sq. inch (psi)	inch of water (in H_2O)	1 psi = 27.70 in H_2O	$\left(\frac{27.70\ in\ H_2O}{1\ psi}\right)$	$\left(\frac{0.03610\ psi}{1\ in\ H_2O}\right)$
	inch of mercury (in Hg)	inch of water (in H_2O)	1 in Hg = 13.61 in H_2O	$\left(\frac{13.61\ in\ H_2O}{1\ in\ Hg}\right)$	$\left(\frac{0.07349\ in\ Hg}{1\ in\ H_2O}\right)$
	bar	pascals (pa) or (N/m^2)	1 bar = 10,000 pa	$\left(\frac{10{,}000\ pa}{1\ bar}\right)$	$\left(\frac{0.00001\ bar}{1\ pa}\right)$
	atmosphere (atm)	bar	1 atm = 1.013 bar	$\left(\frac{1.013\ bar}{1\ atm}\right)$	$\left(\frac{0.9869\ atm}{1\ bar}\right)$
energy (work)	foot-pound (ft-lb)	joule (J) or (N-m)	1 ft-lb = 1.356 J	$\left(\frac{1.356\ J}{1\ ft\text{-}lb}\right)$	$\left(\frac{0.7376\ ft\text{-}lb}{1\ J}\right)$
	calorie (cal)	joule (J) or (N-m)	1 cal = 4.187 J	$\left(\frac{4.187\ J}{1\ cal}\right)$	$\left(\frac{0.2388\ cal}{1\ J}\right)$
	kilocalorie (kcal) or (Cal)	joule (J) or (N-m)	1 kcal = 4,187 J	$\left(\frac{4{,}187\ J}{1\ kcal}\right)$	$\left(\frac{0.0002388\ kcal}{1\ J}\right)$
	kilowatt-hour (kWhr)	kilojoule (kJ)	1 kWhr = 3,600 kJ	$\left(\frac{3.600\ kJ}{1\ kWhr}\right)$	$\left(\frac{0.002778\ kWhr}{1\ kJ}\right)$
	kilowatt-hour (kWhr)	British thermal unit (Btu)	1 kWhr = 2,544 Btu	$\left(\frac{3{,}412\ Btu}{1\ kWhr}\right)$	$\left(\frac{0.0002931\ kWhr}{1\ Btu}\right)$
	kilowatt-hour (kWhr)	kilocalorie (kcal) or (Cal)	1 kWhr = 859.9 kcal	$\left(\frac{859.9\ kcal}{1\ kWhr}\right)$	$\left(\frac{0.001163\ kWhr}{1\ kcal}\right)$
power	kilowatt (kW)	joule per second (J/s)	1 kW = 1,000 J/s	$\left(\frac{1{,}000\ J/s}{1\ kW}\right)$	$\left(\frac{0.001\ kW}{1\ J/s}\right)$
	kilowatt (kW) or (kJ-s)	horsepower (hp)	1 kW = 1.341 hp	$\left(\frac{1.341\ hp}{1\ kW}\right)$	$\left(\frac{0.7457\ kW}{1\ hp}\right)$
temperature	Temperature conversion requires the use of a formula, *not a factor*.			**Conversion Formula 1**	**Conversion Formula 2**
	degree fahrenheit (F)	degree Celsius (C)		(5/9 x (°F-32))	((9/5 x °C) + 32)
	kelvin (K)	degree Celsius (C)		(K - 273.15)	(°C + 273.15)

Reference

Force and Motion

Acceleration	$a = \frac{v_f - v_i}{t}$	v_f is *final speed* in *meters/second*. v_i is *initial speed* in *meters/second*. t is *time* in *seconds*.
Mechanical advantage	$MA = \frac{F_o}{F_i}$	MA is *mechanical advantage*. F_o is *output force*. F_i is *input force*.
Momentum	$p = mv$	p is *momentum* in *kilogram-meter/second*. m is *mass* in *kilograms*. v is *velocity* in *meters/second*.
Newton's Second Law	$a = \frac{F}{m}$	a is acceleration in *meters/second*^{2}. F is *force* in *newtons*. m is *mass* in *kilograms*.
Slope of a line	$slope = \frac{y_2 - y_1}{x_2 - x_1}$	The slope of a line is calculated using two points on that line: (x_1, y_1) and (x_2, y_2).
Speed	$v = \frac{d}{t}$	v is *average speed* in *meters/second*. d is *distance traveled* in *meters*. t is the *time* taken to travel that distance in *seconds*.
Weight	$F_w = mg$	F_w is the *weight force* in *newtons*. m is *mass* in *kilograms*. g is the *acceleration of gravity* (9.8 meters/second^2).

Work and Energy

Work	$W = Fd$	W is *work* in *joules*. F is *force* in *newtons*. d is *distance* in *meters*.
Power	$P = \frac{W}{t}$	P is *power* in *watts*. W is *work* in *joules*. t is *time* in *seconds*.
Kinetic energy	$E_k = \frac{1}{2}mv^2$	E_k is *kinetic energy* in *joules*. m is *mass* in *kilograms*. v is *speed* in *meters /second*.
Potential energy	$E_p = mgh$	E_p is *potential energy* in *joules*. m is *mass* in *kilograms*. g is the *acceleration of gravity* (9.8 meters/second^2). h is *height* in *meters*.

Electricity

Ohm's law	$I = \frac{V}{R}$	*I* is *current* in *amps*. *V* is *voltage* in *volts*. *R* is *resistance* in *ohms*.
Power	$P = V \times I$	*P* is *power* in *watts*. *V* is *voltage* in *volts*. *I* is *current* in *amps*.

Sound and Waves

Frequency	$f = \frac{1}{T}$	*f* is *frequency* in *hertz*. *T* is *period* in *seconds*.
Period	$T = \frac{1}{f}$	*T* is *period* in *seconds*. *f* is *frequency* in *hertz*.
Wave speed	$v = f\lambda$	*v* is *speed* in *meters/second*. *f* is *frequency* in *hertz*. λ is *wavelength* in *meters*.

Light

Index of refraction	$n = \frac{\text{speed of light in air}}{v}$	*n* is the *index of refraction*. The *speed of light in air* is 300 x 10^6 meters/second. *v* is the *speed* in the material in *meters/second*.

Properties of Matter

Density	$D = \frac{m}{v}$	*D* is *density* in *grams / centimeter*. *m* is *mass* in *grams*. *v* is *volume* in *centimeters*.

Heat

Heat gain	$Q = mc\Delta T$	*Q* is *heat* gained or lost in *calories*. m is *mass* in *grams*. *c* is *specific heat* for a substance in calories/grams °C. Δ*T* is *change in temperature* in °C.

Topic	Name	Symbol used in equations	Rounded Value	Exact Value	Unit Symbols	Unit Name
Forces and Motion	Standard acceleration of gravity	g	9.8	9.80665	$m\ s^{-2}$	meter / second^2
	Newtonian constant of gravitation	G	6.7×10^{-11}	6.673×10^{-11}	$m^3kg^{-1}s^{-2}$	meter^3 / kilogram / second^2
	Mass of sun		2.0×10^{30}	1.99×10^{30}	kg	kilograms
	Mass of earth		6.0×10^{24}	5.98×10^{24}	kg	kilograms
	Mass of moon		7.4×10^{22}	7.36×10^{22}	kg	kilograms
	Astronomical unit (average earth-sun distance)	A.U.	1.50×10^{11}	1.50×10^{11}	m	meters
	Average earth-moon distance		3.8×10^{8}	3.84×10^{8}	m	meters
Work and Energy	Mechanical equivalent of heat	J	4.2×10^{3}	4.185×10^{3}	$J\ kcal^{-1}$	Joules / kilocalorie
Electricity and Magnetism	Charge of an electron	e	1.6×10^{-19}	$1.602176462 \times 10^{-19}$	C	Coulomb
Sound and Waves	Speed of sound (20 C, 1 atmosphere)	c_s	343	343	m s-1	meters / second
Light and Optics	Speed of light in a vacuum	c	300,000,000	299,792,458	$m\ s^{-1}$	meter / second
	Plank's constant	h	6.6×10^{-34}	$6.62606876 \times 10^{-34}$	J s	Joules-second
Properties of Matter	Mass of a proton	m_p	1.6×10^{-27}	$1.67262158 \times 10^{-27}$	kg	kilogram
	Mass of a neutron	m_n	1.6×10^{-27}	$1.67492716 \times 10^{-27}$	kg	kilogram
	Mass of an electron	m_e	9.1×10^{-31}	$9.10938188 \times 10^{-31}$	kg	kilogram
Changes in Matter	Avogadro's number	N_A	6.022×10^{-23}	$6.02214199 \times 10^{23}$	mol^{-1}	per mole
	Molar mass of carbon-12	M (^{12}C)	12×10^{-3}	12×10^{-3}	$kg\ mol^{-1}$	kilogram per mole
Water and Solutions	Standard atmospheric pressure	P_s	101,000	101,325	Pa	Pascal (1 atmosphere = 1.01×10^5 Pascals)
Heating and Cooling	Boltzmann constant	k	1.4×10^{-23}	$1.3806503 \times 10^{-23}$	$J\ K^{-1}$	Joules / °Kelvin
	Absolute zero of temperature	0° K	-273	-273.15	°C	°Celsius

A

absorbers – objects that have the ability to absorb radiant energy.

accelerate – to increase speed or change direction.

acceleration – the change of speed over time.

acid – a chemical that contributes hydrogen ions, H+, to a solution.

acid precipitation – rain, snow, or fog that has a pH lower than 5.6.

acid rain – rain that has a pH lower than 5.6.

acoustics – the science and technology of sound.

addition reaction – a chemical reaction in which two or more substances combine to form a new compound.

additive primary colors – red, green, and blue.

air friction – the opposing force created by objects moving through air.

albedo – the percentage of the sun's light reflected from a planet's surface.

alloys – solutions of two or more metals.

alpha decay – radioactive decay that results in an alpha particle (a helium nucleus) being emitted from the nucleus of a radioactive element.

alpha particles – a partially charged particle emitted from the nucleus of an atom during radioactive decay; also called a helium nucleus.

alternating current – an electric current that reverses its direction at repeated intervals; the abbreviation for this is AC.

amperes – the unit for measuring electrical current; the abbreviation is amp.

amplitude – the maximum distance from the average in harmonic motion; amplitude is often a distance or an angle.

anhydrous – means "without water"; describes the state of a hydrate that has lost water through evaporation.

aquifer – an underground area of sediment and rocks where groundwater collects.

Archimedes' principle – a principle that states that the force exerted on an object in a liquid is equal to the weight of the fluid displaced by the object.

atmospheres – the unit used to measure atmospheric pressure; the abbreviation is atm.

atom – the smallest particle of an element that can exist alone or in combination with other atoms.

atomic mass – the average mass of all the known isotopes of an element.

atomic mass unit – defined as the mass of $^{1}/_{12}$ of a carbon-12 atom (6 protons and 6 neutrons in the nucleus plus 6 electrons outside the nucleus).

atomic number – the number of protons that an atom contains.

atomic theory – a theory that states that all matter is composed of tiny particles called atoms.

average speed – how fast something moves over a certain distance.

Avogardo's number – the number of atoms in the atomic mass of an element, or the number of molecules in the formula mass of a compound when these masses are expressed in grams.

B

balance – occurs when the number and type of atoms on the reactant's and product's sides of a chemical equation are equal.

base – a chemical that contributes hydroxyl ions, OH-, to a solution.

battery – a device that uses chemical energy to move electrical charges.

beat – a rapid alteration between loudness and silence.

beta decay – radioactive decay that results in a beta particle (an electron) being emitted from the nucleus of a radioactive element.

beta particles – a negatively charged particle (an electron) emitted from the nucleus of an atom during radioactive decay.

binary compound – a covalent compound that consists of only two types of elements.

Boyle's law – pressure and volume are inversely related.

British thermal unit (Btu) – the quantity of heat it takes to increase the temperature of one pound of water by 1°F. One Btu is equal to 1,055 joules or 252 calories.

brittleness – a measure of a material's tendency to shatter upon impact.

buoyancy – a measure of the upward force a fluid exerts on an object.

buoyant convection– see natural convection.

C

calorie – the quantity of heat required to raise the temperature of one gram of water by 1°C.

carbohydrate – a nutrient molecule composed of simple or complex sugars; it contains four calories of energy per gram.

carbon dating – a technique to find out how old something is; the measure of carbon-14 in a sample that is between a few thousand and 50,000 years old.

cause and effect – the relationship between an event that brings about a result and what happens due to the result.

Celsius scale – a temperature scale on which zero equals the temperature that water freezes (0°C) and 100 is the temperature that water boils (100°C) where *C* stands for Celsius.

Charles' law – the volume of a gas increases with increasing temperature if pressure is held constant.

chemical bond – an attraction between two or more different atoms that binds them together.

chemical change – a change in a substance that involves the breaking and reforming of chemical bonds to make a new substance or substances.

chemical energy – a type of energy stored in molecules.

chemical equation – chemical formulas and symbols that represent a chemical reaction.

chemical formula – a representation of a compound that includes the symbols and numbers of atoms in the compound.

chemical potential energy – the energy that is stored in chemical bonds.

chemical reaction – the breaking of bonds to form new substances (called the products); atoms are rearranged in a chemical reaction.

chemical symbol – an abbreviation that represents the name of an element; used in chemical formulas.

circuit – see electric circuit.

circuit diagram – the diagramatic representation of an electric circuit.

circular waves – waves that move in concentric circles.

closed circuit – a circuit in which the switch is turned to the "on" position, causing there to be no breaks anywhere in the wire.

cochlea – a tiny, fluid-filled bone structure in the inner ear with three tubes and a spiral.

coefficient –a number placed in front of a chemical formula to make the number of atoms on each side of a chemical equation equal.

colloid – a type of mixture in which the particles (atoms or molecules) are between 1.0 and 1,000 nanometers in diameter.

combustion reaction – a reaction in which a substance combines with oxygen, releasing large amounts of energy in the form of heat and light.

compounds – substances made of two or more elements that cannot be separated by physical means.

compression stroke – in a four-stroke engine, the stroke in which the fuel and air are compressed and ignited by a spark plug.

conceptual model – a written description or diagram based on ideas and observations that are used to describe how a process or object works; Sir Isaac Newton's law of universal gravitation is a conceptual model.

condensation – the process by which a substance in its gaseous state loses energy and enters its liquid state; one phase in the water cycle.

conduction – the transfer of thermal energy by the direct contact of particles of matter.

cone cells – photoreceptor cells in the retina of the eye that respond to color.

conservation of atoms – principle that states the number of each type of atom on the reactant's side must be equal to the number of each type of atom on the product's side of a chemical equation.

consonance – a combination of sounds that is harmonious or agreeable.

constructive interference – occurs when waves add up to make a larger amplitude.

continuous – connected to itself.

controlled experiment – when one variable is changed and all the others are controlled or stay the same throughout the experiment.

controlled variables – variables in an experiment that are kept the same throughout the experiment.

convection – occurs when hot air rises upward due to a decrease in density, and then expands, giving off heat.

converge – to bend light so that the rays come together.

converging lens – a type of lens that bends light so that the parallel rays coming in bend toward the focal point.

coulomb – the unit for electrical charge.

covalent bond – a type of chemical bond that is formed when two atoms share electrons.

covalent compound – a compound that consists of atoms that are covalently bonded.

crest – the high point on a wave.

critical angle – the angle at which light is totally reflected back into a material.

current – the quantity that refers to the rate of flow of electric charges; current is measured in amps.

cyan – a greenish, light-blue that is created when red is absorbed and blue and green are reflected.

cycle – a unit of motion that repeats over and over.

D

deceleration – occurs when change in speed, or acceleration, is in the negative direction.

decomposition reaction – a chemical reaction in which a single compound is broken down to produce two or more smaller compounds.

density – a property that describes the relationship between mass and volume.

dependent variable – the variable in an experiment that changes in response to choices made by the experimenter; this variable is plotted on the y-axis of a graph.

destructive interference – occurs when waves add up to make a smaller amplitude.

dew point – the temperature at which air becomes saturated with water.

diatomic molecules – a molecule that has only two atoms of the same element.

diffraction – the process by which waves can bend around corners or pass through openings.

direct current – electrical current flowing in one direction only; the abbreviation is DC.

dissolution reaction – a reaction that occurs when an ionic compound dissolves in water to make an ionic solution.

dissolved – the state in which solute particles are evenly distributed throughout a solvent.

dissolving rate – the length of time it takes for a certain amount of solute to dissolve in a solvent; the dissolving rate can be changed by changing the temperature, or by physical means such as by stirring a solution.

dissonance – a combination of discordant or unsettling sounds.

distance – the length of space between two points.

diverge – bending light so that the rays spread apart.

diverging lens – a type of lens that bends light away from the focal point.

double-displacement reaction – a reaction in which ions from two compounds in a solution exchange places to produce two new compounds.

E

efficiency – the ratio of a machine's output work to input work.

elasticity – a measure of a solid's ability to stretch and then return to its original shape and size.

electric circuits – the structures that provide paths through which electricity travels.

electric motor – a device that uses electricity and magnets to turn electrical energy into rotating mechanical energy.

electrical conductivity – the ability of a material to conduct (or carry) electricity.

electrical conductor – a material that easily carries electrical current.

electrical energy – another term for electricity.

electrical force – the force that charged materials or objects exert on each other.

electrical insulator – a material that poorly conducts current.

electrical symbols – simple symbols used in circuit diagrams.

electrically charged – an object that has an excess amount of either positive or negative charges.

electrically neutral – an object that has equal amounts of positive and negative charges.

electrolytes – chemicals that form ions and conduct current when dissolved in water.

electromagnet – a strong, short-lasting magnet that can be made by inserting iron into a wire coil that is conducting an electric current.

electromagnetic force – the force that exists between electric charges; often described as electrical force or magnetic force depending on how charges interact.

electromagnetic induction – the creation of electric current when a magnet is moved inside a loop of wire; generators are devices that work using electromagnetic induction.

electromagnetic spectrum – the whole range of light (electromagnetic radiation).

electron – a subatomic particle in an atom that is negatively charged and that occupies the energy levels in an atom; electrons are involved in chemical bonds and reactions.

electronegativity – the attraction an atom has for the shared pair of electrons in a chemical bond.

electroscope – an instrument that is used to detect charged objects.

elements – substances that contain only one kind of matter.

emissions – the airborne gases and particles expelled through an operating automobile's tailpipe.

emitters – objects that have the ability to emit radiation efficiently.

endothermic reaction – a reaction in which more energy is required to break the bonds in reactants than is released from the formation of new bonds in the products.

energy – a fundamental building block of the universe; it appears in different forms (i.e., position, motion, or heat) and can travel in different ways (i.e., light, sound, or electricity).

energy level – a region around the nucleus of an atom where electrons are most likely to be found; only a certain number of electrons can be found in each energy level of an atom.

energy transformation – the conversion from one kind of energy to another kind of energy; for example, an energy transformation occurs when potential energy is converted to kinetic energy.

engineering – the application of science to solve technical problems.

engineering cycle – a process used to build devices that solve technical problems. The four steps of the engineering cycle are creating a design, building a prototype, testing the prototype, and evaluating test results.

engineers – people who design technology to solve problems.

English system – a system of measuring that uses, for example, distance units of inches, yards, and miles.

equilibrium – (1) in physics, occurs when the forces on an object are balanced; (2) in chemistry, the state in which the solute in a solution is dissolving and coming out of solution at the same rate.

evaporation – the process by which a substance in its liquid state gains energy and enters its gaseous state; one phase of the water cycle.

excess reactant – a reactant that is not completely used up.

exhaust stroke – in a four-stroke engine, the stroke in which a valve opens and releases exhaust gases.

exothermic reaction – occurs when less energy is required to break the bonds in reactants than is released when bonds are formed to make new products.

experiment – any situation that is set up to observe and measure something happening.

experimental technique – the exact procedure that is followed each time an experiment is repeated.

experimental variable – a variable in an experiment that is changed by the experimenter; the experimental variable is plotted as an independent variable on the *x*-axis of a graph.

external combustion engine – a machine in which the action of heating takes place outside it, as in a steam engine.

F

Fahrenheit scale – a temperature scale on which water freezes at 32 degrees Fahrenheit (or 32°F) and water boils at 212°F.

fat – a nutrient molecule that is composed of carbon and hydrogen atoms, and that contains 9 grams of energy per gram.

first law of thermodynamics – states that energy in a closed system is conserved.

fission – a nuclear reaction that involves the splitting of the nucleus of an atom.

fluorescent – a type of electric light bulb.

focal length – the distance from the center of a lens to the focal point.

focal point – the point at which light rays meet after having entered a converging lens parallel to the principal axis.

focus – the place where all the light rays that have come from an object meet to form an image after having passed through a converging lens.

force – a push, a pull, or any action that has the ability to change motion.

forced convection – occurs when mechanical means is used to force fluid or gas to move.

formula mass – determined by adding up the atomic mass units of all the atoms in the compound; a way to compare the masses of molecules of different compounds.

fossil fuels – hydrocarbon substances including oil, coal, and natural gas that are extracted from the Earth; fossil fuels are used as the primary source of energy in the United States.

free fall – the acceleration of a falling object under the influence of the Earth's gravitational force.

frequency – (1) in harmonics, the number of cycles an oscillator makes per second; (2) in waves, the number of wavelengths that pass a given point in one second.

friction – the force that results from relative motion between objects (like the wheel and axle of a car).

fulcrum – a fixed point on a lever.

fundamental – the name of the first harmonic.

fusion – a nuclear reaction that involves fusing nuclei from two atoms to make a different atom.

G

gamma ray – a photon emitted spontaneously by a radioactive substance.

gear – a wheel with teeth; two or more gears can be connected together to change the speed and/or direction of rotating motion.

generator – a combination of mechanical and electrical systems that converts kinetic energy into electrical energy.

global warming – an increase in the Earth's temperature due to increased carbon dioxide in the atmosphere.

graphical model – a model that shows the relationship between two variables on a graph so that the relationship is easily seen and understood.

gravity – the attractive force that exists between any two objects that have mass.

groundwater – water that collects underground in an aquifer; this water supplies wells and springs.

group of elements – elements that exhibit similar chemical properties; arranged in columns on the periodic table.

H

half-life – the length of time it takes for half an amount of radioactive substance to undergo radioactive decay.

hardness – measures a solid's resistance to scratching.

harmonic motion – motion that repeats itself.

harmonics – (1) frequencies that are multiples of fundamental notes; (2) multiples of natural frequency.

heat – a flow of thermal energy from one object to another object due to a temperature difference.

heat transfer – the transfer of energy in the form of heat from a material at a higher temperature to a material at a lower temperature.

heat-temperature rule – a rule stating that the more heat you add to an object the greater the increase in temperature.

hertz – a unit of one cycle per second used to measure frequency; the abbreviation is Hz.

heterogeneous mixture – a mixture in which every sample of it might have a different composition.

homogeneous mixture – a mixture in which every sample of it has the same composition.

horsepower – a unit of power; one horsepower is equal to 746 watts.

humidity – a measurement of how much water vapor is in the air.

hydrate – a compound that has water molecules chemically bonded to its ions.

hydrated – combined with water or the elements of water.

hydrochloric acid – a highly acidic substance your stomach normally produces to help you break down food.

hydrogen bond – a weak bond between the partially charged positive end of one water molecule and the partially charged negative end of another water molecule.

hydrologic cycle – describes how water moves around the Earth by the processes of evaporation, condensation, precipitation, and transpiration.

hypothesis – a prediction that can be tested by experimentation.

I

image – a picture of an object that is formed using a mirror or lens where light rays from the object meet.

incandescence – the process of making light with heat.

incident ray – the ray that comes from an object and strikes a surface.

independent variable – the variable in an experiment that is manipulated by the experimenter and that causes changes in the dependent variable in the experiment; this variable is plotted on the *x*-axis of a graph.

index of refraction – a ratio that tells how much the speed of light is reduced when it passes through a material.

inertia – the reluctance of a body to change its state of motion.

infrared light – electromagnetic radiation, including heat, with wavelengths longer than the visible spectrum.

input – includes everything you do to make a machine work.

input arm – when you place a lever on a fulcrum, the input arm is the side of the lever where the input force is applied.

input force – the force applied to a machine.

insoluble – a term to describe a substance that does not dissolve in water.

instantaneous speed – the speed of an object at a specific point in its journey.

intake stroke – in a four-stroke engine, the stroke in which air and fuel enter the cylinder.

internal combustion engine – a machine in which the burning process takes place inside the cylinder (the container holding the piston).

investigation – one or more experiences that are all connected to answering the same basic question.

ion – an atom that has an electrical charge.

ionic bond – a type of chemical bond between atoms that gained or lost electrons; a bond between ions.

ionic compound – a compound that is made up of ions.

isotopes – forms of the same element that have different numbers of neutrons and different mass numbers.

J

joule – a unit for measuring work; a joule is equal to one newton of force times one meter of distance; the abbreviation is J.

K

kilocalories – the amount of heat required to raise the temperature of one kilogram of water 1°C; the abbreviation for this is kcal.

kilowatt – a measurement equal to 1,000 watts or 1,000 joules per second.

kilowatt-hour – indicates that a kilowatt of power has been used for one hour.

kinetic energy – energy that comes from motion.

Kirchhoff's current law – states the current into a branch in a circuit equals the amount of current out of the branch.

Kirchhoff's voltage law – states that over an entire circuit, the energy taken out must equal the energy supplied by the battery.

L

latent heat – heat that cannot be sensed with a thermometer; the heat released when vapor condenses into a liquid.

latitude – angular distance north and south from the Earth's equator measured through 90 degrees.

law of conservation of mass – states that the total mass of products of a reaction is equal to the total mass of reactants.

law of conservation of momentum – states that as long as interacting objects are not influenced by outside forces (like friction), their momentum before the interaction will equal their momentum after the interaction.

law of universal gravitation–The force of attraction between two objects is directly related to the masses of the objects and indirectly related to the distance between them.

length – a unit of measurement for distance.

lens – a shape of a transparent material, like glass, that is used to bend light rays.

lever – a stiff structure that rotates around a fixed point called the fulcrum.

limiting reactant – the reactant that is used up first in a chemical reaction.

longitudinal wave – a wave whose oscillations are in the same direction as the wave moves.

M

machine – a type of mechanical system.

magenta – a pink-purple color that is created when green is absorbed and red and blue are reflected.

magnetic field – an area of magnetic force that surrounds magnetic objects.

magnetic force – a force exerted on a particle or object traveling in a magnetic field.

magnetic north pole – the end of a magnetic object that points toward the geographic north pole of the Earth.

Glossary

magnetic south pole – the end of a magnetic object that points away from the geographic north pole of the Earth.

malleability – a solid's ability to be pounded into thin sheets.

mass – a measure of the inertia of an object; the amount of matter an object has.

mass number – the total number of protons and neutrons in the nucleus of an atom.

matter – anything that has mass and takes up space.

measurement– the act or process of measuring in multiples of a specific unit.

mechanical advantage – the ratio of output force to input force.

mechanical system – a series of interrelated, moving parts that work together to accomplish a specific task.

metabolic rate – the rate of energy consumption at all times (resting or awake) within the body.

metric system – a system of measuring that uses, for example, distance units of millimeters, centimeters, meters, and kilometers.

mixture – substance that contains more than one kind of matter.

mole – one set of 6.02×10^{23} atoms or molecules.

molecular formula – includes the symbols for and number of atoms of each element in a compound.

molecule – the smallest particle of a compound that retains the properties of the compound.

momentum – the mass of an object multiplied by its speed or velocity.

monoatomic ions – ions that contain only one type of atom.

musical scale – frequencies of sound that fit into a special pattern.

N

nanometer – a unit of measurement that is equal to one billionth of a meter.

natural (or buoyant) convection – a process that is influenced by gravitational forces and by which hot, less-dense air displaces cooler, denser air.

natural frequency – describes how an object vibrates; for example, a guitar string strummed repeatedly has its own natural force.

natural world– the aspects of the world not created or constructed by people.

negative charge – one of two types of electric charge; the other type is positive charge.

net force – the amount of force that overcomes an opposing force to cause motion; the net force can be zero if the opposing forces are equal.

neutral – (1) a solution that has a pH of 7, meaning it has equal numbers of H+ and OH-, or acidic and basic, ions; (2) when one proton is paired with one electron.

neutron – an uncharged particle found in the nucleus of an atom.

newton – a unit of force; the abbreviation is N.

Newton's first law of motion – states any object at rest will remain at rest unless acted on by an unbalanced force; an object in motion continues with constant speed and direction in a straight line unless acted on by an unbalanced force.

Newton's second law of motion – states that the acceleration of an object is directly proportional to the force acting on it and inversely proportional to its mass.

Newton's third law of motion – states that whenever one object exerts a force on another, the second object exerts an equal and opposite force on the first.

nonpolar – a term used to describe a molecule or covalent bond that does not have partial charges; oils and fats are nonpolar molecules.

normal – a line that is perpendicular to the surface of an object.

nuclear energy – the form of energy that comes from splitting the nucleus of an atom, or fusing two nuclei of an atom.

nuclear reaction – a reaction that involves splitting the nucleus of an atom or fusing two nuclei; these reactions produce much more energy than chemical reactions.

nucleons – the protons and neutrons in the nucleus of an atom.

nucleus – the center core of an atom that contains protons and neutrons.

O

octet – an atom's eight valence electrons.

octet rule – states that atoms form bonds with other atoms by sharing or transferring them to complete their octet and become stable.

ohm – the unit of measurement for electrical resistance; the abbreviation is Ω.

Ohm's law – describes the mathematical relationship present in most circuits.

open circuit – a circuit in which there is a break in the wire so that current cannot flow; a switch turned to the "off" position is one way to cause a break in the wire.

optics – the study of how light behaves.

oscillator – a system that shows harmonic motion.

output – what the machine does.

output arm – of the lever on a fulcrum, the output arm is the side where the output force is applied.

output force – the force a machine applies to accomplish a task.

oxidation number – indicates how many electrons are lost or gained (or shared) when bonding occurs.

P

parallel – lying or moving in the same direction, but always the same distance apart (i.e., never intersecting).

parallel circuit – a circuit in which the current can take more than one path.

pascal (Pa) – the SI unit of pressure. One pascal is equal to one newton of force acting on one square meter of surface.

percent yield – the actual yield of product in a chemical reaction divided by the predicted yield, and multiplied by one hundred to get a percentage.

period – the time for one cycle.

periodic motion – cycles of motion that repeat over and over again; the same as harmonic motion.

periodic table of elements – a table that visually organizes the similarities between all known elements.

permanent magnet – a magnetic object that retains its magnetic properties without external influence.

perpendicular – forming a 90 degree angle with a given edge or surface.

pH – the exact concentrations of H+ ions and OH- ions in a solution.

pH indicator – a solution or object that changes color to identify the pH of a solution.

pH scale – a scale that runs from 0 (strongly acidic) to 14 (strongly basic, or alkaline).

phase – refers to where an oscillator is in its cycle.

photoluminescence – occurs when light energy makes something else give off light.

photoreceptors – rod and cone cells in the retina of the eye that receive light and release a chemical signal that travels down the optic nerve to the brain.

photosynthesis – a chemical reaction performed by plants in which energy from the sun is converted to chemical energy; carbon dioxide is converted to sugar in this reaction.

physical change – change in the physical properties of a substance.

physical models – models that are made of materials and that can be touched and measured; engineers construct scale physical models to test a structure before building it.

pitch – property of a sound determined by the frequency of the waves producing it.

pixel – a dot on your computer screen whose color can change depending on the three numbers your computer assigns to it.

plane waves – waves that move in straight lines.

polar – something that has two poles; a term used to describe a molecule or covalent bond that has partial charges; water is a polar molecule.

polarization – a way of describing the direction (such as vertical or horizontal) that waves of light travel.

polarizer – a partially transparent material that lets through only one polarization of light.

polyatomic ions – ions that contain more than one type of atom.

polymer – a large molecule that is composed of repeating smaller molecules called subunits or monomers.

polymerization – the production of a very large molecule by a series of synthesis reactions.

position – a point in space of an object compared to where it started.

positive charge – one of two types of electric charge; the other type is negative charge.

potential energy – stored energy that comes from position.

potentiometer – a variable resistor.

pounds – English system unit of force.

power – the rate at which work is done.

power stroke – in a four-stroke engine, the stroke in which the ignited fuel expands and pushes the piston back.

precipitate – substance formed when one of the compounds in a double-displacement reaction is insoluble, or does not dissolve in water.

precipitation – water vapor in the atmosphere falling back to Earth in the form of rain, hail, sleet, or snow; one phase in the water cycle.

pressure – a measure of the force felt by the walls of a container.

pressure – the force acting on a unit area of surface.

procedure – a collection of all the techniques you use to do an experiment.

products – substances that are produced in a chemical reaction from reactants.

protein – a nitrogen-containing molecule found in foods that is used to build structural parts of cells and to facilitate cellular reactions.

proton – a subatomic particle identical with the nucleus of the hydrogen atom; found with neutrons in all atomic nuclei; carries a positive charge.

prototype – a working model of a design that can be tested to see if it works.

R

radiant energy – another term for electromagnetic energy.

radiation – (1) the process of emitting radiant energy; (2) a term to describe the particles and energy that are emitted from radioactive substances.

radioactive – a term to describe an atomic state when the nucleus is emitting radiation in the form of particles and energy until it becomes more stable.

radioactive isotope – an unstable isotope of an element that spontaneously undergoes radioactive decay.

ray diagram – a diagram which illustrates how several light rays behave as they go through an optical system.

react – describes how atoms interact when forming a chemical bond with another atom.

reactants – a substance that enters into and is altered in the course of a chemical reaction.

real image – an image formed by rays of light coming together on a surface like a screen or the retina of the eye.

recoil – backward acceleration from the reaction force.

reflected ray – the ray that bounces off an object.

reflection – the bounce of a wave off a surface.

reflectors – objects that reflect light.

refraction – occurs when light passes from one transparent material into another and bends.

relative humidity – the amount of water vapor in the air.

relative mass – a quantity that allows for comparison between amounts of matter that are very small.

research question – a question that is solved through investigation.

resistance – the measure of an object's ability to conduct current.

resistors – components that are used to control current in many circuits.

resonance – an occurrence whereby the natural frequency of a system is exactly in tune with a force applied to the system.

reverberation – multiple echoes of sound.

rod cells – photoreceptor cells in the retina of the eye that respond to differences in brightness.

rolling friction – resistance created when one object rolls over another one.

S

saturated – the state of a mixture in which the maximum amount of solute has dissolved in a solution.

scientific evidence – any observation that can be repeated with the same results.

scientific method – a process that is used to gather evidence that leads to understanding.

scientific model – a method of representing the relationship between variables.

sea breeze – air current created when hot air rises over land due to convection and is replaced by cooler air.

second – a commonly used unit of time; $^1/_{60}$ of a minute.

semiconductor – material between conductor and insulator in its ability to carry current.

series circuit – a circuit in which the current only has one path.

short circuit – a branch in a circuit with zero or very low resistance.

simple machine – an unpowered mechanical device, such as a lever, which has an input and an output force.

single-displacement reaction – a reaction in which one element replaces a similar element in a compound.

sliding friction – resistance created when two surfaces rub against one another.

solar power – radiant energy from the sun that is harnessed for use.

solubility – refers to the amount of solute that can be dissolved in a certain volume of solvent under certain conditions.

solubility rules – a set of rules that identifies whether a combination of ions will dissolve or form a precipitate in water.

solubility value – a number that describes a solute-solvent system; it includes the mass of solute, amount of solvent, and temperature.

solute – the substance in a solution in the smallest amount; the solute is dissolved by the solvent.

solution – a mixture of two or more substances that is homogenous at the molecular level; a solution consists of a solute and a solvent.

solvent – the component of a solution that dissolves the solute and is present in the greatest amount.

sonogram– special kind of graph that shows how loud sound is at different frequencies.

spectral diagram – a diagram that shows the wavelengths and intensities of light emitted from a light source.

speed – describes movement from one place to another over time; distance divided by time.

stable – (1) a term used to describe an atom that has a balance of charge; (2) a non-radioactive nucleus.

standing wave – a wave trapped in one spot.

static electricity – a buildup of either positive or negative charge; consists of isolated motionless charges, like those produced by friction.

strong nuclear force – the force that holds protons together when they are very close together (only 10^{-15} meters apart).

subatomic particles – particles that are smaller than an atom; protons, neutrons, and electrons are subatomic particles.

subscript – a number in a chemical formula that show the number of a type of atom.

substance – a mixture that cannot be separated into different kinds of matter using physical means.

subtractive primary colors – magenta, yellow, and cyan.

supersaturated – condition of a solution when more solute has dissolved than is normally possible at a given temperature.

supersonic – motion that is faster than sound.

surface runoff – water that flows over land until it reaches lakes, rivers, or other surface water areas.

surface water – water contained in places such as lakes, ponds, rivers, streams, and reservoirs.

suspensions – a type of mixture in which the particles (atoms or molecules) are larger than 1,000 nanometers in diameter.

system – a collection of matter and processes that occur in a certain space and can be studied; systems can be open or closed.

T

temperature – the measurement used to quantify the sensations of hot and cold.

tensile strength – a measure of how much pulling, or tension, a material can withstand before breaking.

terahertz – a unit of measurement that is equal to 1,000,000,000 cycles per second.

thermal conductivity – the ability of material to transfer heat.

thermal conductor – a material that easily conducts heat.

thermal energy – energy that comes from heat and the vibration of atoms and molecules.

thermal equilibrium – a state that results when heat flows from a hot object to a cold object until they are at the same temperature.

thermal insulators – materials that are poor conductors of heat.

thermometer – an instrument for measuring the temperature typically by the rise and fall of a liquid in a tube.

thermostat – a device that controls another device based on changes in temperature.

time – a useful measurement of changes in motion or events; all or part of the past, present, and future.

total internal reflection – occurs when light within a material approaches the surface at greater than the critical angle and reflects back.

transpiration – process in which plants open tiny pores on their leaves to gain carbon dioxide but lose water; one phase in the water cycle.

transverse wave – a wave whose oscillation is perpendicular to the direction the wave travels.

trial – each time an experiment is tried.

trough – the low point on a wave.

turbine – an engine whose central driveshaft is fitted with curved vanes spun by the pressure of water, steam, or gas.

Tyndall effect – a way of visually distinguishing colloids from true solutions.

U

ultraviolet light – light of a wavelength shorter than those of visible light but longer than those of X-rays.

unsaturated – a solution in which it is possible for more solute to be dissolved.

V

valence electrons – the electrons in an atom that are involved in the formation of chemical bonds.

variables – factors that affect the results of an experiment.

velocity – describes movement from one place to another over time and in a certain direction.

versorium – the earliest version of today's electroscope.

virtual image – an image formed when rays of light appear to be coming from a place other than where the actual object exists; a virtual image cannot be projected on a screen.

viscosity – a measure of a material's resistance to flow.

viscous friction – resistance created by objects moving in water or other fluids.

visible light – the light you can see in the range between 400 and 700 nanometers.

volt – the measurement unit for voltage.

voltage – the amount of potential energy that each unit of electrical charge has.

W

water cycle – see hydrologic cycle.

watt – the metric, or SI, unit of power.

wavefronts – another term used to describe the crests of a wave.

wavelength – the distance from peak to peak, crest to crest, or trough to trough of a wave.

weight – a force created by gravity.

white noise – an equal mixture of all frequencies, like white is a mixture of all colors.

work – the quantity of force times distance; the result of machines performing tasks.

Y

yellow – a color that is created when blue is absorbed and red and green are reflected.

A

B

C

G

H

I

J

K

L

M

N

O

P

Q

R

S

T

U

V

W

X

Y

Periodic Table of the Elements

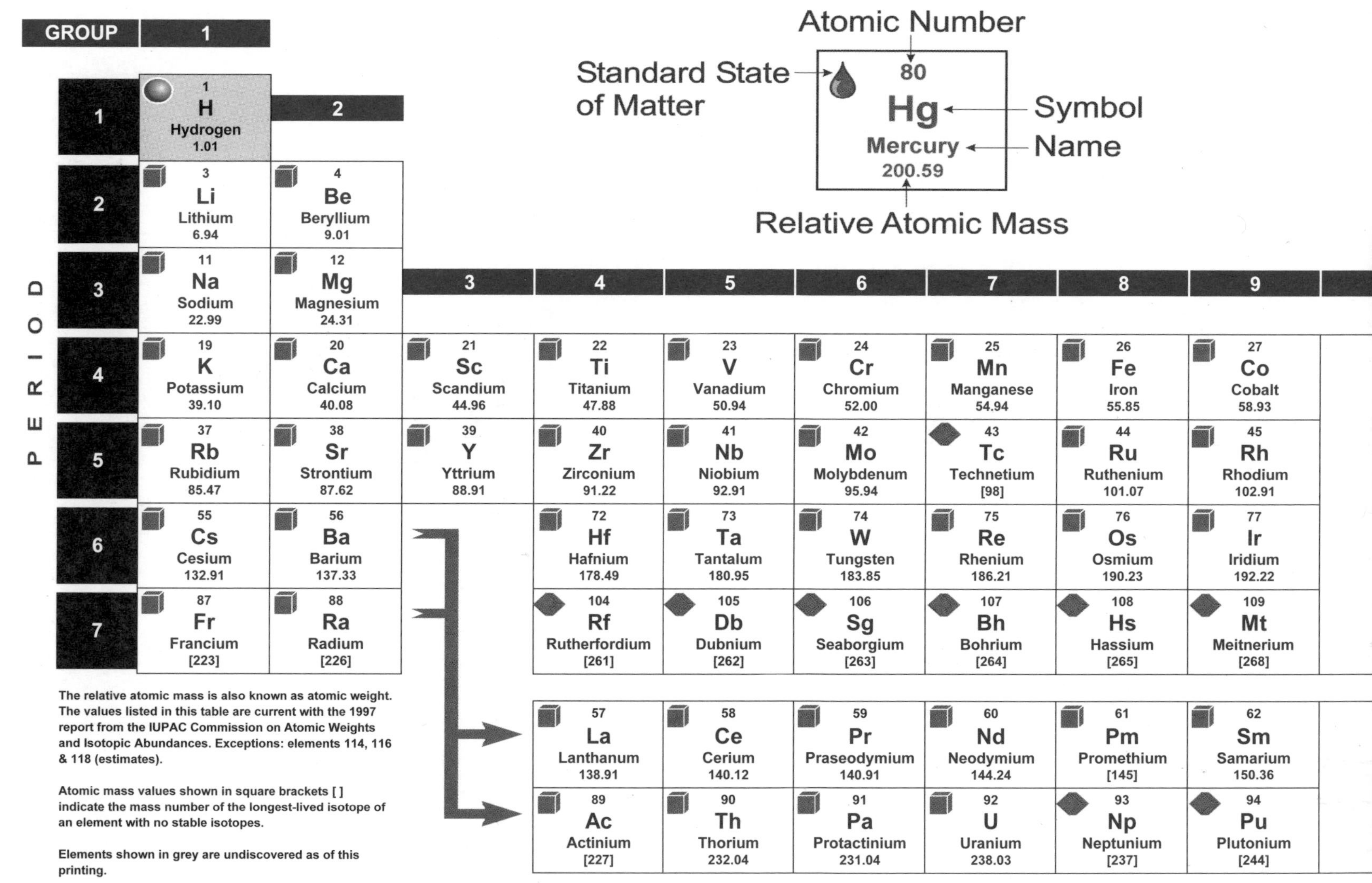

PERIOD \ GROUP	1	2	3	4	5	6	7	8	9
1	1 H Hydrogen 1.01								
2	3 Li Lithium 6.94	4 Be Beryllium 9.01							
3	11 Na Sodium 22.99	12 Mg Magnesium 24.31							
4	19 K Potassium 39.10	20 Ca Calcium 40.08	21 Sc Scandium 44.96	22 Ti Titanium 47.88	23 V Vanadium 50.94	24 Cr Chromium 52.00	25 Mn Manganese 54.94	26 Fe Iron 55.85	27 Co Cobalt 58.93
5	37 Rb Rubidium 85.47	38 Sr Strontium 87.62	39 Y Yttrium 88.91	40 Zr Zirconium 91.22	41 Nb Niobium 92.91	42 Mo Molybdenum 95.94	43 Tc Technetium [98]	44 Ru Ruthenium 101.07	45 Rh Rhodium 102.91
6	55 Cs Cesium 132.91	56 Ba Barium 137.33		72 Hf Hafnium 178.49	73 Ta Tantalum 180.95	74 W Tungsten 183.85	75 Re Rhenium 186.21	76 Os Osmium 190.23	77 Ir Iridium 192.22
7	87 Fr Francium [223]	88 Ra Radium [226]		104 Rf Rutherfordium [261]	105 Db Dubnium [262]	106 Sg Seaborgium [263]	107 Bh Bohrium [264]	108 Hs Hassium [265]	109 Mt Meitnerium [268]

57 La Lanthanum 138.91	58 Ce Cerium 140.12	59 Pr Praseodymium 140.91	60 Nd Neodymium 144.24	61 Pm Promethium [145]	62 Sm Samarium 150.36
89 Ac Actinium [227]	90 Th Thorium 232.04	91 Pa Protactinium 231.04	92 U Uranium 238.03	93 Np Neptunium [237]	94 Pu Plutonium [244]

The relative atomic mass is also known as atomic weight. The values listed in this table are current with the 1997 report from the IUPAC Commission on Atomic Weights and Isotopic Abundances. Exceptions: elements 114, 116 & 118 (estimates).

Atomic mass values shown in square brackets [ ] indicate the mass number of the longest-lived isotope of an element with no stable isotopes.

Elements shown in grey are undiscovered as of this printing.